D0911648

PROFESSIONAL

Xcode® 3

PROFESSIONAL

Xcode® 3

James Bucanek

Wiley Publishing, Inc.

Professional Xcode® 3

Published by
Wiley Publishing, Inc.
10475 Crosspoint Boulevard
Indianapolis, IN 46256
www.wiley.com

Copyright © 2010 by Wiley Publishing, Inc., Indianapolis, Indiana

Published simultaneously in Canada

ISBN: 978-0-470-52522-7

Manufactured in the United States of America

10 9 8 7 6 5 4 3 2 1

No part of this publication may be reproduced, stored in a retrieval system or transmitted in any form or by any means, electronic, mechanical, photocopying, recording, scanning or otherwise, except as permitted under Sections 107 or 108 of the 1976 United States Copyright Act, without either the prior written permission of the Publisher, or authorization through payment of the appropriate per-copy fee to the Copyright Clearance Center, 222 Rosewood Drive, Danvers, MA 01923, (978) 750-8400, fax (978) 646-8600. Requests to the Publisher for permission should be addressed to the Permissions Department, John Wiley & Sons, Inc., 111 River Street, Hoboken, NJ 07030, (201) 748-6011, fax (201) 748-6008, or online at http://www.wiley.com/go/permissions.

Limit of Liability/Disclaimer of Warranty: The publisher and the author make no representations or warranties with respect to the accuracy or completeness of the contents of this work and specifically disclaim all warranties, including without limitation warranties of fitness for a particular purpose. No warranty may be created or extended by sales or promotional materials. The advice and strategies contained herein may not be suitable for every situation. This work is sold with the understanding that the publisher is not engaged in rendering legal, accounting, or other professional services. If professional assistance is required, the services of a competent professional person should be sought. Neither the publisher nor the author shall be liable for damages arising herefrom. The fact that an organization or Web site is referred to in this work as a citation and/or a potential source of further information does not mean that the author or the publisher endorses the information the organization or Web site may provide or recommendations it may make. Further, readers should be aware that Internet Web sites listed in this work may have changed or disappeared between when this work was written and when it is read.

For general information on our other products and services please contact our Customer Care Department within the United States at (877) 762-2974, outside the United States at (317) 572-3993 or fax (317) 572-4002.

Wiley also publishes its books in a variety of electronic formats. Some content that appears in print may not be available in electronic books.

Library of Congress Control Number: 2009942829

Trademarks: Wiley, the Wiley logo, Wrox, the Wrox logo, Wrox Programmer to Programmer, and related trade dress are trademarks or registered trademarks of John Wiley & Sons, Inc. and/or its affiliates, in the United States and other countries, and may not be used without written permission. Xcode is a registered trademark of Apple Computer, Inc. All other trademarks are the property of their respective owners. Wiley Publishing, Inc. is not associated with any product or vendor mentioned in this book.

To my niece, Amber

ABOUT THE AUTHOR

JAMES BUCANEK has spent the past 30 years programming and developing microcomputer systems. He has experience with a broad range of technologies, from embedded consumer products to industrial robotics. His projects include the first local area network for the Apple II, distributed air conditioning control systems, a piano teaching device, miniaturized radio transmitters with temperature probes to monitor the health of livestock — you can't make this stuff up — digital oscilloscopes, silicon wafer deposition furnaces, and collaborative writing tools for K-12 education. James is currently focused on Macintosh and iPhone software development.

When not programming, James indulges in his love of the arts. He has served on the board of directors for local arts organizations and has performed with Ballet Arizona. He earned an Associate's degree from the Royal Academy of Dance in classical ballet, and occasionally teaches at Adams Ballet Academy.

CREDITS

ACQUISITIONS EDITOR
Scott Meyers

PROJECT EDITOR
Christopher J. Rivera

TECHNICAL EDITOR
Michael Trent

PRODUCTION EDITOR
Eric Charbonneau

COPY EDITOR
Kim Cofer

EDITORIAL DIRECTOR
Robyn B. Siesky

EDITORIAL MANAGER
Mary Beth Wakefield

PRODUCTION MANAGER
Tim Tate

VICE PRESIDENT AND EXECUTIVE GROUP PUBLISHER
Richard Swadley

VICE PRESIDENT AND EXECUTIVE PUBLISHER
Barry Pruett

ASSOCIATE PUBLISHER
Jim Minatel

PROJECT COORDINATOR, COVER
Lynsey Stanford

COVER DESIGN
Michael Trent

COVER PHOTO
© tillsonburg/iStockPhoto

PROOFREADER
Josh Chase, Word One

INDEXER
Jack Lewis

ACKNOWLEDGMENTS

THIS BOOK WOULD NOT HAVE BEEN POSSIBLE without the tireless efforts of my many editors. My thanks begin with Scott Meyers, Acquisitions Editor at Wiley Publishing, who made this book possible. I am indebted to my technical editor, Michael Trent, who painstakingly checked every fact, symbol, and line of code for accuracy. I fear I paid a lot more attention to math than English in school; if this book is at all readable, it's due to the talented red pen of my copy editor, Kim Cofer. Eric Charbonneau took mountains of text, tables, and illustrations and transformed them into the cohesive tome you now hold in your hands — or scroll on your screen. Finally, the entire project was held together by the persistent efforts of Christopher Rivera, for whom I am eternally grateful.

CONTENTS

INTRODUCTION

WELCOME TO PROFESSIONAL XCODE 3. The Xcode Development Tools is Apple's free suite of software development resources. The Xcode Development Tools package includes project organizers, editors, utilities, debuggers, software development kits, and documentation.

Xcode is uniquely qualified to produce native solutions both for Apple's Mac OS X operating system and the popular iPhone and iPod Touch devices. If your development plans include Mac OS X or the iPhone OS, Xcode is the *only* rational choice for your development platform.

The size, complexity, and depth of Xcode are both a blessing and a curse. In your favor, you have a wealth of development tools, templates, and documentation, but all that comes at a cost; there's so much to learn and explore that it might take you months — even years — to fully exploit its capabilities. That's where this book comes in.

Professional Xcode 3 takes you on a detailed tour of the Xcode integrated development environment. Besides just explaining features, it will tell what those features are best used for, and give you some sound advice on making your Xcode workflow smooth, effective, and efficient.

It's as important to known what this book is *not* about. This book is not an introduction to programming on Mac OS X or the iPhone. You won't find any "Hello World" projects in these pages. This book is the guide that you'll need after you've built that example project and are ready to build your own. Do you start another project or create a second target? What if you want to share code between two projects? Do you copy the files, use source control, define a source tree, or use project-relative references? Confused? This is the book where you'll find the answers to those questions, the pros and cons of each approach, and some practical advice on which solution is best for you.

WHO THIS BOOK IS FOR

This book is for anyone who wants to get the most out of Xcode. It's for anyone creating multiple projects, large projects, projects that produce multiple products, and projects that need to be built for different deployment targets. It's for anyone working on an open source project, setting up source control, sharing development assets between projects, or collaborating with other developers.

This book is for anyone who wants to write source code efficiently, navigate between files, quickly rename variables, or refactor a class. This book covers the length and breadth of the Xcode editors, their navigation, syntax coloring, and code completion. It describes the many search and replace functions, class browsing, class modeling, and class refactoring.

This book is for anyone who's ever tried to find something in the documentation. It explains the documentation help viewer, research assistant, and quick help. It explains how to search the documentation by topic, symbol name, and how to filter the results by programming language. It shows you shortcuts for jumping from your source code right to the definition or documentation of any function, class, or symbol.

This book is for anyone who needs to debug, analyze, and polish a Mac OS X or iPhone application. It explains how to use the debugger, create and set complex conditional breakpoints, create custom data interpreters, debug on a second computer remotely, and debug full-screen applications. It shows you how to look for inefficient code, track down memory leaks, catch application crashes, and debug an application that's already running.

Finally, this book is for anyone who wants to automate their workflow. This book explains how to add custom script phases to targets, custom code templates in the editor, write breakpoint actions that run during debugging, attach action scripts to their project, and share those solutions with other developers.

WHAT THIS BOOK COVERS

This book covers the Xcode Integrated Development Environment (IDE) application. The *Xcode Development Tools* is the suite of resources that includes the *Xcode* application. Xcode (the application) is your cockpit, your command center, which drives the whole of the rest of your development system. While there are many interesting things you can do with the development tools, this book concentrates on Xcode (the application) and an Xcode-centric workflow. It shows you how to use your compilers, debuggers, linkers, data models, source control, documentation, and automation tools — all without ever stepping outside the Xcode application.

This book covers other important developer tools, particularly those that you'll use in conjunction with Xcode. The most significant are Interface Builder, Instruments, and Shark. All of these tools work hand-in-glove with Xcode, and you'll learn how to seamlessly transition between them.

This book also serves as a guide to additional research. No single book could possibly cover every aspect of Mac OS X and iPhone OS development. Apple produces a vast amount of high-quality documentation. This book often sketches the outline of a common solution, and then points you to the documentation or resource where you can explore the topic more completely.

HOW THIS BOOK IS STRUCTURED

Professional Xcode 3 is broadly organized in the order you typically develop a project. Of course development is never a linear process, but the chapters mimic the general steps you take when producing software:

- ➤ Create a project
- ➤ Populate it with source files and other resources
- ➤ Write code

➤ Edit your code and make global changes

➤ Analyze your code's structure

➤ Look up APIs in the documentation

➤ Design a user interface and connect it to your code

➤ Create data models

➤ Add project targets

➤ Build your project

➤ Debug your project

➤ Analyze its performance

➤ Collaborate with other developers

Each chapter includes a brief introduction to the topic, followed by successively more detailed explanations of the technology. If you want to learn everything about, say, targets you can read Chapter 16 from start to finish. But if you only need to answer the question "should I create a target or a new project," that answer is in the first couple of sections. If you don't need to create a new target, you can move on. Come back later when you need to create a target, or customize an existing one.

I've tried to organize the book topically so that it can serve as a resource for future research. When you first create a data model in Core Data, you probably aren't worrying about developing a migration map to the next version of your data model. But when you do create that second version, I trust that you'll know where to open the book and find the answer. (Hint, it's in the Data Modeling chapter.)

WHAT YOU NEED TO USE THIS BOOK

This book was written for Xcode 3.2. To use Xcode 3.2, you will need the following:

➤ An Intel-based Macintosh computer running Mac OS X 10.6 (a.k.a. Snow Leopard) or later

➤ An Apple developer account (either iPhone or Mac OS X, a free account is sufficient)

➤ For iPhone development, you'll eventually need an iPhone or iPod Touch device and an iPhone developer account — but you can get started without one

➤ At least 10 GB of free disk space

Even though Xcode 3.2 will only run on an Intel-based Macintosh running 10.6, Xcode can produce applications compatible with PowerPC-based systems, Mac operating systems as old as Mac OS X 10.4, and any version of the iPhone OS.

CONVENTIONS

To help you get the most from the text and keep track of what's happening, we've used a number of conventions throughout the book.

As for styles in the text:

- ➤ We *highlight* new terms and important words when we introduce them.
- ➤ We show keyboard strokes like this: Command+A.
- ➤ We show file names, URLs, and code within the text like so: `persistence.properties`.
- ➤ We present code as follows:

```
We use a monofont type with no highlighting for most code examples.
```

SOURCE CODE

As you work through the examples in this book, you may choose either to type in all the code manually or to use the source code files that accompany the book. All of the source code used in this book is available for download at `http://www.wrox.com`. Once at the site, simply locate the book's title (either by using the Search box or by using one of the title lists) and click the Download Code link on the book's detail page to obtain all the source code for the book.

 Because many books have similar titles, you may find it easiest to search by ISBN; this book's ISBN is 978-0-470-52522-7.

Once you download the code, just decompress it with your favorite compression tool. Alternately, you can go to the main Wrox code download page at `http://www.wrox.com/dynamic/books/download.aspx` to see the code available for this book and all other Wrox books.

ERRATA

We make every effort to ensure that there are no errors in the text or in the code. However, no one is perfect, and mistakes do occur. If you find an error in one of our books, like a spelling mistake or faulty piece of code, we would be very grateful for your feedback. By sending in errata you may save another reader hours of frustration and at the same time you will be helping us provide even higher quality information.

To find the errata page for this book, go to `http://www.wrox.com` and locate the title using the Search box or one of the title lists. Then, on the book details page, click the Book Errata link. On this page you can view all errata that has been submitted for this book and posted by Wrox editors.

A complete book list including links to each book's errata is also available at www.wrox.com/misc-pages/booklist.shtml.

If you don't spot "your" error on the Book Errata page, go to www.wrox.com/contact/techsupport.shtml and complete the form there to send us the error you have found. We'll check the information and, if appropriate, post a message to the book's errata page and fix the problem in subsequent editions of the book.

P2P.WROX.COM

For author and peer discussion, join the P2P forums at p2p.wrox.com. The forums are a Web-based system for you to post messages relating to Wrox books and related technologies and interact with other readers and technology users. The forums offer a subscription feature to e-mail you topics of interest of your choosing when new posts are made to the forums. Wrox authors, editors, other industry experts, and your fellow readers are present on these forums.

At http://p2p.wrox.com you will find a number of different forums that will help you not only as you read this book, but also as you develop your own applications. To join the forums, just follow these steps:

1. Go to p2p.wrox.com and click the Register link.

2. Read the terms of use and click Agree.

3. Complete the required information to join as well as any optional information you wish to provide and click Submit.

4. You will receive an e-mail with information describing how to verify your account and complete the joining process.

You can read messages in the forums without joining P2P but in order to post your own messages, you must join.

Once you join, you can post new messages and respond to messages other users post. You can read messages at any time on the Web. If you would like to have new messages from a particular forum e-mailed to you, click the Subscribe to this Forum icon by the forum name in the forum listing.

For more information about how to use the Wrox P2P, be sure to read the P2P FAQs for answers to questions about how the forum software works as well as many common questions specific to P2P and Wrox books. To read the FAQs, click the FAQ link on any P2P page.

1

Installing Xcode

WHAT'S IN THIS CHAPTER?

➤ Installing the Xcode Developer Tools

➤ Choosing the install location and packages

➤ Upgrading Xcode

➤ Removing Xcode

Xcode is part of the Xcode Developer Tools suite developed and distributed by Apple. If you haven't installed it already, read this chapter to find out how to do so. If the tools are already installed, you can skip to the next chapter.

If you've already installed Xcode, be aware that the default installation choices do not include all Xcode components. Features described in some chapters may require you to reinstall the omitted packages before you can use them. Return to this chapter to reinstall, upgrade, or remove the Xcode Developer Tools in your system.

The Xcode Developer Tools encompass a huge amount of material: dozens of applications, scores of utilities, hundreds of sample projects, and thousands of pages of documentations. Despite its scope, the developer tools team at Apple has made it remarkably easy to install this wealth of tools in only a few minutes.

THE XCODE INSTALLER

To install the Xcode Developer Tools, you must be running Mac OS X and have access to an Xcode Developer Tools installer. At the time this book was published, the current version of Xcode was 3.2, which requires that you be running Mac OS X 10.6 (aka Snow Leopard) or later. This entire book was written with, and assumes you are using, Xcode version 3.2 or later. Although the tools require Mac OS X 10.6 or later to run, you can develop code that's compatible with systems as old as Mac OS X 10.4. Some development packages, like the iPhone SDK, may have additional hardware or operating system requirements. The Xcode Developer Tools installer is available from many sources. Many flavors of the Mac OS X operating system installer include a copy of the Xcode Development Tools. Updated versions are occasionally included in the monthly Apple Developer Connection (ADC) DVD for download. First check to see whether you have a recent version of the Xcode developer tools already.

The latest version of the Xcode Developer Tools can always be downloaded from the Apple Developers Connection at `http://developer.apple.com/`. Anyone with an ADC account can download the latest development tools, software development kits, and example code directly from Apple. Online ADC accounts are free and require only that you create an ADC account and agree to the nondisclosure agreement that covers all Apple development technologies. Student, Select, and Premier accounts can be purchased and include many additional benefits. One of these is the monthly ADC mailing, mentioned earlier, which includes regular updates to tools and reference material. Other perks include discounts on hardware used for development and direct access to Apple engineers for technical questions. If you are serious about developing software for Mac OS X or the iPhone OS, you should invest in a paid membership. If you plan to sell your iPhone applications through Apple's App Store, you must have a paid iPhone developer account.

 Apple has never made incremental updaters for Xcode. Every version of Xcode ever released has included a complete copy of the entire suite. As such, there is nothing to be gained by installing an earlier version of Xcode and then upgrading it to a later version. Just install the latest version.

As of this writing, the Xcode developer tools installer is available in two forms. The Xcode download from the Mac Dev Center includes Xcode and all of the resources needed to develop applications for Mac OS X. The iPhone SDK from the iPhone Dev Center includes the entire Mac OS X suite plus additional tools and frameworks for developing iPhone applications. Installing using the vanilla Xcode download enables you to develop applications for Mac OS X. Installing the iPhone SDK enables you develop *both* Mac OS X applications and iPhone applications.

RUNNING THE INSTALLER

To start the installation process, open the XcodeTools or iPhone SDK package. You can find the XcodeTools package in the `Optional Installs` folder of the Mac OS X install DVD, as shown on the left in Figure 1-1. The iPhone SDK package is in the iPhone SDK disk image, as shown on the right in Figure 1-1. Opening the package launches the installer utility.

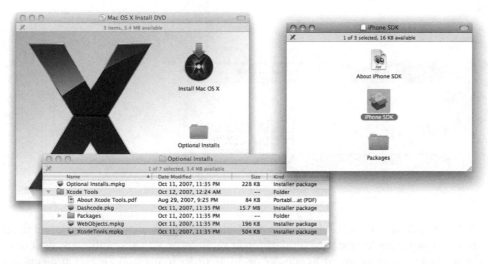

FIGURE 1-1

The installer presents a greeting screen. Click the Continue button. It next presents the software licensing agreement that accompanies the use of the developer tools provided by Apple, and possibly additional licensing agreements for iPhone and other SDKs. The pop-up menu at the top of the window may allow you to read the licensing agreement in other languages. Review the document using the scroll bar. If you like, you can print or save the agreement for review or for your records by clicking the Print or Save button.

After you click the Continue button, a dialog box asks you to confirm that you agree to the terms of the license. Click the Agree button.

If this is your first installation, the installer may prompt you to choose the volume to install. Choose your startup volume. The Custom Install screen, shown in Figure 1-2, selects the packages you want installed and where. By default, the bulk of the Xcode package is installed in the `/Developer` folder of the startup volume. Unless you have a compelling reason to change the installation location, accept the default `/Developer` folder.

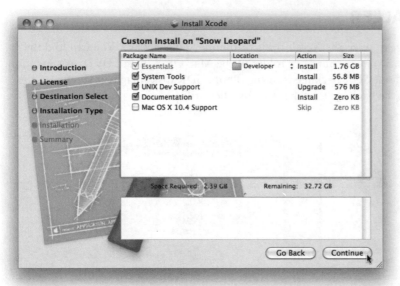

FIGURE 1-2

Beginning with Xcode 3.1, the Xcode tools, documentation, and frameworks can be installed in an alternate location, allowing you to install several different versions of Xcode simultaneously. For example, you may need to keep a copy of Xcode 2.2 or 3.0 in order to maintain legacy projects. To install Xcode in an alternate location, select the pop-up button in the location column and choose a different volume or folder: /Xcode3.1, for example. Note that the UNIX Developer Support package is always installed in the /usr/bin directory, and WebObjects is always installed in /Developer.

The installer will present a default set of packages to install. Alter the set of installation packages by checking, or unchecking, each one in the list. Select a package to display a brief description of its contents.

The following table explains the contents and usefulness of the various Xcode Developer Tools packages.

PACKAGE	DESCRIPTION
Developer Tools Essentials	This package contains the core set of development tools, including the Xcode IDE and all of the Mac OS X SDKs. You must install this package.
iPhone SDK	Includes the compilers, header files, libraries, frameworks, documentation, and emulation tools used to develop iPhone applications.

PACKAGE	DESCRIPTION
System Tools	Installs standalone system analysis tools such as Shark and DTrace components. These can be used independently or from within the Xcode IDE. You should install this package.
UNIX Development Support	Installs a set of compilers and other command-line tools in the /usr/bin directory. Note that these are duplicates of the compilers installed by the Developer Tools Essentials. Install this package if you intend to write shell scripts that perform builds or use makefiles that expect UNIX development tools to be in their traditional location.
Mac OS X 10.4 Support	Installs the compilers and SDKs compatible with Mac OS X 10.4. Install this only if you must produce code that runs on Mac OS X 10.4.

After you choose what you want to install, click the Continue button to start the installation process, shown in Figure 1-3. You will have to supply the account name and password of an administrator when asked.

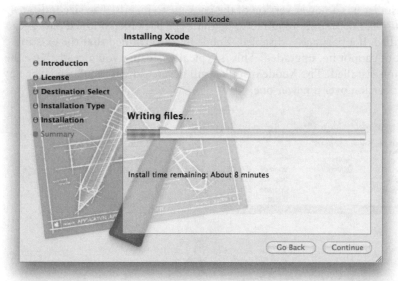

FIGURE 1-3

The bulk of the installation occurs in the /Developer folder, or whatever alternate location you chose, shown in Figure 1-4. Here you will find all of the Xcode applications, command-line tools, example code, and documentation. I recommend that you add the Xcode IDE application to your dock now.

Do not attempt to move or rename this folder or any of its contents. The installer places support files in the system-wide `/Library/Application Support` folder. It installs some special development frameworks, resources, and a few patches into the `/System` folder. UNIX tools and man pages are installed in the `/usr` folder.

After the installer is finished, check out any "About" documents installed for an overview of the developers tools and for any late-breaking news, additions, or corrections.

Congratulations, you've installed Xcode! If you like, you can now skip to Chapter 2.

FIGURE 1-4

UPGRADING XCODE

If you already have an older version of Xcode installed, you'll find some subtle differences when you run the installer again. The installer automatically detects the version of any package that you have previously installed. The packages, shown in Figure 1-5, show which packages will be upgraded, installed, or skipped. An upgrade indicates that the installer has a newer version of the package to install. The size indicates the estimated amount of *additional* disk space required to upgrade the package. Skipped packages will not be upgraded or installed. If a package is disabled, Xcode has determined that the existing package does not need to be, or cannot be, upgraded. This is typically because you already have the most current, or a later, version installed. The Xcode installer will never "downgrade" a package by attempting to install an older version over a newer one.

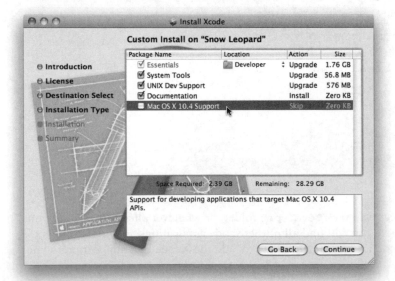

FIGURE 1-5

After you select the packages you want upgraded, click the Continue button. The installer runs much as it does when installing for the first time.

Typically you won't have any problems using your upgraded tools as soon as the installer is finished. However, if you immediately start using some of the performance analysis tools or attempt distributed builds, you may run into problems. These facilities use daemons and system frameworks that may need to be reloaded. Restart your system after upgrading your Xcode tools.

REMOVING AND REINSTALLING XCODE

The Xcode Developer Tools provide the means for completely eradicating itself — the entire suite of tools, support files, libraries, and frameworks — from your system. One really good reason to do this is to perform a clean installation of the tools. Apple often makes pre-release versions of Xcode available to ADC members. As a general rule, you cannot install a release version over a pre-release version even when that release version is newer. You may also have some need to downgrade your installation, something the regular installation process won't allow.

To remove your installation of Xcode, open a Terminal window and enter the following command:

```
sudo /Developer/Library/uninstall-devtools --mode=all
```

If you installed Xcode in a location other than /Developer, adjust the path accordingly. If this file is not present — earlier versions of Xcode used different scripts stored in different locations — refer to the "About" document for the currently installed version to find the appropriate script.

The script must be run from an administrator's account. The sudo command prompts you for the password to that account.

The script uses the receipts left by prior installations of Xcode to surgically remove everything that was previously installed. It also takes care of a few special cases, such as removing symbolic links that get created during the post-installation process.

The --mode argument has four possible values, listed in the following table.

MODE	DESCRIPTION
all	Removes all tools and directories installed by Xcode.
systemsupport	Removes only the UNIX support files (utilities, man pages, and so on) from the startup volume.
unixdev	Removes the compilers and other command-line tools installed by the UNIX Development Support package, described in the previous table.
xcodedir	Removes only the /Developer folder, or its alternative parent location. Equivalent to dragging the /Developer folder to the trash.

After the old copy of the developer tools is removed, you can reinstall whatever version of Xcode you want. The installer treats this as a new installation, installing fresh copies of everything.

After you reinstall the tools, you may need to restart your system. The `uninstall-devtools` script stops processes like the distributed build daemon, but the installer may not restart them again. Removing system frameworks and then replacing them with altered versions can seriously confuse the operating system. Restarting your computer causes all of these resources to be reloaded, reinitialized, and restarted properly.

SUMMARY

You're probably eager to start exploring Xcode, but installing the software first is a necessary evil. As you've seen, the process is relatively painless and quick.

Now, on to the grand tour.

2

The Grand Tour

Starting up Xcode is sort of like walking through the front gates of Disneyland, or onto the campus of a major university, or even a big shopping mall for the very first time. It's vast and you have no idea where to go first. If you just start walking, you'll quickly be lost and disoriented, so you do what every first-time visitor does; you get a map.

Neither Xcode, nor any of those other places, has been intentionally designed to be cryptic or confusing. In fact, they all go out of their way to be as friendly and accommodating as possible. However, the sheer size and complexity of what they offer cause them to be perplexing and frustrating at times. If you take a moment to get a feel for the scope and organization of Xcode, your initial forays will be much more enjoyable. Start by getting your bearings.

THE PROJECT

The central construct in Xcode, both physically and metaphorically, is the *project*. Everything you will accomplish in Xcode begins with a project. In fact, without an open project Xcode won't do much beyond letting you browse the documentation and set some preferences. The spirit of your project is stored in a *project document* on your file system. The project window, shown in Figure 2-1, is the manifestation of that document.

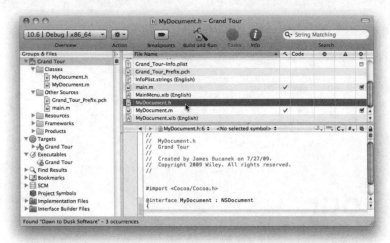

FIGURE 2-1

Because you can't explore much in Xcode without a project, take the time to create one now. You can throw it away later.

Launch the Xcode application and follow these steps:

1. From the Xcode File menu, choose the New Project command (Shift+Command+N). If you've just launched Xcode, click the big Create New Xcode Project button in the Welcome to Xcode window.

2. In the Application group, choose the Cocoa Application template (the options don't matter), as shown in Figure 2-2. Click the Choose button.

3. Enter **Grand Tour** for the project name.

4. Pick a location for the new project and click the Save button.

FIGURE 2-2

Xcode creates a *project folder*, containing a *project document* in addition to the source and resource files generated by the template.

Use this project to explore the various groups in the project window. You can also build, run, and even debug this project right now. Explore the properties of source items, groups, and other objects by Right/Control+clicking them.

The project window is your central workspace. Here you organize and navigate your project's resources, settings, and targets. From here you can initiate builds, launch the application, or start the debugger. Most of the menu commands apply to the currently active project window.

The left side of the project window is the Groups & Files pane. This is where everything that constitutes your project is represented and organized. Resources can be put into groups for better management. Click the expansion triangle to the left of a group's icon to explore its contents.

The right side of the project window is a multipurpose pane. It usually shows the details of the selection made in the Groups & Files pane, but it can also be used as an editor — or you may not even have a right side to your window. Xcode provides different window layouts to suit your work style. Chapter 3 explains these different styles and how to navigate your workspace.

Source Groups

Broadly, the Groups & Files pane contains two kinds of groups. At the top is the project group. This has the same icon and name as the project document. The project group organizes *all* of the source files and resources that make up your project, and is generically referred to as the *source group*. Sources are the files and folders used in your project. This could consist of program source files, headers, property lists, image files, dynamic libraries, frameworks, testing code, and even other projects. None of these constituent parts are stored in the project document itself. The files you will use to build your project exist elsewhere on your file system. The project group only contains *references* to those sources, not the sources themselves. Chapter 5 explains how to create, manage, and organize source references in the project group.

Double-clicking any source item opens it in an editor, assuming the item type is one that can be edited in Xcode.

Smart Groups

The remaining groups are referred to as smart groups. Unlike the project group, which you can organize however you like, the smart groups each represent some specific kind of information about your project. These groups are self-organizing and update automatically to reflect the state of your project.

One of the most important smart groups is the Targets group. This group shows the targets defined in the project. Each product your project produces, typically an executable program, is represented by a target. A target is organized into build phases. Each build phase performs a specific step in the build process, such as compiling all of the source files for a target or copying a set of files into the resource folder of an application bundle. A source is said to be a member of a target if the target includes that source item in any of its phases. Targets can depend on other targets, and they are highly customizable and extensible. Chapter 16 explains the kinds of targets Xcode provides and how to create your own. It also shows you how to organize and customize targets to meet your needs.

The Executables smart group lists the executables (programs that can be launched and run) in the project. Typically, each target produces one executable. The executables in a project can be run or debugged from within Xcode.

Most of the remaining smart groups gather information about your project, collecting them into readily accessible locations. For example, the Find Results smart group contains the history and results of recent searches. The Project Symbols smart group lists all of the symbols defined in your project. You can create your own smart groups that automatically collect source files that meet a certain criteria. If you've ever used smart playlists in iTunes, you are already familiar with this concept.

MENUS

The menus in Xcode are grouped by function. The File menu is where you'll find basic file and project commands. Use these commands to create new projects, files, and groups; close windows; save files; take snapshots; and print.

The Edit menu deals primarily with the editing of source files. The View menu controls the visual appearance of source files, windows, and lists. It also contains a number of file and window navigation commands. The Project menu contains commands specific to the project and its targets.

The Build, Run, Design, and SCM menus contain commands for building the project, debugging an executable program, class and data model design, and source control management, respectively. Each of these topics is covered in its own chapter. The Help menu is the gateway to the ADC reference library and the programming documentation. It also provides a few shortcuts to common topics.

The Window menu is one means of listing, and navigating between, the currently open windows. It also provides access to the organizer, described in Chapter 22.

EDITORS

Xcode includes a sophisticated and flexible set of editors. The one you'll use the most is the text file editor, shown in Figure 2-3. The text editor is context-sensitive, language-aware, and includes auto-completion features. It can automatically format, color, and highlight programming symbols and structures. The editor is integrated into the documentation, build system, and debugger. You can look up a symbol definition, jump to its declaration, review compiler errors, display the value of a variable, or step through your program without ever leaving the editor window. Its extensive editing and navigation features are covered in Chapters 6 and 7.

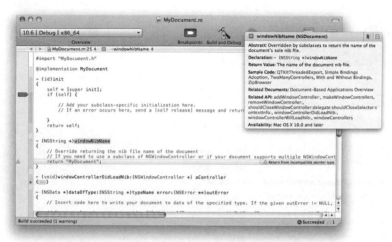

FIGURE 2-3

Xcode includes other kinds of editors, such as the property list editor, that enable you to edit the content of other document types easily. More sophisticated documents, most notably Interface Builder documents, are edited using separate applications that integrate with Xcode. You can also tap your favorite text, image, audio, or resource editor to augment, or replace, the editors provided by Xcode.

Chapter 13 discusses Interface Builder. Chapter 15 explains the data model editor.

SEARCHING, SYMBOLS, AND REFACTORING

Xcode includes many tools for exploring and altering the content and structure of your project. These are useful for finding something specific in your application and for understanding the structure of classes in an application.

The simplest of these tools are the various search commands. You can search a single file, or a group of files, for text patterns ranging from a sequence of characters to complex regular expressions. These commands are covered in Chapter 8.

The Class Browser, shown in Figure 2-4, compiles the classes and data structures in your application into a structured table. Chapter 9 shows you how to use it.

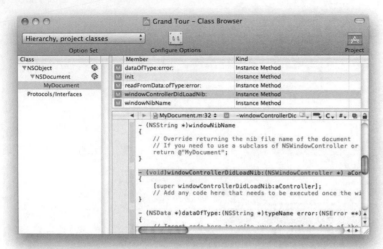

FIGURE 2-4

Chapter 14 introduces you to the class modeler. Like the Class Browser, it constructs a picture of your project's classes and their relationships. Unlike the Class Browser, the picture drawn by the class modeler is — well — a picture. The class modeler produces a graph of the classes in your application (see Figure 2-5). Models can be customized and are dynamically updated as you alter your code.

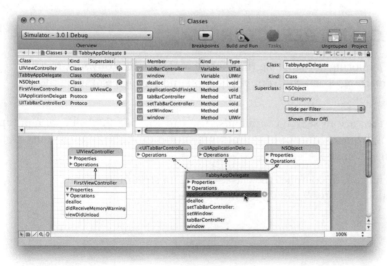

FIGURE 2-5

Chapter 10 describes the refactoring tool. This tool enables you to rename classes and variables intelligently, insert new classes into the hierarchy, relocate methods to a superclass or subclass, and upgrade legacy programming patterns to modern standards.

GETTING HELP

Someone once said, "It's not what you know, it's what you can find out." This sentiment is especially applicable to programming. It is impossible to remember every function name, every parameter, and every data type in the thousands of classes, headers, and libraries available to you. Often the question is not so much which specific function to call as it is "Where do I begin?"

Integrated into Xcode is the bulk of the Apple Developer Connection Reference Library, shown in Figure 2-6. This contains a vast wealth of introductory articles, examples, and programming guidance.

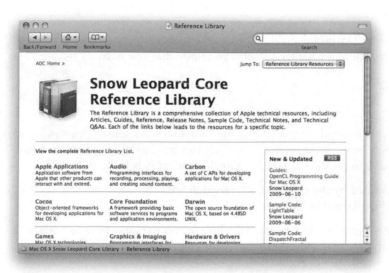

FIGURE 2-6

The Reference Library also includes a detailed, indexed, and searchable database documenting every major API in the Mac OS X and iPhone operating systems, an example of which is shown in Figure 2-7. You can instantly access the symbols in the Reference Library from within your source code or search the documentation interactively.

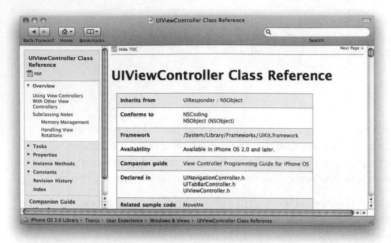

FIGURE 2-7

Being a productive programmer will largely depend on being able to quickly extract what you're looking for from this mountain of detail. Chapter 12 helps you find what you need.

BUILDING

The ultimate goal of any project is to produce something. Building takes the source items in your project and transforms them into a final product. Building can be roughly divided into two activities: defining how to build each product and then controlling what gets built and when.

The "how" portion is largely defined by the targets. Each target defines the steps and sources used to construct its product. This is explained in Chapter 16.

The "what and when" portion is explained in Chapter 17. This chapter explains how to initiate a build process and select exactly what you want to build. Most of the build process is witnessed through the project build window, shown in Figure 2-8.

FIGURE 2-8

Chapter 16 also explains Xcode's system of *build settings* and *build configurations*. Build settings are collections of options that control everything from what warnings the compiler will emit to the names of your executable files. A project contains multiple sets of build settings, forming a layered hierarchy of values. A build setting may apply to the entire project, or only to the files of certain targets, depending on where in the hierarchy the build setting is defined.

Build configurations add another dimension (literally) to build settings. Build configurations make it easy to configure projects that produce subtle variations of the same products, such as debug and release versions. You can also manage not-so-subtle variations; a single project target could produce an application for in-house testing, another version for use by the sales department, and a third variation for the field service engineers.

GETTING IT RIGHT

After your project is built, you then have to verify that it performs the way you intended it to. If any bugs are found, you must locate and correct them.

Xcode is integrated with several debuggers. Launching your application under the control of a debugger, as shown in Figure 2-9, enables you to step through the code in your application, view variables, and even fix bugs and alter data while it's running. The debugger facilities and commands are all explained in Chapter 18.

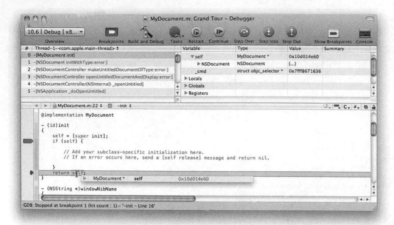

FIGURE 2-9

In addition to the debugger, you can employ unit testing and a cadre of performance and program analysis tools to help you identify, locate, and eliminate unwanted program behavior. Chapter 19 explains the analysis tools. Chapter 20 shows you how to set up your own unit tests.

COLLABORATION AND VERSION CONTROL

You can share projects and project sources with other projects and other developers. You can also configure your project to work directly with a variety of source control systems. Chapter 21 shows you how to create common pools of project resources and how to integrate your projects with a source control manager.

SUMMARY

This should give you some idea of the breadth and scope of the Xcode development environment. As you can see, there's a lot to cover in the subsequent chapters. You're probably anxious to get started, so move on to the next chapter to organize your workspace and learn your way around the interface.

3

Xcode Layout

WHAT'S IN THIS CHAPTER?

➤ Identifying the basic workspace components

➤ Setting up your workspace style

➤ Customizing windows and panes

➤ Getting information about items in your project

Now that you have a bird's eye view of how Xcode is organized, drop a few hundred feet and look at the visual layout of Xcode. In this chapter, you learn how items are organized in the Xcode project window, how to choose a window layout style that you like, how to arrange and customize windows, and how to get information about your project.

The project window, shown in Figure 3-1, represents your project and is your home base in Xcode. All of the components that make up your project are organized here. It is also the central means of browsing your project, allowing you to see the products that your project produces, symbols defined in your project, bookmarks you've saved, and other aspects. All other windows in your project are subordinate to your project window. Closing the project window closes the project and all other windows related to the project.

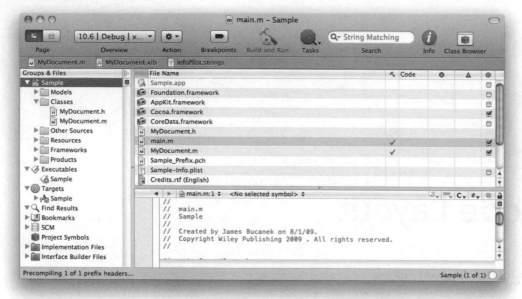

FIGURE 3-1

Project content (source files, property lists, details, log output) is presented in individual windows or in one or more panes that share a single window. Some windows are always organized into multiple panes, like the project and debugger windows. Other windows, like editing windows, usually consist of a single pane, but can often be split into multiple panes if you like. You learn more about this later in this chapter and in Chapter 6.

Broadly, content presented in Xcode can be divided into five categories: the project window, editing panes, Info windows, floating windows, and utility windows.

The project window is unique. It contains the Groups & Files pane and the details pane. These panes do not appear in any other window. Depending on your project layout style, the project window can also include editing panes and present the content of other utility windows.

Editing panes edit the content of source files, and are where you will be spending much of your time during development. Editing panes are often contained in their own window.

Info windows display detailed information about an item in your project. This is where you examine the details and options for each item. You can usually open an Info window by choosing Get Info, either by clicking the toolbar button or choosing View ➪ Get Info. Info windows vary depending on the type of item being inspected. Figure 3-2 shows a typical Info window for the project.

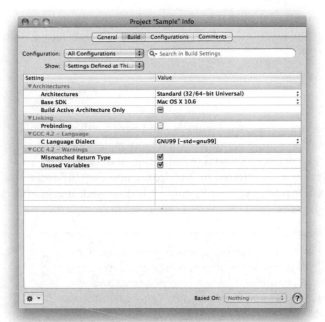

FIGURE 3-2

Xcode also presents transient information in floating windows and tool tips. These include suggested code completions, API documentation, detailed error descriptions, and variable inspectors. An example of a Quick Help window is shown in Figure 3-3.

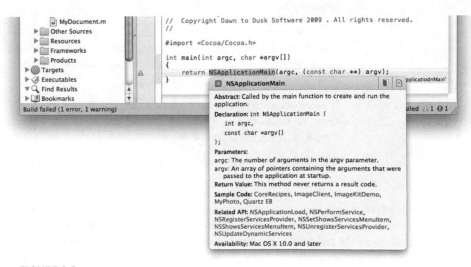

FIGURE 3-3

Utility windows are the catch-all category for all of the other kinds of windows that appear in Xcode. There are windows for browsing the documentation, building your project, debugging your executable, searching multiple files, and so on.

PROJECT LAYOUT

Xcode provides three different strategies for organizing your windows and panes, called a *layout style*. You can change the layout style as often as you like. It doesn't have any material effect on the content or functionality of your project; it just defines its visual organization and navigation. You should have a basic understanding of the layout styles offered by Xcode, because they influence how the project window is organized and where information about its content is displayed. It also affects Xcode's use of separate windows for various tasks.

Xcode saves your layout preferences — open windows, window position, list order, table columns, and other display options — in a per-user, per-layout preference file stored in the project's document. The window positions and display options you establish in one layout will be ignored by other layout styles. Similarly, your view preferences will be independent of those of other users working on the same project (assuming they have a different POSIX account name).

Choosing a Layout

Xcode offers the following three layout styles:

STYLE	DESCRIPTION
Default	All of the project groups and items are in a single browser shared with a combination details and editor pane. Source files may be edited here, or in separate windows. Build, debug, and other tasks open in separate windows.
Condensed	The project window contains only the project groups and items. All tasks, including editing, are performed in separate windows. There is no details pane.
All-In-One	The project and most tasks are confined to a single window.

The Default layout style, which was shown in Figure 3-1, is the traditional Xcode windowing style. The project window contains all of the groups and items in a single browser. The window shares a split pane with item detail and editing panes on the right side. You can view and edit source files immediately in the right pane, or you can open them in separate windows. Build, Debugging, and other tasks appear in their own window. This is a good choice for general development on a moderate-sized screen.

The Condensed layout style, shown in Figure 3-4, could also have been named the "Everything-In-A-Separate-Window" style. The project window contains only the project's group and items. The groups are further subdivided by a tab control at the top of the window. The tab selects between the source groups, the target groups, and all other types of smart groups. This chapter shows you how you can customize this organization a little later. Everything else you work with, or open, appears in a separate window. This is a good style for complex projects and for developers with large monitors.

The descriptively named All-In-One layout style, shown in Figure 3-5, is essentially the opposite of the Condensed style. The project, editing, and all tasks (build results, multifile searches, source control) are contained in a single window. You can switch which view you are working with using one of several tab controls. The tab control in the upper-left corner of the window switches the entire window between the project and debugger views. While in the project view, another tab control above the right editor pane switches the upper portion of the pane between the Detail, Project Find, SCM Results, and Build Results.

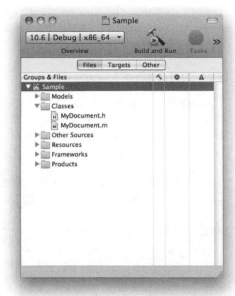

FIGURE 3-4

This is a good style for developers with small monitors or those who want to avoid the clutter of having many different windows open. It can be particularly useful when you're working with multiple projects at the same time — it's often difficult to identify to which project an auxiliary window belongs. This problem is explained in more detail in the "Opening One or More Projects" section in Chapter 4.

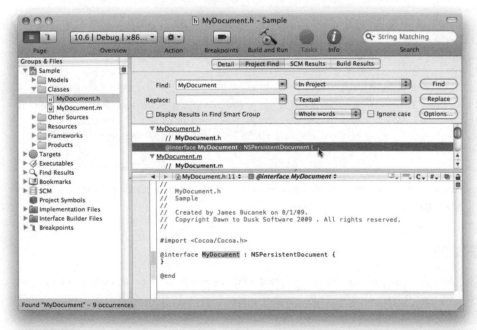

FIGURE 3-5

Despite its name, the All-In-One style does not force everything into a single window. You can still cause selected source files to open in separate windows for more convenient editing. Additionally, Info and Quick Help windows are always separate, regardless of the layout style you are using.

Changing the Layout

Xcode's layout style is global. After you have set it, it applies to all projects that you open. To change Xcode's layout style, choose Xcode ➪ Preferences, and click the General (leftmost) icon at the top of the window (see Figure 3-6).

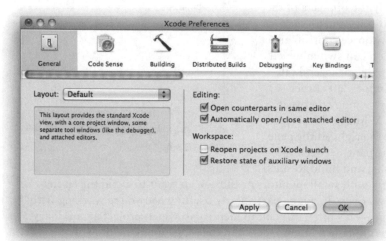

FIGURE 3-6

The global layout style is selected with the Layout pop-up menu. Other options control the behavior for edit panes, whether projects are automatically reopened when Xcode is launched again, and whether open windows are restored when a project is reopened.

 The layout style cannot be changed while there are any open windows that are influenced by Xcode's layout style. If the Layout option in the preferences window is disabled, close all projects and utility windows until it becomes enabled.

The next few sections explain the details of the project window and how the layout styles influence their layout and navigation.

GROUPS & FILES

All of the components of your project are represented as icons in the Groups & Files pane of your project window. Icons with a small grey expansion triangle next to them indicate a group of items. Groups contain items and sometimes other groups.

The very first group is the *project structure group*, or just *project group*. This has the same name as the project and contains all of the project's assets. The remaining groups are called *smart groups*. Smart groups change to reflect the state of the project. Figure 3-7 points out the source and smart groups in a layout.

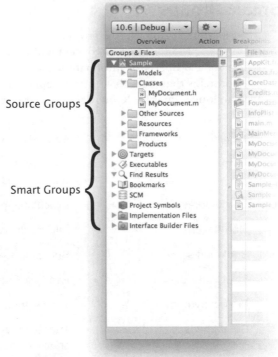

Search for something and the search and its results appear in the Find Results group for future reference. Edit a file checked out from source control and it appears in the SCM group. Check in the changes and it disappears again.

You can expand or collapse the contents of any group by clicking the small triangle next to the group's icon. Holding down the Option key when expanding or collapsing expands or collapses all subgroups as well.

Project Structure Group

The most flexible group is the project structure group. Within this group, you add the source assets (source files, image files, Interface Builder documents, property lists, and so on) that

FIGURE 3-7

will be used to build your project. All of the groups in the project structure group are generically referred to as *source groups*. These can be organized into any arbitrary arrangement of subgroups that you like. When you create a project, Xcode automatically creates source groups for Classes, Other Sources, Resources, Frameworks, Products, and possibly others depending on the project template. Within the Frameworks groups you'll usually find subgroups for Linked Frameworks and Other Frameworks.

How many source groups you create, their names, and how you organize them is entirely up to you. Xcode does not impose any kind of organization or convention when it comes to the project structure group. You are free to put a movie file in the Classes groups or rename the Classes group to "Wonkavator." You can just as easily move all of your assets to the top-level project structure group and delete all subgroups. This is not a bad idea for very small projects, because many small groups can just get in the way.

Although you generally have carte blanche to organize the source groups however you see fit, there is one exception: the Products subgroup. Although Products appears to be just another source group, it's actually a smart group. Products are the end result of targets (see Chapter 16). You cannot delete or rename the Products groups or any of the products contained therein. Products are added, removed, and renamed by editing the targets that define them.

Smart Groups

The remaining groups in the project window are the smart groups. If you have used smart groups in iTunes or Mail lately, this concept will be immediately clear. A smart group contains items that reflect some property or information about your project, and have a fixed or restricted structure. Files or items that meet that criterion appear in the group automatically, and disappear as soon as they no longer qualify. Xcode defines several smart groups, as listed in the following table:

SMART GROUP	CONTENTS
Targets	The targets defined in the project. Expand a target to reveal its build phases. See Chapter 13.
Executables	Executable programs produced by the project.
Find Results	The results of the last several searches that were performed.
Bookmarks	Bookmarks you have created.
SCM	Pending Source Control actions for this project. See Chapter 21.
Project Symbols	The symbols defined in the project.
Breakpoints	The debugger breakpoints set in the project. This group is not shown by default.
Implementation Files	All of the source files (.c, .cpp, .m, .mm, .java, .sh, and so on) in the project.
Interface Builder Files	All of the NIB documents in the project.

Organizing Groups and Their Contents

Reorder your source or smart groups by dragging them to a new position in the list. Reorganize source groups and source items by dragging them to a new position in the source group, or dropping them into another source group. A drop indicator will tell you if are you about to drop the item(s) adjacent the group, or inside it.

You can create a new, empty source group by selecting a source group or file and choosing File ➪ New Group from the main menu, or you can Right/Control+click on a source item and choose Add ➪ New Group. A new group with the name New Group is created inside the selected source group, or in the same group as any selected file, as shown in Figure 3-8. Edit the name of the new group and press Return.

FIGURE 3-8

You can gather an arbitrary set of files or groups and move them inside a newly created group in a single step: select the items and choose the File ➭ Group, or Right/Control+click and choose the Group command. A new group is created, and all of the selected groups and files are placed inside the new group. You have only to name the new group.

You can rename any source group or file by first selecting it and clicking once on the item's name. You can also Right/Control+click an item and choose Rename.

Finally, you can delete a group in one of two ways. The first, and most obvious way, is to choose Delete from either the Edit menu or the Right/Control+click contextual menu. This deletes both the group and its contents. If the group contained file or folder references, you get a confirmation dialog box asking you if you want to delete just the references or the actual files. See Chapter 5 to learn about references.

To delete a group *without* deleting its contents, select a group and choose the Ungroup command from the Right/Control+click contextual menu (there is no main menu command for this). Ungroup dissolves the group and replaces it with the items it previously contained.

Showing and Hiding Groups

You are free to alter which top-level groups are visible in your project window. For example, if you are not using source control you may want to hide the SCM group.

Right/Control+click any top-level group and locate the Preferences submenu. Here you will see all of the top-level groups in your project. Groups that are checked will be visible in the pane. Check and uncheck whatever groups you wish. When you uncheck a group, Xcode asks for confirmation before deleting it. This is somewhat misleading, because the group is not "deleted" in the strictest sense. Check the group in the Preferences menu again and it reappears.

When using the Condensed layout, you have three sets of groups, defined by the Files, Targets, and Other tabs above the group list. Each set is independent of the others, and you can add or remove groups from any tab. I find it convenient to have the Bookmarks group in the Files tab, because most of my bookmarks are shortcuts to places in my source code. Show or hide the groups that make sense to you.

In the Default and All-In-One layout styles, you can also have multiple views of your groups. In these two layout styles, Xcode places a split-pane control just above the group list scroll bar.

Click the split pane icon, as shown in Figure 3-9, to split the list into two lists. You can now alter which groups appear in the upper and lower panes independently. To return to one list again, click the join pane icon just below the split pane icon of the list you want to discard. Unfortunately, Xcode does not remember which groups were visible in the second list the next time you re-split the pane. If you spend time customizing your groups, it's best to leave the pane split, minimizing one or the other as desired.

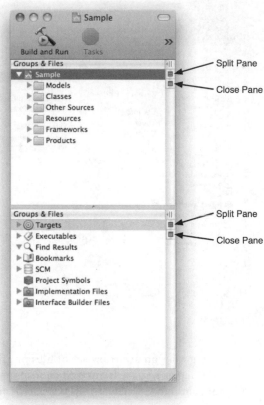

FIGURE 3-9

You can also, rather erroneously, select any top-level group and apply the Delete command as you would a source group. The Delete command merely hides the group and is equivalent to unchecking it in the Preferences submenu.

Making Your Layout the Default Layout

After you've spent some time setting up and customizing the organization, panes, and columns of your project, you can save that layout as the new default for all new projects. Here's how:

1. Customize the layout and organization of a project.
2. Choose the Windows ⇨ Defaults command.
3. Click the Make Layout Default button.

When using the same layout style, all new projects will have the same size, layout, and organization that your current project has right now.

If you've completely trashed the default layout, or you inherited one that you dislike, you can reset the new project layout to the factory settings. To reset the layout, choose the same command but click the Restore To Factory Default button instead. Note that these two commands only apply to new projects using the current Xcode layout style.

Customizing the Implementation and Interface Builder Files Smart Groups

The Implementation Files and Interface Builder Files smart groups automatically collect all of the source files that match a particular naming convention. These groups are actually just predefined custom smart groups, which you can create yourself. The next section will show you how. You edit the criteria of these two by selecting one and choosing the Get Info command. Get Info is available from the File menu, the Right/Control+click contextual menu, and from the toolbar. The Info window for the Implementation Files group is shown in Figure 3-10.

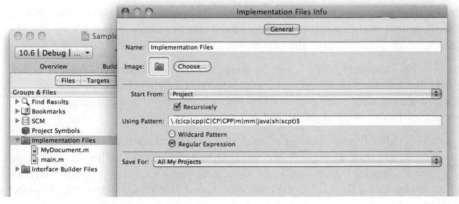

FIGURE 3-10

The really useful settings here are the Start From and Using Pattern settings. You can limit the scope of the smart group's search by setting the source group that it searches, and whether it searches just the files in that group or it and all of its subgroups. The Using Pattern establishes the filename pattern that will cause files to appear in the smart group. If you want header files to appear, but not script files, edit the pattern accordingly. You have the choice of using a shell-like globbing pattern or a regular expression. The changes you make affect all projects.

The rest of the options are really only applicable when creating and customizing your own smart groups, and should probably be left as they are.

Custom Smart Groups

You can create one kind of smart group yourself. This is limited to collecting source files automatically that match a particular pattern. Xcode comes with two of these "simple" smart groups pre-defined: The Implementation Files group and the NIB Files group that were described in the previous section.

Custom smart groups come in two flavors: Simple Filter smart group and Simple Regular Expression smart group. The Filter flavor matches files based on file name "globbing" used in the shell — where the pattern *.c matches all C source files. The Regular Expression flavor matches files using regular expressions — the pattern \.[ch]p{0,2}$ matches file names ending in .c, .h, .cp, .hp, .cpp, or .hpp. See Chapter 8 for an overview of Regular Expressions. The "Searching Lists" section of that same chapter has a brief description of globbing patterns.

Creating a Simple Smart Group

To create your own smart group, choose either the Project ⇨ New Smart Group ⇨ Simple Filter Smart Group or the Project ⇨ New Smart Group ⇨ Simple Regular Expression Smart Group command. A new simple smart group is immediately created, its Info window open and ready to edit. There is no opportunity to cancel here. If you didn't want to create the smart group, delete it (see the "Deleting Custom Smart Groups" section).

Defining a Smart Group

In the Info window, edit the name under which the group will appear in the project window. Click on the Choose… button next to the image, or drag an image into the icon preview, to provide the group with something more evocative than the generic "gear folder" icon.

Start From chooses where the smart group looks for files that match the pattern. Project is the default, and refers to the top-level project structure group. You can also choose to restrict the search to a specific group within the project. The Recursively check box causes the Smart Group to search all subgroups of the Start From group for matches.

The Using Pattern field is either the wildcard or regular expression pattern that will be used to match files. If you selected to create a Simple Filter Smart Group, Wildcard will be selected. If you selected to create a Simple Regular Expression Smart Group, Regular Expression will be selected. You can turn a Filter group into a Regular Expression group, and vice versa, at any time by selecting the other radio button.

The Save For menu determines if the Simple smart group you just created will appear in all projects opened on your system, or only the current project. The All My Projects setting is convenient for Smart Groups you plan to use over and over again, as you can elect to use it in any project just by revealing it in the project's group list.

 Be very careful when creating simple smart groups for all projects. There is no way to individually delete smart groups you've created. A procedure to delete all of the global smart groups is described in the next section, but if you want to delete some and preserve others, you will need to reconstruct them.

Also, be careful when saving a smart group for all projects that have a Start From location that is not the top-level project structure group. There is no clear rule for determining which group will actually be searched in other projects. Those projects might not have a group with that name, or they once did and the group was renamed, or the group has been moved to some other part of the group hierarchy. Any of these conditions can cause a global smart group to search the wrong group for files. When you're creating smart groups that you intend to use in other projects, stick to the top-level project structure group.

You can later open the Info window for any smart group and edit its definition.

One caveat about smart groups is that sometimes they aren't very smart. Although they will usually pick up files that you add to a project, they often fail to update if you rename or remove them from the project. Closing and opening the project will refresh the list.

Using Custom Smart Groups in Other Projects

System-wide smart groups that you define in one project won't automatically appear in other projects. Use the technique described earlier in the "Showing and Hiding Groups" section to add (or remove) your global custom smart group to another project.

Deleting Custom Smart Groups

One unfortunate omission from the Xcode user interface is the ability to delete smart groups that you've created. Like the predefined smart groups, an attempt to delete them only hides them in the list. Even more irksome is that the data structures used to store smart group definitions are opaque, making it impossible to selectively delete smart groups. What you can do is delete all of the smart groups saved in an individual project, or all of the global smart groups available to all projects. If you have smart groups that you want to save and others that you want to delete, you will need to write down the settings for the ones you want to save and recreate them afterwards.

To delete all of the smart groups saved in an individual project, first close the project. Select the project's file icon in the Finder and use the Right/Control+click contextual menu to choose Show Package Contents. Inside the .xcodeproj package, you will find a series of files beginning with your account's short user name where Xcode preserves the layout and window preferences for each user. The file *youraccount*.pbxuser contains the smart group definitions that you've saved in this project. Open the file in a text editor, such as TextEdit or BBEdit, and delete the line that begins with com.apple.ide.smrt.PBXUserSmartGroupsKey. Alternatively, this could also be accomplished via the following command line in the Terminal:

```
james$ cd ~/Desktop/Explore\ Layout/Explore\ Layout.xcodeproj/
james$ mv james.pbxuser james.pbxuser.bak
james$ grep -v PBXUserSmartGroupsKey james.pbxuser.bak > james.pbxuser
```

To delete all of the smart groups saved for all projects, first quit Xcode. Using the Property List Editor (you will find this in the `/Developer/Applications/Utilities` folder), open the `com.apple.Xcode.plist` file in your account's `~/Library/Preferences` folder. Look for an element with the key `com.apple.ide.smrt.PBXUserSmartGroupsKey.ver10`, shown in Figure 3-11.

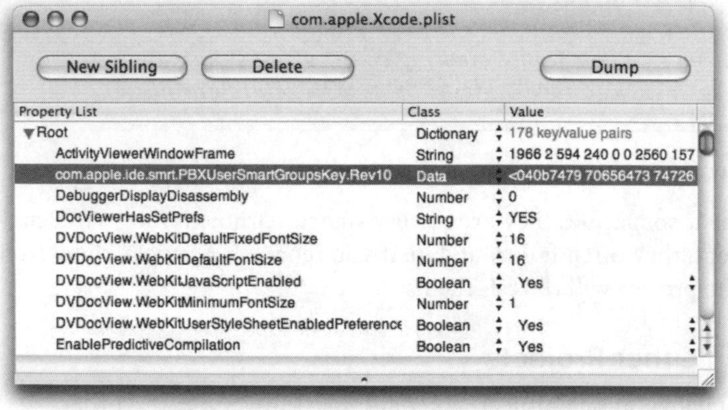

FIGURE 3-11

Delete this element and save the file. The next time you launch Xcode, it will recreate the default Implementation Files and NIB Files groups. All other user-created smart groups will be gone.

DETAILS, DETAILS

Now that you've learned to organize, customize, and navigate the top groups of your project, you're going to start digging into the details of those groups and what they contain. Details about the content of groups are displayed in a table called the details list. The columns of the table display properties about each item.

In the Default and All-In-One layout styles, the details list is displayed in a pane on the right side of the window, as shown in Figure 3-12. The Condensed layout style does not include a details pane in the project window.

The details pane shares its side of the window with an editor pane. If the details list is not visible, choose View ⇨ Detail or View ⇨ Zoom Editor Out to reveal it. You can also drag the divider between the details list and the editor pane.

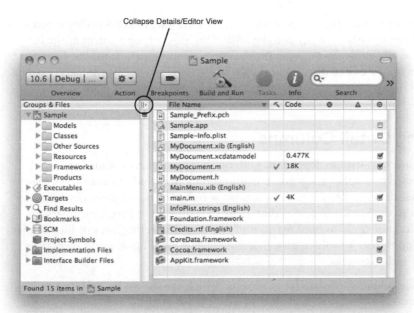

Collapse Details/Editor View

FIGURE 3-12

You can hide the details view and compact the window by double-clicking the expand/collapse control that sits between the Groups & Files list column header and the details list column header, also shown in Figure 3-11. Double-clicking the divider completely collapses the Groups & Files pane, leaving only the details list.

 There are some shortcut commands in the View ⇨ Smart Groups submenu. Each brings the project window to the front and selects the chosen smart group.

The details list always displays the set of source items encompassed by the current selection in the Groups & Files list. Selecting an item in the Groups & Files list displays that item. Selecting a group lists the details of all of the items contained in that group and any subgroups. Selecting a target lists all of the items used to build that target. Selecting combinations of groups and items displays the aggregate union of those sets.

 A few obscure exceptions to this rule exist. For instance, the content of frameworks and bundles are not included in the details list unless the framework or bundle is explicitly selected in the Groups & Files list. This avoids commingling the individual components of a framework, which might include hundreds of header files, with the source files of your project.

The details list is typically used to see the status of an item; for example, to see whether it contains any compiler errors, has been modified, or needs to be built. Double-clicking an item in the list opens that item and is generally equivalent to opening the corresponding item from the Groups & Files list. A few properties can be edited directly in the details list; most notably, the Target column. An item with a check box in this column can be immediately added or removed from the current target by ticking its check box.

Showing and Hiding Detail Columns

The columns shown in the details list are dependant both on the type of items being listed and which columns you've elected to display. Each group contains only one kind of item: The Project group contains source files, the Find Results group contains search results, the Bookmarks group contains bookmarks, and so on. Some properties that apply to source files (Target membership, compiled size, and so on) do not apply to bookmarks and vice versa. Selecting a set of files displays only the detail columns appropriate to source files. Selecting one or more bookmarks displays columns appropriate only to bookmarks.

Within the set of applicable columns, you are free to choose which are shown by enabling and disabling individual columns. To change the columns in a details list Right/Control+click any column header, as shown in Figure 3-13. A pop-up menu shows all the columns and which are currently displayed. Some detail lists have columns that you cannot hide. For example, the Role column in the Targets group cannot be hidden, and does not appear in the pop-up list.

FIGURE 3-13

You can resize columns by dragging the divider line between column headers. Reorder columns by dragging the column header to a new position. The layout for each type of list is remembered separately, so changes to one type of list do not affect others.

Showing Details in the Groups & Files List

In addition to choosing the columns for the details list, you can add selected detail columns directly to the Groups & Files list. Right/Control+click any column header in the Groups & Files list. Not all details apply to all types of items; ones that don't will be blank.

This ability is particularly useful in the Condensed layout style, which does not have a details pane in the project window. For example, in multi-target projects I invariably add the Target Membership column to the Groups & Files list so that I can quickly see (and change) what files are members of the active target.

INFO WINDOWS

The Inspector and Info windows are the third, and finest, level of detail in Xcode. The details list shows basic properties about many items at once, but an Info window tells the whole story. It is where you can inspect and modify every aspect, property, and setting of each item. For some items, that's a lot of information.

You can view the information about an item either in an Info window or in the Inspector palette. Info windows are regular windows. One is shown on the left in Figure 3-14. You can have multiple Info windows open at a time, which is particularly useful for comparing the details of two items. To open the Info window for an item, select the item in the project window, or have an editor window active, and choose the File ➪ Get Info (Command+I) command, click the blue *i* icon in the toolbar, or Right/Control+click the item and choose Get Info from the contextual menu.

Changing the properties of the project, target, or executable is such a common activity that Xcode provides additional shortcuts just for those. When you double-click the top-level project group, individual targets, and individual executables, Xcode opens an Info window — rather than expanding or collapsing their contents like other groups. The Project menu contains three commands: Edit Project Settings, Edit Active Target, and Edit Active Executable. All of these commands just open the appropriate Info window.

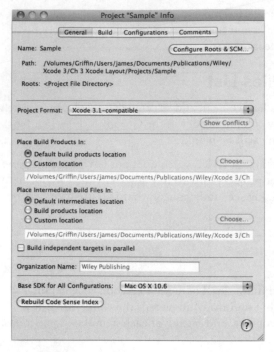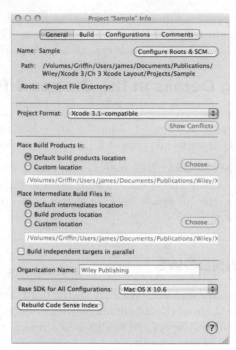

FIGURE 3-14

The Inspector palette, shown on the right in Figure 3-14, is a single floating palette that shows the information for the currently selected item or active window. Getting information about a different item is as easy as selecting the item. The Inspector is always on top of all other windows and disappears when Xcode is not the active application. You can use both the Inspector and Info windows at the same time.

To reveal or hide the Inspector palette, hold down the Option key and select the File ➪ Show/Hide Inspector command (Option+Command+I).

The Inspector and Info windows can display and alter the properties for more than one item at a time. Select multiple items and the Info window presents all of the properties that are common to those items. If you select disparate items, the Info window may only present one or two properties that are common to all, such as the item's Comments. Radically different items result in an Info window that says "Nothing to Inspect."

For each property, Xcode displays the value that is common to all of the items or it presents an indicator that the value of the property varies between the items. Changing the value of the property changes it for all of the items. If the property cannot be logically applied to all items, it is disabled.

> Changes made in the Inspector and Info windows are immediate. There is no opportunity to cancel the change and most changes are not tracked by the Undo facility, so be mindful about making changes that you might want to retract, although there are actually very few changes that you could make in an Info window that aren't easily reversed. The advantage is that you do not have to close the Inspector or Info window for the changes to take effect. This is particularly useful when you're changing values like build settings, because you can edit the setting and build immediately with the new settings. The only exceptions are some text entry fields. You may have to tab out of a field, or switch focus to another control or window, before the change is applied.

TOOLBARS

The toolbar is a standard Macintosh user-interface element. Toolbars can contain command buttons, pop-up lists, search fields, and other controls right at the top of each window, making them immediately visible and quickly accessible. Refer back to Figure 3-1, or almost any other figure of a window, for an example. The items you want in your toolbar are those functions that you use repeatedly and to which you want fast access, as well as settings and conditions that you want to refer to quickly. If you've been using OS X for any length of time, you are undoubtedly familiar with toolbars. If not, here's a crash course on Mac OS X toolbars:

➤ Toolbars can be shown or hidden by clicking the elongated white button at the right side of the window's title bar, or by choosing View ➪ Show/Hide Toolbar.

➤ Toolbars can be customized by choosing View ➪ Customize Toolbar or by clicking the toolbar button while holding down the Command and Option keys.

  ➤ Add, remove, or rearrange items in the toolbar customization sheet by dragging.

  ➤ Choose the icon mode and size at the bottom of the sheet.

➤ You can rotate through the toolbar's icon modes and sizes by repeatedly clicking the toolbar button while holding down the Command key.

➤ All like windows share the same toolbar. Customizing the toolbar of an editor window changes the toolbar for all editor windows.

Almost all toolbar controls implement a command, setting, or function found elsewhere in the Xcode system. Toolbars do not add functionality — they merely add convenience. Some toolbar items are specific to certain windows. For example, the Debugger's toolbar can be populated with all kinds of debug-specific items, which do not appear in other toolbars. Explore the toolbars for each window type to discover what items you can use there.

Although most of the controls you can place in the toolbar are self-explanatory, the following table lists three that might need a little more explanation.

TOOLBAR CONTROL	FUNCTION
Project	An oft-overlooked toolbar shortcut that simply brings you back to your project window, equivalent to View ⇨ Project (Command+0). If you have a lot of editor windows obscuring your screen, it's a quick way back home.
Tasks	The "stop sign" item is used to stop running tasks. Tasks include building, running, and debugging. Click once to stop the most recently started process or application. Hold down the button to reveal a list of running tasks and choose the task you want to terminate.
Overview	The Overview pop-up menu is a combination of the Active SDK, Active Build Configuration, Active Target, Active Executable, and Active Architecture tools. If you work with multitarget projects that produce several executables or have more than three build configurations, this is probably the most useful tool to have in your toolbar.

The project window's toolbar (in the Default and All-In-One layout style) has one oddball tool that you can only add or remove using the View ⇨ Layout ⇨ Show/Hide Page Control command. It adds a tool to the left side of the toolbar that performs the same function as the expand/collapse control that sits between the Groups & Files list column header and the details list column header, as shown in Figure 3-15.

STATUS BAR AND FAVORITES BAR

The thick portion at the bottom of the window's frame (which was visible in Figure 3-1) is not merely decorative — it's the status bar. The status bar displays various progress and status messages for processes like builds and multifile searches. You can hide or show the status bar in most windows using the View ⇨ Layout ⇨ Hide/Show Status Bar command.

You can reveal the Favorites bar in the project window, shown in Figure 3-15, using the View ⇨ Layout ⇨ Show/Hide Favorites Bar command. Here you can place files and bookmarks to which you want convenient access. Drag a file or bookmark into the Favorites bar to add it. Drag it out to remove it.

FIGURE 3-15

Clicking once on a favorites item selects that item in the project window. Double-clicking opens the file. In the case of a bookmark, it jumps to that bookmark location. If you add a source group to the Favorites bar, click and hold on the folder to get a pop-up menu of the files in that group.

ACTIVITY VIEWER WINDOW

The Activity Viewer window is a bit of an odd duck. It's the only window that doesn't really belong to any specific Xcode function, tool, or item. It simply displays the progress of various Xcode tasks. Open it using the Windows ➪ Activity command. It displays the status of background processes such as builds, re-indexing, batch finds, predictive compilation, and similar behind-the-scenes activity. It is most useful for observing Xcode itself. If you're wondering whether the project indexer is finished indexing your project, a quick trip to the Activity window will tell you what's going on. Or, maybe you just want something interesting to look at while building a large project.

SUMMARY

You should now have a good feel for how to get around in Xcode. You know how to choose the visual style that fits your needs, customize the interface a little, organize the items in your projects, and get varying degrees of information about items in a project.

You are now ready to create a working project.

The Project

WHAT'S IN THIS CHAPTER?

- ➤ Creating a project and defining where it's stored
- ➤ Choosing the right project template
- ➤ Juggling multiple projects
- ➤ Configuring project-specific properties

Now that you can navigate around the Xcode interface and customize its view, it's time to learn how projects are created, stored, opened, and closed.

Every project has two essential parts: the *project document* and the *project folder*. The project document, Simple.xcodeproj in Figure 4-1, contains all of the structure, references, layout, settings, preferences, and other attributes that define the project.

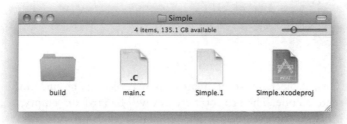

FIGURE 4-1

The folder that contains the project document is the project folder, in this case the `Simple` folder. This is the root location for the project. The project document and project folder usually have the same name, but that's not a requirement, and a project folder can contain multiple project documents.

CREATING A NEW PROJECT

You create a new, empty project using the File ➪ New Project command (Shift+Command+N). This opens the New Project Assistant, shown in Figure 4-2.

FIGURE 4-2

"Empty" is a bit of a misnomer. The New Project Assistant creates a new project using one of the many project templates that are built into Xcode. The project it creates will be far from empty, and may actually have quite a lot in it before you even begin. The templates try to provide the basic framework — a `main()` function, an empty subclass of `NSDocument`, a menu bar with all the standard items, required driver entry points, scores of build settings, and so on — all appropriate to the type of project you are creating. The templates also include the libraries and frameworks a project of that type is expected to need. Some templates go the extra mile and include libraries and frameworks that you're just *likely* to need. These frameworks are referred to by the project, but are not members of any targets. Being included in the project already, it's a trivial matter to add them to a target; this is quite a bit easier than being forced to identify and add the framework yourself.

The Xcode templates give you a huge head start in getting your project going, because so much of the basic groundwork is already done for you. In fact, most projects will build and run (albeit lacking any real functionality) as soon as they are created. Remember that there's nothing done by the templates that will lock your project into a particular technology or configuration. Any project can be modified to produce any other project. You can obtain the same result by starting with an empty project and configuring it appropriately, it's just a lot more work.

Choosing a Template

The first step in creating a new project is to choose the template that most closely matches the type of program or product you want to create. The templates are organized into broad categories on the left. Start by selecting a category, say Mac OS X Application, and a list of project templates appears in a panel on the right.

Many templates include additional options for refining the kind of project you want to create. The Cocoa Application template asks whether your application will be document based, will use Core Data for storage, and whether you plan to include a custom Spotlight Importer plug-in that will integrate your application's data with the Spotlight search facility. The options you choose influence what classes, boilerplate code, and targets are included in your new project.

The Command Line Tool project, pictured in Figure 4-3, has a completely different kind of question. It wants to know in what kind of language you plan to write your command-line tool. The choice here will determine what kind of source files are initially added (C, C++, Objective-C), what headers it will include, and with which frameworks it will link.

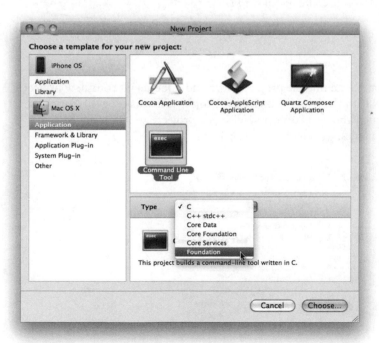

FIGURE 4-3

If you have no idea where to begin, you might want to read more about the kinds of programs you can develop for Apple platforms at `http://developer.apple.com/gettingstarted/`. If you're also working through a programming tutorial, say on iPhone development, the tutorial should indicate which template to choose.

Naming the New Project

After you have selected a project template, click the Choose button. A save dialog box appears prompting for the name and location of the new project. The location you choose determines where the new project folder is created. Inside the newly created project folder, Xcode creates a project document along with whatever additional source files and folders the template defines. This might be a single file or twenty.

The project document and folder will have the same name. Choosing an existing project folder for the location just creates a new project folder inside the existing project folder. If you want to have multiple projects share the same project folder, create a new project outside the existing one, then manually migrate the contents of the new project into the existing one.

 It's possible to "overwrite" a project by creating a new project with the same name and location. In this situation, Xcode warns that you are replacing an existing project. It then proceeds to create new files inside the existing project folder, warning you about template files that will overwrite existing ones. I wouldn't recommend trying this, because the benefits are dubious and it's hard to predict what existing files would be overwritten.

What's in a Name?

The project's name does more than just name the project folder and document. Your new project is customized in numerous places with the name you give the project. The easiest explanation is an example. Say that you are excited about creating a new Xcode project, and your exuberance influences your choice of project names, as shown in Figure 4-4.

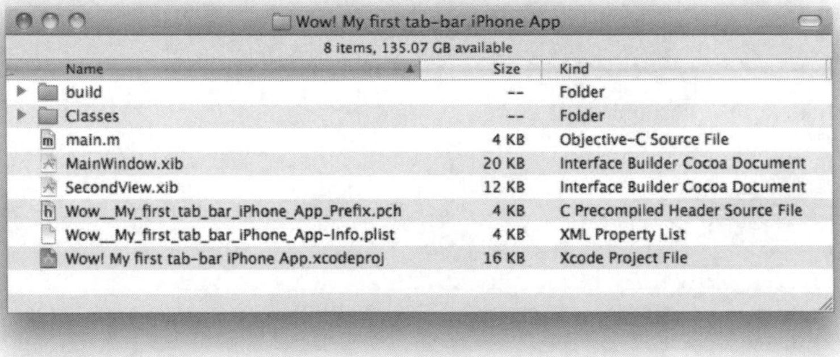

Name	Size	Kind
▶ 📁 build	--	Folder
▶ 📁 Classes	--	Folder
📄 main.m	4 KB	Objective-C Source File
📄 MainWindow.xib	20 KB	Interface Builder Cocoa Document
📄 SecondView.xib	12 KB	Interface Builder Cocoa Document
📄 Wow__My_first_tab_bar_iPhone_App_Prefix.pch	4 KB	C Precompiled Header Source File
📄 Wow__My_first_tab_bar_iPhone_App-Info.plist	4 KB	XML Property List
📄 Wow! My first tab-bar iPhone App.xcodeproj	16 KB	Xcode Project File

Wow! My first tab-bar iPhone App
8 items, 135.07 GB available

FIGURE 4-4

The project folder and documents were created from the iPhone OS, Tab Bar Application template. Looking at the project contents, shown in Figure 4-5, you find some rather convoluted names.

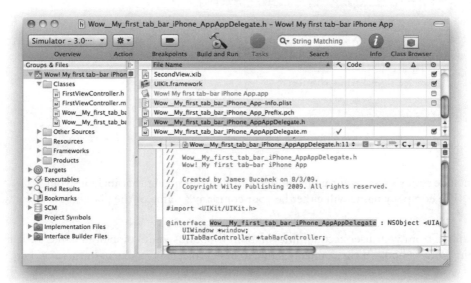

FIGURE 4-5

The project, shown in Figure 4-5, contains a class named `Wow__My_first_tab_bar_iPhone_ AppAppDelegate`. You might be happy living with the goofy application and target names, but really long class names like this will eventually be awkward. You have two choices: You can refactor the class names to something more reasonable, or you can throw the project away and try again.

When creating your project, consider what else you are naming, and what you might want to rename. Ultimately, the name of your project should describe what it produces. I recommend naming your project after the application it produces, and then fixing up class and filenames as needed.

Who's _MyCompanyName_?

Beyond just using the project name to customize file and class names, Xcode uses a number of other values to fill in variables in the project template. Similar substitutions are performed when creating new project files.

If you've created a few projects or files already, you've probably noticed the author credits that get inserted at the beginning of each source file, as shown in Figure 4-6.

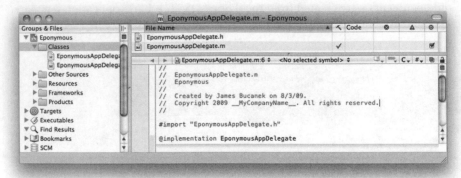

FIGURE 4-6

The comments include today's date, your name, and a copyright statement that includes your company's name. The company name will either be your company's name or the placeholder __MyCompanyName__.

Xcode gets your name from your user account information. It obtains your company's name, rather cleverly, from your address book. If the company name in new projects is incorrect or missing, here's how to fix it:

1. Open the Address Book application.

2. Locate your address card, or create one for yourself if one doesn't exist.

3. Fill in the card's Company field, if empty.

4. Select the card in the Name column and choose the Card ➪ Make This My Card command.

The address book identifies a single card as being "you." You can jump directly to this card using the Card ➪ Go To My Card command. The thumbnail image of your card will show the word "me" in the lower left-hand corner, as shown in Figure 4-7. Xcode uses the company name of this card to customize your source files.

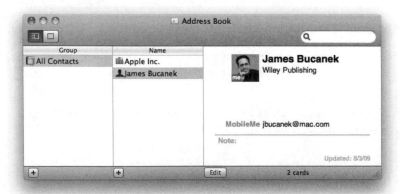

FIGURE 4-7

Older versions of Xcode would obtain your company's name from an obscure ORGANIZATIONNAME macro stored in Xcode's preferences file, which had to be edited manually. Thankfully, those days are behind us.

Closing a Project

To close a project, close the project window or choose Close Project (Control+Command+W) from the File menu. Changes made to the project's structure or attributes are always immediate, so there is no confirmation dialog box asking whether you want to save the changes to your project. However, if any source files in the project have been modified but not yet saved, you are prompted to save or discard the changes made to those.

Closing a project closes all of the windows associated with that project. Windows that contain project content (editor windows, the build window, the Class Browser, and the debugger) are all closed along with the project window. Generic utility windows (Activity Viewer and Help) that do not apply to a particular project remain open.

Opening One or More Projects

To reopen a project, open the project document in the Finder, choose the project from the File ⇨ Recent Projects menu, or choose the project from the Recent Projects list in the Welcome to Xcode window.

Two Xcode preferences, both in the General tab, affect how and when projects are reopened:

➤ The Reopen Projects on Xcode Launch option automatically reopens projects that were open when you last quit Xcode.

➤ The Restore State of Auxiliary Windows option restores the position and size of all the windows that were open when you closed the project. Without this option, only the project window is reopened and any new windows open at default positions on the screen.

You can have several projects open simultaneously, but Xcode focuses on only one project at a time. Whenever a project window, or any project-specific window, is the front (active) window, that project becomes the *active project*. Commands that act on a project, which include most of the commands in the Project, Build, and Debug menus, apply to the active project. You can (usually) tell which project is active by looking at the Window menu.

The Window menu in Figure 4-8 shows two projects — LogInLogOutNotificationTest and Sketch — open at the same time. All of the windows belonging to the LogInLogOutNotificationTest project are listed immediately under the project's name. This includes the project window itself and the main.c source file being edited in a second window. Note that if you are editing a file in a pane of the project's window, the name of the project window changes to

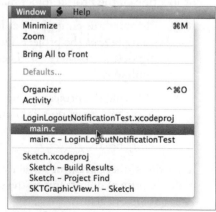

FIGURE 4-8

that of the file, followed by the project name. Therefore, the title of the project window may or may not be the name of the project, depending on its state.

The check mark in the Window menu indicates that main.c is the currently active window and, by inference, LogInLogOutNotificationTest is the currently active project. Selecting a window from the menu brings it to the front, making it, and its project, active. Selecting the name of the project itself brings that project's window to the front.

If the front window does not belong to any project, such as a window containing documentation or the Activity Viewer, things can get a little confusing. Some windows cause Xcode to disable all project-specific commands. In effect, no project is active until you switch back to a window belonging to one of the open projects. Other windows, like the documentation browser, *don't* alter which project is active, but also don't indicate which project was active, so it's impossible to determine easily which project is still active. You might also become disoriented when editing a source file that is shared by two projects. A window belongs to the project you used to open the window, even if the file in that window is part of another project that is also open and active. When in doubt, activate the project window before starting a build or debugging session, or simply keep windows belonging to other projects closed when they are not the focus of your development.

Renaming and Relocating Projects

You can easily rename the project folder or the project document after the project is created. To rename either, first close the project. In the Finder, rename the project folder or project document. Do not alter or remove the .xcodeproj suffix of the project document. Reopen the project by opening the project document. The Project Structure Group in the Groups & Files list will reflect its new name.

The folder containing the project document is always the project folder. Moving a project document to another folder implicitly changes its project folder.

The reason this may be significant has to do with the way in which references to source files are kept. References to files used in your project can be relative to the location of the project folder. There are also other kinds of references, all explained thoroughly in Chapter 5. Changing the name or location of the project folder may affect these references.

➤ Moving the entire project folder to some other location is the safest relocation possible. This only breaks the project if it contains project-relative references to items outside the project folder, or absolute references to items inside the project folder. Both of these conditions are unlikely.

➤ Moving the project document to some other location can be hazardous. The most significant thing this does is change the project folder. Absolute references outside the project folder won't be affected, but *all* project-relative references (both inside and out) will probably break.

Regardless, there are times when you will want to do this. There are very good reasons to have multiple project documents in the same project folder. See the "Build Location" section in Chapter 17 for some of them.

Upgrading Projects

Xcode 3.2 can open and use projects created with Xcode versions as old as Xcode 2.4. Older project formats might not support all of the current features, and Xcode will warn you if you try to use them. See the next section, "Project Settings," about maintaining backward compatibility with older versions of Xcode.

To work with a project created with Xcode versions 1.5 through 2.3 requires that the project be upgraded. When you open one of these old projects, Xcode presents a dialog box like the one shown in Figure 4-9.

If you choose to upgrade the project, Xcode prompts you to provide the name of a new project document. Note that this is just the name and location of the project document — not the project folder — so it should be saved inside the project folder you are upgrading. Xcode will create a new, modern, project document and open it. The project folder will now have two project documents, as shown in Figure 4-10.

FIGURE 4-9

FIGURE 4-10

If you only upgraded the project to view it, dispose of the new project when you are done. Otherwise, trash the obsolete project document. It is unlikely that you will want to keep both project documents, unless you plan to maintain them in parallel.

> *Xcode no longer supports project documents created with versions of Xcode before 1.5, any version of Project Builder (Xcode's ancestor), nor will it import CodeWarrior projects anymore. If you need to start with one of these ancient projects, either download and install Xcode 2.4 or 3.0 and use that as in intermediate step to import/upgrade the old project, or start with a new project and import all of the source files from the old project. It's hard to predict which will be quicker.*

PROJECT SETTINGS

Now that you can create projects, take a look at the attributes of the project itself. Choose Project ➪ Edit Project Settings to open the project's Info window. This is identical to opening the Info window for the project source group. The General tab of a typical project is shown in Figure 4-11.

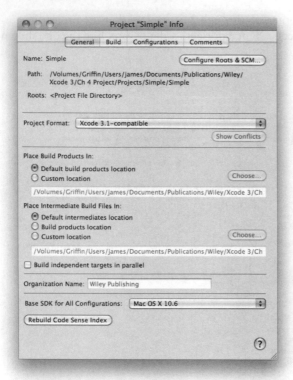

FIGURE 4-11

Here's a brief overview of the General project settings:

➤ The topmost pane shows the location of the project and its source control root directories. Source control and root directories are described in Chapter 21.

➤ The Project Format establishes the earliest version of Xcode that's compatible with this project document. Setting this to Xcode 3.0 means that this project can be opened by Xcode 3.0 and 3.1, but not 2.4. It also means you can't use Xcode features that were added in 3.1 or 3.2 that aren't supported by 3.0. If you lower the format level, there may be features you've already used that aren't compatible with the old version. The Show Conflicts button will describe what features are incompatible.

➤ The next section sets the build locations for this project. Build locations are described in Chapter 17.

➤ The Organization Name is an alternate company name for this project. When you create a new project, Xcode uses the company name in your address book card, as described earlier in "Who's _MyCompanyName_?" To use a different company name in files created just for this project, supply an alternate name here. Clear the field to revert to using your global company name.

➤ The Base SDK defines the default SDK for this project. The Base SDK is described in Chapter 17.

➤ The Rebuild Code Sense Index button flushes and recompiles the project's symbol table, which is used by the editor's auto-completion feature, among others. See the "Code Sense" section of Chapter 7.

The Build tab is where you set the *build settings* that will apply to everything built by this project.

The Configurations tab organizes named sets of build settings called *build configurations*. See Chapter 17 for a detailed explanation of build configurations and build settings.

That last tab is for comments. The project, targets, and most other items in the project have a comments field. This is for your personal use. You can keep whatever information you find useful here — Xcode will store the comments in the project document. You might want to include build instructions for other developers, to-do lists, or just a general abstract about the project and why it exists.

SUMMARY

In this chapter, you learned how to create new projects. More important, you now know how to choose a project template that will get you started in the right direction. You can open, close, rename, relocate, and switch between multiple projects. Finally, you know where to set the project attributes — although most of those attributes won't make much sense until you get to the targets, build, and source control chapters.

Before a project can build something, the project has to contain something to build. These are the project sources and are the subject of the next chapter.

5

Sources

You've learned how to create and reorganize projects. Everything you've learned so far has dealt exclusively with the project document. The project document contains its settings, targets, and preferences, but it doesn't contain any of the assets — files and folders — that will be used to build the project. All of your project's assets, essentially everything to which your project needs to refer, are defined and organized in the project source group. Each item in the source group contains a reference to an actual file or folder in the filesystem.

The most important concept to keep in mind while you're working with source items is this: *Every item in the project group is a reference to a real file or folder.* There are different kinds of source items and there are different kinds of references. Just to make things interesting, source items can refer to other source items, creating references to references.

Source item references in Xcode are *very* flexible, affording you a great deal of latitude to organize your source files and projects in just about any way imaginable. The number of possible combinations, however, can potentially create a lot of confusion and indiscriminately defined references can quickly create a tangled maze of relationships. Once you learn the basic reference types you shouldn't have any problem understanding your project's structure, choosing the correct type for new source items, or straightening out broken ones.

This chapter describes the different types of source items and references, shows you how to add and redefine source items, gives you some strategies for maintaining some sanity in your project's source references, and provides some tips on how to reorganize a project without breaking it, or fixing it if necessary.

REFERENCES

Every file, folder, and framework that you see in the project group of your project's window is a *source item*. Every source item contains a *reference* to a file or folder in the filesystem. Each reference consists of two attributes:

1. Path

2. Reference Type

The path attribute is a POSIX path to a file or folder. The reference type determines where the path originates. The six reference types, their path types, and their origins are listed in the following table.

REFERENCE TYPE	PATH TYPE	PATH ORIGIN
Relative to Enclosing Group	Relative	Location of Enclosing Folder
Relative to Project	Relative	Project Folder
Absolute	Absolute	None
Relative to Build Product	Relative	Active Build Product Folder
Relative to Current SDK	Relative	Current SDK Root Folder
Relative to Xcode	Relative	/Developer

 A relative path can be empty, which means that it refers to the origin directory — equivalent to the identity POSIX path (.).

A *Relative to Enclosing Group* reference, like the one shown in Figure 5-1, is the typical reference type and the one created by default. To view or edit a source item's reference, select the item, open its Info window, and switch to the General tab. The path of an enclosing group reference is relative to the folder referred to by the source group that contains the item. This reference type is the default because it simplifies many aspects of project organization. Ironically, it's also the most difficult to explain, so I'll come back to it after I've described the other reference types.

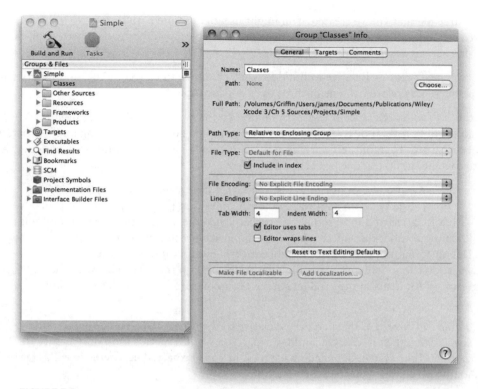

FIGURE 5-1

A *Relative to Project* reference uses a path relative to the current location of the project folder — the folder that contains the project document. The topmost project group always refers to the location of the project folder (you can't change the folder reference of the project group). The origin of these references is dynamic; if you move or rename the project's folder, the origin of the references changes accordingly. Items with this kind of reference are always valid as long as the relative path from the project folder to the source item remains consistent. The most likely candidate for a Relative to Project reference would be a key subfolder inside the project folder. A less common use would be a sister folder outside the project folder that shares a common enclosing folder, or some other near relationship.

Absolute references are the easiest to explain; the path of an absolute reference contains an absolute path to a source file or folder. Absolute references are usually used for referencing system components, such as libraries and frameworks, that never move. You would never use an absolute reference to a source file that you've created. You might use an absolute path to refer to a shared pool of resources on a file server, but source control or source trees would provide a better solution. Both of these alternatives are described in Chapter 21.

The last three reference types — Relative to Build Product, Relative to Current SDK, and Relative to Xcode — define references relative to one of three dynamic locations.

A *Relative to Build Product* reference uses a path relative to the current product build folder. A single target can produce several different products (typically one built for debugging and a different one built for deployment). Each of these variations is defined by a build configuration. Changing the build configuration changes the active project build folder.

If you want to include the product of one target (say, a target that produces a plug-in) as a source item for another target (say an application that includes that plug-in), you would use a source item with a Relative to Build Product reference. When the application is being built with the Debug build configuration, the source item of the application will refer to the plug-in that was built with the Debug configuration. When the application is built with the Release configuration, its source item will automatically refer to the plug-in that was built with the Release configuration. All items in the Product source group (naturally) use Relative to Build Product references.

Similarly, a *Relative to Current SDK* reference is relative to the active SDK being used to build the project — specifically, the SDKROOT build setting. You would use this kind of reference to include SDK resources (like system-supplied image files) in your project. The reference will refer to a different file should you change your base SDK setting.

Last, the *Relative to Xcode* reference is much like the Relative to Project reference. The reference path is relative to the folder where the Xcode tools are installed. Unless you selected an alternate installation location in Chapter 1, this will be /Developer. You would use this reference type if your project were using one of the developer tool resources, like the unit testing framework.

Now, back to the Relative to Enclosing Group reference type. Enclosing group references are those created by default, and the origin of each is the folder referred to by its enclosing group. If all of the references are relative to other references, you might be wondering to what they all refer. To find out, examine any newly created Xcode project. The Simple project, shown in Figure 5-2, uses an enclosing group reference with a path of MyDocument.h.

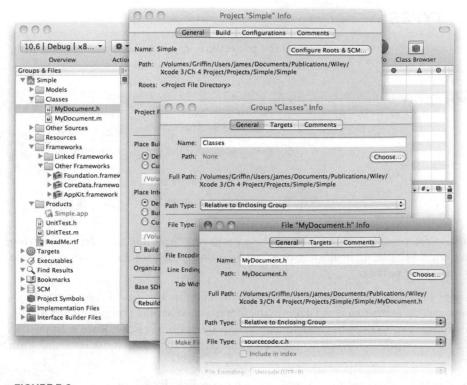

FIGURE 5-2

The file to which it refers is the MyDocument.h file in the folder of its enclosing group — the Classes group. If you examine the Classes source item, it also uses an enclosing group reference with an empty path, meaning that it simply refers to the folder of its enclosing group. Its enclosing group is the Simple project group, whose folder reference is *always* the project folder.

Mystery solved: Every source item reference in the project is relative to its enclosing group, so eventually all references refer (indirectly) to the project folder. The effect is stunningly simple. You can create, rename, and reorganize your project's source groups and items any way you want. No matter how you arrange them, each group eventually refers to the project folder, and all asset files get stored in that one folder.

This is a simple, flat, storage arrangement for the assets of your project; it doesn't require any maintenance and is extremely robust. You use source groups to organize your assets and eschew any attempt to organize the actual files. This project organization strategy is discussed later in the chapter, along with some alternatives.

SOURCE ITEM TYPES

A source item — the generic term for anything in the project group — will be one of the following four types:

SOURCE ITEM TYPE	REFERENCE
Source File	Any file used to build the project
Source Group	A folder that members of the group can refer to
Source Folder	A folder used to build the project
Framework	A folder containing a framework

A *source file* item is a reference to a data file. It can be a program source file, a header, an Interface Builder document, an XML file, an image file, or a font — it doesn't matter. Every source file item refers to exactly one file or package.

You've already spent some time working with *source groups*. They are the logical containers of the project. Each source group refers to a real folder on the filesystem. What the group contains (in the project structure group) is entirely up to you and may have little or no correspondence with the files in that folder. The folder to which it refers is of primary interest to subitems that use enclosing group references.

Two more source item types also refer to a folder but much more directly. A *source folder* item is very much like a source file item, but the folder to which it refers defines its content. The visual differences between a source group and source folder are slight, but their behavioral differences are profound.

Figure 5-3 shows two projects. In the one on the left, the Help item is a source *group* containing three items (`index.html`, `help.css`, and `background.png`). In the project on the right, the Help item is a source *folder* containing three files. Do they look the same? In a black-and-white illustration it's going to be hard to tell the difference. The source group (left) is yellow in the Xcode interface, whereas the source folder (right) is blue. Looking at the attributes of the two items, as shown in Figure 5-4, reveals that the item on the right is of type "folder."

FIGURE 5-3

FIGURE 5-4

The key difference is this:

> ➤ A source group is a logical container for other source items.

> ➤ A source folder *is* a source item.

To put it another way, a source group is a folder within your project, while a source folder is a folder in the filesystem. Although Xcode lets you browse the contents of both, a source folder is treated as a single source object. The contents of the folder are not treated as separate source items. This means that they can't be individually included in a target or otherwise referred to in the project, nor do they have attributes or references.

Source folders are not that common, but are handy when you have a prepopulated folder structure that you need to treat as a single entity in a target or build phase. Typical examples would be a folder of HTML help files or a precompiled database.

You can see this difference in the interface. Look again at Figure 5-2. A target membership attribute appears next to the source folder, but not next to any of its items; a source folder is a single object that can be a member of a target. The situation for the source group is reversed. A source group is never a member of a target; it's only a container for other source items, which have their own target membership attributes.

TIP TO REMEMBER

Like smart groups, the items in a source folder item dynamically reflect the contents of its folder. Add a file to the folder and it appears in the source folder item — well, sometimes. Xcode can be lazy about updating its display. Collapse and re-expand a folder item to see any changes made to the folder.

How you add a source folder item to your project isn't particularly obvious. It's described later in this chapter in the section "Adding Existing Items," under the subsection "Recursively Creating Groups and Creating Folder References."

Finally, a *framework* item is yet another kind of folder item. The only difference between a framework item and a folder item is that Xcode automatically recognizes framework folders and integrates them into the project. It indexes the headers of the framework, includes the framework symbols in auto-completion, and correctly links to the dynamic libraries in the framework. In the project, treat it as you would a single library to which your project links. Xcode takes care of the details.

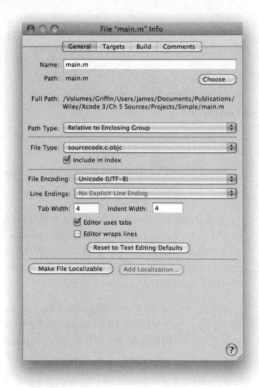

SOURCE ITEM ATTRIBUTES

You already know how to see the source item's attributes in its Info window, as shown in Figure 5-5. This section explains how to edit an item's reference. You can do this individually or for a group of items.

The Name field contains the name of the item. If the item can be renamed, this field is editable. The name of a file, folder, or framework item is always the same as the item's actual filename. Editing the name of a file, folder, or framework item *renames the actual file or folder*. A source group's name is independent of the folder it refers to, and renaming a source group merely renames it in the project document.

FIGURE 5-5

Setting an Item's Path

The Path and Path Type fields define the item's reference, and are what most of this chapter has been about so far. The Full Path field displays the ultimate (resolved) path to the file or folder. This is how

Xcode interprets the path using the given reference type. You can change the reference type using the pop-up menu. Xcode recalculates an equivalent path.

If you want to see the file or folder to which an item refers, Control/Right-click the source item in the project and choose Reveal in Finder.

To change the path, click the Choose button. Select a file or folder from the browser. For file, folder, and framework items, the name of the item changes to match that of the newly selected file or folder.

Selecting a new path for a source group also renames the source group to the name of the chosen folder. If you want the group to have a different name, edit it after choosing the folder.

Source Item Type and Encoding

The next section in the Info window is the item's type. This is an internal categorization based on the file's file type and extension so that Xcode knows how to treat the item. It is used to determine whether an item can be included in a target, and in what phase of the target the item should be. It determines how, or whether, Xcode will display the item in an editor window and what language and syntax coloring should be used.

You can change how Xcode treats an item by selecting a different type. Normally Xcode sets the type correctly, but on rare occasions you might need to change it if, say, Xcode identifies a file as being `text.xml` when it's actually `text.plist.xml`. The type attribute only affects Xcode's handling of the file. The operating system, external build systems, and compilers still interpret the file based on its type and extension. That is, changing the type of an `.m` file from `source.c.objc` to `source.c.cpp` will *not* cause the file to be compiled as a C++ file.

The File Encoding, Line Endings, and Tab attributes apply only to text files and are disabled for all other types. The File Encoding defines the expected binary format for the characters in the file. Change this setting if the assumption is wrong. The Line Endings attribute is also an assumption, but one that is largely superfluous; most Xcode editors determine what line endings are being used when the file is opened.

Changing the File Encoding for a text file presents the dialog box shown in Figure 5-6. The Convert button interprets the file using the previous encoding, and then rewrites the file using the new encoding. Use this option if the encoding of the file was correct and you want to change the format of the file to a different encoding. The Reinterpret button simply changes the encoding attribute in the source item, leaving the file unaltered. Select Reinterpret if the encoding attribute of the file was incorrect, and you're changing it to what it should be.

The Tab Width, Indent Width, and Editor Uses Tabs options (see Figure 5-5 again) are explained in the next chapter. Normally, you will want to use the same settings for all files, but you can change them for an individual file here, or by using the View ➪ Text ➪ Tab Settings command while editing the file. Click the Reset to Text Editing Defaults button to restore the file's settings to the defaults set in the editor preferences.

FIGURE 5-6

The Make File Localizable and Add Localization buttons are used to create multiple, locale-specific versions of a file. Many files can be localized so that language- and location-specific information in the file can be customized for different regions and populations. File localization is also covered in the next chapter.

Changing Attributes for Multiple Items

In Chapter 3, you learned how to use the Inspector palette or an Info window to display the aggregate attributes for multiple items. Settings that are common to all of the items are shown. If all of the items have the same value for a particular setting, that value is displayed. If a value differs for some items, the value displayed is some kind of Mixed value, as shown in Figure 5-7. For check boxes, this displays as a dash. Changing any of the settings in a multi-item Info window changes that setting for all of the items to the same value.

FIGURE 5-7

Some settings behave a little differently when they are changed for multiple items. This is particularly true of the Path attribute. You wouldn't want Xcode literally to set the same path attribute for multiple items; all of the items would suddenly point to the same file or folder! Instead, the Choose button in a multi-item Info window enables you to choose the folder that *contains* all of the items. The name of each item is not altered, and a new path for each is constructed by combining the chosen folder and the item's file or folder name. This is an efficient way of setting the location for any number of source files at once. Note that this can cause item references to be broken if the folder chosen does not contain one or more of the items.

You use this ability of Info windows later in this chapter to reorganize some large projects and fix the properties of targets.

ORGANIZING SOURCES

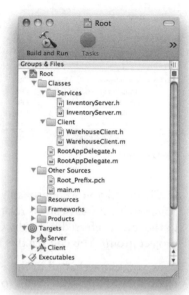

FIGURE 5-8

This section presents several strategies for organizing source items and references in a project. To illustrate how references can be configured, start with the very simple project pictured in Figure 5-8.

This project is, ostensibly, an Objective-C project for inventory management. It consists of four primary source files: main.m, RootAppDelegate.m, InventoryServer.m, and WarehouseClient.m. The three class files have matching header files, and there is a precompiled header file along with other Interface Builder documents and property lists in the Resources group.

This section reorganizes this project four different ways, using different types and combinations of references. All of these projects are available for download at http://www.wrox.com. Open the Root, Root2, Root3, Root4, and RootRot projects as you work through this section. These aren't functional projects, and make no attempt to be. They exist solely to demonstrate various source item reference strategies. As you work through these different schemes, keep the following in mind:

➤ Source *items* and *groups* are objects in the project. Source *files* and *folders* are the physical items in the filesystem.

➤ Every source item has a reference to its source file or folder.

➤ The name of a source group, and its location in the project structure group tree, can be completely independent of the name and location of the folder to which it refers. The name of all other types of source items is always the same as the file or folder to which it refers.

➤ The folder referred to by the topmost project structure group (also known as the project group) is always the project folder.

Default References

In Chapter 3, you created, renamed, and deleted source groups. You then moved groups around and moved source files into and out of groups. If you used what you've learned in Chapter 3 to create the example project shown in Figure 5-8, you would end up with a project folder that looks like Figure 5-9.

FIGURE 5-9

In Chapter 3 you were probably unaware that every group you created had a folder reference. The `InventoryServer.m` file is relative to the folder referred to by the Services group, which is relative to the folder referred to by the Classes group, which is relative to the folder referred to by the Root project group. You can see this by examining any source item's reference.

Now you know that all of these source items and groups use enclosing group references, which mean they all indirectly refer to the project folder. This is why all of the files are in the same folder (see Figure 5-9).

Whenever you create a new group using the File ➪ New Group command, Xcode creates a group with an empty path and an enclosing group reference. The net effect is a kind of "null" folder reference that always refers to the same folder as its parent group.

Thus, the default organization of Xcode projects places all of the source files directly in the project folder. You are free to reorganize the hierarchy of your source groups and items to any depth you want; the organization of the actual files will remain flat. For small- to medium-sized projects that are self-contained and have no duplicate filenames, this is the easiest organization. It is uncomplicated and shouldn't cause any surprises. Better yet, you don't have to worry about source group folder references. If your project falls into this category, feel free to skip ahead to the next section now and come back here when your projects get more complex.

However, if you want to control the physical organization of the files in your project, or your project source files are already organized into multiple folders, read on.

Sharing a Subfolder

Often, source files are already organized into a hierarchy of folders. They may have been organized this way in a former project, for source control, or by an obsessive programmer — we know who you are. The next few variations of the Root project present different techniques for grafting a source group structure onto an existing folder structure.

Figure 5-10 shows a reorganization of the source files by type. All of the programming source files in the Root2 project have been moved into a `Source` folder and the application bundle resource files have been moved into a `Resources` folder.

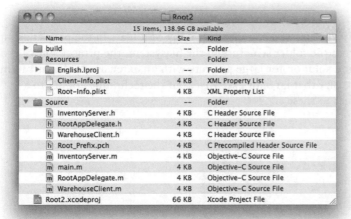

FIGURE 5-10

The folder references for the Classes, Other Source, and Resources groups were changed from enclosing group to project relative. The paths of the first two groups were both set to Source. The Resources group's path was set to Resources.

> **TIP TO REMEMBER**
>
> If you want to quickly browse the properties of several source items, open up the Inspector palette (Option+Command+I). The Inspector follows the current selection, so just click each source item to review its path and reference type.

This is a variation of the default references you looked at in Root. Instead of lumping everything together in the project folder, a few key folders are designated as gathering places for a broad collection of assets. The Source folder contains all of the program source files. In the project, the Classes, Services, Client, and Other Sources groups all refer to the same folder. This allows fine-grained organization within the project structure group, using a coarser folder structure.

This is a good organization for a medium-sized project whose files are grouped by type, where you just want to keep the main project folder uncluttered, or there is some other logical reason for subdividing the files. A good application of this approach would be for a project that produced multiple targets (that is, a client and a server). The project might have broad subfolders like Common, Client, and Server, whereas the project structure group would have more detailed groups, like Utilities, Network Services, Logging, Database, and so on.

By establishing a few key high-level groups anchored to a specific subfolder, then using default subgroups, you keep much of the flexibility of Xcode default source group arrangement, while imposing a modest amount of structure on the actual files.

Everything is Relative

Another approach is to mirror the structure of a complex hierarchy of folders in the project group. Rather than being disconnected from the folder structure in the filesystem, the project source groups mimic them verbatim. This is a good solution for large projects with an extensive folder hierarchy. The folder structure in Figure 5-11 isn't that large or extensive, but the technique applies to a hundred folders as easily as it applies to these six.

FIGURE 5-11

In this scheme, each source group uses its path to point to a specific subfolder within its enclosing group's folder. In earlier projects, all of the source groups using an enclosing group reference type have had empty paths — referring to the same folder as their parent group. These groups all have paths that refer to a subfolder of the enclosing group and have the same name as the folder to which they refer. The end result is a source group structure that parallels the folder structure in the filesystem.

In Figure 5-12, the Source group refers to the Source folder within the folder of its enclosing group. Its enclosing group (Server) refers to the Server folder within its enclosing group, which is the project folder.

FIGURE 5-12

A few of the source items in the Root3 project are listed in the following table to illustrate the relationships.

ITEM	REFERENCE TYPE	PATH	COMPLETE PATH
Root3	*Fixed*	*project*	.../Root3
Client	Enclosing-group	Client	.../Root3/Client
Resources	Enclosing-group	Resources	.../Root3/Client/Resources
Source	Enclosing-group	Source	.../Root3/Client/Source
Server	Enclosing-group	Server	.../Root3/Server
Resources	Enclosing-group	Resources	.../Root3/Server/Resources
Source	Enclosing-group	Source	.../Root3/Server/Source
Warehouse-Client.m	Enclosing-group	WarehouseClient.m	.../Root3/Client/Source/WarehouseClient.m
Root-Info.plist	Enclosing-group	Root-Info.plist	.../Root3/Server/Resources/Root-Info.plist
main.m	Enclosing-group	main.m	.../Root3/Server/Source/main.m

As you develop the project, it's pretty easy to maintain the relationship between the source groups and the filesystem folder structure. New and imported files are automatically added to the correct folder. If a folder is reorganized or renamed, making the same change to its source group keeps all enclosing references valid.

You might think that setting up all of these references would be tedious — especially for the imagined project containing hundreds of source files. Fear not. Xcode's import process, described a little later in this chapter, will create any number of nested source groups — exactly like those described here — with a single command.

Outside the Box

Conveniently, all of the references so far have been to folders inside the folder of the enclosing group or project, but this does not have to be the case. Figure 5-13 shows the project group and the files in project folder for Root4.

FIGURE 5-13

You'll notice that the project includes a Client group that contains two source files (WarehouseClient.h and WarehouseClient.m) that aren't in the project folder, so where do these files come from? The answer can be found in the Client group's properties, as shown in Figure 5-14.

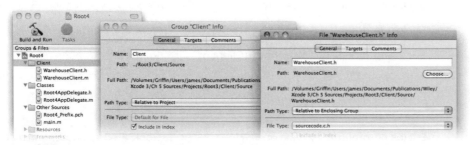

FIGURE 5-14

The Client group uses a project relative reference. Its POSIX path refers to a subfolder of Root4's sister project, Root3. The Root4 project has included files outside its project folder, just as if it owned them. Some selected source item references are listed in the following table.

ITEM	REFERENCE TYPE	PATH	COMPLETE PATH
Root4	*fixed*	*Project*	.../Root4
Client	Project-relative	../Root3/Client/Source	.../Root3/Client/Source
WarehouseClient.h	Enclosing-group	WarehouseClient.h	.../Root3/Client/Source/WarehouseClient.h
WarehouseClient.m	Enclosing-group	WarehouseClient.m	.../Root3/Client/Source/WarehouseClient.m
Root4AppDelegate.h	Enclosing-group	Root4AppDelegate.h	.../Root4/Root4AppDelegate.h

Although it's easier to create a single project with multiple targets, as you see in Chapter 16, this isn't always possible. If you must create multiple projects that need to share common assets, relative paths that refer to sister project folders is one way to share a single source file.

A popular use for this scheme is to set up "libraries" of source files (that is, a Utilities folder full of commonly used C functions or classes). Any number of projects can include selected files from the shared Utilities folder, without duplicating source files, or incurring the added complexity of creating a formal framework or dynamic library.

 A more robust solution to sharing folders amongst multiple projects is to use source trees. See Chapter 21 if you have this type of folder structure.

This technique can also be used to create "shell" projects. Suppose you have a large project written for Linux in an Eclipse project folder. You can create an Xcode project that uses source group paths that refer to the folders inside the Eclipse workspace folder. The Xcode project wouldn't have to contain anything beyond the project document and any project-specific files.

The disadvantage to this technique is that it creates a rather fragile project structure:

➤   If the first project's folder were renamed, the references in the second project would break.

➤   If either project were moved without the other, the references would break.

➤   If the folder structure of the first project were reorganized, the references in the second project would break.

Ideally, project folders are self-contained and autonomous. The only references they have to assets outside the project folder are to system frameworks that never change location. When the ideal isn't practical, you can use relative paths to include shared assets outside the project's folder.

Bad References

It's just as important to know what kind of references you should *not* create. I left this last project open overnight, and some mischievous pixies snuck in and decided they would have a little fun with it.

At first glance, the RootRot project looks pretty much like project Root3. All of the references are valid, and the project builds and runs — at least on my computer. Things can't be all bad, can they? The following table lists a few of the references in the project.

ITEM	REFERENCE TYPE	PATH	COMPLETE PATH
RootRot	*fixed*	*project*	.../RootRot
Client	Absolute	.../RootRot/Client	.../RootRot/Client
Source	Enclosing-group	Database	.../RootRot/Source/ Database
WarehouseClient.h	Enclosing-group	../Source/ WarehouseClient.h	.../RootRot/Client/Source/ WarehouseClient.h
main.m	Project-relative	Server/Source/main.m	.../RootRot/Server/Source/ main.m
Resources	Project-relative	../Root3/Server/Resources	.../Root3/Server/Resources
Root-Info.plist	Enclosing-group	Root-Info.plist	.../Root3/Server/Resources/ Root-Info.plist

Here's some of what's going on in the RootRot project:

➤ The Client source group uses an absolute path. If you copied this project to your system — or moved it anywhere other than where the project was originally created — the project won't build because Client won't refer to a valid folder, and all items that refer to Client's folder will be broken.

➤ The WarehouseClient.h item was moved from the Source group to the Resources group. Xcode conveniently "fixed" the path of the item so that it still refers to the WarehouseClient.h file that's in the sister directory to Resources. If the location or name of the Source folder ever changed, this reference would break.

➤ main.m uses a project relative path. If the location or name of either the Server or Source folder changed, the reference would break. On the other hand, this item could be moved anywhere in the project structure group and would still refer to the main.m file.

➤ The second Resources group has been changed to a project relative reference that refers to the Resources folder in the Root3 project. None of the references for its subitems (like Root-Info.plist) has been altered. Because they all use enclosing folder references, they all now refer to items in Root3's, not RootRot's, project folder. This could create a great deal of confusion.

Although Xcode provides you very flexible structures for organizing and referring to your project's assets, you can see that this flexibility can be abused. If you checked out a project like RootRot to a new directory, you'd probably end up spending more time trying to figure out what's wrong with the project than you would building it.

Best Practices

Here are some simple tips for keeping your project group functional and tidy:

- ➤ Use enclosing group references unless there's a compelling reason to use some other reference type.

- ➤ Avoid references to items outside your project folder.

- ➤ Use project relative references to point to top-level folders within the project folder that aren't likely to move, or to top-level folders outside the project that contain assets shared with other projects.

- ➤ When referring to assets included in an SDK or the Xcode tool, use the appropriate SDK or Xcode reference type.

- ➤ Never use absolute references for anything except system frameworks or other reasonably static assets, like a shared repository of development resources on a file server.

- ➤ Learn to use source trees (see chapter 21).

- ➤ If your asset is a product, or any part of a product, that's produced by a target, *always* use a product relative reference (or an enclosing folder reference that refers to a product relative reference).

CREATING NEW SOURCE FILES

In this section you learn how to add new files to a project. You've already created source groups. This section describes how to create new files and add them to your project. The next section shows you how to import existing files and folders into a project.

Unless your project is trivial, you will soon want to create new source files. The File ⇨ New File command creates a new source file based on a file template of your choosing, and adds that file as a source item to your project. The item is added to the currently selected group, or the group that contains the currently selected item. The first step to creating a new source file is to choose the location in the project where you want it added. Now choose File ⇨ New File (Command+N) or Right/Control+click a source item and choose Add ⇨ New File.

Figure 5-15 shows the New File Assistant where you choose a file template. Most templates are self-explanatory. Source file templates produce skeletal files with some basic comments and appropriate `#include` or `#import` statements. The C++ and Objective-C class file templates declare an empty class with the same name as the file.

FIGURE 5-15

Many templates have other options that can be selected before creating the file.
For example, the Objective-C template has an option to choose the base class for the new class.
The UIViewController class template will optionally produce a companion NIB document
containing the UIView for the new controller. Choose your desired options and click the Next
button. This presents the dialog box shown in Figure 5-16.

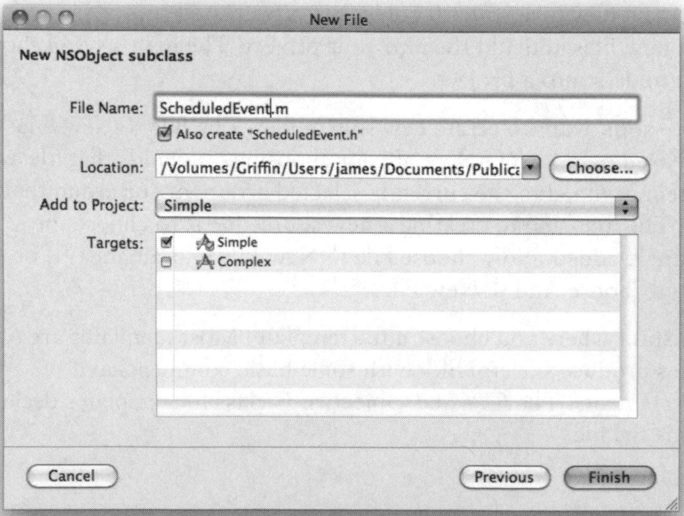

FIGURE 5-16

In the File Name field, edit the name of the file. Be careful not to alter the file's extension. If the template is for a source file type that normally has a companion header file (C, C++, and Objective-C templates), Xcode offers to create both files at the same time. Uncheck this option if, for some exceptional reason, you want Xcode to skip the creation of the companion header file.

The Location field displays the path to the folder where the new file will be created. This is always the folder referred to by the source group where the new item will be created. New file references are always relative to the enclosing group. Think twice before navigating to another folder, because Xcode will construct a relative path from the group's folder to the new file. Review the RootRot project again, if you need a reminder of why that's probably a bad idea.

If you do decide to change the location, enter the path or click the Choose button to select an existing folder. You can also create an arbitrary number of new folders at the same time by appending the paths of the nonexistent folders to the path. Before the new folders are created, a dialog appears that asks whether you really want to create them. Alternatively, you can use the New Folder button in the Choose browser to create any number of new folders before selecting the final one.

The Add to Project option (see Figure 5-16) selects the project to which the new source item will be added. The default is the active project, but you can choose another open project or "none." Selecting none creates the file, or files, but does not add any new source items to the project. That's one situation where changing the file's location field won't have unexpected consequences.

The Targets list shows all of the targets that accept the type of file being created. Only targets in the project selected in the Add to Project pop-up menu are considered; the list will be empty if the project is "none," or if no targets in the selected project accept the type of file being created.

Each target in the list has a check box next to it. If checked, the newly created source item is added to that target. If you are creating both a source file and its companion header file, checking a target adds both files to the target — unless the target only accepts one of the two types. This can actually be a hazard for targets that accept both types, because you often want to add the source file to a target but not the header. The "Ridding Targets of Unwanted Files" section has a trick for quickly getting unwanted headers out of a target.

Once the new file has a name, a location, a project, and a list of targets, click the Finish button to create the file and add its source item to the project. The new file opens automatically in an editor window.

If you try to create a file that already exists, Xcode warns you with the dialog box shown in Figure 5-17.

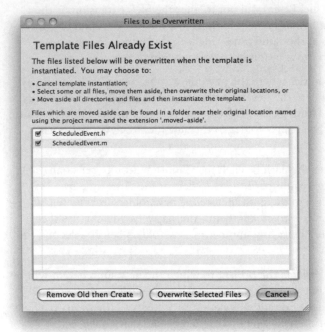

FIGURE 5-17

You have three choices, obtusely explained in the dialog box. The first choice, which is probably the best, is to cancel the operation.

Your second choice is to check the boxes next to the files you want to replace and click the Overwrite Selected Files button. Despite the fact that the button says "Overwrite," the checked files are not overwritten. They are first moved to a new subfolder named with a numeric suffix and the extension .moved-aside, as shown in Figure 5-18. The folder will be in the same folder where the new files are being created.

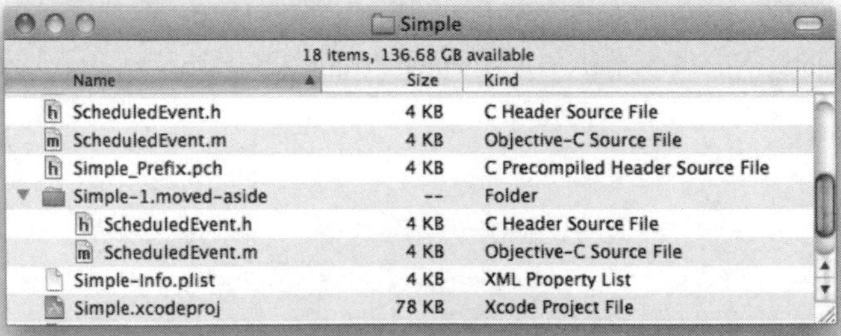

FIGURE 5-18

The third choice is to click the Remove Old Then Create button. The action of this button is equivalent to first checking all of the files listed and clicking the Overwrite Selected Files button. When the dialog box is first presented, all of the files are checked, making the action of the two buttons identical.

After the files are moved aside, new files are created in the same location from the template. If there were already source items for these files, you now have duplicate source items. Make note of the new source items (which will be selected) and remove the duplicates.

The files that were moved aside are no longer referred to from the project. You can examine the files, recover what you want, and then trash them along with the spontaneously generated folder that contains them.

CREATING AN EMPTY FILE

The File ⇨ New File command performs several common steps and can be a great time saver, but sometimes you just want an empty file that doesn't have a name, isn't based on a template, isn't added to a project, and isn't included in one or more targets. The File ⇨ New Empty File command (Command+Control+N) does exactly that. In fact, the New Empty File command is very similar to the New command found in most text editor applications. It opens an empty, untitled, editor window. The content of the new window is not associated with a file until it is saved.

The first time it is saved, Xcode kindly offers to add the new file to the active project. You can accept or decline. If you accept, you are presented with the same options you're given when you add any existing source file to a project. These options are explained fully in the next section.

ADDING EXISTING ITEMS

You won't create every file in your project from scratch. There will be many occasions when you have an existing file or document that you want to add to your project — and you certainly don't write the frameworks you link to.

At some point, you are going to need to add existing files, folders, and frameworks to your project. Essentially, you select the filesystem items you want to add and Xcode creates new source items in your project group that refer to those items. Once the references are created, those files become assets of your project.

Selecting the Items to Add

You have basically two ways of selecting the items to add to your project: start in Xcode or start in the Finder.

The first is to use Xcode's Project ⇨ Add to Project command (Option+Command+A). Just as you did when creating new files, begin by selecting the source group that will contain the new source items, or an existing source item within that group, and then choose the Add to Project command from the Project menu. You can also Right/Control+click a source item and choose Add ⇨ Existing

Files. Xcode presents an open file dialog box to select the file, files, or folders to be added. This is a multi-selection dialog box; use the Command or Shift key while clicking items to select more than one file or folder. Xcode creates a new item reference for every item you select in the dialog box. Figure 5-19 shows two new source files being added to a project. Note that items already referred to in the project are disabled (grey) and can't be added again.

FIGURE 5-19

The second method is more direct. Select any group of items in the Finder (or any application that lets you drag files) and drag them into the source group of your project. A drop indicator shows you where in the source group the new item, or items, will be created — exactly as it does when you're dragging items around in the tree.

The only significant disadvantage of the drag-and-drop method is that Xcode permits you to create duplicate items to files that are already referred to in the project.

 One quirk to be aware of when using the drag-and-drop technique, at least when dragging from the Finder, is that symbolic links and aliases are not resolved. The source item created will refer to the alias, not to the file or folder to which the alias resolves.

As soon as Xcode knows where to create the new source items in the project and what files will be used to create those items, it presents the dialog box shown in Figure 5-20.

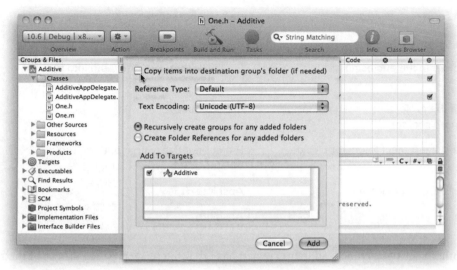

FIGURE 5-20

This dialog box contains several controls that determine what kind of source items are created, the type of references they will have, and where the final source files will reside. The effect of these options is often interconnected; some options behave differently depending on the choices you make for other options.

Copying Items into the Destination Group's Folder

Check the Copy Items into Destination Group's Folder (If Needed) option to make physical copies of the original files or folders inside the group's folder. The group's folder is the folder referred to by the group to which the new source items are being added. If you select this option, all of the files and folders being added are first copied into the group's folder. Each source item created refers to the copy made in the group's folder, not the original. Note that items contained inside a subfolder of the group's folder are *not* considered to be in the group's folder. Files or folders in any other folder on the filesystem are copied; if you've selected files already in your project this will create duplicate source files. Use this option only to import sources from locations outside of the project folder.

The "(If Needed)" qualifier is there because this option is ignored if the files are already in the enclosing group's folder. Well, not entirely ignored. Due to a long-standing bug in Xcode, this works with files but not folders. If you check this option when you're adding a folder to a group whose folder already contains that folder, Xcode displays an error that it can't copy the folder to itself. No harm will come of this, but you will have to perform the operation again, this time turning the Copy option off.

Reference Type

The Reference Type option controls what type of reference each new source item will have. The choice you make applies to all items being added. Choosing the special reference type of Default individually selects a reference type best suited for each item's location, as listed in the following table.

LOCATION OF EXISTING FILE OR FOLDER	DEFAULT REFERENCE TYPE
In the enclosing group's folder	Enclosing-group
Inside any subfolder in the enclosing group's folder	Enclosing-group, with a path into the subfolders
Anywhere inside the project folder but not inside the enclosing group's folder	Project-relative
Anywhere outside the project folder, but inside /Users	Project-relative, with a path that refers outside of the project folder
Anywhere outside the /Users folder	Absolute
Another volume	Absolute

If you select any other type of reference, all items created have that reference type regardless of their location.

Text Encoding

The Text Encoding option applies only to source items created for text files. It sets the text encoding for the file, which determines how the bytes in the file are translated into characters when the file is opened for editing. Normally, you wouldn't need to change this for regular program source files. The gcc compiler always assumes plain ASCII text, so all program source files must be ASCII text files. Change this option if you are adding things like XML files that are in UTF-8 or UTF-16 encoded Unicode, or text files in any other ISO encoding. You can always change the encoding later if you need to. See the "Source Item Attributes" section earlier in this chapter on how to change the encoding of a file.

Recursively Creating Groups and Creating Folder References

The two radio buttons, Recursively Create Groups for Any Added Folder and Create Folder References for Any Added Folders, determine whether folders added to the project will create source groups or folder items.

With the Recursively Create Groups radio button selected, adding a folder creates a source group. After that, every file and folder in that folder is recursively added to the new group using the same settings. The folder reference of the new group points to the folder that was added, using the reference type selected. The recursively added items get the same treatment.

If the reference type is Default — all of the recursively added items will (by definition) have enclosing-group references regardless of the reference type or location of the first new group. Does that organization sound familiar? Look again at the Root3 project. Each source group refers to a single subfolder in the folder of its enclosing group, and every source item refers to a file in the folder of its enclosing group. When you use these Add to Project settings, Xcode turns an entire folder hierarchy into an equivalent tree of source groups and source items with a single command.

If, instead, you choose Create Folder References for Any Added Folders, Xcode does not recursively process the contents of the folders being added. Instead, it creates a single source folder item as described in the "Source Item Types" section earlier in this chapter. Adding an existing folder and choosing this option is the only way of creating a source folder item.

Adding the New Items to Targets

At the bottom of the dialog box is a list of targets defined in the project. If you check the box next to a target, Xcode attempts to add each source item created to that target. The key word is "attempts." Some targets only accept, or understand, certain types of source items. An item is added to a target only if the target accepts that type of item.

When everything is set, click the Add button to add the items to the project.

Adding a Framework

Xcode has a special interface just for adding frameworks. Right/Control+click the source group where you want the framework added and choose the Add ⇨ Existing Framework command. A framework picker dialog box appears, like the one in Figure 5-21.

Xcode assembles a list of all known frameworks and libraries. Choose one or more from the list and click Add. If you're having trouble finding what you're looking for, the pop-up menu at the top will narrow the list to a specific class of library or framework.

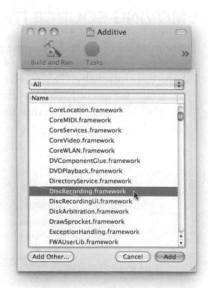

To add a framework that isn't one of the standards, use the Project ⇨ Add to Project command, exactly as you did in the previous section, and select the framework folder. Make sure the Copy Items into Destination Group's Folder option is *not* checked. Xcode will recognize that you're adding a framework and create the correct framework source item.

FIGURE 5-21

Adding an Open File

Xcode can open an arbitrary file into an editor window. The file does not have to belong to a project. You can add the file of any open editor window to the current project by selecting the Project ⇨ Add Current File to Project command. A dialog box presents the same set of options that the Project ⇨ Add to Project command does.

Ridding Targets of Unwanted Files

It is very easy, when you're adding lots of new source files to a project, to end up with files in targets where they don't belong. This most often happens when you're adding source and header files at the same time. Targets that compile C source into object files (native targets) normally only accept C, C++, or Objective-C source files. Trying to add the companion header files to those targets at the same time does nothing, but some native targets have a Copy Files phase that accepts any kind of file. The end result is that all of the .h files get added to the target's Copy Files phase, and the target dutifully copies all of the headers files in your project into the final application. This is probably not what you want.

To fix this, select the project structure group in the Groups & Files list to display all of the files in the project in the details window (choose View ➪ Details if you are using the Condensed layout style). In the details list, click the icon (file type) column to sort the items by type. Click the first header file in the list, then scroll down and Shift-click the last one to select all of the header files in the project. Now choose File ➪ Get Info to get an aggregate Info window for all of the header file items. Switch to the Targets tab and uncheck all of the targets. This removes all of the header files from all of the targets in your project.

You can adapt this technique to make similar changes in other types of files.

REMOVING SOURCE ITEMS

Removing source items from your project is just about as easy as you would imagine it would be. Select one or more source items and press the Delete key, choose Edit ➪ Delete, or Right/Control+click ➪ Delete. Xcode presents a dialog box, as shown in Figure 5-22. The Delete References button only removes the source item (reference) from your project structure group. The Also Move to Trash button removes the source item *and* moves the file(s) it refers to the system Trash folder.

FIGURE 5-22

REORGANIZING SOURCES

This section walks you through reorganizing the files in a project. This usually entails rearranging the actual files and then altering the source item references to agree.

When you're working with source item references, it's useful to know when an item's reference is valid and when it's broken. Whenever Xcode discovers that a reference no longer refers to a file or folder, the item in the source group turns red. Figure 5-23 shows invalid references for the Two.h, Two.m, and main.cpp items.

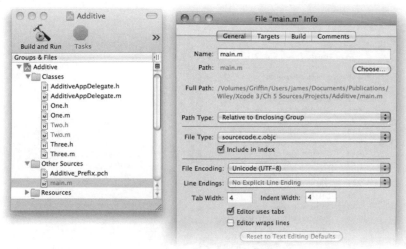

FIGURE 5-23

Again, this is hard to see in black-and-white. Red items are usually a clue that the item's reference needs to be fixed — but not always. Whenever you create a new project or target, a source item is created for the product that *will* be produced. Until you successfully build the target, its product doesn't exist and its product item in the source tree will be red. This is perfectly normal and expected.

You can fix a reference in two ways: open the Info window for the item and correct its Path attribute, or put the file or folder the item is pointing to where the reference expects it to be. Xcode immediately recognizes that the reference is valid again, and changes the item's color back to black.

The next three sections present typical project item reorganization chores, and the steps you need to follow to keep your source item references valid.

Moving Files

The ReorganizeMe1 project, shown in Figure 5-24, has two subfolders: Main and Flipside. You decide that the SpinningWidget class files need to be moved from the Main group to the Flipside group.

FIGURE 5-24

To relocate the two files, follow these steps:

1. Open the ReorganizeMe1 project.

2. Drag the `SpinningWidget.h` and `SpinningWidget.m` items from the Main group into the Flipside group.

3. Control/Right-click the Main source group and choose Reveal in Finder.

4. In the Finder window, move the two source files, `SpinningWidget.h` and `SpinningWidget.m`, from the `Main` folder into the `Flipside` folder.

5. Switch back to the project window. Notice that the two source items are now red. Select *both* items and choose File ⇨ Get Info.

6. In the multi-item Info window, click the Choose button. Select the `Flipside` folder and click Choose. The item references are now valid again.

Whenever you move a source item, Xcode adjusts the path (never the reference type) of the item so it continues to refer to the same file or folder. This is convenient in one sense, because it allows you to reorganize your source items freely without breaking any references. The disadvantage is that it permits you to create convoluted item references with relative paths through parent folders and an organization that no longer reflects the organization of the physical files.

All of the items in this exercise use enclosing-group references. When you moved the two source file items from one group to the other in step 2, Xcode recalculated new paths starting from the new group back to the old one's folder. If you had stopped and looked at the attributes of the two items after step 2, their paths would have been `../Main/SpinningWidget.h` and `../Main/SpinningWidget.m`. This also explains why the two items were still valid after the move.

In step 4, you moved the actual files. As a result, the files were no longer in the `Main` folder and the source item references broke. When you switched back to the project window, Xcode displayed the two items in red.

In steps 5 and 6, you examined the attributes of the two items in a multi-item Info window and used it to point both items to their respective files in the Flipside folder. Remember that when you select a new path for *multiple items*, you're selecting the *parent folder* for every individual item — you're not setting every item to the same path. The path for each was recalculated using a relative path to the Flipside folder (which is nothing, because the enclosing group's folder is the Flipside folder) and their respective filenames. The references are once again valid.

Rearranging Folders

Now you are going to relocate entire folders. This demonstrates the principle advantage of using enclosing-group references in your project.

ReorganizeMe2 has a Source folder that contains two subfolders: Product and Order. The project is about to grow into a client and server. The source files for the client and server are to be kept apart, and the common code moved into a shared tree. Follow these steps:

1. Open the ReorganizeMe2 project.

2. Select the Order group. Control/Right-click the Order group and choose Reveal in Finder. In the Finder window, create three new folders inside the Source folder: Common, Client, and Server. Drag the Product and Order folders into the Common folder.

3. Switch back to the project window. Select the Product and Order groups and choose Project ⇨ Group to enclose them in a new group. Name the group Common. Use the File ⇨ New Group command to create new groups named Client and Server in the Source group.

4. Select the Common group. Control/Right-click the Common group and choose Get Info. In the Info window, click the Choose button and select the Common folder in the project. Click Choose to change the path.

5. Repeat step 4 for the Client and Server groups, choosing the Client and Server folders, respectively.

The Order and Product source groups refer to the Order and Product subfolders in their enclosing group's folder. Moving the Order and Product folders into the newly created Common folder broke the references to those folders, and all the references of the items they contained.

In step 3, the new groups Common, Client, and Server were created with enclosing group references that referred to the folder in the source group (remember that this is the default for all newly created source groups). Although the Order and Product groups are now enclosed in the Common group, they still indirectly refer to the same location and are still broken.

In step 4, you changed the Common group's folder from the Source folder to the new Common subfolder. As soon as that happened, the references in the Order and Product folders were valid again.

Step 5 simply prepared the other two groups, Client and Server, so they reference files in their respective folders.

When you're using enclosing-group references, it is usually easier to rearrange folders than it is to move individual files around. Xcode only adjusts the path of the group being moved. Items within that group are not adjusted and continue to have the same relative relationship to their enclosing group. After the parent group references are fixed, all of the child references are valid again.

Reorganizing by Re-adding

You can see how using the multi-item Info window and relative references can save a lot of time when changing references for large trees of groups and files. If you're moving just a few folders around, that's probably the best way, but even this can be a fair amount of work if you're making a lot of changes at once.

Another technique is simply to throw the whole thing away and let Xcode rebuild all of the relationships from scratch. Start with the ReorganizeMe3 project. All of the items in this project have enclosing-group references.

ReorganizeMe3 has several subfolders: Database, Product, Order, ShoppingCart, and Utilities. Create three new folders in the Source folder: Common, Client, and Server. Move the Database folder into the Server folder. Move the ShoppingCart folder into the Client folder. Move the Product, Order, and Utilities folders into the Common folder. The file structure should now look like Figure 5-25.

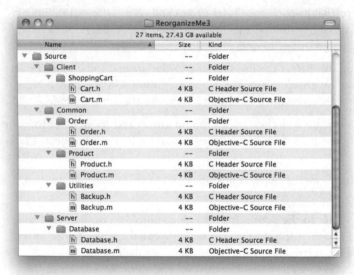

FIGURE 5-25

Now follow these steps:

1. Open the ReorganizeMe3 project.

2. Select the Source group. Control/Right-click the Source group and choose Delete. In the dialog box, click Delete References.

3. Select the Project Structure group. Choose Project ➭ Add to Project. Select the Source folder and click the Add button.

4. In the Add to Project dialog box, uncheck the Copy option, set Reference Type to Default, and select Recursively Create Groups for Any Added Folders. Click the Add button.

Remember that the project document doesn't contain any of the source material for your project; just references to those files. In step 2, you deleted all of the references to the source files in this project — but just the references; the original source files are still in the project folder.

In steps 2 and 3, you used the Add to Project command to re-create new groups and source file items that match the reorganized folder hierarchy exactly.

If you have major asset reorganization to do, the fastest and easiest way to rectify your groups and source items might be simply to start over. This might inadvertently include other files, or place files in targets that don't belong there, but these aberrations can usually be dealt with swiftly.

 Why you would not want to let Xcode rebuild all the groups and items? Deleting the source items also deletes any other attributes associated with those items. File encoding, custom tab settings, specific target membership, comments, and build options are lost when the source items are deleted. The newly created source items will all have default attributes. If you need to preserve attributes for a large number of source items, you probably have no choice but to reorganize the groups and folders "the hard way," using one of the first two techniques.

SUMMARY

You should now have a clear understanding of how Xcode refers to source files in a project. As you work with Xcode, keep these key concepts in mind:

➤ Every source item has a path to the file or folder to which it refers.

➤ A path can be absolute, relative to the project folder, or relative to the folder of the enclosing group.

➤ File, folder, and framework items have the same names as the source files or folders to which they refer. Renaming the source item renames the physical file or folder. In contrast, the name of a source group is independent of the folder to which it refers.

➤ The path and reference type of an item can be changed in an Info window. A multi-item Info window can change the location or reference type for several items at once.

➤ Moving an item in the source tree adjusts its path so that it continues to refer to the same file or folder.

Now that you can add new and existing source files to your project, you will undoubtedly want to edit them. Editing text is the topic of the next chapter.

Editing Text

WHAT'S IN THIS CHAPTER?

- ➤ Understanding editing windows and panes
- ➤ Navigating text and jumping between files efficiently
- ➤ Editing and reformatting text
- ➤ Using syntax-aware display and completion features
- ➤ Editing other types of files (Rich Text Format, property lists)

In the introduction, I mentioned that Xcode doesn't really do much of the actual development work. Most of the heavy lifting is performed by external tools — compilers, linkers, debuggers, and others — that are not part of the Xcode application, but Xcode does provide one critical tool that is integral to every developer's workflow: the text editor. You will spend far more time editing source files than doing almost any other single task. Learning how to edit efficiently and navigate your source files quickly will greatly enrich your productivity.

If you've spent any time at all using Mac OS X, you're familiar with the basic text editing concepts and commands. This chapter explores the powerful, and some obscure, extensions that Xcode adds to the core text editing facilities. It shows you a variety of techniques and shortcuts for navigating, editing, and reformatting text. Xcode also supplies a rich set of language-aware code formatting, coloring, and auto-completion features that make writing source code much more productive. Finally, this chapter touches on a number of ancillary topics like file encoding, localization, the spelling checker, and printing.

Xcode has, what seems like, a thousand features to aid your development, but this also means that there are a thousand features to learn — some of which are rather obscure. The more you learn about the ins and outs of the text editor, the more productive you'll be, but you can't learn them all in one sitting. Here's how I suggest you approach this chapter:

➤ Skim this and the next chapter to get a general idea of what the Xcode editor has to offer.

➤ Learn to use:

  ➤ The Functions menu (see "Jumping to Functions, Breakpoints, and Bookmarks")

  ➤ The Jump to Definition and Documentation shortcuts (see the "Most Productive Shortcuts" sidebar)

  ➤ The Jump to Counterpart command (Option+Command+up arrow)

  ➤ The code completion feature (see "Code Completion" in Chapter 7)

➤ Once you become comfortable with those, return to this chapter to explore more advanced features.

WINDOWS AND PANES

Editing in Xcode occurs in an editor pane. An editor pane can be part of a multi-pane window, like the project window in the Default style, or it can be the sole content of a separate editor window. Figure 6-1 shows a file being edited in three panes: once in the project window, again in the editor pane of the project find window, and again in an independent editor window.

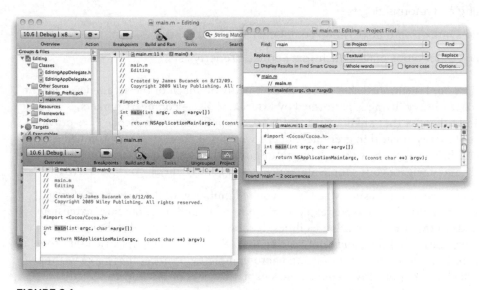

FIGURE 6-1

Editing Panes

Xcode editing panes are homogeneous. The features, functions, and capabilities are identical regardless of where they appear. This imparts one extremely useful feature: No matter where a source file appears in Xcode, you have the full power of the Xcode editor at your disposal.

The text of a file that appears in a search window, the debugger, or the object browser can all be edited immediately without any need to locate the file or open another window. The same file can appear in multiple editing panes at once. Changes made to one are reflected in all.

Opening a File in a Separate Window

To edit a file in a separate editor window, double-click the source file item in the project window. If the file already appears in an editing pane of another window, you can force it to open in a new window by choosing the Open in Separate Editor command. This command can be accessed from the File menu by holding down the Option key (Option+Command+O) or by Right/Control+clicking a source file in the project group. Selecting this command while an edit pane is active opens another window containing the same file.

Editor Panes in Multi-Pane Windows

The editor pane of a multi-pane window usually tracks some other selection in the window. For example, selecting a class in the class browser displays the source of the class's header in its editor pane. Clicking a line found in the Project Find window displays the file where the line was found in that window's editor pane, and so on.

The Project Window's Editor Pane

The editor pane of the project window is no exception, but the behavior is a little more complex. When you're using the Default and All-In-One Xcode styles, the project source list shares a window with the details list and an editor pane. Figure 6-2 shows all three panes visible at once.

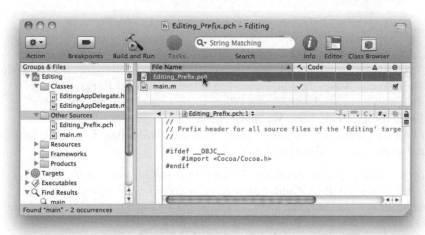

FIGURE 6-2

Selecting a single file in either the Groups & Files list or the details list immediately brings the contents of that file into the editor pane — that is, if the editor pane is visible. As you saw in Chapter 3, the details list and the editor pane share the same area in the project window. You can adjust the division between the two by using the divider bar, the View ➪ Zoom Editor In/Out command, or the Editor button in the toolbar.

 The Editor toolbar button is shown in Figure 6-2, but is not part of the default project window toolbar. Choose View ➪ Customize Toolbar to add an Editor button to your toolbar.

All three configurations of the details list and editor pane are shown in Figure 6-3. On the left, only the details list is visible. On the right, only the editor pane is visible. In the center, both share the same area. The divider between them can be dragged to the top to fill the area with the editor pane, to the bottom to hide it, or anywhere in between. Double-clicking the divider alternately collapses the editor pane so it is completely hidden, or restores it to its previous location — which could be at the top, completely hiding the details list.

FIGURE 6-3

The View ➪ Zoom Editor In/Out command (Command+Shift+E) is the complement to double-clicking the divider bar. Instead of alternately collapsing and restoring the details pane, it alternately expands or restores the editor pane. When the editor pane is hidden or shares the area with the detail window (left and center in Figure 6-3), the Zoom Editor In command expands the editor pane so that the details list is completely hidden. When the editor pane is expanded, the command changes to Zoom Editor Out and restores the previous position of the divider bar. The Editor button in the toolbar is equivalent to the Zoom Editor In/Out command in the menu.

Holding down the Option key turns the command into Zoom Editor In/Out Fully. When used in a multi-pane window like the project window, Zoom Editor In Fully collapses all other panes. This would be equivalent to expanding the editor, and then collapsing the Groups & Files list so only the editor pane is visible. Zoom Editor Out Fully runs the editor pane back down and re-expands the Groups & Files list. Using the All-In-One window style, this is a quick way of pushing everything else aside in order to see the code, and may be more convenient than opening the file in a separate window.

Normally, the division between the details list and the editor pane stays put until you change it. When the editor pane is collapsed, this requires two commands to edit the contents of a file. You must first select the file in a list, and then resize the divider or use the Zoom Editor In command before the editor pane is visible. If you find yourself doing this often, enable the Automatically Open/Close Attached Editor option in the General pane of the Xcode Preferences. Checking this option causes the editor pane to expand automatically whenever a single source file is selected in the Groups & Files or details list.

Using a Group Editor Window

Xcode, like most document-based applications, creates a new window for every file you open in a separate window. If that statement sounds ridiculously obvious, bear with me. It can, however, restrict all files to a *single* separate editing window. This mode is accessible only through the toolbar Grouped/Ungrouped control, shown in Figure 6-4.

FIGURE 6-4

If the control shows as Ungrouped, opening a new file in a separate editor creates a new window. There is no practical limit on the number of separate editor windows you can have open at a time. Clicking the button toggles the mode and establishes that window as the "group" editing window. In this mode, opening a file simply changes the file being displayed in the active pane of the group editor window; no new windows are created. This mode can be used to avoid window clutter. The setting of this mode does not affect any other windows that have already been created, and only one window can be designated as the group editor window at a time.

Opening Files from the Filesystem

Xcode also lets you open files in the traditional manner by picking a file in the filesystem. It will also respond to open document requests from the Finder or any other application. Xcode understands the formats of many file types that it doesn't "own." You can cause Xcode to open a file that would normally launch another application by dropping the file into Xcode's icon in the dock, as shown in Figure 6-5.

FIGURE 6-5

Opening an editable file using the traditional File ⇨ Open command (Command+O) opens the file into the editor pane of the project window or a new editor window — which one you get is somewhat difficult to determine in advance. If Xcode has a project window open, Xcode may open the file in the editor pane of the project window. Otherwise, the file is opened in a new editor window. Opening any file that is already displayed in an Xcode window brings that window to the front. Although you can select multiple files in the open dialog box, the side effect of some display rules, like the Grouped mode, can result in only one of the selected files being displayed in an editor pane.

Open Quickly by Filename or Symbol

An extremely useful command for finding and opening a file is the File ⇨ Open Quickly (Command+Shift+D) command. Enter all or the beginning of any filename or symbol into the Open Quickly dialog box field, as shown in Figure 6-6. Xcode locates all of the files with that name or that define that symbol. This includes all of the files in your project and all of the frameworks to which your project links. Double-click the file (or select it and press Return) in the list to open it.

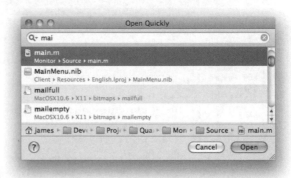

FIGURE 6-6

 If you have text selected in the editor when you invoke the Open Quickly command, it's used as the default search. This makes it really easy to open a header file (select the #include *filename, then press Command+Shift+D) or find the file that defines almost any symbol.*

Closing and Saving Editor Panes

Close any window using the File ⇨ Close (Command+W) command, or click the close button in the window's title bar. File ⇨ Close Project (Command+Control+W) closes the current project and all windows that belong to that project. The File ⇨ Close File "*filename*" command (Command+Shift+W) closes all windows currently editing the named file.

TIP TO REMEMBER

Hold down the Option key and click the close button of an independent editor window, or choose File ⇨ Close All. This closes it and all other editor windows for that project, but not the project or any other type of window. This is really useful when you've been editing for a while and have dozens of editor windows piled up on the screen.

Because Xcode enables you to edit a source file in multiple windows simultaneously, there isn't a one-to-one correspondence between a window and a file. Unless you use the Close File *"filename"* command, closing a window does not necessarily force you to save the changes made to that file. Even closing all of the visible panes where a file was being edited might not force the changes to be written. The changes are held in memory until committed in response to another command. Files that have been modified but not yet saved appear grey in the project window. In Figure 6-7, the PromiseListViewController.h, PromiseListViewController.m, and DueDatePicker.h files have been edited but not saved.

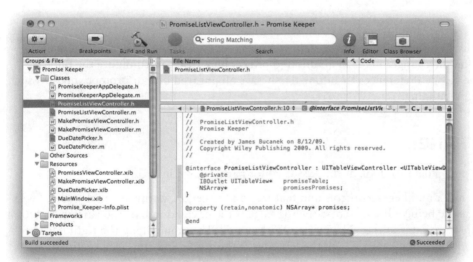

FIGURE 6-7

The File ⇨ Save (Command+S) command immediately writes the changes made in the active editor pane to the file. The File ⇨ Save All (Option+Command+S) command presents a dialog box, like the one in Figure 6-8, that lists all of the unsaved files. Select the files to save and click the Save All/Selected button.

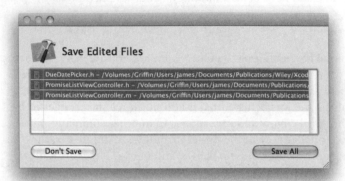

FIGURE 6-8

Some actions cause the Save All window to appear automatically. Closing a project forces you to save or abandon the changes made in all unsaved project files. You can configure the Build commands in the Xcode Preferences to automatically save all unsaved files or prompt you for which ones to save before building.

THE EDITOR PANE

It's now time to take a detailed look at the Xcode editor pane, shown in Figure 6-9.

The editor pane has a number of controls and features. In the center, naturally, is the editor with the content of the file being edited. Across the top edge is the navigation bar, the various functions of which are explained later in the "Navigating Within a File" section. Along the right edge are the scrollbars and split pane controls. On the left edge is the gutter and ribbon, explained later in the "Gutter" section. The line running down the right side of the main editing region is the page guide. Depending on your display preferences and the kind of file being edited, some of these features may not be visible. See the "Display Options" section to find out how to enable or disable them.

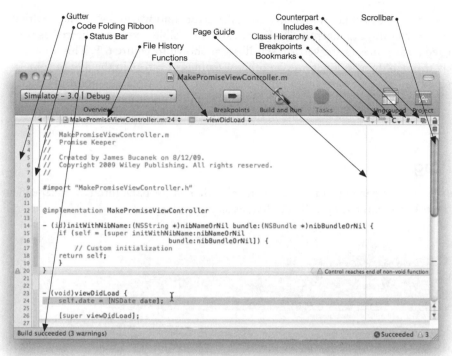

FIGURE 6-9

The active pane always has a blinking text cursor or a shaded text selection.

You might get the idea that the text insertion cursor and the current text selection mentioned throughout this book are separate concepts. In reality, they are usually equivalent. The blinking text cursor is logically a text selection of zero characters. Both indicate the current location in the file. At times the behavior of a command is different when the selection is empty (when the text cursor is visible), but unless stated explicitly to the contrary, if you read one assume it applies equally to the other.

Scrollbars

The scrollbar controls are standard and shouldn't surprise anyone who has used a modern graphical user interface. Xcode enhances their basic behavior with a few extras.

Holding down the Option key when you click the arrow buttons scrolls the window slightly less than one screen's worth of text.

The editor is scroll-wheel aware, although a scroll-wheel is not an Xcode-specific feature. If your mouse, trackball, or trackpad has a scroll-wheel, the active editor pane will respond to it. I personally consider a multi-button trackball with a scroll-wheel an indispensable development tool.

The gutter, described in more detail later, indicates compiler errors and warnings for the text that is visible in the window. Warnings and errors above or below the visible text are indicated as thin black (warning) or red (error) lines in the vertical scrollbar, as shown in Figure 6-9. This allows you to scroll quickly through the window to reveal other warnings or errors in the file. In your System Preferences, the Appearance pane has a Jump to the Spot That's Clicked option. If selected, clicking in the empty part of the scrollbar jumps immediately to that point in the file. Though this is a system-wide preference change, it makes jumping to relative locations in source files particularly convenient.

Split-Pane Editing

Above the scrollbar is the split pane button. Clicking it splits that editor pane into two independent panes, one above the other, separated by a divider bar, as shown in Figure 6-10.

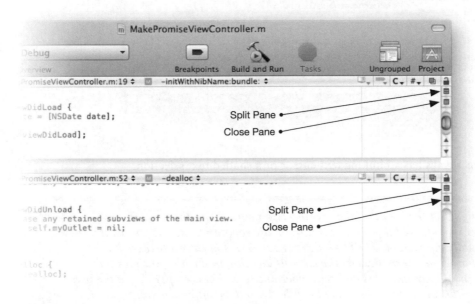

FIGURE 6-10

You can achieve the same effect using the View ⇨ Split *filename* Vertically command (Command+Shift+"), which splits the pane with the active text selection or cursor. Each new pane contains a split pane and a close pane button. The split pane button splits the pane again. The close pane button closes that pane; the adjacent pane assumes its space.

Holding down the Option key splits the pane horizontally, as shown in Figure 6-11. Choosing to split a pane horizontally or vertically only works for the first pane. After a pane is split horizontally, all subsequent splits are horizontal regardless of whether you select a horizontal or vertical split. The same is true for vertical splits. (This is considered a bug by the Xcode development team and may be fixed in a future version.)

FIGURE 6-11

Unlike the pane divider between the editor pane and the details list, the divider between editing panes does not respond to a double-click. However, it is possible to drag the divider all the way to one edge if you want to hide a pane from view. Drag it back out to the middle again, or close the visible pane, to reveal the hidden pane.

The panes that result from a split are truly independent editing environments. The "Jumping to Other Files" section explains how to switch from one file to another in the same pane. You can do this with split panes, which allows you to edit two or more different files in a single editor window — very handy for editing a code file and its header in the same window. Notice back in Figure 6-11 that the right pane is displaying the MakePromiseViewController.m file and the left pane is editing its companion .h file.

Gutter

The gutter is the shaded bar running down the left edge of the editor pane. If it is not visible, enable it by selecting Show Gutter in the Text Editing pane of the Xcode Preferences. The gutter, shown in Figure 6-12, can display a variety of annotations.

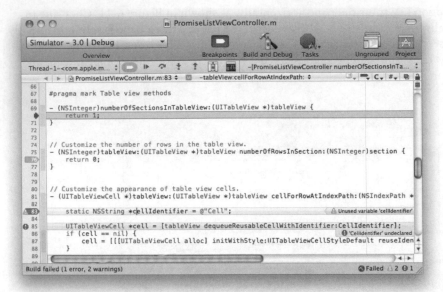

FIGURE 6-12

The gutter displays errors or warnings for a particular line, breakpoints, the current execution location of the debugger, and (optionally) line numbers. The display of line numbers is set in the Xcode Preferences. Warnings and errors are indicated by the yellow caution and red stop-sign symbols. Breakpoints show up as wide blue tabs. Active breakpoints are dark blue. Inactive ones are light grey. A large red arrow indicates where program execution is currently paused in the debugger.

Clicking an error or warning icon in the gutter toggles its description in the text, enabling you to hide error descriptions selectively — which can be a bit distracting if you're trying to fix the problem.

Clicking a breakpoint alternately enables or disables the breakpoint. You can set new breakpoints by clicking anywhere in the background of the gutter. Breakpoints can only be set in file types that Xcode recognizes as program source (C, C++, Objective-C, Java, AppleScript, and so on). You cannot set a breakpoint in XML or other types of non-program text files. You can relocate breakpoints to another line by dragging them there, or delete them by dragging them out of the gutter. Right/Control+click a breakpoint, or in the gutter, to add, remove, edit, or review breakpoints. Double-clicking a breakpoint opens the Breakpoints window. See Chapter 18 for more about breakpoints.

Navigation Bar

The navigation bar, shown in Figure 6-13, occupies the top edge of the editor pane and contains several status and navigation controls. You can hide the navigation bar of the active editor pane with the View ⇨ Hide Navigation Bar command, and reveal it again with View ⇨ Show Navigation Bar.

FIGURE 6-13

The following table lists the functions of the navigation bar controls.

CONTROL	FUNCTION
File History	Jumps to a file that has been edited in this pane
Functions	Jumps to a function, definition, or marker in the file
Bookmarks	Jumps to a bookmark set in the file
Breakpoints	Jumps to a breakpoint set in the file
Class Hierarchy	Jumps to related class definitions
Included Files	Jumps to an included file, or a file that includes this file
Counterpart	Jumps to the counterpart of this file
Lock	Locks or unlocks the file

The Lock button toggles the lock (read-only) attribute of the file. If you lock a file, or the file was locked when it was opened, the editor will be in display-only mode. If you attempt to change the document, Xcode warns you that you cannot edit the file. You can override this mode in the dialog box and make changes to the document, but that does not change the permissions of the file and you will not be able to save changes until the file is made writable. Unlocking a file automatically switches the editor to its normal editing mode. See the option Save Files As Writable in the "Display Options" section of this chapter.

Numerous Xcode features rely on knowledge about your program's symbols and source files obtained from the Code Sense index. This includes features like jumping to a symbol definition, the Class Hierarchy menu, Included Files menus, and auto-completion — just to name a few. By default, Code Sense is enabled for all projects so this shouldn't present an obstacle, but if any of these features aren't working, see the "Code Sense" section in Chapter 7. You may need to turn on Code Sense or reindex your project.

All of the other navigation controls are explained in the "Navigating Within a File" section, later in this chapter.

DISPLAY OPTIONS

The appearance of an editor pane can be customized in a number of different ways and a variety of options determine how the text itself is interpreted and displayed. The following table lists the principal display options.

DISPLAY OPTION	COMMAND	EFFECT
Line Wrap	View ⇨ Text ⇨ Wrap Lines	Wraps lines wider than the window to the next line
Show Control Characters	View ⇨ Text ⇨ Show Control Characters	Makes control characters visible
Show Spaces	View ⇨ Text ⇨ Show Spaces	Makes space (ASCII 32) characters visible
Show Issues	View ⇨ Message Bubbles ⇨ Show Issues	Shows message bubbles in the gutter
Navigation Bar	View ⇨ Layout ⇨ Show Navigation Bar	Shows the navigation bar
Status Bar	View ⇨ Layout ⇨ Show Status Bar	Shows the status bar
Toolbar	View ⇨ Show Toolbar	Shows the toolbar

Text Wrapping

The View ⇨ Text ⇨ Wrap Lines command toggles between wrapped and unwrapped editor modes. With line wrapping turned on, lines that exceed the width of the window are split at some convenient point and continued on the next line in the editor. When line wrapping is off, long lines simply continue off the right edge of the editor pane. If one or more lines exceed the width of the editor, a horizontal scrollbar appears at the bottom of the pane.

Invisible Characters

Control characters and the space character are normally invisible. Two more commands in the View ⇨ Text menu, Show Control Characters (Command+Shift+6) and Show Spaces, make those characters visible. Show Control Characters is particularly useful for finding gremlins — illegal control characters in a source file. This option does not show any of the normal control characters: tab, newline, or return. Show Spaces marks the location of each ASCII space character with a spacing bracket. Select either command again to toggle them back off.

The font and size of the text used for all editor panes are set in the Fonts & Colors tab of the Xcode Preferences. These settings are described in the "Syntax Coloring" section of Chapter 7.

Global Display Options

Several global settings control the appearance of editor panes for all windows. These are in the Text Editing tab of the Xcode Preferences, as shown in Figure 6-14.

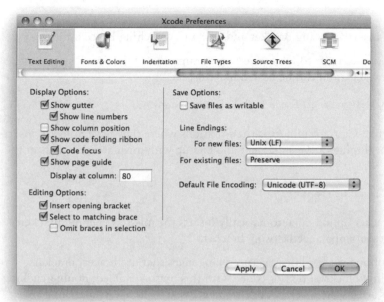

FIGURE 6-14

Editor Pane Display Options

Show Gutter enables the display of the gutter in regular editor panes. Without the gutter, you cannot see or set breakpoints or find where the execution of the application is currently paused. Because of this, the gutter is automatically displayed whenever you start a debugging session, and is hidden again when the debugging session ends. The editor pane in the Debugger window always shows a gutter.

Show Line Numbers displays the number of each line in the gutter. The Show Gutter option must be enabled for line numbers to be visible.

Show Column Position adds a column number to the filename of the current file in the history control of the navigation bar. The navigation bar must be visible for this option to have any effect. When this option is enabled, the name of the current file indicates both the line and column number of the current insertion point or the beginning of the text selection. If the option is disabled, only the file's name and line number are displayed.

The code folding ribbon is described in the "Code Folding" section of Chapter 7. The Code Focus option actively highlights the code block your cursor is currently hovering over. You may find it amazingly useful or merely annoying — perhaps both.

Turning on the Show Page Guide option causes a vertical line to be drawn at the column number specified in the Display at Column field. Some coding styles require all program text to fit within a certain number of columns. If you are adhering to such a coding style, or are formatting text for a fixed-width output device, the page guide is very useful. Note that the page guide is based on the em-width of the font (traditionally, the width of a capital *M*) and is only accurate when you're using fixed-width fonts.

Editing Options

The Editing Options consist of Insert Opening Bracket and Select to Matching Brace options.

The Insert Opening Bracket option is a gift to Objective-C programmers. Objective-C statements are enclosed between square brackets, and can be nested like this:

```
[self setDelegate:[[[MyDelegate alloc] init] autorelease]];
```

A persistent problem for Objective-C programmers is the situations where they have failed to insert enough opening braces at the beginning of the statement and end up with mismatch brackets at the end, like this statement:

```
[[MyObject alloc] init] autorelease];
```

Turning the Insert Opening Bracket option on automatically inserts the missing opening bracket whenever the programmer types an unbalanced closing bracket.

The Select to Matching Brace option is useful in structured languages that use braces, brackets, parentheses, and quotes to delimit blocks of text or code. With this option enabled, double-clicking any of the following characters selects the block of code/text enclosed by it and its matching delimiter:

```
{ [ ( ' " ) ] }
```

For example, double-clicking a single or double quote selects a string. Double-clicking an open parenthesis selects the parenthetical statement it encloses. Double-clicking a curly brace selects an entire block of code. The editor takes nested delimiters into account.

The Omit Braces in Selection option refines this feature by determining whether the text selected will include the delimiters in the selection, or just the text between the delimiters.

Save Options

The Save Options are an eclectic set of options that deal with file permissions and line endings. The Save Files as Writable option causes Xcode to set the POSIX write permission of a file when it is saved. With this option off, Xcode preserves the POSIX write permissions the file had before it was saved. That is, if the file were read-only it will be left read-only. When opening a read-only file, Xcode puts the editor pane in display-only mode. Any attempt to change the file is met with a warning, as shown in Figure 6-15. This is mostly to prevent you from trying to edit read-only files that belong to frameworks.

FIGURE 6-15

Clicking the Allow Editing button puts the editor pane in its normal editing mode, but it does not change the permissions of the underlying file. In this state, Xcode refuses to save the file from the Save All window. However, you can save the file by using the File ⇨ Save command directly or by starting a Build with the Always Save option selected. Xcode temporarily makes the file writable, writes the changes, and then restores the read-only permissions of the file. The editor pane remains editable.

Set the Save Files as Writable option and Xcode will *not* restore the read-only permissions after a save, leaving the file writable. After the save, the file will behave like any other writable file.

This behavior applies to the POSIX write permissions for the file. The other method of making a file unwritable is to set its POSIX immutable flag. (On an HFS filesystem, this flag is synonymous with the HFS locked attribute.) You can set or clear this flag by using the Lock button in the navigation bar, or in the Get Info window for the file in the Finder. The POSIX immutable flag is never overwritten by Xcode, making it a more secure method of preventing changes to a file than merely denying write permission. A locked file behaves the same as a file that lacks write privileges, except that File ⇨ Save does not change the status of the immutable flag or write to the file. Instead, Xcode displays a simple error dialog box explaining that it cannot write to the file. To make changes to the file, you must first click the Lock control in the navigation bar to unlock the file.

File Encoding

The remaining options in the Text Editing tab deal with line endings and character encoding. Under Line Encodings, the For New Files option determines the line endings for files created in Xcode. The choices are to end each line with a single LF character (Mac OS X or UNIX format), a single CR (Mac OS 9 and earlier format), or a CR+LF sequence (Microsoft DOS format). Unless you have some specific reason to use CR or CRLF line endings, all text files should be written using LF. The For Existing Files option determines the line encoding for files that are saved in Xcode. If this option is set to something other than Preserve, any file saved in Xcode will have its line encoding automatically converted into the selected format. The Preserve setting saves the file in whatever line encoding format it had when it was opened.

Use the Default File Encoding option to choose the character encoding that will be used for any file where Xcode does not know its character encoding. This applies to existing text files being added to a project, or any text file opened in Xcode that does not belong to an open project. If an open project contains a source file item that refers to the file being opened, the character encoding recorded in that source item is used.

NAVIGATION WITHIN A FILE

You'll probably spend more time moving around in your source code than you'll spend writing it. Programming just isn't a linear activity. One rarely sits down and types out a function of any consequence from start to finish. Knowing how to move around your source code quickly and decisively will greatly enhance your efficacy.

Cursor Movement

Start with just moving around in a single source file. The following table lists the key combinations that simply move the cursor around in the text.

 All of the key combinations in this chapter are based on the key binding set named "Xcode Defaults." This is the default set when Xcode is installed. Key bindings — the mapping of key combinations to actions — are extremely flexible and can be customized extensively. Xcode includes key binding sets that approximate the key combinations used in BBEdit, Metrowerks' CodeWarrior, and the venerable MPW system. You are also free to devise your own key binding sets. See Chapter 23 for a complete description of key bindings and how to alter them. If you have changed the key bindings in the Xcode Preferences, you may want to set them back to the Xcode Default set while working through this chapter.

KEY COMBINATION	CURSOR MOVEMENT
Right arrow, Control+F	Next character
Command+right arrow, Control+E	End of line
Option+right arrow	End of next word
Control+right arrow	End of next subword
Left arrow, Control+B	Previous character
Command+left arrow, Control+A	Beginning of line
Option+left arrow	Beginning of previous word
Control+left arrow	Beginning of previous subword
Up arrow, Control+P	One line up
Command+up arrow	Beginning of document

KEY COMBINATION	CURSOR MOVEMENT
Option+up arrow	Previous beginning of line
Down arrow, Control+N	One line down
Command+down arrow	End of document
Option+down arrow	Next end of line
Option+Page Up	One page up
Option+Page Down	One page down

Memorize this table or earmark this page in the book. It will save you an immense amount of time navigating your source code. The most important thing to remember is that the amount of cursor movement increases depending on the modifier key used with the left or right arrow keys, as shown in Figure 6-16. These are, in increasing order or magnitude: none, Control, Option, and Command.

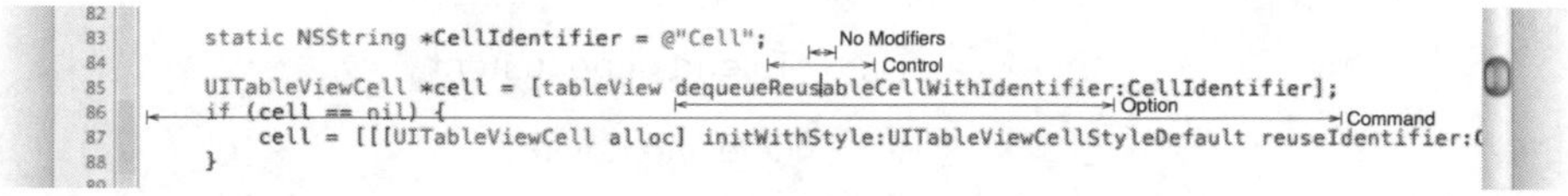

FIGURE 6-16

A word in Xcode is a run of letters, numbers, or the underscore character. A subword is a capital letter followed by a run of lowercase letters, a run of numbers, a run of uppercase letters, or a run of underscore characters between subwords. Leading and trailing underscore characters do not count as subwords.

Emacs

You may have noticed a few odd synonyms for some of the cursor movements, like Control+P to move up one line, or Control+E to move to the end of the line. Xcode key bindings emulate a number of the standard Emacs editor commands. If you're used to using Emacs, you will want to explore the key bindings in the Xcode Preferences to see what Emacs control sequences are supported. This book doesn't go into all of the Emacs commands that are supported by Xcode, but the following table provides a couple of examples.

KEY COMBINATION	ACTION
Control+Space	Sets the mark from the current position
Control+X Control+X	Swaps the current position with the mark

Emacs maintains the concept of a "mark," which is simply a saved location in the file, much like a bookmark. You can set the mark by pressing Control+spacebar. You can also "swap" the mark with the current cursor position or selection by pressing Control+X Control+X (that's Control+X twice in a row). The current cursor position or selection becomes the new mark, and the cursor position or selection is moved to the previous mark. This can be very handy when copying and pasting between two different sections of the same file.

Scrolling

Besides the scrollbar controls, key combinations also exist that scroll the text without changing the current cursor position or selection, as listed in the following table.

KEY COMBINATION	SCROLL MOVEMENT
Page Up, Control+up arrow	One page up
Page Down, Control+down arrow	One page down
Home	To beginning of document
Command+Home	One line up
End	To end of document
Command+End	One line down
Command+J	Jump to Selection

These can often result in scrolling the text so that the current cursor position is no longer visible. Every cursor movement includes an implied request to scroll the window so that the new cursor position is visible. To scroll the window so that the current cursor or selection is visible again, use the Edit ⇨ Find ⇨ Jump to Selection (Command+J) command.

Jumping to Functions, Breakpoints, and Bookmarks

The navigation bar provides several tools for navigating to locations within the current file, as shown in Figure 6-13.

All of these controls are drop-down menus. Select an item in the menu and the cursor moves immediately to that location in the file. Keyboard shortcuts also exist for these menus, as listed in the following table. Using one of the shortcuts drops the menu down. You can then navigate the menu with the up and down arrows or by typing the first few letters of the desired item. Press Return when the desired item is highlighted. Press Esc to dismiss the menu.

KEYBOARD SHORTCUT	NAVIGATION MENU
Control+1, Control+Option+1	File History
Control+2, Control+Option+2	Functions
Control+3	Class Hierarchy
Control+4	Bookmarks
Control+5	Breakpoints
Control+6	Included Files

The File History, Class Hierarchy, and Included Files menus are described a little later in the "Jumping to Other Files" section. The remaining menus navigate within the current file.

Functions

The Functions menu, shown in Figure 6-17, parses the definitions in the source file and dynamically builds a list of functions, classes, methods, types, defines, and markers. This is one of the syntax-aware editing features of Xcode and only works when you're editing file types that Xcode recognizes as being program source files.

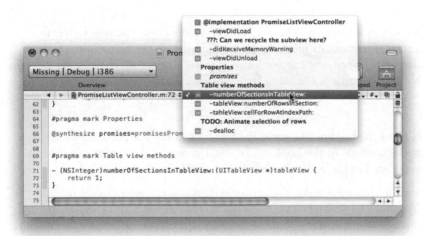

FIGURE 6-17

The menu includes an item for each of the following that Xcode discovers in your source code:

➤ A class, method, or function (declaration or definition)

➤ A type (`typedef`) declaration

➤ `#define` directives

➤ `#pragma mark` directives

➤ Any comment that contains the (case-sensitive) text:

  ➤ `MARK:`

  ➤ `TODO:`

  ➤ `FIXME:`

  ➤ `!!!:`

  ➤ `???:`

Normally, the menu is in the order that the declarations appear in the file. Hold down the Option key when clicking the menu or using the keyboard shortcut to sort the items in alphabetical order. Method names in Java and Objective-C classes are sorted as though their names were fully qualified (for example, `MyReader::isEOF`), so all of the methods for a class cluster together in the list, subsorted by method name. You can choose to switch the default order by setting the Sort List Alphabetically option in the Code Sense pane of the Xcode Preferences. When this option is set, the list is sorted alphabetically by default and in file order when the Option key is used.

Declarations are italicized in the menu. Declarations can be excluded by turning off the Show Declarations option in the Code Sense pane of the Xcode Preferences.

The most flexible means of adding arbitrary entries to the Functions menu is to insert a `#pragma mark` directive to your source code, as shown in Figure 6-17. The statement `#pragma mark -` adds a menu divider.

Finally, the Functions menu acts as a location indicator. Whenever the cursor or selection is in a definition or the body of a class, function, or method, the menu indicates the name of the current location. When the menu is popped open, the current location is indicated with a check mark. If the cursor position is not within any definition, the message "<No Selected Symbol>" is displayed.

Bookmarks

The Bookmarks menu lists all of the bookmarks set in the file. It does not list bookmarks set in other files. Use the Bookmarks window or the Bookmarks smart group in the project window to see those. Bookmarks are always listed in the order they appear in the file.

To set a bookmark, position the cursor or make a selection and choose the Edit ⇨ Add to Bookmarks (Command+D) command or Right/Control+click a text selection and choose Add to Bookmarks. This presents a bookmark name dialog sheet. The default name of a new bookmark will be its location in the file, which you can change if you want something more descriptive. Bookmarks are stored in the project document; you can only set bookmarks in files that are assets of an open project.

Breakpoints

The Breakpoints menu jumps to any breakpoints set in the file. Each breakpoint is displayed as the function or method name containing the breakpoint plus a line number.

Jumping to Other Files

Just as important as being able to move around quickly within a file is the ability to move quickly between files. You've already seen how to open and browse files from the project window, but Xcode provides a variety of other ways to switch directly from one file to another.

MOST PRODUCTIVE SHORTCUTS

Before I get into some of the more mundane ways of navigating between files, let me point out probably the two most useful shortcuts in Xcode:

SHORTCUT	COMMAND	EFFECT
Command+double-click	Edit ⇨ Find ⇨ Jump to Definition	Quickly jumps to the source code where the symbol is defined.
Option+double-click	Help ⇨ Quick Help	Opens the symbol's documentation in a Quick Help window.

The double-click action selects the word or symbol at your cursor location, so these shortcuts perform two actions simultaneously: select the symbol and jump to its definition or documentation. These shortcuts are described in this and the help chapters, but they're so useful that I encourage you to take a moment to memorize them now.

File History

The File History menu in the navigation bar maintains a list of the files that have been displayed in *that* editor pane, as shown in Figure 6-18. Select a file from the list and the pane switches to that file. The keyboard shortcut for the File History menu is Control+1.

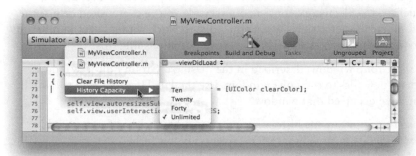

FIGURE 6-18

File history is maintained individually for each editor pane. Even multiple panes within the same window have their own history. For the editor pane in the project window, or when you're using the Grouped window mode, this can be quite a long list. For separate editor windows, it tends to be just the file that is being edited. All new panes have an empty history, and closing a pane discards the history for that pane. The only exception is when Xcode saves the state of a window in the project document. It always does this for the project window, and it saves the state of other open windows if the Save Window State option in the General preferences is set. Thus, the history of the project window's editor pane is always preserved and so is, possibly, the state of all open editor windows.

To limit (or not) how much file history is retained, the File History menu has two special items, as previously shown in Figure 6-18. The Clear File History item does just that. It forgets all previously visited files except the current one. The History Capacity item sets the limit for the number of files in the list. The capacity defaults to Unlimited. For most editor panes, this isn't an issue because they rarely get past two. For editor panes, like those in the project window that are constantly being reused, you may want to limit the size of the history, or the list may become unwieldy. Like the file history itself, this setting is stored separately for each editor pane and is saved in the window's state.

The two arrow buttons to the left of the File History menu move through the history list, like the previous and next buttons in a browser. The File History menu lists each file in alphabetical order, but the history buttons are really a browser-like history of the locations that have been visited, in the order that they were visited. Clicking the Previous button takes you to the location previously visited, not the file above the current one in the menu. It is unlike the File History menu in two other respects: it remembers your location within each file, not just files. This appears as a filename and line number, such as "main.c:27." A file and location may occur more than once. The history and the menu are both limited to the number of items set in the History Capacity menu.

Aggregate History

Hold down the Option key when popping up the File History menu to see the aggregate file history. The aggregate file history is a combined list of the history items from every open window. Be careful about using the feature too liberally with multiple projects open, because the list will include files from all of your projects. You can easily open the project window for project A and switch to a source file that belongs to project B.

Adding an Arbitrary File to the History

Xcode windowing options tend either to open all files in a single editor pane, or every file in a separate window. Consequently, the file history consists of every file you've ever visited or just the file opened in that window. There are some times when you'd like to work with a select number of files in a single, separate, editor window. You have three ways of accomplishing this.

The first method is to use the Group window, described in the "Using a Group Editor Window" section earlier. This directs all new files to the same window. Use the File History menu to switch between all of the files that have occupied that window.

The second method is to use the aggregate file history to switch to a file that has been visited in some other editor pane. Once the file is brought into the current window, it becomes part of its history. This is the simplest way of adopting a file that is, or has been, opened elsewhere.

The last method is to drag a file and drop it directly into the navigation bar, as shown in Figure 6-19. This switches the editor pane to that file and adds it to its history.

FIGURE 6-19

The source of the drag can be a source item in the project window, a file from the Finder, or the file icon in the title bar of a document window. This technique can only be used to add one file at a time.

Included Files

The Included Files menu is another syntax-aware feature for C and C-like language files. Each `#include` or `#import` directive that it finds is listed in the top portion of the menu, as shown in Figure 6-20. Selecting an item from the list jumps to that file. The keyboard shortcut is Control+6.

FIGURE 6-20

When used in a header file, the Included Files menu also lists the files that include this file at the bottom of the menu. In Figure 6-20, the current file, `MyViewController.h`, includes one header file, `UIKit.h`, and is included by two other files in the project, `AppDelegate.m` and `MyViewController.m`.

Switching Between a Header and its Source File

The convention for C, C++, and Objective-C languages is to place the declarations for functions and data types in a header file with an `.h` or `.hpp` filename extension, and write the implementation of those functions in a source file of the same name. If you use this convention, Xcode lets you quickly jump back and forth between the two using the View ➪ Switch to Header/Source File (Option+Command+ ↑) command, or click the Counterpart button in the navigation bar. Your editor focus switches immediately to the companion header or source file.

Whether the counterpart file opens in a new editing window depends on your layout style and the setting of the Open Counterparts in Same Editor option in the General pane of the Xcode preferences.

Jumping to a Definition

As mentioned earlier in this section, one of the most useful navigation tools in Xcode is the Edit ➪ Find ➪ Jump to Definition command. This command doesn't have a keyboard combination. To access it quickly, double-click a word in a source file while holding down the Command key.

Jump to Definition uses the syntax-aware symbols table to index all of the class, function, type, and constant names that are defined in your project. Command+double-clicking a word, or selecting a symbol name and choosing Edit ➪ Find ➪ Jump to Definition, immediately jumps to the implementation of that function or method, or to the definition of that class, type, or constant. If the current selection *is* the function or method implementation, it jumps to the declaration of that function or method.

If there are multiple symbols with the same name, or if you choose a class name with multiple implementations, Xcode pops up a list of the possible matches, as shown in Figure 6-21. Select the desired symbol and the editor jumps there.

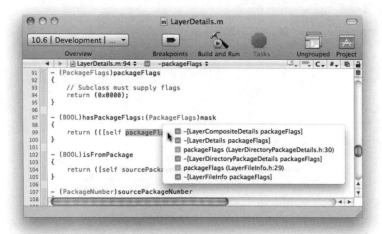

FIGURE 6-21

Code Sense indexing must be enabled for this feature to work. See the "Code Sense" section in Chapter 7.

EDITING

All of the standard text selection and editing features supplied by the operating system's text editing framework work in Xcode. If you need a refresher on the basics, refer to the Mac OS X Help. The following sections highlight a few obscure features that are particularly useful when editing source code. In addition, Xcode adds its own set of features and commands.

Selecting Text

All of the standard text selection gestures work in Xcode. Click and drag to select some text. Hold down the Shift key to extend a selection. Selecting text by dragging is dependent on timing; see the "Drag and Drop" section later for an explanation.

The standard Mac OS X text editor is sensitive to word boundaries when extending text selections. It's an obscure quirk that most people don't notice, but may impact your coding. When you Shift-click to extend a selection, Xcode examines the other end of the selection (the end not being moved). If that end lies on a word boundary, the end being extended snaps to word boundaries. If the stationary end is in the middle of a word or between non-word characters, the extended end can be positioned at any character. This makes it very quick and easy to extend a selection to include additional words or symbols, because you don't have to select the edge of the word; dragging anywhere into the word will suffice. If you start with a selection on a word boundary, and want to extend it to a non-word boundary, extend the selection using the keyboard (Shift+right arrow or Shift+left arrow) instead. This might be a good time to review the cursor movement modifiers back in the "Cursor Movement" section.

Selecting Columns

One of the more obscure features of the editor is the ability to select columns of text. You can select all of the characters between two column positions across multiple lines by holding down the Option key and dragging out a selection. Figure 6-22 shows a column selection. Hold down the Shift and Option keys to extend or contract an existing column selection.

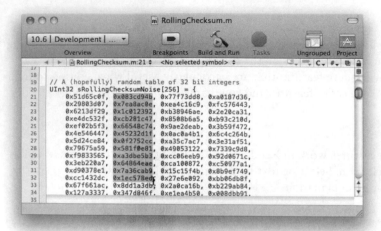

FIGURE 6-22

You can copy the selected characters to the clipboard or delete them. If you copy the selection, the clipboard will contain the selected characters of each line on separate lines. Lines that have no characters selected (lines shorter than the first column) are not included. You cannot paste into a column selection or otherwise replace a column with multi-line content.

Selecting Code Blocks

The Edit ➪ Format ➪ Balance command, also on the Right/Control+click contextual pop-up menu, selects the contents of a C or Java style block of code surrounded by square brackets or curly braces. The command looks outward from the current selection to find the nearest block delimiter, then selects all of the text between it and its matching delimiter. It will correctly account for escaped quote characters and nested blocks.

This command is similar to, and independent of, the Select to Matching Brace option in the Text Editing pane of the Xcode Preferences, described earlier in the "Editing Options" section. This command, however, works only with braces and brackets.

Jumping to a Line or Character

The Edit ➪ Go To Line (Command+L) command lets you jump to a specific line or character position in a text file. Selecting the command opens the Goto window, as shown in Figure 6-23.

Enter the position within the file that you want to select. The radio buttons determine whether the position will be interpreted as a character offset or a line number.

FIGURE 6-23

Press the Return key and that line or character is selected in the file and the Goto window closes. Alternatively, you can click the Select button. This also selects your chosen position, but leaves the Goto window open. If you check the Auto-Update option, the position in the Goto window continuously updates to reflect your current position within the file.

Deleting Text

The text editor provides several useful variations of the standard delete key for deleting text adjacent to the insertion point, as listed in the following table.

KEY COMBINATION	DELETES
Delete, Control+H	One character to the left of the cursor
Control+Delete	From the cursor to the beginning of the previous subword
Option+Delete	From the cursor to the beginning of the previous word
Command+Delete	From the cursor to the beginning of the line
Delete-right, Control+D	One character to the right of the cursor
Control+delete-right	From the cursor to the end of the next subword
Option+delete-right	From the cursor to the end of the next word
Control+W	From the cursor to the current mark

The Delete key, just above the Return key (sometimes labeled ⌫), deletes to the left. The delete-right key (⌦), typically found on extended keyboards near the Home and End keys, deletes to the right. Either can delete a single character, subword, word, or line.

The delete keys follow the same pattern that the right and left arrow keys do. The amount they delete increases depending on the modifier used: either none, Control, Option, or Command. The one exception is the combination of Command+right-delete, which doesn't work; use Shift+Command+right-arrow to select to the end of the line, and then press the Delete key.

Control+H and Control+D are Emacs synonyms for Delete and delete-right. Use these if you prefer or if you don't have a delete-right key on your keyboard. These control key equivalents cannot be combined with the Option or the Control key modifiers. The Emacs-centric Control+W command deletes from the current cursor location to the location of the mark, previously set with Control-spacebar or Control+X Control+X.

Drag and Drop

A text selection can be dragged around within a document, between documents, and between Xcode and other applications.

A text selection and a text drag use the same gesture: click, move, and release. The difference is in the timing. To drag out a new text selection, press down the mouse button and move the mouse immediately. The cursor remains a text cursor. To start a drag, press down the mouse button and wait. After a very short delay (less than a second) the cursor turns into an arrow. You are now dragging the text selection. You can customize this delay to suit your mousing speed. See the discussion of the `NSDragAndDropTextDelay` expert setting in Chapter 23.

Press down the Option key before dropping the text to make a copy. Dragging between documents always performs a copy. Dragging from other applications inserts the text equivalent of the object being dragged. Dragging file icons from the Finder or the project window inserts the URL of the file, not the contents of the file itself. To insert the contents of a file, open that file in Xcode, choose Edit ⇨ Select All, and drag the text into your document.

Most lists, displays, and fields in Xcode can be the source of a drag even when they are not editable. How useful this is will vary, but keep it in mind before you reach for a yellow pad to write something down. You might simply be able to drag it somewhere to keep it. Drag any text selection to the desktop or an open Finder window to create a clipping file containing that text. This is a handy way of saving or "setting aside" a chunk of code while you experiment.

Font and Text Styles

Program source files are plaintext files that do not include any font, style, color, or other typographic information. Logically then, the commands and tools in the Edit ⇨ Format ⇨ Font and Edit ⇨ Format ⇨ Text menus are inapplicable — even if they're enabled. The font and style used for the text is set globally, as explained earlier in the "Display Options" section.

When you use Xcode's RTF (styled text) editor, the commands in these menus perform as expected.

Saving Files

All editor panes, except for ones just created with the File ⇨ New Empty File command, are associated with a physical file. Editing only changes the copy of the text held in memory. A file is not actually altered until the editor pane is saved, which writes those changes back to the file. Several variations of the Save command exist in Xcode, as listed in the following table.

COMMAND	ACTION
Save (Command+S)	Writes the contents of the editor pane to its file.
Save As... (Shift+Command+S)	Enables you to create a new file and writes the text to that new file. The new file becomes the file associated with that pane. If the original file was referred from a project, the path and name of that source item is also updated to refer to the new file. The original file is not altered, and the project no longer has a reference to it. Use this command to rename a file while preserving a copy of the original.
Save a Copy As (Shift+Option+Command+S)	Like Save As, this command enables you to choose a new file, write the contents of the editor pane to it, and leave the contents of the original file untouched. But that's where it stops. The file associated with the editor pane is not changed, and it still refers to the original file. A subsequent Save command writes any changes to the original file. Nothing in the project is altered. This command is useful for making a snapshot of a file, or for quickly creating a new file that is a copy of an existing one without altering the project.

COMMAND	ACTION
Save All (Option+Command+S)	This command presents a dialog box, shown in Figure 6-8, that lists all modified file buffers being held in memory. You can choose to save all, or only some, of them in a single command. The Save All dialog box was described earlier in this chapter in the "Closing and Saving Editor Panes" section.

The Revert to Saved (Command+U) command is the opposite of the various Save commands. Instead of writing the changes to the file, it discards any changes made since the file was opened or saved and re-reads the text from the file. Xcode presents a warning beforehand, shown in Figure 6-24, ensuring that you really do want to abandon all the changes you've recently made. You cannot recover these changes once the Revert to Saved command has executed.

FIGURE 6-24

Undo

Xcode's undo features work pretty much the way they do in most modern applications, but a couple of differences exist. Undo history is maintained on a per-file basis. Until the file is saved and all editing panes that contain it are closed, Xcode maintains the undo history for the file, and all editing panes showing the same file share the same undo history.

Each atomic editing action is recorded as a step in the undo history. An "atomic" action would be typing some sequence of regular text characters, navigation, auto-completion, using the Tab key, deleting text, cutting, pasting, or any other menu command that changes the contents of the text buffer.

The Edit ⇨ Undo command (Command+Z) reverses the effect of the most recent action recorded in the history. The original action is then remembered on the redo list. As you repeatedly use the Undo command, each change made to the file is undone, depleting the undo history and adding to the redo list.

Undoing a Cut or Copy command does not restore the previous contents of the system's clipboard. It only restores the state of the editor pane prior to the Cut command.

The Redo command performs the complement of the Undo command. It takes the most recent action moved to the redo list, performs it again, and adds it to the undo history. Together, the Undo and Redo commands are like a time machine, allowing you to step forward and backward through the history of the file's changes until you find the state of the file you want.

Any new change made to a file erases the redo list. If you go back in time and make a different choice, you can no longer visit the future that contained the original choice. The Revert to Saved command empties both the undo and redo information for a file.

The Save command does not alter the undo or redo information for a file. This means it is possible to undo changes made to a file *after* it has been saved. Whenever you try to undo the last action that occurred before a file was saved, Xcode presents a dialog box like the one shown in Figure 6-25.

FIGURE 6-25

Some developers find this dialog box annoying. Chapter 19 explains how to set the `XCShowUndoPastSaveWarning` advanced setting to disable that warning.

SHELL SCRIPTS

If you've been around the Macintosh platform long enough to remember MPW (the Macintosh Programmer's Workshop), you may be missing one of its more intriguing features. Every text window in MPW was a "live" worksheet, capable of executing any MPW command. In fact, MPW made no real distinction between a text document and a shell window. This made for some interesting possibilities.

Xcode resurrects this ability, in a fashion, with the hidden Execute Script command. This command is normally bound to the Control+R key combination. It doesn't appear in any of the menus. Select any text and press Control+R. The selected text is executed in your default shell (bash, by default). The output of those commands is inserted into your text file immediately after the selected script, as shown on the right in Figure 6-26.

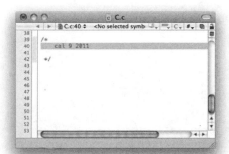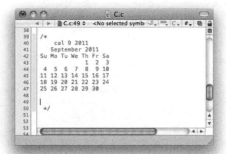

FIGURE 6-26

The current directory is always set to the active project folder prior to execution, so you can refer to project files using project folder–relative paths. A new instance of the shell is used for each invocation, so aliases and shell variables are not persistent. Note that the shell's stdin is set to /dev/null, making it impossible to use commands that prompt for user input, such as sudo.

SPELL CHECKING

Programmers are notoriously bad spellers. Thanks to the Cocoa underpinnings of Xcode, the editor inherits the standard Mac OS X spelling checker. The spelling checker is great for correcting comments and documentation, thus avoiding the scorn and ridicule of the documentation department that is inevitably populated with English majors and spelling bee champions. The spelling checker is essentially useless for code. Avoid adding program symbols or language keywords to your user dictionary. Your login account has only one user dictionary, and filling it with programming symbols defeats its usefulness in other applications.

Interactive Checking

Start the interactive spelling checker with the Edit ➪ Spelling ➪ Show Spelling & Grammar (Shift+Command+:) command. This opens the Spelling and Grammar palette (see Figure 6-27).

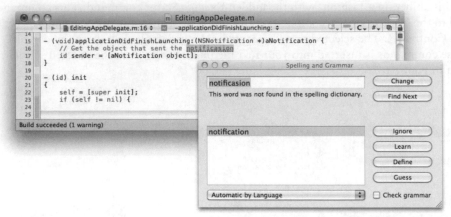

FIGURE 6-27

Checking starts at the text cursor or the beginning of the current selection. Checking is not limited to the text selection; it just starts there. The next word that the spelling checker suspects is misspelled is highlighted in the text and displayed in the entry field of the palette. Above the suspect word is a list of suggested corrections.

The Ignore button adds the suspect word to the temporary ignore list. The spelling checker ignores this word, and assumes that it is spelled correctly, until the next editor session. Use this to teach the spelling checker temporarily about correctly spelled words, without permanently adding them to the dictionary.

The Find Next button skips this word and goes looking for the next suspicious word. The spelling checker still considers the word to be misspelled.

You can immediately replace a word with a suggestion from the Guess list by selecting the suggestion and clicking the Change button, or by double-clicking a suggestion in the list. You can replace the word with any arbitrary text by editing the contents of the text field before clicking the Change button.

If the spelling checker cannot guess the correct spelling of the word, you can help it by editing the suspect word and telling it to guess again using the Guess button. For example, the spelling checker cannot guess that you mean "exhausted" if you've actually typed "eghosted." Replacing the "g" with an "x" and clicking the Guess button, as shown in Figure 6-28, gets the word close enough for the spelling checker to find the correct word.

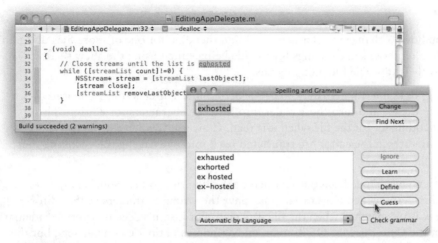

FIGURE 6-28

The pop-up at the bottom of the palette lets you choose a different language. The Learn and Ignore buttons take the word currently in the entry field and either add or remove it from your user dictionary. To remove a word you previously added, you have to type or paste it into the field before clicking the Ignore button. Your user dictionary is shared by all applications that use the Spelling Checker interface, so add to it wisely and sparingly.

Checking One Word

You can invoke the spelling checker without bringing up the spelling checker palette with the Edit ⇨ Spelling ⇨ Check Spelling (Command+;) command. This command starts at the current location in the file and finds the next suspect word, which it highlights. That's it. Edit the word in the editor pane or use the command again to find the next suspect word.

This is probably the most useful spell checking command for programmers. After writing a long comment, position the cursor at the beginning of the comment and press Command+;. The spelling checker will skip to the first suspect word in the comment. Once you've corrected all of the English words in the comment, simply go back to writing code.

Checking While Typing

The Spelling menu has an option to Check Spelling as You Type. If selected, words that you just typed or edited are spell checked and highlighted automatically. Note that this does not spell check the entire document, or text that you paste or drag. It only checks the word that your cursor was just in or adjacent to. The word that the cursor is currently in or adjacent to is *never* highlighted (because it is assumed that you are in the process of changing it).

You may find this feature useless and annoying when you're editing source code, because practically every "word" in your program is going to be tagged as misspelled. However, if you are writing a large amount of documentation in Xcode, you might find it helpful to turn it on temporarily.

FILE ENCODING

Chapter 5 showed you how to change the character and line encoding for one or more files using an Info window. You can alter those same settings for the file being edited using the View ➪ Text ➪ Line Ending and View ➪ Text ➪ File Encoding menus.

Changing these settings does not, immediately, alter the actual file. The encodings are used to interpret the bytes in the file and turn those codes into Unicode characters for editing. This translation uses the encoding set for the file when it is read. Conversely, when the file is later saved, the Unicode characters in the editor are translated back into bytes using the encoding that is set then.

Problems can arise when you change from one character encoding to another. Some characters cannot be represented in certain encodings or you may have the wrong characters in the editor because the encoding was mismatched when the file was read. For instance, the registered trademark symbol (®) appears in the Unicode, Mac OS Roman, and Windows Latin 1 character sets, but the binary code used to represent it in a text file is different for all three. If the file was written using Windows Latin 1 encoding and you read the file into the editor using Mac OS Roman encoding, the editor displays some other symbol because the value in the file is not the Mac OS Roman value for the registered trademark symbol.

When you change the encoding for a file, Xcode asks if it should convert or reinterpret the characters in the file, as shown in Figure 6-29.

FIGURE 6-29

The Convert button actually does very little beyond remembering the new encoding for the file. The characters are already in their universal form in memory. The "conversion" doesn't actually occur until you save the file. The bytes in the file were read using the old encoding, and will eventually be written using the new encoding. Use this option if the characters in the file are correct and you simply want to save the file using a different encoding. The one thing the Convert button does do is check that all of the characters in the file can be written using the new encoding. Xcode does not allow characters in an editor pane that cannot be encoded when it is saved. If the document contains characters that are illegal in the new encoding, the conversion is not allowed.

Use the Reinterpret button when the encoding is incorrect and the editor has misinterpreted the bytes in the file. If a file containing the registered trademark symbol is encoded using Windows Latin 1, and read using Mac OS Roman, the character that appears in the file is "Æ." To correct this, change the encoding to Western (Windows Latin 1) and click the Reinterpret button. The contents of the file are read again, this time using the Windows Latin 1 encoding, and the ® symbol appears instead. To save this file using Mac OS Roman encoding, change the encoding again — this time using the Convert button.

The Reinterpret button must re-read the bytes in the actual file. The binary encoding of characters is not maintained in memory — only the Unicode characters are. If changes have been made to a file, the Reinterpret button warns you that all unsaved changes will be lost when the file is reinterpreted, as shown in Figure 6-30. You can choose to discard all unsaved changes or cancel. To preserve and reinterpret the file including all of the changes that you've made, cancel the reinterpretation, save the file using the old encoding, and change the encoding again.

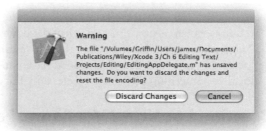

FIGURE 6-30

As mentioned earlier, Xcode won't allow you to convert a file if the resulting document would have characters that cannot be encoded. Likewise, the editor won't let you insert a character into a document if the file's encoding won't support it. If you try, you get a warning like the one in Figure 6-31.

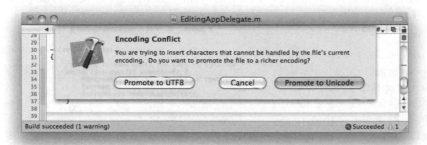

FIGURE 6-31

You have the choice of converting your document to Unicode (really Unicode-16) or Unicode-8. Unicode-16 is the "raw" Unicode encoding used internally by the editor. Unicode-16 writes or stores each character as a 16-bit integer word. Most editors, compilers, and other ASCII-oriented programs are not compatible with Unicode-16. Unicode-8 writes the common ASCII (0–127) characters as single bytes and encodes higher-value Unicode characters using a complex system of escape values. Unicode-8 is compact, compatible with many applications, and backwards-compatible with plain ASCII text. If given this choice, convert your document to Unicode-8.

If you don't want to use Unicode-8 or Unicode-16, cancel the insertion. Convert the file to an encoding that supports the characters you are trying to insert, and insert them again.

LOCALIZING FILES

One of the hallmarks of the Macintosh is the ability of programs to transform themselves to accommodate the language, currency, and time conventions of different countries and populations. This is generically referred to as localization. Xcode supports localization of individual project files. It does this by maintaining multiple copies of the file, one for each locale.

Your locale — the locale that your Xcode development system is currently set to — is called the *development region*. You should always start by creating the version of a file for your development region. When you localize a file, the original file becomes the version for the development region. You can then create variations of the file for other regions.

Normally, you only localize resource files like string lists, images, and NIB documents. Localization requires runtime support, and is usually done for files that are copied into the deployment bundle. The bundle is organized so that all versions are copied into the bundle and the appropriately localized version of the file is loaded based on the locale of the current user. Though it is possible to localize something like a source file, only the development region's version will be compiled.

Creating Localized Versions of a File

To prepare a file for localization, open the Info window for the file's item and click the Make File Localizable button. The file's source item is turned into a group and the existing file becomes the localized version for the development region. In the project structure group, the source item becomes a kind of source group. The top-level item acts as a proxy for the development region's version of the file, equivalent to the original file; that is, opening the item opens the localization for the development region. To open or change settings for an individual locale, expand the group and deal with each version separately.

After you initially localize the file, you can add more localizations by opening an Info window for either the item group, or any specific localization, and clicking the Add Localization button. Enter the name of the localization, or choose one from the pop-up menu, as shown in Figure 6-32. A new file is created by duplicating the current file. The new file becomes the localized version for that region.

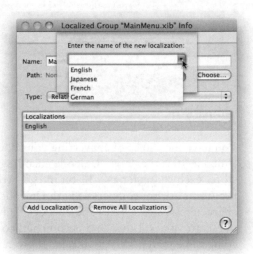

FIGURE 6-32

In the project folder, Xcode creates an .lproj subfolder for each localization. All of the files localized for English are in the English.lproj subfolder, all the files localized for French are in the French.lproj subfolder, and so forth. When the file is first localized, a localization folder for the development region is created in the same location, and the file is moved into the .lproj subfolder. The Multiglot project, shown in Figure 6-33, shows the organization of the project and project folder after the MainMenu.nib and InfoPlist.strings files have been localized for English, French, and Spanish.

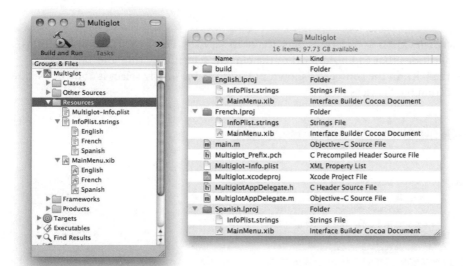

FIGURE 6-33

Removing Some or All Localizations

To remove a single localization of a file, select the specific localization within the file's group and delete it like you would any other source item.

To remove all localizations of a file, open the Info window for the localized group or any specific localization. Click the Remove All Localizations button. The localization for the development region is moved from the .lproj subfolder back to its original location. The localized group in the project is replaced with a simple source file reference again. Any additional localized versions of the file are left in their respective .lproj folders, but are no longer referred to in the project. If you later localize the file again, Xcode will *not* automatically pick up the other localized versions. However, if you add a localization for a region that already has a file in its .lproj subfolder, the file is not replaced and it becomes the localization for that region.

PRINTING

Rudimentary printing of editor panes is provided through the File ➪ Print (Command+P) command. The Print command prints the contents of the editor pane, using the editor's font. The gutter, page guide, and other annotations are not printed. Lines wider than the page are always wrapped to the next line; the Wrap Lines setting of the editor pane is ignored. The Use Colors When Printing option in the Font & Colors tab of the Xcode Preferences controls whether editor and syntax coloring is applied to the printout.

The text is printed at 72 dpi, which means that it will probably be unacceptably large. Use the scaling feature of the page setup to reduce the size of the text. A scale between 50% and 75% makes for a very readable and compact listing. For an even more compact listing, set the scaling between 80% and 100% and select a two-up page layout.

SERVICES

Xcode, like all well-written Cocoa applications, has access to services. Services are small functions provided by other applications that can be applied to the current selection within another application. To open the URL in the source file shown in Figure 6-34, simply select it and choose the Open URL command from the Services menu.

FIGURE 6-34

What services you have in your Services menu depends entirely on what applications and plug-ins you have installed.

SUMMARY

As you can see, Xcode's editor provides a lot of features designed to make your editing sessions fluid and productive. Learning to use the various navigation controls will make moving around within a file, and between files, quick and efficient.

Though the editor provides many useful features for editing and formatting your code, there's a lot more that it can do for you. The next chapter describes the many syntax-aware features of the editor.

7

Syntax-Aware Editing

WHAT'S IN THIS CHAPTER?

➤ Using and customizing syntax coloring

➤ Folding code blocks

➤ Accepting code completion suggestions

➤ Inserting text macros

In Chapter 6, you learned a lot of editing features specifically designed to make writing source code easier, but most of these features are just textual aides that know little or nothing about your code and symbols.

Xcode's syntax-aware features pick up where the basic text editing aides leave off — with some overlap between them. *Syntax-aware editing* means that the editor analyzes your source code and uses that knowledge to highlight your code's structure and symbols, offer suggestions, and make intelligent changes.

You've already encountered a few syntax-aware features. The Balance command, which finds a matching brace or bracket, understands the block structure, string format, comment syntax, and other details of your programming language.

This chapter describes the various syntax-aware editing features and tools available in Xcode. Xcode can know a lot about your code's structure, and its vocabulary is quite broad; it understands languages from ADA to XML. The code analysis is performed continuously and in the background. It won't get in the way of your development, and it's almost always up-to-date.

CODE SENSE

Code Sense is the technology that analyzes your code continuously while you write it. It assembles and maintains a database, called the *Code Sense index*, of the classes, variables, methods, functions, structures, types, data models, and constants defined in your application. It also tracks class inheritance and file references. Many of the syntax-aware features described in this chapter rely on Code Sense.

Code sense updates its index incrementally, analyzing only the function or method that you're editing and the source files that have been saved recently. Updates are typically quite fast — on the order of a few seconds. This means that Code Sense recognizes local variables in the method you're editing almost instantly, and changes to classes, methods, functions, and types as soon as you save the file.

> *If a symbol doesn't appear to be in the Code Sense index (that is, you can't jump to its definition, or it doesn't appear in the auto-completion list), save all of your source files to disk (File ⇨ Save All, Option+Command+S). If the symbol still fails to appear within a reasonable amount of time, compile your code and check for syntax errors. Code Sense may not be able to index source files that won't compile.*

Enabling Code Sense

You enable Code Sense globally for all projects in the Code Sense panel of the Xcode preferences, as shown in Figure 7-1.

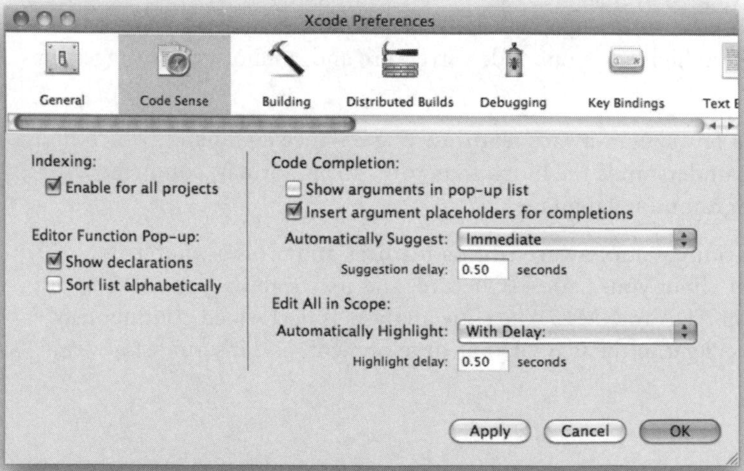

FIGURE 7-1

The Enable for All Projects option turns all Code Sense–dependent features on or off. This includes some syntax coloring, code completion, jump to definition, the Included Files and Class Hierarchy navigation menus, the Symbols smart group, and the Class Browser. The only real motivation for disabling Code Sense is to avoid the CPU, memory, and disk space required to maintain it, but these seem like small prices to pay for the enormous benefits that Code Sense provides. I would recommend disabling it only if absolutely necessary.

Code Sense works by interacting intimately with the compiler. This also requires that all the source items are members of a "native" target. Native targets are targets that Xcode knows how to build (see Chapter 16), and by extension it knows what compilers will be used to compile each source file. External (non-native) targets defer the actual build process to some external program, such as Make or Ant. Items in external targets cannot use Code Sense.

> **TIP TO REMEMBER**
>
> *If you would like to use Code Sense in a project that requires the use of an external target, you still can. Simply create an additional native target that includes all of the source files and libraries you want Code Sense to see. Code Sense indexes all of the native source files referred to in a project. You never have to build that target; it just has to be defined.*

Because Code Sense works silently in the background, it's sometimes hard to tell whether a symbol isn't in the Code Sense index or whether Code Sense just hasn't reindexed it yet. The Window ➪ Activity window tells when Code Sense is working and how far along it is. If Code Sense isn't working, and a symbol isn't in the index, either there's a syntax error preventing Code Sense from indexing your source files or the index needs to be rebuilt.

Reindexing a Project

If you suspect that the Code Sense index has gotten out of synchronization with your project, open the Info widow for the project (Project ➪ Edit Project Settings). At the bottom of the project's Info window, shown in Figure 7-2, is a Rebuild Code Sense Index button. Clicking it flushes the index for that project and queues Code Sense to index the entire project. For large projects, this could take some time.

The Code Sense index is stored in your account's ~/Library/Caches folder. If the Code Sense index is ever deleted or is not in synchronization, Xcode automatically rebuilds it.

FIGURE 7-2

SYNTAX COLORING

The most visible and passive of the syntax-aware editing features is *syntax coloring*. It uses a basic knowledge of a language's syntax to colorize the text of source code so that keywords, comments, literals, symbols, and other language elements are displayed in distinctive colors, fonts, or styles. The intent is to make it easier to read the code by highlighting the functionality of elements in the source.

Customizing Syntax Coloring

You control the colors that syntax coloring uses, or whether syntax coloring is done at all, in the Fonts & Colors tab of the Xcode Preferences, shown in Figure 7-3.

FIGURE 7-3

Each entry in the table controls the color, and possibly the font, used to display a category of editor element. The entire collection is collectively referred to as a *theme*. Xcode provides several themes that you can choose from, and you can create your own. The major categories are described in the following table.

You can control syntax-aware coloring globally with the Use Syntax-Based Formatting and Color Indexed Symbols options. Turning the first option off disables all syntax coloring. With syntax coloring enabled, the second option determines whether only basic language elements are colorized, or whether project symbols in the Code Sense index are also colorized.

In addition to the syntax coloring, this preference pane also establishes the font and color scheme used in all editing panes. This includes the background color of the pane and the color used to highlight selected text. The list is broadly organized into three groups of entries:

➤ The Background, Selection, Insertion Point, and Plain Text categories apply globally to all text editor panes.

➤ The categories Comments through Attributes affect recognized language elements when the Use Syntax-Based Formatting option is enabled.

➤ The remaining categories change the color of recognized symbols when the Color Indexed Symbols option is enabled.

Text that isn't colorized — either because it's not one of the recognized categories or you've turned off the Use Syntax-Based Formatting or Color Index Symbols options — is displayed using the Plain Text color and font.

CATEGORY	DESCRIPTION
Background	The background color for all editor panes. Make sure that it contrasts well with the colors chosen for text selections, the insertion point, and text. Any element that's the same color as the background will be invisible.
Selection, Insertion Point	The colors used to indicate the current text selection and insertion point.
Plain Text	The color, font, and size for all text that's not colorized using one of the other categories.
Comments	Comments in the source code. For C, Java, and similar languages this means text enclosed by /* and */ character sequences, and the text following a //. For property lists and shell scripts, comments are lines that begin with #. AppleScript denotes comments between pairs of (* and *) and after --.
Documentation Comments	Java's JavaDoc and Darwin's HeaderDoc tools scan source code files and generate documentation for a program or library. Both rely on specially formatted comments that begin with /** or /*! and contain annotations and keywords.
Documentation Comments Keywords	JavaDoc and HeaderDoc comments can also include any number of keywords that identify the different parts of the comment. For instance, the @param keyword is used to document a single parameter of a function call.
Strings	String literals contained between pairs of double quotes. Xcode interprets escape characters; it won't be confused by strings such as "North Carolina (the \"Tar Heel\" State)".

continues

(continued)

CATEGORY	DESCRIPTION
Characters	Character literals contained between single quotes.
Numbers	Numeric constants. Xcode recognizes decimal, octal, and hexadecimal numbers that begin with `0x`. It does not recognize numeric Unicode constants.
Keywords	The standard keywords for the language. Obviously, this will vary wildly from one language to the next. For C-like languages, words such as `for`, `if`, `else`, and `then` are keywords. The word `register` is a keyword in a C++ source file, but not in a Java file. For shell scripts, the keywords are the bash built-in commands.
Preprocessor Statements	Preprocessor directives used by C-based languages, such as `#include` or `#define`. Xcode understands multi-line preprocessor statements.
URLs	Any valid URL.

Font & Color themes provided by Xcode are not editable. To create a customized theme, begin by clicking the Duplicate button to make a copy of any existing theme. To delete a custom theme, select it as the current theme and click the Delete button. If you attempt to edit a built-in theme, Xcode alerts you and gives you the opportunity to duplicate it.

To customize an element, select the category (or categories) in the list and apply any of the text styling commands found in the Edit ⇨ Format menu. As a shortcut, double-clicking a font name opens the Font palette, and double-clicking a color opens the Color-picker palette. Font styles (bold, italic, underline, strikethrough) are generally ignored, unless the font family has variants for specific styles like bold or italic. You can only set the color of the background, selection, insertion point, and index symbol types; these categories don't use a font, or will use the font of the Plain Text category.

Changing Syntax Coloring for a Single File

Syntax coloring is naturally dependent on Xcode knowing in what language your source file is written. By default, Xcode uses the file's type (see the "Source Item Attributes" section in Chapter 5) to determine this. The vast majority of time this is correct. If, for any reason, Xcode guesses wrong, you can manually specify that it use a different language when interpreting the file by selecting the correct language (or None) from the View ⇨ Syntax Coloring menu, as shown in Figure 7-4.

FIGURE 7-4

When Default is selected, the language Xcode has chosen is displayed as a dash in the menu of available languages.

For files that belong to a project, this setting is stored in the project document and is persistent. Otherwise, the selection is lost when the editor pane is closed.

CODE FOLDING

Code folding highlights blocks of structured text and allows them to be collapsed — or "folded" — so that you can concentrate on the higher-level structure of your code. Code folding is supported in all C-like languages (C++, Objective-C, Java) and XML, as shown in Figure 7-5. To see and use code folding, you must have the Show Code Folding Ribbon option turned on in the Text Editing pane of the Xcode Preferences.

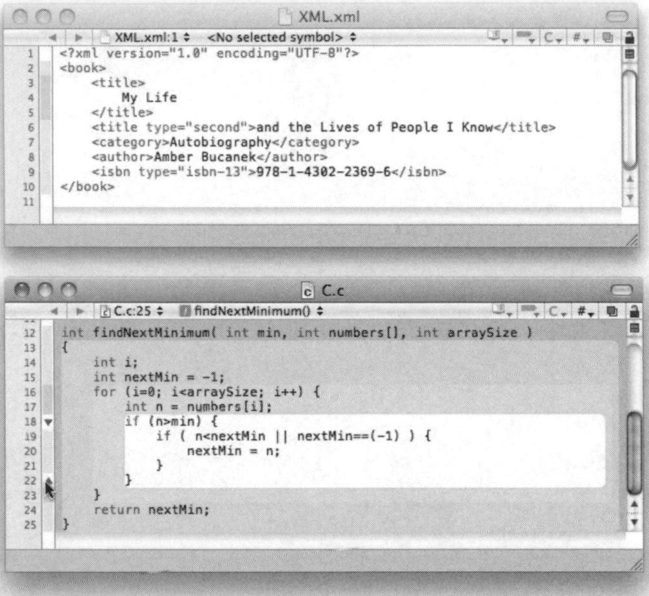

FIGURE 7-5

The code folding ribbon appears between the gutter and the text. The depth of the blocks in your text is graphed using gradations of grey; the darker the ribbon, the deeper the text in that line is nested. Hovering your cursor over the ribbon presents collapse controls for the block of text that begins on that line.

Code Focus

Code focus highlights a block of text in the editor, making it easier to see what the block encompasses, as shown in the bottom window in Figure 7-5. Code focus appears when you hover your cursor over the code folding ribbon. Uncheck the Code Focus option in the preferences to disable this behavior.

If you find code focus really useful, even temporarily, and are tired of moving your cursor over the code folding ribbon, you can have code focus follow your current text selection by choosing View ➪ Code Folding ➪ Focus Follows Selection (Control+Option+Command+F). Now, the code focus animation will continuously highlight the block containing the current selection or insertion point. Invoke the command a second time to toggle the feature off again.

Folding Code

You have four ways to fold a block of code, listed in the following table.

ACTION OR COMMAND	EFFECT
Collapse button in ribbon	Collapses highlighted block
View ⇨ Code Folding ⇨ Fold	Collapses block containing the current selection
View ⇨ Code Folding ⇨ Fold Methods/Functions	Collapses the outmost block of every method or function
View ⇨ Code Folding ⇨ Fold Comment Blocks	Collapses all multi-line comments

Folded code is collapsed and replaced with an ellipsis placeholder, as shown in Figure 7-6.

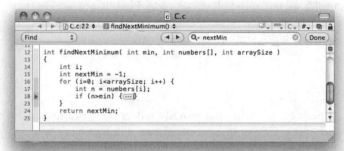

FIGURE 7-6

The Fold command folds the block containing the current text selection or insertion point, and is the only fold action that uses the current selection. The Collapse button folds the highlighted block in the ribbon, and the other two commands apply globally to the entire file.

Folding comment blocks only applies to multi-line comments (like /* ... */). The command does not recognize, or fold, successive lines of single-line comments (//).

Have no fear; the text in the folded region is still there. Including a folded block placeholder in a text selection includes all of the text in that block, just as if it weren't folded.

Unfolding Code

You have six ways to unfold code, listed in the following table.

ACTION OR COMMAND	EFFECT
Expand button in ribbon	Expands collapsed block
View ➪ Code Folding ➪ Unfold	Expands blocks contained in the selected text or in the selected block
View ➪ Code Folding ➪ Unfold Methods/Functions	Expands the outmost block of every method or function
View ➪ Code Folding ➪ Unfold Comment Blocks	Expands all multi-line comments
View ➪ Code Folding ➪ Unfold All	Expands all collapsed blocks
Display any text in a collapsed block	Expands the block containing the text

The first four actions are symmetric complements to the code folding actions in the previous section. In addition, the Unfold All command unfolds all collapsed blocks of code. Finally, any action that you take that causes some text to be selected or revealed — searching for text or jumping to a symbol definition — automatically expands the block so that the text is visible.

INDENTING TEXT

Over the years, programmers have developed coding styles that visually reflect the structured nature of the languages in which they are programming. One of these conventions is indenting. These conventions have become so common and consistent, that many can be automated.

Indenting is accomplished by starting a line with tab or space characters. Using spaces to indent lines is the most predictable method, but creates unnecessarily large files. Tab characters are more efficient, but are problematic because there is no standard that dictates how many column positions a tab character represents. If you decide that tab stops should be every four columns and you open a text file from a programmer who thought tabs should be every eight columns, the text won't line up correctly. You'll achieve the greatest compatibility by adopting four-column tab stops, which seems to be the most common setting these days. You can also alter the tab width for individual files. The default tab settings for files are configured in the Indentation tab of the Xcode Preferences.

Xcode's tab width, indenting, and auto-formatting behaviors are all set globally in the preference's Indenting pane, shown in Figure 7-7. The tab widths are default for files, but individual files can override these global settings. The remaining options in this preferences pane are global and apply to all source files.

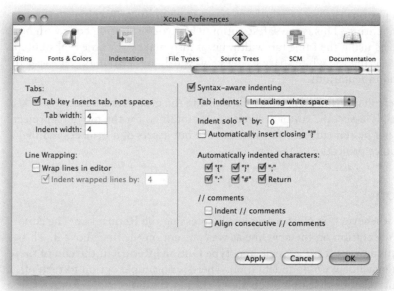

FIGURE 7-7

Setting Tab Width and Indent Width

Xcode makes a distinction between the width of the tab stops and the amount by which each line of code is indented. The two numbers do not have to be the same. The Tab Width setting, shown in Figure 7-7, determines the width of the tab stops in characters. The Indent Width setting is the number of columns' worth of white space added to the beginning of a line to indent it one level. Xcode uses the most efficient combination of spaces and tabs that it can. If the indent width is an integer multiple of the tab width, only tab characters are used to indent lines. If not, a combination of tabs and spaces is used to achieve the desired indentation. Say you have a tab width of 8 and an indent width of 4. To indent a line one level requires four space characters. Indenting two levels would cause these spaces to be replaced by a single tab.

The global tab and indent width settings can be overridden for an individual file either in the Info window for the file, or by choosing the View ➪ Text ➪ Tab Settings command, both of which are shown in Figure 7-8.

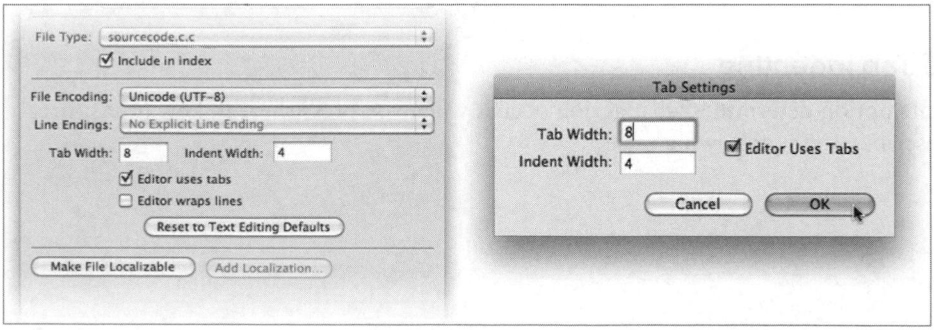

FIGURE 7-8

The Editor Uses Tabs option permits the use of tab characters to indent lines. Turning it off forces Xcode to use spaces for all indenting. This is the safest option when you're sharing code with other programmers who might not be using the same tab width, but it also makes your files substantially larger. I also think it makes deleting the white space in lines awkward, and also makes it easier to inadvertently align text at odd indentations.

The Reset to Text Editing Defaults button returns the file to using the global settings in the Indentation preferences panel. File-specific editor settings are maintained for the file in its project document. The settings will not be remembered for files that are not assets of a project, and the settings are independent of other projects.

Automatic Indentation

Automatic indenting occurs whenever you start a new line by pressing the Return key. The editor inserts the same amount of indentation on the new line as was present on the line above it. This feature is always active. To circumvent it for a single line, type Option+Return at the end of the line. Option+Return starts a new line with no indentation. There is no simple option to turn off auto-indentation globally, but it can be defeated by changing the key binding for the Return key, as explained in Chapter 23.

Syntax-Aware Indentation

Enabling Syntax-Aware Indenting in the Indentation pane of the Xcode Preferences turns on a number of additional features that will aid you in indenting source code and forming code blocks. You can have Xcode do any of the following:

➤ Automatically indent lines when you press the Tab key

➤ Automatically indent code blocks

➤ Automatically create a balanced code block when you type a { character

➤ Automatically re-indent a line when you type one of several punctuation characters

➤ Automatically indent C-style comments

Each feature can be independently configured or disabled, as desired.

Syntax-Aware Tab Indenting

The Tab Indents option determines what action occurs when you press the Tab key. It has three settings, as described in the following table.

TAB INDENTS SETTING	TAB KEY ACTION
In Leading White Space	When the text cursor is at the beginning, in, or immediately to the right of any white space at the beginning of the line, pressing the Tab key causes the entire line to be indented one level. When not in this leading non–white space portion of the line, the Tab key inserts a single tab character.
Always	Regardless of where the cursor position is within the line, pressing the Tab key causes the line to be re-indented.
Never	Tab key inserts a tab character.

The In Leading White Space setting is the most useful when you're programming in block-structured languages. At the beginning of the line, pressing the Tab key indents the line. Within the line, typically at the end of a statement where you want to begin a comment, the Tab key simply inserts a tab character.

> *"White space" refers to the non-graphic, printable characters in the Unicode character set. Practically, that means the tab, space, and end-of-line characters, but, technically, it also includes characters like the non-breaking space (Unicode 0x00A0). White space characters get their name from the fact that they cause subsequent characters in the file to be shifted to new lines or column positions, but are not themselves visible. In other words, they just leave a white space on the page.*

Note that the first two settings are not variations on one another. Xcode has two indentation functions: indent and re-indent. Indent increases the indentation level of a line by inserting more white space. Re-indention looks at the indention of the line with respect to the indentation of the line that precedes it, and uses syntax-aware rules to determine what its indentation level should be. Repeatedly indenting a line continues to shift the line further and further to the right. Repeatedly re-indenting a line does nothing. Until you change the contents of the line, or the preceding line, Xcode repeatedly reformats the text to the same indentation level.

You can circumvent the settings for the Tab key at any time by using Option+Tab or Control+I. Option+Tab always inserts a tab character, regardless of the syntax-aware tab settings. Control+I always performs a re-indent of the currently selected line, or lines, and is the same as the Edit ➪ Format ➪ Re-indent command.

Indenting Solitary "{"

Returning to the Indentations tab of the Xcode Preferences (see Figure 7-7), the Indent Solo "{" option determines what happens when an opening brace is the first non–white space character of a line. The option determines how much the line will be indented relative to the previous line. This is independent of the Indent Width setting, but if non-zero it's typically the same value — the Horstmann style illustrates an exception. The following table illustrates some popular coding styles that can benefit from this option. The table assumes an indent width of 4.

STYLE	INDENT SOLO "{"	EXAMPLE

Allman	0	`if (a==b)`
		`{`
		`    foo();`
		`}`

Whitesmiths	4	`if (a==b)`
		`    {`
		`    foo();`
		`    }`

GNU	2	`if (a==b)`
		`  {`
		`    foo();`
		`  }`

Horstmann	0	`if (a==b)`
		`{   foo();`
		`}`

The indentation amount is always relative to the indentation of the previous line, *not* the indentation level of the line containing the leading { character. In other words, if the Indent Solo "{" setting is 4 characters and the line was already indented four characters more than the previous line, a leading { changes nothing. In fact, the indentation level could decrease if the Indent Solo "{" setting is lower than the nominal indentation amount for the line.

Automatically Close { ... } Blocks

The Automatically Insert Closing "}" option does two things when you type a { character: it inserts a line with a matching } ahead of the cursor, and then it advances to the next line as if the Return key had been pressed. The effect is simple: typing a { creates a balanced block with the cursor positioned at the first line of the block. Figure 7-9 shows an `if` statement before and after a single { character was typed.

Controlling When Automatic Indentation Occurs

The Automatically Indented Characters setting selects the characters that trigger an automatic re-indentation of the current line. When a character in the set is checked, typing one of

FIGURE 7-9

those characters is the same as invoking the Edit ➪ Format ➪ Re-indent command after typing the character. Note that this is a *re-indent*, not an indent; Xcode reinterprets the line using its syntax-aware rules and determines the appropriate indentation level for the line based on its new content. This may, or may not, change the indentation of the line. This re-indentation occurs *after* the character has been inserted. Thus, the Return key calculates the indentation of the new line it just created, not the line the Return key was pressed on.

Indenting Comments

The two // Comments options apply to C/C++-style comments when a line is re-indented. They are not applied when comments are being typed. The Indent // Comments option treats // comments like any other program statement and indents them to the same level as the surrounding code. If off, // comments are left at whatever indentation level the programmer typed them. The Align Consecutive // Comments option indents a // comment that appears alone on a line to the same indentation level as the // comment in the previous line. This is most significant when // comments are started to the right of a program statement and continued in another // comment on the next line.

The following three listings illustrate the effects of the two comment formatting options:

No // Comment Formatting

```
int main (int argc, char * const argv[])

{

// Check the environment

    char * server_addr = getenv("SERVER");

    if (server_addr==NULL)

        exit(3);            // terminate immediately

                // returning a status of 3
```

Indent // Comments Only

```
int main (int argc, char * const argv[])

{

    // Check the environment

    char * server_addr = getenv("SERVER");

    if (server_addr==NULL)

        exit(3);            // terminate immediately

    // returning a status of 3
```

Indent // Comments and Align Consecutive // Comments

```
int main (int argc, char * const argv[])

{

    // Check the environment

    char * server_addr = getenv("SERVER");

    if (server_addr==NULL)
```

```
    exit(3);            // terminate immediately
                        // returning a status of 3
```

When you use both comment formatting options, you should get in the habit of inserting a blank line before starting a new C/C++-style comment on its own line. Otherwise, it may get indented to the level of the comment on the previous line.

Re-indenting Text

As mentioned earlier, re-indenting text uses the language-specific rules to determine the appropriate indentation level for each line. This can happen automatically as you type, depending on which syntax-aware indentation options you have enabled, or manually when you use Control+I or the Edit ➪ Format ➪ Re-indent command. It also happens whenever text is pasted from the clipboard.

You can always manually alter the indentation level of a line, or lines, using the Edit ➪ Format ➪ Shift Right (Command+]) and Edit ➪ Format ➪ Shift Left (Command+[) commands. These either increase or decrease the indentation of every line in the selection by indentation width. Lines that are already at the left margin cannot be decreased any further. This is just a manual adjustment of the amount of white space at the beginning of the line. A subsequent re-indent recalculates the appropriate indentation level based on the language rules, undoing any effect of Shift Right or Shift Left.

CODE COMPLETION

The most sophisticated feature of syntax-aware editing is Code Completion, Xcode's auto-completion technology. Code completion analyzes the context of the code you are typing and interactively offers suggestions for completing the statement. Code completion supports the C, C++, Objective-C, Objective-C++, Java, and AppleScript languages. It works by assembling a list of symbol names from the Code Sense index that would be appropriate at that point in your code. If you are starting a new statement, the appropriate symbols will include any global variable, function, class name, or language keyword, but if you typed a class or structure name, the appropriate symbols would be only the member functions or instance variables in that class or structure. Figure 7-10 shows the available completions for the CGSize structure nested inside a CGRect structure.

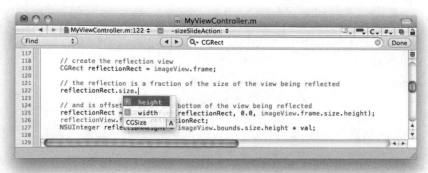

FIGURE 7-10

Code completion uses the context, scope, and type of variables found in the Code Sense index. Consequently, code completion is very accurate and is not easily fooled by namespace, scope, or preprocessor macros.

Accepting Suggestions

Code completion appears in two forms: suggestions and completion lists. Suggestions appear ahead of your typing, as shown in Figure 7-11. In this example I typed the text NSDic and code completion suggested the rest.

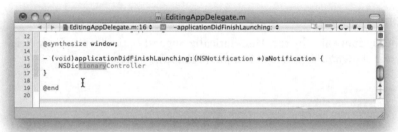

FIGURE 7-11

The portion of grey text to the right of the insertion point is the suggestion. You can accept a suggestion by pressing the Tab key. To ignore a suggestion, just keep typing.

The highlighted portion of the suggestion is what will be inserted if you press the Tab key. Xcode recognizes that many symbol names are very similar. In the code in Figure 7-11, you might want to type NSDictionary or NSDictionaryController. If you wanted NSDictionary, press Tab once (to accept the NSDictionary portion) and continue typing. If you wanted NSDictionaryController instead, start by pressing the Tab key once to accept the tionary suggestion. Code completion immediately returns with all of the suggestions that begin with NSDictionary, which include NSDictionaryController, as shown in Figure 7-12. Pressing Tab a second time accepts the Controller suggestion and the classname is complete.

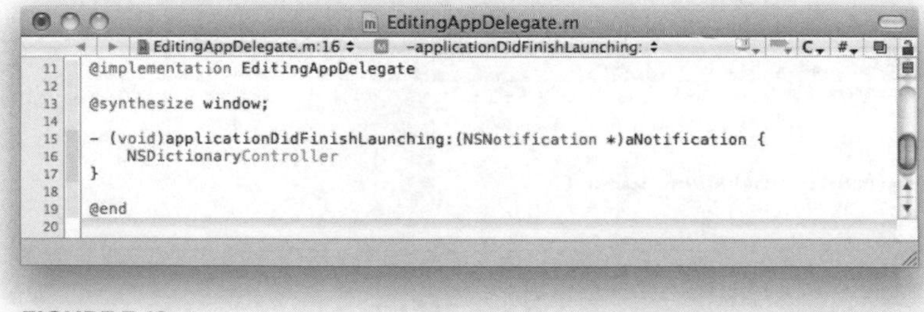

FIGURE 7-12

This successive refinement of suggestions permits you to narrow down your choice quickly from huge families of class and constant names that share common prefixes.

 Symbol completion is case-insensitive and retroactively corrects the case of what you've already typed. In the example in Figure 7-11, I could have just as easily typed nsdic instead of NSDic. If I accepted Xcode's suggestion of NSDictionary, the case of the letters I had already typed would have been changed to agree with the symbol. If I ignored the suggestion, the text would have reverted to its original lowercase form.

Suggestion Display Settings

The appearance of suggestions is controlled by the Automatically Suggest option in the Code Sense panel of the preferences, as was shown in Figure 7-1. The possible settings are:

➤ Never

➤ Immediately

➤ With Delay

Never means suggestions never appear while you're typing, but those suggestions and the completion lists are still available. Immediately and With Delay automatically present suggestions either all the time, or only after you've stopped typing for a moment. Suggestions never appear unless Xcode thinks it can make a reasonably accurate guess about what you're typing. For example, thousands of symbols begin with NS in the Cocoa framework. Typing NS will not present any suggestions. Neither will typing NSFile — almost 100 symbols begin with NSFile. But typing NSFileW will suggest either NSFileWrite or NSFileWrapper, followed by the two dozen or so symbols that begin with those prefixes.

Getting Another Suggestion

At any time — even when a suggestion isn't being presented in your text — you can prompt Xcode to offer the next suggestion in its list of candidates by choosing Edit ⇨ Next Completion (Control+.). This command inserts the next suggestion in the list, sort of on a trial basis, as shown in Figure 7-13. While a suggestion appears ahead of your insertion point in grey text, Next Completion inserts the suggestion but remembers what it inserted.

```
EditingAppDelegate.m
EditingAppDelegate.m:16    ~applicationDidFinishLaunching:                    C  #

11   @implementation EditingAppDelegate
12
13   @synthesize window;
14
15   - (void)applicationDidFinishLaunching:(NSNotification *)aNotification {
16       NSDictionaryController
17   }
18
19   @end
20
```

FIGURE 7-13

If you like the suggestion, just keep typing — the suggestion is already part of your text. If you don't, choose Edit ➪ Undo (Command+Z) or choose Next Completion again. Next Completion erases the previous suggestion and inserts the next one. You can do this repeatedly, cycling through every suggestion until you find the one you want.

Using Completion Lists

Choose Edit ➪ Completion List (Esc) to see the entire list of possible completions. You can do this at any time; you don't have to wait for Xcode to make a suggestion first. The completion list menu shows every possible completion based on the context of your current insertion point. A completion list for an NSNotification object is shown in Figure 7-14.

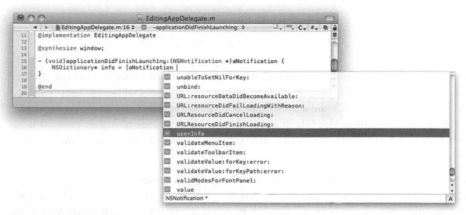

FIGURE 7-14

The list can be extensive. In this example, it includes every method of NSNotification, every method of its NSObject superclass, and every category of NSObject. The list can be navigated using the mouse or keyboard (up arrow, down arrow, home, end, page up, page down). You can also continue to type; the completion list will refine itself as you do. Press Tab or Return to accept the currently selected suggestion from the list, or Esc again to close the list.

 Code completion requires some practice. Don't get discouraged at first. Once you become used to the "rhythm" of suggestions and the keyboard shortcuts to accept, pick, and reject suggestions, coding even the longest symbol names becomes rapid and accurate.

The typical technique is to use the completion list as a guide to what symbols exist. Type enough of the first portion of the symbol you want, until the list becomes short enough to use the keyboard arrows to select the desired symbol from the list. Then press Tab or Return to insert the suggestion.

Completion Arguments

When Xcode completes a function or method name, it inserts placeholders for its arguments, as shown in Figure 7-15.

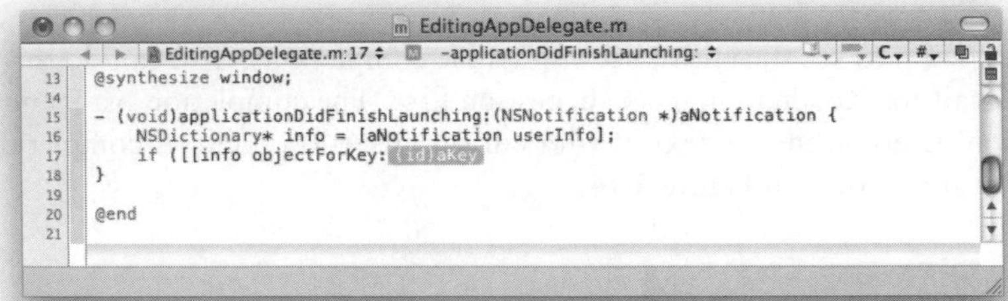

FIGURE 7-15

After the completion, the first placeholder is selected automatically. To provide a value for the first placeholder just begin typing — with code completion, of course. The special Edit ⇨ Select Next Placeholder (Control+/) command finds the next placeholder in the file and selects it. To finish the method or function call, repeatedly replace the placeholders with the required arguments. You don't have to replace them in any particular order, and you can leave placeholders in your code indefinitely.

The Show Arguments in Pop-Up List option of the Code Sense Preferences pane (see Figure 7-1) controls whether argument placeholders appear in suggestion or the completion list. C, C++, and Java programmers should turn this option on. These languages use method overloading and without the argument placeholders it's impossible to distinguish between multiple functions that differ only in their argument types. Objective-C programmers, on the other hand, will probably want to turn this off because Objective-C method names are unique and tend to be descriptive of their argument types.

TEXT MACROS

Text macros are another kind of auto-completion. These are text fragments that can be inserted whenever you need them. The text macros supplied by Xcode include a variety of common control structures and programming conventions, the kind that programmers tend to reuse repeatedly. This section discusses how to use text macros.

Text macros are organized by language in the Edit ⇨ Insert Text Macro menu. Select the desired macro, and its contents are inserted into the editor pane. When using the menu, you can choose any macro you want, but it really only makes sense to choose a macro that is appropriate to the language you're writing in.

Text macros can contain placeholders, just like code completions for methods and functions. They may also contain a special placeholder that is replaced by the current selection in the editor. For instance, on the left in Figure 7-16 the statement `free(byteArray);` is selected. After you select Edit ⇨ Insert Text Macro ⇨ C ⇨ If Block, the text is replaced with the code on the right. If you don't have anything selected, a `statements` placeholder is inserted instead.

 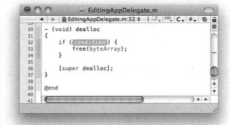

FIGURE 7-16

Like function arguments inserted by code completion, the first placeholder in the macro is automatically selected. Use the same Select Next Placeholder (Control+/) command to jump to any additional placeholders.

Code completion can also insert text macros. Each text macro has a name property. These names appear in the completion list alongside other top-level function and symbol names. The following table lists a few of the text macros — accessible via code completion — that will save you a lot of typing.

CODE COMPLETION NAME	INSERTS
init	Skeleton Objective-C `-(id)init` method
dealloc	Skeleton Objective-C `-(void)dealloc` method
if/for/while/do/switch/case	C control blocks
@try	Objective-C `@try`/`@catch`/`@finally` block

Unlike the menu, only those macros appropriate to your file's language appear. Selecting one inserts the entire text macro. Because you have to be typing the name of the macro to invoke code completion, you cannot simultaneously select text to replace the `statements` placeholder. If you want to use this feature, you have to invoke the macro by using the menu.

Macros can have several variations. Inserting the C ⇨ If Block macro inserts a simple conditional block guarded by a conditional. Without editing anything, select the macro from the menu again. The second time, the simple conditional block is replaced by a compound `if/else` statement with two blocks. The following code listing shows these two iterations. Some HTML macros have four or more variations for a single macro.

First Use of Edit ⇨ Insert Text Macro ⇨ C ⇨ If Block

```
int foo( int bar )

{

 if (<#condition#>) {

        <#statements#>

 }

 }
```

Immediately Selecting Edit ⇨ Insert Text Macro ⇨ C ⇨ If Block Again

```
int foo( int bar )

{

 if (<#condition#>) {

        <#statements#>

 }

 else {

        <#statements#>

 }

 }
```

When inserting macros from code completion, use the Edit ⇨ Next Completion (Control+.) command to cycle through the variants of a text macro.

> *The text* <#statements#> *in these listings appears as a single* statements *placeholder in the Xcode editor. If you save the file, it will contain the text* "<#statements#>" *where the placeholder is. If you add text to your file using this form (that is,* <#name#>*), it won't appear as a placeholder, but the Edit ⇨ Next Completion command will jump to it like any other placeholder.*

EDITING SYMBOL NAMES

The editor provides a small, eclectic set of shortcuts for finding and editing symbol names. These are referred to collectively as the "Edit All in Scope" feature, although that's just one of its functions. This feature is enabled in the Code Sense pane (see Figure 7-1 again) of the preferences and can be set to Never, Immediate, or With Delay. When enabled, hovering your cursor over a symbol name that's selected or is at the current insertion point presents a pop-up menu button, as shown in Figure 7-17.

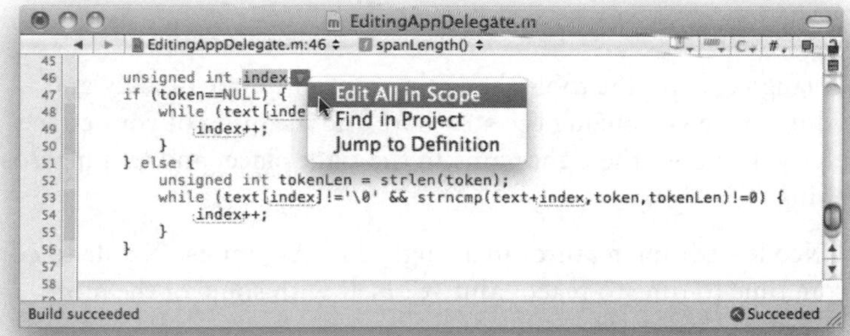

FIGURE 7-17

Clicking this button presents three commands. The Edit All in Scope command is a quick means of renaming all occurrences of that symbol within the block of code that contains it. To use it, choose Edit All in Scope and type a replacement name. The editor highlights all occurrences of the symbol so you can see what is about to be changed, and then simultaneously replaces all occurrences as you type. The results are shown in Figure 7-18.

FIGURE 7-18

Alternatively, you can also select a symbol name and choose the Edit ⇨ All In Scope (Control+Command+T) command. Use the command if you're in a hurry or have set the Edit All in Scope setting to Never.

The Find in Project command makes the current symbol the search text and opens the Find in Project window. Learn more about searching projects in Chapter 8. The Jump to Definition command is the same one described in the "Jumping to a Definition" section in Chapter 6.

SUMMARY

Xcode's editor provides powerful, language-specific tools that help you write code quickly and accurately. Code coloring and folding make visualizing the structure and meaning of your code much easier. Code completion helps you choose the right name in the right place, and text macros save you from many repetitive coding tasks.

You probably won't absorb all of Xcode's editing features in a single day. As you use Xcode to edit files, revisit these two chapters from time to time to reacquaint yourself with some of the more esoteric features.

Though the editor provides a number of navigation features that will jump to predetermined or saved locations, sometimes you just need to go looking for something, or replace occurrences of one thing with something else. The next chapter explains how.

Searching

WHAT'S IN THIS CHAPTER?

➤ Searching and replacing text in a single file

➤ Searching and replacing text across multiple files

➤ Using advanced search patterns

➤ Using search history to repeat searches and revisit results

➤ Learning search shortcuts and tricks

A lot of development is spent just looking for things: finding all occurrences of a particular constant, looking for a message in a string, finding where a family of symbols is defined, and so on. Learning to use Xcode's find and replace features can save you a lot of tedious work.

Xcode provides five basic facilities for finding, and potentially replacing, text and code definitions in your project:

➤ Single file search

➤ Multi-file search

➤ Definition search

➤ Syntax-aware refactoring

➤ Edit All in Scope

Taking the last two first, the Edit All in Scope feature was described in the "Editing Symbol Names" section of Chapter 7. Refactoring, which can change (aka find and replace) symbol names intelligently, is described in Chapter 10. All of the remaining tools are described in this chapter.

Single and multi-file search tools search the text files in your project for text patterns or regular expressions, and optionally replace them, either individually or *en masse*. You can also search your project's symbol definitions (Code Sense index) intelligently to locate the code that defines a symbol.

Xcode keeps a history of your searches and their results, making it easy to repeat a search or revisit the result of a former one. Finally, a lot of shortcuts and tricks exist for performing all kinds of find and replace actions swiftly and effortlessly.

SEARCHING AND REPLACING TEXT IN A SINGLE FILE

The single file search bar appears at the top of the active editor pane whenever you choose either the Edit ⇨ Find ⇨ Find (Command+F) or the Edit ⇨ Find ⇨ Find and Replace (Control+Command+F) command, as shown in Figure 8-1.

FIGURE 8-1

The search bar has two modes: the find mode appears when you choose the Find command. The replace mode appears when you choose the Find and Replace command. You can change between modes using the pop-up menu on the left, or by choosing one of the alternate search commands. Dismiss the search bar by clicking the Done button or pressing the Esc key.

Setting Search Options

The search bar contains a search pattern field, previous and next match buttons, a search options menu, and clear button, all shown in Figure 8-2.

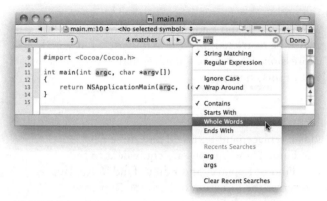

FIGURE 8-2

Type the text pattern you want to find in the search field and use the next or previous button to jump to the next (or previous) occurrence of that pattern in the file. The commands Edit ⇨ Find ⇨ Next (Command+G) and Edit ⇨ Find ⇨ Previous (Shift+Command+G) are synonymous with the next and previous buttons, respectively.

The search menu, also shown in Figure 8-2, has a number of options that control the search behavior and how the search pattern is interpreted, as shown in the following table.

SEARCH OPTION	EFFECT
String Matching	Search pattern is a literal string.
Regular Expression	Search pattern is a regular expression.
Ignore Case	Letters in the search pattern match both upper- and lowercase text.
Wrap Around	If there are no more occurrences of the search pattern in the file, the next and previous commands continue searching from the beginning or end of the file, respectively.
Contains	Search string matches any sequence of text in the file.
Starts With	Search string only matches text that starts at a word boundary.
Whole Words	Search string only matches text that starts and ends at word boundaries.
Ends With	Search string only matches text that ends at a word boundary.
Recent Searches	A menu of recent search patterns.
Clear Recent Searches	Clears the Recent Searches menu.

The String Matching and Regular Expression options are mutually exclusive. The word boundary options (Contains, Starts With, Whole Word, and Ends With) apply only to String Matching. Regular Expression searches can also be restricted to word boundaries, but you'll have to include that as part of the regular expression. Read more about regular expressions in the "Regular Expression Search" section later in this chapter.

Replacing Text

Switching the search bar to replace mode adds a replacement text field and three new buttons: Replace All, Replace, and Replace & Find. These buttons are equivalent to the commands Edit ➪ Find ➪ Replace All, Edit ➪ Find ➪ Replace, and Edit ➪ Find ➪ Replace and Find Next. Holding down the Shift key reverses the direction of both the Replace and Find Next command and button. The commands and their effect are listed in the following table.

COMMAND	EFFECT
Replace All	Replaces all occurrences of the pattern with the contents of the replacement text field. The current text selection is ignored.
Replace	Replaces the current text selection with the replacement text field. The current selection, or insertion point, doesn't have to match the search pattern; it's unconditionally replaced.
Replace and Find Next/Previous	Perform a Replace, and then find the next (or previous) occurrence of the search pattern.

All replacements performed by Replace All occupy a single step in the file's undo history. Performing an Edit ➪ Undo immediately afterwards restores all replaced text with the original pattern. Replace and Replace and Find Next/Previous replace one occurrence at a time.

If you searched for text using a regular expression, you may want to read the section "Replacing Text Using Regular Expressions" later in this chapter.

SEARCHING AND REPLACING TEXT IN MULTIPLE FILES

Every open project has a single Project Find window. Choose the Edit ➪ Find ➪ Find In Project (Shift+Command+F) command to open the Project Find window for the active project. The Project Find window, shown in Figure 8-3, consists of three principal parts.

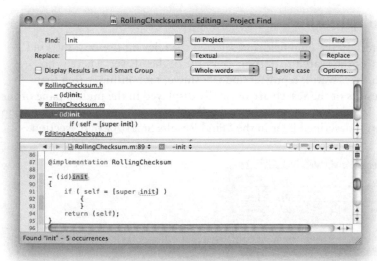

FIGURE 8-3

At the top of the window are the search and replace options. The middle pane displays a summary of search results. The bottom pane is an editor that jumps to a selected search result.

The find and replace fields, search options, and buttons are functionally equivalent to those in the editor's search bar. In addition, there are controls to select the set of files to be searched along with some special search options.

To the right of the Find and Replace fields are three pop-up menus. The top one selects the batch find options set to use, which essentially determines the set of files to search. Normally, this is set to In Project, which searches all of the source items in the project. The Options button lets you alter the batch find options and define your own sets. Batch find options are described later in the section "Batch Find Options."

The middle pop-up menu selects how the Find field is interpreted and can be set to one of:

➤ Textual

➤ Regular Expression

➤ Definitions

➤ Symbols

The first two choices, Textual and Regular Expression, are the same as the String Matching and Regular Expression search options described earlier for single file searches. In addition, you can search your project's Code Sense index for definitions or symbols. Those search types are described later in the "Symbol Search" section.

The bottom pop-up selects between the four textual search modes: Contains, Starts With, Ends With, and Whole Words. Like the single file search, word boundary options apply to all search types except Regular Expression. The Ignore Case option works the same way it does in the editor's search bar.

Finding a Pattern in Multiple Files

Once you've entered a search pattern in the Find field and selected the relevant options, the Find button searches for every instance of the search pattern in every file of the file set. There is no direction (for example, forward or backward); a project find is a single, monolithic search that produces a list of matches. The results of the search are normally displayed in the middle pane of the window, as shown in Figure 8-4. If they are not, make sure the Display Results in Find Smart Group option is *not* checked. This option is described later in the "Find Results Smart Group" section.

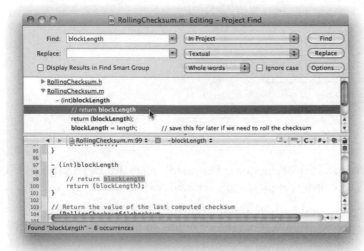

FIGURE 8-4

Every file that contains the search pattern is listed in the results pane as a group. The individual lines within each file that match the pattern are listed below each file. Use the disclosure triangle next to the file to collapse or expand the group, temporarily hiding all of the "hits" in a specific file. The text that matched the search pattern is displayed in bold text. A single line may appear more than once if the search patterns occurred several times in that line.

Select any line in the search results list and the matching text is immediately displayed in the editor pane at the bottom of the window. You can resize the divider between the list and the editor pane, or collapse it by double-clicking it. This is a full-featured editor pane, supporting all of the built-in editing features described in Chapter 6 — including its own single file search bar.

> **TIP TO REMEMBER**
>
> *You can "peek" at an excessively long line — one that extends beyond the right edge of the window — in the search results list by hovering your cursor over the line.*

 Recalling an earlier search pattern from the search history also recalls the search results for that pattern. See the section "Search History" for more about recalling previous search patterns.

With the search results pane active, the up and down arrow keys move from one search result to the next, allowing you to skip quickly to each found pattern, revealing its context in the editor pane.

Replacing Text in Multiple Files

The Replace button replaces some or all of the occurrences listed in the find results with the text in the Replace field. Regular Expression searches can use replacement variables (see the section "Replacing Text Using Regular Expressions" later in this chapter). The selected text lines in the results list determine which occurrences are replaced. If no source lines are selected, all listed occurrences are replaced. If one, or more, text lines is selected, *only those occurrences* are replaced. Note that selecting a file group in the list has no effect and is not considered an occurrence. Use the Edit ➪ Select All command to select all visible (not collapsed) lines in the results list. Select a subset using the Shift and Command keys while clicking lines in the list.

Clicking the Replace button presents a dialog box like the one in Figure 8-5. Make a habit of reading the confirmation dialog box before committing to the replace. It is very easy to accidentally replace all occurrences when you just wanted to replace one, or a subset of the occurrences when you wanted to replace them all. The latter usually happens when you perform a search, browse the results (leaving text lines in the results list selected), and then perform the replace — mistakenly thinking that Xcode will replace them all.

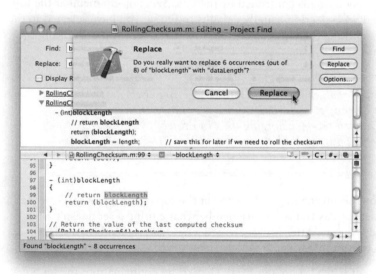

FIGURE 8-5

Batch Find Options

Which files the Find command in the Project Find window searches for is determined by the batch find options. Batch find options are stored in sets. You select a set using the top pop-up menu control in the Project Find window. By default, the set is In Project. This set searches all of the files referred to by the project, excluding those in frameworks. Clicking the Options button presents the Batch Find Options window, shown in Figure 8-6.

FIGURE 8-6

The batch find options set you are modifying is controlled by the Find Sets pop-up menu at the top of the window. Be careful: the Find Sets selection usually defaults to the set you have selected in the find window, but might not. After clicking the Options button, first make sure you are editing the correct set before changing anything.

Batch find options sets are global; changing the settings for an existing set changes its definition for all *projects. The best advice is never to change any of the settings in the predefined sets — changing the "In Project" set to search frameworks really defeats the purpose of having a set named "In Project." If you want to define a special set of options, create a custom set; it's easy to do.*

Create additional batch find options sets using the Add button at the top of the window. Give the new set a name and then edit its settings as you see fit. Remember that editing a set doesn't alter the set selected in the Project Find window. After you've created a new set, remember to select that set in the Project Find window in order to use it.

The Delete button deletes the current batch find options set. There is no confirmation; the set is deleted immediately and permanently for all projects.

The four check boxes at the left enable one of four sets of files; the union of those sets defines the complete set of files that will be searched — subject to some additional filtering. The possible sets are:

➤ The Search in Open Documents option includes any file open in any editor pane.

➤ The Search in Open Projects option includes files to which open projects refer. Which files, and from which projects, is defined by the next two radio button groups.

➤ The first group determines which files are included, and can be set to Selected Files in This Project, All Files in This Project, All Open Projects, or This Project and Referenced Projects. Normally, it is set to All Files in This Project and only searches the files in the current project. If you typically work with multiple projects that are related, using All Open Projects or This Project and Referenced Projects lets you search the files in all open or related projects. Selected Files in This Project requires that you first select the specific files you want to search in the project source group.

➤ The second radio button group considers whether the project source file reference is part of a framework. Project Files and Frameworks includes all source files to which the project refers, including all of the source files in any frameworks. Project Files Only excludes the headers and source files contained in frameworks. Frameworks Only searches only the headers and source files in the frameworks, ignoring the source files of the project itself.

➤ The Search in Included Files option adds any files included by files to the set.

➤ The Search in Files and Folders option adds the arbitrary list of files and folders immediately underneath the option to the set. Add a file or directory by clicking the plus (+) button below the list, or simply drag files and folders into the list. Remove items from the list by selecting them and clicking the minus (–) button or pressing the Delete key. Each batch find options set has its own list of additional files.

On the right are filtering options that refine the set of files to search:

➤ The All Candidate Files option doesn't exclude any files; it searches all of the text files defined by the other options.

➤ The Source Files Only option limits the search to candidate files that contain source code. Text files such as documentation, RTF, XML, and HTML are skipped.

➤ The Filter Files Using regex Patterns option allows you to filter the candidate set of files by filename and extension using regular expressions.

When filtering using regular expressions, each enabled (checked) regular expression in the patterns list is applied to each candidate filename. If the filename matches all of the checked expressions, it's included in the search. If not, it's ignored. The key points to keep in mind when editing the regular expression pattern list are:

➤ The pattern list is global. Changing a pattern's definition changes it for every batch find options set in every project.

➤ A batch find options set uses only those patterns that are enabled (checked) for that set. Each set remembers which patterns it uses.

➤ A candidate filename must match *all* of the checked patterned. In other words, the set of files to search is formed by the intersection (logical AND) of the file sets defined by each regular expression.

➤ The Include/Exclude option inverts the sense of the regular expression: when set to Include, a file is a member if it matches the expression. When set to Exclude, a file is a member if it *does not* match the expression.

Add a pattern to the list using the + button below the list; remove patterns using the - button. Check the pattern (to enable it), and then double-click the pattern to edit it, as shown in Figure 8-7.

FIGURE 8-7

 Each batch find options set remembers which patterns it uses, but the patterns themselves are a global list, shared by all sets of every project. This allows you to share patterns with other sets and projects easily, but also means that if you edit a pattern you're changing the rule for every batch finds options set everywhere. When in doubt, create a new pattern.

To the left of each pattern is the Include/Exclude control that determines whether the pattern must match (or not match) a filename to be included in the set.

For a file to be included in the search, its name must satisfy all of the checked regular expression patterns in the list. If the list has the two patterns `Include \.m$` and `Include \.h$` both checked, then no files will be searched; there is no filename that will match both `\.m$` and `\.h$`. In general, use at most one `Include` pattern to define the principle group of files to consider, and then use additional `Exclude` terms to winnow out unwanted files.

SEARCH PATTERNS

The various Find commands all apply a search pattern to the text of your files in order to find the text that matches the pattern. Xcode gives you a lot of flexibility in specifying the parameters of your search, from a simple, unanchored literal text string to complex regular expressions. This section describes some of the finer points of the three kinds of search that Xcode performs.

Textual or String Search

Searching for a string, also referred to as a textual or literal string search, is the simplest type of search. The search scans the text of a file looking for the exact sequence of characters in the search pattern field.

You can refine the search by requiring that a pattern be found on a word boundary. The options are described in the following table.

SEARCH MODE	STRING MATCHES
Contains	Matches the string pattern anywhere in the text. This option turns off word boundary restrictions.
Starts With	Matches text starting with the character immediately after a word boundary.
Ends With	Matches text ending with the character immediately preceding a word boundary.
Whole Words	Matches text only if both the first and the last characters of the matched text begin and end on word boundaries.

The Ignore Case option causes case differences between the text and the string pattern to be ignored. With this option on, the letters *a* or *A* in the pattern will match any *a* or *A* in the text, interchangeably. Likewise, the letter *ü* will match either *ü* or *Ü* in the text, but not *u*, *ù*, *ú*, or *û*. Matching is based on the Unicode rules for letter case. This option has no effect on punctuation or special characters. These must always match exactly.

Regular Expression Search

For those of you who have been living in a cave since the 1960s, regular expressions are strings of characters that describe patterns of text. Using a textual match, described in the previous section, the pattern "c.t" would match the literal text "c.t" in a file. In a regular expression the period character (.) is instead interpreted as a pattern that means "match any single character." Thus, the regular expression "c.t" describes a sequence of three characters: The letter *c*, followed by any character, followed by the letter *t*. This pattern would match the words "cat," "cut," and "cot," as well as the text "c.t."

Regular expressions are an expansive topic; entire books have been written on the subject. The following primer should give you a basic introduction to the most useful regular expressions. It should also serve as a handy reference to the patterns and operators supported by Xcode.

Regular Expressions

In simplified terms, regular expressions are constructed from patterns and operators. Patterns define a character to match, and operators augment how those patterns are matched. The key concept to keep in mind is that operators do not, by themselves, match anything. A pattern matches something and an operator must have a pattern on which to operate.

Patterns

Every pattern in a regular expression matches exactly one character. Many patterns match a special character or one character from a set of possible characters. These are called meta-character patterns. The most common are listed in the following table.

PATTERN	MATCHES
.	Matches any character.
\character	Quotes one of the following special characters: *, ?, +, [, (,), {, }, ^, $, |, \, ., or /.
^	Matches at the beginning of a line.
$	Matches at the end of a line.
\b	Matches a word boundary.
\B	Matches a non-word boundary.
[set]	Matches any one character from the set. Sets are explained in more detail a little later.

Any single character that is not a meta-character pattern, nor a regular expression operator, is a literal pattern that matches itself. The string cat is, technically, a regular expression consisting of three patterns: *c*, *a*, and *t*. This expression would match the word "cat," which is a really long-winded way of saying that anything that doesn't contain any kind of special expression will match itself just as if you had searched for a literal string.

The . pattern is used quite often with operators, but it can always be used by itself as was demonstrated in the previous "c.t" example.

Another useful pattern is the escape pattern. Most punctuation characters seem to have some special meaning in regular expressions. If you need to search for any of these characters — that is, use the character as a pattern and not an operator — precede it with a backslash. The pattern \. matches a single period in the text. The pattern \\ matches a single backslash character.

The four patterns ^, $, \b, and \B are called *boundary patterns*. Rather than match a character, like regular patterns, they match the location *between* two characters. The first two match the positions at the beginning and end of a line, respectively. For example, the regular expression ^# matches a single pound-sign character only if it is the first character on the line. Similarly, the expression ;$ matches a single semicolon only if it is the last character on a line.

The \b pattern matches the word boundary between characters. In Textual search mode, you used the Whole Words option to require that the first and last characters of the pattern "one" was found between two word boundaries. The equivalent regular expression is \bone\b. The \B pattern is the opposite and matches the position between two characters only if it is not a word boundary. The regular expression \Bone matches "done" but not "one."

The last pattern is the set. A set matches any single character contained in the set. The set `[abc]` will match *a*, *b*, or *c* in the text. The expression `c[au]t` will match the words "cat" and "cut," but not the word "cot." Set patterns can be quite complex. The following table lists some of the more common ways to express a set.

SET	MATCHES
`[characters]`	Matches any character in the set.
`[^set]`	Matches any character *not* in the set.
`[a-z]`	Matches any character in the range starting with the Unicode value of character *a* and ending with character *z*, inclusive.
`[:named set:]`	Matches any character in the named set. Named sets include `Alphabetic`, `Digit`, `Hex_Digit`, `Letter`, `Lowercase`, `Math`, `Quotation_Mark`, `Uppercase`, and `White_Space`. For example, the set `[:Hex_Digit:]` matches the same characters as the set `[0123456789abcdefABCDEF]`. Named sets often include many esoteric Unicode characters. The `:Letter:` set includes all natural language letters from all languages.

The `[`, `]`, `-`, and `^` characters may have special meaning in a set. Escape them (`[X\-]`) to include them in the set as a literal character. Sets can be combined and nested. The set `[[:Digit:]A-Fx]` will match any character that is a decimal digit, or one of the letters *A*, *B*, *C*, *D*, *E*, *F*, or *x*.

A number of special escape patterns also exist, as listed in the following table. Each begins with the backslash character. The letter or sequence that follows matches a single character or is shorthand for a predefined set.

META-CHARACTER	MATCHES
`\t`	Matches a single tab character.
`\n`	Matches a single line feed character.
`\r`	Matches a single carriage return character.
`\uhhhh`	Matches a single character with the Unicode value *0xhhhh*. `\u` must be followed by exactly 4 hexadecimal digits.
`\Uhhhhhhhh`	Matches a character with the Unicode value *0xhhhhhhhh*. `\U` must be followed by exactly 8 hexadecimal digits.
`\d, \D`	Matches any digit (`\d`) or any character that is not a digit (`\D`). Equivalent to the sets `[:Digit:]` and `[^:Digit:]`.
`\s, \S`	Matches a single white space character (`\s`), or any character that is not white space (`\S`).
`\w, \W`	Matches any word (`\w`) or non-word (`\W`) character.

Operators

Although patterns are very flexible in matching specific characters, the power of regular expressions is in its operators. Almost every operator acts on the pattern that precedes it. The classic regular expression .* consists of a pattern (.) and an operator (*). The pattern matches any single character. The operator matches any number of instances of the preceding pattern. The result is an expression that will match any sequence of characters, including nothing at all. The following table summarizes the most useful operators.

OPERATOR	DESCRIPTION
*	Matches the pattern 0 or more times.
+	Matches the pattern 1 or more times.
?	Matches the pattern 0 or 1 times.
|	Matches the pattern on the left or the right of the operator. A|B matches either *A* or *B*.
{n}	Matches the pattern exactly *n* times, where *n* is a decimal number.
{n, }	Matches that pattern *n* or more times.
{n,m}	Matches the pattern between *n* and *m* times, inclusive.
*?, +?, ??, {n, }?, {n,m}?	Appending a ? causes these operators to match as few a number of patterns as possible. Normally, operators match as many copies of the pattern as they can.
(regular expression)	Capturing parentheses. Used to group regular expressions. The entire expression within the parentheses can be treated as a single pattern. After the match, the range of text that matched the parenthesized subexpression is available as a variable that can be used in a replacement expression.
(?flags-flags)	Sets or clears one or more flags. Flags are single characters. Flags that appear before the hyphen are set. Flags after the hyphen are cleared. If only setting flags, the hyphen is optional. The changes affect the remainder of the regular expression.
(?flags-flags: regular expression)	Same as the flags-setting operator, but the modified flags only apply to the regular expression between the colon and the end of the operator.

The four repetition operators (*, +, ?, and {n,m}) search for some number of copies of the previous pattern. The only difference between them is the minimum and maximum number of times a pattern is matched. As an example, the expression [0-9]+ matches one or more digits and would match the text "150" and "2," but not "one" (it contains no digits).

The ? modifier makes its operator parsimonious. Normally operators are "greedy" and match as many repetitions of a pattern as possible. The ? modifier causes repetition operators to match the fewest occurrences of a pattern that will still satisfy the expression. As an example, take the line "one, two, three, four." The expression .*, matches the text "one, two, three," because the .* can match the first 15 repetitions of the . pattern and still satisfy the expression. In contrast, the pattern .*?, matches only the text "one," because it only requires three occurrences of the . pattern to satisfy the expression.

Use parentheses both to group expressions and to capture the text matched by a subexpression. Any expression can be treated as a pattern. The expression M(iss)+ippi matches the text "Mississippi." It would also match "Missippi" and "Mississississippi." You can create very complex regular expressions by nesting expressions. The expression (0x[:Hex_Digit:]+(,\s*)?)+ matches the line "0x100, 0x0, 0x1a84e3, 0xcafebabe." Dissecting this expression:

➤   0x[:Hex_Digit:]+ matches a hex constant that begins with 0x followed by one or more hex digits.

➤   The (,\s*)? subexpression matches a comma followed by any number of white space characters, or nothing at all (the ? operator makes the entire expression optional).

➤   Finally, the whole expression is wrapped in parentheses such that the + operator now looks for one or more repetitions of that entire pattern.

Finally, you can use the flag operators to alter one of the modes of operation. Flags before the hyphen turn the flags on; flags after the hyphen turn the flags off. If you're only turning one or more flags on, the hyphen can be omitted. The first version of the operator sets the flag for the remainder of the expression. The second version sets the flag only for expression contained within the operator. The only really useful flag is case-insensitive mode:

FLAG	MODE
i	Case-insensitive mode. If this flag is set, the case of letters is not considered when matching text.

You can set or clear the i flag anywhere within an expression. When you set this flag, expressions match text irrespective of case differences. The case sensitivity at the beginning of the expression is determined by the setting of the Ignore Case option in the Find window. The expression one (?i)TWO (?-i)three will match the text "one two three," but not "ONE TWO THREE."

Finally, whatever regular expression you use, it cannot match "nothing." Double negative aside, the expression cannot match an empty string; if it did, it would theoretically match every position in the entire file. The solitary expression .* will match any number of characters, but it will also match none at all, making it an illegal pattern to search for. If you try to use such a pattern, Xcode warns you with a dialog saying "Regular expression for searches must not match the empty string."

Try Some Regular Expressions

If you're new to regular expressions, I recommend that you try a few out to become comfortable with the concepts. Start with the source file shown in Listing 8-1.

Available for
download on
Wrox.com

LISTING 8-1: Example file text

```
#define ONE      1
#define TWO      2
#if ONE+TWO != 3
    #warning "Math in this universe is not linear."
#endif


/////////////////
// Static data //
/////////////////

static Number series[] = {
        { 1, "one",     0x1 },
        { 2, "two",     0x0002 },
        { 3, "three",   0x0003 },
        { 4, "four",    0x0004 },
        { 5, "five",    0x0005 },
        { 6, "six",     0x0006 },
        { 7, "thirteen",0x000d }
    };


/////////////
// Methods //
/////////////

/*!
 *  @abstract Establish the logical Set used by the receiver
 *  @param set The set to use. Will be retained by receiver. Can be null.
 */

- (void)setSet:(Set*)set
{
    [workingSet autorelease];   /* release any old set we might still be using */
    workingSet = [set retain];  /* retain this set */
}

/*!
 *  @abstract Get the set being used by this object.
 *  @result The logical set used by this object. If none, an empty set is returned.
 */

- (Set*)getSet
{
    if (set!=null)
        return set;
    return [[[Set alloc] init] autorelease];
}
```

Open the file and choose Edit ➪ Find ➪ Find to display the search bar. Set the search mode
to Regular Expression, clear the Ignore Case option, and set the Wrap Around option. Search
repeatedly for the following regular expressions:

- ➤   `one`

- ➤   `\bone\b`

- ➤   `\bSet`

- ➤   `\BSet`

- ➤   `[.*]`

- ➤   `\[.*\]`

- ➤   `/+`

- ➤   `/{2}.*`

- ➤   `/\*.*\*/`

- ➤   `^#\w+`

- ➤   `".*"`

- ➤   `".{3,5}"`

- ➤   `".{1,10}",\t+0x[0-9a-f]{4}`

- ➤   `".{1,10}",\s*0x[0-9a-f]{1,4}`

- ➤   `ONE|TWO`

- ➤   `(?i:ONE)|TWO`

Searching for `one` found "one" and "none" but not "ONE." There were no special regular expression patterns or operators, making the search equivalent to a simple textual search. The expression `\bone\b` required that the *c* and *e* start and end on word boundaries, making it equivalent to a textual search in Whole Word mode.

Using variations of the word boundary pattern, `\bSet` searched for text where the *S* starts a word, and is equivalent to a textual search in Begins With mode. `\BSet` specifies just the opposite and has no textual search equivalent. It only found the text "Set" when the *S* did *not* begin a word.

The expression `[.*]` matched any single period or asterisk in the file. Operators lose their meaning within a set and become just another character. In contrast, `\[.*\]` searched for an open bracket, followed by any sequence of characters, followed by a close bracket. By escaping `[` and `]` they are no longer treated as defining a set and instead are simple literal patterns that match a single bracket character. Now that they are not in a set, the `.` and `*` characters assume their more common meanings as a pattern and operator.

`/+` matched one or more slash characters. Most would be C++-style comments, but it would also match a single /. The expression to match a C++-style comment is `/{2}.*`. This matches two consecutive slash characters followed by anything else up to the end of the line.

`/\*.*\*/` matched the more traditional C-style comments in the file. Note that the two literal `*`'s had to be escaped to avoid having them treated as operators.

`^#\w+` matched a pound sign following by a word, but only if it appears at the beginning of the line. The pattern found "#define", "#if", and "#endif", but not "#warning".

`".*"` matched anything between double quotes. In the pattern `".{3,5}"` this was limited to anything between double quotes that was between three and five characters long.

`".{1,10}",\t+0x[0-9a-f]{4}` is a complex expression designed to match statements in the Number table. If you opened the text file in the example projects, you'll notice that it failed to match the lines containing "one," "four," and "thirteen." It misses "one" because the `0x[0-9a-f]{4}` expression requires exactly 4 hexadecimal digits following the "0x" and that line only has 1 digit. The line with "four" is missed because the white space between the comma and the "0x" turns out to be spaces, not tabs. The line with "thirteen" is missed because there are no tabs at all between the comma and the hex number. The pattern `".{1,10}",\s*0x[0-9a-f]{1,4}` corrects all of these shortcomings. If you're typing in the text for this example by hand, use the Tab key and temporarily turn on the Tab Key Inserts Tab, Not Spaces option found in the Indentation pane of the Xcode preferences.

The expression `ONE|TWO` found either the text "ONE" or "TWO," but not both. The `(?i:ONE)|TWO` expression demonstrates altering the case-sensitivity of a subexpression. It matched "ONE," "one," and "TWO" but not "two."

Learning More about Regular Expressions

Xcode uses the ICU (International Components for Unicode) Regular Expression package to perform its regular expression searches. This chapter explained many of its more common, and a few uncommon, features. There is quite a bit more; although much of it is rather obscure. Should you need to stretch the limits of regular expressions in Xcode, visit the ICU Regular Expressions users guide at `http://icu.sourceforge.net/` for a complete description of the syntax.

Replacing Text Using Regular Expressions

When searching using regular expressions, it is possible for the replacement text to contain portions of the text that was found. The parentheses operators not only group subexpressions, but they also capture the text that was matched by that subexpression in a variable. These variables can be used in the replacement text.

The variables are numbered. Variable 1 is the text matched by the first parenthetical subexpression, variable 2 contains the text matched by the second, and so on. The replacement text can refer to the contents of these variables using the syntax \n, where n is the number of the subexpression. The variables in the replacement text can be used in any order, more than once, or not at all.

For example, take the text "one plus two equals three." The regular expression `(\w+) plus (\w+) equals (\w+)` matches that text. Because of the parentheses, the text matched by each `\w+` subexpression can be used in the replacement. The replacement text `\1+\2=\3` replaces the original text with "one+two=three" as shown in Figure 8-8.

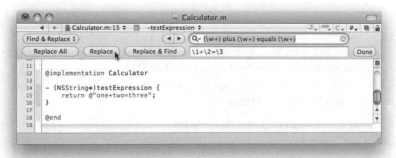

FIGURE 8-8

Regular expression replacement patterns are extremely useful for rearranging repetitive statements. Use the following code snippet as an example:

```
static Number series[] = {
        { 1, "one",       0x1 },
        { 2, "two",       0x0002 },
        { 3, "three",     0x0003 },
        { 4, "four",      0x0004 },
        { 5, "five",      0x0005 },
        { 6, "six",       0x0006 },
        { 7, "thirteen", 0x000d }
    };
```

Using the regular expression mode, find the pattern:

```
\{ ([0-9]+), (".*?")
```

and replace it with:

```
{ \2, \1
```

The text of subexpressions ([0-9]+) and (".*") were captured and used in the replacement text to reverse their order in the table. This replaced { 1, "one",   0x1 }, with { "one", 1, 0x1},. Note that the replacement text had to include everything outside of the subexpressions.

Here are some details to consider when using regular expression replacement variables:

➤ There are only nine variables (\1 through \9). If the regular expression contains more than nine parenthetical subexpressions, those expressions are not accessible. Variables that do not correspond to a subexpression are always empty.

➤ If parentheses are nested, they are assigned to variables in the order that the opening parentheses appeared in the expression.

➤ If a subexpression is used to match multiple occurrences of text, only the last match is retained in the variable. Using the text "one, two, three;" the regular expression ((, *)? (\w+))+ matches the three words before the semicolon. A replacement pattern of 1='\1' 2='\2' 3='\3' results in the text "1=', three' 2=', ' 3='three'" because:

  ➤ Variable \1 contains the last occurrence of the outermost subexpression.

  ➤ Variables \2 and \3 each contain the last occurrence of the nested subexpressions.

  ➤ The values of the first two occurrences are lost.

Symbol Search

The Project Find window includes two special search modes: Definition and Symbol. Instead of searching the text of your project's files, these modes search the symbol names in the project's Code Sense index. These syntax-aware search modes locate symbol names that appear in the compiled portion of your source code. Their principle advantage is that they won't match other superfluous occurrences of a symbol's name, specifically those in comments.

Both symbol search modes use literal string search mode, the word boundary option, and the ignore case option, to find the symbols in the Code Sense database.

> *For the definition and symbol search modes to be accurate, the Code Sense index must be up-to-date. That usually requires that all of your source files be first saved to disk. Some Code Sense information, particularly class and method definitions, is not updated until the files are saved. Get into the habit of performing a File ⇨ Save All (Option+Command+S) before starting a symbol search. Also note that syntax and other compiler errors may prevent the indexer from compiling an accurate database.*

Definitions Search

A *definitions search* finds all of the symbol definitions matching the string search pattern. A definition is where a class, method, function, or variable is defined or implemented, as shown in Figure 8-9. It will not find references to a symbol.

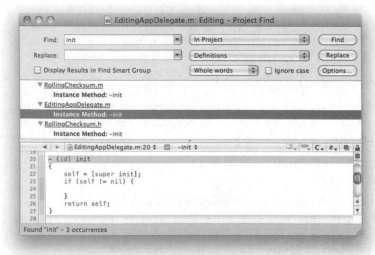

FIGURE 8-9

When performing a definitions search, the results list shows the type of the symbol and the symbol name found, rather than the line of text in the file.

The search is limited to those files in the batch find options set.

Symbol Search

A symbol search finds all of the compiled occurrences of a symbol in your project. The scope of this search mode is not defined by the batch find options set; it searches the compiled instances of symbols in your project. This does not include anything in your linked frameworks, because linked frameworks are not a compiled by your project.

Figure 8-10 illustrates one of the big advantages of using the symbol search mode. The figure shows finding all compiled references to the willUpdateCalculator:field: method. Three are shown here: a reference to its selector constant, a method invocation, and the method's definition. Notice that the occurrence of the text "willUpdateCalculator:field:" in the comment is not part of the search results.

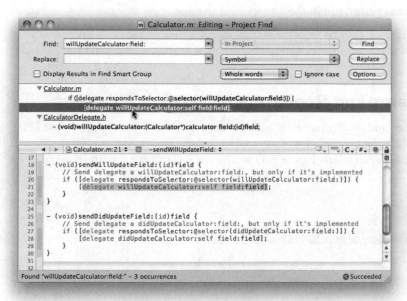

FIGURE 8-10

Here are a few things to keep in mind when searching symbols:

> ➤ A symbol search matches the entire expression that contains the symbol. Often this is just the symbol name (in the case of a variable of function). But in the example in Figure 8-10, the text matched is delegate willUpdateCalculator:self field:field, which is clearly more than just the symbol name.

➤ Symbol names are the complete, fully qualified, symbol in the program. If you perform a symbol search using the Whole Words option, searching for "openFile" will not find the method `openFile:`, and "willUpdateCalculator:" will not find the method `willUpdate-Calculator:file:`. Use the Starts With or Contains option instead.

➤ The definition and symbol search modes only find literal references to symbols in your source code. For example, if the preprocessor macro `CHECKPOINT` expanded to code that referred to the variable `testCount`, a symbol search for `testCount` would not match a line containing the `CHECKPOINT` macro, even though (technically) a `testCount` variable reference occurs at that point in the code.

SEARCH HISTORY

As you find and replace text in your project, Xcode keeps a short history of the following:

➤ Recently used search patterns

➤ Recently used replacement patterns

➤ The results of searches performed in the Project Find window

Retrieving search history makes it easy to repeat a search or replacement that you've previously done, perform a new search that's a minor variation of a previous search, and review search results even after the text that generated those results has changed.

Recent Search Patterns and Replacement Text

Both the single file search bar and the Project Find window keep a history of the recently used search patterns and the replacement text that was associated with it. Figure 8-2 showed the Recent Searches menu in the single file search bar. Figure 8-11 shows the recent search pattern menu in the Project Find window.

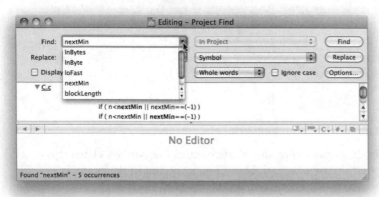

FIGURE 8-11

In the single file search bar, previously used search and replacement patterns are paired; choosing a previously used search pattern also recalls the replacement text it was associated with. The search pattern and replacement text fields in the Project Find window are independent of each other. You can independently recall a previously used search pattern or a previous replacement text.

New search and replace patterns are added to the top of each list, but are never duplicated in the list. Reusing a search pattern does not move it back to the top of the list.

Xcode remembers the mode used by a search pattern (Textual, Regular Expression, Definitions, or Symbol), but none of its options (word boundaries, ignore case, wrapping). If you recall a regular expression, the mode will automatically switch to Regular Expression, but if you check the Ignore Case option and then recall a previous search pattern that option will still be set.

Recent Search Results

The Project Find window also remembers the last set of search results for each pattern. Recalling a previous pattern also recalls its last result set. Previous result sets are also preserved in the Find Results Smart Group, described in the next section.

Be careful about recalling old searches or editing files between the time you did the find and the replace. The history of search results is a set of original locations. Like the single file Replace command, the Replace button inserts the replacement text at those locations even if the text no longer matches the search pattern.

The safest practice is to get into the habit of rerunning the Find again after recalling any earlier search results or after editing any files.

On the other hand, this particular "feature" can save the day. If you make a mistake in the replacement text, you can perform another replacement to correct it *even if a new find won't find those occurrences anymore.*

Global Search Patterns

The current search pattern is shared globally with all projects and with the Mac OS X operating system. Entering a search pattern makes it the search for every search bar and Project Find window in Xcode. In addition, the Mac OS X operating system has a global search term variable shared by all applications. Applications that use this variable will set, or honor, the search pattern in Xcode. For example, search for something in BBEdit, then switch back to Xcode. Whatever you searched for in BBEdit will be the current search pattern in Xcode, and vice versa.

The search pattern, replacement text, and search results history is local to each project and persists only as long as the project is open.

FIND RESULTS SMART GROUP

Every find executed in the Project Find window adds its results to the Find Results smart group in the project window, as shown in Figure 8-12.

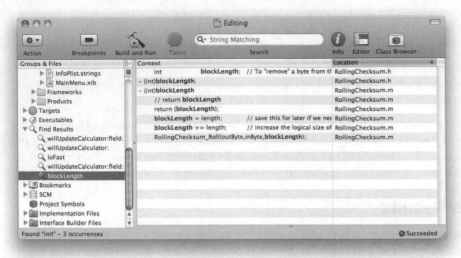

FIGURE 8-12

Select an item in the Find Results smart group and the details pane lists the location (filename and line number) and the line or symbol definition that was found. Selecting a "hit" from the list displays that location in the project window's editor pane. You can also double-click the item or use the View ➪ Open In Separate Editor command to open the file in a new window, at the location of the line or symbol. Selecting an item in the group and pressing the Delete key disposes of the search results.

Unlike the recent search results in the Project Find window, the Find Results smart group remembers the results of every search performed — not just the last one for each search pattern.

If you check the Display Results in Find Smart Group option of the Project Find window, the Find Results smart group becomes your primary means of browsing the results of a search. With this option checked, the results list in the Project Find window disappears. When a find is executed, the project window becomes active and the results of the search are automatically selected. This option really only makes sense when using the All-In-One style. Leave this option unchecked to stay in the Project Find window and review the search results there.

SEARCH SHORTCUTS

Searching and replacing text during development is very common, and often repetitive. Xcode provides a number of shortcuts to keep your keystrokes and mouse clicks to a minimum. The following table lists some handy shortcuts — either keyboard shortcuts or combination commands that perform a sequence of common actions. Most apply to the text selected in the active editor pane, but those that aren't will also function in the Project Find window. Many of these same commands appear in the contextual pop-up menu in the editor pane.

TIP TO REMEMBER

Pressing the Return key while the active text selection is in either the search pattern or replacement text fields performs an Edit ⇨ Find ⇨ Next command.

ACTION	SHORTCUT
Make the selected text the search pattern	Edit ⇨ Find ⇨ Use Selection for Find (Command+E)
Make the selected text the replacement text	Edit ⇨ Find ⇨ Use Selection for Replace (Control+Command+E)
Make the selected text the search pattern and immediately find the next occurrence in the file	Edit ⇨ Find ⇨ Find in File
Make the selected text the search pattern and immediately find all occurrences using the Project Find window	Edit ⇨ Find ⇨ Find in Project
Search for the selected text in the project using a literal string search	Right-click ⇨ Find In Project ⇨ As Text
Search for the selected text in the project's definitions	Right-click ⇨ Find In Project ⇨ As Definition
Search for the selected text in the project's symbols	Right-click ⇨ Find In Project ⇨ As Symbol
Find the next occurrence of the pattern in the file	Edit ⇨ Find ⇨ Next (Command+G)
Find the previous occurrence of the pattern in the file	Edit ⇨ Find ⇨ Previous (Shift+Command+G)

Another useful combination command is the Edit ⇨ Find ⇨ Replace and Find Next/Previous command. It performs the same function as the Replace & Find button in the editor's search bar, but has no keyboard shortcut in the default Xcode bindings.

SEARCHING LISTS

A third kind of search tool is located in the toolbar, as shown in Figure 8-13. This quick search field quickly winnows any details list to only those items that match the term in the search field.

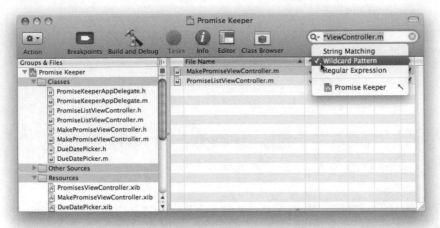

FIGURE 8-13

The list could be a list of files in the project, a list of bookmarks, the project symbols, or even the results of a project search. In short, whatever you have listed in the details pane can be filtered using this search field.

In most contexts, the search field operates in one of three modes — String Matching, Wildcard Pattern, or Regular Expression — as described in the following table. Select the mode by clicking the magnifying glass at the left end of the field. The current mode is displayed in grey when the field is empty, so you know what mode it is in before you enter anything.

SEARCH MODE	DESCRIPTION
String Matching	Performs a simple textual search.
Wildcard Pattern	Wildcard patterns use the so-called "globbing" characters used by the shell. The characters * and ? will match any string or a single character, respectively. A set of characters can be defined with the set syntax: [chars]. For example, the pattern *.h will match all of the header files in a file list. Don't confuse wildcards with regular expression operators.
Regular Expression	The same regular expressions described earlier in this chapter.

In some contexts, the search field may have special modes specific to the type of list being displayed. The Project Symbols smart group displays the list of indexed symbols in the details list. When you're displaying the symbols list, the search modes change to Search All, Search Symbols, Search Kind, and Search Location. Choosing a setting other than Search All limits the search to a particular column in the table.

To use the search field, simply type something into it. Whatever you enter is immediately used to reduce the details list to only those items that match the search term. Figure 8-14 shows the effect of entering a variable name while the details list displays contents of the Project Symbols smart group. The options in the search menu also changed. When searching the symbols smart group, you can search by name, type, or file location. Because the mode was set to Search All, the search pattern "check" found the symbols `checkSpelling:` and `checksum`, but also found every symbol in the `RollingChecksum.m` file.

FIGURE 8-14

Clearing the contents of the search field, or clicking the X button at the right end of the field, cancels the search and restores the details list to its voluminous, uncensored, state.

 The quick search field is particularly handy when digging through the results of a search; the results of a search can be further narrowed without the need to compose a more complex search. Execute a broad search in the Project Find window, switch to the Find Results smart group, and then enter a second search term in the search field. Only those lines that match both terms are listed.

SUMMARY

You should now have at least a basic understanding of the file and project search tools. Regular expressions are a powerful tool, but using them is often more art than science. If you are new to using regular expressions, be patient. After you grasp the fundamentals of regular expressions, you will be in possession of a very powerful development tool. Don't forget the quick search field; it comes in very handy when you're wading through large projects.

The next chapter looks at progressively more sophisticated ways of renaming and restructuring your code using the Refactoring tool.

Class Browser

WHAT'S IN THIS CHAPTER?

➤ Opening and navigating the class browser

➤ Switching class browser display options

➤ Customizing the class browser display

➤ Jumping to source code and documentation

In the previous chapter, you saw how to search the Code Sense index for symbols and definitions. The class browser provides a much more structured way of exploring your project's Code Sense database; it builds a structured summary of your project's classes that describes their methods, instance variables, and inheritance. You can open it at any time, and it's always up-to-date — or at least as current as your Code Sense index. It's one of my favorite development tools, and I use it incessantly to review classes, untangle inheritance, and jump to their definitions.

Chapter 14 shows you some additional high-level tools for analyzing your classes graphically. The best part about the class browser is that it's free. You don't have to do anything special to your project beyond turning on Code Sense. Once the Code Sense index for your project is built, the class browser is ready to go.

NAVIGATING THE CLASS BROWSER

Choose the Project ➪ Class Browser (Command+Shift+C) command to open the class browser window, shown in Figure 9-1. You'll also find a Class Browser button in the toolbar of many windows.

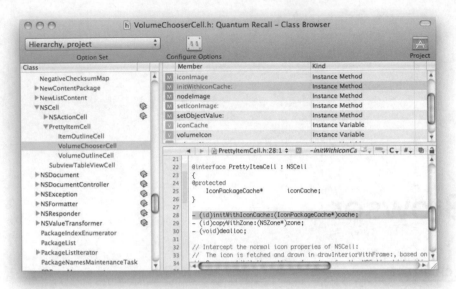

FIGURE 9-1

The class browser's toolbar typically includes the Option Set control and the Configure Options button. The Option Set menu and Configure Options button work like the Project Find window's batch find options set, described in Chapter 8. The pop-up menu lets you select the named set of browser options, and the Configure Options button allows you to alter the options in a set or create new sets. This chapter covers option sets and the browser options shortly.

Browsing Classes

The class browser is broadly divided into three panes. The pane on the left is the class list. This lists all classes, interfaces, and protocols defined in the project. These can be organized in a hierarchy — a superclass becomes a group that contains all of the subclasses that inherit it. Expand or collapse groups using the triangle to the left of the class name. Hold down the Option key to recursively collapse or expand all subclasses. Alternatively, you can list the classes in alphabetical order. Java class names include the package so that similarly named classes in different packages can be distinguished easily. Classes defined in your project appear blue. Classes defined in frameworks are black.

Selecting a class in the list displays the member elements of that class in the details pane on the right, and the source that defines the class in the editor pane below it. The details pane lists the member elements, grouped by type. Members defined in the class are black, and inherited members (if shown) are grey. Member functions and methods are listed first, followed by variables. Class (static) members are listed before instance members. You can reorganize and resize the table columns by dragging in the column headers, but you cannot change the sorting order.

Selecting any member in the details list displays its declaration in the editor pane below it. Double-clicking either the class name or a member jumps to that location in a new editor window.

Getting Class Documentation

If online documentation is available for a class, a small book icon appears to the right of the class name. Clicking the book icon jumps to that class's documentation in the help viewer, as shown in Figure 9-2.

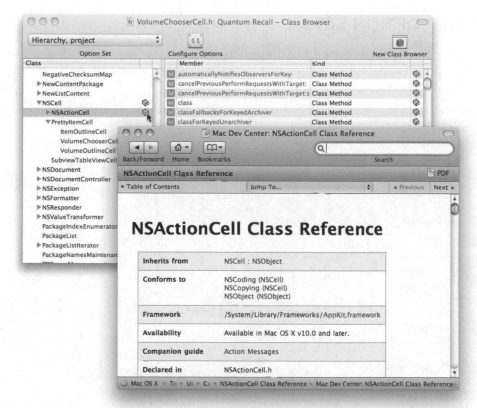

FIGURE 9-2

Opening Multiple Class Browsers

Normally, there is one class browser window for each project. It is possible to open multiple class browser windows using the New Class Browser button in the toolbar of the class browser window itself — not to be confused with the Class Browser button that appears on most other windows. This button isn't in the default set of toolbar buttons; to use it you must add it to your toolbar. See the "Toolbars" section of Chapter 3 if you're unsure how.

Figure 9-3 shows the New Class Browser button. Multiple browser windows permit you to view different aspects of your classes simultaneously, so consider adding the New Class Browser button to your class browser's toolbar (View ➪ Customize Toolbar).

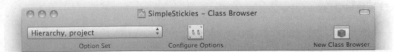

FIGURE 9-3

CLASS BROWSER OPTION SETS

The class browser comes preconfigured with four option sets. These four sets of options display just those classes defined in the project or all classes visible to the project. The classes can be organized in a hierarchy or listed alphabetically irrespective of relationships.

Click the Configure Options button to edit the configuration of a set. This displays the class browser options configuration sheet, shown in Figure 9-4.

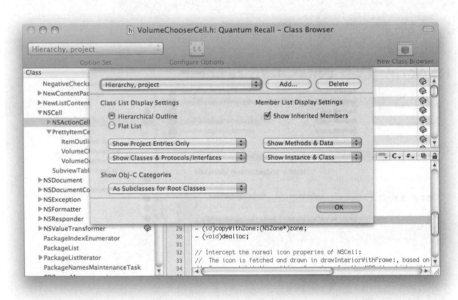

FIGURE 9-4

Select the set of options to edit using the pop-up menu at the top of the sheet. You can edit the predefined sets, but avoid making any changes that run counter to their descriptive names. Changing the Hierarchy, Project Classes set to display only framework classes in a flat list is guaranteed to cause confusion. If you want to make significantly different sets of browser options, create new sets using the Add button. With the Delete button, you can delete sets you don't care to use.

 Like the Project Find window, the class browser option sets are shared among all projects. Make changes to them judiciously.

The left side of the sheet contains the Class List Display Settings, which consist of four options that determine which classes are included in the class browser, and how those classes are organized in the class list.

➤   The first option has two choices: Hierarchical Outline groups subclasses within their super-class in a tree, and Flat List simply sorts all of the class names alphabetically.

➤   The next option has three possible settings that determine what classes are included in the list. Show Project and Framework Entries includes all classes and members defined in the project source and any classes defined in any referenced frameworks. Show Project Entries Only excludes classes defined in the frameworks, and Show Framework Entries Only lists only those classes defined in the frameworks. When you use the Hierarchical Outline display, an exception is made for superclasses. Superclasses of a class, regardless of where they are defined, are always included in the hierarchical display as the parents of that class. This also affects the display of inherited class members. If a project class inherits a method or variable from a framework class, and Show Project Entries Only is selected, those inher-ited members are not listed.

➤   The third option also has three possible settings: Show Classes & Protocols/Interface, Show Classes Only, and Show Protocols/Interfaces Only. This control determines whether only the class definitions, only protocols/interface definitions, or both are included in the class list. If both are included, protocols and interfaces are grouped together at the bottom of the class list. In the hierarchical view, they are listed under the title Protocols/Interfaces. In the list view, each is prefixed with the "Prot:" text.

➤   The last option applies only to Objective-C and determines how Objective-C categories are organized in the class list. For those not familiar with Objective-C, a *category* is a way of defining a set of methods for a class where the definition and implementation of those methods is completely outside the definition of the class itself. In other words, it's a way of "attaching" methods to a class without subclassing, just as if those methods had been defined in the class itself. (If the C++ and Java programmers in the audience are scratch-ing their heads wondering how this is possible, the magic occurs at run time — all message dispatching in Objective-C is dynamic, so new method handlers can be added to any class during program execution.) The problem is that categories don't fit in the neat hierarchy of classes and interfaces, because they are neither.

  ➤   The As Subclass setting treats the category as if it were a subclass in the hierarchy. The category appears as a subclass of the attached class with a "Cat:" prefix. This makes it clear which class the category was written for, but is somewhat misleading because the category is *not* a subclass. The methods defined by the category are defined in that class and inherited by any subclasses — neither of which will be reflected in the class browser. If you're looking for the methods in a class, you have to browse not only that class but all of its categories, and any categories of its superclasses as well.

  ➤   The second alternative is the As Subclasses for Root Classes setting. This treats a category as though it was a subclass of the root object of the class it is attached to (almost invariably NSObject). Although this is also a fabrication, it has the advan-tage that categories are easy to find because they end up grouped together at the end of NSObject's subclasses. More important, the methods defined by a category correctly appear in the attached class and any of its subclasses. This is probably the most useful setting.

➤ The final choice, Always Merged into Class, is the most accurate in that it merges the category methods into each class just as though those methods had been defined in that class. The categories themselves are not shown anywhere in the class list. To discover which methods of a class are defined by a category you must refer to the source declaration of each method.

On the right are three controls that influence the amount of detail presented about each class:

➤ The Show Inherited Members option causes the members of a class to include all inherited members. Inherited members are displayed in grey, and the members defined or overridden in the class are black.

➤ The Show Methods & Data, Show Methods Only, and Show Data Only options display all members of the class, or only methods, or only instance variables, respectively.

➤ The Show Instance & Class, Show Instance Only, and Show Class Only options further refine the class details such that it lists all class members, or only instance members, or only class members. The term *class* is really an Objective-C term, where it refers to messages that can be sent to the Class object, as opposed to regular messages that would be sent to an instance of that class. In C++ and Java, class refers to static members and variables. Note that so-called static nested classes are regular classes and will appear in the browser hierarchy within their superclass.

BROWSER SHORTCUTS

Xcode provides an internal editing action (Reveal in Class Browser) that jumps from the currently selected symbol in the editor to its entry in the class browser. In Xcode's default key bindings, this action (sadly) isn't bound to any keyboard shortcut. If you find the Reveal in Class Browser shortcut useful, add a key binding for the action in the Key Bindings preferences. Key bindings are explained in Chapter 23.

SUMMARY

The class browser is a powerful tool for illuminating the class structure of any project. Learning to use it effectively will help you understand and navigate your code. In some ways, it is both a search tool and a documentation tool. Object-oriented programs were once said to be self-documenting. Although this is rarely true, being able to see the class structure of a project can provide insights into its organization that code comments and documentation often fail to provide.

With the ability to find text, symbols, and class information, you're ready to start making serious changes to your code. The next two chapters help you make those changes intelligently and safely.

10

Refactoring

WHAT'S IN THIS CHAPTER?

➤ Renaming classes, types, methods, functions, and variables

➤ Reorganizing code and restructuring classes

➤ Modernizing your code

Despite our best efforts, class and data structures don't always endure. New features, requirements, operating system evolution, and improvements elsewhere in your application may cause you to revisit the design of your existing class and data architecture. You may need to reorganize the hierarchy of your classes, migrate functionality from one class to another, take advantage of new language features, or simply rename a variable so that it more accurately reflects its purpose. These kinds of changes are referred to as *refactoring* your code.

Making structural changes to your code using the editor and the search and replace tools can often be tedious, time consuming, and error prone. In the days before refactoring, I would often rename or relocate an instance variable by simply changing its declaration, and then hunting down and correcting all of the compilation errors that resulted — not the most productive way to spend an afternoon.

Fortunately, Xcode now provides a refactoring tool that helps you make many common structural changes to your application, quickly and succinctly. It uses the Code Sense database and an inherent knowledge of C and Objective-C syntax to intelligently rename symbols, reorganize classes, and streamline code. This chapter describes the kinds of changes the refactoring tool performs and the steps required.

Refactoring is formally defined as a change to the internal structure of your program that doesn't change its external, or functional, behavior. The reality is that any change, no matter how careful, can have unintended consequences. The section "Refactoring Pitfalls" discusses some of these potential problems, how to address them, and some best practices.

REFACTORING WORKFLOW

To refactor something in your project, follow these general steps:

1. Select the symbol or code fragment to refactor.

2. Choose the Edit ⇨ Refactor (Shift+Command+J) command to open the refactoring tool window.

3. Select the type of refactoring to perform, provide whatever additional information is required, and choose options.

4. Preview the refactoring.

5. Commit the refactoring.

The process begins by selecting the specific symbol name or code fragment in the editor that represents what you want to refactor. Once selected, choose the Edit ⇨ Refactor command to present the refactoring tool window, as shown in Figure 10-1.

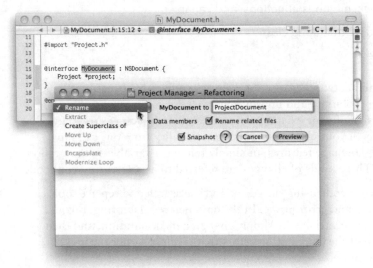

FIGURE 10-1

The refactor tool determines which refactoring methods, called *transformations*, can be applied to the selected text. Select your desired transformation from the pop-up menu on the left, as shown in Figure 10-1. What transformations are available will depend entirely on the nature and context of the selection. Xcode offers to rename or create a superclass if a class name is selected. A selected block of code could be extracted or possibly modernized.

Refactoring uses the Code Sense index. This means that Code Sense must be enabled, up-to-date, and it must be able to make sense of your code. As a general rule, don't refactor code that won't compile — especially code that contains syntax errors that might prevent Code Sense from interpreting its meaning. See Chapter 7 if you need to turn Code Sense on or reindex your project.

Once the transformation is chosen, supply whatever additional information, if any, the transformation requires. For a rename transformation, you'll need to supply the symbol's new name. Other transformations might require several pieces of information.

Some transformations present options, typically used to control what additional, non-code changes are made. For example, renaming a class presents two options: one will also rename KVC references to that class found in Interface Builder documents and Core Data models. The other option will automatically rename the source files that contain the class's definition so that they continue to match the class name.

After you've prepared the transformation, start the process by clicking the Preview button. The process scans your entire project and prepares a list of proposed changes. At this point no changes have actually been made. You can preview the changes using the differences browser, as shown in Figure 10-2. It may also present a list of warnings that should be considered.

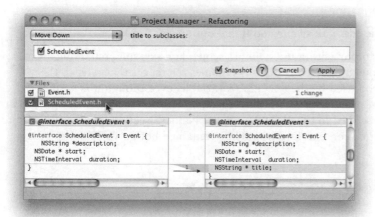

FIGURE 10-2

You can elect which of the changes you're going to allow the refactoring tool to make using the check boxes next to each file in the list. Uncheck a file, and Xcode will not make any of the proposed changes contained therein.

You also have the option of an added safety net, in the form of a project snapshot. Checking the Snapshot option makes a snapshot of your entire project before making any of the proposed changes. This also has the advantage of being able to selectively reverse unwanted changes on a change-by-change basis. See Chapter 11 for more about snapshots.

Once you've defined and previewed the transformation, click the Apply button to commit the changes. When finished, the Refactor window closes and returns you to your (now modified) project.

C AND OBJECTIVE-C TRANSFORMATIONS

As of this writing, the refactoring tool only refactors C and Objective-C source code; C++ and Java programmers are just out of luck. The next few sections describe the specific transformations that the refactoring tool provides, along with some examples.

Rename

The rename transformation is the simplest and most flexible. It will rename any of the following:

- ➤ Global, instance, parameter, and automatic variable names
- ➤ Function names
- ➤ Typdef, structure tag, and enum names
- ➤ Class names
- ➤ Method signatures

To rename a symbol, follow these steps:

1. Select a symbol name or at least one token of an Objective-C message name.

2. Choose the Edit ➪ Refactor command.

3. Select the Rename transformation.

4. Supply a replacement name and choose any additional option.

All of the rename transformations occur within the symbol's scope. For example, renaming an integer variable from c to i, as shown in Figure 10-3, only renames references that refer to the selected variable. Refactor is not confused by the unichar c variable, even though it is nested within the block of code where int c is declared. In this respect, refactoring is more intelligent than the Edit All in Scope command described in the "Editing Symbol Names" section of Chapter 7. Edit All in Scope only analyzes the textual context, and would have renamed both c variables to i.

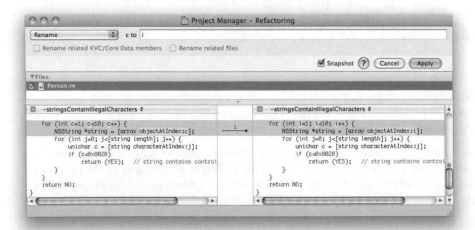

FIGURE 10-3

Renaming method signatures is particularly accurate and flexible. For example, when renaming an Objective-C method name, Xcode picks up the entire method signature and asks that you supply a replacement. You can change any, or all, of the method name tokens and the refactoring tool will make the appropriate changes in the code. In the example shown in Figure 10-4, the method `scheduleDate:time:room:` is being renamed to `scheduleStartingAt:duration:room:`. The replacement method name must match the number and order of the original arguments.

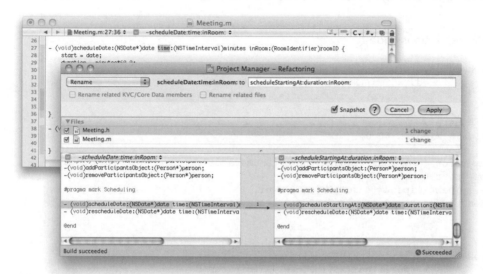

FIGURE 10-4

TIP TO REMEMBER

The refactoring tool can be used as an intelligent multi-file search for instance variables and method names. Select a variable or method and rename it to something else, and then preview — but don't commit — the refactoring. In the preview, the rename transformation will find all references to a variable, ignoring symbols with the same name in other contexts. Similarly, the rename transformation can quickly locate all instances of a complex Objective-C message name, even one that's split across multiple lines.

When renaming a class, you are given the additional option of renaming any source files with the same name. By tradition, the files that define the `Hue` class are named `Hue.h` and `Hue.m`. Renaming the `Hue` class to `Color` would also rename the files to `Color.h` and `Color.m`, and update any `#include "Hue.h"` and `#import "Hue.m"` statements to match.

The Rename Related KVC/Core Data Members option extends the refactoring beyond the scope of your source code. It scours NIB documents and Core Data models for any references to the class, method, or variable being remained. This option will update class inheritance, member names, outlet connections, actions, and bindings. If you have any NIB document or Core Data models that refer to your class, I highly recommend checking this option.

Extract

Reusable, modular code is the hallmark of efficient programming. Often, however, code that could be organized into its own method or function is originally embedded in a larger function — often because you don't realize its utility until later. Take the situation shown in Listing 10-1. Here, the programmer is writing a new rescheduleStartingAt:duration: method, when she realizes that the loop she is about to write is identical to the one in scheduleStartingAt:duration:inRoom:.

Available for
download on
Wrox.com

LISTING 10-1: Repetitious code

```
- (void)scheduleStartingAt:(NSDate*)date
                  duration:(NSTimeInterval)minutes
                    inRoom:(RoomIdentifier)roomID
{
    start = date;
    duration = minutes*60.0;
    room = roomID;
    NSEnumerator *e = [participants objectEnumerator];
    Person *participant;
    while ( (participant=[e nextObject])!=nil ) {
        [participant updateCalendarEvent:self];
    }
}

- (void)rescheduleStartingAt:(NSDate*)date
                    duration:(NSTimeInterval)minutes
{
    start = date;
    duration = minutes*60.0;
    NSEnumerator *e =
}
```

Ideally, the loop that sends update events to all of the meeting participants should be isolated in its own method. Then, rescheduleStartingAt:duration: and scheduleStartingAt:duration: inRoom: can reuse the logic. This transformation is called an extraction.

To extract a block of code, follow these steps:

1. Select the block of code you want to reuse.

2. Choose the Edit ➪ Refactor command.

3. Choose the Extract transformation.

4. Decide whether you want the code to extract into a C function or an Objective-C method.

5. Supply the name of the new function or method.

Figure 10-5 illustrates our programmer exacting the enumeration loop in Listing 10-1 into its own method.

The extract transformation lifts a local fragment of code and puts it into its own Objective-C method or C function (your choice). In the example shown in Figure 10-5, our programmer is extracting the enumeration loop into a new method named -(void)updateParticipants. The original code is replaced with a message that invokes the new method. After the extraction, the rescheduleStartingAt: duration: can now be completed with a single [self updateParticipants]; statement.

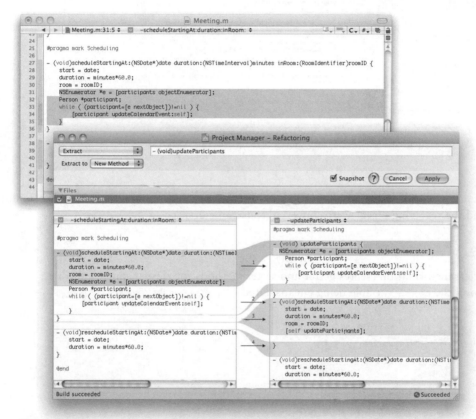

FIGURE 10-5

 The formatting of extracted code can be a bit erratic. After extraction, select the new method and reformat it by typing Control+I.

When extracting code, Xcode analyzes the scope of all of the variable references within the code block. Any variable that isn't in scope when the code is relocated to its own method (or function) is converted into a parameter. In the previous example, both the participants and self instance variables are still accessible in the new updateParticipants method. If you choose to extract this code into a C function, or the loop refers to any automatic variables declared earlier in the method, those references will be converted into parameters, as shown in Figure 10-6.

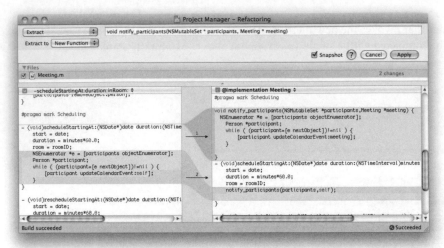

FIGURE 10-6

The function `notify_participants(...)` in Figure 10-6 has no object context, so the collection of participants and the receiving object were converted to parameters.

Encapsulate

The encapsulate transformation creates getter and setter methods for class instance variables. Figure 10-7 shows the `tasks` variable being encapsulated.

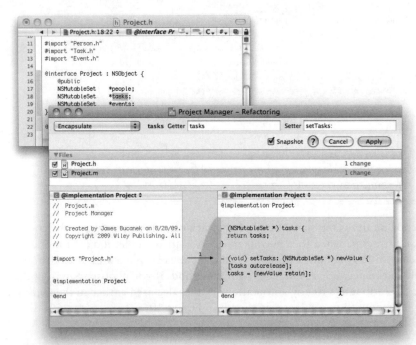

FIGURE 10-7

To encapsulate an instance variable, follow these steps:

1. Select the name of the instance variable.

2. Choose the Edit ▷ Refactor command.

3. Choose the Encapsulate transformation.

4. Optionally edit the getter and setter method names. Xcode generates a matched pair of KVC-compliant method names, but you can change them if you want.

The encapsulate transformation generates a getter and setter method for the instance variable and then replaces any existing references to the variable with messages (that is, `ivar` with `[object ivar]` and `ivar=...` with `[object setIvar:...]`).

As of this writing, a number of unfortunate limitations keep the encapsulate transformation from being truly useful, except in a narrow set of circumstances. For the specifics, see the "Encapsulate" portion of the "Refactoring Pitfalls" section, later in this chapter.

Because of these issues, I recommend using the encapsulate transformation only when:

➤ You are *not* using Objective-C 2.0.

➤ You are using managed memory (not garbage collection).

➤ You have just added an instance variable and want to create getter and setter methods for it, but have not yet used the variable in any code. If you've already used the variable in your code, you will need to carefully review the memory management of the object afterwards.

➤ Your property does not need to be thread-safe.

In any other circumstances, I'd recommend using Objective-C `@property` and `@synthesize` directives instead. See the "Updating a Project to Objective-C 2.0" section later in this chapter.

Create Superclass

The create superclass transformation creates a new class definition and inserts it between an existing class and its original superclass. This is most useful when you need to create a more abstract superclass for an existing class whose functionality needs to be partitioned. To create a superclass, follow these steps:

1. Select the name of the existing class.

2. Choose the Edit ▷ Refactor command.

3. Choose the Create Superclass transformation.

4. Supply a new class name and choose whether the new class should be defined in the existing file or defined in a new set of source files with the same name.

Xcode changes the inheritance of the existing class so that it is now a subclass of the new class, which is a subclass of the original superclass. If you asked Xcode to generate new class files, those files are added to the project and appropriate `#import` directives are inserted into the original files, as shown in Figure 10-8.

FIGURE 10-8

In the hypothetical project management program, you decide that you need an intermediate class between the very abstract Event class and the very specific Meeting class. The create superclass transformation quickly defines a new ScheduledMeeting class, changes the superclass of the Meeting class, and then creates and adds all the necessary project files.

Move Up and Move Down

After applying a create superclass transformation, or simply creating a new subclass, you may want to migrate properties or functionality from a class to its superclass or vice versa. That's what the move up and move down transformations do.

To move an instance variable or method to a superclass or one of its subclasses, follow these steps:

1. Select the instance variable declaration or method name.

2. Choose the Edit ⇨ Refactor command.

3. Choose either the Move Up or Move Down transformation.

4. Select the desired options:

   a. If moving an instance variable up, you may also elect to move related methods — any method that refers to the variable — to the superclass.

   b. If moving down, the Refactor tool presents a list of the immediate subclasses of the class; choose which subclasses will get a copy of the variable or method.

Using the project management example again, the `start` and `duration` properties in the Meeting class need to be migrated to the new ScheduledEvent superclass, as shown in Figure 10-9.

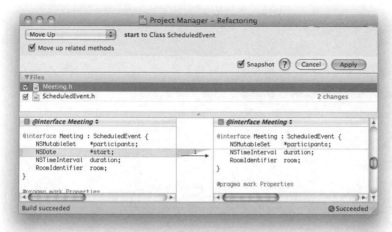

FIGURE 10-9

This transformation is rarely without consequences; you must migrate the instance variables `start` and `duration`, along with any related methods, one at a time. This will also require that some of the methods be recoded, and you'll probably want to create an abstract `scheduleStartingAt:duration:` method in the new superclass. You could do this using two transformations: extract the code that sets the schedule in `scheduleStartingAt:duration:inRoom:` into its own method, then perform a move up transformation to migrate it to the ScheduledEvent superclass.

 Like encapsulate, the move up and move down transformations know nothing about Objective-C 2.0 properties. If you move an instance variable up or down, you'll have to manually relocate any `@property` *and* `@synthesize` *directives.*

Modernize Loop

Objective-C introduces the much-appreciated fast enumeration syntax. Fast enumeration provides a succinct syntax for processing the objects in a collection that's both fast and robust. Prior to Objective-C 2.0, programmers used a variety of `for` and `while` loop patterns. The modernize loop transformation attempts to convert a legacy `for` or `while` loop into its equivalent using fast enumeration syntax.

To modernize a single loop, follow these steps:

1. Select an entire `for` or `while` statement, including the statement or block of code that it controls. Do not include any statements before or after the loop, even if they include loop initialization.

2. Choose the Edit ⇨ Refactor command.

3. Choose the Modernize Loop transformation.

The process begins by selecting the entire for loop statement and block, as shown in Figure 10-10.

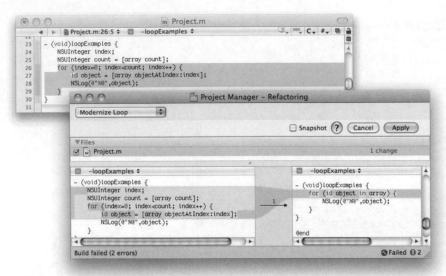

FIGURE 10-10

Loop modernization only transforms `for` loops that meet these criteria:

➤ The loop iterates through the contents of an NSArray.

➤ Uses the message [`collection objectAtIndex:index`] to obtain each object.

➤ Starts with the first object in the collection.

➤ Each object is processed in order, without skipping objects (this does not preclude exiting the loop early using a `break` statement).

➤ Each iteration processes a single object, without trying to access any other objects in the collection at the same time.

When the modernize loop transformation updates a `while` loop, it replaces the traditional NSEnumerator pattern shown in Figure 10-11 with its modern equivalent.

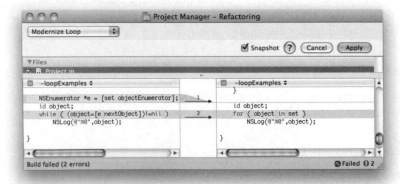

FIGURE 10-11

Loop modernization only transforms `while` loops that meet these criteria:

➤ The `while` loop iterates through the objects in a collection using an NSEnumerator object.

➤ Uses the message `[enumerator nextObject]` to obtain each object.

➤ Starts with the first object in the collection.

➤ Processes each object, in order, without skipping objects (this does not preclude exiting the loop early using a `break` statement).

The second and third points mean that you can't use refactoring to modernize a loop that uses `-reverseObjectEnumerator`.

An often-overlooked feature of fast enumeration is that the modern NSEnumerator class also conforms to NSFastEnumeration. The implication is that any enumerator object can be treated as the collection object in a fast enumeration statement. Consider the following code:

```
NSEnumerator* e = [collection reverseObjectEnumerator];
for ( id obj in e ) {
...
}
```

The enumerator acts as a proxy for its collection. The statement loops through the objects returned by the enumerator. This is particularly useful with enumerators that return a subset of a collection or process objects in a different order, like -[NSDictionary keysSortedByValueUsingSelector:].

It should be noted that this trick does not improve the performance of your application; a fast enumeration using an enumerator object isn't any faster than using the enumerator object directly. In other words, you don't get the "fast" part of fast enumeration; you just get the convenience of a concise syntax.

UPDATING A PROJECT TO OBJECTIVE-C 2.0

The Edit ➪ Convert to Objective-C 2.0 command is specifically designed to ease that transition of legacy projects to Objective-C 2.0. It, optionally, performs two transitions on every source file in your project:

➤ Modernize Loops

➤ Convert instance variables to properties

To update your entire project to Objective-C 2.0, follow these steps:

1. Choose the Edit ➪ Convert to Objective-C 2.0 command.

2. Select either, or both, of the Modernize loops or Use properties transformations.

The modernize loops transformation is the same one described in the previous section, just applied globally to every Objective-C source file in your project.

The use properties transformation converts simple instance variables to Objective-C 2.0 properties. Is does this by

➤   Adding a `@property` directive for each instance variable.

➤   Adding a `@synthesize` directive for each instance variable that does not already have KVC-compliant getter and setter methods with the same name.

REFACTORING PITFALLS

As mentioned at the beginning of the chapter, any change to an application — no matter how seemingly inconsequential — can occasionally have profound effects on its behavior. Although the refactoring logic is quite intelligent, it isn't omniscient. It makes mechanical replacements that are reasonably expected to be functionally equivalent, but may not be.

Many of these pitfalls can be avoided by refactoring your application defensively and with the assumption that any transformation could introduce a bug. Try to follow these best practices when refactoring:

1.   Your project should build successfully and function correctly before beginning any refactoring.

2.   Make use of the refactoring preview; diligently review each proposed change before committing the transformation. Disable any changes that aren't appropriate.

3.   Always make a project snapshot. They are easy to discard later.

4.   After the transformation, make sure the project still builds. Fix any compilation errors that appear.

5.   If you have any unit tests defined, run them.

Each transformation carries some specific pitfalls. The next few sections highlight common issues that you're likely to encounter when refactoring.

Rename

➤   Renaming a method only renames the occurrences of that method defined by a single class. If that method overrides an inherited method, the inherited method in the superclass is *not* renamed. If you need to rename an inherited method, you must rename the same method in all other classes.

➤   Conversely, renaming a method could change it from a unique method to one that now overrides a method in its superclass.

Encapsulate

➤   Encapsulate only generates getter and setter methods. It does not produce `@property` or `@synthesize` directives. If you're using Objective-C 2.0, just write `@property` or `@synthesize` directives instead of trying to use encapsulate.

➤ The getter and setter methods assume that you are using traditional managed memory, not garbage collection. Though this will work in a garbage collection environment, it still generates more code than is optimal. Again, `@property` or `@synthesize` directives are a better solution. The `@synthesize` directive automatically adapts to your chosen memory management model.

➤ Existing memory management is overlooked, which can create over-retain and over-release issues. For example, encapsulating the `ivar` variable will replace the two statements `[ivar release]; ivar=nil;` with the statements `[[self ivar] release]; [self setIvar:nil];`. This results in `ivar` being released twice: once in the code and again in the setter.

➤ The visibility of the original instance variable remains unchanged. If it were `@public` before the transformation, it's still public afterwards. After the transformation, change the visibility of the instance variable to `@protected` or `@private`.

➤ The setter method generated is not thread-safe.

Move Up

➤ Moving an instance variable to its superclass does not migrate its `@property` or `@synthesize` directives.

➤ The visibility of a variable is not retained. A `@private` variable could become `@protected` or `@public`.

➤ If you migrate related methods, you could migrate methods that now refer to properties defined only in the subclass. This requires either migrating those other properties as well, or redesigning the methods.

➤ The refactoring tool warns you if the superclass already has a variable or method with the same name, but it won't prevent you from applying the transformation. The result will be a class with duplicate methods.

➤ You can only migrate a variable or method to its immediate superclass.

Move Down

➤ Moving an instance variable to one of its subclasses does not migrate its `@property` or `@synthesize` directives.

➤ The visibility of a variable is not retained. A `@private` variable could become `@protected` or `@public`.

➤ The refactoring tool warns you if any of the subclasses already have a variable or method with the same name, but it won't prevent you from applying the transformation. The result will be classes with duplicate methods.

➤ You can only migrate a variable or method to one or more of its immediate subclasses.

Modernize Loop

➤ The modernize loop transformation is generally safe, because it simply refuses to be applied unless the control loop meets its rather strict prerequisites. It is still possible, however, to trick the refactoring tool into transforming a loop that contains abnormal behavior hidden in preprocessor macros.

Use Properties

➤ The use properties transformation may produce `@property` directives whose attributes (that is, `assign`, `retain`, `copy`, `nonatomic`) do not agree with the implementation of the existing getter or setter methods. Review each new `@property` directive and confirm that your getter and setter fulfill the property contract, correcting one or the other as appropriate.

➤ The transformation will not create `@synthesize` directives for properties that already have KVC getter and setter methods, even if the getter and setter methods use generic patterns. You may want to delete simplistic getter and setter methods before converting your project and let the transformation insert the more modern `@synthesize` directives.

➤ Unlike the encapsulate transformation, use properties will not replace direct references to instance variables (`ivar=...`) with property "dot" syntax (`self.ivar=...`) or getter and setter messages (`[self setIvar:...]`). You will need to search your code for direct instance variable references and determine which should be replaced with property accessors.

➤ No attempt is made to reduce the visibility of the existing instance variables. After the transformation, consider making the instance variables `@private`. This will also help identify direct references to the variable outside the class.

SUMMARY

Changing the structure of your application isn't always as simple as moving a definition or performing a global search and replace. The refactoring tool makes short work of many common code changes, quickly and as intelligently as possible. This doesn't relieve you of the need to confirm the veracity of those changes, but it does relieve you of much of the tedium involved in making them.

Before every transformation, the refactoring tool gives you the option of making a snapshot of your project. The next chapter explains what snapshots are and how to use them in other circumstances.

11

Snapshots

WHAT'S IN THIS CHAPTER?

➤ Taking snapshots of your entire project

➤ Reviewing snapshots and comparing them with your working files

➤ Managing and restoring snapshots

If you're like me, you hate to throw away code. Most code, especially the stuff that works, is a hard-won commodity that represents time, effort, expertise, and creativity. The best way to improve your code, however, is to experiment with new approaches — which often means abandoning or discarding the code you've already written. Making copies of your source files or saving snippets of old code as comments is both awkward and time consuming. Enter snapshots. Snapshots let you have it both ways: you can keep your existing code while simultaneously replacing it with new, experimental code.

In simple terms, a *snapshot* is an archived copy of the source files in your project. It quickly preserves their current state so you are free to make changes to your project — even radical ones — secure in the knowledge that you can always revert back to the saved version at any time. You can make as many snapshots as you like. You can easily see what changes you've made, as shown in Figure 11-1, by comparing your working project files to those in a snapshot. You can revert your changes to any previous snapshot on a change-by-change basis, by file, or perform a wholesale restore of the entire project.

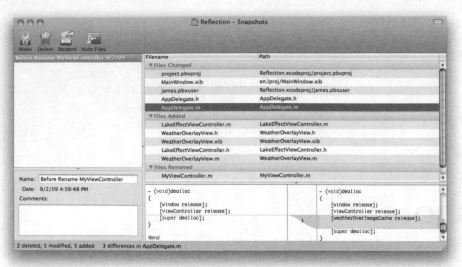

FIGURE 11-1

Snapshots encourage experimentation by making it easy to save and contrast existing code with new code. There's very little risk in rewriting a collection loop to improve performance when Xcode will preserve the previous implementation. Take a snapshot, rewrite the loop, and test its performance. Is it an improvement? Keep the new code. Not an improvement? Restore the saved snapshot and move on or try a different approach. It's that simple.

Snapshots resemble a source control system, but shouldn't be treated as one. Each snapshot is (conceptually) a complete and independent copy of your entire project. Snapshots are not deltas, so they won't preserve a history or audit trail of your changes — although you can compare two snapshots. Snapshots are cached on your local filesystem; they cannot be transferred to another user, nor is any snapshot information preserved in the project itself. Snapshots are intended to be a spontaneous method of marking your progress. Snapshots can be used independently of, or in addition to, the source control management features. See the "Source Control vs. Snapshots" section of Chapter 21 about issues that can arise when mixing snapshots and source control operations.

TAKING SNAPSHOTS

You have four ways of taking a snapshot:

➤ Choose the File ➪ Make Snapshot (Control+Command+S) command

➤ Add a snapshot from the snapshot window

➤ Take a snapshot via the refactoring tool

➤ Restore a snapshot

Snapshots occur immediately; there are no dialogs or other overt indications that a snapshot was taken. Each snapshot has a name and an optional description; but when initially added all snapshots are given a generic name that describes how the snapshot was made (menu command, snapshot window, refactor transformation, or restore) and the date. If you want to make a snapshot memorable, rename it or add a comment to the freshly created snapshot in the snapshot window (File ⇨ Snapshots).

When Xcode takes a snapshot, it preserves the project source files contained within your project folder. If you have added source items to your project whose files are located outside of your project folder, those files will not be included in the snapshot. If you want resources outside of your project folder (like other projects) to be included in your snapshots, consider relocating your project's root folder (see Chapter 21) or use the snapshot feature of the organizer (see Chapter 22).

The minimal user interaction is intended to make snapshots a seamless part of your development workflow, not another interruption to it. On modern computer systems, snapshots are fast and inexpensive. Get into the habit of taking a snapshot before starting any atomic change to your project. Taking snapshots should become second nature, just as many developers save their files at strategic times. You will want to visit your snapshots occasionally to dispose of old and intermediate snapshots.

MANAGING SNAPSHOTS

Snapshots are managed in the snapshot window (File ⇨ Snapshots). The snapshot window is typically collapsed and shows only the summary of snapshots, as shown in Figure 11-2. Click the Show Files button in the toolbar to display change information that was shown in Figure 11-1.

The snapshot window is the central interface for browsing, commenting, examining, comparing, and deleting your snapshots. These actions are explained in the following sections.

Commenting on Snapshots

Snapshots are initially named by the method they were taken (via the main menu, before a refactoring, and so on)

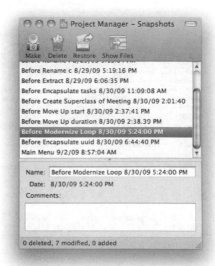

FIGURE 11-2

and when. If you want to give a snapshot a more memorable name, or make some notes about it, select the snapshot and edit the information as shown in Figure 11-3.

Remember that the snapshot represents the project as it was before you make any additional changes. Make your comments from the perspective of how the project was (for example, "Performance baseline before any optimization"), not how it will be (for example, "Adding new slider animation"). That way, the comments will make more sense later.

FIGURE 11-3

Examining Snapshots

You can examine the differences between a snapshot and the current state of your project by selecting a snapshot and expanding the snapshot window, as was shown in Figure 11-1.

The right side of the snapshots window will contain one or two panes:

➤ A list of file changes

➤ A differences browser

When you select a snapshot, the files that have been changed, added, or removed to the project since that snapshot was taken are listed on the right. Selecting a file in the list presents a differences viewer pane that shows the specific changes that were made. Both are shown in Figure 11-4.

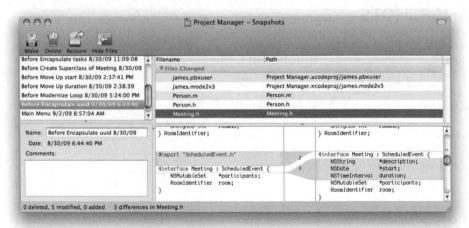

FIGURE 11-4

When you select a single snapshot, the differences shown are all the changes that have occurred since that snapshot was taken.

If you select exactly two snapshots, as shown in Figure 11-5, the file list shows the differences between those two snapshots.

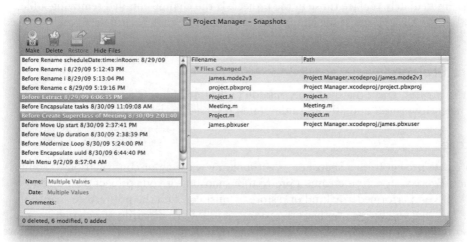

FIGURE 11-5

Restoring Changes

You can discard your changes and recover your original code from a snapshot in one of three ways.

Restore Individual Changes

To recover an individual change, locate the change by selecting the snapshot and a file. Locate the original text in the differences browser. The original (snapshot) version will be on the left and your current version will be on the right, although you can change this in the Xcode preferences. Select and copy the original code to the clipboard, open the file in your project, and paste over the modified code.

 The differences viewer can normally update the files directly, exchanging or combining changes directly. For some reason, this feature is disabled in the snapshots window.

Restore Individual Files

To restore all of the changes made to an individual file, and this includes adding and removing a file, select the snapshot, select one or more files in the file list, and click the Restore button in the toolbar.

The snapshot files immediately replace those in the project. If the change entailed removing a file, that file is added back to the project. If the change was adding a file, that file is deleted and removed from the project.

Restore an Entire Project

To restore an entire project, select the snapshot, but don't select any files. Clicking the Restore button restores the entire project and all files to the state preserved in the snapshot.

Undoing a Restore

If restoring your entire project from a snapshot — without any warning or confirmation — sounds hazardous, it's not. Every restore first creates a pre-restore snapshot of your project, forming a sort of redo stack. If you performed any kind of restore by mistake, find the pre-restore snapshot and restore that. Yes, this will create another pre-restore snapshot. To discard your changes permanently, restore from a snapshot and then delete the pre-restore snapshot created by the restore.

DELETING SNAPSHOTS

Deleting a snapshot is the one truly destructive snapshot action. To delete one or more snapshots, select them in the list and click the Delete button in the toolbar. Xcode confirms that you want to delete the selected snapshots, as shown in Figure 11-6.

If you want to delete all snapshots for every project at once, follow these steps:

➤   Quit Xcode

➤   Locate and discard the file ~/Library/ Application Support/Developer/Shared/ SnapshotRepository.sparseimage

FIGURE 11-6

SUMMARY

Taking snapshots encourages experimentation, spontaneously illustrates your changes, and reduces the chance of errors should you decide to revert to a previous incarnation of your code. Using snapshots is easy and fast, and should become a regular part of your workflow.

The next chapter looks at the many ways of browsing and searching through the huge amount of documentation that Xcode includes.

12

Help and Documentation

WHAT'S IN THIS CHAPTER?

➤ Browsing the Xcode, API, and developer documentation

➤ Searching for symbols, topics, and keywords

➤ Navigating help documentation

➤ Learning handy help shortcuts

➤ Using quick help to get fast answers

➤ Installing new documentation sets and keep them up to date

Modern operating systems are staggering in their size and complexity. The sheer quantity of application program interfaces (APIs) available to a developer can be overwhelming at times. There are scores of frameworks and libraries, each consisting of literally thousands of classes, methods, functions, and constants. Often, just finding the correct method or constant can be your most difficult programming task.

To help you navigate this jungle of symbols, Xcode provides integrated help and documentation. You can browse and search developer documentation. All of the major APIs are indexed, allowing you to call up the documentation for any symbol almost instantly.

This chapter gives you an overview of what help resources are available, shows you how to navigate the documentation, and explores a number of different search techniques.

A lot of the documentation features are nice to know but aren't critical for day-to-day development. If you want just the essentials from this chapter, read the following sections:

➤ Navigating Documentation

➤ Searching Documentation

➤ Documentation Shortcuts

The documentation provided with Xcode, along with additional material available through subscription, include:

- API Reference Documents
- Technology Guides
- Developer Articles
- Technical Notes and Q&As
- Release Notes
- Sample Code

While programming, you're most likely to be using the API reference documents. These are the documents that describe the details of each individual class, method, function, and constant. You'll normally find these by searching or using one of the documentation shortcuts.

When you're just getting started or learning a new technology, the guides and articles are the best place to begin. Find these by browsing the documentation sets.

You can also browse the documentation sets for technical notes, release notes, and technical Q&As, but you're more likely to find them when searching or through a link from another article.

Xcode used to include numerous sample projects as part of the Xcode tools installation. Now, those sample projects — and many more — have references in the documentation sets, but the actual project code must be downloaded. See the "Sample Projects" section later in this chapter.

THE DOCUMENTATION WINDOW

The main interface for all Xcode help is the Help and Documentation window, shown in Figure 12-1, which this chapter refers to simply as the *help window*. You have various ways of opening it, but the simplest is to choose the Help ⇨ Developer Documentation (Command+Option+Shift+?) command. Most of the other commands in the Help menu — Help ⇨ Xcode Help (Command+Shift+?), Help ⇨ Xcode Quick Start, and Help ⇨ Xcode Release Notes — all open the help window to some predetermined content; these are essentially built-in bookmarks.

> *If you've used the help window in earlier versions of Xcode, you may find the new one somewhat perplexing. It's actually a substantial improvement and has a pleasantly simplified interface.*

The help window, shown in Figure 12-1, has three basic parts. At the top is the help window's toolbar. It contains some essential controls, so make sure it's visible or your interactions with the help window will be extremely limited. The main pane that occupies most of the lower-right portion of the window is the documentation browser. It's a WebKit view and acts much like any standard web browser.

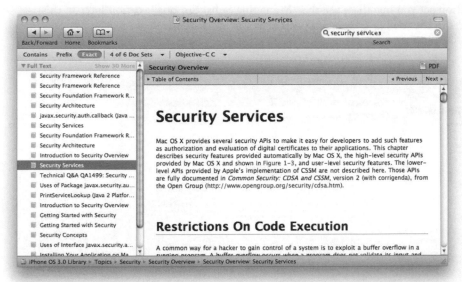

FIGURE 12-1

The search control bar underneath the toolbar, and the search results sidebar to the left, appear only when you are searching the documentation. The help window has two basic modes: browse only and search. When you enter any search term into the toolbar search field, the search control bar and search results sidebar appear. Clear the search term and they disappear again.

There's a special search tool for looking up the "man" (manual) pages that are part of the BSD operating system. It has its own command and toolbar control (see Figure 12-2). Man page searches are described in the "Man Pages" section, later in this chapter.

It's possible to create more than one help window by opening a link in a new Xcode help window. See the section "External Links" to learn how.

Browsing Documentation

The easiest way to use the help window is as a browser. Like any browser, you need a place to start and Xcode provides several:

➤   Most of the Help menu items load preset documentation pages

➤   The "Home" page for each of the documentation sets

➤   Bookmarks

Help ⇨ Xcode Quick Start is a great place to start in general. For questions about Xcode itself, the Help menu provides direct links to Xcode's documentation (Help ⇨ Xcode Help), and the latest release notes (Help ⇨ Xcode Release Notes).

Each documentation set you install — see the "Managing Subscriptions" section later in this chapter — appears in the toolbar's Home pop-up menu, as shown in Figure 12-2.

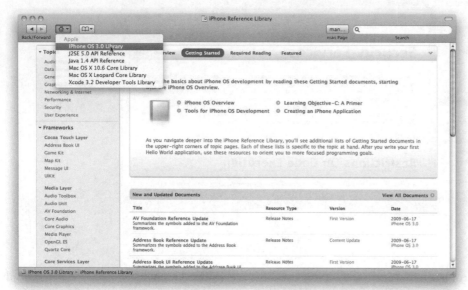

FIGURE 12-2

If you want to explore the documentation of a particular operating system or technology, start at its home page. Over the years, most of the articles, technical notes, and other introductory material available from Apple's developer web site has migrated into the Xcode documentation sets — in much the same form.

Bookmarks are described later in the "Bookmarks" section.

Navigating Help Documents

As mentioned, the documentation browser is essentially a web page browser, so all of the standard elements (links, images, embedded video, scrolling) all work exactly as you would expect. The help window only adds two features to the browser: history and bookmarks. The back (Command+[) and forward (Command+]) history buttons are in the toolbar and act as you would expect them to. All other navigation is provided by the content of the documentation pages themselves — mostly via HTML and JavaScript. Thus, the organization and navigation of pages changes depending on the kind of documents at which you're looking, and can evolve as the documentation content is updated.

As of this writing, there are a couple of consistent themes. The document home pages or collection pages, as was shown in Figure 12-2, tend to list related documents and often have a table of contents on the left that let you jump to different sections. Some even have search, filter, and sorting features, like that shown in Figure 12-3.

FIGURE 12-3

The API documentation, as shown in Figure 12-4, adds a number of navigation tools. The navigation bar across the top lets you toggle the table of contents for the group of documents. The table of contents contains links that jump to various sections and related documents. It often contains high-level section titles that can be individually expanded or collapsed.

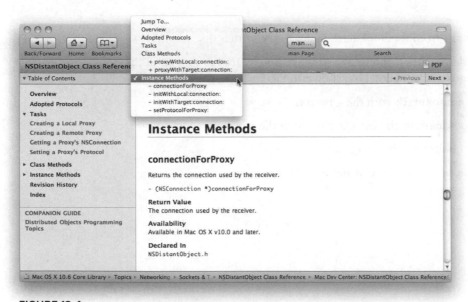

FIGURE 12-4

The pop-up navigation menu, also shown in Figure 12-4, lets you jump directly to various sections within the page and is organized very much like the functions menu in the text editor. Finally, the Previous and Next links at the upper-right link to the previous and next page within that document section; these are not history navigation buttons. When reading multi-page articles, use them to move sequentially through the material.

Bookmarks

Choose the Find ➪ Add to Bookmarks (Command+D) command, or choose the Add Bookmark For '. . .' command from the Bookmarks toolbar control to create a bookmark to the current document. Figure 12-5 shows adding a bookmark to the File Manager Reference page. You can bookmark a page, but you can't bookmark a particular anchor within a page. Bookmarks are added to the Bookmarks toolbar control and are independent of the Bookmarks smart group in your project.

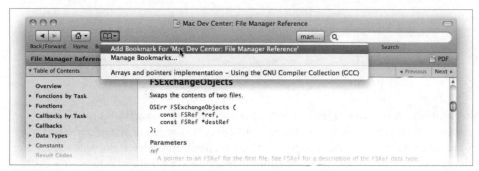

FIGURE 12-5

Choose a bookmark from the Bookmark menu to revisit that document.

To manage your bookmarks, choose the Manage Bookmarks command in the Bookmarks toolbar control. In the bookmarks dialog box, shown in Figure 12-6, you can:

➤ Remove a bookmark with the – button.

➤ Add a bookmark to the current page with the + button.

➤ Reorder bookmarks by dragging.

➤ Rename a bookmark title by double-clicking.

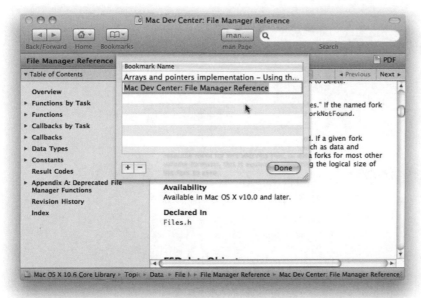

FIGURE 12-6

External Links

Documentation pages may contain links to external sources (outside the `/Developer/ Documentation` folder). These include:

➤ Links to supplementary documents on Apple's web site

➤ The PDF version of a document

➤ Feedback and bug reporting links

➤ Links to related standards (ISO, W3C, and so on)

➤ File archives (ZIP files, disk images, and so on)

➤ Multimedia (iTunes University, and so on)

Most external links are handed off to your operating system and are handled according to your system preferences; an HTML link will most likely open in your default browser, a file link may download the file to your `Downloads` folder, a PDF link may download the document and open it using the Preview application, and a podcast may launch iTunes.

A number of contextual commands are accessible by Control/Right-clicking a link or selection, as shown on the left in Figure 12-7, or anywhere else in a page, as shown on the right.

FIGURE 12-7

These commands are:

COMMAND	ACTION
Open Link	Same as clicking the link
Open Link in New Window	Creates a second Xcode help window with the contents of the link
Copy Link	Copies the URL of the link to the clipboard
Open Link in Browser	Sends the URL of the link to your default browser
Find Text in Documentation	Enters the link or selected text as the search term (see the "Searching Documentation" section later in this chapter)
Open Page in New Window	Creates a second Xcode help window with the same content
Open Page in Browser	Sends the URL of the current page to your default browser

The "in New Window" commands are the only way of creating multiple help windows. The original help window remains the principal help window for your project; shortcuts, for example, are always directed to the principal help window.

Opening a link or page in your browser is a great way of keeping multiple documentation pages open at once. Modern browsers, with their tabs and workspace sets, can be much more effective at organizing, remembering, and managing multiple help documents than the simple Xcode help window.

SAMPLE PROJECTS

A special kind of external link is found in sample project pages. Recently, the Xcode developer tools suite has moved away from providing sample projects as part of the installation to providing links to sample projects in the documentation, going so far as to cross-reference each API with the example projects that use it. Figure 12-8 shows the ButtonMadness sample project page. I got to this page from the `insertMenu:atIndex:` method reference document.

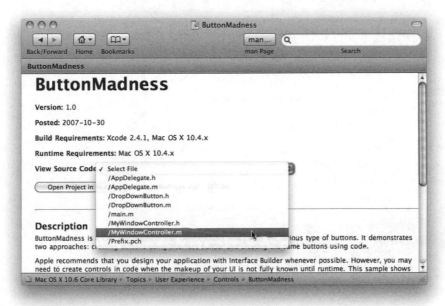

FIGURE 12-8

You have two ways of exploring a sample project. The first is simply to view the source files in the help window using the pop-up menu, also shown in Figure 12-8.

The other method is to click the Open Project in Xcode button. You'll be prompted for a location on your disk. Choose a location and Xcode downloads the project archive to the selected folder, extracts the project files, and opens the project. If it did anything more for you, you'd be obligated to tip it afterwards.

SEARCHING DOCUMENTATION

Browsing the ADC documentation is great way to get an overview of a technology or work through a tutorial. During actual development, however, you usually just want to find something specific — and you want to find it in a hurry. The simplest way is to enter a search term into the search field.

Search Field

The help window's search field is in the toolbar, as shown in Figure 12-9. Entering anything into the search field activates the help window's search mode and adds two additional sets of controls.

FIGURE 12-9

The search control bar appears underneath the toolbar and a search results sidebar appears on the left of the content area. These controls let you refine the search and browse its results.

Your search term is instantly and simultaneously used to search the documentation in three ways:

➤ API Symbols

➤ Article Titles

➤ Article Text

The results of each search appear in its own group in the search results sidebar. Each group always shows the most likely matches. If there are more, you can expand the results list by clicking one of the Show More Results buttons.

The API symbols group only searches the Application Programming Interface index of the documentation. These are the class, method, function, variable, and constant names documented in the API reference material. If you're looking for some specific framework or symbol, this is where you are mostly like to find it.

The article title and text groups search the titles and complete text of every article, technical note, guide, and reference page for a match. If you are trying to find a description of a particular technology or topic, these are the search groups you are most likely to find it in.

A search term can contain multiple keywords and operators. The search field recognizes the following operators:

OPERATOR	MEANING
(...)	Logical group. Treats the terms between the parentheses as a single term.
!	Not. Inverts the sense of the search term.
&	And. Requires that the term on the left and right are both found. This is the default when you're searching for multiple keywords.
|	Or. Matches if either the term on the right or the term on the left is found.
+	Required word. Equivalent to just searching for a keyword.
–	Unwanted word. Excludes any results that contain that keyword.
*	Wildcard. Creates a keyword that matches a partial word (for example, `menu*` or `*Notification`).

For example, the following search term locates all articles that contain the word "services," and either the word "sync" or "system," but do not contain the word "audio":

```
(sync | system) services -audio
```

Every symbol in the API index is considered to be a single word. No multi-keyword search will ever match an API symbol, even if the symbol contains all of the keywords.

Clearing the search field hides the search control bar and the results sidebar again.

Search Control Bar

The search control bar further refines how the search keywords are applied, and the scope of what's searched. The search control bar has three controls, all shown in Figure 12-9.

Word Boundary

The word boundary control determines how each search keyword must match a symbol or word in the documentation:

WORD BOUNDARY SETTING	MATCH RULE
Contains	Keyword can appear anywhere in the word
Prefix	Keyword must match the beginning of the word
Exact	Keyword must match the whole word

The prefix setting is most useful when searching the API reference documents for symbols. It allows you to type the beginning of a known symbol and quickly narrow down the list of symbols you're looking for. Contains and Exact apply equally to API and text searches.

 The wildcard operator may defeat or interact with the word boundary setting. For example, searching for menu* *using the Exact setting is the same as searching for* menu *with the Prefix setting.*

Documentation Sets

You can limit which sets of documentation Xcode searches by selecting them in the Doc Sets control, shown in Figure 12-10.

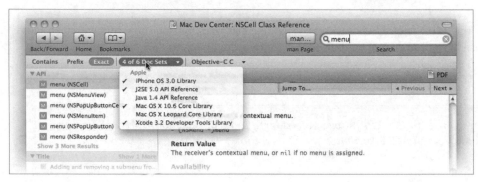

FIGURE 12-10

Select only the platforms or technologies that you're using for development right now. That limits the scope of your searches to just the documentation that's appropriate for your development. If you are doing cross development that targets several versions of an operating system, you might also want to uncheck the modern documentation sets. That way, you're unlikely to accidentally use an API that only exists in the more recent OS.

Language Sets

The language sets control, shown in Figure 12-11, further limits your API symbol searches to only those symbols defined in the selected languages. For example, if you're programming in Objective-C, check C and Objective-C. If you're programming in JavaScript, uncheck everything except JavaScript. If you're programming in Objective-C++, you may want to check C, C++, and Objective-C.

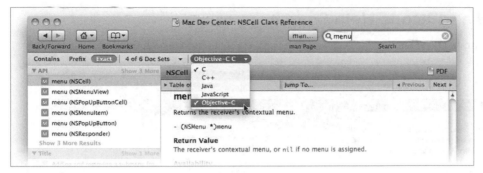

FIGURE 12-11

Text Search

The help document browser includes a simplified text search tool, very much like the single file search tool described in Chapter 8, for searching through the text of the current document. Press Command+F to reveal the search tool, as shown in Figure 12-12.

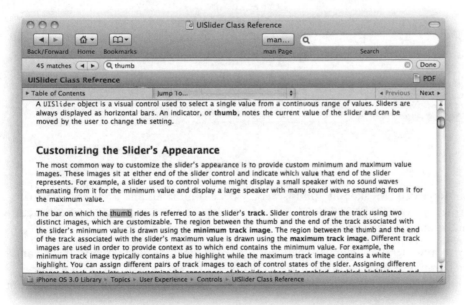

FIGURE 12-12

The document search tool has no options, but responds to the same Find Next (Command+G) and Find Previous (Shift+Command+G) commands that the single file search tool does. Click the Done button to dismiss the tool.

Command and Xcode Help Search

To find a command or a particular Xcode help topic, enter a term directly into the help menu's search field, as shown in Figure 12-13.

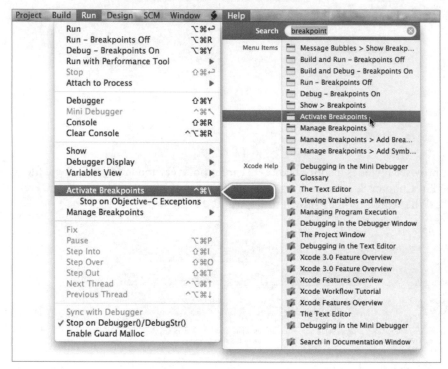

FIGURE 12-13

In Figure 12-13, the keyword "breakpoint" finds several Xcode commands and a variety of help documents. Hovering over one of the commands results reveals that command in the menu structure so that you can find it again in the future.

This is a great way to find menu commands. There are a *lot* of commands in the Xcode menus, and it's easy to lose track of where they are. Also, it seems that every new release of Xcode moves or renames about a third of the commands, so even seasoned Xcoders need to reorient themselves from time to time.

The lower portion of the menu lists the Xcode help document topics that match the search term. These open the help window to a specific Xcode help document.

Finally, the Search in Documentation Window command at the very bottom of the menu opens the help window and performs the same search, for those times where you don't find what you're looking for in the menu.

DOCUMENTATION SHORTCUTS

A number of shortcuts are available for accessing the help window and for quickly looking up key terms. The global shortcuts are:

SHORTCUT	ACTION
Option+Shift+Command+?	Opens the help window
Control+Shift+Command+?	Opens the quick help window
Shift+Command+?	Activates the Help menu

These three shortcuts are available almost universally in Xcode. The quick help window is described in the "Quick Help" section a little later in this chapter.

The next few sections describe other kinds of documentation shortcuts and how to access them.

Editing Shortcuts

You will most likely want to consult the documentation for a particular function or method while editing code. With a symbol name selected in the text editor pane, you have the following menu command and shortcuts available to you:

SHORTCUT	ACTION
Option+Shift+double-click	Searches for symbol in documentation
Option+double-click	Opens quick help window for symbol
Control/Right-click ⇨ Find Text in Documentation	Searches for selected text in documentation
Help ⇨ Find Documentation for Selected Text	Same as Find Text in Documentation

The two most useful shortcuts are the Option+Shift+double-click and Option+double-click gestures. These immediately select the word (symbol) underneath the cursor and search for its definition in either the help window or the quick help window (described in the next section).

Quick Help

The quick help window, shown in Figure 12-14, is a miniature help window that presents a succinct summary of a single API symbol. It operates in two modes: transient and persistent.

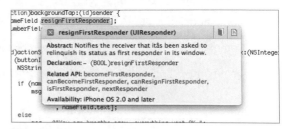

FIGURE 12-14

The quick help window has two action buttons, in addition to the standard title bar, resize, and close controls. The button with the little book jumps to the full API documentation for that symbol in the standard help window — equivalent to any of the other symbol search shortcuts mentioned in this section.

 If you have upgraded from an earlier version of Xcode, quick help replaces the Research Assistant. The "Persistent Quick Help" section described how to keep the quick help window open, where it acts very much like the Research Assistant did.

The optional header button jumps to the definition of the symbol in the framework's header (.h) file. This is equivalent to the Edit ⇨ Find ⇨ Jump to Definition (Command+double-click) shortcut.

Transient Quick Help

Quick help is intended to be just that: quick. When summoned from the editor using the Option+double-click shortcut, it appears immediately adjacent to the symbol in question. Pressing the Esc key, or clicking anywhere in the editor pane, dismisses the quick help window and returns you to your coding.

Persistent Quick Help

If you summon the quick help window and then move or resize it, or open it using the Help ⇨ Quick Help (Control+Shift+Command+?) command, the quick help window becomes persistent; it will not automatically close when you return to editing. Instead, it acts more like an inspector palette, constantly updating its content based on the current text selection.

If you find yourself referring to the quick help window a lot, consider letting it be persistent. If you have limited screen real estate or, like me, only like to see it open when you need it, use the Option+double-click shortcut to open it on demand and press Esc to close it again.

Documentation Shortcuts

The help document browser responds to the following standard shortcuts, although — oddly — most are not associated with any of Xcode's menus:

SHORTCUT	ACTION
Command+[	Previous page in history
Command+]	Next page in history
Command+F	Find text, or find next

SHORTCUT	ACTION
Command+G	Find next
Shift+Command+G	Find previous
Command+D	Add bookmark

MAN PAGES

UNIX man pages are another source of documentation that is loosely integrated with Xcode. The C functions (section 3) of the man pages are included in the API search index. Looking up or searching for a POSIX C function displays the man page for that function, but the man pages for shell commands (section 1), file formats (section 5), system utilities (section 8), along with third-party man pages are not indexed and cannot be found through the help window.

To review any man page installed in your system, choose the Help ⇨ Open man Page command, which presents the dialog shown in Figure 12-15. There is also a man . . . toolbar button that you can add to your help window's toolbar.

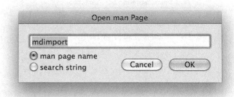

FIGURE 12-15

The man page name option invokes the man command with your search term and presents the resulting man page in the help window.

The search string option invokes the apropos (man -k) command. This searches all of the short descriptions in the man page database for the given keywords and presents the results in the help window. Each result is linked to its man page, so review the search results and click the entries that interest you.

CUSTOMIZING HELP

The Documentation pane of the Xcode preferences, shown in Figure 12-16, allow you to customize three things: what documentation sets you subscribe to, what information is presented in the quick help window, and how small the documentation text fonts are allowed to be.

FIGURE 12-16

Managing Subscriptions

Any or all of the documentation sets installed in /Developer/Documentation can be maintained through an RSS feed. Xcode can query these RSS feeds to determine if there are any updates to the documentation sets. If new documentation is available, Xcode will offer to (or will automatically) download the updated documentation and install it. Downloading documentation from Apple's servers requires that you provide your developer connection account ID and password, as shown in Figure 12-17. This information will be saved for future updates. Installing new files in your /Developer folder also requires an administrator's authorization.

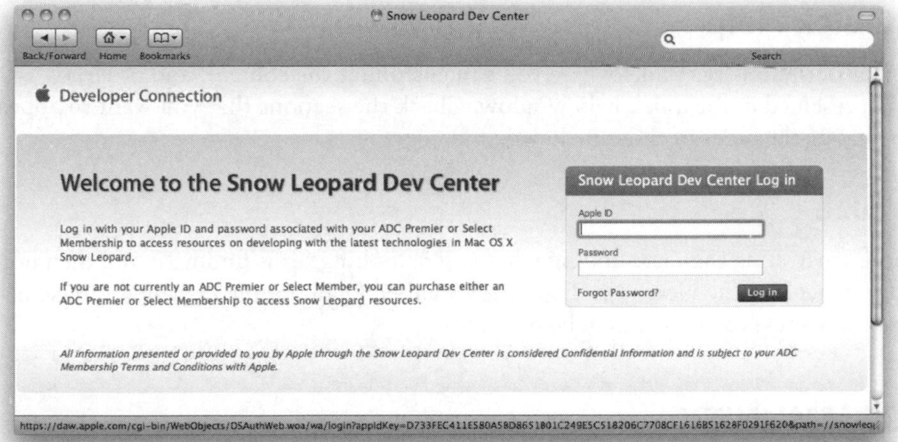

FIGURE 12-17

The Check For And Install Updates Automatically option instructs Xcode to periodically check for, and install, new documentation updates. If left unchecked, you will want to manually check for updates occasionally using the Check and Install Now button, preferably when you have a high-speed Internet connection — documentation updates can be quite large. In Figure 12-16, you can see that the iPhone OS 3.0 and Snow Leopard Library documentation sets are in the process of being downloaded. Be patient; even with a fast network pipe, large documentation sets can take an hour or more to download and install. If you're wondering what the progress of the update is, check Xcode's Activity window, as shown in Figure 12-18.

FIGURE 12-18

A number of documentation sets have subscription feeds, but are disabled by default. In Figure 12-16, the original iPhone OS Library, Java Library, and some other sets are not installed. Click the Get button to download, install, and activate the RSS feed for that document set. If you're curious about where the files for a particular document set are installed, the address of its RSS feed, and other information, click the small *i* (Info) button next to the set name.

You cannot delete any of the preinstalled document sets from Apple, but you can install additional sets generated by you or a third party. The details of generating and installing your own Xcode-compatible documentation is amply described in the article "Using Doxygen to Create Xcode Documentation Sets," which is part of the Xcode documentation set.

Customizing Quick Help

To the right of the subscriptions is a panel where you can customize the content, and order, of information that is presented in the quick help window. Check the sections that you want to appear. Click and drag to change the order of those included.

Limiting Font Size

The only thing more frustrating than not finding what you're looking for is finding it and then not being able to read it. Checking the Never Use Font Sizes Smaller Than option lets you establish a minimum font size for all text that appears in help windows.

THE XCODE COMMUNITY

This chapter has focused on the help and documentation resources accessible through the Xcode interface, but one of the most valuable resources for Xcode users is *other Xcode users*.

In addition to supplementary developer information at Apple's Developer Connection web site, you'll also find a variety of mailing list and discussion forums. You can see the complete list of the mailing lists at `http://lists.apple.com/mailman/listinfo`. Of particular interest is the Xcode-users mailing list. This list is populated by Xcode users from all over the world and is a phenomenal resource for solving problems with Xcode. I tapped the talented and helpful individuals of this list several times while writing this book. I would strongly urge you to join the Xcode-users list.

As with many Internet discussion groups, members contribute their time and knowledge as a courtesy to others and to support the community of Xcode users. Many are professional software engineers with busy schedules and none of them are obligated to help you. Be respectful of their time and efforts by adhering to these guidelines:

➤   The list does not exist to solve your problems for you. Post questions only when you've read all the available documentation (which should include this book), searched the list archives for similar questions, and tried all of the solutions you can think of.

➤   Be clear, concise, complete, and courteous.

➤   Give something back. The list is a community of members helping members. If you know the answer to a question, or have a helpful suggestion, take the time to post it. You can't expect others to help you if you never help anyone else.

➤   The list is not your personal soapbox. It's not a forum for rants and personal opinions. If you want to provide feedback to the Xcode developers, use one of the feedback links on Apple's website or file an enhancement request via the bug reporter (available to registered developers). In my experience, the Xcode development team is very open to suggestions that will improve Xcode.

➤   The list is not Apple support. If you need technical, sales, or developer support from Apple, contact the appropriate party through ADC. Apple engineers have been known to monitor and answer questions on the list, but they cannot provide you with any kind of official support through the list.

SUMMARY

Xcode includes a massive amount of documentation, and a variety of tools for working with it. You've seen how to search for keywords and symbols, and find API documentation from within the class browser and directly from within your source code. You can even add you own documentation, if you need to.

You may still not find what you are looking for in the local documentation. Remember to avail yourself of the Apple Developer Connection web site (`http://developer.apple.com/`). Apple's online resources contain many more articles, documents, and sample code than could ever be downloaded and stored locally, and these resources are updated constantly.

13

Interface Builder

➤   Creating nib documents

➤   Adding objects to a nib document

➤   Configuring and connecting objects together

➤   Defining and creating custom objects

➤   Customizing Interface Builder

Interface Builder is a graphical user interface editor. Interface Builder and the Xcode IDE work hand in glove to create a fluid, dynamic, and (nearly) seamless workflow for designing and implementing your user interface objects. Getting the most out of Interface Builder is essential to any Mac or iPhone development project.

Interface Builder has a long history. Interface Builder and Project Builder (later renamed Xcode) trace their lineage all the way back to NeXT, where they were originally conceived. Twenty years later, the roles of these two applications remain largely unchanged — a testament to the vision of its creators. You write your code (controller) in Xcode using text editors and compilers. You design your interface (view) in Interface Builder using graphical design tools and object inspectors.

Although this is not a book about programming, it's very difficult to describe how to use Interface Builder without understanding what Interface Builder does and the technologies that allow it to work. This is a common source of confusion for new developers, particularly those coming from other development environments. If you fall into this category (or don't know whether you fall into this category), read through the sections "What Is Interface Builder?" and "Interface Builder Workflow." Readers comfortable with Interface Builder concepts can skip ahead to the sections that describe specific features.

WHAT IS INTERFACE BUILDER?

In a nutshell, Interface Builder, shown in Figure 13-1, edits a graph of archived objects stored in a data file. That's a terse statement, but it accurately captures the key concept behind Interface Builder. Specifically, Interface Builder edits the contents of a nib document. A nib document contains archived objects — also called serialized, marshaled, or freeze-dried objects. The nib document is transformed into a nib file when the project is built. At run time, you "load" a nib file; this un-archives (de-serializes, un-marshals) the graph of objects, creating instances of objects with preset properties, indistinguishable from objects created programmatically.

NIB originally stood for NeXT Interface Builder document, but Apple has officially rechristened the extension Interface Builder Document. *Although modern nib documents are actually XIB (XML Interface Builder) files, the terms "nib," "nib file," and "nib document" are used genetrically to describe all Interface Builder documents, regardless of their actual format. The term "nib document" is used here when talking about the document file (or bundle) that you edit in Interface Builder, while "nib file" usually refers to the binary deployment file loaded by your application.*

FIGURE 13-1

By editing an archived data file, Interface Builder allows you to define complex graphs of interconnected objects, customize them in a myriad of ways, and do all of that using visual design tools. At run time, the entire set of objects is instantiated, initialized, and connected together with a single code statement — or no code at all, for nib files loaded automatically by the framework. This improves your productivity and the robustness of your applications in a number of ways:

➤ Your application code is less brittle because, simply, there's less code — sometimes no code at all.

➤ It's easier, faster, and more rational to create an interface design using a graphical design tool rather than hard-coding values in your program. Should the coordinates of your input text field be (314,20,276,22) or (20,314,22,276)?

➤ NIB files are more efficient. An archived object data stream is generally far more compact than the code required to create, initialize, configure, and connect that same set of objects.

➤ Changes to your interface often don't require any code changes. This minimizes debugging and reduces the chance of introducing unexpected errors.

➤ Your interface can be redefined based on the location and language of your user, or for any other reason you choose. Multiple nib files that represent the same, or similar, interfaces can be dynamically selected at run time to change the look and feel of your application. The operating system automatically loads the correct nib file for your user's language and locale. You can selectively load nib files programmatically based on any criteria you define.

Almost as important as what Interface Builder is, is what Interface Builder is not:

➤ Interface Builder is not a template editor.

➤ Interface Builder is not a code generator.

➤ Interface Builder is not a compiler.

If you've come from a development environment where the graphical user interface design tools create scripts, layout information files, generate source, or insert binary code into your application, set those concepts aside. Interface Builder edits archived objects, or specifically data, that just happens to describe objects. Everything you do in Interface Builder will be from the perspective of objects, their properties, and their relationships — the same way you design with objects in your code. The result (the nib file) is just data. It's data during development; it's data at build time; and it's still data in your finished application. Only when the data is un-archived does it become objects in your application.

Code vs. Interface Builder

To provide an unambiguous example, consider the following two programs. The first program, shown in Listing 13-1, creates a window and populates it with some controls.

Available for download on Wrox.com

LISTING 13-1: Creating a Window Programmatically

```
- (void)makeNewRecordWindow
{
    NSRect frame = NSMakeRect(100.0,100.0,349.0,123.0);
    newRecordWindow = [[NSWindow alloc]
                        initWithContentRect:frame
                                  styleMask:(NSTitledWindowMask|
                                             NSClosableWindowMask|
                                             NSMiniaturizableWindowMask)
                                    backing:NSBackingStoreBuffered
                                      defer:YES];
    NSView* windowContentView = [newRecordWindow contentView];
    frame = NSMakeRect(253.0,12.0,82.0,32.0);
    NSButton* okButton = [[NSButton alloc] initWithFrame:frame];
    [okButton setTitle:@"Create"];
    [okButton setButtonType:NSMomentaryLightButton];
```

continues

LISTING 13-1 *(continued)*

```
    [okButton setBezelStyle:NSRoundedBezelStyle];
    [windowContentView addSubview:okButton];
    frame = NSMakeRect(171.0,12.0,82.0,32.0);
    NSButton* cancelButton = [[NSButton alloc] initWithFrame:frame];
    [cancelButton setTitle:@"Cancel"];
    [cancelButton setButtonType:NSMomentaryLightButton];
    [cancelButton setBezelStyle:NSRoundedBezelStyle];
    [windowContentView addSubview:cancelButton];
    frame = NSMakeRect(20.0,90.0,130.0,13.0);
    NSTextField* titleField = [[NSTextField alloc] initWithFrame:frame];
    [titleField setStringValue:@"Record Name:"];
    [titleField setEditable:NO];
    [titleField setSelectable:NO];
    [titleField setBordered:NO];
    [titleField setDrawsBackground:NO];
    [windowContentView addSubview:titleField];
    frame = NSMakeRect(20.0,60.0,309.0,22.0);
    NSTextField* nameField = [[NSTextField alloc] initWithFrame:frame];
    [windowContentView addSubview:nameField];

    [newRecordWindow makeKeyAndOrderFront:self];
}
```

The Interface Builder document that creates an identical window was shown in Figure 13-1. The code needed to create, initialize, and display the window defined by the nib document shown in Figure 13-1 is shown in Listing 13-2.

Available for
download on
Wrox.com

LISTING 13-2: Creating a Window Stored in a Nib File

```
- (void)makeNewRecordWindow
{
    [[NSBundle mainBundle] loadNibNamed:@"NewRecord" owner:self];
    [newRecordWindow makeKeyAndOrderFront:self];
}
```

The two different –makeNewRecordWindow methods, shown in Listing 13-1 and 13-2, accomplish exactly the same thing. After the method returns, the objects that are created, their relationships, properties, and inter-object references are the same.

It should be obvious that the window design in Figure 13-1 is far easier to comprehend and manipulate than the code in Listing 13-1. For example, a button object could be repositioned simply by dragging it to a new location. This is vastly simpler, and more predictable, than trying to edit the coordinate constants in Listing 13-1 — assuming you could find them.

This brings me to one last, but important, benefit of using Interface Builder:

➤ Your application doesn't give up any control or features by using nib created objects. You are free to programmatically manipulate objects created by a nib file just as you would objects created programmatically. You can define as much, or as little, in the nib file as appropriate. Many nib files define nothing more than a container object that's later populated programmatically.

The Three C's of Interface Builder

Interface Builder lets you do three things:

➤ Create instances of objects

➤ Configure object attributes

➤ Connect objects together

You can create instances of any of the multitude of predefined objects provided in Interface Builder's library, or you can create instances of classes that you've defined yourself. Creating objects is described in the section "Creating Objects."

You edit the attributes (properties) of object instances in a variety of ways, but the result is ultimately the same; the property values you select become part of the archive data stream and are used to initialize the object when it's created at run time. This is covered in the sections "Selecting Objects" and "Configuring Objects."

Finally, and probably what Interface Builder is most famous for, is the ability to *connect* objects. A connection is just IB-speak for an object reference. In Interface Builder, you make a connection by dragging an outlet or action from one object to another. At run time, the connection sets an instance variable of the referring object to point to the object that you connected it to. It's that simple. The effect of connecting the outlet `inputField` to an NSTextField object would be equivalent to writing the code:

```
self.inputField = [NSTextField new];
```

You can learn the many different ways of connecting objects in the section "Connecting Objects."

That's it! That's all Interface Builder does. With the mystery of Interface Builder out of the way, I can now show you how Interface Builder integrates into Xcode and your development workflow.

INTERFACE BUILDER WORKFLOW

Interface Builder is (technically) a standalone editor. You can launch Interface Builder and use it to create, edit, and save nib documents. Except in a few rare cases — say where you might want to use Interface Builder to "hack" an existing nib document — you're most likely to use Interface Builder as an adjunct editor for an Xcode project.

Editing NIB Documents in an Xcode Workflow

The typical workflow when using Xcode and Interface Builder is shown in Figure 13-2.

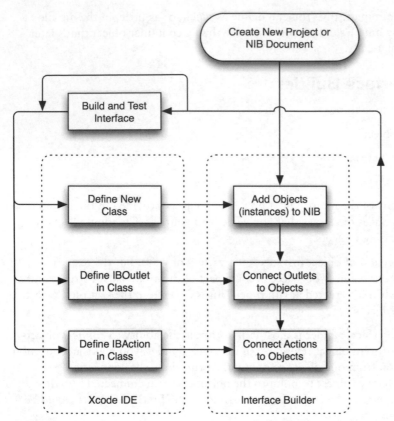

FIGURE 13-2

Interface Builder isn't a compiler, but it does observe and interpret your project's class declarations. It understands the classes, inheritance, properties, and methods that you declare and synchronizes those with your nib document. Your development workflow might proceed like so:

1. Xcode: Define a new view controller class.

2. Interface Builder: Create a nib document to define the objects in the interface.

3. Interface Builder: Add some input text field objects to the interface.

4. Xcode: Add some instance variables to the view controller class that will refer to those input field objects.

5. Interface Builder: Connect the input field objects to the instance variables.

6. Xcode: Create an action method.

7. Interface Builder: Add a button to the interface and connect its action to the controller's new method.

8. And so on . . .

As you can see, you'll jump back and forth between Xcode and Interface Builder quite a lot while working on your interface. A number of features and shortcuts for making this workflow nearly seamless are covered at appropriate places in this chapter.

Simulating an Interface

During interface design and development, you'll often want get an approximate idea of how your interface will look and behave. Building and running your application is the obvious way to test it, but sometimes that's not convenient; projects under development are often in a state where they can't be built and tested.

Interface Builder provides an interface simulator, which you can launch using the File ➪ Simulate Interface (Command+R) command. The simulator loads your nib document in a neutral application environment consisting only of the standard framework objects supplied by the operating system. All custom objects, outlets, and actions are reduced to their base class behavior or are ignored.

Figure 13-3 shows an iPhone interface design and the same nib document running in the iPhone simulator. Interface Builder uses the iPhone simulator for Cocoa Touch documents. Cocoa documents are presented in a Cocoa simulator built into the Interface Builder application. When you're done with the simulation, choose the Quit command.

FIGURE 13-3

The simulator presents your interface using the standard framework objects, sans any programmatic enhancements provided by your application. The results can be quite rich or stunningly dull. Consider a custom view object that's drawn by your application; the simulator will present a blank white square.

The simulator provides canned data for list, table, and browser views (the names of cities, in the example shown in Figure 13-3). Editable text fields are editable; date pickers are pickable; and so on. The simulator is good for checking window resizing behavior, multi-tab views, table column resizing, and the like. Most buttons and application-specific menu items will be non-functional, of course.

Some interface objects can automatically record position and other state information in the user defaults for your application. For example, the NSWindow object can record its position and size when closed and a check box button can be bound to a user defaults property. The next time the application/simulator is launched, the position of the window and the state of the button will be restored from the user defaults.

Interface Builder provides a "scratch pad" user defaults file for each simulated nib document. This transient set of preferences can be set to be periodically, or manually, erased from the Simulator tab of the Interface Builder preferences. Erasing the preferences clears all user default values, as though the application was being run for the first time.

Building Your Project from Interface Builder

If you look at the workflow diagram in Figure 13-2, you'll see that it's very typical to write code, make connections in Interface Builder, switch back to Xcode, and then build and test your application.

Interface Builder provides a shortcut: the File ⇨ Build and Go in Xcode (Shift+Command+R) command switches back to Xcode, builds your project, and launches it.

INTERFACE BUILDER'S INTERFACE

This section starts with a brief tour of Interface Builder's interface. One reason it will be brief, and also one of the reasons Interface Builder is so easy to use, is that there are basically only three interface elements: the nib document window, the inspector palette, and the library palette. All three are shown in Figures 13-4 and 13-5.

FIGURE 13-4

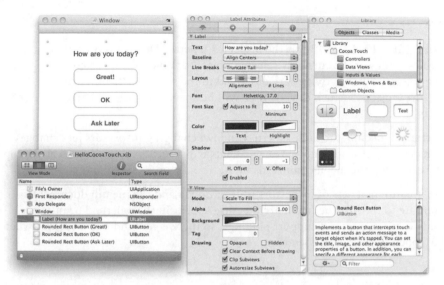

FIGURE 13-5

Figure 13-4 shows a Cocoa nib document, and Figure 13-5 shows a Cocoa Touch (iPhone/iPod) nib document. When you open a nib document, the contents of the file are represented abstractly in the nib document window, as shown in the lower left of Figures 13-4 and 13-5. Nib documents contain objects, and those objects are shown here either as icons, hierarchically, or in a browser. You select which view you want to see in the toolbar. Figure 13-6 shows the contents of a nib document in all three views. The icon view only shows the top-level objects. You will also find a few special objects listed; these are described later in the section "Placeholder Objects."

FIGURE 13-6

The two important palettes are the inspector palette and the library palette, both described next. Most of the other windows you'll be working with will be view windows. View windows present your view objects (approximately) as they will appear in your application: a window is shown as a window, a menu as a menu, a button as a button. You can edit your objects in either the nib document or manipulate their visual representation in a view window. The effect is the same.

Inspector Palette

Shown in the middle of Figures 13-4 and 13-5 is the inspector palette. The inspector palette shows the properties and settings of the currently selected object (or objects). It's where you customize and connect objects. These activities are described in the sections "Configuring Objects" and "Connecting Objects." Much of your time will be spent using the inspector palette to fine-tune your objects.

Several different inspectors all occupy the same palette window; changing inspectors just changes the view of the single inspector palette window. You can change inspectors using the tabs at the top of the inspector window or using the menu commands in the Tool menu.

You'll notice that there are different sets of inspectors for the Cocoa and iPhone nib documents. Only inspectors appropriate to the nib document architecture appear in the palette. For instance, the iPhone OS (as of this writing) does not support bindings, so there is no bindings inspector when working with a Cocoa Touch (iPhone) nib document.

Library Palette

On the right in Figures 13-4 and 13-5 is the library palette. The library palette is your source for new objects and other resources. Creating a new object is described in the section "Creating Objects." The library is organized into groups, selectable using the tab control at the top of the palette window. To create a window, for example, just drag a window object out of the library palette and drop it anywhere in the screen. To add a button to that window, drag a button object off the palette and drop it into the window.

The library palette's Classes view lists all of the classes that Interface Builder knows about. While many of these classes are represented in the Objects view, the Classes view also includes all custom classes you've defined and is organized by name rather than by function. Either view can be used as a source of new objects.

 In addition to missing inspector palettes, the active nib document architecture may cause other Interface Builder interface elements to appear or disappear. Carbon nib documents, for example, do not support creating objects with arbitrary types (classes), so there will be no Classes tab in the Library palette when a Carbon document is active.

The Media tab represents content files (mostly images) to which objects can refer in your nib document. These include system resources, like standard button icons and sounds, as well as any resources you've added to your project.

The library palette presents each list in one or more panes. In the objects list, the top portion lets you browse and select categories of objects. The individual objects in the selected categories are displayed in the middle pane. The bottom pane presents interesting information about the selected objects. The layout of the list can be controlled with the pop-up menu at the bottom of the palette. The other lists have similar features and controls.

If you know the name, or part of the name, of the class or media object you're looking for, type it into the search field at the bottom of the window, as shown in Figure 13-7.

Multiple NIB Document Windows

Like Xcode projects, Interface Builder always has one active nib document. Also like Xcode, the Window ➪ Document (Command+0) command brings forward the currently active document window.

To aid you in identifying the view windows contained in that nib document, Interface Builder dims any view objects that are not part of the active nib document. Figure 13-8 shows two nib documents: one containing a Cocoa window and menu and the other containing

FIGURE 13-7

a Cocoa Touch view. The Cocoa document is active. This dims all of the windows belonging to the other nib document.

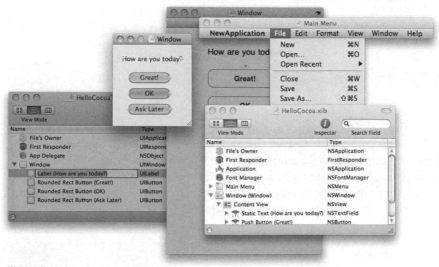

FIGURE 13-8

CREATING A NIB DOCUMENT

Interface Builder edits nib documents, so the first thing you must do is create a nib document. If you created your project in Xcode using one of the standard templates, you probably already have a nib document in your project. Open the nib document in the source group and Xcode launches Interface Builder. Also, many new file templates in Xcode also create companion nib documents. For example, creating a new iPhone view controller class in Xcode also adds its associated nib document to the project for you.

If you already have a nib document, or created a new one using Xcode, you can skip this section. Come back when you need to create one.

Choosing a Template

If you need to create additional nib documents, launch or switch to Interface Builder and choose the File ⇨ New command. Interface Builder presents the template assistant shown in Figure 13-9.

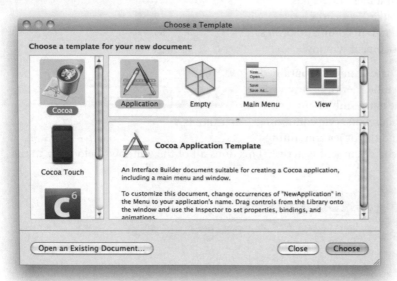

FIGURE 13-9

Choose a template from the list. The templates are organized into groups, depending on the SDKs you have installed. This can include Cocoa, Cocoa Touch (iPhone/iPod), Carbon, and IB Kit (Interface Builder Kit) groups. All of the templates in the Cocoa group create a Cocoa nib document; Carbon group templates create Carbon nib documents, and so on. You cannot change or convert between document types, so make sure you choose a template from the correct group. The following tables provide a brief summary of the templates.

COCOA TEMPLATES	CONTENTS
Application	Makes a Cocoa nib document containing a standard Cocoa application menu bar and an empty window. This template is appropriate for a "single window" (non-document based) application. However, you should rarely need this template — all Xcode project templates for Cocoa applications already include a nib document containing the same thing.
Empty	Creates an empty Cocoa nib document.

COCOA TEMPLATES	CONTENTS
Main Menu	Contains a standard application menu bar. Again, you're unlikely to use this template unless you're creating alternate menu sets for your application.
View	Contains a single NSView object. Useful for defining a subview. You can populate it to include any combination of standard and custom view objects (you can change the class of the view object to one of your own).
Window	Creates a Cocoa nib document containing a single, empty, NSWindow object.

COCOA TOUCH TEMPLATES	CONTENTS
Application	Creates a Cocoa Touch nib document containing a UIWindow and an application delegate object. Again, you should rarely need this template — the Xcode project templates for an iPhone application will already include a nib document containing a much more specific set of objects appropriate to the type of application you're creating.
Empty	Creates an empty Cocoa Touch nib document.
View	Contains a single UIView object. Useful for defining a complete view, subview, or a reusable cell (in the iPhone framework, a cell is a subclass of UIView). You can expand it to include any combination of standard and custom view objects.
Window	Creates a Cocoa Touch nib document containing a single, empty, UIWindow object.

CARBON TEMPLATES	CONTENTS
Application	Creates a Carbon nib document containing a Carbon application menu bar and an empty window. This template is appropriate for a "single window" (non-document based) application.
Dialog	A single Movable Modal window.
Empty	An empty Carbon nib document.
Main Menu	Contains a standard application menu bar. Again, you're unlikely to use this template unless you're creating alternate menu sets for your application.
Window	A single Carbon window.

Interface Builder still supports legacy Carbon nib documents, but support for Carbon (pure C) programming and technologies is being systematically removed from both the operating system and the Xcode development tools in favor of the more modern Cocoa technologies. This chapter focuses almost exclusively on development in a Cocoa environment. For more information about Carbon nib documents, refer to the Carbon Resources Programming Guide *at* `http://developer.apple.com/mac/library/documentation/Cocoa/ Conceptual/LoadingResources/CarbonNibs/`.

IB KIT TEMPLATES	CONTENTS
inspector	Creates a Cocoa nib document containing an inspector palette subview. Use this template to create your own extensions to Interface Builder. See the "Customizing Interface Builder" section for more details.
Library	Creates a Cocoa nib document containing the NSView objects used to present a custom Interface Builder object in the library palette.

When you have selected your desired template, click the New button. Alternatively, you can avoid creating a new file and open an existing document by clicking the Open an Existing Document button. This option is here mostly because Interface Builder presents the new document assistant whenever you start Interface Builder without opening a document, or when you close all of the document windows, thus providing a quick method to either create a new nib document or open an existing one.

Adding a New Nib Document to a Project

When you save a newly created nib document for the first time, Interface Builder looks to see whether it is saved inside the project folder of *any* project currently open in Xcode. If it is, Interface Builder offers to add it to that project through the dialog shown in Figure 13-10.

Select the targets you want the nib document to be included in and click the Add button.

If you plan to localize your nib document, follow these steps:

1. Create the new nib document for the development (that is, your) localization.

FIGURE 13-10

2. Save the file in the project folder and let Interface Builder add it to the project.

3. Close the nib document in Interface Builder.

4. Localize the nib document in Xcode as described in the "Localizing Files" section of Chapter 6.

TIP TO REMEMBER

If your project already has .lproj folders (because other files have been localized), you can save your new file directly into the .lproj folder of the appropriate language. Xcode treats the nib document as if it has already been localized. You can skip the step of localizing the file, and jump right to adding new localizations.

OPENING SISTER LOCALIZATIONS

In addition to the obvious ways of opening a nib document — opening it from Xcode or the Finder, the File ⇨ Open command, or the File ⇨ Open Recent menu — Interface Builder has a shortcut for opening other localizations of the same file.

The File ⇨ Open Localization menu lists all of the other language variants of the currently active nib document. Interface Builder detects when a nib document is located in an .lproj localization folder. It then finds all sister .lproj folders containing the same document and adds them to this submenu. This allows you to quickly switch between localizations of the same file. The Open All command opens all localizations at once.

CREATING OBJECTS

The first "C" of Interface Builder is creating objects. Objects are easy to create: drag an object from the library palette into your nib document or view window.

Creating an object is as easy as dragging an instance out of the library item and dropping it into your nib document window, as shown in the middle in Figure 13-11. You can also drop a view object directly into a view window, as shown on the left in Figure 13-11 — as long as it's an object appropriate for that view.

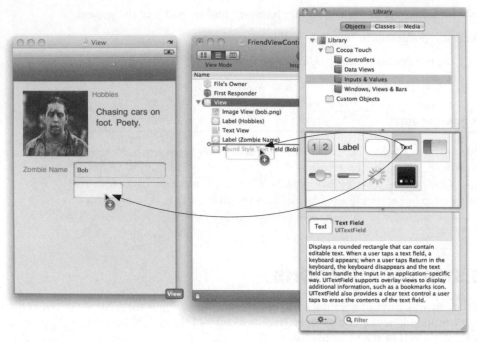

FIGURE 13-11

Using either technique, subview objects can be inserted directly into the view hierarchy. When dropping into the nib document window, drop the object inside the appropriate view. When dropping a new object in a view window, it's implied that the new object will be inserted into a container view, even if that container is just the window object. Interface Builder highlights and identifies the container that will receive the new object. Figure 13-12 illustrates how the location of the drop determines which superview will receive the new object.

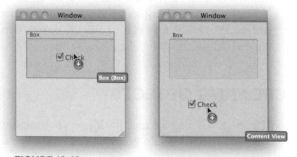

FIGURE 13-12

In all cases, containers *only* accept certain object classes (or their subclasses). For example, you cannot add an arbitrary object (such as NSObject) inside a view container, no matter where you attempt to drop it.

The library palette will only create objects in its repertoire. See the section "Custom Classes" later in this chapter to learn how to create objects with custom classes.

Here are a few shortcuts and tricks for creating objects in Interface Builder:

➤   Create a new window by dragging a window object out of the library palette and dropping it anywhere on the screen.

➤ To create an unattached view (NSView, UIView, and so on) object, drag a new view object into the nib document window to create a top-level object. Double-click the new object to open it in a view window where you can edit its content.

➤ You *cannot* create a top-level Cocoa application menu bar object using the NSMenu object in the library palette. (It will create *a* menu bar, but it won't be *the* application menu bar.) Should you ever need to create one, use the Cocoa Main Menu template to create a new nib document that contains a full application menu bar object, copy it into your nib document, and then edit it as desired.

COPYING, DUPLICATING, AND DELETING OBJECTS

Another way of creating an object that should not be overlooked is to duplicate an existing object. This can save a lot of time when creating groups of similarly configured objects. The following actions create copies or delete objects in your nib document:

➤ Edit ⇨ Cut

➤ Edit ⇨ Copy

➤ Edit ⇨ Paste

➤ Edit ⇨ Delete

➤ Delete key

➤ Edit ⇨ Duplicate

➤ Option+drag

➤ Drag an object from one nib document to another

Holding down the Option key while dragging objects, or selecting the Edit ⇨ Duplicate command, duplicates the selected objects, inserting the copies wherever they are dropped or making them siblings of their originals, respectively.

If you repeatedly use complex objects or layouts in your projects, you can save preconfigured objects in the library palette. See the section "Saving Custom Objects" toward the end of this chapter.

SELECTING OBJECTS

Before you can examine or change the attributes of an object, you must select it. This sounds simple — and it usually is — but there is some subtlety to selecting objects in Interface Builder of which you'll want to be aware.

There are two places to select Interface Builder objects. All objects appear in the nib document window and can be selected there. View objects can optionally appear in a view window, approximately as they will appear in your application. Selecting a view object is equivalent to selecting the same object in the nib document window.

Objects in the Nib Document Window

Selecting objects in the nib document window is simple and straightforward: select the object or objects with which you want to work using any of the three view modes. The icon view only allows you to select top-level objects, and the browser mode only lets you select multiple objects within the same branch of the hierarchy. I tend to use the list view most of the time. All of the standard Mac OS X icon/list selection gestures work here: Click, Shift+click, Command+click, and dragging out a rectangle.

 Selecting a container object does not select any of the objects that it contains. If you want to edit the attributes of a view and all of its subviews simultaneously, you must explicitly select both the container view and its subview objects.

The advantage of selecting objects in the nib document window is that they are unambiguous. The nib document window lists each and every object defined in that document. Of course, the nib document window is the only place you can select objects that don't have a visual representation.

The disadvantage is that it may sometimes be difficult to distinguish between different objects in the list. For example, a nib document that defines five untitled radio-button objects simply shows five identical radio-button icons, whereas in a view window, each radio button object appears as a radio button, at the position it will be in that window. See the "Identity" section to learn how to name objects so they are easier to find in the nib document window.

Object Order

The order in which subobjects appear in the nib document window list defines their order in the nib document. Often the order of objects is completely immaterial. Within a view container, the order defines the Z-order of the subviews — the order in which the objects overlap. The first object in the list will be behind all of the objects that come after it. You can reorder objects in the document window by dragging them to a new position in the list, or you can use any of these commands on view objects:

➤ Layout ➪ Send to Front (Option+Shift+Command+F)

➤ Layout ➪ Send to Back

➤ Layout ➪ Send Forward

➤ Layout ➪ Send Backwards

Object order is different from object position (see the "Moving and Resizing Objects" section).

View Objects

View objects in the nib document window may also appear as "themselves" — an approximate representation of that class of view object at run time — in a separate view window. For example, a view window containing the menu of your application lets you see, select, and edit the contents of your menus, more or less as the menu items will appear in your application. A single NSView or UIView object will appear in a window where you can resize it, add subviews, and customize its appearance. If the view object is, itself, a window object, the view window represents that window object in the nib document.

View objects do not have to appear in a view window. Any view window can be closed, tidying up your workspace. To reveal it again, double-click the view object in the nib document window. The view object, or the view window that contains it, will open again. This will also select the view object in the view window. Unless the view window is representative of an actual window object in the nib document, the view window is just a convenient container provided by Interface Builder. For example, the position of the view window that contains a menubar object is superfluous.

Selecting Multiple View Objects

Select a single view object by clicking it. You can select multiple view objects by dragging out a selection rectangle. Any view objects whose position intersects the selection rectangle will be selected, as shown in Figure 13-13.

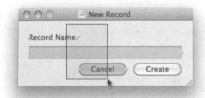

FIGURE 13-13

When single-clicking an object, the selection can be modified using one of the following keyboard modifiers:

> Holding down the Shift key adds the object to the set of currently selected objects.

> Holding down the Command key toggles the selection of the object: an unselected object is selected (same as Shift), and a selected object is unselected.

Selecting Interior View Objects

Some objects, like tab and split pane views, are containers for other view objects. To select a container object, click any unoccupied region within the container. To select an object within the container, click directly over that object. Figure 13-14 shows two different selections: on the left, the button object contained in the box object is selected; on the right, the box object itself is selected.

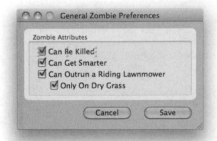 

FIGURE 13-14

Sometimes, selecting a container is inconvenient or impossible (a split view with an invisible divider might not have any unoccupied region on which to click). Normally when you click a view object, Interface Builder selects the most specific object in the visual hierarchy at the clicked coordinate. This is the so-called "inside out" selection strategy.

Holding down the Command key while clicking reverses this logic. Interface Builder selects the outermost container that occupies the clicked coordinate. In the example shown in Figure 13-14, clicking the Can Get Smarter radio button selects that NSButton object. Holding down the Command key while clicking same button selects its enclosing NSBox object.

Drilling Into View Objects

Tables and many other kinds of nested views support a selection technique called *drilling*. The first time you click the object, you select the container object. Single-click again, and the selection "drills down" into the object hierarchy.

Using the table view object in Figure 13-15 as an example, imagine positioning your cursor over the middle Text Cell object. Clicking four times slowly — remember these are all single-click actions — produces the following selections:

1. The first click selects the scroll view object.

2. The second click selects the table view object nested inside the scroll view.

3. The third click selects the second table column object of the table view.

4. The fourth click selects the text cell object used to draw the cells of the second column.

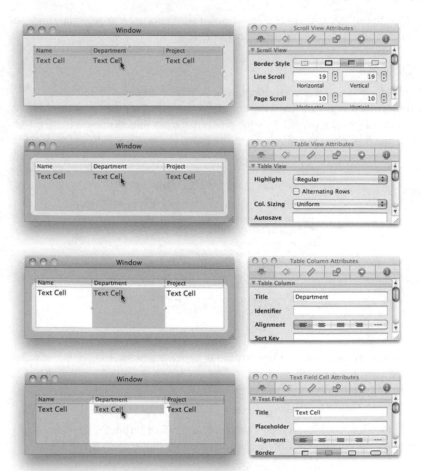

FIGURE 13-15

The same technique works with the column header objects of the table. Most view objects that form a similar hierarchy can be drilled into, such as any scroll view. Of particular note is the cell object nested inside each control view object. It's not always obvious, but every control view (button, slider, and so on) is actually two objects: a controller object and a cell object that provides its look and feel.

Object Selection vs. Object Focus

There's a subtle difference between selecting a view object and having a view object that's the current focus of Interface Builder. Click once to select a container object. Click again to make it the focus. Figure 13-16 shows the difference. On the left, the Box view object is selected. On the right, the box view has the current focus.

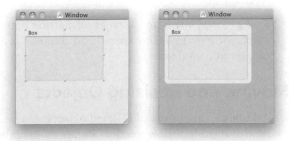

FIGURE 13-16

For many commands, there's no difference between these two states, but for some, notably Edit ⇨ Paste, there's a big difference. If there were two button objects on the clipboard, choosing the Edit ⇨ Paste command while the box object was selected (left) would just paste two buttons into the window. If the box object is the focus (right), the Paste command would insert the two buttons inside, making them subviews of the box object.

Adjusting the Selection

A number of commands change the selection. When selecting and unselecting multiple objects, don't neglect these perennial favorites:

- ➤ Edit ⇨ Select All (Command+A)
- ➤ Edit ⇨ Select None (Shift+Command+D)

The following four commands let you shift the selection to a different object relative to the currently selected object, or objects:

- ➤ Tools ⇨ Select Parent (Control+Command+↑)
- ➤ Tools ⇨ Select Child (Control+Command+↓)
- ➤ Tools ⇨ Select Previous Sibling (Control+Command+←)
- ➤ Tools ⇨ Select Next Sibling (Control+Command+→)

The Tools ⇨ Select Parent command selects the container object of the currently selected object or objects. Tools ⇨ Select Child selects the first object contained within the currently selected object. Taken together, these two commands allow you to either "walk up" or "drill down" into the object hierarchy.

The Next and Previous Sibling commands shift the selection to the next, or previous, object in the same container object. These commands navigate by object order (Z-order), not position.

CONFIGURING OBJECTS

Objects in Interface Builder wouldn't be much use if you couldn't bend and shape them to your needs. Most of your time in Interface Builder will be spent editing objects, and you have many different ways to do that. The overt aspects (visible text, placement, and size) of view objects can be manipulated directly: drag an object around to reposition it; double-click the text of an object to change it.

Less obvious attributes, such as formatting options and bindings, are manipulated in the inspector palette. A few specialized commands also exist for aligning objects and grouping objects in containers.

Moving and Resizing Objects

An object, or a group of selected objects, can be repositioned in a view window simply by dragging it to another location, as shown in Figure 13-17. Depending on the layout, some objects may not be repositioned. For instance, an object in one half of a split view always occupies that entire space. It cannot be repositioned, because its location and size are determined by the split view. Altering the position of the split view or its divider is the only way to change that object's position in the window.

FIGURE 13-17

Interface Builder displays guidelines as an object is dragged. When the object is released, it "snaps" to nearest guideline. See the "Guides" section to find out how to control these automatic guidelines or create your own.

The arrow keys nudge the selected objects one pixel in any direction. Hold down the Shift key to nudge them 10 pixels at a time.

Dragging the handles on the edge of an object resizes it. Some objects cannot be resized, or can only be resized in certain directions. For example, the height of a button is fixed in Cocoa. You can only change its width. Using the resize handles, you can only resize one object at a time.

> **TIP TO REMEMBER**
>
> Holding down the Command and Options keys while resizing a container view, such as a window or box view, resizes its subviews too. The subviews are resized according to their resize behavior. This is the same effect that you get when resizing a container view using the Size inspector. Both the Size inspector and resize behavior are described later in the "Size" section.

Sizing Objects to Fit

Choose Layout ➪ Size to Fit (Command+=) to shrink (or expand) objects to their minimum/optimal size. The Size to Fit command determines the minimum dimensions required to display the object's content — typically its title. A button or text field shrinks down so that the object is exactly the size needed to display the title or text. A box shrinks so that it is just larger than all of the objects it contains. Some objects don't respond to the Size to Fit request.

Clipped objects are objects that are too small to display their content, and appear with a grey + symbol, indicating that there's more to the view than will be visible, as shown in Figure 13-18. The usual culprits are buttons and pop-up menu objects that are too narrow to display their title or selection.

The two commands Tools ➪ Select Next Object With Clipped Content (Command+K) and Tools ➪ Select Previous Object With Clipped Content (Shift+Command+K) will help you find clipped objects. These two commands find, and

FIGURE 13-18

select, an object that is sized too small to display its content. A quick Command+K, Command+= will remedy that.

Making Objects the Same Size

Use the Layout ➪ Same Size command to set multiple objects to the same size. Start by selecting the object that is already the desired size. Shift+click to select the additional objects to be resized. Choose the Same Size command. All of the additional objects are set to the size of the first object selected.

Aligning Objects

In addition to the automatic guides that appear when you drag or resize an object, the alignment commands provide a number of methods for aligning objects in a view. All of the alignment commands are found in the Layout ➪ Alignment submenu:

➤   Layout ➪ Alignment ➪ Align Left Edges

➤   Layout ➪ Alignment ➪ Align Right Edges

➤   Layout ➪ Alignment ➪ Align Top Edges

➤   Layout ➪ Alignment ➪ Align Bottom Edges

➤   Layout ➪ Alignment ➪ Align Vertical Centers

➤   Layout ➪ Alignment ➪ Align Horizontal Centers

➤   Layout ➪ Alignment ➪ Align Baselines

➤   Layout ➪ Alignment ➪ Align Vertical Centers in Container

➤   Layout ➪ Alignment ➪ Align Horizontal Centers in Container

The first seven commands all reposition two or more selected objects so that the desired edge or center of every object is at the same coordinate.

The last two commands can be applied to a single object or a group of objects contained within another view. These commands position the object, or objects, so that it is centered in its superview. When used with a group of objects, the group is treated as a whole; the relative position of the objects in the group remains the same and all objects are moved equally so the group is centered in the superview.

View Bounds Indicators

The two aids for visualizing the actual location of view objects in an interface are as follows:

➤ Layout ⇨ Show Bounds Rectangles

➤ Layout ⇨ Show Layout Rectangles (Command+L)

These two commands draw a thin blue (bounds) or red (layout) line to indicate the exact coordinates occupied by the objects in a view, as shown in Figure 13-19. The layout rectangle will also include a line showing where the text baseline of the object lies, for those objects that display text.

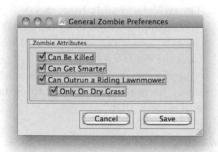

FIGURE 13-19

The distinction between the layout and bounds rectangles is primarily of interest to Cocoa developers. The bounds of a Cocoa Touch view is invariably the same as its layout rectangle, so turning on the layout rectangle indicator is sufficient.

Relative Position Indicators

Holding down the Option key while one or more objects are selected reveals the spatial relationship between objects. With the Option key held down, let the mouse pointer hover over some other object, the unoccupied area in a container, or the window itself. Interface Builder illustrates the relationship between the two. In Figure 13-20, the check box button is selected and the cursor is hovering over the push button while the Option key is held down.

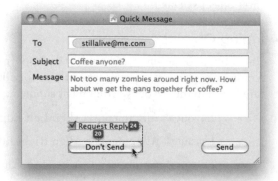

FIGURE 13-20

Subviews

A number of view objects types are containers for other view objects. The container is the superview and the view objects it contains are its subviews. Every view has its own size and position within its superview and can itself contain any number of subviews. This nesting of objects is reflected in both the nib document window and in how the objects are displayed at run time.

You have two ways of moving an object into, or out of, a container view:

➤ In the nib document window, drag the object out of one container into another.

➤ Use one of the Embed commands.

The embed commands are found in the Layout ➪ Embed Objects In submenu. These commands are:

➤ Layout ➪ Embed Objects In ➪ Box

➤ Layout ➪ Embed Objects In ➪ Custom View

➤ Layout ➪ Embed Objects In ➪ Scroll View

➤ Layout ➪ Embed Objects In ➪ Split View

➤ Layout ➪ Embed Objects In ➪ Tab View

➤ Layout ➪ Embed Objects In ➪ Matrix

➤ Layout ➪ Embed Objects In ➪ Submenu

Each command creates a new container view object in the same superview as the selected objects, and then moves those objects from their current container into the newly created subview. Figure 13-21 shows the effect of selecting four radio buttons and using the Layout ➪ Embed Objects In ➪ Box to wrap them up in a new NSBox object.

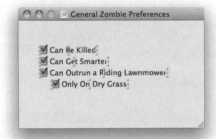 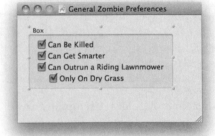

FIGURE 13-21

All of these commands are essentially a shortcut for these steps:

1. Use the library palette to create a new container view.

2. Select the sibling views you want the new view to contain.

3. Drag the sibling views into the container view (Edit ➪ Cut, Edit ➪ Paste would also work).

The inverse of all of these commands is the single Layout ➪ Unembed Objects command. This command deletes a container view and replaces it with the subviews it formally contained.

Guides

Laying out a window or dialog box so that it is functional and aesthetically pleasing is no small feat. To help you space and align items in your layout, Interface Builder provides two kinds of guides. A guide is a vertical or horizontal line at some coordinate that aids you in aligning objects.

Whenever you position an object by dragging, the boundary of the object "snaps" to that coordinate whenever it is near a guide.

Aqua guides are relative to the edges of other objects, which include containers, in the layout. These distances are based on the Aqua interface design standard. For example, the suggested distance between a button and the edge of a window is 20 pixels. Dragging the button, or resizing the window as shown in Figure 13-22, automatically places Aqua guides 20 pixels from the edges of the window and nearby objects.

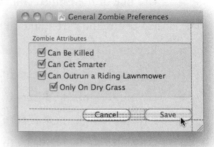

Aqua guides are very intelligent, but they don't know everything. You should still refer to the Human Interface Guidelines in making layout decisions. For example, the Human Interface Guidelines suggest that buttons that destroy data should be farther away from buttons that save data or cancel an operation. Interface Builder has no way of knowing what the buttons in your layout do, and are therefore limited in what suggestions they can offer.

FIGURE 13-22

Apple's Human Interface Guidelines are so important that Interface Builder has a built-in shortcut to them. Choosing the Help ➪ Human Interface Guidelines command opens the Apple Human Interface Guidelines *document in Xcode. You can also find this document in Apple's Reference Library or view it online at* `http://developer.apple.com/documentation/UserExperience/ Conceptual/OSXHIGuidelines/.`

User guides are the other kind of guides. User guides are fixed guides that you can position anywhere in a layout. Objects dragged near a user guide snap to it just as they would snap to an Aqua guide. The Layout ➪ Add Horizontal Guide (Command+_) and Layout ➪ Add Vertical Guide (Command+|) commands create a new vertical or horizontal guide in the current window. Position the cursor over the guide and drag it to the desired location, as shown in Figure 13-23. While you drag the guide, the distances to the opposite edges of the window are displayed on the guide.

You can disable guide snapping temporarily or permanently:

➤ Hold down the Command key while dragging an object to temporarily disable guide snapping.

➤ Choose Layout ➪ Snap to Guides to turn all guide snapping off. Select the command again to turn it back on.

To delete a user guide, drag it outside the window bounds.

FIGURE 13-23

Inspector Palette

The inspector palette is where the nitty-gritty details of your objects are manipulated. The inspector palette (see Figure 13-1) is a floating window that constantly shows the attributes for the currently selected object or objects. The palette is organized into different panels, selectable using the tabs at the top of the palette or any of the "Inspector" commands in the Tools menu. Each inspector configures some aspect of the object. The possible inspector panels are:

INSPECTOR	USE
Attributes	Edits the class-specific properties.
Effects	Sets Core Animation effects for a Cocoa object.
Size	Establishes the size, position, orientation, resizing behavior, minimum/maximum size, and other visual layout attributes.
Bindings	Binds selected properties of a view object to properties of other objects.
Connections	Creates and inspects the connections between the object and other objects.
Identity	Defines the class, name, and identity of the object.

Which inspectors appear depends on the type of nib document you are editing. A Cocoa document presents all of these inspectors, whereas a Cocoa Touch document shows only the Attributes, Size, Connections, and Identity panels.

In the case of the bindings panel, the difference is significant. Cocoa Touch does not support bindings, so there's no binding panel at all. On the other hand, the effects panel is also missing; but that's because in the Cocoa framework Core Animation layers are an optional element of NSView objects. In Cocoa Touch, all view objects are animation layers, so many of the attributes you'd set in the effects inspector in Cocoa are set in the Attributes inspector in Cocoa Touch.

You'll find yourself switching between the various inspector panels often. I suggest learning to use the keyboard shortcuts Command+1 through Command+6. The numbers correspond to the tab positions at the top of the inspector palette window, so in Cocoa the connections inspector is Command+5, whereas in Cocoa Touch the same inspector is Command+3.

The following sections briefly describe the various inspector panels, however a complete description requires an understanding of the framework classes and their behaviors, which is far beyond the scope of this book.

Attributes

This panel is common to all nib document types and edits the class-specific attributes of an object. The attributes that are available, and what those attributes mean, vary wildly from one object to another. Figured 10-24 shows the attributes panel for three different objects.

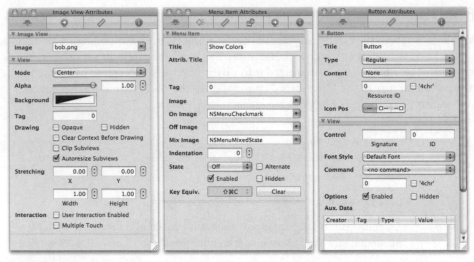

FIGURE 13-24

The best place to look for descriptions of object attributes is in the API documentation for that class or structure. The title bar of the inspector changes to indicate the kind of object being inspected. In the left two inspectors in Figure 13-24, the documentation for the image view (UIImage) and menu item (NSMenuItem) classes explain every detail of the attributes for those objects. If you're unsure about the specific class of an object, see the "Identity" inspector section.

The attributes in the inspector panel are organized into groups based on the object's class inheritance. For example, a UIButton object inherits from UIControl, which inherits from UIView, UIResponder, and NSObject. When editing a UIButton, the inspector shows three groups of attributes: Button, Control, and View. Each group contains the attributes defined by the respective class (UIButton, UIControl, UIView). The UIResponder and NSObjects don't define any Interface Builder editable properties, so there is no group for those classes.

The organization of groups makes it clear to which domain each attribute belongs. You can collapse one or more groups of attributes to save screen real estate, or if perhaps you're just not interested in them.

 A few non-object attributes have begun to sneak into Interface Builder's inspector panel of late. Specifically, the attributes for Cocoa Touch (iPhone) views include a new "Simulated User Interface Elements" group. These are not attributes of a UIView object; they are used solely to present the view in a simulation of its superview environment at run time. Interface Builder remembers these attributes, but they aren't properties of any object at run time.

The pane on the right in Figure 13-24 is for a Carbon Button object. Carbon objects are more obtuse because the Carbon interface is C, not Objective-C, so each object type doesn't have a simple one-to-one relationship with a class. The best place to start is the User Experience documentation collection in the Carbon group of the Reference Library. The *HIView Programming Guide* should give you an overview of the Carbon view model. The "Handling Carbon Windows and Controls" document explains how control events are handled in Carbon applications. In brief, the C interface that lets you control something about a window structure (like passing the `kWindowIgnoreClicksAttribute` constant to `CreateNewWindow`) corresponds to an attribute in the panel (the Ignore Clicks option).

Connections

The connections inspectors let you review, establish, and destroy connections between objects, as shown in Figure 13-25. Connections are the third "C" of Interface Builder, and are described in detail in the "Connecting Objects" section, a little later in this chapter.

Briefly, the connections inspector shows the connection outlets defined for the object, and to what each of those is connected (if anything). If you click a connected connection, Interface Builder highlights the object to which it's connected.

Size

The size inspector lets you set the position, size, and related attributes for most view objects. All view objects have a rectangular region defined by its location in its superview and its size. The controls in the size inspector, as shown in Figure 13-26, allow you edit any of those values numerically. Setting an object's position numerically is sometimes easier that attempting to position or resize the object using the mouse, but has the same effect. The dimensions of some view objects are fixed, in which case those values will not be editable.

FIGURE 13-25

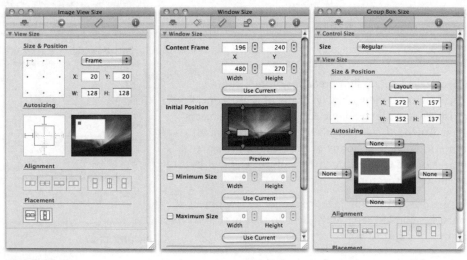

FIGURE 13-26

Two common controls let you define the position and size of the object in various ways. The little square graph to the left of the size and position fields lets you choose the origin to use, and the pop-up menu above lets you specify either the layout bounds or the frame bounds of the object. These alternative coordinate schemes are just conveniences provided by Interface Builder; however you enter the coordinates, they will be translated into frame bounds in the superview's coordinate system. That's what gets used to initialize the object at run time.

> *Some objects, such as labels, have a size attribute that determines the size of its text, whereas other objects set their text size in the attributes inspector. If you can't find a size-related property in the attributes inspector, check the size inspector, and vice versa.*

Resizing a container view — any view that contains other view objects — using the Size inspector also resizes its subviews according to their resize behavior, which is explained next. To resize a container view without resizing its subviews, resize the view using your mouse as described in the "Moving and Resizing Objects" section.

Many view objects have a resize behavior. You'll need to consult the documentation for the class of objects you're editing, but in general the edges of an object can be optionally fixed ("anchored") relative to the corresponding edge of its superview, and its vertical and horizontal dimension can be either fixed or variable ("springy").

Interface Builder thoughtfully provides a resize preview animation. The animation is active whenever your cursor is over the inspector palette window. It shows a simulation of the effects of resizing the object's superview. This lets you quickly visualize how your settings will affect how your object is resized. Note that this is only accurate when using Cocoa or Carbon's built-in resizing behavior, which could be overridden in your code.

The remaining attributes (window type, initial position, background color, minimum/maximum size, and so on) will be specific to the type of object you're editing.

Effects

The effects inspector lets you assign predefined filters and animation effects to Cocoa view objects. Many of these same effects (like transparency) are available for Cocoa Touch objects too; but in Cocoa Touch, *all* view objects are inherently drawn using Core Animation layers, so many of these capabilities are permanent features of the Cocoa Touch view object and can be found in the attributes inspector.

In Cocoa, using a Core Animation layer to render a view object is optional and must be enabled separately. You do that in the effects inspector, as shown in Figure 13-27.

FIGURE 13-27

Enabling Core Animation effects is simple:

1. Select the view, or views, that should use a CALayer to perform rendering. Checking the box next to an object sends it a `-setWantsLayer:YES` message when the object is created. This creates a CALayer object and attaches it to the NSView object.

2. The remainder of the inspector allows you to set common properties of the CALayer (transparency, drop shadow), attach system-supplied image filters (sharpen, blur, color adjustment), and assign default transitions for its subviews (page curl, ripple, swipe).

Bindings

Bindings are actually a third kind of connection (see the "Connecting Objects" section later in this chapter). Unlike traditional connections, bindings are set symbolically. This is for practical reasons; bindings can be very complex and don't lend themselves to the point-to-point specificity of regular Interface Builder connections.

A lot of programming in the Model-View-Controller paradigm is rote: create a property, write a getter method, write a setter method, have the setter method notify its view object when it changes, write an action method to let the view object change the property, wash, rinse, repeat. Bindings attempt to alleviate much of that tedium (and bugs) by providing standard tools to connect model objects with their visual representations. These concepts are described in the documentation for Cocoa Bindings at `http://developer.apple.com/mac/library/documentation/Cocoa/Conceptual/CocoaBindings/`.

As of this writing, the Cocoa Touch (iPhone) framework does not support bindings — sadly. There will be no bindings panel when editing a Cocoa Touch or Carbon nib document.

The Bindings panel, shown in Figure 13-28, contains the properties of an object that can be bound to a controller, data model, or any object with an observable property (technically, the property must be Key Value Observing–compliant). You bind properties of view objects to properties of other controller objects in the nib document. See the sections "Custom Classes" and "Placeholder Objects" about connecting nib document objects to your custom controller classes.

What makes bindings so brilliant is that creating the binding is often all you have to do. If your object's property is KVO-compliant (and most should be), you simply create a binding and you're finished. The binding framework takes care of all of the necessary Model-View-Controller communications needed to update your property whenever the view is changed, and automatically update the view whenever the property is changed (programmatically or otherwise). If you do have to write supporting code, it's usually just to make your property KVO-compliant.

FIGURE 13-28

In this context, the terms attribute *and* property *are equivalent. Interface Builder uses the term "attribute," whereas Objective-C and Key Value Coding use the term "property," but the two are interchangeable here.*

Creating a binding might seem daunting at first, but it is a fairly straightforward procedure:

1. Start by choosing the attribute you want to bind. This is often the `value` attribute of the view, that is, the information the view displays (a setting, a number, a string, an image, and so on). You can also bind many other attributes of a view object to a property. For example, binding the `enabled` attribute of a button or pop-up menu enables or disables that control simply by setting a Boolean property in your controller object. Bindings can control the current selection, the title, the color, or even the font attributes of a view object.

2. Expand the binding group to expose its settings, enable the binding by checking the Bind To check box, and then select the controller object you want to bind to. The pop-up list will include all bindable objects in your document. You cannot create a binding to an arbitrary object in your application, unless that object happens to be the File's Owner object. See the section "Placeholder Objects" for more about the File's Owner object.

3. If the object you selected in step 2 is a subclass of NSController, choose the Controller Key to bind to. This is essentially the first element in the Model Key Path (see step 4), but it's convenient because Interface Builder knows the list of standard bindable properties of the various NSController subclasses; you just select one from the pop-up menu. If you need to bind to a non-standard property, enter that property's name instead.

4. Enter the path of the property to bind to in the Model Key Path field. The path is a Key Value Coding path that's relative to either the object selected in step 2 or (in the case of an NSController) the object specified by the value of the controller key in step 3. Leave the field blank if the controller key (step 3) *is* the value you want to bind to. Either way, it's a fully functional KVC path. It's normally a simple property name, but it can contain complex paths (for example, "mother.birthday.reminderDate") and KVC operators (such as "notifications.@count"). To bind to the value of the object itself, use the path "self."

5. The remaining settings are all optional. You can provide a transformer object that will translate between the two objects, along with many choices for how the binding is configured, and what placeholder values are used.

You can learn more about bindings by reading the *Introduction to Cocoa Bindings* at `http://developer.apple.com/mac/library/documentation/Cocoa/Conceptual/CocoaBindings/`.

Identity

The identity inspector edits the identity of the object: what it is and how it appears in the nib document window. It also edits some miscellaneous properties that, in earlier versions of Interface Builder, were in separate inspector panels.

The two most important things you can change in the identity inspector are the class of the object and how it identifies itself in Interface Builder.

Changing the class of an object is how you create instances of custom classes. This is explained in detail in the "Custom Classes" section, but in a nutshell you begin by creating a generic object that's a superclass of your custom class, and then use the identity inspector to change the class of the object to yours. In Figure 13-29, a UIImageView object was added to the nib document. In the Xcode project, a subclass of UIImageView called ZombiePortraitView was created. Interface Builder will now allow you to change the class of the object to from UIImageView to ZombiePortraitView. At run time, an instance of ZombiePortraitView is constructed, initialized, and inserted into the view.

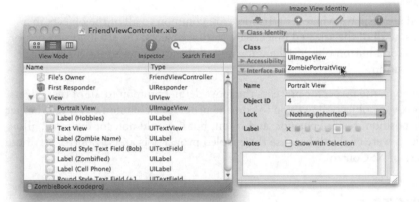

FIGURE 13-29

The other really useful feature of the identity inspector is the ability to assign custom descriptions and labels to objects in your document. In Figure 13-29, the UIImageView is given a custom name and a color label, which makes it much easier to identify in the document window. The Object ID is assigned by Interface Builder and cannot be changed.

> **TIP TO REMEMBER**
>
> There's a shortcut to renaming objects in the nib document window: click the name of the object and edit it directly.

The Lock control lets you disable editing of certain properties in the attributes, size, and other inspectors. You can lock all attributes, localizable attributes, or non-localizable attributes. This is particularly handy when you're performing localizations. Localizing a nib document often entails duplicating one locale and then editing the localizable attributes. Locking non-localizable attributes keeps you from accidentally changing any attributes that shouldn't be altered. Also see the "Document Locking" section later in this chapter.

 If you try to make a change to an object, and you just get a big floating padlock symbol instead, it's because you've locked some aspect of your object that is preventing that action.

The identity inspector has also become a dumping ground for obscure attributes that don't fit neatly into any of the other inspectors. Depending on the nib document architecture and object type, you might find an accessibility attributes group, a tool tips group, a help system identity group, or a dynamically defined object attributes group in the inspector. If you're trying to find an attribute that you think should be editable in Interface Builder, but can't find it, poke around in the identity inspector; it might be there.

Inspecting Multiple Objects

Generally, the inspector palette displays whatever attributes are common to all of the objects in a multi-object selection. Thus, if all of the selected objects are button objects, the attributes inspector presents all of the attributes for a button object. Changing any of the attributes in the inspector updates that value in every button.

If the selection is heterogeneous, the inspector presents the most detail common to all of the objects. Selecting a button and a box view object allows you to edit the properties common to both: whether the views are hidden, their position, resize behavior, and so on, but it would not, for example, allow you to set whether the objects were enabled, because the enabled property is an NSControl attribute and NSBox is not a subclass of NSControl.

CONNECTING OBJECTS

Connections are probably Interface Builder's defining feature. To restate, a connection is little more than an object reference: one object has an instance variable that points to another object. Interface Builder allows you to set that variable to point to another object simply by dragging a connection line from one to the other. There are two principal kinds of connections in Interface Builder:

➤ *Outlets* are simple instance variable references from one object to another. An outlet gives one object direct access to another object. Outlets allow you to weave arbitrary graphs of objects in a nib document.

➤ *Actions* are a Cocoa-specific duo consisting of an object reference (an outlet) and a message identifier (an Objective-C selector). Taken together, they define the object that will receive the message and exactly what message it will receive. Actions are sent almost exclusively by view objects in response to some user-initiated action, such as a mouse click, key press, touch gesture, and so on. Actions are how you "wire" your interface objects to your controller objects that will ultimately do the work.

Interface Builder outlets and actions are standard features of hundreds of preexisting classes in the Cocoa and Cocoa Touch frameworks. It's like having a huge collection of Lego blocks, ready to be connected together to form whatever you can imagine. In addition, you can add outlet properties and action methods to your own classes and then connect them to other objects exactly the same way. See the section "Custom Classes" for a complete description of creating and connecting your own objects in Interface Builder.

 In the sections that follow, the term "this object" means "the currently selected Interface Builder object, which is the subject of the active inspector palette."

Interface Builder provides no fewer than five different techniques for setting connections — evidence of how central connections are to the Interface Builder paradigm. I introduce them one at a time in the new few sections. All connections are the same. The different techniques are simply progressively more sophisticated shortcuts. Learn the basic ones first, and then explore the shortcuts as you spend more time making Interface Builder connections.

Connections Inspector

The connections inspector, introduced earlier, shows the outlets and actions sent by the object. Figure 13-30 shows the connections inspector for three different kinds of objects.

FIGURE 13-30

The Outlets group is where the outlets of the object are viewed, set, and broken. The Sent Actions group (Cocoa) or Events group (Cocoa Touch) lists the kinds of events that will trigger an action. Cocoa control objects only have one kind of event, so the list is the object that will receive the action and the action message sent. Cocoa Touch objects have many different kinds of events that cause an action message to be sent. Each one can be individually connected with a recipient/message pair. All of these groups contains connections "from" this object; in other words, object references maintained by this object that refer to other objects.

The Received Actions and Referencing Outlets groups are the complementary perspective to the Outlets, Sent Actions, and Events groups. Interface Builder thoughtfully cross-references all of the outlet references and sent actions configured from any *other* object in your nib document, and lists those references in these two groups. The Referencing Outlets group shows you all the other objects that have outlets connected to this object. The Received Actions group lists all of the action methods that this object defines, and shows you which objects are configured to send them.

Some events, and the Received Actions and Referencing Outlets groups, may have multiple connections for a single outlet or action. These will be collected together in the single connection. Use the disclosure triangle to expose multiple connections and manipulate them individually.

Don't confuse connections with containers. A container object has *implicit* references to the objects it contains. A connection is an *explicit* reference, identified by name, and deliberately set between two objects.

Connecting an Outlet

The simplest and most basic way to set an outlet connection is from the connections inspector of the object that defines the outlet. To set a connection, click the connection circle next to the outlet in the Outlets group and drag it to the object you want it connected to. You can choose any representation of the target object you can find in Interface Builder; you can drag it to the object in the document window (as shown), or its visual representation in a view window. The left side of Figure 13-31 shows how the docMenu outlet of the NSApplication object is being connected to an NSMenu object in the nib document.

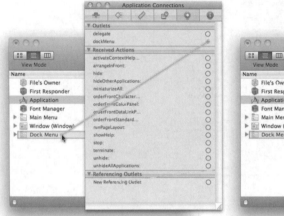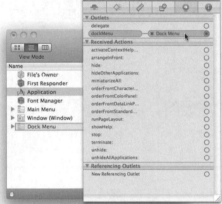

FIGURE 13-31

After releasing the mouse button, the connection is established, as shown on the right of Figure 13-31. The object outlet shows the name of the object to which it is connected. When the nib document is loaded at run time, the NSApplication's docMenu outlet property will point to a new instance of NSMenu. That's all there is to making outlet connections!

Interface Builder only allows connections to objects of the correct class. Interface Builder knows the class of each object, the action methods it implements, and the class of each outlet property. Interface Builder only permits connections to objects that are members of the outlet's class, and only creates action connections with messages that are implemented by the receiver. If an outlet or action doesn't appear in a list, or you think Interface Builder is ignoring your request to create a connection, it's most likely that you're trying to create an invalid connection.

Exploring and Breaking Connections

Hovering the cursor over a connection highlights the object it is connected to, also shown on the right in Figure 13-31.

To clear a connection, click the close (x) button next to the connection. You can also overwrite a connection by simply connecting the outlet to a different object. Unconnected outlets are ignored when the nib document is loaded, which typically means they will contain a `nil` value.

Connecting Another Object to This Object

The Referencing Outlets group contains a special New Referencing Outlet connection. It's an abstract outlet that lets you create connections *to* this object by setting an outlet in another object.

In Figure 13-31, the inspector palette was focused on the NSApplication object that defines the `docMenu` outlet. What if the inspector was focused on the NSMenu object instead? While you could switch the selection to the NSApplication object and then drag its `docMenu` outlet back to the NSMenu object, the New Referencing Outlet connection provides a more efficient route. The left side of Figure 13-32 shows the New Referencing Outlet being dragged from the NSMenu object to the NSApplication object.

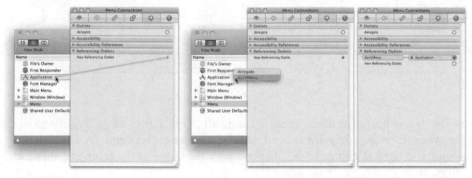

FIGURE 13-32

When the mouse button is released, Interface Builder presents a menu of all possible outlets that could refer to this object, as shown in the middle of Figure 13-32. Clicking one of the outlets sets the outlet *in the object you dragged to*, to this object.

After being set, the connection appears in this object's Referencing Outlets group. The result is identical to having set the outlet from the NSApplication object, but you weren't forced to first change your object focus.

If you want to set that same outlet in another object, drag the connection circle next to the new referencing connection to that object. This time, Interface Builder does not prompt you to choose which outlet; the outlet will always be the same as the one previously set. Remember the distinction between the two:

➤ Creating a New Referencing Connection lets you choose which outlet to set.

➤ Creating a referencing connection from an existing referencing connection will set the same outlet in the chosen object that is set in the other objects.

Creating a new referencing connection will not replace any other connections to this object, so new connections will accumulate in the group — although, you might be overwriting outlets that were previously connected in some other object.

Connecting an Action

Creating an action connection is only slightly more complicated than creating an outlet connection, owing to the fact that it involves two pieces of information: the receiving object and the message to send.

You create an action connection almost exactly as you would an outlet connection. In the sent actions or events group, drag a connection circle to the receiving object, as shown in the left of Figure 13-33.

FIGURE 13-33

When you release the mouse button, a menu appears listing all of the action methods defined by the receiver. Select the action message you want to send and the connection is complete. The finished connection, shown on the right of Figure 13-33, displays both the name of the receiving object and the message it will receive.

Action connections are explored and broken exactly the same way as outlet connections.

Connecting an Action to This Object

Just as with the Referencing Objects group, an object's Received Actions group lists the other objects that have actions connected to this one. Unlike the Referencing Objects group, the list of actions is fixed; it's the action methods implemented by this object. An object can only receive action messages that it has implemented. (Sending a message that isn't implemented is a run time error.)

It works pretty much the same way the Referencing Objects group does. To configure an object to send an action to this object, select the connection circle next to the action that you want this object to receive, and than drag it to the object that you want to send it.

If the sender is a Cocoa object, you're done. If it's a Cocoa Touch object that generates multiple events, you must now select which event you want to trigger that message, as shown in Figure 13-34.

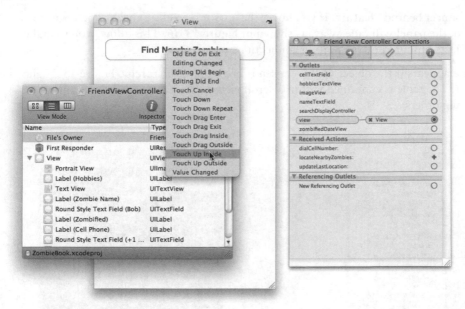

FIGURE 13-34

Pop-Up Connections Panel

Technically, you've learned everything you need to know to create, explore, dissolve, and cross-reference connections in your nib document, but creating connections is such a common activity that Interface Builder provides a number of additional shortcuts.

In the earlier techniques you set connections by:

1. Selecting an object.

2. Selecting the connections inspector panel.

3. Dragging the desired outlet or action to the target object.

Pop-up connection panels, shown in Figure 13-35, eliminate step 2 of that procedure. Pop-up connection panels are floating panels that appear over an object when you Right/Control-click an object.

Click the close button or press the Esc key to dismiss the panel.

A pop-up connections panel is identical to the connections inspector for that object — the only difference is that you didn't have to open the connections inspector. All of the controls work exactly the way they do in the connections inspector, with a couple of added features.

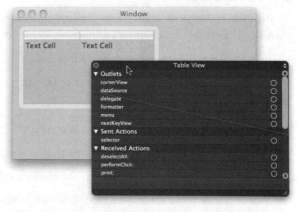

FIGURE 13-35

The first is the "connect behind" feature. If you hover the cursor over the panel as you begin to make a connection, the panel will fade away, as shown in Figure 13-36. This allows you to make connections to objects obscured by the pop-up connections panel.

The second feature appears if the object you've chosen is in an object hierarchy. Figure 13-37 shows a table view object. The table is contained within a scroll view and a window, and contains a column view (among others).

FIGURE 13-36

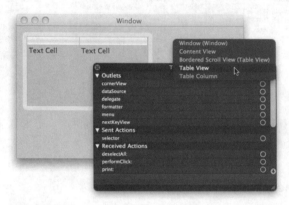

FIGURE 13-37

The pop-up connection panel for the table includes a small set of arrow buttons at the right edge of the panel's title. Clicking those arrows, as shown in Figure 13-37, brings up a menu of the objects in the hierarchy at the coordinate that you originally clicked. This is the same sequence of objects that you would get by "drilling down" at that point in the interface.

Selecting one of the other objects in the menu refocuses the pop-up connections panel to that object, allowing you Right-click one object and then set a connection for one of its containers or subobjects.

Quick Connection

A quick connection is Interface Builder shorthand. It creates a connection between two objects with a single gesture. To create a connection (outlet or action) between any two objects:

1. Right/Control-click the source object.

2. Hold down the mouse button and drag to the destination object, as shown in Figure 13-38.

3. Release the mouse button.

4. Select the outlet or action to connect.

The direction of the drag is the same that you use in the Outlets, Sent Actions, and Events groups:

➤ Drag *from* the object with the outlet *to* the object you want the outlet connected to.

➤ Drag *from* the object that sends an action *to* the object that implements the action.

When you release the mouse button, a menu appears with every outlet and action connection that's possible between those two objects. Select the outlet or action and the connection is complete.

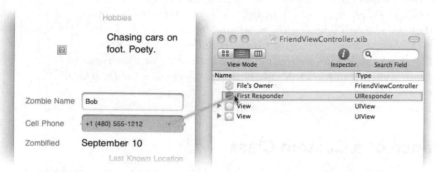

FIGURE 13-38

There's a limitation when making quick connections from Cocoa Touch objects. When you create an action connection, the action is *always* connected to the Touch Up Inside event. In other words, you can't use a quick connection to select both the event to connect to and the action message to send. Use the pop-up connections panel if you need to connect an action to some event other than Touch Up Inside.

The real power of connections and actions emerges when you define your own outlets and action messages. This is explained in the next section.

CUSTOM CLASSES

Interface Builder would only be mildly useful if all it could do was create, configure, and connect instances of the predefined framework objects found in the library palette. The power of Interface Builder explodes when you can define your own classes, outlets, and actions, and then use Interface Builder to create instances of your custom objects, configure them, and then connect them just like any other nib document object. Using Interface Builder you can:

➤ Add instances of your custom classes to a nib document.

➤ Define outlets in your custom classes that will be recognized by Interface Builder.

➤ Define action methods in your custom classes that will be recognized by Interface Builder.

Interface Builder recognizes when a nib document belongs to an open Xcode project. It then interfaces with Xcode to extract information about your class definitions and incorporate that into the document. It does this quickly, quietly, and transparently in the background. All you have to do is define your class. By the time you've saved your class files and switched to Interface Builder, your class definitions will have been assimilated and are ready to instantiate, configure, and connect.

Save your source files! Interface Builder only considers class definition files that have been saved to disk. Get into the habit of saving all files (Option+Command+S) before switching from Xcode to Interface Builder. This ensures that Interface Builder has the most current knowledge about your project's class definitions. If a class or property doesn't appear in Interface Builder, make sure your source files don't have any syntax errors. Also make sure the Synchronize With Xcode option is checked in the Interface Builder preferences.

Creating an Instance of a Custom Class

You can add an instance of practically *any* class you've defined in your project to a nib document. To create an instance of a class, follow these steps:

1. Define the class in Xcode.

2. Save the interface file(s) that define the class.

3. In Interface Builder, find the generic superclass object for your class in the library palette and create an instance of it.

4. Select the new object.

5. In the identity inspector, change the class of the object from its generic class (for example, NSObject) to your specific class (such as MyObject).

Figure 13-39 shows the class of a generic NSObject being changed to MyAppDelegate, a custom class defined in the active Xcode project.

At run time, an instance of your class is created instead of the generic object that was in the library palette. The library palette object you choose will depend on the superclass of your custom object. In general, follow this rule: choose the *most specific* class in the library palette that your custom class inherits from.

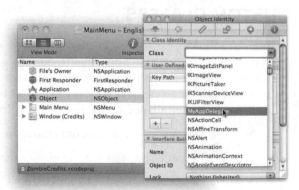

FIGURE 13-39

For example, if your class is a custom subclass of NSTokenField, then create an NSTokenField object before changing its class to yours. Interface Builder understands that your object is a subclass of NSTokenField and will present all of the attributes, connections, and actions defined by its superclasses (NSTokenField, NSTextField, NSControl, and NSView), in addition to any outlets and action methods that your subclass defines.

The library palette provides a short list of truly generic classes that — as themselves — don't do much of anything useful. They are included in the library palette solely so you can create custom subclasses of them:

GENERIC LIBRARY OBJECT	CLASS
Object or External Object	NSObject
View Controller	NSViewController or UIViewController
Custom View	NSView
View	UIView

Create an (External) Object when you subclass NSObject directly, or subclass any class that isn't represented in the library palette.

 Anything means anything. *Interface Builder will let you change the class of a generic NSObject instance to any class that exists, even ones defined in the frameworks. There's no NSMutableArray object in the library palette, but there's nothing stopping you from creating a generic Object instance, changing its class to NSMutableArray, and connecting it to an outlet. At run time, the nib document will gladly create and connect an instance of NSMutableArray.*

The most obvious applications of custom objects in a nib document are to:

➤ Create a controller object and connect it to all of its view objects.

➤ Create a custom delegate object and connect it to the `delegate` outlet of whatever objects (application, windows, tables, and so on) it should augment.

➤ Create custom subclasses of NSView or UIView and position them in superviews.

I'm sure you can think of a million other uses. The basic principle is this:

➤ If you need to create an object that will connect to, or be connected from, other objects in a nib document, consider creating the object in the nib document.

Now that you know how to create instances of your own classes, or replace instances of library objects with your own custom subclasses, you'll want to start creating custom connections. To do that, you need to define outlets and actions in your class.

Adding Custom Outlets to Your Class

Adding outlets to your own class is simple:

1. Declare a settable property (or instance variable) that stores an object pointer.

2. Include the `IBOutlet` modifier in the property's type.

All IBOutlet marked properties will appear as outlets in the object's connections inspector. In Figure 13-40, the class MyAppController declares an aboutWindow property that refers to an NSWindow object.

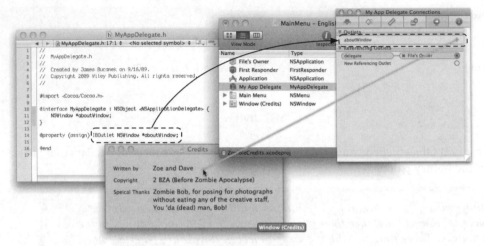

FIGURE 13-40

If you're using Objective-C 2.0, the preferred place to declare a property as an IBOutlet is in the @property directive, as was shown in Figure 13-40. You can still use the IBOutlet type modifier in the instance variable declaration if you're not using Objective 2.0 or do not include a @property directive. Interface Builder will recognize either.

I should note that the IBOutlet type really isn't a type; it's just tag for Interface Builder. As of this writing, IBOutlet is a preprocessor macro that's replaced with nothing at compile time.

Renaming a property by editing its declaration can confuse Interface Builder. For example, if you renamed aboutWindow *to* creditsWindow *after having connected* aboutWindow *to the NSWindow object in your nib document, the nib document will now contain a connection to a non-existent property. (In Interface Builder this will appear as a connection with a warning symbol next to it.) Rename outlet properties and action methods using the Refactoring tool (see Chapter 10), which can find and rename any nib document references as well.*

Adding Custom Actions to Your Class

Creating actions is about as simple as creating outlets:

1. Define a method that conforms to the prototype –(void) *anyMethod*: (id) *sender*.

   a. The method must have a void return type.

   b. The method should expect a single object reference as its only parameter.

2. Replace the return type in the declaration with `IBAction`, as in
`-(IBAction)`*myAction*`:(id)`*sender*.

In Figure 13-41, an action method has been added to MyAppDelegate. The action appears in the connections inspector, where it can be connected to view objects. In this case, the button's action is configured to send MyAppDelegate a `-closeAboutWindow:` message when the user clicked the button.

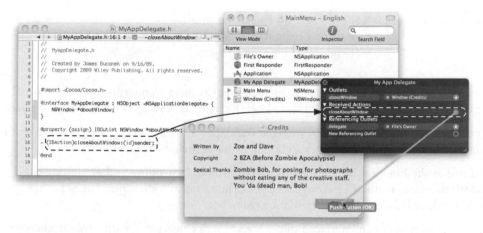

FIGURE 13-41

When your object receives an action, the `sender` parameter refers to the object that sent the message, providing it some context. In the case shown in Figure 13-41, `sender` refers to the "OK" NSButton object the user clicked. Note that this is a convention of the Cocoa framework, it's not a strict requirement. If you send action messages yourself, you can pass some other object, or even `nil`, as you see fit. Many action methods simply ignore the `sender` parameter.

Initializing Custom Objects at Run Time

For the most part, nib files contain archived (serialized) versions of Cocoa objects, but the nib file loading mechanism makes some concessions, and relaxes a few of the normal rules of object archiving in order to make the nib file content as flexible and convenient as possible. Specifically:

- ➤ Custom objects in a nib file are *not* required to conform to NSCoding protocol.

- ➤ Most custom objects are initialized using a simple – `init` method, rather than the formal – `initWithCoder:` used to decode archived objects.

This means that your custom objects don't have to conform to NSCoding in order to be instantiated from a nib file. It also means that any object that can be validly constructed with `[[`*Class* `alloc] init]` can be added to a nib file.

The following table describes exactly how objects in a nib document are constructed at run time:

OBJECT TYPE	DESCRIPTION	INITIALIZER
Custom View Objects	A custom subclass of NSView.	`-initWithFrame:`
Non-View Custom Objects	A custom subclass of NSObject that is not a subclass of NSView.	`-init`
Interface Builder Classes	Any class that appears in the library palette, or a custom subclass of an object that appears in the library palette.	`-initWithCoder:`

Constructing custom view objects with `-initWithFrame:` makes them compatible with the normal programmatic initialization of NSView objects (`-initWithFrame:` is NSView's designated initializer).

All non-view custom objects are constructed with the standard `-init` message. This means that you don't have to make your class conform to NSCoding in order to include it in a nib file.

The objects defined in the Interface Builder palette all conform to NSCoding and are initialized using the standard decoding method `-initWithCoder:`. The attribute values that you set in the inspector panels are decoded from the archive data stream.

If you create a custom subclass of an Interface Builder object that's constructed with `-initWithCoder:`, your class will initialize itself with `-initWithCoder:` too. That's the only way that attributes set for its superclasses can be read at run time. Custom NSObject subclasses can be initialized with `-init` because there are no editable properties for custom classes — only outlets and actions. Nothing needs to be read from the archive stream during initialization.

After the objects in the nib file are constructed, two more things happen:

1. All of the connections are set.
2. Every object receives an `-awakeFromNib` message.

If your object needs to perform any additional initialization, especially any initialization that depends on connections, it should implement a `-(void)awakeFromNib` method.

PLACEHOLDER OBJECTS

A subject I've been avoiding is what those other, mysterious, objects in your nib document — like File's Owner and First Responder — are. These are special *placeholder objects*. They represent objects that will exist before the nib document is loaded.

Now that you understand connections and custom objects, explaining the role of placeholder objects is simple. Placeholder objects allow you to create connections between the objects in your nib document and objects that already exist in your application. This allows you to create connections to objects outside the set of objects in the nib document.

The most important placeholders to understand are the File's Owner and the First Responder. The remaining placeholders represent miscellaneous singleton objects supplied by the frameworks.

File's Owner

File's Owner

When a nib file is loaded, one object is designated as its *owner*. What object that is depends on who's doing the loading. The following table lists the owner objects of common nib files loaded by the Cocoa frameworks:

FILE'S OWNER	NIB DOCUMENT
NSApplication	Main application interface
NSDocument	Document window
UIViewController	Interface view

For example, when you design a UIVewController object, the controller is associated with a nib document. When the controller needs to construct its view objects, it loads its nib document passing itself as the file's owner. In the nib document, the class of the File's Owner object is UIViewController, exposing all the outlets and actions defined by your controller to the nib document objects. For example, when the nib is loaded, the controller's `view` outlet is connected to the new UIView object that contains the controller's interface. After the nib file is loaded — as if by magic — the UIViewController now has an instance variable that points to a complete set of interface objects.

You can exploit the nib file's owner object to great effect in two ways. The first is use the identity inspector to change the class of the File's Owner object to your custom subclass. This happens naturally with NSDocument and UIViewController objects — you virtually never use the base class of these objects. Once you've changed the File's Owner to your subclass, your outlet and actions appear, ready to be connected.

The other approach is to load the nib file yourself. When you load a nib file with a message like `+[NSBundle loadNibNamed:owner:]`, you can pass whatever object you want as the file's owner. Thus, you have the ultimate control on what object is available to make connections.

The caveat under all circumstances is that the actual class of the file's owner *must agree* with the class in the identity inspector of the nib document. When you're making connections in the nib document, the class of the file's owner is assumed to be correct. It's up to you to make sure the actual owner is a compatible object at run time.

First Responder

First Responder

The *first responder* is a placeholder object used to make action connections. The Cocoa frameworks have a concept called the responder chain. Briefly, it's a list of active view objects that's determined by the current state of the user interface. Fluctuations in the chain affect what actions are acted upon, and what objects receive those actions.

When you connect an action to a specific object, you create an explicit connection. The object will always send the action to the object it's connected to; there's no ambiguity.

An object that has a message identifier (Objective-C selector) but no object reference (nil) is said to be connected to the first responder. It really isn't connected to anything at all, but at run time the recipient of the action will be determined dynamically by passing the message to the current responder chain. (If you're curious, an object with no action connection has a NULL message identifier.)

You create a first responder connection by connecting the action of an object to — yes, you guessed it — the First Responder placeholder. When you do, it creates a connection with a valid message identifier and a `nil` object reference.

The conundrum for the first responder placeholder object is that it doesn't know what actions the dynamic responder chain actually responds to — that's determined at run time. So, the first responder placeholder object simply pretends to respond to *every* action message Interface Builder knows about. When you connect an object to the first responder, you'll see a huge list of actions. This is perfectly normal. Select the action that you expect the chain to respond to at run time.

Other Placeholders

Any other placeholder objects that you find will invariably be singleton objects supplied by the framework. The most common are:

Application   Font Manager   Shared User ...

PLACEHOLDER	OBJECT
Application	The single NSApplication object created for every Cocoa application.
Font Manager	The single instance of NSFontManager returned by +[NSFontManager sharedFontManager].
Shared User Defaults	An instance of NSUserDefaultsController for creating bindings directly to the user defaults.

If the single NSApplication object is actually an instance of your NSApplication subclass, you can change the class of the placeholder object in the identity inspector. This gives your nib document direct access to the custom outlets and actions in your application.

 It's far more common to create your own application delegate object, implement your custom outlets and actions there, create an instance of your delegate in the nib document, and then connect the delegate object to the `delegate` *outlet of the vanilla NSApplication object.*

DECOMPOSING AN INTERFACE

This isn't about feature rot, but it does concern nib document bloat. It's easy to add new interface elements (utility windows, subviews, alternate views) to an existing nib document, so we often do. The result can be a nib document that loads many objects that the application doesn't need immediately. This isn't typically a problem for desktop applications, but on small hand-held devices (like iPhones and iPods), nib document bloat can slow initial load times and degrade the perceived performance of your application.

To help you break up large nib documents, Interface Builder provides the File ⇨ Decompose Interface command. This command simply takes every top-level object in your nib document that isn't interconnected with other objects, and copies it into a new (untitled) nib document window. How many new nib documents get created will depend on how many top-level object groups are defined.

In Figure 13-42, a view controller's nib document defines a view with a single table. It also defines a number of table view cell layouts that are employed based on table content. Loading all of these cell views takes time, even though the table might end up using only one or two.

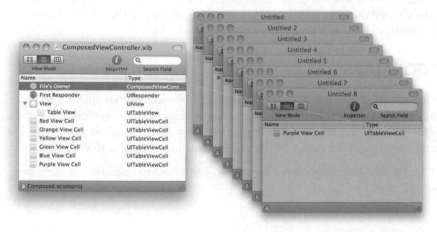

FIGURE 13-42

After decomposing the interface, Interface Builder has created nine new nib document windows. The ones that contain a single table view cell layout can now be saved and added to the project. The original copies of the individual cell views would be deleted and the code in the controller would be rewritten to lazily load each table cell view as needed. The result is a table view that loads quicker, and may potentially use less memory.

IMPORTING AND EXPORTING CLASSES

Until recently, it was possible to define new classes, complete with outlets and actions, entirely within Interface Builder. The idea was that you could design your interface, classes, connections, and actions before ever writing a single line of code.

Thankfully, those days are behind us. The idea of designing classes in Interface Builder might seem like a nice one, but it falls victim to the problems that plague other design tools that generate code: how to keep the classes you define in the interface design tool in synchronization with the source code of the application. If that fails, you end up with a nib document that contains classes, outlets, and actions that don't actually exist in the application.

The modern incarnation of Interface Builder eliminates these problems by eliminating round-trip editing. You define your classes, outlets, and actions in the Xcode project, and then switch to Interface Builder to create, configure, and connect them together. It's demonstrably the fastest and easiest way to work, and it keeps your project in perfect synchronization with your nib document.

Nevertheless, a few vestiges of the old methodology still lurk in Interface Builder. The commands File ⇨ Read Class Files and File ⇨ Write Class Files will import or export class definitions from/to a text file.

To export a class, choose one or more objects in a nib document and choose File ⇨ Write Class Files. Interface Builder will generate skeleton class definitions that include every outlet and action method Interface Builder is aware of. It does not include any attribute properties.

To import a class, choose File ⇨ Read Class Files and select one or more class definition (.h) files. Interface Builder will interpret these, locating all of the `IBOutlet` and `IBAction` declarations, and add the class to its internal model of known classes. You can now create custom instances of the class that will include the defined outlets and actions. It's up to you to ensure that those classes, with those outlets and actions, exist at run time.

NIB DOCUMENT FORMATS

Both Xcode and Cocoa have evolved over the years. The format of nib documents has changed to accommodate that evolution, adding new features and capabilities — along with compatibility issues. The biggest recent change in Interface Builder has been the support for a new XML-based nib document. The XML document is compiled to produce the binary NIB file that's actually deployed with your application.

Choose the Window ⇨ Document Info (Option+Command+I) command to open the nib document's info window, as shown in Figure 13-43.

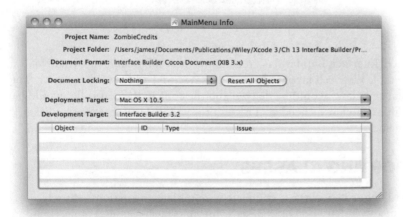

FIGURE 13-43

Here you can set and verify a number of different compatibility settings.

Document Format

The Document Format tells you what kind of format the nib document uses. The basic types are Cocoa, Cocoa Touch, and Carbon. If the nib document was created recently, it will probably be in the new XML (XIB) format. If not, it will be in one of the legacy (NIB) file formats.

You can't change the type of a nib document; the type is fixed when the document is created.

XIB nib documents are stored as XML documents. When your application is built, the XML representation is compiled (via the `ibtool`) into a binary form suitable for deployment. If you are still using one of the legacy nib document bundles, the binary portion of the nib document is simply copied into your application's bundle.

You can use the `ibtool` command-line tool to extract information, convert between storage formats, and perform other manipulations. For example, the following command converts the legacy MainMenu.nib bundle into a modern XIB document:

```
ibtool --upgrade MainMenu.nib --write NewMainMenu.xib
```

Use Xcode's Help ➪ Open man Page command to review the documentation for `ibtool`.

Document Locking

The Document Locking controls are exactly the same as those in the identity inspector, but apply to every object in the document. If you've individually locked some objects, the Reset All Objects button will clear all locked objects in the nib.

Checking Deployment Compatibility

The Deployment Target performs some basic deployment compatibility checks on the objects in your nib document. As operating systems evolve, so do the features and capabilities of the objects in your nib document. Setting the minimum anticipated deployment target for the nib document presents any possible conflicts or incompatibilities that might exist when the nib document is loaded on an older system, as shown in Figure 13-44.

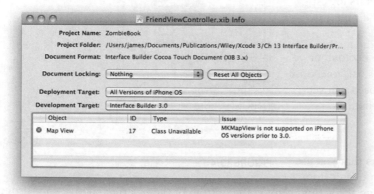

FIGURE 13-44

Compatibility conflicts can be notes, warnings, or errors. In Figure 13-44, the error tells you that the MKMapView class did not exist prior to iPhone OS 3.0. If this nib document were loaded using an older iPhone OS, it would fail to create the necessary objects, possibly failing to load altogether. The solution would be to either restrict this application to iPhone OS 3.0 or later, or prepare two nib documents: one to load on iPhone OS 3.0 and a second one (without an instance of MKMapView) for earlier systems.

Keeping Backward Compatibility

The Development Target setting lets you define the earliest version of Interface Builder that you want the nib document to be compatible with. This is important if you are working on projects that are being maintained using an older version of Xcode. Though it would be nice if everyone were always using the latest version of Xcode, sometimes that's not practical. Setting this option warns you if any properties of the nib document are incompatible with earlier versions.

CUSTOMIZING INTERFACE BUILDER

Interface Builder can be customized in a few small, and one very significant, ways.

Customizing the Library Palette

There are number of ways to customize the look and content of the library palette. The typical library palette, shown on the left in Figure 13-45, has three panes: the library group, the objects in the selected groups, and a description of the selected object.

You can collapse the group list down to single pop-up menu by dragging the upper pane separator to its highest position. You can eliminate the description pane by dragging the lower separator to its lowest position. Both are shown on the right in Figure 13-45.

Choose the action menu at the bottom, or Right/Control-click the objects list, to choose the display style. You can choose from very compact to extremely verbose listings.

Creating Custom Groups

If you have a number of objects that you use regularly, you can collect them in a custom group. Choose New Group from the action menu at the bottom of the palette and give your group

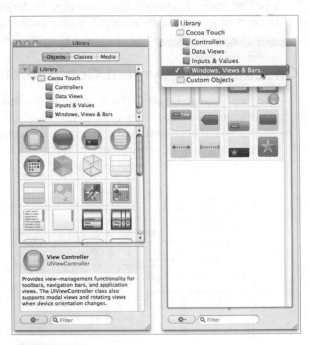

FIGURE 13-45

a descriptive name. Items can be added to your group by dragging them from the other library groups into your group. To remove items, select them and choose the Remove From Group command. To delete the entire group, choose Remove Group.

You can also create smart groups using the New Smart Group command. A smart group collects objects automatically based on some criteria that you define, as shown in Figure 13-46.

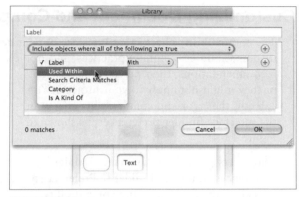

FIGURE 13-46

Saving Custom Objects

You can also preconfigure one or more objects, and then save them in the library palette for use again later. To save custom objects:

1. Create an interface with one or more objects.

2. Customize, configure, and connect them.

3. Drag the objects from your nib document back into either the Custom Objects group or your own custom group, as shown on the left in Figure 13-47.

4. Provide a name and some details for the saved objects, as shown on the right in Figure 13-47.

The custom object, or objects, are saved in the library and can be re-created like any standard object. To delete a custom object, select it and choose Remove From Library in either the action menu or by Right/Control-clicking the item.

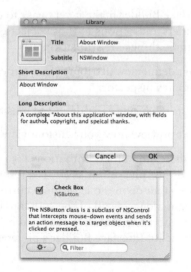

FIGURE 13-47

Customizing Document and Compatibility Checking

The compatibility checks that Interface Builder performs are done based on known incompatibilities, common practices, and Apple's recommendations. You might not agree with these recommendations, their perceived severity, or they might not apply to your projects. You can edit the error and compatibility checks in the Interface Builder preferences, as shown in Figure 13-48.

The Alerts panel of the Interface Builder preferences (Interface Builder ➪ Preferences) lists all of the document and compatibility checks that Interface Builder performs. Next to each is a severity, which you can change. Set the severity to Ignore and Interface Builder will stop checking that issue. In Figure 13-48, I'm raising the severity of an invalid outlet connection, because I consider that to be a profound programming error (although at run time the connection is simply ignored).

FIGURE 13-48

At the bottom is the Alert When Saving option. Set it to the minimum severity that you want to be alerted to every time you save your nib document.

Developing Custom Interface Builder Objects

Xcode and Interface Builder make it very easy to define and create custom objects. It's almost trivial to add outlets and actions to those objects, which you can connect to other objects in the nib document, but three things are still lacking:

➤ You can't define new attributes for your custom objects, or edit your object properties using the attributes inspector.

➤ Your custom objects can't define actions that they send.

➤ You can't preview how your custom view object will look in Interface Builder.

The solution to these, and other, limitations is to create an Interface Builder Plug-In. An Interface Builder Plug-In, or just plug-in for short, is a resource bundle that you create — probably as a separate project — that defines one or more custom objects that will appear in the Interface Builder library palette right alongside all of the standard objects. In fact, most of the objects you see in Interface Builder's library palette are provided by plug-ins. You can see (and change) those plug-ins in the Plug-Ins panel of Interface Builder's preferences window, as shown in Figure 13-49.

A plug-in object can have attributes, editable using the attributes panel. It can have a simulated representation, so you can see how it will look in Interface Builder, and it can embody many of the advanced features of the built-in objects: intelligent alignment guides, embedded objects, size restrictions, and so on.

If you decide you want to create your own Interface Builder Plug-In, start with the Interface Builder Plug-In template in Xcode. You'll also find the IBKit Interface Builder templates convenient for adding additional object definitions to an existing plug-in. A rough sketch of how an Interface Builder Plug-In is developed is as follows:

FIGURE 13-49

1. Create an Interface Builder Plug-In project.

2. Define a nib document that will present the object in the library palette.

3. Define a nib document that contains the controls that will appear in its attributes panel.

4. Prepare an abstract description of the object that describes its properties, outlets, and actions.

5. Write an object simulator that Interface Builder will use to draw instances of your object in Interface Builder.

6. Build your plug-in and add the finished product in the Plug-Ins preferences panel.

These steps, and many other details, are described in the *Interface Builder Plug-in Programming Guide*, included in the developer tools documentation.

SUMMARY

Interface Builder provides a rich environment for designing menus and windows, but it goes beyond that, letting you define classes, create custom objects, and connect those objects together at runtime, all without having to write a single line of code.

You'll quickly become addicted to designing your application interfaces and object relationships using Interface Builder. If you like seeing your interface design graphically, you'll enjoy the next chapter, where you learn how to visualize your classes graphically.

14

Class Modeling

WHAT'S IN THIS CHAPTER?

➤ Graphically modeling classes

➤ Learning the basics of the Xcode modeling tools

➤ Customizing diagrams and filtering out extraneous detail

To be an effective object-oriented programmer, you must have a clear mental picture of the classes in your application and their relationships. Sometimes this "picture" is hard to form, because class relationships can be both complex and abstract. The class browser, discussed in Chapter 9, uses the project's index to list your project's classes. Although this helps, it still doesn't present a bird's-eye view of your application's structure. Enter class modeling. Class modeling performs the same function as the class browser, but in a much more visual and customizable way.

You model classes by creating a class model document. The document can include any set of classes; this could be your entire application or just a set of functionally related classes. Xcode then graphs those classes, as shown in Figure 14-1. The class model tracks, and instantly reflects, any changes made to your source files. Unlike data modeling, discussed in the next chapter, the class modeler is not an editor. You cannot design or alter the declarations in a class model and then transform that model into code. In other words, the class modeler is not a UML design tool.

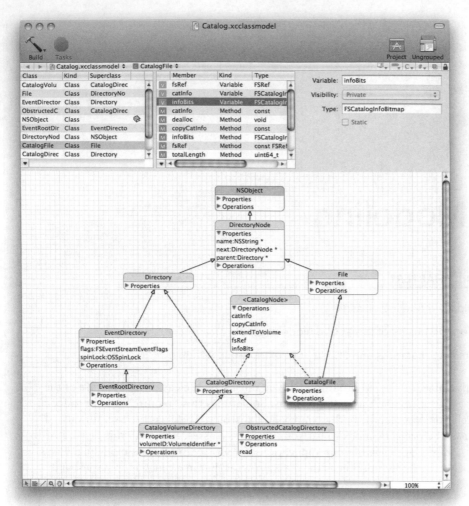

FIGURE 14-1

Class models are really useful when:

> ➤ You want to maintain a clear picture of a complex set of classes.

> ➤ You're considering refactoring a group of classes.

> ➤ You're trying to assimilate a set of classes written by another developer or team.

> ➤ You want to clearly document a set of classes for other developers.

If you're not in any of those circumstances, don't skip to the next chapter just yet. There's one more reason why you should learn to use the class modeler:

> ➤ The class modeling tools use nearly the same interface as the data modeling tools.

The data modeling tools, described in the next chapter, build on the interface elements you learn in this chapter. The data modeling tools are used to create Core Data models — something in which you should *definitely* be interested. At the very least, skim this chapter to learn the basics of creating, browsing, navigating, editing, and customizing models. That knowledge will serve you well in Chapter 15.

CREATING A CLASS MODEL

A class model is stored in a class model document. The documents themselves are extremely lightweight, containing little more than a list of source files. Think of a class model document as just another "view" into your project.

The information about your classes is gleaned from the project's Code Sense index. This exposes two very important prerequisites of class model documents:

➤ *Your project must be indexed for class modeling to work.*

➤ *The project containing your classes must be open.*

If Code Sense indexing is turned off, turn it on in the Code Sense panel of the Xcode Preferences. If your project is currently being indexed in the background, class modeling starts working as soon as the index is complete.

Class model documents cannot be used outside the context of a project. You cannot open a class model document unless the project that it refers to is also open. Although it is possible to create class model documents outside of your project, it is not advisable. If you are intent on keeping a class model, it should be stored in your project's folder, added to the project's source group, and only opened when the project is open.

For small projects, I tend to create a Models source group and store my project's class model documents there. For larger projects, like the one shown in Figure 14-2, I organize my classes into functional groups, and then store the class model document in the group that contains the classes it models.

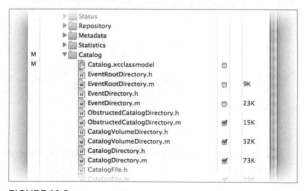

FIGURE 14-2

Creating a New Class Model Document

You add a class model document to your project much as you would any new source file:

1. Choose File ➪ New File.

2. Choose the Class Model document template.

3. Give the class model document a name.

4. Ignore the project targets.

5. Select the source files and source groups that you want to model.

You begin by using the File ➪ New File (or any equivalent) command. If you have any questions about that process, see the "Creating New Source Files" section in Chapter 5.

Next, select the Class Model document type from the list of file templates, as shown in Figure 14-3. You will find the Class Model template under the Mac OS X "Other" group. Class model documents are universal, applying equally well to iPhone and other project types. Give the document a name. Xcode will want you to select the targets the class model document should be included in, as it does for any new project file; don't check any targets in the list. Class model documents are for reference only; they shouldn't be included in any build targets.

FIGURE 14-3

After naming your new document, Xcode presents the model's file tracking dialog box, shown in Figure 14-4.

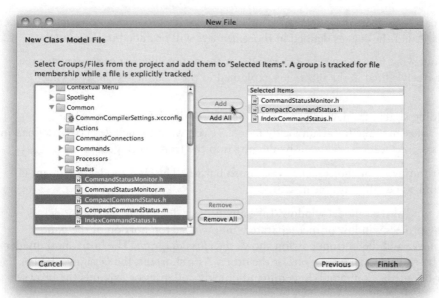

FIGURE 14-4

On the left are all the source groups and files defined in the project. On the right is the list of files or groups that will be tracked by the new model. Select the source files, or source groups, that you want to model on the left and click the Add button to include them in the model. You can do this all at once or incrementally. The Add All button adds every single source file *and* group in your project. This is usually excessive and is not recommended; it's only useful in the case where it's more succinct to specify the files and groups you *do not* want to track.

If you have added too many sources, select them in the list on the right and click the Remove button. Remove All removes all of the sources, so you can start over.

You can add any kind of source file that you like, but the class modeler is only interested in class definitions. For Objective-C and C++, this will typically be the class's header (.h) file. In Java, the .java file that defines the class should be added. The class modeler creates a model using every class definition that it finds in those files. Files that contain non-class declarations, libraries, and so on are ignored. There's no harm in adding those files to the model, but there's no point either. It also makes no difference how many source files define the same class; a class appears in the model only once.

Here are the key points to keep in mind when building the tracking list for a class model:

➤ Adding a source group to a model implicitly tracks every source file contained in that group. If the contents of the group change, so do the files in the model.

➤ You can add both a source file and the group that contains that source file to the model. One reason for doing this would be to avoid having a class disappear from a model if it were moved outside its current source group.

➤ Frameworks can be added. A framework is, logically, a source group that contains a number of header files. All of the classes defined in those headers will be added to the model.

➤ Don't fret about what files to include, or exclude, at this point. The list of sources for the model can be freely edited in the future (as explained in the "Changing the Tracking" section).

Be judicious when adding system frameworks, because these typically define scores, if not hundreds, of classes. This can make for an unwieldy model. If you want to include classes defined in frameworks, add the specific headers you want by digging into the framework group.

After assembling your initial list of choices, click the Finish button. The class model document is added to the project and Xcode displays the new model.

Figure 14-1 showed a typical class model window. Like any project document, a class model pane can appear in the project window or in a separate window. The top portion of the pane contains the *class browser* and the bottom portion shows the *class diagram*. The horizontal divider between the two can be resized to show just one or the other. As a shortcut, the Design ➪ Hide/Show Model Browser (Control+Command+B) command quickly collapses or expands the browser portion of the pane.

Creating a Quick Model

The Quick Model command is a fast way of creating an ephemeral model for a select group of classes, and is an alternative to the more formal procedure for creating class model documents that was just described. Follow these steps to create a quick class model:

1. Select one or more source files or groups in an open project. You can do this in the project source group or in the details list.

2. Choose Design ➪ Class Model ➪ Quick Model.

The Design ➪ Class Model ➪ Quick Model command immediately constructs a class model from the selected sources. The new model window is not associated with a class model document and nothing is added to your project.

Use the Quick Model command to gain quick insight into the class structure of an application. When you are done with the model, simply close it. If you made no modifications to the model, it just goes away. If you did, Xcode treats it like any unnamed document window and prompts you to save it. As mentioned earlier, class model documents are useless outside the context of the open project. If you don't want to keep the model, discard the changes or just save the file as is. The document is a temporary file, so just saving the file doesn't preserve it — it will still be deleted once you're finished with the diagram.

If you later decide you want to save the quick model as a permanent class model document, choose the File ➪ Save As command, and save the class model document in your project's folder. You will then need to add the new document file to your project. See Chapter 5 for one of the many ways of adding a source file to your project.

CLASS MODEL BROWSER

The upper pane in the class model is the class model browser, as shown in Figure 14-5. On the left is the list of classes being tracked by the model. Selecting a class displays the class's members in the middle list. Selecting an item in either list displays additional information about that item in the details pane on the right. You can use the dividers between these sections to resize them, within limits.

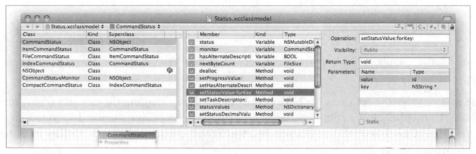

FIGURE 14-5

 To avoid any confusion, the term "class browser," or just "browser," in this chapter refers to the class model browser, not the class browser discussed in Chapter 9.

Class modeling can be used to model C++, Java, and Objective-C classes. The terminology used in class modeling tends to be neutral:

➤ *Properties* refer to instance or member variables of a class.

➤ *Operations* refer to class methods, functions, or messages.

➤ *Protocols* refer to either Objective-C protocols or Java interfaces.

➤ *Categories* are Objective-C categories.

➤ *Packages* are Java packages.

Not all modeling concepts apply to all languages. Categories only appear when modeling Objective-C classes. Package names only appear when you're modeling Java classes. Multiple-inheritance can only occur with C++ classes.

You can customize the browser display a number of different ways. In the lower-left corner of both the class and member lists is a pop-up menu that will alter a list's display. The choices for the class list, shown on the left in Figure 14-6, are Flat List and Inheritance Tree. Flat List lists all of the classes alphabetically. Inheritance Tree lists the classes in a hierarchical browser.

FIGURE 14-6

The list options for the members list lets you select between Show All Members, Show Properties, and Show Operations.

You can resize and reorder the columns for both lists as desired by dragging the column separators or headers. Right/Control-click the column titles to control which columns the list displays, also shown in Figure 14-6. Check only those columns you want to see. The menu for both lists includes a Show All Columns command.

CLASS MODEL DIAGRAM

In the lower portion of the pane is the class diagram, as shown in Figure 14-7, and is class modeling's raison d'être. The diagram presents a graphic visualization of the class relationships. Note that the browser and diagram show much of the same information, just in different ways.

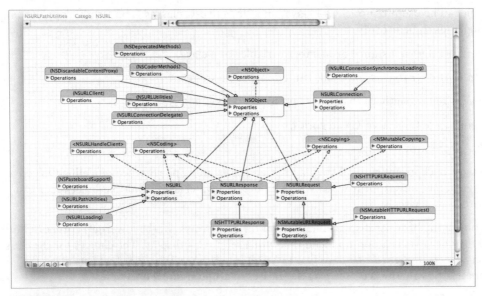

FIGURE 14-7

The entire class model diagram is contained on a variable number of pages that look like graph paper. The number of pages automatically expands to encompass the diagram.

Nodes

Entities in a class model diagram are represented as nodes. At the top of each node is its title. Nodes may optionally show additional detail — quite a bit of detail, if you like. The form and color of the title indicate its type, as listed in the following table:

NODE TITLE	COLOR	NODE TYPE
PlainTitle	Blue	Class
<TitleInBrackets>	Red	Objective-C protocol or Java interface
(TitleInParentheses)	Green	Objective-C category

The background color of framework classes is darker than that of classes defined in your application.

Lines between nodes denote inheritance. The arrow points to the superclass, interface, or category from which the node inherits, conforms, or extends. The possible combination of arrows and lines is listed in the following table:

LINE AND ARROW TYPE	RELATIONSHIP
Solid line with an open arrow	Points to the superclass or category that the class inherits
Dashed line with an open arrow	Points to the interface or protocol that the class adopts
Solid line with no arrow	Indicates an attached annotation node

The compartments below the title detail the members of the class. The Properties member lists the instance variables and the Operations member lists the methods or functions. You can completely hide these details by "rolling up" the node, and reveal them again by rolling them down. You accomplish this by using the Design ⇨ Roll Up Compartments and Design ⇨ Roll Down Compartments commands. The command applies to the currently selected node or nodes. You can also access those same commands by Right/Control+clicking selected nodes. If no nodes are selected, the commands change to Roll Up All and Roll Down All.

The lists within the compartments can be individually expanded or collapsed by clicking the disclosure triangle to the left of the compartment title. To collapse or expand all the compartments at once, select a node or nodes and choose either the Design ⇨ Collapse Compartments or Design ⇨ Expand Compartments command. When no nodes are selected, the commands change to Design ⇨ Collapse All and Design ⇨ Expand All. Figure 14-8 shows a variety of node states: the categories on the left have been rolled up, the classes have been selectively expanded, and the categories on the right have been fully expanded.

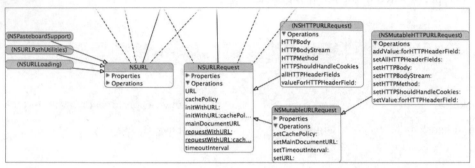

FIGURE 14-8

The members of a class may optionally display their visibility (private, protected, or public), type, return type, or method parameters. All of these display options are set in the General tab of the diagram's Info window. With the selection tool, click anywhere on the background of the diagram so that no nodes are selected, and then choose File ⇨ Get Info (Command+I). Switch to the General tab and the various display options appear at the top of the window, as shown in Figure 14-9.

The Show Visibility option refers to the scope or accessibility of class members, indicated by a small icon next to each member. The possibilities are as follows:

FIGURE 14-9

VISIBILITY/SCOPE	SYMBOL
Private	red circle
Package	orange triangle (pointing down)
Protected	yellow triangle (pointing up)
Public	green square

The Show Property Type option includes the variable type after each class property. Show Operation Return Type shows the return value type of each operation. This may appear before or after the operation name, depending on the language being modeled. The Show Operation Parameter List option includes the entire parameter list of each operation, and can make for some very wide class nodes.

The Show Package option applies only to Java. If you select this option, the package name appears below the name of the class or interface in the node's title compartment.

Figure 14-10 shows a diagram with all the display options turned on (left) and off (right). Static, also known as class, operations are underlined. This is one display option that is not customizable.

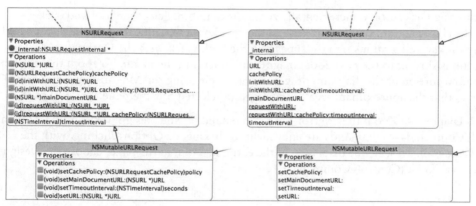

FIGURE 14-10

Tools

Five tools, listed in the following table, are displayed in the palette in the lower-left corner of the class diagram. To use a tool, click it. The currently selected tool is highlighted, and the cursor reflects the current tool whenever it is in the class diagram pane.

TOOL	DESCRIPTION
Arrow	Selection tool. Used to select elements, move, expand, and resize nodes. This is the default tool.
Note	Note tool. Creates annotation nodes.
Line	Line tool. Connects nodes.
Magnifying Glass	Zoom tool. Enlarges or shrinks the diagram display.
Hand	Drag tool. Pans the diagram around in the window.

Choose the Arrow tool whenever you need to select, move, resize, or otherwise manipulate the nodes in a diagram.

The Note and Line tools are described later in the "Adding Annotations" section.

The Magnifying Glass and Hand tools are ways of navigating the diagram, and are described in the next section.

Navigation

Moving around the class diagram is pretty straightforward. You can use the scroll bars at the bottom and right side of the pane to scroll the diagram. You can also select the Hand tool and drag the diagram around.

Reduce or magnify the diagram by selecting a magnification amount in the zoom control in the lower-right corner of the pane. You can select a specific magnification from between 10 and 1600 percent.

Use the Magnifying Glass tool to incrementally zoom the diagram. Select the tool and click anywhere in the class diagram pane to increase to the next zoom magnification in the menu. Hold down the Option key and a minus sign (–) appears in the tool. Click with the Option key held down and the diagram is shrunk to the next zoom magnification level in the menu. To zoom the diagram to fit an arbitrary portion of the diagram, drag out a rectangle using the Magnifying Glass tool. The image zooms so that the approximate area of the diagram selected fills the pane.

The Design ➪ Diagram ➪ Zoom In (Control+Shift+Command+=) and Design ➪ Diagram ➪ Zoom Out (Control+Command+–) commands are equivalent to clicking, or Option+clicking, with the Magnifying Glass tool. To scale the display to fit the entire diagram in the pane, choose the Design ➪ Diagram ➪ Zoom To Fit (Control+Command+=) command.

Selecting

You can select class nodes in a variety of ways. Selecting a class also causes the diagram to scroll if the selected class is beyond the edge of the visible diagram.

Click a node to select it. Drag out a rectangle using the Arrow tool to select all of the nodes that intersect the rectangle.

Class selection in the diagram and browser are linked. Selecting a class in the browser selects the same class in the diagram, and vice versa. The Functions menu in a class diagram lists all of the classes in the model, as shown in Figure 14-11. Choosing one selects that class in both the browser and diagram, and scrolls to make both visible.

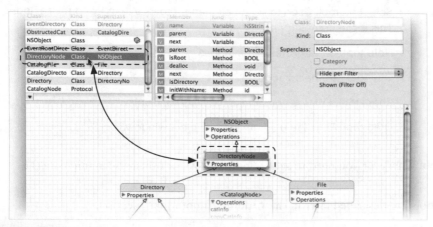

FIGURE 14-11

You can add class nodes to the selection by holding down the Shift key while clicking unselected nodes or dragging out a selection rectangle. Nodes can be individually removed from a selection by clicking a selected node while holding down the Shift key. It may be necessary to click the background area or the edge of a node; clicking the node's title or a member may not deselect it.

You can also type the first few letters of a class name. When listed alphabetically, the first class that matches the characters typed is selected.

Quick-Jump to Source

Double-click any class or member in the class browser, and Xcode jumps to its declaration in the source code.

In the class diagram, Right/Control+click on a node, as shown in Figure 14-12, and choose one of the commands:

➤ Go to Declaration

➤ Go to Definition

➤ Go to Documentation

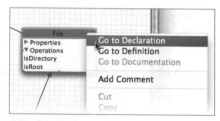

These same three commands can be found in the Design ⇨ Class Model submenu. If an individual property or operation in the node is selected, Xcode jumps to that specific instance variable or method. Otherwise, you are taken to the class's definition, implementation, or documentation.

If a class or method appears in the API documentation, a small "book" icon appears next to its name in the browser. Clicking the book icon jumps to its documentation, and is the same as choosing the Design ⇨ Class Model ⇨ Go to Documentation command.

FIGURE 14-12

EDITING A CLASS MODEL

"Editing" a class diagram is limited to customizing its appearance. As mentioned at the beginning of this chapter, you can't alter the definition of a class in a class model. Class modeling is strictly a visualization tool. Any changes you make will be (mostly) cosmetic. That said, you can alter the layout and appearance of the class diagram significantly, which can profoundly influence its effectiveness as a programming aid.

Moving Nodes

The main point of class diagrams is to visually represent the relationship between classes. Creating a pleasing and readable distribution of class nodes is, therefore, paramount to creating a useful class model. Xcode provides a variety of tools and techniques by which you can reshape a class diagram. The inheritance lines between class nodes are permanent fixtures and will follow the nodes as you reposition them. In fact, organizing the diagram such that all of the inheritance lines are visible and unambiguous will be your biggest challenge.

You can move nodes individually, or in groups, by selecting and dragging them to a new position. You can also use the arrow keys on the keyboard to move selected nodes.

A variety of alignment commands are found in the Design ⇨ Alignment ⇨ Align menu. Most of these are self-explanatory, and apply to the currently selected nodes. You must have at least two nodes selected for the alignment commands to work. These same commands are located in the Alignment submenu of the node's contextual menu in the diagram.

Automatic Layout

Xcode provides two algorithms for automatically rearranging class nodes: hierarchical and force-directed. Select the set of nodes you want laid out — or select none to rearrange them all — and choose the desired layout command from the Design ⇨ Automatic Layout menu. Hierarchical layout, shown in Figure 14-13, produces graphs where sister nodes (two nodes that inherit from a common node) are distributed horizontally. For large collections of classes that all descend from the same class (NSObject, for instance), this can create very wide diagrams.

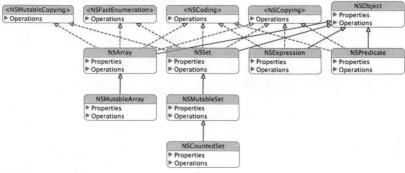

FIGURE 14-13

Force-directed layout tends to put progenitor classes in the middle of the diagram, with descendants radiating outward. Imagine that all of the nodes are negatively charged particles that are equally repelled by all other nodes. Imagine that the lines connecting the nodes are elastic bands. Now, pick up the root nodes of the model and let the remaining nodes hang like a mobile. This is, approximately, the effect of force-directed layout. The diagram in Figure 14-13 is the same diagram shown in Figure 14-12, reorganized using force-directed layout.

FIGURE 14-14

Hierarchical layout is the most predictable and produces extremely easy-to-see relationships, but it can produce unwieldy results for large collections of classes. Force-directed layout produces compact graphs, but they are often unintuitive. The release notes for Xcode also warn that the algorithm used to generate force-directed layouts is "unbounded," meaning that it can take an indeterminate amount of CPU time to compute the layout of a large and complex diagram.

Xcode uses hierarchical automatic layout when a model is first created, and whenever the tracking for the model is changed. Automatic layout uses the current size of each node, and tries to create layouts such that nodes do not overlap. Locked nodes (see the "Locking Nodes" section) can interfere with this goal.

Resizing Nodes

You can resize nodes using the resize "handles" that appear on the edges of the node when it is selected. Choose the Design ⇨ Diagram ⇨ Size ⇨ Size to Fit command to resize selected nodes such that their height and width are exactly enough to show their entire names and all exposed members. The height of a node does this automatically whenever the compartments are rolled up, rolled down, expanded, or collapsed. The width, however, is never automatically adjusted. If you want the width to be sufficient to show all members, have those compartments expanded before using the Size to Fit command.

You can also set the height or width of multiple nodes so that they are all identical. Begin by selecting a prototype node. Select additional nodes by holding down the Shift key. The Size ⇨ Make Same Width and Size ⇨ Make Same Height commands set the width or the height of all selected nodes so that they are identical to the dimension of the prototype node.

Locking Nodes

Locking a node prevents it from being moved or resized. To lock or unlock a node, or nodes, use the Lock and Unlock commands in the Design ⇨ Diagram or the node's contextual menu. Locking is very useful for preserving the layout of a subgroup of nodes, while you add, remove, or rearrange other nodes around them.

Grid and Grid Alignment

As an aid to positioning and sizing nodes, Xcode provides an optional grid. The grid is drawn in light gray behind the diagram, as shown in Figure 14-15.

When you're dragging nodes around, their position will normally "snap" to the nearest grid line. To enable or disable grid snap, choose the Design ➪ Diagram ➪ Turn Grid On/Off command in the main menu or simply Right/Control+click on the background of the diagram.

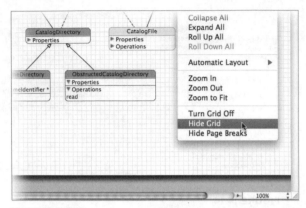

FIGURE 14-15

Use the Design ➪ Diagram ➪ Hide/Show Grid command to hide and reveal the grid. Grid snap is independent of its visibility.

Page Layout

A class diagram occupies a series of pages. Like a WYSIWYG word processor or spreadsheet, Xcode extends the graph area in page increments to accommodate the size of the diagram. Drag a node off the edge of the page, and a new page appears. A solid gray line indicates the boundary between pages. If you plan to print a diagram, you can use the page guides to ensure that nodes don't straddle two or more pages. If they are unimportant, the page guides can be hidden using the Design ➪ Diagram ➪ Show/Hide Page Breaks command.

The size of a page is controlled using the File ➪ Page Setup command. By default, Xcode sets the page magnification to 80 percent and the orientation to landscape. Smaller magnification values shrink the size of the node, allowing you to fit more nodes on a page. Consider passing out reading glasses if you reduce the page magnification below 50 percent.

Changing the Tracking

You can add or remove classes to and from a class model at any time. Click the diagram background, so that no nodes are selected, and then choose the File ➪ Get Info command. This opens the Info window for the class model. Switch to the Tracking tab. In it, you will find the list of source files and groups the class model is tracking. To remove files or groups, select them in the list and click the – button at the bottom of the window.

 Changing the tracking may add, remove, or replace existing nodes. This may cause customized diagrams to lose some of their customization. At the very least, any change will perform an automatic hierarchical layout, undoing any hand-arranged node positions. Save your document before changing your document's tracking — or better yet, take a snapshot or check it into source control first.

To add new sources, click the + button. This presents the sheet shown in Figure 14-16. Select the additional sources you want added to the model and click the Add Tracking button.

FIGURE 14-16

 In its current incarnation, Xcode occasionally exhibits problems constructing class models. The symptom is missing inheritance between classes, protocols, or categories. If this happens, try removing the subclass and adding it back to the model following the classes and other nodes it inherits from. If that doesn't work, create a new, empty, model. Add classes in batches, starting with the superclasses, in such a way that you never add a class unless all of the superclasses and interfaces or protocols from which it inherits are already in the model. An easy way of accomplishing this is to keep the Class Browser window visible behind the diagram's Info window. That way, you can easily refer to the hierarchical arrangement of classes as you add them to the model.

Adding Annotations

Beyond altering its appearance, the only real content that can be added to a class diagram is an annotation node. Create annotation nodes by dragging out a rectangle using the Note tool, or by choosing the Design ⇨ Class Model ⇨ Add Comment command. An annotation node has a page-like, or sticky-note-like, appearance, as shown in Figure 14-17.

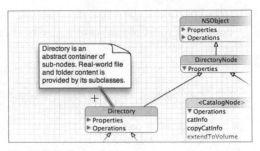

FIGURE 14-17

The content of the node is free-formed text. Double-click the node to enter text edit mode. All of the typographical formatting features in the Edit ⇨ Format ⇨ Font and Edit ⇨ Format ⇨ Text submenus can be used, which gives you an immense amount of formatting control. Even the text rulers and tab stops work, although they seem a little silly in an area only big enough for a sentence or two.

Annotation nodes can be connected to any number of other regular nodes, but not another annotation node. To connect an annotation node to a class node, use the Line tool to drag out a line between the two nodes. To remove a connection or an annotation node, select the line or node and press the Delete key or choose Edit ⇨ Delete.

Customizing Colors and Fonts

You can customize the text color, font, size, and style of nodes in the Appearance tab of the Info window. Choose File ⇨ Get Info with one or more nodes selected to alter the appearance of those nodes. With no node selected, the Info window allows you to set the default settings for new nodes; the default settings apply only to new nodes created by adding additional classes to the model.

Figure 14-18 shows the Appearance tab. The three categories — Name, Property, and Operation — address the three compartments of each node. Changing the color changes the color of the text. Changing the font, by clicking the Set button to the right of each sample, allows you to change the font face, style, and size of the text of each compartment.

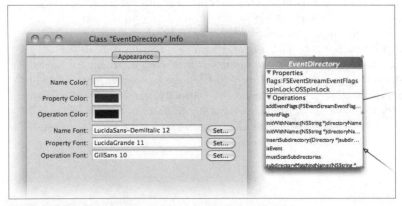

FIGURE 14-18

You can change the background color used in the title to distinguish between different types of nodes — in a roundabout way. Drop a color from any color source onto a node to change its background color. Probably the easiest way to get a color source is to choose Edit ⇨ Format ⇨ Font ⇨ Show Colors to display the color picker. Dial a color, and then drag the color sample at the top of the picker into the node. Figure 14-19 shows nodes with customized colors.

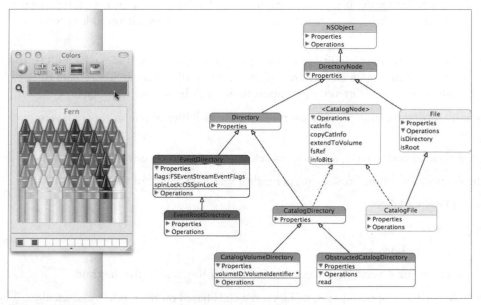

FIGURE 14-19

Hiding Classes and Members

One of the primary uses of a class diagram is to maintain a high-level vision of class relationships — but sometimes there can be so many classes, class members, protocols, and categories that its essence is obscured by the details. You can regain some perspective by selectively hiding superfluous classes and members. You can do this on a per-class basis or automate it using rules.

You might want to hide classes or certain members of classes for many reasons:

➤ Private or protected members that shouldn't be exposed

➤ Internal utility or helper classes

➤ Base class methods, like -(NSUInteger)hash, that don't add anything significant to the description of the classes

➤ Unrelated or superfluous classes that happen to be defined in the same file as important classes

➤ Categories that are unrelated or are used to hide private methods

Selectively hiding classes and class elements lets you pair down the diagram to *exactly* the detail you want to see. For example, an Objective-C class that can be archived probably implements `initWithCoder:` and `encodeWithCoder:`. Having these methods listed in every single class node really doesn't impart any useful information.

Why you would want to hide elements also depends a lot on your goals. If you're using a class model as an aide to developing your code, you'll probably want to see all of the private and protected members. If your intent is to provide a class model to other developers as a means of documenting how your classes relate and their public functionality, private and protected variables probably shouldn't be visible.

You can individually control the visibility of classes, protocols, categories, and packages. Or, you can create rules to determine which classes are visible automatically. You can also create rules to determine the visibility of properties and operations; those can't be set individually.

Start by manually setting the visibility of classes. To set the visibility of one or more classes manually:

1. Select a node or nodes in the diagram, or select one or more classes in the class list.

2. In the details pane of the browser (upper right), set the visibility of the class or classes to:

- ➤ Hide per Filter
- ➤ Always Show
- ➤ Always Hide

Choosing Always Show or Always Hide fixes the visibility of the class in the diagram.

Selecting the Hide per Filter option shows, or hides, the class based on the model's classes filter. When this option is selected, a line of text below the control indicates the visibility of the class based on the filter. There is also a Hidden column available in the class list of the browser. Right/Control+click the class column titles and reveal the Hidden column in the table. Click the box in the row of each class to selectively hide (checked), show (unchecked), or filter it (indeterminate).

You can create class, property, and operation filters in the General tab of the diagram's Info window. Make sure no nodes are selected, and then choose File ⇨ Get Info (Command+I) to open the Info window. At the bottom of the Info window are three filter settings, shown in Figure 14-20.

To enable a filter, check the box next to the desired filter. If disabled (or the filter rule is left empty), the filter will not hide any nodes in the diagram.

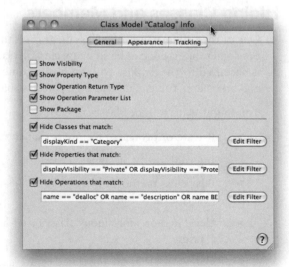

FIGURE 14-20

If you're conversant in Mac OS X's predicate language, you can edit the predicate statement directly in the text field. If you're like me and need some help constructing the condition statement, click the Edit Filter button. Xcode presents a predicate editor, as shown in Figure 14-21.

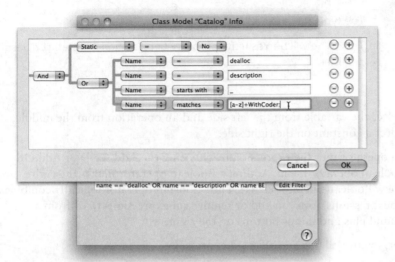

FIGURE 14-21

The predicate editor allows you to graphically create arbitrarily complex conditional statements. The predicate editor is described in more detail in Chapter 15, but here's the short version.

An expression is built from basic conditionals. A condition consists of three parts: variable, operator, and value. Variables are properties of each node or member in the class model, and the set of variables is fixed. For properties and operations, the variables are Name, Visibility, Type, and Static. For classes, the variables are Name, Kind, Superclass, Language, and Project Member. These variables are described in the following table:

VARIABLE	DESCRIPTION
Name	The class or member's name.
Kind	The type of the class node in the diagram: Class, Protocol, Interface, or Category.
Superclass	The name of the class that the class or category extends.
Language	The language in which the class was defined: C++, Java, or Objective-C.
Project Member	This value will be Yes if the class is defined in the project.

continues

(continued)

VARIABLE	DESCRIPTION
Visibility	The visibility or scope of the property or operation: Public, Package, Protected, or Private.
Type	The type of the variable.
Static	This value will be Yes if the property or operation is a static or class member.

To configure a conditional, select the variable from the left side and an operation from the middle, and then enter a value or a select a constant on the right side.

You can insert a new Boolean operator into the expression by choosing the Add AND or Add OR item in either a variable or Boolean operator menu. Adding a Boolean operator makes the entire subexpression one term in a new Boolean operator clause. Each Boolean operator logically combines the results of two or more subexpressions. You can add or remove subexpressions to or from a Boolean operator using the round plus and minus buttons on the right.

To remove a Boolean operator, remove all but one of its subexpressions.

You can negate a conditional or Boolean operator by selecting the Add NOT item. This inserts a negation operator, which you can remove again by choosing Remove in its menu.

Figures 14-22, 14-23, and 14-24 present a practical example that uses three predicate formulas to filter a class diagram. The goal is to hide much of the minutia — simple framework classes, common methods, private instance variables, and so on — that would otherwise clutter the diagram.

The Hide Classes rule, shown in Figure 14-22, hides the NSObject base class and every immediate subclass of NSObject that is *not* defined in the current project.

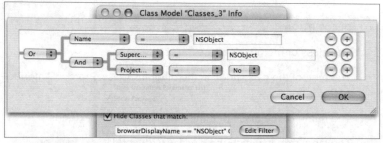

FIGURE 14-22

The Hide Properties rule, shown in Figure 14-23, hides all properties that are private or whose name begins with an underscore (_) character.

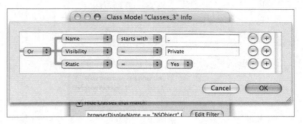

FIGURE 14-23

The Hide Operations rule, shown in Figure 14-24, hides the following methods in every class:

➤ `-dealloc`

➤ `-compare:`

➤ `-description`

➤ Any method that starts with an underscore character

➤ Any method whose name ends in `WithZone:`

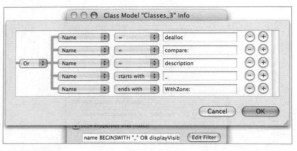

FIGURE 14-24

SUMMARY

Class modeling is a powerful analysis tool. You can use it to understand the structure of someone else's code, or classes that you haven't visited in a while. Because class models instantly reflect changes in your code, class modeling is a great tool for watching as your code develops and is a powerful aid when it comes time to reorganizing a set of classes. Class model annotations are a convenient way of highlighting key concepts and communicating them to other developers. Class and member filtering lets you tailor how much detail is revealed, keeping the focus on the important aspects of the class model.

In this chapter, you've seen how powerful visual modeling can be. In the previous chapter, you saw how easy and efficient visual editing of run time objects can be. The next chapter combines these two technologies, allowing you to visually design your data model objects.

15

Data Modeling

➤ Create a data schema

➤ Define entities, properties, and relationships

➤ Migrate between data schema versions

➤ Quickly create a user interface

Data modeling is a visual tool for defining data objects and their relationships, called a data schema. A schema defines entities that contain properties. Properties can be values or relationships to other entities. The data modeling tools in Xcode let you create and edit a data model, as shown in Figure 15-1. The data model then becomes a resource that can be used by your application at run time.

To use data modeling effectively, you must have a rudimentary understanding of Core Data. If you are not familiar with Core Data, start by perusing the *Core Data Programming Guide*. You can find it in the Xcode documentation, or you can browse it online at `http:// developer.apple.com/mac/library/documentation/Cocoa/Conceptual/CoreData/`.

This book is not about database development or Core Data programming, but like the chapter on Interface Builder, it's difficult to explain how to use the data modeling tools without describing what you're doing and why. This chapter focuses on the Xcode tools you use to develop and maintain data models. In the process, I'll explain the data model's relationship to the run time environment and touch on some best practices. Just know that the modeling tools are the tip of the Core Data iceberg; Core Data can be extended *extensively* with custom code — all well beyond the scope of this book. If you have questions, refer to the *Core Data Programming Guide*.

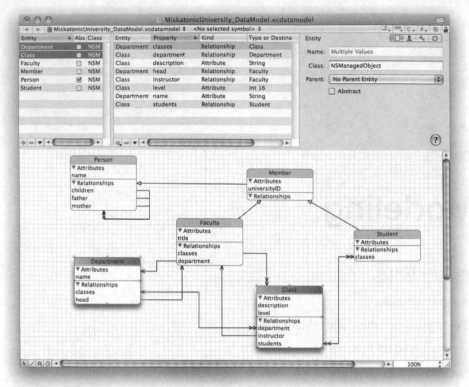

FIGURE 15-1

TECHNOLOGY

Data modeling in Xcode has similarities to both class modeling and Interface Builder.

The user interface for data modeling is essentially the same as what you've used for class modeling, with one very important difference: in data modeling, you actually create and edit the objects in the data model. It is a true editor, not just a fancy visualization tool.

 The user interface for data modeling is almost identical to the interface used for class modeling; so similar that discussion of the common features has been omitted from this chapter. If you haven't read Chapter 14, I strongly urge you to at least browse through the "Class Model Browser," "Class Model Diagram," and "Editing a Class Model" sections. For the most part, simply substitute the words "entity" for "class" and "property" for "member."

From a conceptual standpoint, data modeling is most like Interface Builder: you graphically define objects and relationships. These definitions are stored in a data file that is included in the application's bundle. At run time, the data is read and objects are created. In Interface Builder, the objects are archived in a nib document. In data modeling, the data schema is deployed in a mom (Managed Object Model) file, produced by the data model compiler.

Entities (the containers you define in a data model) are essentially class definitions: They define the form from which any number of instances are created. Unlike Interface Builder, you don't define the instances in the class model. Instances are created dynamically to represent the records in your database. The number of instances of the Employee entity that get created is a function of how many employee records are read or created at run time. A human resources application that tracks employees might create 50,000 Employee objects for a large company or none at all when used by a sole proprietor.

Every instance of an entity becomes an instance of an NSManagedObject at run time. If you need to add functionality to your entities — beyond what's possible using the data modeling tools — you can define your own subclasses of NSManagedObject to be used instead. The "Creating NSManagedObject Subclasses" section toward the end of this chapter explains how that's done.

TERMINOLOGY

One of the things that can be immediately confusing about data modeling is the terminology. The data schema concepts are so much like classes and objects that it's hard to see why the same vocabulary isn't used. The reason is largely historical: Database design and computer programming had independent origins. Later, the two embraced many of the same concepts, ultimately merging to form Object-Oriented Database Management Systems (ODBMS). Though many of the concepts of object-oriented programming (OOP) and object-oriented databases (OODB) are the same, they retain their original lexicons.

Despite their resemblance, significant differences still exist between entities and classes, and the different monikers help reinforce that. Just keep these two principles in mind:

➤   At development time, you are designing a database.

➤   At run time, managed objects are created to contain the data in that database.

The following table defines common terms used in Core Data and data modeling:

TERM	DEFINITION
Entity	An entity defines a container of properties. An entity can also contain other auxiliary data such as user-defined values and predefined fetch requests. Defining an entity is similar to defining a class or a table in a database. At run time, instances of an entity are embodied by instances of NSManagedObject.
Property	The generic term for a member of an entity. The properties of an entity can be attributes, relationships, or predefined queries.

continues

(continued)

TERM	DEFINITION
Attribute	A value in an entity. In a class, this would be an instance variable. In a database, this would be a field. Values store primitive, atomic values such as strings and integers.
Relationship	A connection between an entity and other entities. Relationships can be one-to-one or one-to-many. A Person entity might have two relationships, mother and father, both of which would be one-to-one relationships. The same entity might have a cousin relationship. This would be a one-to-many relationship that connects that entity to all of its cousins — which might be dozens or none at all. Relationships can be defined in the actual storage using any number of techniques, but typical database tools would use foreign keys or junction tables.
Inverse Relationship	If entity A has a relationship to entity B, and entity B has a reflexive relationship back to entity A, these two relationships are considered to be the inverse of each other. The data modeler can recognize inverse relationships, and uses that to simplify the data model diagram and to highlight bidirectional connections.
Fetched Property	A fetched property is like a relationship in that it connects an entity to some other set of entities. Unlike a regular relationship, fetched properties are based on a fetch request. A Person entity might have a relationship called `siblings`. It might then define a fetched property named `sisters`, which would be defined as all of the siblings where `sex == "female"`.
Fetch Request	A fetch request is a predefined query, usually created with the predicate builder. A fetch request defines some criteria, such as `person.age < 21`, that can be used to filter entities.

CREATING A DATA MODEL

If you started your Xcode project using one of the Core Data application templates, your project already has a data model document, and you can skip to the next section.

> *If you're new to Core Data, I highly recommend that you start by creating your first data model via one of the Core Data project templates — if only to examine what it does. There's a modest amount of "plumbing" that has to be connected before your data model will work at all. Specifically, NSManagedObjectContext, NSPersistentStoreCoordinator, and NSManagedObjectModel objects have to be created, configured, and shutdown properly. The Core Data project templates do all of these basics already and make a great place to start.*

Create a new data model and add it to your project by choosing the File ⇨ New command. Choose the Data Model template — you'll find it in the Resource subgroup of either the iPhone OS or Mac OS X groups. Give the document a name and decide in what targets the model should be included. Unlike class models, data models produce a product and should be included in the targets that will use it. Clicking Next presents a dialog box like the one shown in Figure 15-2.

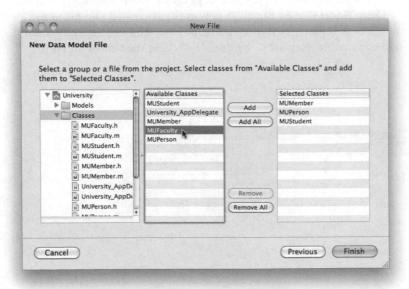

FIGURE 15-2

If your project already has classes that represent your data model, or you've already started your Core Data design by creating subclasses of NSManagedObject, Xcode can import your class definitions and — as best as it can — use those to create an equivalent set of entities. If you're starting your data model from scratch, just skip this step.

On the left are the project's source files and groups. Select a set of sources, and Xcode scans those source files for class definitions. The classes it finds are listed in the center column. Click the Add All button to add them all to the data model, or select specific classes and use the Add button to add them selectively. Repeat this process until you've added all of the classes you want included in the model. If you add too many classes, select them in the right column and click the Remove button to forget them.

Click the Finish button to create the model and add it to the project. For every class added to the Selected Classes list, Xcode creates an entity with that class name and implementation. As mentioned earlier, entities based on classes other than NSManagedObject must ultimately be a subclass of NSManagedObject. In other words, you can use your existing classes as the basis for your new data model, but before your application will work you'll have to change those classes so they are subclasses of NSManagedObject. The section "Creating NSManagedObject Subclasses" explains both how to subclass NSManagedObject and why you might *not* need to.

Creating Entities

The first thing to do is create entities — if you haven't already. Underneath the Entity list are plus (+), minus (–), and disclosure buttons. Click the plus button to create a new entity. Alternatively, choose Design ⇨ Data Model ⇨ Add Entity. A new entity is created and given a generic name. Edit the name in the details pane, as shown in Figure 15-3. You can also edit a name by double-clicking an entity name in the browser list or by double-clicking the title of an entity node in the diagram.

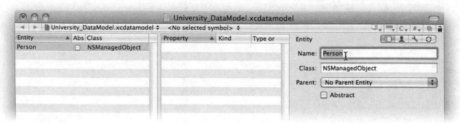

FIGURE 15-3

In the upper-right corner of the details pane is a small tab control that switches between several different groups of settings. The different groups are similar to the different inspectors in Interface Builder; each edits a particular aspect of the entity (or property). The leftmost settings tab is the details pane of primary interest. I'll also discuss some of the migration tab (wrench icon) settings later in this chapter. You can find descriptions of the other settings in the *Core Data Programming Guide*.

Newly created entities have a class of NSManagedObject. If the entity is implemented by a custom class, enter the name of your custom class in the Class field. At run time, an instance of that class is created instead.

Like classes, entities can inherit from other entities. You can define common properties of several entities in a superentity, with subentities filling out the differences. If an entity extends the definition of another entity, select its superentity in the Parent menu. A superentity that exists only as a base for subentities — one that is never used on its own — can be marked as Abstract. Abstract entities are never created at run time.

To delete one or more entities, select them and click the – button, press the Delete key, or choose Edit ⇨ Delete.

Creating Properties

Entities aren't too interesting until they contain something. To add properties to an entity, begin by selecting the entity in the browser or diagram. The list of existing properties appears in the middle column of the browser. Click the + button below the Properties list and choose the Add Attribute, Add Relationship, or Add Fetched Property command. If you don't see this menu, choose Show All Properties from the disclosure menu to the right of the − button. Alternatively, you can choose the Design ⇨ Data Model ⇨ Add Attribute (Control+Command+A), Design ⇨ Data Model ⇨ Add Relationship (Control+Command+R), or Design ⇨ Data Model ⇨ Add Fetched Property commands from the main menu.

> *Interestingly, you can select multiple entities and add a new property to every one using any of the Add Property commands. For example, selecting three classes and choosing Add Attribute adds a new attribute to all three classes. So if you needed to add a* tag *attribute to eight different entities, you could do it with a single Add Attribute command by selecting all eight entities before you began.*

Adding any property creates the kind of property you chose and gives it a generic name. Edit the name, type, and other specifics of the new property in the details pane. To rename a property, you can also double-click its name in either the browser list or in the diagram. All property names should begin with a lowercase letter. The three principal kinds of properties are described in the following sections.

Attributes

Attribute properties contain discrete values, and are the basic building blocks of your data. The types of data that Core Data supports are listed in the Type menu. Select the data type for the attribute from the list. Depending on which type you select, additional validation fields appear, as shown in Figure 15-4. The validation settings are used to determine if the value stored, or attempting to be stored, in this attribute is allowed.

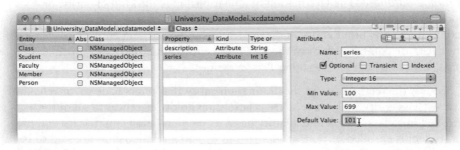

FIGURE 15-4

The scalar numeric types (Integer, Decimal, Float, and Date) define minimum and maximum values. String attributes can have minimum and maximum lengths. Alternatively, string attributes can be matched against a regular expression. If the regular expression matches the string, the string is valid. Other types, like Boolean and Binary Data, have no constraints.

An attribute can be Optional. If this is checked, the attribute is allowed to be completely absent (nil) when stored. Entities — like most databases — make a distinction between no value (nil) and a neutral or default value like zero or a zero-length string. Attributes that are *not* optional must be set before the entity can be stored.

The Default Value is the value given to an attribute when a new instance of the entity is created. If left blank, the initial value will be absent (nil).

The Transient option is used for attributes that are not persistent (that is, they aren't saved). As long as the instance of the entity's object exists in memory, the attribute will hold its value, but when the entity is stored for later retrieval, transient properties are discarded.

One reason for using transient attributes is to model data types that Core Data doesn't understand. A transient attribute can use the Undefined data type, allowing you to use any kind of value your application needs. In order to store the value, you also include one or more persistent attributes in the entity that the undefined type can be translated into. The persistent attributes store the value in the database, which can be converted back into the special type when needed. For example, you might define a custom class that represents a direction (course, azimuth, and velocity). Core Data does not know how to store your object, but your object can be easily converted into three Double attributes that Core Data can store. You can read more about non-standard attributes at http://developer.apple.com/mac/library/documentation/Cocoa/ Conceptual/CoreData/Articles/cdNSAttributes.html.

Relationships

Relationships connect an instance of an entity to some number of other entities, and put the "relational" in *relational database*. The Destination of a relationship is the kind of entity, or entities, the relationship contains. By definition, all entities stored by a relationship must be the same. The destination can be any other entity in the model, including abstract entities or even itself. Self-referential references are common. For instance, a Person entity might have children and parent relationships, both of which refer to other Person entities.

The Inverse menu chooses the relationship in the destination entity that refers back to, or reflexively includes, this entity. A Class entity with a students relationship holds references to all of the Student entities enrolled in a class. The Student entity has a classes relationship that lists all of the Class entities a student is enrolled in. The students and classes relationships are said to be inverses of each other. Any Class that refers to a Student will find itself in the list of classes that student is enrolled in. Data modeling does not create inverse relationships automatically. You must create both complementary relationships yourself. Setting the inverse relationship simplifies the data model diagram and highlights the symmetrical nature of the relationships, as described in the "Data Model Diagram" section later in this chapter.

Relationships come in two flavors: *to-one* and *to-many*. By default, a relationship is a to-one relationship, meaning that the relationship refers to exactly one other entity. A `mother` relationship in a Person entity would be a to-one relationship because every person has exactly one mother. (For the purposes of this discussion, I'll use nominal biological mothers and ignore boundary conditions such as adoption and cloning.) A to-many relationship stores a variable number of references to other entities. Define a to-many relationship by checking the To-Many Relationship option in the details pane, as shown in Figure 15-5. A `children` relationship in a Person entity would be a to-many relationship. A person could have none, one, or many children.

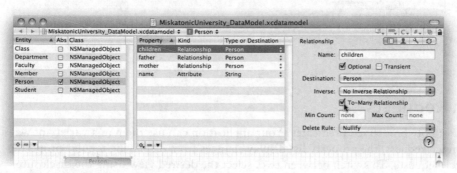

FIGURE 15-5

To-many relationships can be bounded, enforcing that the number of entities referred does not fall outside a set range. Use the Min Count and Max Count fields to set those bounds. An example would be a `livingParents` relationship, which would have a minimum count of 0 and a maximum count of 2.

Like attributes, relationships can be Optional. This means that the relationship may be empty. On a to-one relationship, it means that that the relationship might be `nil` — logically equivalent to a to-many relationship with a minimum count of 0 and a maximum count of 1.

Relationships also have a Delete Rule. The Delete Rule determines what happens when an entity is removed from a relationship — or even if it is allowed to be removed. The meanings of the different settings are explained in the *Core Data Programming Guide*.

Adding Fetched Properties

Fetched properties are like relationships in that they define a set of related entities. Unlike relationships, they don't store actual references to other entities. Instead, they define a predicate (such as a rule or criteria) that determines what entities are included. Like relationships, you must select a destination entity. To define the predicate to use, click the Edit Predicate button. The predicate builder uses the context of the destination entity, so don't forget to select the destination before editing the predicate. The textual version of the predicate you define is displayed in the Predicate field but is not directly editable there, as shown in Figure 15-6.

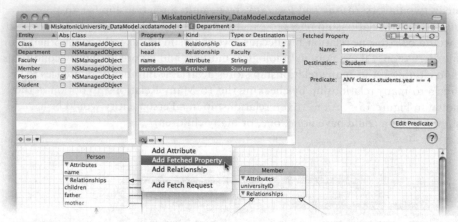

FIGURE 15-6

Adding Fetch Requests

Fetch requests are simply predefined predicates. Your application can use them in a variety of ways. When you add a fetch request, the property list display changes from displaying regular properties to listing only fetch requests. To switch between two, select the desired view using the disclosure triangle at the bottom of the properties list. See the "Data Model Browser" section for more details.

DATA MODELING INTERFACE

The interface used by data modeling is so similar to the interface used for class modeling that it would be a waste to reiterate it all here. Instead, this section just points out the differences between class modeling and data modeling. Before reading this section, you should familiarize yourself with the class modeling interface if you have not already done so. Class modeling was described in detail in Chapter 14.

Data Model Browser

The data model browser lists the entities on the left, the entity properties in the middle, and the details pane on the right, as shown in Figure 15-7.

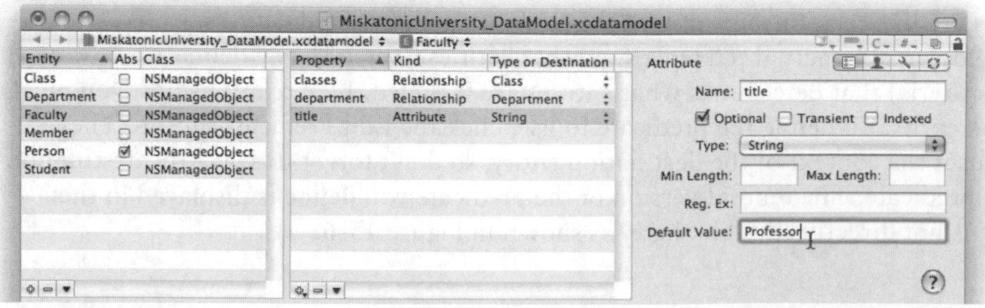

FIGURE 15-7

Selecting an entity in the Entity list displays the properties or fetch requests in the center list. Selecting multiple entities displays a combined list of all properties of the selected entities. The use of the + and – buttons has already been described in the "Creating Properties" section.

The disclosure triangles below each list control how each list is displayed. Similar to the class browser, the Property list has the choices of Show All Properties, Show Attributes, Show Relationships, and Show Fetched Properties. These four choices let you display all standard property types, or limit the display to a single type. The fifth choice, Show Fetch Requests, shows only fetch requests. The formats of the fetch request and property lists are different and are mutually exclusive; the browser can't display both properties and fetch requests at the same time.

Details Pane Views

The details pane shows the settings for the selected entity or property. If you have multiple entities or properties selected at once, the details pane displays the settings common to all of those items, if there are any. Changing a setting that applies to all of the selected items alters all of those items at once.

The details pane has four different inspectors that you select using the small tabs in the upper-right corner of the pane. Figure 15-8 shows the four different panes. From left to right, they are General, User Info, Configurations, and Synchronization.

FIGURE 15-8

General Pane

The General pane displays the settings and controls for the selected entity or property. The format of this pane varies depending on what items are selected in the browser and even on what settings have been selected.

User Info Pane

The User Info pane lists the user info dictionary attached to an entity or property. The dictionary cannot be attached to fetch requests. A user info dictionary is simply a list of key-value strings associated with the entity or property. These values are stored in the data model and can be retrieved at run time by your application for whatever purpose you need.

Configurations Pane

Configurations are named collections of entities and apply only to entities. Using configurations, a data model can contain many different combinations of entities. Your application can then selectively load a data model that contains only the set of entities that it needs. For example, an application for professional photographers might have entities for Image, Thumbnail, Keyword, ModelRelease, CopyrightOwner, and PriceSchedule. That same application, running in "amateur" mode, might only want a data model that includes Image, Thumbnail, and Keyword. This can be accomplished in a single data model by creating two configurations, "Professional" and "Consumer," including all of the entities in the "Professional" configuration, but omitting ModelRelease, CopyrightOwner, and PriceSchedule from the "Consumer" configuration.

Create new configurations by clicking the + button at the bottom of the pane. Select one or more entities and put a check mark next to the configurations they belong in. To delete a configuration, select it and click the – button or press the Delete key.

You'll also find versioning, migration, and miscellaneous storage settings in the Configurations pane. The Renaming Identifier is described later in the "Migrating Data Schemas" section.

Synchronization Pane

The synchronization settings let you integrate your Core Data model with Sync Services, a framework for synchronizing data changes with remote data sets. You can learn more about Sync Services in the *Sync Services Programming Guide* included in the Xcode documentation, or online at `http://developer.apple.com/mac/library/documentation/Cocoa/Conceptual/SyncServices/`.

Data Model Diagram

Nodes in a data model represent entities. The compartments of entity nodes are Attributes, Relationships, and Fetched Properties (see Figure 15-9). The Fetched Properties compartment appears only if fetched properties have been defined for the entity. Fetch requests are not visible in the data model diagram.

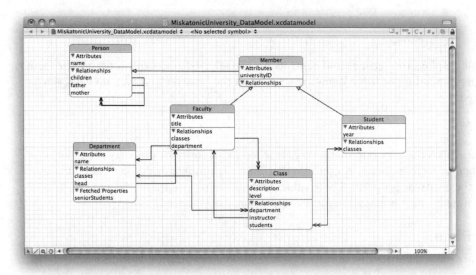

FIGURE 15-9

Lines between entities describe relationships and inheritance. The shapes of the arrowheads indicate the kind of relationship, as listed in the following table:

LINE	RELATIONSHIP
Single arrowhead	To-one relationship. The arrow points to the destination entity.
Double arrowhead	To-many relationship. The arrow points to the destination entity.
Hollow arrowhead	Inheritance. The arrow points to the superentity.

If two relationships have been flagged as being inverse relationships, the data model diagram represents both relationships as a single line with two arrowheads. This greatly improves the readability of the diagram.

Inheritance and unidirectional relationship lines begin at their source and point abstractly toward the destination entity. For inverse relationships, Xcode draws the line precisely from one complementary relationship property to the other.

Selecting a node or attribute in the diagram selects the same in the browser. Selecting a relationship line in the diagram selects the relationship in the browser. If the line represents two inverse relationships, both relationships are selected along with the entities that contain them.

Like class modeling, you can customize the appearance of nodes. You cannot, however, filter the entities or properties that are displayed.

Tools

The Arrow, Magnifying Glass, and Hand tools work exactly as they do in class modeling. There is no Notes tool in data modeling.

Use the Line tool to create relationships between entities. Select the Line tool and drag from one entity to another. A new relationship is created in the entity where the drag began. To create a relationship between an entity and itself, click the entity. Follow the steps in the earlier "Relationships" section for editing its details.

Duplicating Entities and Properties

You can copy entities and properties to the clipboard. From there, you can paste them into the same or different data models. You can also duplicate entities in the data model diagram by holding down the Option key while dragging an entity to a new location. Duplicated entities are given names with numeric suffixes.

Predicate Builder

The predicate builder allows you to construct predicates — logical expressions used to find, select, or filter data — graphically. The predicate editor is based on the Cocoa Predicate framework. You can find both an introduction and a complete description of predicates in the Reference Library under Cocoa ➪ Data Management ➪ Predicates Programming Guide, or you can find it online at
`http://developer.apple.com/mac/library/documentation/Cocoa/Conceptual/Predicates/`.

You can invoke the predicate builder, shown in Figure 15-10, from a variety of places. It is even used in class modeling to determine what classes and members are displayed. The predicate builder is context-sensitive. That is, the pre-assembled set of values used to construct the expression will be garnered from the entity or its destination, as appropriate. Using the predicate builder will be easier and more productive if you have first defined the entire context surrounding the predicate before you begin editing it. Specifically, you should define the types of attributes and any relationships between entities before trying to edit a predicate.

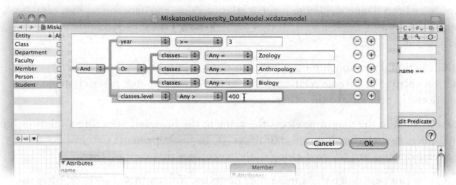

FIGURE 15-10

Simple expressions are constructed from keys (which specify the variable or attribute), operators, and values. You can combine simple expressions using logical operators. The textual form of the expression in Figure 15-10 is `year >= 3 AND (ANY classes.department.name == "Zoology" OR ANY classes.department.name == "Anthropology" OR ANY classes.department.name == "Biology") AND ANY classes.level > 400`.

Simple Expressions

The key menu selects the attribute you want to compare. The keys listed will be the attributes of the entity that the predicate is being built for. To select something more complex than a simple attribute, choose the Select Key item from the menu. This presents a key browser, shown in Figure 15-11.

The browser shows the same attributes, but also includes the relationships defined for the entity. A Key Value path is like a directory path, in that it can specify an attribute of an entity related to an entity. For example, in the university data model, students are enrolled in a class. That class is taught by a faculty member, who belongs to a college. In a Class entity, the Key Value path `instructor.department.name` specifies the name of the department of the faculty member that teaches the class.

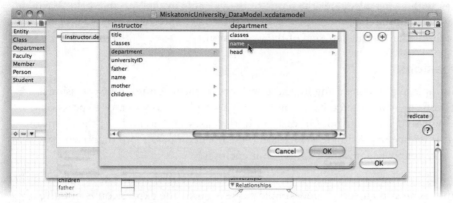

FIGURE 15-11

The type of the variable selected determines the operators and values that can be used in the expression. A Boolean variable presents only two operators (equals and does not equal) and two values (yes and no) to complete the expression. A string value presents numerous operators, all appropriate to matching string values. Select the desired operator from the operator menu.

The selected operator further refines the type of value that will be used in the comparison. Some operators, such as the "within" operator, have more than one value. Normally, the value is a constant. Type the value of the constant into the field. The text entered in the constant field must agree with the type of data on the other side of the operator. You cannot compare a Decimal attribute with the string "zero."

The value can also be another attribute (specified by a key) or a variable. Variables are values defined at run time and exist in an environment space associated with the predicate. Variables appear as $VAR_NAME in a predicate expression. To change the constant field to a variable or key, Right/Control-click in the background of the expression and select Constant, Variable, or Key from the contextual menu, as shown in Figure 15-12. This is usually easiest to do by Right/Control-clicking just to the immediate right of the value field. Some choices may be disabled, depending on the data type of the key or the operator selected.

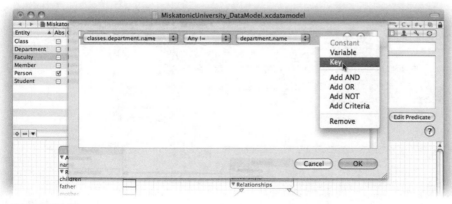

FIGURE 15-12

To compare the key with a variable, enter the name of the variable in the Variable field. Variable names cannot be verified in the data model, so make sure they are spelled correctly. You select a key value just as you would a key on the left side of the expression.

Compound Expressions

You can combine simple expressions using logical operators to form compound expressions. Compound expressions are constructed by encompassing a simple expression, or expressions, within one of the logical operators: And, Or, or Not. In the cases of And and Or, the operator must encompass at least one other simple expression but can encompass more than two. The Not operator is unary and simply negates the expression it encloses.

You have two ways of inserting logical operators into a predicate expression. The + button at the right of every simple expression inserts a new simple expression. If the expression is not already enclosed in a logical operator, a new logical operator is inserted (AND, by default). If a logical operator already encloses the expression, that operator is expanded to include the new expression.

The Add AND, Add OR, Add NOT, and Add Criteria commands are located on every key, logical operator, and Right/Control-click menu in the predicate builder. Selecting Add Criteria is identical to clicking a + button. The other three commands insert a new logical operator enclosing the expression. When you insert a new AND or OR operator, a new simple expression is also created and inserted below the existing expression. Remember that AND and OR operators must enclose at least two expressions. Add Criteria creates a logical operator only when it has to. The other three — Add AND, Add OR, and Add NOT — *always* insert a new logical operator. You can change a logical operator from AND or OR and back again using its menu.

Drag expressions, even entire subexpression trees, to rearrange them in the tree. You can click and drag any portion of an expression's background, but it's often hard to miss the control areas of the pop-up menus. The most reliable drag point is the left end of the line that runs through the middle of the expression, or at the root of an expression tree.

Figure 15-13 shows an OR expression being dragged to a different location in the expression tree. Dragging does not create new logical operators. However, if a logical operator contains only two expressions, dragging one of them to another subexpression deletes it — just as if you had deleted the expression.

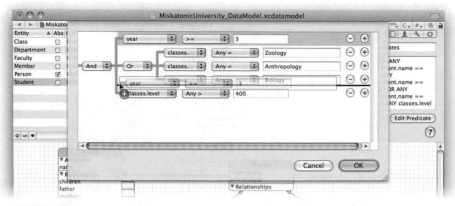

FIGURE 15-13

Use the – button to the right of the expression to delete it. You can delete expressions and NOT operators by choosing the Remove command from any of the expression menus. You cannot delete the logical operators AND and OR directly. To delete an AND or OR operator, delete or remove all but one of the expressions the operator encompasses.

Textual Expressions

Every expression constructed by the predicate builder has a textual representation as well. It is this textual version of the expression that you see in the data model browser. You can also enter predicate expressions directly, or you can insert textual subexpressions in the predicate builder. You may elect to do this because entering the expression directly is often easier than building one graphically, or because you want to use specialized functions or non-trivial Key Value paths.

To enter an expression directly, type the formula into the Predicate field, double-click the predicate expression in the fetched properties list, or add an Expression term in the predicate editor, as shown in Figure 15-14. The expression must be a valid predicate expression. As long as the predicate builder is open, the expression will be displayed just as you entered it.

 Be careful when pasting expressions that the predicate builder can't represent. It is possible to enter expressions, or later change the definition of an entity, resulting in an expression that cannot be edited. If you find yourself in this situation, copy the textual representation of the expression in the browser, delete the fetched property or request, and then create a new one by pasting the (modified) expression into the Expression field.

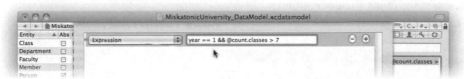

FIGURE 15-14

When you close the predicate builder, the predicate is compiled and stored as archived Predicate objects in the data model. When you edit that predicate again, the predicate editor reinterprets the expression and creates a minimal representation of it. Consequently, the expression in the predicate builder may look different when you edit it again, but will logically represent the same statement. Figure 15-15 shows the expression previously shown in Figure 15-14, after it was saved and reopened.

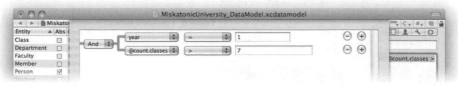

FIGURE 15-15

CREATING AN INSTANT INTERFACE

Xcode can create an "instant interface" from a data model. An instant interface produces a functional Cocoa user interface that allows you to enter and edit data in your data model. This can be a huge time saver if you are just getting your application going or just need a minimal interface in which to view or edit your data. You often have some portion of a working data model, but no data and little or nothing that resembles an application.

To create an instant interface, you'll first need a window to put it in: open a nib document in Interface Builder that already has a Cocoa window in it, create a new nib document, or add a new window object to an existing nib document.

You can now initiate the interface builder process from either Xcode or Interface Builder:

➤ To use Xcode, arrange the window so that it is visible on the screen alongside your data model window in Xcode. Switch back to the data model window. Select the Pointer tool. While holding down the Option key, click and drag an entity from the data model diagram and drop it into the Interface Builder window. When you start the drag, a shadow of the entity with a + sign follows the cursor. If it does not, you are not dragging a copy of the entity.

➤ To use Interface Builder, drag a Core Data Entity object (you'll find it in the Core Data group) from the library palette into the window. A browser appears. Select the project, data model, and entity for which you want to generate the interface.

Xcode now asks you if you want an interface that represents one or many entity objects. Entry fields are created for each attribute. For a collection of entities, Fetch, Add, and Delete buttons can be created along with a table listing all of the instances in the collection. Figure 15-16 shows the instant interface created for many Faculty entities.

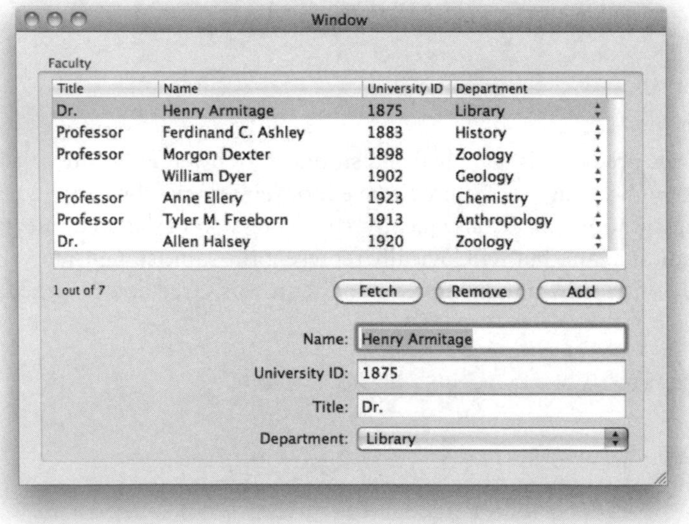

FIGURE 15-16

Amazingly, the entire interface is produced without any code. The interface is constructed using bindings and Interface Builder connections. If nothing else, it's a testament to the power of bindings. A little time spent exploring these bindings can be very educational.

MIGRATING DATA SCHEMAS

The problem with persistent data is that it is, well, persistent. Data written to a data file might exist for years, even decades, while your application continues to evolve. Unless your data model is trivial, or you have exceptional foresight, a time will come when you need to change your data model, such that the data model of your application no longer agrees with the structure of the existing database. When this happens, your application is no longer able to read the previously written data. The important thing to remember is this:

➤ A data schema *must* agree with the format and organization of the information in the data store. Any discrepancies make the two inoperable.

To help circumvent this inevitable disaster, Core Data supports *data model versioning*. Instead of simply changing your data model, you create a new one — a version. When your new application attempts to access its old data, Core Data locates the previous data schema version, uses that to read the data, and then transitions the data from the old schema to the new one; a process called *data migration*.

Make backups of your existing (working) data stores before beginning any migration project. You probably won't get it right the first time, which might leave you with an incorrectly migrated data store.

This section describes the data modeling tools that let you configure versions, define mappings between versions, and provide hints for Core Data to use during migration. You should read the *Core Data Model Versioning and Data Migration Programming Guide* for more in-depth information, as well as the programmatic requirements.

Core Data migration requires code to be added to your application; it won't happen automatically, even after you've followed all of the steps in this section. See the Core Data Model Versioning and Data Migration Programming Guide *for the code needed to request or initiate a data migration.*

Creating a New Version

The first step in any migration strategy is to create a new version of your data schema. With your current data model open, or selected in the source group, choose Design ➪ Data Model ➪ Add Model Version. A copy of the model will appear in your project, as shown in Figure 15-17.

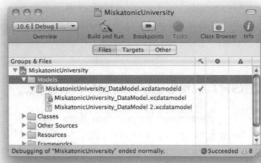

FIGURE 15-17

If this is your first alternate version, your single data model document becomes a group containing the original and all subsequent versions. This parallels the organization of localized resources, which appear as a group containing their individual variants.

When compiled, all of the versions will be combined into a single managed object model (mom) bundle, providing your application with run time access to all versions. One version is designated as the current version, indicated by a check mark (see Figure 15-17). To change the current version, open or select the desired data model document and choose Design ➪ Data Model ➪ Set Current Version.

Be careful not to build your data models twice. When you create the first new version of your data model, your mom document deployment changes from building a single `.mom` *file to packaging multiple* `.mom` *files inside a nested* `.momd` *bundle. The* `.momd` *bundle is built by the data model (*`.xcdatamodeld`*) group that appears in your project. The data model source group should be included in the target — that group compiles all your versions and deploys a single bundle. The individual* `.xcdatamodel` *source files inside the group should not be included in the same target. If you include both, the application's bundle will contain duplicate data models — one inside the bundle and one outside. Core Data will (by default) attempt to merge these, and your application will abort with obscure errors like* "`Can't merge models with two different entities named 'User'.`" *You may need to perform a Build ➪ Clean to erase any stray deployments of the old model. Chapter 16 explains target membership.*

Each version has an arbitrary version identifier string that you assign. Open the data model, ensure that no entities or properties are selected, and choose the File ➪ Get Info command. In the data model's info window, switch to the Versioning tab and assign the model a version identifier, as shown in Figure 15-18.

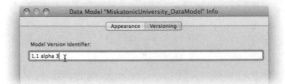

FIGURE 15-18

Now make the needed modifications to the newly created data schema version. The next two sections will help you configure the migration from the old schema to the new one.

Adding Lightweight Migration Hints

If you are using Mac OS X 10.6 or later, Core Data provides a lightweight migration strategy for data models with only superficial changes. If you are using an earlier version of Core Data, or if you make signification changes to your data model, you'll need to create a mapping, as described in the next section.

Lightweight migration has several advantages:

➤ You don't have to create a migration mapping.

➤ You might not have to version your data model.

➤ It's fast.

Core Data can migrate from one schema to another as long as the changes are limited to:

➤ Adding new attributes to an entity

➤ Making a required attribute optional

➤ Making an optional attribute required *and* providing a default value

➤ Renaming an entity

➤ Renaming an attribute

As long as your data schema changes are confined to this set of changes, you can use lightweight migration.

Renaming an entity or attribute requires you to create a data model version and provide Core Data with a little extra assistance. In the configurations inspector of the entity or attribute is a Renaming Identifier, as shown in Figure 15-19.

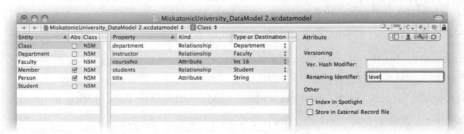

FIGURE 15-19

If you need to rename an entity or attribute, first create a new version of your data model. In the new version, rename the element and then set this field to the element's previous name. This tells Core Data which entity or attribute in the old schema corresponds to the new one.

If you didn't rename any entities or attributes, you can use lightweight migration without creating a new version of your data schema. See the Data Migration Guide *for the cases where you don't need to create a data schema version.*

Creating a Migration Mapping

A migration mapping transitions the data from one schema to another. You can initiate a migration programmatically or let the Core Data framework perform it automatically, as needed. In either case, the migration proceeds in roughly the following phases:

1. The versions of the old and new data schemas are identified and a suitable mapping is found.

2. The old data store is opened and a new data store is created.

3. Objects are created from the old data store.

4. The mapping is used to create new objects in the new data store, and then insert copy/convert the old attributes into new attributes.

5. The relationships between old objects are replicated in the new objects.

6. The new objects are written to the new data store and the old objects are discarded.

The Core Data framework provides many of the basic tools needed to map one data schema to another, and most of these can be configured in Xcode's mapping model tool. If you need a more sophisticated translation, almost every phase of the migration can be influenced with custom code.

To create a data model mapping, follow these steps:

1. Create a new data model version. You must have at least two versions to create a mapping.

2. Choose the File ➪ New File (or any equivalent) command.

3. Select the Mapping Model template (in the Resource group).

4. Give the mapping document a name. I tend to name my mappings after the model and the versions it translates between, such as `Accounts2to3.xcmappingmodel`.

    a. Choose the project to which to add the mapping document.

    b. The location for the new document should be inside your project's folder, preferably with the other data model documents.

    c. Choose the targets. Each target must also include both of the data models in question.

5. Xcode presents a dialog box similar to the one shown in Figure 15-20.

    a. In your project's files, locate and select the old data model file. You will need to expand your data model group, because you have more than one version.

    b. Click the Set Source Model button.

    c. Select the new data model file.

    d. Click the Set Destination Model button.

Xcode constructs a new mapping model document, and fills in the translations that look obvious to it. Your job is to supply anything that's missing or needs to be customized.

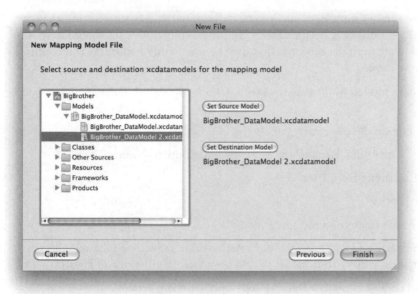

FIGURE 15-20

The mapping model document window, shown in Figure 15-22, is organized very much like the data model browser: the left column lists the entity mappings. Selecting an entity mapping displays the property mappings for that entity mapping in the middle column. On the right is a details pane where you set the specifics for the selected entity or property mapping. You can add or remove mappings using the + and – buttons/menus at the bottom of the columns.

 Order is sometimes important. Entity mappings are performed in a specific order, and if you have mappings that depend on previous mappings then that order may be significant. To change the order, first sort the entity mappings column by order (the # column). You can then drag entity rows into the sequence you desire.

Most of the details concern how entities are mapped to other entities, and how the attributes of new objects are determined using the content of old objects.

One field of note is the Custom Policy property of an entity mapping. A custom migration policy object is a subclass of NSEntityMigrationPolicy. It receives a series of messages as the various migration phases are performed, allowing you to inject custom code into the process. Enter the name of your custom subclass of NSEntityMigrationPolicy into the field. Core Data creates an instance of your class and lets it participate in various aspects of entity migration.

An example serves as a good explanation. Let's say you have a Core Data project that is just getting started. You begin by defining a User entity that has `firstName`, `lastName`, `location`, and `email` attributes.

It's a good start, and you've entered some data into your database, but you quickly realize that `location` is vague and really should have been `country`, and the e-mail addresses should have been a separate table so you can relate multiple accounts that use the same e-mail address. You continue development, following these steps:

1. Open the current data model. Make sure it's saved. Choose Design ➪ Data Model ➪ Add Model Version.

2. Open the new data model (`BigBrother_DataModel 2`).

3. Select the User entity mapping. Rename the `location` attribute to `country`.

4. Remove the `email` attribute from User.

5. Create a new Email entity.

6. Add an `emailAddress` attribute to the new entity.

7. Return to the User entity and add a new to-one relationship, name it `email`, and choose Email as the destination entity. Your model should now look like the one in Figure 15-21.

8. Save the model and choose Design ➪ Data Model ➪ Set Current Version.

9. Make whatever code and nib document changes are needed to work with your new data model.

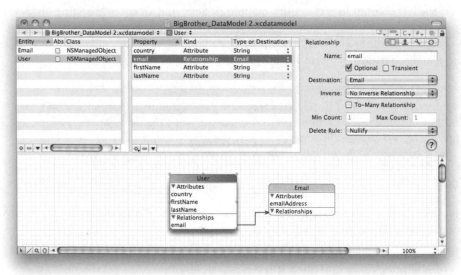

FIGURE 15-21

At this point, you've created a new version of your data schema and application. Unfortunately, the data you already entered is in the old version and can no longer be read. Launching your application at this point would simply result in Core Data errors.

You construct a mapping to convert the data in the old schema into the new one:

10. Choose File ➪ New File, select the Mapping Model template, and name it `BigBrother1to2.xcmappingmodel`.

You then edit your migration mapping to fill in the missing pieces:

11. Handle the attribute rename by selecting the UserToUser mapping, and then selecting the `county` attribute mapping. Set its value expression to `$source.location`. This copies the value of the `location` attribute from the old User to the `country` attribute in the new User.

12. Select the Email entity mapping. Change the source from nothing to User. This now creates a new Email entity for every User entity in the old database. (There are now two mappings for the User entity, so every old User object is processed twice — once to make a new User and again to make a new Email.)

13. Select the `emailAddress` attribute mapping of the new UserToEmail mapping. Enter a value expression of `$source.email`. This copies the `email` attribute of the old User entity into the `emailAddress` attribute of the new Email entity.

14. Select The UserToUser entity mapping, and then select the `email` attribute mapping. Under the Auto Generate Value Expression, enter a KeyPath of `$source` and Mapping Name of UserToEmail, as shown in Figure 15-22. This sets the `email` relationship in the new User object to the single object created by the UserToEmail mapping (that is, the new Email object).

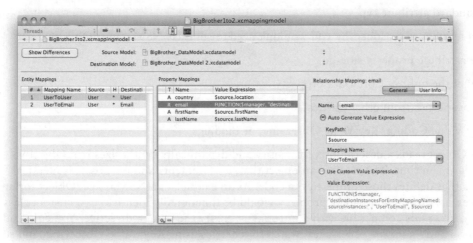

FIGURE 15-22

15. Add the following code to your application's data store setup:

```
NSDictionary *options = [NSDictionary dictionaryWithObjectsAndKeys:
                            [NSNumber numberWithBool:YES],
                            NSMigratePersistentStoresAutomaticallyOption,
                            [NSNumber numberWithBool:YES],
                            NSInferMappingModelAutomaticallyOption,
                            nil];
```

16. Pass the newly created `options` object in the `-addPersistentStoreWithType:configuration:URL:options:error:` message during startup.

Your application is now ready to run. When it starts, Core Data detects that your current data model does not agree with the structure of your existing store. It automatically finds the older version of the data schema that does, finds the mapping that maps between those two models, applies the mapping, and updates your data store.

CREATING NSMANAGEDOBJECT SUBCLASSES

The beginning of this chapter mentioned that the entities you define in your data model exist as instances of NSManagedObject at run time. Quite often, NSManagedObject is more than sufficient for your needs.

You might, however, need a class with more specialized functionality for many reasons:

➤ Localized business logic in the entity object

➤ Specialized or complex validation

➤ Custom pre- or post-processing of attribute changes

➤ Non-standard attribute types

There are also a number of reasons why you wouldn't need to subclass NSManagedObject:

➤ Provide attribute property storage

➤ Use any of the built-in Core Data property features

➤ Inherit properties from other entities

➤ Use Key Value Coding, Key Value Observing, or Bindings

An NSManagedObject reads a description of its entity and dynamically synthesizes real Objective-C accessor methods at run time. The result is an object that, for all intents and purposes, is identical to a custom class that defines those properties in code. As an example, an NSManagedObject for an entity that defines a string `name` attribute property would be functionally identical to a custom class that implemented accessors compatible with a `@property NSString* name` directive. You can send either object `-name` and `-setName:` messages, watch for changes using Key Value Observing, and so on. Ask yourself if you really need to subclass NSManagedObject before continuing.

To create a custom implementation class for an entity, start by subclassing NSManagedObject. You cannot use just any arbitrary class; your class must be a subclass of NSManagedObject. The easiest way to get started is to use the Managed Object Class file template. This template appears only when you have a data model open and (optionally) one or more entities selected prior to choosing the File ⇨ New command. Select the Managed Object Class template from the New File assistant and click the Next button.

Unlike most other new file templates, the Managed Object Class does not ask for a filename. The filename is generated from the names of the entities. You do need to choose a location for the files and the targets in which the Objective-C source files should be included. When you are done, click the Next button, and Xcode presents the pane shown in Figure 15-23.

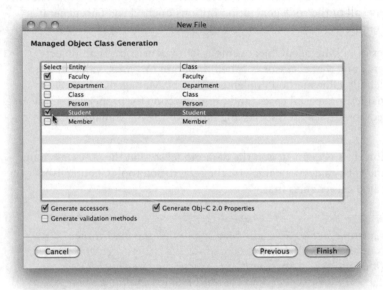

FIGURE 15-23

Check the entities for which you want to create custom implementation classes. By default, the entities that were selected in the model are already checked, but you are free to alter that here. You then need to pick any of the code generation options:

➤ Generate Accessors

➤ Generate Obj-C 2.0 Properties

➤ Generate Validation Methods

The Generate Accessors option generates standard accessor methods for every property defined in the entity. These methods will be Key Value Coding, Key Value Observing, and Bindings compliant.

The Generate Obj-C 2.0 Properties option augments the Generate Accessors option by producing modern Objective-C 2.0 @property and @synthesize directives, instead of emitting boilerplate Objective-C code. This option does nothing if the Generate Accessors option isn't also selected.

The Generate Validation Methods define validation methods for every attribute defined. You can keep the ones you want and delete the ones you don't need to override.

As of this writing, the Generate Obj-C 2.0 Properties object mysteriously defeats the Generate Validation Methods option. If you want Xcode to produce stub methods for validating your properties, leave the Generate Obj-C 2.0 Properties option off. You can easily replace the simplistic getters and setters with `@property` *and* `@synthesize` *directives later.*

If the plan for your NSManagedObject subclass is to add special functionality, and not to customize the behavior of its properties, leave all of the code generation options unchecked. This generates empty subclasses of the selected entities.

Core Data accesses the properties of NSManagedObject using a set of heuristics. If an object has an accessor defined for an attribute, that accessor is called to obtain or set the value. If not, the value is obtained using the default value method implemented in NSManagedObject. Only define accessor and instance variables for special cases, and omit any code for properties you want handled normally by NSManagedObject. See the Subclassing Notes of the NSManagedObject documentation for more details.

After your custom implementation class is defined, edit the data model so that the new class name is specified in the Class field of the entity's details pane. Use the refactoring tool (Chapter 10) if you want to rename any of the generated class names first.

The inheritance of your custom classes does not have to parallel the inheritance of your entities. For example, say your data model defines the entity Vegetable, which inherits from Crop, which inherits from Plant. You then create custom NSManagedObject subclasses, MyCrop and MyVegetable, and assign those to the Crop and Vegetable entities, respectively. Here's the surprising bit: MyVegetable isn't required to be a subclass of MyCrop. It might seem strange, and I can't imagine many practical uses, but it's perfectly valid from Core Data's perspective.

Of course, you don't have to use the Managed Object Class template. You are free to write your own subclass of NSManagedObject. It makes no difference to Xcode. Note that the accessor methods generated by Xcode include explicit calls to -willAccessValueforKey:, -didAccessValueForKey:, -willChangeValueForKey:, and so on. This is because NSManagedObjects disable the normal automatic messaging for Key Value Observing. You need to be mindful of this fact when implementing your own methods, which is another good reason to start with those generated by the template.

EXPORTING CLASS METHODS

The Managed Object Class template is a great time saver, but it's a one-shot tool. You can't modify your entity and use the template again. Doing so will either overwrite or replace the previous class files — a dialog box warns you that Xcode is about to replace the class files and asks what you want to do with the old ones. You either have to replicate your previous customizations or copy and paste from the old implementation.

If you are simply adding new properties to an entity, there's an easier way. Xcode will produce the same accessor methods that the template creates, but copy them to the clipboard instead. It will do this for any selected property, or properties, in the data browser. Select one or more properties and choose any of the following commands:

➤ Design ⇨ Data Model ⇨ Copy Method Declarations to Clipboard

➤ Design ⇨ Data Model ⇨ Copy Method Implementation to Clipboard

➤ Design ⇨ Data Model ⇨ Copy Obj-C 2.0 Method Declarations to Clipboard

➤ Design ⇨ Data Model ⇨ Copy Obj-C 2.0 Method Implementation to Clipboard

Switch to the implementation or header file for the class, as appropriate, and paste in the new methods.

IMPORTING DATA MODELS

To import the data model in a compiled .mom document, open a data model document and choose the Design ⇨ Data Model ⇨ Import command. Select a compiled .mom document, and Xcode disassembles the file and adds the entities that it finds to the model.

If you're trying to import a .mom document contained in an application bundle, it's a bit tricky because Xcode's open file dialog won't let you select files inside a package. To do that, first open the contents of the application package in the Finder by Right/Control-clicking and choosing the Show Package Contents command. In Xcode, choose Design ⇨ Data Model ⇨ Import, and then drag the .mom file from the open Finder window into the open file dialog. Alternatively, press Shift+Command+G in the open file dialog and enter the path of the file or application bundle folder. Note that Shift+Command+G works in almost any Mac OS X open file dialog, and it supports POSIX shell-style pathname completion.

SUMMARY

Data modeling is a powerful tool. You can start incorporating the power of Core Data into your application in a matter of minutes, simply by creating an entity or two. Like class modeling, it is also a visualization tool, so you never lose sight of the "picture" of your data model throughout the course of your development. Instant interfaces make getting your application up and running quickly even easier. As your data schema evolves, versioning and migration tools will keep your data coming right along with you.

16

Targets

Targets are the engines of Xcode. They define the steps that will transform your source code and resource files into a finished product. Targets can be very complex or ridiculously simple. Xcode comes with targets that automatically take care of the myriad details needed to produce standard products such as application bundles, or you can take complete control and choose a target that abdicates all of the responsibility for building a product to you.

The purpose of a target is to produce something. Most targets produce *a* product. There are different types of targets, depending on what kind of product is being produced. Each target refers to the source files and resources required to produce its product, along with the instructions on how those source files get transformed, how the product is assembled, and the order in which all of those things happen.

Targets appear in the Targets smart group of the project window, as shown in Figure 16-1. Most project templates come with a target already defined, appropriately configured for that project type. If you stick to developing simple applications and tools you may never need to add a target to an existing project. Nevertheless, understanding what a target is and does is a prerequisite to customizing one and is fundamental to understanding the build process as a whole.

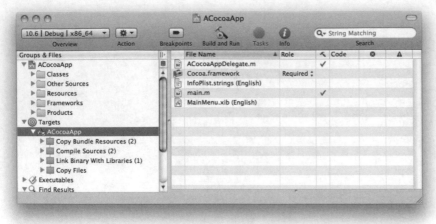

FIGURE 16-1

TARGETS VS. SUB-PROJECTS

Anytime you have a project that makes two or more products, you have a very important decision to make: you can add a new target to your existing project or you can create a new project. Which you choose will have far reaching consequences on your project's structure and maintenance. My advice is always: add a new target to your existing project unless there is a compelling need to confine the product in its own project.

In other words, if you can't think of a good reason to make it a separate project, make it a target. Managing, editing, building, and testing a project with multiple targets is generally easier and more efficient than separating the parts into individual sub-projects. The following table lists some of the pros and cons of adding a target to a project versus creating a sub-project:

CONCERN	TARGET	SUB-PROJECT
Project Folders	Targets share the same project and build folders.	Projects generally have independent project folders, but you can place multiple project documents in the same project folder. If separate, source references between them will have to extend outside the project folder. If shared, they must be configured to either peacefully share build folders or use independent build folders.
Source Items	Targets can refer to or share any of the project's source items.	Projects cannot share source items. Any common items will have to be defined twice, and maintained in parallel.

CONCERN	TARGET	SUB-PROJECT
Source Files	The source files referred by source items are inherently shared by all targets.	Source files can be shared through duplicate source items, but Xcode may not recognize them as being the same file.
Build Settings	Each target has its own build settings, but shares the common build settings for the project.	Projects have independent build settings. Build settings common to multiple projects must be maintained in parallel.
Build Configurations	All targets share the same matrix of build configurations.	Build configurations in sub-projects must be coordinated so that they match, or appropriate default configurations defined.
Source Control	All source items in a project share the same source control management repository.	Source control for separate projects must be configured independently, but could (potentially) share the same SCM repository, or a branch therein.
Xcode Management	All targets and source items belong to the open project.	Common items shared by two open projects belong to one or the other, but not both. This can sometimes lead to some confusion about which project is active.

The Ideal Single-Project Project

A single-project project is one where everything produced by the project is contained in a single project folder and described in a single project document. A separate target produces each product of the project. Target dependencies determine the build order. They all share the same source control management, object browser, project search window, build configurations, and smart groups. Examples of this kind of project are:

- ➤ A Cocoa application project that contains an embedded Spotlight indexing plug-in
- ➤ A project that produces a pair of applications, like a client and server
- ➤ A project that builds a suite of POSIX command-line tools

In each of these projects, the benefits of keeping everything in a single project are clear:

- ➤ Targets easily share common source files
- ➤ Centralized build settings and configurations
- ➤ Unified source control management and snapshots
- ➤ Multi-file searches across all targets
- ➤ A single Code Sense index

It is likely that these kinds of projects will need to share common source files, header files, and other resources. They are also likely to all use the same, or a similar, set of build settings. Changing a source file or build setting will correctly rebuild all dependent targets.

The Ideal Multi-Project Project

The kind of project that should be subdivided into multiple projects are those where you want to explicitly isolate one from the other. Idea examples would be:

➤ A Cocoa application that uses an open-source processing engine

➤ A suite of applications where each component is being developed by a separate team of engineers

➤ A framework used by other applications

In the first situation, you have your Cocoa application and another large collection of source files that belong to an open source project. The open source project is probably under its own source control management system, it might require special compiler settings to build, and probably includes a large number of internal functions that your application shouldn't use directly.

Frameworks are particularly well-suited to being sequestered into separate projects because frameworks are specifically designed to be development resources. A project using the framework has access to its API (in the form of header files), resource files, and even documentation without the need to explicitly include those files in the project.

In these situations, it's advantageous to isolate the open source code, individual applications, or frameworks into their own projects, which you can then make your project targets dependent on.

The Project in the Middle

Often, your decision won't be so cut and dried. A good example would be a project that produced a service, like a streaming media server, and a desktop application to control and configure that server.

There may not be that much code, if any, shared by the two products. It isn't clear that they need to be built using a common set of build settings, or whether having separate build settings might not be an advantage. Is each version of the desktop application intimately tied to specific versions of the server, or are the two loosely interoperable? Does one team of programmers work on the server and another on the desktop application?

These are the questions you need to ask when deciding on whether to start a second project or not. If you can't decide, start with a single project and multiple targets. It's much easier to split a project into two than trying to combine two projects into one. To split a project, start by making a copy of the entire project folder. Rename the project document, and then delete all "B" assets from project A and all "A" assets from project B.

THE ANATOMY OF A TARGET

Targets consist of several interrelated parts: dependencies, build phases, build settings, build rules, and a product, as described in the following table. Different target types may include all, some, or only one of these parts. All of the components are described in detail later in this chapter.

COMPONENT	DESCRIPTION
Dependencies	The other targets on which this target depends.
Build phases	Defines the steps required to build a target. Each phase defines a procedure and the source files involved.
Build settings	Variables available to the build phases that can be used to customize the build.
Build rules	Rules that define how files of a particular type are compiled or transformed.
Product	The end result of the target.

You edit most of these parts using various tabs in the target's Info window or via the Inspector palette. To open a target's Info window, select the target and choose Get Info from the File menu or the Right/Control-click contextual menu. For native targets (which are explained later), you can just double-click the target or select it and press the Return key. If the target you want to edit is the active target, use the Project ➪ Edit Active Target '*TargetName*' (Option+Command+E) command.

Every target has a name. You can change the name of a target by selecting the target group in the project window and choosing Rename from the Right/Control-click contextual pop-up menu. You can also edit it in the General tab of the target's Info window.

Target Dependencies

A target may depend on other targets. A target dependency is a target, either in this project or an external project, which must be built before this target can be built. Target dependencies appear in the target group before the target's build phases — an allusion to the order of build events. They are also listed in the General tab of the target's Info window.

A target build phase may also maintain its own set of internal dependencies. These are the implicit dependencies between intermediate files and the source files used to produce them. These are calculated by the target and are not under your control. Whenever possible, a target only recompiles files affected by changes made since the last build. You can see the internal dependencies at work in the details pane of the project window. The small hammer column displays a check mark for files that need to be rebuilt.

Target Build Phases

A target can have one or more build phases. You can see a target's build phases by expanding the target's group in the project window, as shown in Figure 16-2. Build phases define the broad order in which steps will occur during a build. For example, all of your C source files must be compiled into object files before those object files can be linked together. All of the object files must be linked together before the final executable can be copied into the application's bundle, and so on.

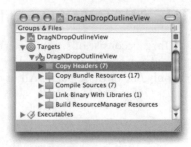

FIGURE 16-2

The order of steps *within* a build phase is entirely up to that phase. The order within some phases is fixed, whereas others are very dynamic. A build phase that compiles a gaggle of source files may compile them in alphabetical order or in the order in which they were most recently modified. It may compile them one at a time or compile twenty at a time using a network of distributed build servers. Intelligent build phases try to optimize the order whenever possible. Your only guarantee is that all of the work performed in a phase will be completed before the next phase begins.

Target Membership

Here's an important concept about targets and *target membership*: a source item is a member of a target if, and only if, it is included in one or more build phases of that target.

You see the target membership of items in your project — usually as a check box — in many places: its Info window, in the details pane, in the source group, when you add an item to your project, and elsewhere. It might seem like target membership is a Boolean property of the individual source items, but it isn't. The targets that refer to an item imply its target membership.

Changing an item's target membership has the following effects:

➤ Adding an item to a target adds that item to the (hopefully) appropriate build phase of the target.

➤ Removing an item from a target simply deletes all references to that item from all build phases of the target.

➤ If a target is disabled for an item, it means that no build phases in that target are compatible with that item's type.

For most targets, adding and removing an item from a target is a simple and predictable operation. In the case of a target that contains two or more build phases compatible with an item, you might need to fix the target membership in the target — a simple add might not insert the item into the correct phase, or phases. This is described in detail in the "Files in a Build Phase" section, later in this chapter.

Target Build Settings

If a target includes build settings, you can edit those settings in the Build tab of the Info window or Inspector palette for that target, as shown in Figure 16-3.

FIGURE 16-3

Targets can also have multiple sets of settings called build configurations. The project itself has multiple sets of build settings. Because build settings and build configurations are not unique to targets, the editing of build settings, the management of build configurations, and how they all interact with each other are explained in Chapter 17.

Target Build Rules

Targets that compile files have a set of build rules. Build rules tell a target what compiler or translator to use when building each source file. The build rules can be modified in the Rules tab of the target's Info window, shown in Figure 16-4. Each rule is a pairing of a file type, which you select using the Process menu, and a compiler, which you select using the Using menu. If necessary, you can define your own rules or redefine standards.

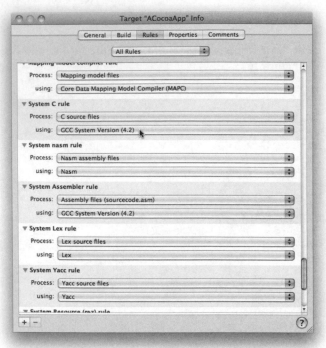

FIGURE 16-4

Target Product

Most targets produce a product. The kind of product produced is determined by the type of the target. Application targets produce applications, library targets produce libraries, command-line targets produce UNIX executables, and so on. A special type of target, called an aggregate target, doesn't produce anything itself. It exists solely to group other targets so they can be treated as a single target. In other words, it's a target that "produces" other targets.

TARGET TYPES

It's difficult to classify target types in Xcode neatly, because the types form a kind of spectrum. However, the spectrum of target types can be roughly divided between the native and non-native targets. Native targets are at one extreme of the spectrum. They are sophisticated, are tightly integrated into Xcode, are highly configurable, have a flexible number of build phases, and produce complex products (like frameworks). At the other extreme is the non-native external target. An external target simply launches some external process with the understanding that said process will do whatever is necessary to build the target. Xcode doesn't know what an external process will do, what files it depends on, or even if it produces anything. An external target has no build phases and is not configurable (from within Xcode). In between these two extremes are target types such as aggregate targets and the legacy Jam-based targets. The sophistication of these target types varies. They may have some of the same parts as native targets but are usually simpler and are not as tightly integrated into Xcode.

The type of a target is displayed in the General tab of the target's Info window. You cannot change the type of a target. If you find you are using the wrong target type, you must delete the target and create a new target of the correct type.

Native Targets

The native target types in Xcode are Application, Command-Line Tool, Dynamic Library, Static Library, Framework, Bundle, Kernel Extension, and IOKit Kernel Extension. Native targets are easily identified by their colorful and emotive target icons. Application targets have a small application icon, Command-Line Tool targets are represented by a little terminal screen, Framework targets have a toolbox icon, and the remaining targets appear as plug-ins. Native targets usually have a full complement of parts (build phases, settings, rules, and dependencies). Native targets that include an `Info.plist` file in their product also include a set of properties. See the "Properties" section, later in this chapter, for more details.

External Targets

An external target defines a build target that is produced by some external process. This was designed to permit Xcode to integrate with existing workflows based on build tools like Make or Ant. The target is little more than a placeholder. It specifies the tool that will perform the build and the arguments that are passed to it, as shown in Figure 16-5. Xcode has no knowledge of what files the process requires, what it does, or what it will produce. You cannot add project files or build phases to an external target. The section "Java and Other Jam-Based Targets" has more information.

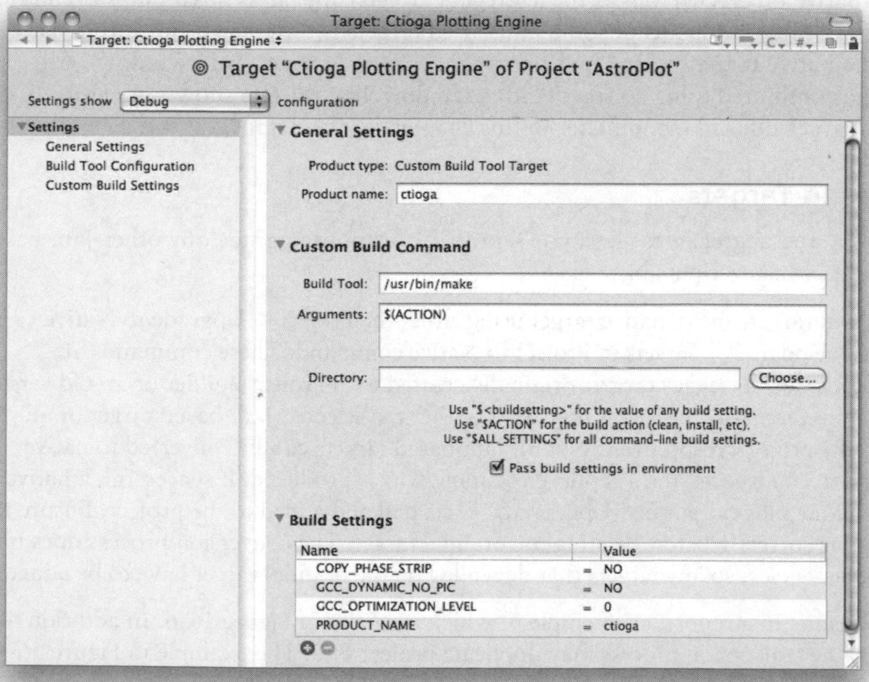

FIGURE 16-5

Aggregate Targets

Aggregate targets, as the name implies, group several targets together using dependencies. An aggregate target that depends on several different targets can be used to build all of those targets as a unit. Suppose you have developed a suite of BSD command-line tools, each produced by a separate target. To build all of these tools at once, you would create an aggregate target, say it's named "Tools," that depends on all of the Command-Line Tool targets. Now whenever you want to build all of the tools, you simply build the one Tools target. Likewise, you might have applications or other projects that depend on having all of those tools built. Making those targets dependent on the single Tools target is much easier to maintain than adding each tool target to every target that depends on them.

Aggregate targets can also be used for utilitarian purposes. Aggregate targets don't produce a product, but they can still be made to do useful work by adding Copy Files or Shell Script build phases. These build phases are executed whenever the target is built, regardless of whether it has any dependencies. See the section "Build Phases" for more details about adding build phases to a target.

Java and Other Jam-Based Targets

Xcode still includes support for the legacy Jam build system, which it inherits from its predecessor, Project Builder. A Jam-based target is a non-native target; the target's build logic is external to Xcode, and the target's configuration isn't integrated with the rest of Xcode. Jam-based targets are used to implement the external and aggregate target types, and to support legacy targets that were created in Project Builder or obsolete versions of Xcode.

Using Jam-Based Targets

All Jam-based, non-native targets (as well as the aggregate targets) appear as a red bull's-eye in the Targets smart group. Editing the details of some Jam-based targets is different from editing native targets (you configure native targets using the different panes in the target's Info window). All Jam-based targets are configured using a target editing window, like the one shown in Figure 16-5. See the "Jam-Based Target Editor" section later in this chapter for the details.

Upgrading Jam-Based Targets

Except for the external and aggregate targets, you'll probably want to upgrade any other Jam-based targets to native targets whenever possible.

Convert your Jam-based targets into a native target using either the Project ➪ Upgrade to Native Target or the Project ➪ Update All Targets in Project to Native command. These commands are enabled whenever Xcode detects legacy targets originally created with Project Builder or an old version of Xcode. These commands run a conversion process on either the selected Jam-based target or all non-native targets in the project, respectively. Not all Jam-based targets can be converted to native targets. If the conversion is unsuccessful, a report explaining why is produced. If successful, a native target with the same name plus the suffix "(Upgraded)" is created and added to the project. Ensure that the new target functions correctly before deleting the original target. The conversion process does not create new target dependencies, so any targets that depended on the original target have to be edited.

The conversion also results in a report, an example of which is shown in Figure 16-6. In addition to making a new target, the conversion process may duplicate project files. The example in Figure 16-6 shows that a duplicate of the `Info-StockMarketTicker.plist` file was made and was named

`Info-StockMarketTicker__Upgraded_.plist`. Delete the original `.plist` file when you delete the original target. You may also want to rename the new `.plist` file, which requires editing the new target's settings to match.

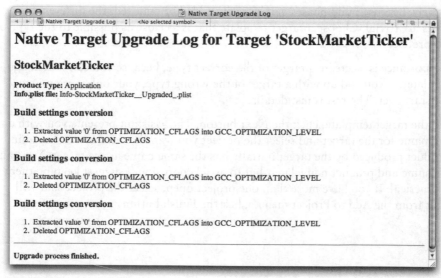

FIGURE 16-6

CREATING A TARGET

Creating a target is much like adding a new file to your project. Choose the Project ⇨ New Target command. Alternatively, Right/Control+click the Targets group and choose the Add ⇨ New Target command. Either method presents the New Target assistant, shown in Figure 16-7.

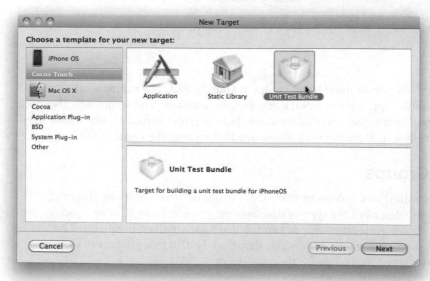

FIGURE 16-7

Choose a target template from the list. You'll immediately notice that there are far more templates than target types. Many of the templates produce targets of the same type, but are preconfigured for different purposes. For example, the Aggregate, Copy Files Target, and Shell Script Target templates all create an aggregate target with no build phases, one Copy Files build phase, or one Run Script build phase, respectively. Because build phases can be easily added or removed, the differences among these templates are trivial. Choose a target template that is as close as possible to the type of product you want to produce.

What is of utmost importance is to create a target of the correct type, because you cannot change the type of the target later. If you end up with a target of the wrong type, your only option is to delete the target and start over. The rest is just details.

After you've selected the target template, click the Next button. The assistant presents you with a dialog box to enter a name for the target and select the project you want it added to, as shown in Figure 16-8. The product produced by the target initially has the same name as the target. You can alter both the target name and product name later, but to avoid confusion, I suggest keeping them the same whenever practical. If you have more than one project open, select the project that will receive the new target from the Add to Project menu. Click the Finish button.

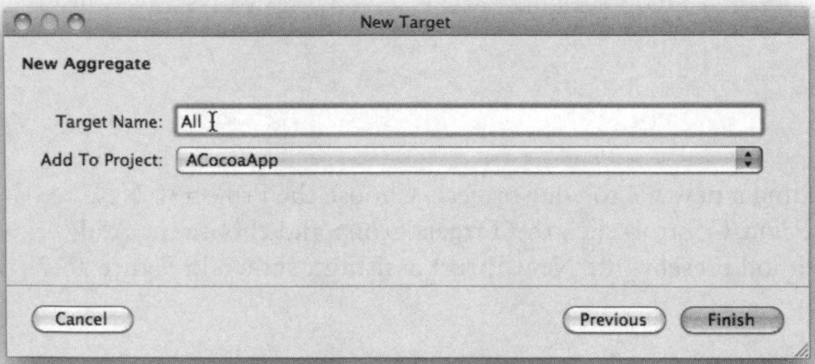

FIGURE 16-8

Some templates will also add one or more support files to your project. For example, almost any target the produces a bundle (application, framework, plug-in, unit test, and so on) will also need a `Info.plist` file to describe its contents. Adding a new bundle target automatically adds a new `Info.plist` file to your project, typically with a filename that mimics the name of the target.

Target Template Groups

Target templates are organized into groups to make them easier to locate. Start by choosing the group that most closely describes the type of development you are doing (Cocoa, Cocoa Touch, BSD), and then choose your template. Be careful of similarly named templates. The Application template in the Cocoa group produces a significantly different product than the Application template in the Cocoa Touch group.

Cocoa Touch Templates

Templates in the Cocoa Touch group create targets suitable for producing iPhone applications, static libraries, and unit tests. These are similar to the targets in the Cocoa group, but have different compiler settings and link to different frameworks.

TEMPLATE	DESCRIPTION
Application	A native iPhone or iPod Touch application target. The template adds an `Info.plist` file to your project.
Static Library	A native Static Library target that produces a static library file.
Unit Test Bundle	A unit test bundle, linked to the Foundation framework. Also adds an `Info.plist` file to your project. See Chapter 20 for more information about unit testing.

Cocoa Templates

Use these targets, listed in the following table, to produce Mac OS X applications, libraries, and shell tools.

TEMPLATE	DESCRIPTION
Application	A native Application target that produces an application bundle linked to the Cocoa framework. This template adds an `Info.plist` file to your project.
Dynamic Library	A native Dynamic Library target that produces a `.dylib` library file, itself linked to the Cocoa framework.
Framework	A native Framework bundle target. This template adds an `Info.plist` file to your project.
Loadable Bundle	A native Bundle target that produces a generic bundle linked to the Cocoa framework. This template adds an `Info.plist` file to your project.
Shell Tool	A native Command-Line target that produces a BSD executable binary.
Static Library	A native Static Library target that produces a static library file, itself linked to the Cocoa framework.
Unit Test Bundle	A native Bundle target configured to produce a unit test written using the Cocoa framework. See Chapter 20 for more information about unit testing. This template adds an `Info.plist` file to your project.

The Loadable Bundle is the catch-all template for creating virtually any kind of bundle. If you can't find a template for the particular type of bundle (application, plug-in, and so on) that you're trying to create, start with the Loadable Bundle template.

Application Plug-In Templates

The only template currently in this group is the Automator Action template:

TEMPLATE	DESCRIPTION
Automator Action	A native Bundle target that includes a Compile AppleScript Files phase, suitable for producing Automator Action bundles. This template adds an `Info.plist` file to your project.

BSD Templates

The BSD templates, listed in the following table, create targets that produce flat BSD executable or library files.

TEMPLATE	DESCRIPTION
Dynamic Library	A native Dynamic Library target that produces a `.dylib` library file.
Object File	A native Object File target that compiles a single module using the BSD APIs.
Shell Tool	A native Command-Line target that produces a BSD executable binary.
Static Library	A native Static Library target that produces a static library file.

System Plug-Ins Templates

The two templates, listed in the following table, create the specialized targets used to produce kernel extension bundles.

TEMPLATE	DESCRIPTION
Generic Kernel Extension	A Kernel Extension target that produces a kernel extension bundle.
IOKit Driver	An IOKit Kernel Extension target that produces a kernel extension bundle.

Other Templates

The targets listed in the following table create empty or placeholder targets. None of these targets produces a product, although the process launched by an external target is expected to build something.

TARGET	DESCRIPTION
Aggregate	An empty Aggregate target.
Copy Files	An Aggregate target with a single Copy Files build phase.
External	A Jam-based External target. External targets run some external process (like make) to build the target. They cannot have build phases.
Shell Script	An Aggregate target with a single Run Script build phase.

Legacy

If you upgraded an earlier version of Xcode, your installation may contain additional target templates that have since been removed from the Xcode Developer Tools. These might include Java Applet, Carbon, and other deprecated targets. For the most part, Xcode still supports these legacy target templates, but may not in the future.

Duplicating Targets

You can also create a new target by duplicating an existing one. This is especially useful if you need a new target that is very similar to one that already exists. Select the target in the Targets smart group. In the Right/Control+click contextual menu choose the Duplicate command. A duplicate of the target is created with the suffix "copy" appended to the target's name. Note that the new target is an exact duplicate except, of course, for its name. If the original target produced a product, the new target will produce the same product. Assuming you want the targets to build separate products, remember to edit the settings of the target so the two products don't overwrite one another.

Deleting Targets

To delete a target, select the target in the Targets smart group. Press the Delete key or choose Delete from the Right/Control+click contextual menu. Xcode presents a warning that removing a target will also remove the reference to it in any targets that depend on it. Click the Delete button to acknowledge the warning and delete the target.

BUILD PHASES

Build phases define the steps that must occur in order to build a target. Build phases tend to paint with a broad brush. Targets typically have one Compile Sources build phase that compiles *all* of the source files for that target, even if that includes source files from many different languages. Consequently, targets rarely have more than three or four build phases.

Use the disclosure triangle next to the target's name in the Targets smart group to reveal the build phases for the target, as shown in Figure 16-9. The list of files on which a build phase will operate, or depends, is referred to as the phase's input files. Selecting a build phase lists the input files in the details pane of the project window. Alternatively, you can use the disclosure triangle on a build phase to list the input files in the Groups & Files list. The number of input files is listed in parentheses after the name of the build phase. Note that this applies only to build phases that process files using Xcode's internal build system. The input files listed for a build phase include only those source files that you have explicitly added to the build phase. Intermediate files produced by another build phase are not listed or counted.

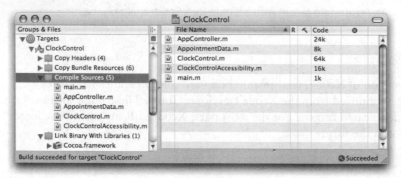

FIGURE 16-9

Build phases occur in the order in which they appear in the target. Build phases can be reordered by dragging a build phase to a new position in the target. Be *very* careful when doing this. The reason build phases exist is because build steps have to occur in a specific order for the build to be successful — you can't link code before it's compiled. About the only time you'll find yourself reordering build phases is if you add your own build phase and need that phase to occur before or after another phase. You can also reorder the files that a build phase includes. For some build phases, this may be a significant change. For others, the order of files is superfluous. You cannot drag build phases into other targets, nor can you copy them via the clipboard.

New build phases are simple to add. Select a target and choose a new build phase from the Project ⇨ New Build Phase menu or Right/Control+click an existing target or build phase, and choose an item from the Add ⇨ New Build Phase menu. Not all build phase types can be added to all target types. An aggregate target can only contain Copy Files and Run Script build phases. An external target cannot have any build phases. The New Build Phase menu lists only those phases appropriate to the selected target. After you've added the build phase, drag it to set its order in the target and then configure the new phase as desired.

To remove a build phase, select it and press the Delete key or choose Delete from the Right/Control+click contextual menu.

Files in a Build Phase

Every build phase has a set of preferred source file types. A Compile Sources phase prefers the source file types it has build rules for (.c, .cpp, .m, .l, and so on) — build rules are described later in the "Build Rules" section. The Copy Bundle Resources phase prefers the resource files one typically copies into an application's bundle (`.tiff`, `.icn`, `.png`, and so on). When you add a source file to a target, the file becomes an input file for the first phase that prefers that file type the most. If a target contains both a Copy Headers phase and a Copy Files phase, adding an `.h` file to that target adds the file to the Copy Headers phase. The Copy Headers phase is more specific than the Copy Files phase, and prefers `.h` files more than the Copy Files phase does. If a target contains only two Copy Headers phases, adding an `.h` file adds it to the first Copy Headers phase in the target, because both phases prefer an `.h` file equally.

Adding Items to Targets

You typically add files to targets via the targets list that appears when the file is created, added to the project, in the Info window for the file, or using the target check box column in the project window. This is usually foolproof and effective, allowing Xcode to choose automatically the appropriate phase to add the file to. If a target has no phases that prefer a source file's type, that file cannot be added to that target using any of the aforementioned dialogs.

Precisely Controlling Target Phase Membership

Using the target group, you have more precise control over what input files are included in what phases, and you can occasionally break the rules. You can add a source file to a build phase by dragging the file into that phase and dropping it. Figure 16-10 shows the `Image1.png` file being added to the Copy Bundle Resources phase.

You can move or copy a file from one phase to another. In the previous example, where there was both a Copy Files and a Copy Headers phase, you may really have wanted a specific header file to be in the Copy Files phase, not the Copy Headers phase. Just adding the file to the target puts it in the Copy Headers phase. Grab the file in the Copy Headers phase and move it into the Copy Files phase. Hold down the Option key before dropping it, and Xcode duplicates the reference, adding the file to both phases.

FIGURE 16-10

Using drag and drop, you can include a file in more than one phase and you can include the file in phases that don't prefer it. Let's say you have developed a Java application that dynamically produces executable Java code by manipulating a source file template and then compiling it. You want the Java source template file, `GenericTransformTemplate.java`, to be included in the application's bundle as a resource file. To accomplish this, drag the `GenericTransformTemplate.java` file into the Copy Bundle Resources phase. When the application is built, this Java source file is copied into the resource bundle of the finished application, something that would normally never happen.

Removing an Item from a Target

You can remove a source file from a target by selecting it and pressing the Delete key or choosing Delete from the Right/Control+click contextual menu. You will receive a warning from Xcode asking if you want to delete the item. Don't panic. You are only deleting the phase's reference to the source file, not the source file itself.

If you have added a source file to any phase of a target, Xcode indicates that it is a member of that target. Removing (unchecking) a target in a target list removes that file from every phase it is included in.

 It's possible to create a paradox if you have manually forced a source file to be included in a target that has no phases that prefer that file type; the target for that source file will indicate that it is a member, but the check box control for the target will be disabled (because there are no phases that prefer that type). To remove a file from a target under these circumstances, you must delete the file directly from the build phase or phases.

Build Phase Types

There are nine build phase types: Compile Sources, Compile AppleScripts, Link Binary With Libraries, Copy Headers, Copy Bundle Resources, Copy Files, Build Java Resources, Build ResourceManager Resources, and Run Script.

Compiler Phases

The Compile Sources phase is the most sophisticated of the build phases. It is responsible for compiling any kind of source file. The kinds of sources files it will compile and what compiler it will use for each are determined by the build rules for the target, described later in the "Build Rules" section. The Compile Source phase understands a vast array of build settings that apply to the compilers. It parses all of these and makes the appropriate adjustments to the parameters passed to each compiler.

The Compile AppleScripts phase is similar to Compile Sources, but it only compiles AppleScript source files. The Build ResourceManager Resources phase is another specialized compiler phase just for resource definitions files. It compiles and merges legacy .r and .rsrc files to produce a resource file in the product's bundle, or inserts them into the resource fork of the product file. You're not likely to run across any ResourceManager Resource phases unless you're working on older Carbon projects.

The Link Binary With Libraries phase is the companion to the Compile Sources phase. It takes whatever intermediate files were produced by the Compile Sources phase and links them together, along with whatever libraries and frameworks they need. The input files to the link phase are the external libraries and frameworks that the object files (from the previous phase) need to be linked to.

Copy Phases

The Copy Headers, Copy Bundle Resources, and (legacy) Build Java Resources phases are specialized versions of the Copy Files phase. Their sole purpose is to copy files into the product's bundle.

Copy Headers is designed for use with framework and library targets. It uses the "role" of its input files, be they public or private, and copies them to the appropriate location in the output project. The role of a header is set using the role column of the details pane with that file or phase selected.

Copy Bundle Resources copies any input file into the Resources folder of the product's bundle. This is the phase to use if you want a literal copy of a file stored in your bundle's resource folder for access at run time. This phase is also responsible for constructing and copying the Info.plist file into the product's bundle. (See the "Properties" section later in this chapter for more about how to configure the Info.plist file.)

The Copy Files phase is a utilitarian phase that copies all of the phase's input files or folders to the destination of your choice. That destination is set in the Info window of the phase, as shown in Figure 16-11. The destination location can be either an absolute path or a path relative to the product's location. For targets that produce a bundle, predefined locations are provided that will target many of the standard locations in the product's bundle. An absolute path is just that. Use this to copy files to a particular installation or test location.

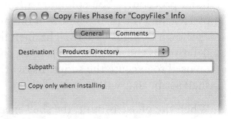

FIGURE 16-11

Relative paths require a bit of an explanation. The build location — the location to which the product of a target will be written — is unique for each build configuration. If you have two build configurations, Debug and Release, every target will produce two different products: a Debug product and a Release product. The remaining paths in the destination menu are all relative to the product's output directory. The choices are the output directory itself or one of the standard folders inside a bundle, assuming the target produces a bundle. (See Chapter 17 for a complete explanation of build locations and build configurations.) The path field can be left blank for any choice other than Absolute. Any folders that do not exist when the phase executes are automatically created.

The path can also contain build variables using the form $(BUILD_VAR). The macro will be substituted for its actual value when the build phase runs. By using build variables in the path, you can customize the normal destination location calculated by Xcode.

Speaking of build locations, remember when Chapter 5 mentioned that product-relative references are based on the active build configuration and target? This fact is most applicable to product file references used as input files to a Copy Files phase. Product references also change based on the active build configuration, making both the source and destination locations of the phase variable. An example would be an application that includes a BSD executable in its bundle. A Copy Files phase could be used to copy the project-relative product produced by the BSD target into the resource bundle being produced by the application target. Both the source (product reference) and the destination (application bundle) are variable. When built using the Debug build configuration, the Debug version of the BSD product is copied into the Debug version of the application bundle. When the Release configuration is active, the Release version of the BSD product is copied into the Release version of the application bundle.

If the Copy Only When Installing option is set, the copy phase is only executed when the build is being performed with the install option set. You can do this from within Xcode by turning on the DEPLOYMENT_LOCATION build setting or passing the install option to the xcodebuild tool. Both of these are described in Chapter 17.

Script Phase

The Run Script phase is the "backdoor" by which you can interject virtually any custom build procedure. You configure a Run Script phase using the Info window of the phase, as shown in Figure 16-12. The Shell field determines the shell, or interpreter, that will be used to execute the script. Below that is the shell script that will be executed.

When the phase is built, the shell executable is put on a so-called "she-bang" line (#!/path/to/shell) and the remaining script is appended to it. The whole thing is written into an executable script file and run using the sh tool. One side effect is that the zeroth argument to the script will be the path to the temporary script itself, which makes it relatively uninformative.

The Shell field can be any valid interpreter. It could be perl, ruby, awk, or php. It doesn't matter, as long as the given interpreter can execute the script file. Most of the build settings are transferred into environment variables before the script is executed, so your script has unfettered access to your build settings.

FIGURE 16-12

If you're interested, or are having trouble with the build settings passed to your script, check the Show Environment Variables In Build Log option. This option dumps the entire shell environment prior to execution into the build log for later analysis.

Checking the Run Script Only When Installing option prohibits the script from running unless the DEPLOYMENT_LOCATION build setting is turned on or the install command is passed to the xcodebuild tool.

Xcode, of course, has no idea what your script will do, what files it needs, or what it produces. Assuming that the script produces some output files from some input files, Xcode would like to optimize the build by skipping this build phase if the modification dates of the output files are newer than the input files. You can satisfy Xcode's curiosity by manually setting the Input Files and Output Files for the phase. Click the + button to add an input or output file to the list. When the new entry appears, enter the file's path. Sadly, you can't drag a source file from the project window into the list. However, once an entry is created you can drag a source file into the field and then edit the path. It can be an absolute path or a path relative to the project directory. The script is run only if the modification date of one or more of the input files is more recent than the oldest output file. If either list is empty, the script runs every time.

The files in the Input Files list are not *passed to the script as parameters, nor are they piped to it via* stdin. *They are used by Xcode solely to determine if the script should be run. It is up to the shell script to read the listed Input Files and produce all of the files promised in the Output Files. If you want to reuse a script in multiple targets and need a variable list of input or output files, define them in a custom build setting.*

BUILD RULES

Build rules define the transformation of source files into their compiled results. The compiler phase uses the target's build rules to determine which compiler should be used to compile each source file. For example, a build rule might specify that all C source files (C, C++, and Objective-C) are compiled using the gcc compiler.

A build rule applies to all the files of a specific type. The type of a file is determined by its extension *or* the file type assigned to that source file. A file's type is typically in agreement with the filename extensions, but it doesn't have to be. You can change the file type of a .java source file to sourcecode.cpp. The Compile Sources phase will then apply the sourcecode.cpp rule to that file as if it were a C++ source file — probably without much success.

You'll probably never need to alter the build rules in Xcode. However, there are several reasons why you might want to:

➤   Force Xcode to use an older, newer, or custom compiler.

➤   Add a rule to compile a source type that is not normally compiled by Xcode.

➤   Add a pre- or post-processing script to every compilation.

➤   Define your own transformation.

You can examine and alter the build rules, previously shown in Figure 16-4, for a target in the target's Info window. When it comes time to compile an input file, the file is tested against each rule starting from the top of the list. The first rule that matches a particular input file is the rule used to compile that file.

 Each target has one set of build rules, shared by all of the build phases in that target. You cannot create different rules for different phases of the same target.

Every set of build rules includes a set of system rules that cannot be edited. The system rules are always at the bottom of the list. You can add your own custom rules to a target. These custom rules can only be added to the top of the list and are always evaluated before any of the system rules. If you define a rule that matches the same type of file as a system rule, your custom rule is used instead. Click and drag the title of a custom rule to reorder it in the list.

Creating Custom Build Rules

To add a new rule, click the + button at
the bottom of the screen. A new, undefined
rule is created. Another way to create a
new rule is to modify one of the system
rules; Xcode balks and warns you that you
cannot edit system rules, as shown in
Figure 16-13. Click the Make a Copy
button and Xcode duplicates the system as
a new custom rule, which you are free to alter.

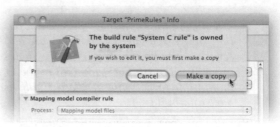

FIGURE 16-13

Choose the type of file that the rule will
process from the Process menu. This can
be one of the Xcode file types, as set in the
source file's properties, or it can be a filename
pattern. To match a filename pattern, choose
the Source Files With Names Matching
option at the bottom of the menu and a
filename pattern field appears, as shown in
Figure 16-14. Enter the filename pattern,
such as `*.xml`. This field is a globbing
pattern like you would use in the shell; it
is not a regular expression. The pattern is
case-sensitive. By using filename patterns,
it is possible to partially override system
rules. For example, the "C source files"
type encompasses C (`.c`), C++ (`.cpp`), and

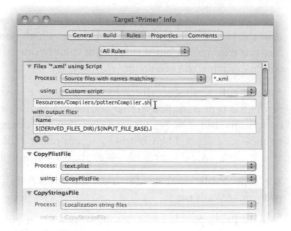

FIGURE 16-14

Objective-C (`.m`) files. By creating a custom rule that matches only `*.c` files, you can redirect plain C
files to an alternate compiler while allowing C++ and Objective-C files to "fall through" and match
the default system rule for compiling any kind of C file.

*In Xcode 3.0 and 3.1, if you want to use a particular version of the compiler, say
gcc 3.3 instead of gcc 4.0, you should create a custom build rule that overrides
the system build rule for C files. In other versions of Xcode the GCC_VERSION
build setting selects the desired compiler. That setting was deprecated in Xcode
3.0, but is supported again in Xcode 3.2 (with many new choices).*

*If you choose to redefine the C compiler by creating a custom build rule, you
must duplicate the rule in every target. Currently, there is no means by which
you can edit the build rules for the entire project; you must create a new build
rule in every target that compiles C source files. Modify the System C rule to
quickly create a custom C rule, and then select the desired compiler.*

A less refined approach is to use the `gcc_select` *tool to change the default gcc
compiler for your entire system. This will change the default compiler for every
project you build on your system. See* `man gcc_select` *for details.*

Customizing the Build Rule Compiler

With the file type selected, choose the compiler that will process each file of this type with the Using menu. This can be one of the standard Xcode compilers or you can direct compilations to your own script or tool by choosing the Custom Script item. When you choose a custom script as the compiler additional fields appear, as previously shown in Figure 16-14. The first field is the path and filename of the script to execute. The path can be an absolute path or a path relative to the project folder. The With Output Files control lets you specify what files are produced when your compiler is executed. The naming of output files is dynamic and requires build rule variables, described in the next section.

Build Rule Variables

When your custom script or tool is executed, the following occurs:

➤ The current directory is set to the project's folder.

➤ Environment variables are created that describe the file that Xcode wants processed and where Xcode expects the output file, or files, to be written.

➤ The rule's script or tool is executed.

Note that no parameters are passed to the script. The script must determine what to process by examining its environment variables. If you're using an existing compiler or other tool that expects the input file to be in an argument, you will need to write a "wrapper" script that extracts the environment values and passes them to your compiler. The following table lists the key environment variables passed to a custom build script when it is executed:

ENVIRONMENT VARIABLE	DESCRIPTION
INPUT_FILE_PATH	The full path, including the filename, to the source file being processed.
INPUT_FILE_DIR	Just the directory portion of INPUT_FILE_PATH, without the filename.
INPUT_FILE_NAME	Just the filename portion of INPUT_FILE_PATH, without the directory.
INPUT_FILE_BASE	The base name of the file; in other words, the value of INPUT_FILE_NAME without any filename extension.
INPUT_FILE_SUFFIX	Just the filename extension of INPUT_FILE_NAME.
DERIVED_FILES_DIR	The complete path to the directory where Xcode expects the intermediate files to be written. Intermediate files are kept between builds and used to determine if the source file needs to be compiled again by comparing the modification dates of the two.
TARGET_BUILD_DIR	The complete path to the target's product directory; in other words, where the final product of this target is being constructed.

The following is a simple shell script that demonstrates the use of a custom build rule script. In this example, the project includes XML files that define patterns of text. The project contains an SXL transform file that converts an XML file into a LEX file describing the pattern. The details are unimportant. The key ingredients are that there is *some process* that converts the input file into one or more output files and the shell's environment variables tell the script where the source and destinations are.

```bash
#!/bin/bash

# Xcode compile script
# Run the input file through the java XSLT transformer
# The KeyPatternToLEX.sxlt file contains a transform that
#  will convert the pattern record into LEX syntax.

XSLT = "Source/Transforms/KeyPatternToLEX.sxlt"
IN = "$INPUT_FILE_PATH"
OUT = "${DERIVED_FILES_DIR}/${INPUT_FILE_BASE}.l"

java org.mycompany.patterns.Transformer "$XSLT" "$IN" > "$OUT"
```

Writing the Build Rule's Output Files

If the files produced by the script go into the target's product, they should be written to the appropriate location in `TARGET_BUILD_DIR`.

If the script produces intermediate output files, it should write those to the `DERIVED_FILES_DIR` directory. Intermediate output files are files that will be consumed later in this phase. If a compiler produces one or more intermediate output files, Xcode takes those files and runs them back through the build rules. It continues this process until no rule matches the files. This example defined a rule that takes an XML file and produces a LEX source file. When built, Xcode will run the XML file though the custom build script, producing a LEX source file. That LEX source file will be run through the rules again. This time, it will match the LEX rule that will compile the LEX file into a C source file. That C source file is again run through the build rules, this time matching the System C rule, and ultimately producing an object file.

This brings up an interesting conundrum. Xcode has no idea what a custom build script produces or where. You have to communicate that to the build rule by listing the files that the script will produce. Under the With Output Files section in the build rule, enter the filename that will be produced by the script. You can use any of the environment variables listed in the previous table. For this example, the output file is `$(DERIVED_FILES_DIR)/$(INPUT_FILE_BASE).l`, which agrees with the output filename in the script. The syntax for using environment variables in the output files list is `$(VAR_NAME)`, which may be different than the syntax required by your script's interpreter. If the script produces more than one file, say a matched pair of `.h` and `.c` files, add more files by clicking the + button immediately below the list.

A Build Rule Example

Assume a hypothetical application, called PrimeRules, that needs a precompiled table of prime numbers. You've already written a shell script that generates the C source code for a table of prime numbers between 2 and some arbitrary limit. Now you could run that script manually, capture the output, save it as a file, and add that to the project. If the maximum number ever changed, you'd have to repeat the process. The solution is awkward, and the generated C table could (potentially) be huge.

What you'd like is simply to set the maximum prime number somewhere in the project and have the build automatically generate the table of primes, compile it, and link the results into your application. One solution is to use a custom build rule:

1. Start with a Command Line project that produces a BSD executable.

2. Add the compilePrimeTables.sh shell script to your project. (Not strictly necessary, but you'd want to check it into source control and make it obvious that it's part of the project.) The script should not be included in any targets.

3. Add a new build rule to the PrimeRules target, as shown in Figure 16-15. The rule takes *.primetable files and uses the compilePrimeTables.sh script to transform them into C source files.

4. Create a new knownprimes.primetable file and add it to the project. Edit the file; it should contain nothing except a single number.

5. Add the knownprimes.primetable file to the PrimeRules target by dragging it into the target's Compile Sources build phase.

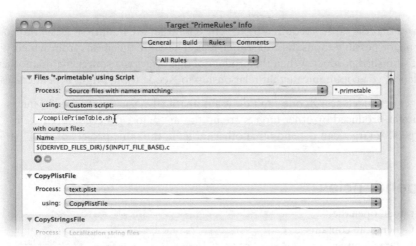

FIGURE 16-15

The project is now finished, and should look something like the one in Figure 16-16.

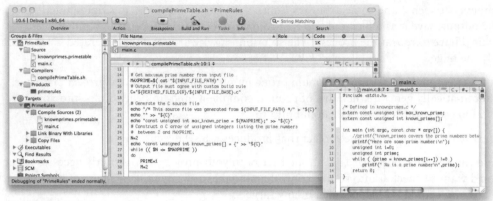

FIGURE 16-16

When the PrimeRules target is built, the Compile Sources phase runs each of its source items through the build rules for the target. The `main.c` file gets compiled as you would expect. Because of your custom build rule, the `knownprimes.primetable` file runs the `compilePrimeTables.sh` script, which produces an intermediate `.c` file. The intermediate file is run back through the rules again, and is eventually compiled by the C compiler.

The two final object files, `main` and `knownprimes`, are linked together to form the finished executable.

DEPENDENCIES

A target dependency ensures that the targets required by the current target are built first. Basic targets produce *a* product from one, or possibly thousands, of source files. These are the atoms from which you assemble your project's finished product. When the product of one target is a source file in another target, it creates a dependency; you communicate that relationship to Xcode using target dependencies.

You must define your target dependencies; Xcode can't do it automatically. You create dependencies to guarantee that source items produced by other targets are up-to-date before proceeding, as well as to order and group targets. A target can depend on another target in the same project or in a different project.

Adding Target Dependencies

To add a dependency to a target, open the target's Info window. The General tab contains the Direct Dependencies list. Drag a target, or targets, from the project's Groups & Files list into the list. Or, you can click the + button just below the list and Xcode presents a list of targets from which to choose, as shown in Figure 16-17. Select one or more targets from the list and click the Add Target button. To remove a target, select it in the list and click the – button.

FIGURE 16-17

Xcode (cleverly) prevents you from creating circular dependencies. Targets in the list that contain a dependency to the target you are editing, either directly or indirectly through other targets, are disabled and cannot be added.

After you've added target dependencies, they also appear along with the other build phases of the target. This brings up the second way of creating target dependencies; you can add dependencies by dragging one target directly into another target's group.

Logically, all dependent targets are built before any of the target's build phases begin, and the order in the target group reflects this. Just as you can reorder build phases, you can reorder dependent targets to control the order in which they are built. However, you cannot move a dependent target *after* a build phase.

Adding Project Dependencies

You can also make a target dependent on a target in a different project. This is called a *cross-project dependency*. Before you can create a cross-project dependency, you must first add the sub-project to your project using any of the techniques described in Chapter 5. The easiest methods are to use the Project ⇨ Add to Project command and choose the sub-project's document (.xcodeproj). You can also simply drag the project document from the Finder into the source group. The Add to Project dialog box prompts you to select the targets for the sub-project, which you can ignore — regardless of which targets you select, the sub-project will not be added to any targets. What appears in your source group is a project reference group, illustrated with a small Xcode project icon. Expand the contents of the sub-project group and you will find all of the products (not the targets) that the sub-project produces, as shown in Figure 16-18. These source items are references to the products produced by the sub-project; use them the same way you would use the product items produced by the project itself.

FIGURE 16-18

After you've added the sub-project, it appears in the list of potential target dependencies as a group of targets, as shown in Figure 16-19. Select and add any of the cross-project targets. When a cross-project target is listed in the target's dependencies, Xcode lists the target name and the project that contains it.

FIGURE 16-19

Some potentially important differences exist in how a project target and a cross-project target are built. The primary consideration is the build settings that will be used. Every target in the same project shares the same set of build configurations, so the Deployment version of one target always depends on the Deployment version of its dependent target. This is not necessarily true of cross-project targets, which might have a completely different set of build configurations. See Chapter 17 for a discussion on how Xcode handles build settings in other projects as well as shared build locations.

Strategies for Target Dependencies

Target dependencies serve a number of purposes. They:

➤ Construct products

➤ Control build order

➤ Aggregate targets

The most common reason for a project to have multiple targets is because it produces multiple products. These are often intermediate products that are later combined into a final product by another target. For example, an application that includes two executable BSD command-line programs in its resource bundle requires three targets: an application target and two command-line targets. To produce the bundle, the application target depends on the other two command-line targets. The products of the two command-line targets are added to the application's Copy Bundle Resources phase. Whenever the application target is built, Xcode ensures that the two command-line tools are built first; then during the Copy Bundle Resources phase, it copies the two tools into the final product while constructing the application's bundle.

Large projects can be made more manageable by isolating common code into libraries or separate projects, which can be built using a single target. All of the other products that rely on that common code will have a dependency on that single target. Whenever any of those products are built, Xcode first makes sure that the common library target is built first.

Target dependencies also impose order on the build process. All dependent targets must be completely and successfully built before a target begins to build. In the "Build Rules" section, you added rules to turn XML files into object files. The assumption was that the individual source files and their outputs are all independent of each other. It didn't matter which source files, or in what order, Xcode decided to build these files. Often, as in the case of C source files, this doesn't matter, but what if it did? In the Copy Bundle Resources phase example, used earlier, the phase clearly expects all of the source items to be built already. You solve this by moving the compilation of the prerequisite files into another target, and then create a target dependency to ensure that these are all built beforehand.

Aggregate targets depend on other targets, but don't build anything themselves. An aggregate target effectively groups other targets so that you, or another target, can build multiple targets by referring to a single target. When you build in Xcode, you always build the single active target. If your project produces several products, which aren't dependent on one another, you can create an aggregate target to build them all at once. Let's say you have a project that produces two applications, a client and a server. To build both the client and server at once, create an aggregate target that depends on both. Setting the active target to the aggregate targets causes both applications to be built using a single build command.

By combining target dependencies, you can create large trees of targets. It would not be uncommon to have an aggregate target that builds five applications, each of which depends on a single common framework, which in turn depends on building several libraries. The Xcode build system is intelligent and eliminates all excess building of targets. Building that single top-level aggregate target will only cause the common framework target to be built once. As Xcode progresses through the build, it knows what targets have already been built. Before the first application is built, Xcode first builds the framework target, which in turn builds its dependent targets. However, the other four applications can then be built without rebuilding the framework target.

BUILD SETTINGS

Most targets have their own set of build settings, accessible in the Build tab of the target's Info window. Build settings are a collection of named values (key/value pairs) used to customize a target's behavior. You can edit any of the predefined build settings. You can also define your own variable names and assign them any value you choose. All build settings are accessible by the target and all of its build phases.

Xcode defines a large number of predefined build settings, and the Xcode-supplied build phases expect specific variables with strictly defined values. As an example, the INFOPLIST_FILE setting tells the Copy Bundle Resources phase where to get the Info.plist file for the bundle. The GCC_UNROLL_LOOPS setting tells the Compile Sources phase to pass the -funroll-loops flag to the gcc compiler. There are hundreds of predefined settings. This chapter explores some of them, some are covered in the "Building Projects" chapter, and still others in the "Debugging" chapter. Many are specific to the compiler or linker. For more details, consult the build settings help or your compiler's documentation.

A target can have more than one complete set of build settings. Each set is called a build configuration. By using build configurations, you can use a single target to produce variations of the same product. In addition to targets, both the project and individual files define their own build settings; the build settings for a target form one layer in the build settings hierarchy. Target build settings are part of a larger system of build variables, inheritance, and build configurations, discussed in Chapter 17.

JAM-BASED TARGET EDITOR

As I mentioned earlier, the external target type, as well as some legacy targets, use the Jam build system. If you need to configure an external target, or have inherited an old project that you can't easily upgrade, you'll need to read this section.

In the Jam build system, a target editor window performs the same functions as that of the Build Settings tab, the properties editor (see the next section), and the build phase Info windows found in Xcode. Double-click a Jam-based target or select it and press Return to open its target editor window, as shown in Figure 16-20. Jam-based targets still have an Info window, which you can open using the Get Info command, but it only permits editing of the target's name, dependencies, and comments.

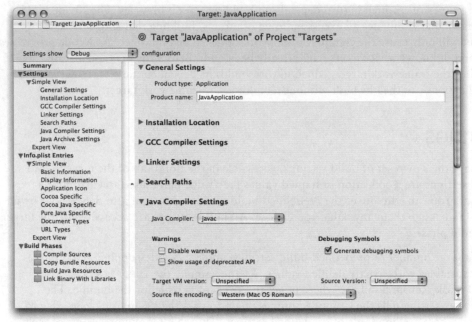

FIGURE 16-20

If you have used Project Builder in the distant past, this interface will look very familiar to you. In fact, it *is* the interface used in earlier versions of Xcode. The Jam-based settings window isn't quite as flexible, intelligent, or well integrated into Xcode as its native cousin. Nevertheless, most of the settings that you would find in the Info window of a native target are here, just in a different organization.

The settings that are available depend on the type of target. Generally, every target has a Settings group that controls the build settings for that target. Similar to the panes in the Info window, the settings are subdivided into groups for easier browsing. Selecting an individual setting or a group of settings reveals them in the right pane. Edit any of the settings as needed. At the bottom of each major section of settings is an Expert View group. This displays all of the setting in their raw form. You can also edit any of the settings here, or add your own build variables. The editing of settings in expert view is not intelligent, so be careful that the values you enter here are valid. A field that expects to be either YES or NO may not be happy if you set it to 1. Also, custom variables only appear in the expert view.

A build configuration menu has been added to the target editor to make the Jam-based settings compatible with the newer Xcode system of build configurations. Select the build configuration you want to work with from the Settings Show Configuration menu. All changes will be applied to that configuration. However, the target editor interface is not really build-configuration savvy. Unlike the settings editor for native targets, it does not highlight settings that differ from the project build settings. You can't view a combined display of all of the build settings, nor can you set a build setting for all configurations at once. If you need to change a build setting in a Jam-based target for all build configurations, you must enter it separately for each configuration.

Also in this window are the target's build phases. You can manipulate the build phases of a Jam-based target in its settings window or from the project window, as described earlier in the chapter for native targets.

Finally, if the target produces a bundle the Jam-based target editor also defines all of the `Info` `.plist` settings for the product. You can define simple property values in the expert view, which become tagged values in the product's `Info.plist` file.

PROPERTIES

Native targets that produce an `Info.plist` file as part of their product have a Properties tab in their Info window, as shown in Figure 16-21.

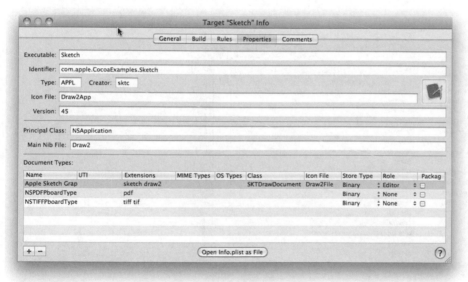

FIGURE 16-21

Each field in the Properties tab becomes one of the standard properties in the `Info.plist` file. For example, the Executable field becomes the `CFBundleExecutable` property in the `Info.plist` file. The Identifier field becomes the `CFBundleIdentifier` property, and so on. Make sure these values are correct, because Xcode does not check their validity. Depending on the type of product, any or all of these values may be superfluous. The Runtime Configuration Guidelines at `http://developer.apple.com/mac/library/documentation/MacOSX/Conceptual/BPRuntimeConfig/` has more details.

At the bottom of the pane are the document types that your application creates, owns, understands, or works with. This information is used by Launch Services to relate document files with applications. Each line defines a single document type. You can add or delete document types using the + and – buttons at the bottom of the pane. Double-click any field in the list to edit it.

The Version field contains the version of your application, bundle, or framework. This is not, however, the version number that will appear to the user in the Finder's Get Info window. To set that, you need to define the CFBundleShortVersionString property.

Now you're probably wondering where to set the CFBundleShortVersionString property. Actually, scores of other properties have meaning in an Info.plist file that do not have a convenient user interface in the Properties tab. To set any of the less common properties, click the Open Info.plist as File button at the bottom of the pane. This button opens the Info.plist file in an editor window — this is the same as opening the Info.plist file from the project source group — as shown in Figure 16-22. Here you can edit the property values in the document, much like you do the build settings; the only significant difference is that the property lists are hierarchical. The values that you set here will become the Info.plist file when the bundle is assembled. You'll notice that all of the values you set in the Properties tab also appear in the Info.plist file editor. Each field in the Properties tab corresponds to a specific Info.plist key. You can change the values in either place.

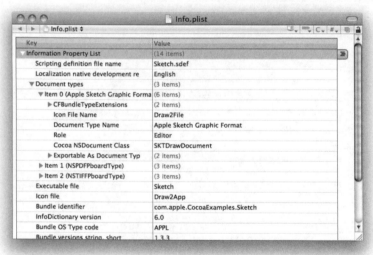

FIGURE 16-22

You'll also notice that the Info.plist file includes variable values, like ${PRODUCT_NAME}. As you will see in the next chapter, the Info.plist file can be additionally processed by the gcc compiler. Together, these allow you to use build setting variable names, conditional statements, and preprocessor macros in your Info.plist file — making it more of a template than a literal data file.

If you need to "freely edit" the contents of a Info.plist file, Right/Control-click the source item in the project and choose Open As ➪ Source Code File. This opens the same file in its raw XML format. Being able to freely edit an Info.plist file has its downside: you can, quite easily, alter the file so that it is no longer a valid XML file. If you do this, Xcode refuses to display the file in the Properties tab or editor. Correct the syntax of the file and the familiar properties interface returns.

PRODUCTS

Most targets produce a product. Targets that produce a product create a product source item in the Products group, as shown in Figure 16-23. In this sense, the Products group is more like a smart group than a source group.

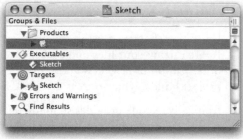

FIGURE 16-23

You use a product source reference just like you would any other source file item. For example, to include a command-line tool produced by a Shell Tool target in the bundle of a Cocoa application, you would do the following:

1. Make the Cocoa application target dependent on the Shell Tool target.

2. Add a Copy Files build phase to the Cocoa application target.

3. Configure the build phase to copy its source file(s) into the Resources section of the application bundle.

4. Drag the `shelltool` product from the Products group and drop it into the Copy Files build phase of the Cocoa application target.

When the application target is built, the shell tool target will be built first. The product of that build will then be copied into the final application bundle.

Like any source reference, the product reference turns red if the product that it refers to doesn't exist. Unlike source references, this isn't necessarily a bad thing. It just means that the product hasn't been built yet.

As explained in Chapter 5, the path type of a product is relative to the build product. Each build configuration has a different product location, so the product references change whenever the active build configuration changes. This means that if you add a product reference to to a target, the file the reference points to will change whenever you change the active build configuration. This is normally exactly what you want. When your build configuration is set to Debug, all product references refer to the Debug version of those products.

You cannot change the reference type of a product reference, nor can you rename or delete a product reference. To change a product you must edit the target that produces it. To delete a product you must delete the target that produces it.

All native targets that produce a product have a Product Name build setting. This setting defines the name of the product the target will produce. Changing this build setting changes the name of the product, renames the product reference in the source group, and updates any other targets that refer to it.

EXECUTABLES

Targets that produce executable programs also create an executable. Executables appear in the Executables smart group, which was also shown in Figure 16-23. Opening the Info window for an executable allows you to define the run time environment used when the executable is launched from within Xcode. Executables, and custom executables, are explained in Chapter 18.

SUMMARY

Up to this chapter, most of the organization of your project has been for convenience and clarity. Reorganizing your files and source groups has little impact on what your project builds, but the organization of targets literally shapes the end result of your project. Targets define what your project builds, what sources are used, how those sources are compiled, and in what order.

Ironically, Xcode provides so many templates with preconfigured targets that you may never need to deal with targets much beyond tweaking a few build settings, but a keen understanding of targets, their component parts, and how they can be interlinked is critical to constructing and maintaining complex projects.

If targets are the engine of your project, then the build commands are the fire that drives them. The next chapter looks at firing up those targets, controlling when and how they are built.

17

Building Projects

WHAT'S IN THIS CHAPTER?

➤ Starting and stopping builds

➤ Selecting a build target and settings

➤ Navigating build transcripts, warnings, and errors

➤ Understanding build settings and build configurations

➤ Editing build settings

➤ Distributing builds to a workgroup

Building projects is Xcode's ultimate ambition. It might not be yours — you probably want your finished application to run flawlessly and be wildly popular. While Xcode does provide additional tools for debugging and performance analysis that are covered in subsequent chapters — sorry, it can't do much about your application's popularity — its central purpose is to faithfully compile and assemble your finished application.

This chapter explains how to choose what you want built and how to start, stop, and customize the build process. This chapter also explains build settings and build configurations, which are used to customize everything from compiler options to packaging, so your products come out just the way you want them to.

Starting a build is relatively simple, and is described first. After that, the chapter covers targets selection, the build window preferences, and build locations. Builds often don't go flawlessly, so the next sections describe how to dig into the details of your build transcript and navigate any warnings or errors.

The bulk of this chapter explores the build settings: a multi-dimensional hierarchy of named values that control everything from the name of your application to what compiler errors are important. Knowing how to organize, find, edit, and customize your build settings is critical to using Xcode effectively. This is followed by a section describing some of the more important build settings.

Finally, I describe how to distribute your builds to a network of other Xcode users for improved productivity.

STARTING AND STOPPING A BUILD

To build your project, choose one of the Build commands:

➤ Build ➪ Build (Command+B)

➤ Build ➪ Build and Analyze (Shift+Command+A)

➤ Build ➪ Build and Run (Command+Return)

➤ Build ➪ Build and Run - Breakpoints Off (Command+R)

➤ Build ➪ Build and Debug - Breakpoints On (Command+Y)

➤ Or from Interface Builder, File ➪ Build and Go in Xcode (Shift+Command+R)

The Build ➪ Build command builds the currently active target of the currently active project using the currently active build configuration. The section "Selecting the Active Target and Build Configuration" describes how to change these.

The Build ➪ Build command simply builds the active target and stops. All of the remaining commands first build the active target, and then perform some other action, like running the active executable, starting the debugger, or initiating performance analysis tools. These are all shorthand commands for common sequences that you'll repeat every day; the command Build ➪ Build and Run is identical to choosing Build ➪ Build followed by Run ➪ Run. The build performed in all cases is identical.

These same commands can be invoked from toolbar buttons, as shown in Figure 17-1, if you find that more convenient. Xcode provides three build buttons for toolbars: Build, Build and Run/Debug, and the Build (menu). The Build and the Build and Run/Debug buttons are the same as the Build ➪ Build, Build ➪ Build and Run - Breakpoints Off, and Build ➪ Build and Debug - Breakpoints On commands, respectively. Holding down the Option key turns the Build and Run button into the Build and Debug button, shown in the lower portion of Figure 17-1.

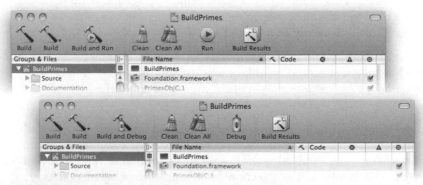

FIGURE 17-1

The Build button with the drop-down triangles is a combination of a Build button and a drop-down menu of build and clean commands. The clean commands are described later in the "Clean Builds" section. Click it quickly to execute the Build command. Click and hold to select one of the other commands. This toolbar button is useful if you want to keep Build, Clean, and Clean All buttons in your toolbar, but are short on toolbar space.

The progress and results of the build are displayed in the build window for the project. The build window is covered in detail in the "The Build Window" section. The progress of a build also appears in the Activity Viewer window, and in the status bar — at the bottom of many Xcode windows. The status bar shows a one-line summary of the build's progress, as shown in Figure 17-2. At the right end of the bar is a small round progress indicator with Xcode's estimate of how much of the build has been completed.

Precompiling 3 of 3 prefix headers...   Brick House (3 of 3)

FIGURE 17-2

When the build is finished, a completion statement replaces the progress message. If the build is successful, the message "Build succeeded" is displayed. If not, the message indicates that the build failed, possibly with an explanation of why. It may also include a count of the number of errors or warnings that were encountered.

> *On systems with multiple processors, multi-core processors, or in a distributed build workgroup, Xcode will attempt to perform build tasks within a single target in parallel. By default, Xcode completes all of the phases in a target before building the next target. If you have many relatively independent targets, consider enabling the Build Independent Targets In Parallel option found in the General tab of the project's Info window (see Figure 17-13). Xcode will then build dependent targets in parallel, whenever possible.*

You can build only one target in a project at a time, but you can start a build in multiple projects simultaneously.

Selecting the Active Target and Build Configuration

All of the previously described build commands begin a build based on what's "active" at that time. These five items define what the "active" target of the build is:

➤   The current project

➤   The active target

➤ The active build configuration

➤ The active architecture

➤ The active SDK

The current project is implied.

The active target is set using the Project ➪ Set Active Target menu, or from the toolbar — toolbar controls are described a little later. Xcode only builds a single target. If you need to build multiple targets you must create target dependencies to first build the subordinate targets, or create an aggregate target to group several targets into one, as described in Chapter 16.

 Changing the active target may also change the active executable. The active executable is the executable product that will be launched by any of the Run, Debug, or Analyze commands. See Chapter 18 for more about executables.

The active build configuration is set using the Project ➪ Set Active Build Configuration menu (or via the toolbar). The active build configuration defines which set of build settings should be used to build the active target. Build settings and configurations are described later in this chapter.

The active architecture and SDK can be set using the Project ➪ Set Active Architecture and Project ➪ Set Active SDK menus. These settings are actually overrides of standard build settings. You can effect the same changes by setting them in the Xcode interface or by editing the appropriate build setting for the active configuration. These settings are handy, because you often want to build against a different SDK or for a different device architecture without having to alter your build settings.

The active SDK settings have an explicit Use Base SDK setting, which defers to the Base SDK setting in your active build configuration. If you've selected a specific SDK in your build settings, the menu will let you choose a newer, but not an older, SDK with which to build.

In projects with multiple products, build configurations, and deployments, switching between different targets, build configurations, and architectures becomes a common activity. Xcode provides an entire family of toolbar controls to make those tasks easier, and to make the currently active settings readily visible. The toolbar in Figure 17-3 show all of the individual toolbar controls for build settings.

FIGURE 17-3

From left to right in Figure 17-3, the toolbar controls display and let you set the active target, executable, build configuration, architecture, and SDK. As you can see, this consumes a fair amount of toolbar space, so either remove the toolbar controls you don't change often (ever), or consider the more compact Overview control, shown in Figure 17-4.

The Overview toolbar control displays a compact summary of the current SDK, build configuration, target, executable, and architecture. Its drop-down menu lets you individually change any of those settings. How many settings are displayed in the Overview control depend on what other

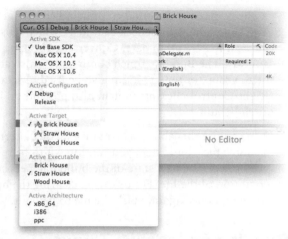

FIGURE 17-4

individual build setting controls — that is, those shown in Figure 17-3 — you've added to your toolbar. It always shows the active SDK, build configuration, and architecture settings but might not include the active target or executable if you also have individual target and executable controls in the same toolbar.

Controlling the Build of Individual Items

Xcode is constantly reevaluating what items need to be built. It does this in the background whenever changes are made to your project or to any of its source files — it doesn't wait until you start a build to decide. Whenever Xcode has decided that a source file needs to be rebuilt, it sets the item's build flag and marks it in the build (hammer) column of the details pane, as shown in Figure 17-5.

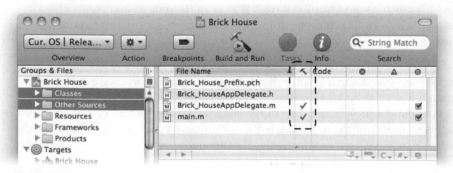

FIGURE 17-5

A check mark in the build column indicates that the source file will be built in the next build. You can manually uncheck that item, which tells Xcode to ignore the changes and treat the file as if it were up to date. Conversely, checking an unchecked item tells Xcode to rebuild it anyway. The Build ➪ Touch command — also accessible by Right/Control-clicking a source item, group, or target — can also be used to set the build flag of one or more source files. Right/Control-clicking an item also presents an Untouch command, treating the item as already built.

You can use this ability as a more exacting alternative to a clean build, described later. By checking a source file's build flag, you can force it to be rebuilt, even when Xcode is convinced that it doesn't need to be. The new state of the build flag persists only until Xcode decides to reevaluate the condition of the file. For example, clearing the build flag for a file and then modifying it causes Xcode to, once again, mark the file to be built.

Building an Inactive Target

Although the build commands in the main menu and toolbar always apply to the active target, there is a shortcut for immediately building any of the other targets in your project. Control/Right+click a target in the target's smart group. In the contextual pop-up menu for the target you will find Build, Build and Start, Build and Debug, and Clean build commands. Selecting any of these is equivalent to making that target active, starting a build, and then switching back to the previously active target.

CLEAN BUILDS

A "clean" build is a build that constructs everything in the product solely from the project's source files. You might think this would be true of every build, but it isn't. Xcode, like most Make systems, keeps all of the intermediate files that were produced during previous builds. It reuses these intermediate files to reduce the work required for subsequent builds: a C source file is compiled into an object file, which is later linked to form an executable. The C file is the source and the executable is the product, but the object file is an intermediate file. Xcode normally only recompiles the source file when its modification date is later than the intermediate object file. Likewise, the executable is only re-linked if one or more of the intermediate objects are newer than the latest executable.

Xcode does this to avoid recompiling everything in the project and all of its libraries and frameworks every time you make a single change. For large projects the difference can be a 20-minute build versus a 5-second build. However, it's possible for Xcode to become confused. The classic example is to build a project and then to replace a source file with an earlier version. The source file is different and needs to be recompiled, but its modification date is still earlier than the intermediate object file. Xcode does not recompile the file and much consternation ensues. Other actions, such as deleting or renaming components in a project, can also leave obsolete intermediate files behind.

Some build systems have a "build clean" option that simply ignores the state of intermediate files and recompiles everything. In Xcode, this is a two-step process using the Clean (Command+Shift+K) command or Clean All Targets command followed by a new build. These two commands delete the product and all intermediate files generated by that target. The next time a build is executed, everything in the target will need to be rebuilt. The Clean command only applies to the active target. The Clean All Targets command cleans out all targets in the project. Both present the dialog box shown in Figure 17-6.

FIGURE 17-6

Remember that the product will also be deleted, so you probably don't want to clean a target while your application is still running.

If you check the option Also Remove Precompiled Headers, the precompiled headers for the target are also deleted. Precompiling the system headers is a lot of work, so saving the precompiled headers will save a fair amount of time on the next build. Because the precompiled headers for most projects consist of *just* the headers from the system frameworks, they are also unlikely to have changed or be out of synchronization. On the other hand, it is also possible to include your own headers and symbols in your precompiled headers and, though rare, system frameworks do change from time to time. In any case, clearing the headers is the safest choice.

The other option is Also Clean Dependencies. If checked, any targets the active target depends on are also cleaned.

It's worth noting that running the Clean command is not equivalent to deleting the contents of your build folder, and is one reason that Xcode provides a command to do this. There are two potential pitfalls to avoid here: the Clean command might not erase all intermediate items, and deleting the build folder might have unintended consequences. The build folder is also the repository for other project support files, possibly files from other projects. The support files are used to provide auto-completion, data modeling, predictive compilation, and other intelligent features of Xcode. Problems can arise if you impulsively delete these support files while Xcode is running. Conversely, if you issue a Clean command after removing a target the products of the target you deleted won't be removed, because they are no longer part of the project.

If you want to ensure that everything in your project is clean, and do so in a way that won't confound Xcode, follow these steps:

1. *Close the project.*

2. *Trash the project's build folder.*

3. *Re-open and build the project.*

Xcode automatically re-creates the build folder, along with whatever support files it needs. The build folder is normally the folder named "build" inside the project folder — unless you've relocated it. The "Build Locations" section explains how to change or identify a project's build location.

PARTIAL BUILDS

There are a few commands for compiling a single file without committing a full build. These commands are:

➤ Build ⇨ Compile (Command+K)

➤ Build ⇨ Preprocess

➤ Build ⇨ Show Assembly Code

Each is enabled whenever you are editing, or have selected, a program source file that belongs to the project. Selecting one of these commands compiles the file using the current, or only, target that compiles that file.

The Compile and Preprocess commands are quick ways of checking that this source file compiles, without waiting for any other files or dependent targets to be built. The Preprocess command only runs the file though the compiler looking for errors. It does not replace the object code last compiled for the file, nor does it perform any other build-related steps.

The Show Assembly Code command is a little different. It compiles the source file using flags that cause the compiler to output assembly source code for the file instead of a compiled object file. This can be instructive if you need to examine the actual machine code produced by the compiler. The assembly source file exists in the build directory and will be overwritten by the next Show Assembly

Code command or the next time a clean build is run. If you want to compare the assembly code differences between two versions of your source code, you'll have to save or copy the first one before producing another.

Xcode also includes a feature called Predictive Compilation. You turn this on in the Build tab of the Xcode preferences, explained a little later in this chapter. When this feature is enabled, Xcode quietly compiles sources files that you have, or are still, editing in the background. It does this to optimize the build process by trying to compile as many source files as it can *before* you request a build. Unless you've just made sweeping changes to a project, it's likely that most of your source files will already be compiled before the build begins.

While Xcode is precompiling your source files, it saves the precompiled object files in a temporary cache. Predictive compilation never overwrites any of the intermediate object files in your build folder until you start a build. When you do finally begin the build, Xcode makes one last check to see whether each precompiled object file is still up to date. If it is, Xcode quickly replaces the intermediate object file in the build folder with the one it precompiled — skipping the need to compile the source file again. If the precompiled object file is not up to date, it is discarded and the build proceeds normally.

THE BUILD WINDOW

The build window is your central control for builds, as shown in Figure 17-7. Choose Build ➪ Build Results (Command+Shift+B) to open the build window for the active project. From the build window, you can start and stop builds, monitor a build's progress, browse errors and warnings, read the detailed build logs, and even correct errors without switching to another window.

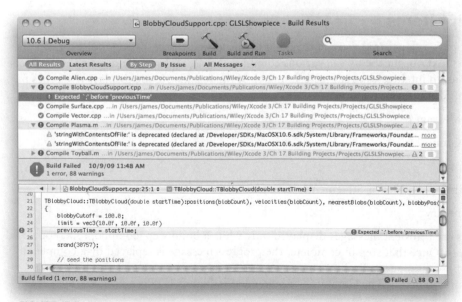

FIGURE 17-7

The build window's toolbar can contain a number of build-related buttons and controls. The more useful are the controls to display and change the active target and build configuration (described earlier), the various Build buttons, and the Clean and Clean All buttons. Note that the Build button turns into a Stop Build button whenever a build is in progress.

The build window is divided into two panes. The upper pane displays progress messages and the build transcript. The lower pane is an editor pane that will automatically focus on the source file associated with the selected issue in the transcript.

The items in the transcript pane can be filtered and organized in different ways using the controls in the ribbon at the top of the pane. The three groups of controls are as follows:

➤ Choosing All Results shows the results of all recent builds for this project. Switching to Latest Results hides the results of previous builds.

➤ Choosing By Step or By Issue either groups together the issue, warning, and error messages produced in the step that produced them, or by the type of issue. See the section "Message Groups" for more details.

➤ The Messages control is a drop-down menu that lets you filter the items it the build transcript so that it shows:

  ➤ All build steps and messages

  ➤ Only issues — essentially any message other than completed build steps

  ➤ Only error and warning messages

  ➤ Only error messages

  ➤ Only static analyzer messages

Build Transcript Items

The build transcript is a structured view of the build log produced by the Xcode tools. It takes the (often voluminous) text output the by the various compilers, tools, and scripts; digests it; compacts it; and presents it as an intelligent, organized summary of the results. Xcode displays five types of messages in the build transcript window:

➤ Progress Messages

➤ Message Groups

➤ Build Steps

➤ Issue, Warning, and Error Statements

➤ Build Summary

Progress messages are transient messages displayed only while a build step (compile, link, copy, and so on) is in progress. Once that step in complete, the progress message is replaced by a completed build step or it simply disappears. Progress messages appear as grey text and let you follow the activity of your build in detail. The CompileXIB statement in Figure 17-8 is a progress message.

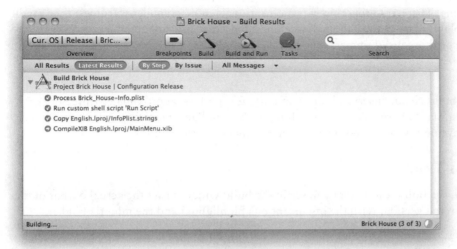

FIGURE 17-8

The persistent items that appear in your build transcript are the results of the build. These are described in the following sections, and are shown in Figures 17-7 and 17-8.

A build step appears for each completed step in the build, distinguished by a green check mark. If the step is associated with a specific source file, selecting the step displays that file in the editor pane.

Message Groups

Anytime a build transcript item encompasses one or more submessages, it becomes a message group. Use the disclosure triangle to expand or to collapse the group.

The build results of each target are contained within a group for that target. Collapse the target group if you want to hide (or ignore) the build results for that target.

The Choosing By Step or By Issue switch above the build transcript determines whether build issues (warnings, errors, and similar notices) are grouped by step or by type:

➤ By Step groups build issues together in the step where they occurred. If a single source file produced an error and two warnings, those three issues are grouped in the single Compile step that built that file.

➤ By Type groups build issues together by type. If three different source files each contained a call to a deprecated method, all three messages are grouped together under a single "is deprecated" group.

Issue, Warning, and Error Statements

The items of most interest in the build transcript are the *issues*. These are the warnings, errors, and other informational messages that tell you what is, or could be, wrong with your project.

Issues are decorated with an icon indicating their type and severity. You can selectively filter out lesser issues, using the Messages control above the pane, so that the transcript only shows you the more severe problems. There are programmers who routinely ignore compiler warnings; they might set the filter to display Errors Only, hiding all warnings and other informational messages. I trust that you're *not* one of those programmers, but we know they're out there.

Build Summary

At the end of each build Xcode inserts a build summary. It's a tall — approximately three lines high — message summarizing the success, or failure, of the build and the time it was started. The build summary conveniently delineates between the results of multiple builds.

Transcript Item Text

As mentioned early, the build results that you see in the build window isn't the actual output of the build. It's an interpreted version, with the important bits highlighted and the minutia hidden.

Sometimes, however, the details of what went wrong are buried in that minutia. When this happens, you'll want to examine the raw output of the build process. There are three techniques for digging into the details of the build transcript.

See the Entire Message

Sometimes the build message is too long to fit on a single line, or is abbreviated for clarity. In either case, hovering the cursor over the text of the message shows the complete message in a tooltip.

Issues that are too long for a single line may also have a "more" link at the right edge of the window, as was shown in Figure 17-7. Clicking this link expands the message into multiple lines so you can read the entire message. A "less" link appears in the expanded message, which will return it to its compact state.

Reveal the Source Build Output

To the right of some messages is a *reveal transcript* button, as shown in Figure 17-9. Clicking it reveals the source build output that the message, or messages, were constructed from.

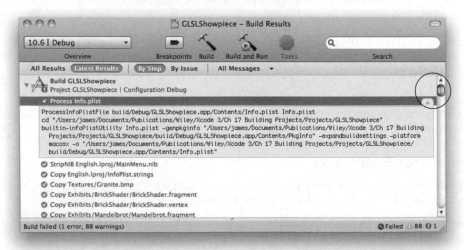

FIGURE 17-9

Right/Control+clicking any message in the build transcript reveals two commands: Expand All Transcripts and Collapse All Transcripts. These commands reveal, or hide, the transcripts for every message in the window.

Extract Some or All of the Build Log

Right/Control+click any message in the build transcript and choose either the Copy or the Open These Latest Results as Transcript Text file command. The Copy command copies the raw build log output associated with the selected message to the clipboard.

The Open These Latest Results as Transcript Text file command — possibly a nominee for the longest command name — exports the entire log from the latest build to a new editor window, where you can sift through it for clues. This is particularly useful when looking for problems that don't produce build transcript messages.

Navigating Errors and Warnings

Having a concise summary of the problems in your project is only half the battle. You have to get to the source of the problems and fix them. Xcode provides a number of navigation shortcuts for quickly getting to the root of your build issues.

Build Window Editor Pane

The build window editor pane is probably the simplest and quickest way to fix small problems. Select any single message in the build transcript; the associated source file (if it has one) is immediately displayed in the editing pane, with the suspect text selected. Use the editor to fix the problem and move on.

 The View ➪ Zoom Editor In and View ➪ Zoom Editor Out commands work equally well in the build window as they do in the project window. Double-clicking the divider bar between the editor and the build transcript also expands or collapses the pane.

Jumping to the Source

Double-click any build issue and Xcode jumps right to the location in the source file that generated the problem. You will be transported to either the project window or a separate text editing window, depending on your layout preferences.

Issues from the build are used to annotate your source code, so it's easy to see the location of the issue, a description of the problem, and any other issues in the same file. The section "Message Bubbles" describes this in more detail.

Jumping to the Next Warning or Error

If your build resulted in a large number of errors, you have my condolences. You also have a couple of commands that will quickly navigate to the next error or warning:

➤ Build ➪ Next Build Warning or Error (Command+=)

➤ Build ➪ Previous Build Warning or Error (Shift+Command+=)

These two commands jump immediately to the next warning or error in the build transcript. If the build window is active, it jumps to next issue in the list and reveals it in the editor pane of the build window. If you are currently in a separate editing window, the commands skip to the next issue in that file, or opens the next file with a problem.

Message Bubbles

Though message bubbles were mentioned briefly in Chapter 6, this is where they become useful — or annoying, depending on the circumstances. Each build issue that's associated with a particular location in a source file appears as a message bubble at that location. A build issue indicator appears in the gutter, and a message bubble describing the issue appears to the right of, or below, the suspect text, as shown in Figure 17-10.

FIGURE 17-10

While having the description of the problem appear right where the problem lies is exceptionally handy, the message bubbles can get in the way of serious editing — particularly when several errors occur on a single line. There are a number of ways to hide, and later reveal, them if they become a hindrance:

➤ Click on the issue's icon in the gutter

➤ View ➪ Message Bubbles ➪ Hide/Show Issues (Shift+Command+H)

➤ View ➪ Message Bubbles ➪ All Issues

➤ View ➪ Message Bubbles ➪ Errors & Warnings Only

➤ View ➪ Message Bubbles ➪ Errors Only

➤ View ➪ Message Bubbles ➪ Analyzer Results Only

Clicking an issue's icon in the gutter toggles the display of that single message bubble. The remaining commands selectively hide or reveal all of the message bubbles, or message bubbles of a particular class. The command settings change the message bubbles display for *all* windows and are remembered between builds.

 All of the commands in the View ▷ Message Bubbles menu are also available in the Right/Control+click contextual menu of the editor pane.

BUILD PREFERENCES

The Build tab in the Xcode Preferences, as shown in Figure 17-11, is where you'll find a number of global build preferences.

FIGURE 17-11

Establishing Common Build Locations

The Place Build Products In and Place Intermediate Build Files In options define the default build locations projects. If you have special build locations that should be used for all projects, set them here. Otherwise, leave them set to Project Directory and With Build Products. The meanings of these locations are described in the "Build Locations" section, later in this chapter.

Automating Build Window Behavior

The Build Results Window options let you choose when the build window for the project is automatically opened and closed. The choices for automatically opening the build window are:

➤ Always

➤ Never

➤ On Errors

➤ On Issues

The Always and Never choice will, or will not, automatically open the project's build window whenever a build is started, respectively. The other two choices open the build window only when the build concludes with one or more errors or issues, respectively.

There is also a set of choices for automatically closing the build window at the conclusion of a build. These choices are:

➤ Never

➤ Always

➤ On Success

➤ On No Errors

➤ On No Issues

The Never choice leaves the build window alone. The remaining choices will automatically close the build window at the end of every build, only if the build is successful, only if there are no errors, or only if there are no issues, respectively.

If you like to follow and interact with the build process in the build window, I suggest settings the open option to Always and the close option to either On Success or On No Issues. This will open the build window at the beginning of the build and close it automatically if successful, or leave it open if there were problems.

If you want to let your builds run quietly in the background, set the open option to On Issues and the close option to Never. With this configuration, the build will run quietly until it completes or encounters a problem. If issues arise, the build window will automatically open to show them to you.

Other Global Build Options

The Continue Building After Errors option permits phases like Compile Sources to continue compiling source files even after one has failed. It's usually more efficient to concentrate on fixing the errors of just one file at a time, so stopping the build as soon as a compilation fails makes sense. However, there are rare occasions when an error in a second file is the root cause of the error in the first, in which case you'll want Xcode to show them all. Or maybe you simply prefer to fix as many errors as you possibly can before building again. For any of these cases, turn this option on. This is a global setting that affects all projects.

The Use Predictive Compilation option enables anticipatory compilation of source files while you are editing them, which was explained in the "Partial Builds" section earlier in this chapter.

Handling Unsaved Files

The For Unsaved Files option, on the right, controls the automatic saving of source files in the project before a build begins. You have four choices:

➤ Ask Before Building presents a standard Save All dialog if there are any unsaved source files. (See Chapter 6 for information about the Save All dialog window.)

➤ Always Save automatically saves all open source files without asking.

➤ Never Save builds the project without regard to unsaved changes in source files.

➤ Cancel Build simply blocks the build from starting if there are files with unsaved changes.

If you choose Cancel Build, there's almost no indication that the build was canceled — besides the obvious fact that it didn't start. I recommend using either the Ask Before Building or Always Save; the Never Save choice is a very hazardous one, and will inevitably result in your making a change to a file and then building your product *without* that change. This can be immensely frustrating during development.

The automatic save options only save files belonging to the active project. This is a concern if your project contains cross-project target dependencies. If you have other projects open and have modified files in those projects, starting a build in your active project will not *save the files belonging to those other projects. If you are using multiple projects with cross-project dependencies, you should cultivate the habit of manually saving all of your files before beginning a build.*

BUILD LOCATIONS

When you start a build, Xcode (hopefully) begins producing a lot of files. The build locations determine where those files get written. There are two build locations. The product location is where the final products of a target are written. The intermediate files location is where all of the derived and intermediate files, like individual object files, are saved between builds.

Wherever the build location is, it has the same structure. Within the product location folder, Xcode creates one product folder for each build configuration. Build configurations are discussed later in this chapter, but you should know that build configurations can produce variations of a single product. Xcode keeps each variant separate by creating a folder for each, as shown in Figure 17-12. In this example, there are two versions of the Brick House application: one built using the Debug build configuration and a second using the Release configuration.

Within the intermediate files location, Xcode creates a single .build folder for each project. Within that folder are individual subfolders for each build configuration. Again, these are used to separate the intermediate files produced by a single target built with different build configurations. This location is also used by the project to store its project and symbol index files.

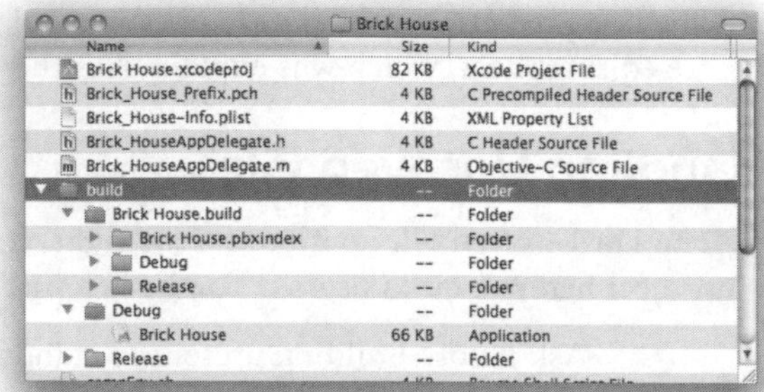

The product and intermediate files location can be the same location or different locations. As was shown in Figure 17-9, both the product and intermediate files locations are the same, so all of the build subfolders coexist in one place.

The default for a new installation of Xcode is to use a build folder within each project's folder as the location for both products and

FIGURE 17-12

intermediate files. Technically, the build location is set to $(SRCROOT)/build (SRCROOT is a build variable set to the path of your project's folder). This is a foolproof setting and works fine for all independent projects of any size or complexity. You many never have to change this setting.

 The various build locations and intermediate directory structures are actually controlled by a group of build settings. As you'll see later in this chapter, you have a great deal of control over build settings and can customize many of the standard build location paths. However, I suggest that you don't attempt to do that; changing build paths can have many unexpected consequences. Set the build location using the settings provided in the General tab of the project's Info window, and let Xcode define the rest of its build locations relative to those.

There are, however, some very good reasons why you might need to alter these locations. The most obvious is to resolve cross-project product references. All product references in Xcode are relative to the product location. Within a single project this will never fail, because all of the targets in a project share a single build location — another reason for why single-project projects are easier to maintain. Two projects that have separate build locations, however, cannot refer to each other's products because their build locations will be different.

Say you have two projects. Project A builds a static library that Project B needs to link to. In the target of the Project B you create a dependency on Project A (to make sure it's up to date before linking), and then add the product of Project A to the link phase of Project B. With the default Xcode build locations, the link phase fails with a "library not found" error. Why? Because Xcode is expecting the library to be in the products location of Project B, along with the rest of the products, but it isn't. It's in the products location of Project A where it was produced.

This problem extends beyond Xcode. An application that loads plug-ins may be expecting those plug-ins to be in the same folder as the application. If the plug-ins are produced by a different project, they could be somewhere else when you test your application. Or maybe your project files are on a (relatively) slow network volume and you'd like your intermediate files written to your (relatively) fast local hard drive. The point is that there are lots of reasons for relocating your build folders.

The straightforward way of fixing these and similar dilemmas is to define a common build location, so the products from all projects are written to the same location. Products produced by Project A will be accessible to Project B just as if targets in Project B had produced them.

So where do you change the build locations for a project? The first option is to change the global build locations in the Build tab of the Xcode Preferences, as previously shown in Figure 17-11. The defaults are to use the project folder for the products location and to use that same location for the intermediate files. You can specify a different location for the products folder by clicking the Customized Location radio button and then entering an absolute path to the desired location, or by clicking the Choose button and browsing to a folder.

The intermediate files location can be the same as the products location, or it can be independent. Again, select the Customized Location and choose a location. Unfortunately, you can't set a common location for the products while keeping the intermediate files location relative to the project.

The problem is that you just redefined the build locations for *every* project you open with this installation of Xcode. (That's not entirely true, but the caveat will have to wait a moment.) This may never be a problem, but there are some serious pitfalls to watch out for. The biggest problem is project and product name collisions. The intermediate and index files for a project are kept in a `.build` folder derived from the project's name. If you have two or more projects with the same name, they will all try to use the same index and intermediate build files. Just as bad is the situation of two or more projects that produce products with identical names. The product of one project will simply overwrite the product of the other project. These consequences can range from amusing to disastrous.

Alternatively, you can set the build locations for an individual project. You do this through the Info window of the project, as shown in Figure 17-13.

The choices for the Place Build Products In setting are:

➤ Default Build Products Location

➤ Custom Location

The default option refers to the setting in the Xcode Preferences pane you saw earlier. The custom option lets you to specify an absolute path by entering it into the field below the radio button, or by clicking the Choose button. Whenever you create a new project in Xcode, its build location is set to use the default products location. Changing the global preference changes the build location for all projects that use the default location, but it doesn't affect projects with custom locations.

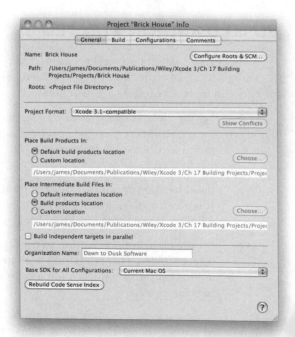

FIGURE 17-13

Similarly, the Place Intermediate Build Files In setting has three choices:

➤ Default Intermediates Location

➤ Build Products Location

➤ Custom Location

The default location refers to the global default, which could be the project location or a custom location. The Build Products Location is whatever location was chosen for the products — in other words, whatever location was ultimately decided on by the build products location settings. Finally, the custom choice allows you to select an arbitrary location.

> *Whenever you change the build locations for a project, do a little housecleaning. Close the project and delete all of the project's build folders. This saves disk space and you won't have, potentially, thousands of orphaned files cluttering up your development folder. Xcode automatically re-creates whatever build folders it needs.*

Xcode conveniently uses the two custom location path fields to preview the location of your build folders. If you select anything other than Custom Location, the disabled path field will display the actual path that Xcode intends to use — calculated using the project's folder location, the project location settings, and global location settings in the Xcode Preferences.

BUILD LOCATION STRATEGIES

Although you might have other reasons, the primary reason for redefining build locations is to share a single location with two or more projects. The three basic strategies for sharing build locations between multiple projects are as follows:

➤ Set the global build location to an absolute path and have all projects use the default location. This is ideal for reusing libraries and frameworks, and for sharing them between multiple projects or developers.

➤ Set the global build location to use a project-relative build folder, and then override the build location specifically for the projects that need to share a build location. This is a good solution for sharing build products between a limited number of projects for a single user, without abandoning local build folders for your remaining projects.

➤ Set the global build location to use a project-relative build folder and then share a single project folder. This is a handy trick for subdividing a single, self-contained, project into multiple projects while avoiding most of the build location issues inherent with the other two solutions.

The first solution is the simplest, and is probably the best choice when you're dealing with a large number of projects or developers. You'll have to decide what a "large number" is, but keep in mind that many professional software teams use a common build location to share built products. At the very least, maintenance is easier if your projects don't override the build location defined in the Xcode Preferences. Any change that needs to be made can be made in one place: the Xcode Preferences.

The second solution sets the custom build location only in those projects that need to share built products. Although this would appear to be the most concise solution, you are going to have problems sharing those projects with other developers. Project-specific custom build locations are absolute paths stored in the project document. Give that project to another developer, and the project won't build if the path to its build location doesn't exist on their system. More than likely, it won't — unless you've colluded with the other developer beforehand to ensure that it does. Using the single build location defined in the Xcode Preferences (the first strategy) works because the only information stored in each project document is a flag to use the global build location defined by the current user — a location that can be different for every developer. This is, in a fashion, similar to the philosophy of source trees described in Chapter 21 and requires only that all of the developers have a custom build location defined in their preferences.

On the other hand, defining a centralized build location for all projects prevents any project from using the project folder for its build location. After you set the Xcode Preferences to a custom build location, you lose the convenience of using the local build folder for all of your projects. If you have *just a few* projects that need to share built products, and you don't need to share those projects with other developers, consider setting the build location for those projects individually. The rest of your projects can continue to use their local build folder.

The third option is somewhat of a trick, but works well for small, self-contained, projects. When you place two or more projects in the same project folder, they all share the same local build folder without having to define a custom build location in Xcode or any of the projects. There's no configuration required and the projects build regardless of the current Xcode preferences.

When you're considering your options, think about *why* you need to break up your work into multiple projects. If the goal is to reuse libraries and frameworks or share projects with other developers, then one of the aforementioned solutions will meet your needs. However, if you are subdividing your project merely for the sake of organization, consider for a moment if you even need separate projects. You may be able to achieve the same goals using multiple targets, source groups, and build configuration files in a single project, eliminating all multi-project problems and complexities.

BUILD SETTINGS

Build settings have been mentioned numerous times, so you'll probably be glad to finally be getting around to finding out about them in detail. At the risk of sounding monotonous, build settings are a set of named values used to customize the build process.

So what are build settings used for? Build settings are used by targets to determine what and how to construct their product, by the compile phases to control various compiler options, and by Xcode itself to control where files are written. Build settings are passed to compile scripts and external build processes, so those scripts and tools can make decisions and alter their behavior based on those settings. You can define your own settings, passing those values to the compiler and your own custom build scripts. A better question might be "what are build settings *not* used for?"

Later sections enumerate some of the more important build settings and describe what they do. For now, all you need to know is that build variables are named values, usually written as SETTING_ NAME = value — although it's unusual to actually write build settings yourself. To understand the interface for build settings, you need to understand how build settings are related to other build settings and how build configurations group them. The two key concepts to understand are:

➤ Build settings are a hierarchy of named values collections

➤ Build configurations are distinct sets of build settings

As you work through the next few sections, keep these core concepts in mind. Build settings and configurations are notorious for confounding new Xcode users. If you grasp these basic relationships, you'll be using them like a pro in no time.

Build settings form a layered hierarchy. Each layer has its own collection of build settings. A value in a higher layer overrides the value with the same name in lower layers. The layers, from top to bottom, are Command Line, Target, Target Configuration File, Project, Project Configuration File, Xcode Default, and Environment. Figure 17-14 shows the layers and their order.

The top layer is formed by the command-line parameters passed to the xcodebuild tool. This is significant *only* if you are building Xcode projects from the command line. When you're building from within the Xcode application, this layer does not exist and can be ignored. "The xcodebuild Tool" section, later in this chapter, explains how to override build settings using the command line.

The next layer is the build settings for the current target. Most targets have a set of build settings. Aggregate targets do not have any configurable build settings — it is assumed that an aggregate target doesn't actually build anything.

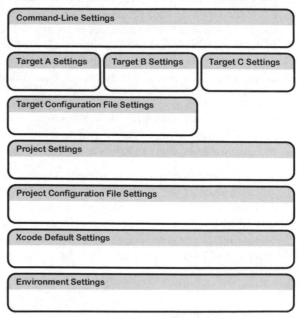

FIGURE 17-14

Every target with build settings can also inherit a set of build settings from an Xcode configuration file. An Xcode configuration file is just another set of build settings stored in a source file. Creating and adding configuration files to your project is covered a little later in the "Configuration Settings Files" section. If a target is based on a configuration file, the settings in that file form the next layer in the hierarchy. If the target is not based on a configuration file, this layer is ignored. Multiple targets can be based on the same configuration file.

The next layer is the project layer. The project build settings are set in the project's Info window. As the name implies, there is only one set of project build settings. Like a target, the project itself can be based on an Xcode configuration file. If used, this configuration file forms another layer below the project build settings.

Below the project layer is a fixed set of build settings provided by Xcode itself. These are the default values for all projects, and comprises most of what you see when you go to edit build settings. This layer also includes the build settings that Xcode generates dynamically, like the SRCROOT setting that contains the path of the project. At last count, there were more than 200 default build settings.

Finally, the bottom layer is the environment layer. These are values found in Xcode's or xcodebuild's process environment. You can set these in the shell or as explained later in the "Environment Settings" section. Environment variables are a way of passing build settings to many or all projects.

For the most part, the important layers — that is, the layers you will be working with on a daily basis — are the target and project layers. The remaining discussion often glosses over the other layers; just remember that if those layers are present, they behave just like any other layer.

The Scope of Build Settings

Each set of build settings has a scope, or lifetime, as described in the following table. Build settings that are out of scope when a particular target is being built are inaccessible and irrelevant.

BUILD SETTING LAYER	SCOPE
Command-Line	Present for the duration of the build started using the xcodebuild tool.
Target and Target Configuration File	Present during the build phases of the target.
Project and Project Configuration File	Present while building any target in the project.
Xcode Defaults and Environment	Always present.

Any build settings established using the command-line arguments passed to the xcodebuild tool exist for the duration of the build. This may span the building of many targets.

The build settings for a target only exist while files in that target are being processed. If dependencies cause another target to be built, the build settings used for the dependent target are the build settings belonging to that dependent target. Targets do not inherit, or in any way pass, their build settings to the build phases of other targets.

The project build settings exist whenever a target in that project is being built. If a dependency causes a cross-project target to be built, that target will be built using the project build setting belonging to the external project. Projects do not inherit or pass build settings to other projects.

Environment build settings are constant throughout a build. The environment settings used during a build are those that existed when Xcode or the xcodebuild tool was launched. When those build settings get created and their values are beyond Xcode's control.

Build settings are passed to custom scripts and tools via the environment. Scripts and external build tools are free to alter any of the build settings that Xcode passes to them. However, changing them does not alter the build settings in the project. This is consistent with the UNIX model of shell variables: altering a variable in a sub-shell does not alter that value in its super-shell. External build tools can pass custom or modified build settings to other builds using the command-line and environment layers.

Build Setting Evaluation

Every named build setting used by a target, script, or tool forms, essentially, an expression that Xcode converts into a value. The rules for evaluating build setting expressions are pretty simple, and most of the time are trivial. For simple build settings — those that don't refer to other build settings — the rule is this:

➤ The highest layer that contains a build setting defines its value

If more than one build setting layer contains a value with the same name, the value defined by the top layer is used. Take a look at the build settings shown in Figure 17-15 as an example.

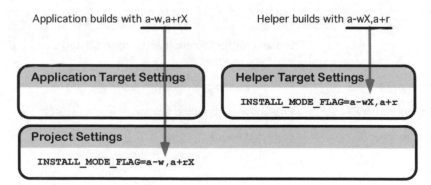

FIGURE 17-15

The INSTALL_MODE_FLAG setting is used to set the access permissions of executable product files. The default value of a-w,a+rX gives all users read and execute rights to the file, which is appropriate for most applications. However, this application includes a self-installing helper tool — an executable that will be copied to another location and executed there. For security purposes, you don't want the program file in the application bundle to be executable, because it should never be launched from within the bundle. To accomplish this, the INSTALL_MODE_FLAG build setting is set to a-wX,a+r in the HelperTool target.

When the Application target is built, the four sets of build settings — Command-Line, Application Target, Project, and Environment — are assembled. Only the project layer defines an INSTALL_MODE_FLAG setting, so the value used when building the Application target is a-w,a+rX. When it comes time to build the HelperTool target, the build sets that are in scope — which this time includes the HelperTool target settings but not the Application target set — are assembled. This time, both the HelperTool target and the project define a setting named INSTALL_MODE_FLAG. The definition of INSTALL_MODE_FLAG in the target set is in a higher layer than the project, so the value from the HelperTool target is used. When it's all finished, the project produces an application that can be launched along with a BSD program file that can be read but not directly executed.

Build Setting Value Substitution

As you can see, the scope and precedence of build settings are pretty simple. That is, until build settings start referring to other build settings. This simultaneously makes build settings more powerful while significantly complicating how build settings are resolved.

The $(VAR_NAME) syntax enables a build setting to refer to any other build setting. For example, the Other C++ Flags (OTHER_CPLUSPLUSFLAGS) build setting is normally set to the value $(OTHER_CFLAGS). This build setting effectively sets the Other C++ Flags setting to match the Other C Flags setting, so that any extra compiler flags you set for C compiles will also be used when compiling C++ files. Any custom C flags, regardless of what layer they are defined in, are automatically passed to the C++ compiler as well.

Figure 17-16 illustrates the order and rules used to resolve build setting references.

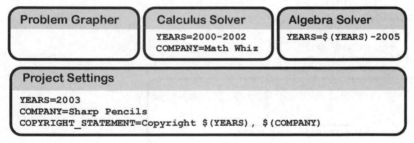

FIGURE 17-16

This project produces three applications: Problem Grapher, Algebra Solver, and Calculus Solver. Each application includes a copyright statement. Sharp Pencils wrote Problem Grapher and Algebra Solver, and Math Whiz wrote Calculus Solver.

The project defines a COMPANY setting containing a company name and a YEARS setting defining a span of years. It also defines a COPYRIGHT_STATEMENT setting that forms a complete copyright statement using the values of the other two build settings.

When the Problem Grapher target is built, the value of the COPYRIGHT_STATEMENT setting is constructed by substituting the values of the YEARS and COMPANY settings where their references appear in the value, as illustrated in Figure 17-17. Ultimately, the value of COPYRIGHT_STATEMENT is Copyright 2003, Sharp Pencils.

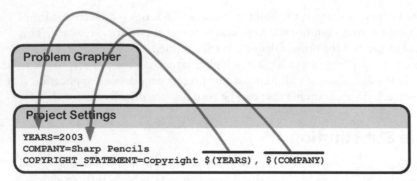

FIGURE 17-17

When the Calculus Solver target is built, things get a little more interesting. When Xcode resolves the references to YEARS and COMPANY, it finds values set in the Calculus Solver target (which is now in scope) that override the values in the project, as shown in Figure 17-18. Using those values instead, the COPYRIGHT_STATEMENT setting now resolves to Copyright 2000-2003, Math Whiz. Notice how a value defined in a higher layer can alter a definition defined in a lower one.

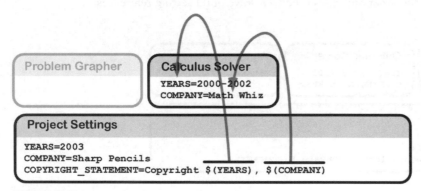

FIGURE 17-18

Next is the Algebra Solver target. This target is interesting because the YEARS setting contains a self-referential value. That is, the value of YEARS refers to the value of the YEARS setting. Xcode resolves self-referential references by obtaining the value of the setting from a *lower layer* of build settings. When the COPYRIGHT_STATEMENT setting refers to the YEARS setting, Xcode finds it in the Algebra Solver target setting. When Xcode constructs the value for the YEARS setting for that target, it finds a reference to the YEARS setting. Xcode recursively searches for another definition of the YEARS setting, but ignores layers at or above the layer containing the reference, as shown in Figure 17-19. Ultimately, the $(YEARS) reference in the target's YEARS setting is replaced with the YEARS value set in the project, resulting in a value of 2003-2005.

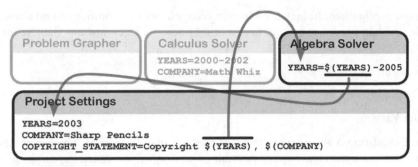

FIGURE 17-19

Recursive references are particularly useful for amending Xcode build settings. For example, the OTHER_CFLAGS build setting defines additional arguments that are passed to the gcc compiler. If you defined just a set of flags in your target, it would override whatever the value of this setting might be in the project. Instead, you can define the value of this setting as $(OTHER_CFLAGS) —myflag in the target. The argument —myflag is merely appended to whatever the project or environment setting was, rather than replacing it. As described earlier, whatever your OTHER_CFLAGS ultimately resolved to would be transferred to OTHER_CPLUSPLUSFLAGS, even if the augmentation of OTHER_CFLAGS occurred in an higher layer.

 The special reference $(inherited) *is the same as* $(VAR), *where* VAR *is self-referential, as in* MY_ARGS=--verbose $(inherited).

If there were no lower layers that contained a YEARS setting, the reference $(YEARS) would be replaced with an empty string. In fact, any reference to an undefined or out-of-scope build setting is replaced with nothing. Referring to an undefined build setting does not cause a build error or produce any kind of warning.

References to environment variables are treated like references to any other build setting. However, references *in* environment variables are a special case: references in an environment variable cannot refer to any non-environment layer build setting. In this example, the COPYRIGHT_STATEMENT setting could not be defined solely as an environment setting. If it was, the $(YEARS) and $(COMPANY) references would only be substituted if there were YEAR and COMPANY settings in the environment layer as well. Any values for YEAR and COMPANY in any other layer would be ignored.

Conditional Build Settings

There's a special kind of build setting that creates an additional quasi-layer of settings: conditional build settings. A conditional build setting is keyed to some other combination of build settings. If those other build settings match a given pattern, it substitutes a different value for that setting. The general textual form for conditional build settings is:

```
BUILD_SETTING[condition=pattern] = value
```

This isn't a general-purpose mechanism. In fact, Xcode only recognizes three conditions and these conditions are only evaluated and passed to certain native build phases. The conditions that Xcode evaluates are:

➤ arch (Processor Architecture)

➤ sdk (Software Development Kit)

➤ variant (Product Variant)

The pattern portion of the condition is the name of the architecture, sdk, or variant. The pattern can include a "*" wildcard character to match groups of possible condition values. A setting can have multiple conditionals, as in SOME_SETTING[sdk=iphonesimulator*][variant=debug] = YES.

Consider the following build setting and variant:

```
GCC_USE_INDIRECT_FUNCTION_CALLS = NO
GCC_USE_INDIRECT_FUNCTION_CALLS[arch=ppc*] = YES
```

When the target is being built for any non-PowerPC architectures (Intel, Arm, and so on) the conditional build setting doesn't match the pattern and is ignored; in these cases GCC_USE_INDIRECT_FUNCTION_CALLS evaluates to NO. Whenever the target is compiled for any PowerPC architecture (ppc, ppc64, ppc7400, ppc970, and so on) the condition matches the pattern (ppc*) and the build setting evaluates to YES.

Logically, conditional build settings create another layer, immediately above the current layer, with alternate build settings that are only in scope when their condition patterns are satisfied. You cannot refer to conditional build settings in references; they're simply alternate settings that supersede the base setting under certain circumstances.

Conditional build settings cannot be used by custom build rules or Run Script phases. Furthermore, only those build settings that apply to native compilation phases can be made conditional.

The possible values for each condition change from release to release, but the Xcode build settings editor knows what they are and will let you choose them from a menu. If you want to know what patterns are available, take a peek by creating a conditional build setting — described later in the "Create a Conditional Build Setting" section — then look at the resulting build setting statement by copying it to the clipboard.

Variable Build Settings

Variable build setting names are an alternative to conditional build settings. This works by using a build setting value as all, or part, of a build setting name. Consider the following build settings:

```
VALUE_FOR_COND_1 = YES
VALUE_FOR_COND_2 = NO
VALUE_FOR_COND_3 = MAYBE
MY_CONDITION = 2
MY_VALUE = $(VALUE_FOR_COND_$(MY_CONDITION))
```

Build setting values are evaluated recursively. The expression $(VALUE_FOR_COND_$(MY_CONDITION)) is first replaced with $(VALUE_FOR_COND_2), which then evaluates to NO. Thus, setting the MY_CONDITION setting to 2 ultimately causes MY_VALUE to be NO. Setting it to 3 would cause MY_VALUE to be MAYBE.

This isn't quite as flexible or sophisticated as using conditional build variables, but it works with all build settings. Using this technique, you can create a set of related build setting and then select one of them via the value of another setting.

BUILD CONFIGURATIONS

Build configurations are complete sets of build settings. If you imagine build settings forming a two-dimensional tree of build settings, each build configuration creates a new plane of build settings in a third dimension. Each named build configuration represents an independent collection of build settings for the project and all of its targets.

The previous example had a project for four sets of build settings: one set for the project and three sets for the targets. If that project had three build configurations — named Alpha, Beta, and Release — it would actually contain 12 complete sets of build settings, as shown in Figure 17-20.

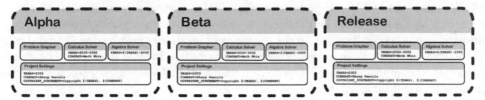

FIGURE 17-20

While you are editing your project or target build settings, keep this in mind: every target and project has an independent set of build settings for each named build configuration.

Only the build settings for the active build configuration, which you choose using the Project ⇨ Set Active Build Configuration menu, are in scope.

This lets you create build settings for a target or project that changes depending on which build configuration is active. If you create a new target, that target gets a set of build settings for each configuration in the project. If you create a new configuration, a new set of build settings is added to the project and every target. Think of build settings as values written on a sheet of paper. Every page is a build configuration. Add a configuration, and you create a completely new page of build settings for everything in your project. When you build, you choose which page of build settings to use.

If you have used Xcode or Project Builder in the distant past (prior to Xcode 2.1), read this section carefully. Older versions of Xcode used a system of build settings and build "styles." There was only one set of build settings for each target. Each build style could then selectively override specific build settings. Although the two systems are effectively similar, the interface and conceptual structure of build styles and build configurations are significantly different.

You might be worried at this point that a complex project with five targets and four build configurations would have an unmanageable number of build settings — at least 25 complete sets of build settings, in all. Don't worry. Xcode provides several tools for visualizing build settings as a whole, editing build settings in multiple configurations at once, and moving build settings between layers. Each of these are covered shortly.

The most common use of build configurations is to alter the compiler and linking options when producing an application for different purposes. For debugging, the application needs to be compiled with certain code optimizations turned off (code optimizations can interfere with source-level debugging) and with debug information included. Conversely, the released version of your application needs to be fully optimized, but does not need to include any debugger data — the end user doesn't need it and it significantly increases the size of the application. You may also need to produce an application that's between these two extremes for performance testing. For that, you'll want an application that is fully optimized (just like the final version), but also includes all of the information used by the debugger to identify functions and variables.

This use of build configurations is so common that these are exactly the build configurations provided by Xcode templates. All Xcode project templates include two configurations, named Debug and Release. The default values for the build configurations set the compiler and linking options to those you would typically want. In the Debug configuration, optimization is turned off, debugging symbols are enabled, as are useful debugging features like Fix and Continue. The Release configuration has just the opposite settings. Optimization and normal linking are turned on, and all of the debugging aides are disabled.

EDITING BUILD SETTINGS

Now that you understand the hierarchy of build settings and build configurations, you should now be able to make sense of the interface for editing build settings.

Select a project or target and open its Info window; the easiest way is to double-click the project or target icon. Switch to the Build tab and a list of build settings is displayed, as shown in Figure 17-21.

The name of each setting is in the Setting column and its value is listed in the Value column.

The Configurations pop-up menu selects which set of build settings you are seeing or editing. You can choose a specific build configuration, or whatever configuration is currently active.

The special All Configurations choice merges the build settings from all of your

FIGURE 17-21

configurations into the single list. *Changing a setting in this mode changes that setting in every build configuration.* A setting with values that vary between configurations displays `<Multiple values>` for its value.

Filtering Build Settings

Build settings are organized into groups to make it easier to find the settings you're looking for. You can filter out uninteresting settings by name or value by typing something into the search field. By default, the search field will match any setting's name, title, value, definition, or description. Use the search field's menu to limit the scope of the search, if necessary. For example, type "gar" into the search field to quickly locate the Objective-C Garbage Collection settings.

The Show menu can be set to one of three choices:

➤ All Settings

➤ Settings Defined at This Level

➤ User-Defined Settings

When All Settings is chosen, the list shows every build setting that Xcode knows about. This will be far more build settings than are set in the level (project or target) you are editing. Those actually defined at this level are displayed in bold. The settings in normal text are those inherited from lower levels, showing you all of the existing settings that you might want to redefine at this level.

To narrow your focus to just the build settings defined in this level, change the Show setting to Settings Defined at This Level. All of the inherited settings are hidden.

User-Defined Settings is the same as All Settings, but filters out all of the standard settings that Xcode knows about. The resulting display lists only custom build settings that you've defined. Again, the settings in bold are defined at this level and non-bold values are inherited from lower levels.

Viewing Names and Definitions

Every build setting has a name and an optional title. The name is the actual variable name defined in the collection, like `OTHER_CFLAGS`. Its title is a more human readable title supplied by Xcode, like "Other C Flags." Build settings that Xcode does not recognize are always displayed using their name, which naturally includes all user-defined settings.

You can have Xcode list build settings by name or by title. Right/Control+click any build setting — anywhere in the row, but it can't be an empty row. The pop-up menu has two commands:

➤ Show Setting Names/Titles

➤ Show Definitions/Values

The first command toggles the Title column between displaying the title of the setting and its name, both shown in Figure 17-22.

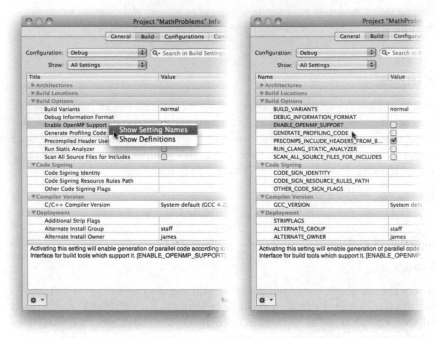

FIGURE 17-22

The second command toggles the Value column between displaying the resolved value for the setting and its actual definition, as shown in Figure 17-23.

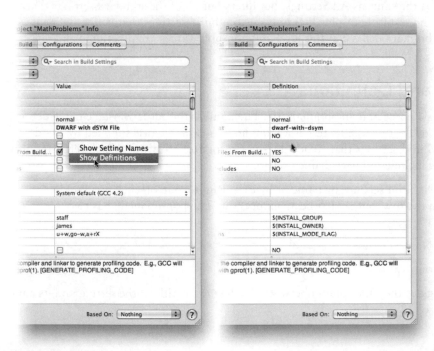

FIGURE 17-23

Values are resolved using the current level and any lower (inherited) levels; build settings that refer to values in higher levels, like our YEAR example earlier, won't display the correct build time value in the Info window. This is rare, however. Most of the time, the values expressed in the Info window are exactly what they will be at build time. You can test references by editing other build setting layers and immediately see the results.

A Peek-A-Boo Build Script

When editing complex sets of interrelated build settings, it's sometimes difficult to tell what the end result will be. If you're wondering what value a particular build setting gets resolved to at build time, add a custom Run Script phase to your target, like this:

1. In the target of interest, add a new Run Script build phase.

2. Edit the phase's script so it's something like:

```
echo 'The build settings containing TEST:'
env | fgrep -i TEST | sort
exit 0
```

When your target is built, it will run the script, dumping all of the environment variables that contain the word "test" to the build transcript, which you can examine in the build window.

This works because, before running an external script or tool, Xcode resolves every build setting that's currently in scope and converts each one into an environment variable. This environment is then passed to the child process.

If you already have a Run Script phase that's doing something, consider checking the Show Environment Variables in Build Log option of the build phase. This option dumps all of the environment variables (which includes the build settings) to the build transcript prior to running the script.

There are a million variations on these techniques. Just keep in mind that if you ever want to know exactly what a build setting's value is, dump it from a script.

Changing Build Setting Values

Editing build settings values depends somewhat on the display mode, as explained in the earlier section "Viewing Names and Definitions." When the values of settings are displayed, Xcode shows — whenever possible — an intelligent setting control. This is true for Boolean values, lists, and values that have a known set of acceptable values. All three are shown in Figure 17-24.

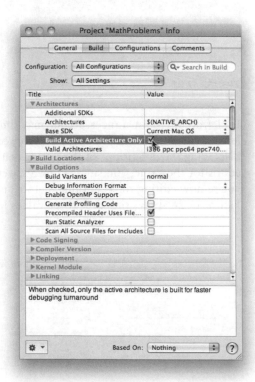

FIGURE 17-24

In Figure 17-24, the Build Active Architecture Only setting is a Boolean value that appears as a simple check box. Tick the box to set it to YES and untick it to set to NO.

Xcode recognizes that the Valid Architectures settings is a list. Double-clicking the value cell presents an editable list, as shown on the right in Figure 17-25. Add, remove, and edit members of the list in the dialog sheet. Xcode assembles the list into a single space-delimited value.

The Debug Information Format setting is known to have three valid settings, which Xcode presents as a pop-up menu, as shown on the left in Figure 17-25. Select the one you want and Xcode substitutes the correct value. Notice that the value is not the same as the description. Like build setting titles, Xcode has a known set of values for which it substitutes more easily read titles.

FIGURE 17-25

Under other circumstances, Xcode may simply present you with a free-form editing dialog, or let you edit the value directly in the value cell of the table. This can happen because you're displaying the definitions of the settings rather than their values, Xcode doesn't have a specialized editor for the value, you single-click a selected value rather than double-click, and so on. Either way, you're now editing the raw value, before any references have been resolved and sans any translation. Figure 17-26 shows the same three values in Figures 17-24 and 17-25 being edited in their raw form.

FIGURE 17-26

Changing a build setting defines that build setting in the level where you edited it, even if you set it back to its inherited value. Once a build setting is defined, it remains defined at that level until you delete it (see the section "Deleting a Build Setting"). This is a problem when you change a build setting for a target, change it back to its default, and then edit the same build setting in the project build settings. You might think you are now changing that setting for all targets, but the target where the build setting is still defined won't change because its setting — with the old value — overrides the one in the project.

Finally, there's an Edit Definition At This Level command in the action pop-up menu in the lower-left corner of the Info window. It has the same effect as double-clicking a setting.

Creating a Conditional Build Setting

As mentioned earlier in the "Conditional Build Settings" section, certain build settings can be conditional. That is, they will take on different values under specific combinations of SDK and processor architecture.

To create a conditional build setting, select a build setting that's defined at this level and choose the Add Build Setting Condition command from the action menu. The variant appears underneath the existing setting, as shown in Figure 17-27.

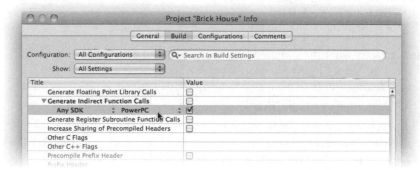

FIGURE 17-27

The conditional setting is defined by two pop-up controls that let you choose the circumstances under which the conditional setting is used. Choose an SDK, processor architecture, or combination using the pop-up menus. The Xcode interface does not let you choose a variant condition, nor can you use wildcard conditions to match multiple conditions. To do that, you'll have to use a configuration settings file, described later in this chapter.

Creating a Custom Build Setting

To create a new build setting for your own purposes, simply choose the Add User-Defined Setting from the action menu at the bottom-left corner of the Info window. A new build setting is added to the table, and Xcode lets you edit its name and value, as shown on the left in Figure 17-28.

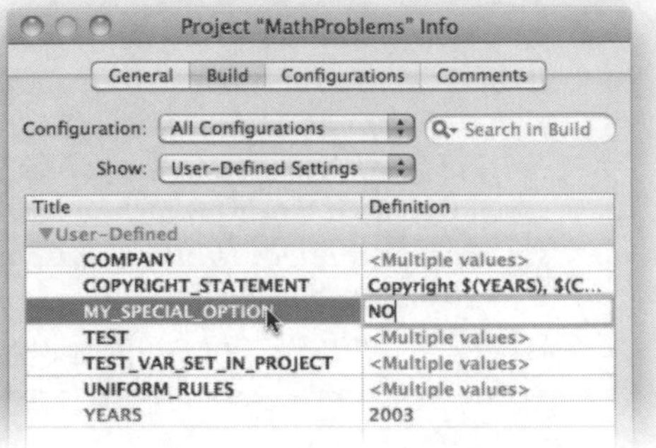

The name cannot duplicate any existing build setting, and once created you can't rename it. To rename a user-defined setting, delete the old setting and create a new one.

Build setting names must conform to the C macro naming convention and are traditionally all uppercase. If they don't, Xcode presents the warning dialog shown in Figure 17-29. Xcode will allow you to create multiple settings that differ only in case, but settings may be case-insensitive in some circumstances, so avoid doing that whenever possible.

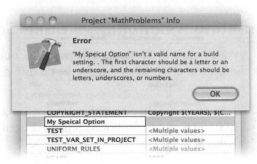

FIGURE 17-28

FIGURE 17-29

Deleting a Build Setting

To delete a build setting, select the setting in the list and choose the Delete Definition At This Level command from the action menu, or simply press the Delete key.

Deleting a build setting does exactly what the command says: it deletes the definition of that build setting *at this level*. Build settings defined by Xcode or in other levels continue to exist. If you're showing all settings, the build setting will turn from a bold setting (one defined at this level) to a normal setting (one inherited from some lower level).

The only time deleting a build setting will make it totally disappear is when you're deleting the only definition of a user-defined setting. Naturally, if you have the Info window set to show only settings defined at this level it will also disappear, but the setting still exists elsewhere.

Switching Between Build Configurations

Most of what's been discussed so far about editing and creating build settings has assumed that that you only have one build configuration. A project with three build configurations means that there are three sets of build settings for each target.

As mentioned earlier, you select the build configuration you are editing using the Configuration pop-up menu at the top of the Build tab. To edit the build settings for a particular configuration, select that configuration from the list. You can also select the Active (*name*) item. The Info window always shows and edits whatever the active build configuration is. Changing the build configuration using Project ⇨ Set Active Build Configuration immediately changes the build settings in the Info window to match.

One of the most useful views is the All Configurations view. When you select this view, the Build tab shows a composite view of all of the settings from all configurations. It does this the same way items in a multi-item Info window are displayed. Settings with values that are different between configurations are displayed as `<Multiple values>`. Boolean options whose values are set with a check box show a hyphen.

You can quickly scan the list to see which settings differ between configurations. More importantly, when you are in this view, any change you make to a setting sets that value in every configuration of the target or project. This mode is extremely useful for setting project and target settings in multiple configurations simultaneously, but it also requires some care. You can easily overwrite settings that were created for a specific configuration. It is also easy to unintentionally create new build settings. In the All Configurations view, editing the value of a setting also creates that setting (with the same value) in *every* configuration that did not previously contain that setting. Similarly, deleting a setting in the All Configurations view deletes that setting from every configuration.

EDITING BUILD CONFIGURATIONS

You manage build configurations in the Configurations tab of the project's Info window, shown in Figure 17-30. The Edit Configuration List shows the build configurations defined in the project. You can get to this by opening the Info window for the project. You can also jump there by selecting the conveniently placed Edit Configurations item in the Configuration menu of any build settings editor.

You create a new configuration by selecting an existing configuration and clicking the Duplicate button at the bottom of the pane. Remember that a build configuration represents a complete set of build settings for every target and for the project itself — you really wouldn't want to create a completely empty set of build settings. Select the configuration that is closest to the settings you want for your new configuration, duplicate it, and then go fix the differences in the build settings of the project and each target.

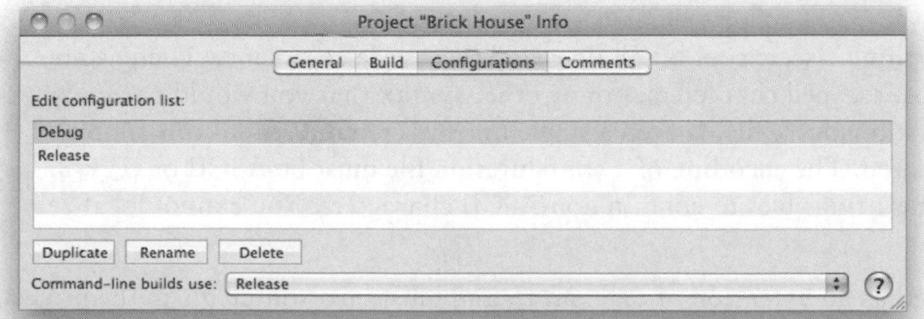

FIGURE 17-30

To delete a build configuration, select it in the list and click the Delete button. A project must have at least one build configuration, so you can't delete them all. You can rename a build configuration using the Rename button or by double-clicking the configuration's name.

At the bottom of the pane is a default configuration selection, declared as the Command-Line Builds Use setting. Use this to select the default build configuration for the project. This setting may be significant when building cross-project targets or when you're building a project using the `xcodebuild` tool.

When you're building a project directly within the Xcode application, the active build configuration unambiguously determines the build configuration that will be used. However, subprojects and projects built with the `xcodebuild` tool are not always as definitive. When a cross-project dependency causes a target in another project to be built, Xcode *tries* to use the build configuration in the external project with the same name as the one it is using for the current target. What if a build configuration with that name doesn't exist in the other project? Likewise, when using the `xcodebuild` tool, you are not required to specify which build configuration you want to use, forcing Xcode to choose for you. In both of these situations, Xcode uses the default build configuration you've specified in your project. If the default configuration is set to "none," the default build configuration is undefined and unpredictable; fix this by choosing a configuration from the menu.

CONFIGURATION SETTINGS FILES

Target and project build settings can be based on a configuration settings file. A configuration settings file is nothing more than a specially formatted text file containing a collection of build settings. The following code demonstrates a configuration settings file that defines the same build settings used in an earlier example:

```
COMPANY = Sharp Pencils
YEARS = 2003
COPYRIGHT_STATEMENT = "Copyright $(YEARS), $(COMPANY)"
```

The format of the file is simple. Each line contains a build setting variable name, an equals sign (=), followed by the setting's value. Any amount of white space before or after the = and at the end of the line is ignored. Placing quotes around values with special characters is optional. Everything between the = and the end of the line, ignoring any leading or trailing white space, becomes the value for the setting.

The file cannot contain anything else, except blank lines and C++-style comments. There is no support for multi-line values, escaped characters, or any other syntax that you would normally associate with a property list or source file. If even a single line fails to conform to this simple format, the entire file is ignored. The encoding of a configuration file must be ASCII or UTF-8. UFT-8 allows configuration settings files to contain non-ASCII characters. You cannot localize configuration settings files.

A configuration settings file has an extension of `.xcconfig` and must be a source file in the project, although it should not be included in any targets. After you've added a configuration settings file to your project, you can set any target or project build settings to be based on that configuration settings file by selecting it in the Based On menu as shown in Figure 17-31.

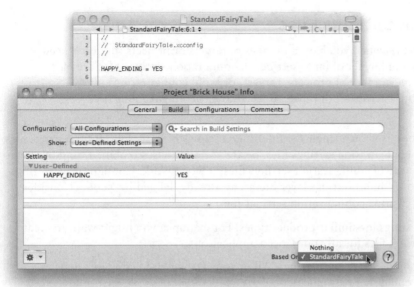

FIGURE 17-31

The build settings in the configuration settings file form a layer of build settings immediately *below* the target or project layer you've adopted them in. The Based On option is build configuration specific, so you can use different configuration settings files for each configuration. A project or target that is based on a configuration settings file can still override any of the settings in the file by defining its own setting — exactly as it would override a setting from any lower layer of build settings.

 The All Configurations view may not display a <multiple values> *value for the configuration file of the target or project. Changing the Based On setting while you're in the All Configurations view dutifully sets the configuration file for all configurations to the new choice.*

Adding a Configuration Settings File

Create an empty configuration settings file and add it to your project by choosing the File ➪ New File command. Find and choose the Xcode Configurations Settings File template. Give the file a name and add it to your project. When asked, do not add the file to any targets. Configuration settings files are not input files to the target's build phases; they are only used to populate the build settings.

If you already have a configuration settings file that exists but hasn't been added to the project, simply add it to the project like any other source file. See Chapter 5 for a quick refresher on adding source files. Again, do not add the configuration settings file to any targets when adding it to the project. Configuration settings files are part of the build infrastructure; they are not the thing being built.

Using Configuration Settings Files

Use configuration settings files when you have a number of targets or projects that each need a uniform, or at least very similar, set of build settings. Configuration settings files are most useful when you have a large number of projects, targets, or build configurations, and maintaining common settings across all of those projects/targets/configurations becomes cumbersome.

Targets and projects can be based on a single configuration settings file. Configuration settings files cannot be linked to other configuration settings files, nested, or otherwise combined, so don't try to design a hierarchical structure of configuration settings files; it won't work. Configuration settings files are only an adjunct to the build settings layer hierarchy already defined by Xcode. Consider these best practices when creating configuration settings files:

➤ Common build settings for similar product types. For example, you might want to create a configuration settings files for all your Cocoa applications.

➤ Regularly used compiler or debug settings. All of your Debug build configurations in different projects could share a single `MyFavoriteDebugSettings.xcconfig` file.

➤ Build settings that are maintained externally or that can be generated programmatically. Build settings containing things like company product codes could be generated or updated by an external process.

Keep in mind the project or target can override anything defined in the settings file on which it is based. Settings files don't have to contain exactly the values needed by all of the targets, projects, or configurations that are based on it. They only need to define the preferred values for the settings you regularly set. Think of them as your own layer of defaults, much like Xcode's default settings layer.

MOVING BUILD SETTINGS AROUND

Eventually, you'll discover that you have a build setting in a target that really needs to be in the project build settings or a build configuration file. Moving build settings around couldn't be easier, although it may not be immediately obvious as to how.

The trick is to use the clipboard. You can cut, copy, and paste build settings between build settings panes and configuration files. When Xcode copies a build setting to the clipboard, it places a textual representation of the build setting in the clipboard using the format required by configuration files. Because of this, you can copy build settings from a build settings pane and paste them into another build settings pane, a configuration settings file, or vice versa.

Pasting in a build settings pane replaces any other settings defined with the same name. Cutting a build setting is equivalent to copying the setting to the clipboard and then deleting the setting. Note that cutting an inherited setting results in a copy, because there's no setting to delete at this level. Copying a value in the All Configurations view may result in copying the value `<Multiple values>`, which you'll have to edit.

ENVIRONMENT SETTINGS

The environment layer of build settings must be set up outside of Xcode and they must be set before the Xcode application or xcodebuild tool are launched. Xcode uses any environment variable that conforms to the build settings naming convention. Specifically, a variable name must begin with a letter or underscore and contain only letters, numbers, or underscore characters. All letters should be uppercase.

How you set environment variables before launching the xcodebuild tool depends on the calling process. Shells such as bash and tcsh typically use some form of "export" command. For Perl, C, Java, or similar programming languages, environment variables are usually assembled into a collection that is passed to the function that launches the tool. Regardless of how it is accomplished, whatever environment values are passed to the xcodebuild tool will be accessible to the build phases of each target built.

> *The beginning of the "Build Settings" section stated that target and project build setting are never inherited or passed to other targets or projects. This may not always be true if your build involves shell scripts. Whenever Xcode starts an external process — a custom build script or external tool — all of the build settings for that target are resolved and passed to that process as environment variables. If that external process causes another Xcode target to be built using the* xcodebuild *tool, that build inherits all of the build settings as environment settings, regardless of their original scope. Thus, a setting that is defined as a target setting in one project can appear as an environment setting in a second if the second target was built by the first target using a custom build script or external build tool.*

How you set environment variables for use with the Xcode application itself isn't immediately obvious. That's because you don't normally think of GUI applications of having an "environment" the way shell and BSD tools do. In fact, OS X provides a simple — albeit obscure — technique for defining whatever environment variables you want. These variables are available to all running applications. You can read more about it at http://developer.apple.com/mac/library/qa/qa2001/qa1067.html.

The magic file is named ~/.MacOSX/environment.plist. The .MacOSX folder is an invisible folder in your login account's home directory. The environment.plist file is an XML property list file containing a list of key/value pairs. Each pair defines an environment variable that gets defined when you log in. All applications you launch include these variables in their environment.

You can edit the environment.plist file using the Property List Editor application or any good text editor. However, you might prefer to use a little utility called RCEnvironment, shown in Figure 17-32, which is available free from Rubicode at http://www.rubicode.com/Software/RCEnvironment/. It's a System Preferences panel that lets you edit your environment.plist file very much like you would edit build settings in Xcode. Remember that changes only take effect when you log in. After making changes, remember to save the file, log out, and then log back in again.

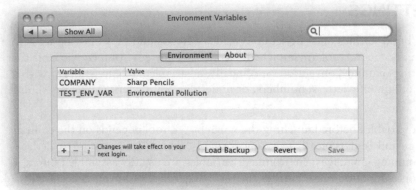

FIGURE 17-32

CUSTOMIZING THE BUILD

Using build settings, and a few specialized Xcode settings, it's possible to customize hundreds of details about your build.

There are literally hundreds of build settings — and the number grows with each release of Xcode. Finding the build setting you're looking for can sometimes be a challenge. The build settings tab displays a description of the selected build setting, and is the first place to look when you're hunting for a build setting or wondering what a build setting does. You can also set the search field to search the descriptions of build settings, which might also help you find what you're looking for.

The next few sections cover many common ways of customizing your build process and products. A few are special features of the Xcode application, but most are configured using build settings.

The later sections cover some of the more important build settings, especially ones that control the build process itself and ones that might have non-obvious relationships. This book can't possibly explain them all. The following sections hit the highlights and point you toward the documentation for the rest.

Per-File Compiler Flags

The per-file compiler flags setting is a special place where the compilation of a single source file can be modified. These are literal command-line arguments, set for a particular source file and target, and passed to the compiler only when *that* source file is compiled. Each source file has a separate compiler flags setting for each target in the project, so you can specify one compiler flag when the file is being compiled for one target and a different compiler flag when it is compiled for another. There are no templates or documentation for these options in Xcode. You will need to consult the compiler's documentation to compose your argument list correctly.

Open the Info window for a source file. If the source belongs to the active target, a Build tab appears in the Info window, as shown in Figure 17-33. You can only edit the compiler flags for the active target. To edit the compiler flags for a different target, you must close the Info window, choose a new active target using the Project ⇨ Set Active Target menu, and then open the Info window for the source file again.

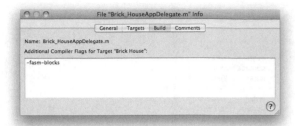

FIGURE 17-33

Per-file compiler flags are like build settings in that they have a specific scope; they are only passed to the compiler when that specific file is being compiled for a specific target. In terms of customizing the build process to your needs, compiler flags can be thought of as the very highest layer of build settings, overriding even the compiler settings in the command-line layer. Just keep in mind that compiler flags settings are not part of the build settings architecture: they are not named variables, cannot refer to other build settings, are not added to the execution environment, and are not accessible to build scripts or external processes. They are a feature supplied by the Compile Sources phase as one more way of fine-tuning the build process.

Personally, I try to avoid per-file compiler flags when possible. It's an obscure feature that's difficult to document and correlate to the source file. These per-file compiler flags are stored in the project document as part of source item, which presents another potential problem; removing the source item or adding the file to another project will discard its settings.

Today, many compiler options can be specified in the source file itself using `#pragma`, `__attribute__`, and other compiler-specific syntax. My first choice would be set any module-specific compiler options in the source file, and use per-file compiler flags only as a last resort.

Cross-Development

In Xcode, cross-development refers to developing a program for use in one or more different versions of Mac OS X. It does not mean cross-platform development, or writing a program that runs on a multitude of different operating systems or architectures. Cross-development allows you to produce a program that runs on a specific range of operating system versions (Mac OS X 10.3.4 through Mac OS X 10.5.0, for example). You can also produce applications that run only on a specific version or an application that will run on any version that supports the features it requires.

Installing Cross-Development SDKs

Before you can even think about doing cross-development, you have to install the cross-development SDKs. The standard Xcode Developer Tools installation includes recent cross-development SDKs, but SDKs for older operating systems may be optional installs, as shown in Figure 17-34. If you did not install the SDKs when you installed Xcode, quit Xcode and run the latest Development Tools installer again. At the Custom Install screen, choose the optional Cross-Development support package or packages.

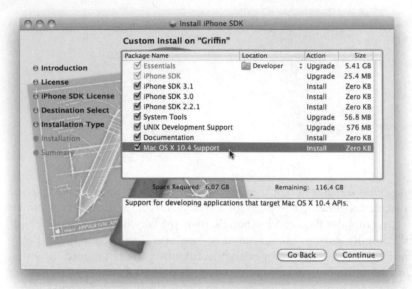

FIGURE 17-34

To use cross-development, you need to choose two boundaries: the earliest version of the operating system that your application can run on, and the latest version of the OS that it utilizes.

Choosing a Target SDK

The latest OS version that your project uses is called the *Target SDK*. For example, you might be writing and developing your application using Mac OS X 10.6, but your application only uses features and APIs that were present in Mac OS X 10.5, which should allow it run smoothly on both. In this situation, your target SDK should be set to Mac OS X 10.5. The Target SDK setting is set for the entire project in the project's Info window, as shown in Figure 17-35. You can set it using the Base SDK build setting for individual build configurations, or use the General tab to set it for all configurations, as shown at the bottom of Figure 17-35.

When you set the target SDK, the compiler and linker will fail if you refer to symbols, functions, or types that did not exist when that version of the operating system was released. Understand that this in no way prevents your application from running on later versions of the operating system.

FIGURE 17-35

It simply means that Xcode compiles your source code using the headers and frameworks defined by an older version of the OS. This ensures that you're unlikely to use any newer APIs or constants that might cause your application to fail when run on an older OS. There may be other reasons it won't run, but the Target SDK isn't one of them.

 It should be noted that the iPhone provides two target SDKs for each major release of the iPhone OS: a native device SDK and a companion simulator SDK. When you build your iPhone or iPod Touch application for the simulator, you're building your application using a different set of frameworks than those used by the actual device. Be aware that there are some subtle differences between the two, and you should thoroughly test all aspects of your application on a real iPhone or iPod.

Choosing a Deployment Target

The other boundary is the deployment target, set using the Mac OS X Deployment Target (MACOSX_DEPLOYMENT_TARGET) or iPhone OS Deployment Target (IPHONEOS_DEPLOYMENT_TARGET) build setting, as shown in Figure 17-36. This sets the *earliest* version of the operating system your application will successfully run on. Whereas the Target SDK setting is purely a build time setting, the Deployment Target setting is both a development setting and a run time setting. At build time, this setting flags certain framework and library references as *weak*. A weak library reference lets your application link to a function that was introduced in a later OS, but still load on an earlier system that lacks that function. (That doesn't mean you can successfully call that function in the legacy environment, it just means the program will load and start running without it.) This setting is also included in the Info. plist of your application bundle and tells the operating system not to allow your application to load if the minimum operating system requirement is not met. This may not have anything to do with what features your application uses; maybe you have simply never tested your application on Mac OS X version 10.4 and you don't want anyone else trying.

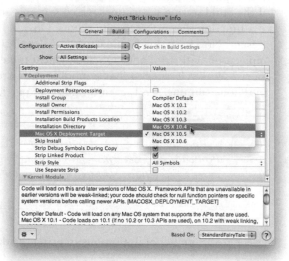

FIGURE 17-36

Both of these boundaries have defaults that are set for new projects. The default for the Target SDK is Current OS. In other words, it compiles and links using the operating system frameworks and libraries currently installed on your development system. The default for the Deployment Target is Compiler Default, which really means "none." The operating system will do its best to load and link your application to the available APIs at run time. Your application will fail to load if it has "hard" links to APIs that don't exist.

Cross-Development Building

So how does this all work? When you installed the SDKs, you put a complete set of system frameworks for each major version of the operating system in the /Developers/SDKs folder. Each folder contains a complete copy of the headers, frameworks, and dynamic libraries that shipped with that version of the operating system, except that all of the executable code has been removed; so-called "stub" libraries.

When you choose a Target SDK in the project, Xcode sets the SDKROOT build settings. This is the path used by the compiler and linker to read all of the system headers and libraries your program links to. (I recommend not trying to change its value using a build setting.) When you set the Target SDK for iPhone OS 3.0, it is just as if you were writing and compiling your program on an iPhone running 3.0. The compilers and linkers know nothing about new features added in later versions of the OS, and will complain if you try to use them. This should prevent you from using any features unique to the iPhone OS version 3.1, which might make your app incompatible with 3.0.

Cross-Development Deployment

The Deployment Target is a little more complicated. The headers in the SDK use the MACOSX_ DEPLOYMENT_TARGET and IPHONEOS_DEPLOYMENT_TARGET settings to define special macros. These macros identify API symbols that did not exist in earlier versions of the operating system. The value of the build setting determines which symbols are affected. For example, say your application refers to a function that was added in iPhone OS 3.0. If run under iPhone OS 2.2.1, that function isn't present. Normally this would cause your application to fail before it even started. By compiling your application with an iPhone OS deployment target of 2.2.1, it tells the compiler and linker to make a special weak reference to that symbol in the system framework. Your program will load and run on an iPhone running 2.2.1, even though that particular routine isn't present in the 2.2.1 frameworks.

 Calling a missing function is still a very bad idea. *You'll have to add code to your application to determine conditionally whether that function is available — hint, a weak reference to a missing symbol will be NULL — and avoid calling it when it's not.*

There are a number of limitations to using the deployment target. Here are a few:

➤ Cross-development is only supported for native targets.

➤ Weak linking only works in Mac OS X 10.2 and later, and even then not all cross-development features are available in 10.2.

➤ You cannot use the system's umbrella header file as your program's prefix file. That is, you can't set your project's prefix file to /System/Library/Frameworks/Carbon.framework/ Headers/Carbon.h. That's because this isn't the correct header if you've chosen a different

SDK. Create your own header that does nothing but include the current framework header, as follows, which will automatically include the `Carbon.h` header from whatever SDK you have selected:

```
#include <Carbon/Carbon.h>
```

A number of other, more obscure limitations and caveats exist. To find out about them, refer to the *Cross-Development Programming Guide* included with the Xcode documentation, or online at `http://developer.apple.com/mac/library/documentation/DeveloperTools/Conceptual/cross_development/`. Also check out the SDKExample project. This demonstrates how to use weak linking for functions in a newer version of the OS, and then check to see if those functions are available at run time.

Building Universal Binaries

Prior to 2004, Xcode only produced PowerPC executable binaries. That's because this was the only processor architecture that Mac OS X supported. Since then, Apple Computer has added two new architectures to its OS pantheon (64-bit PowerPC, Intel 32- and 62-bit), along with new processors (ARM) for its consumer lines of iPhone and iPod Touch products. Xcode can compile your program for any or all of these architectures when you build your project. It does so by repeatedly compiling your application, once for each architecture, and then storing all of the resulting versions in a single multi-architecture binary (MAB) file — a file format that Mac OS X has supported for a long time. Binaries that contain executable code for multiple architectures are referred to as Universal Binaries.

Choosing the Architecture Set

To determine which architectures you want to build, set the Architectures (`ARCHS`) build setting; you will find it in the Architectures group. When you click the setting name, an architectures pop-up menu appears. Select the architecture, or architecture set, that you want to build.

The Architectures (`ARCHS`) setting is a space-delimited list of architectures to be built. Xcode supplies a number of build settings that contain predefined sets of useful architecture lists, such as `ARCHS_STANDARD_32BIT`, which will build only the 32-bit variants of the processors that Mac OS X deploys on (that is, PowerPC and Intel). The pop-up menu simply defines the `ARCHS` setting to equal one of these built-in settings, that is, `ARCHS = $(ARCHS_STANDARD_32_BIT)`. The standard architecture macros supplied by Xcode are listed in the following table:

BUILD SETTING	DESCRIPTION
ARCHS	The list of architectures to build
ARCHS_STANDARD_32_64_BIT	Standard architectures for mixed 32-/64-bit deployment
ARCHS_STANDARD_32_BIT	32-bit only architectures
ARCHS_STANDARD_64_BIT	64-bit only architectures

When you're building your project for release, ARCHS should define the list of architectures your application supports.

For development, however, building multiple architectures is a waste of time; you typically test on the system that you're developing on, and you can only run and test code compatible with the architecture of your development system. That's why the ARCHS build setting for the Debug build configuration is normally set to $(NATIVE_ARCH), which is described next.

Your Native Architecture

The NATIVE_ARCH build setting is the name of the architecture of the machine Xcode is currently running on. Setting ARCHS to $(NATIVE_ARCH) causes Xcode to only build the single, native architecture when compiling applications and is intended for debugging. A number of variations of this build setting are listed in the following table:

BUILD SETTING	DESCRIPTION
NATIVE_ARCH	Generic architecture of your development system
NATIVE_ARCH_32_BIT	Development architecture in 32-bit mode
NATIVE_ARCH_64_BIT	Development architecture in 64-bit mode, if available
NATIVE_ARCH_ACTUAL	The specific architecture currently running

For example, on the development system I'm using right now, NATIVE_ARCH is i386 (Intel), and NATIVE_ARCH_ACTUAL is x86_64 (because I'm running on a 64-bit capable system).

The Valid Architectures

The ARCHS setting is always tempered by the VALID_ARCHS build setting. This setting does not appear in the Xcode interface, but defaults to the list of architectures that Xcode knows how to build. Xcode *only* builds the architectures listed in this setting. If you redefined VALID_ARCHS to ppc ppc64 it would limit the project to producing only 32-bit and 64-bit PowerPC binaries, even if other project settings requested other architectures.

> *If you're trying to create a conditional build setting and don't know what value to use in the* arch= *statement, use the shell script trick described in the "A Peek-A-Boo Build Script" section to dump all of* ARCH *variables. There you will find the exact architecture names that Xcode recognizes.*

Finally, recompiling your program for another architecture is no guarantee that it will work. Subtle differences in pointer sizes and byte order can cause your application to fail. If you need to build a specific architecture for debugging and testing, set ARCHS to that specific architecture. Refer to the "Universal Binary Programming Guidelines" and the "64-Bit Transition Guide" in the Xcode documentation for additional details.

Selected Build Settings in Detail

Build settings, like so many other details in software development, are easy to find — as long as you already know where to look. The catch-22 occurs when you're trying to find something and don't know what it is or where to find it. The following sections highlight hand-selected build settings that you should be familiar with, or are notoriously difficult to find in the documentation.

When listing Xcode-defined build settings, this book uses the form "Full Title (NAME)" to describe each setting. Use its title when you're looking for a setting in the Xcode documentation. Use its name when referring to build settings in scripts or in build-setting value expressions. Remember that copying a build setting will place its definition (NAME=value) on the clipboard.

> *Build settings fall roughly into two categories: modifiable build settings that alter the behavior of the build process and informational build settings created by Xcode. The latter are not intended to be changed. They are for use in other build setting values, custom scripts, and external processes and provide you with information about what is being built and how. Changing an informational build setting can lead to undesirable results.*

Browsing the build settings in the Build tab of the target or project can be very instructional. The major build settings are described here. If you see a build setting that's not covered in this chapter, search the Xcode documentation for its name. The Xcode release notes cover most new and existing build settings. There is also a Build Setting Reference document included in the Xcode documentation that describes many of these same settings.

Products

The Product Name (PRODUCT_NAME) setting is, quit literally, the name of the product produced by the target. To change the name of your target's product, edit this build setting. Note that the final product name is actually a little more complicated if it includes an extension or is in a wrapper (bundle), but these are tacked on by other build settings.

Info.plist Files

These settings control how the Info.plist file is generated for targets that produce bundles, as described in the following table.

BUILD SETTING	DESCRIPTION
Info.plist File (INFOPLIST_FILE)	This is the file in your project that will become the Info.plist file for your product.
Preprocess Info.plist File (INFOPLIST_PREPROCESS)	If this flag is set, then INFOPLIST_FILE is run through the gcc preprocessor. This allows you to use preprocessing macros and #if statements in your source Info.plist file.

continues

(continued)

BUILD SETTING	DESCRIPTION
Info.plist Preprocessor Prefix File (`INFOPLIST_PREFIX_HEADER`)	If your `Info.plist` file is preprocessed, this prefix file is read by the compiler first.
Info.plist Preprocessor Definitions (`INFOPLIST_PREPROCESSOR_ DEFINITIONS`)	Space-separated list of macro definitions passed to the compiler when preprocessing the `Info.plist` file. Use this as an alternative to, or as an adjunct to, using a prefix file.

Search Paths

The search path settings determine where compilers and linkers look for headers and other files referred to only by their name or partial path. Each build setting is a space-separated list of paths. If a path itself contains a space or some other special character, it must be quoted in the list.

Each path specifies a folder to search. If the path ends in `**`, Xcode also searches any subfolders for the file it is looking for. Xcode always searches each folder for the file first, before looking in any subfolders.

Many of the paths in these settings refer to headers and libraries in the system framework folders. These would be paths that start with `/System/Library/Frameworks`. When you're building using a Target SDK, Xcode automatically prefixes any system framework path with `$(SDKROOT)` so that it correctly refers to the corresponding folder in the current SDK.

BUILD SETTING	DESCRIPTION
Header Search Paths (`HEADER_SEARCH_PATHS`)	The paths where the gcc compiler and other tools will look for included files. System paths are prefixed with `$(SDKROOT)`.
Library Search Paths (`LIBRARY_SEARCH_PATHS`)	The folders where the linker will look for libraries. System paths are prefixed with `$(SDKROOT)`.
Framework Search Paths (`FRAMEWORK_SEARCH_PATHS`)	Paths for frameworks, used mostly to locate framework headers. System paths are prefixed with `$(SDKROOT)`.
Rez Search Paths (`REZ_SEARCH_PATHS`)	Paths for the Rez resource compiler
Always Search User Paths (`ALWAYS_SEARCH_USER_PATHS`)	In C, the directives `#include "file.h"` and `#include <file.h>` use different search paths to locate the file, distinguishing "user" from "system" headers. Making this build setting `YES` causes both directives to use the same search path.

Precompiled Headers and Prefix Headers

Precompiled headers are a saved compiler state containing all of the definitions defined in some source headers. It takes quite a bit of time to interpret and construct the type, class, and constants defined in a large group of headers, yet most headers do not change at all between builds. By saving the compiled form of a commonly used set of headers, the compiler avoids the need to repeat that work for every source file in your project.

You begin by creating what's called a prefix header with an extension of .pch. This is a source file that does nothing but include (#include) the headers to which you want access in all of the source files in a target. A typical prefix header is shown in the following code:

```
#ifdef __OBJC__
    #import <Cocoa/Cocoa.h>
#endif
```

You can also include other global defines or headers that you expect every source file to need and you do not expect to change often, if ever. Xcode compiles this file first, and then automatically *prefixes* it to every source file it compiles. It is just as if you manually inserted #include "MyPrefixHeader.h" as the first line of every source file in your project. Most application project templates already include a prefix header, so look in your project before creating a new one.

BUILD SETTING	DESCRIPTION
Prefix Header (GCC_PREFIX_HEADER)	The header to include at the beginning of every source file.
Precompile Prefix Header (GCC_PRECOMPILE_PREFIX_HEADER)	When set to YES, this causes the prefix header to be precompiled and saved between builds. If you use prefix headers, this should be turned on.

C Compiler

The gcc compiler is by far the largest consumer of build settings. Most apply to specific settings for the gcc compiler. You can browse them in the build settings editor under the GNU C/C++ Compiler category. Most are self-explanatory. You can refer to the gcc man page or the gcc manual at http://gcc.gnu.org/onlinedocs/ for more in-depth description of the various options and switches.

The following table describes some of the more commonly customized C compiler build settings.

BUILD SETTING	DESCRIPTION
Preprocessor Macros (`GCC_PREPROCESSOR_DEFINITIONS`)	A space-separated list of macro definitions that will be predefined by gcc before each source file is compiled. Identical to inserting a `#define MACRO value` statement at the beginning of each file. The form for each definition in the list is either `MACRO` or `MACRO=value`. If the definition contains special characters, it needs to be surrounded by quotes.
Preprocessor Macros Not Used in Precompiled Headers (`GCC_PREPROCESSOR_DEFINITIONS_NOT_USED_IN_PRECOMPILED_HEADERS`)	Just like Preprocessor Macros, but these are defined *after* the prefix file is included. If your prefixed headers do not need the definitions defined on the gcc command line, they should be in this build setting. Otherwise, Xcode must recompile your prefix headers whenever these values change.
`GCC_VERSION`	Selects the version of the gcc compiler to use (GCC 4.x, LLVM, Clang). This setting was deprecated for a while, but is back in vogue again. Be aware that the effects of this setting can be overridden by build rules.
Other C Flags (`OTHER_CFLAGS`), Other C++ Flags (`OTHER_CPLUSPLUSFLAGS`)	These are open-ended build settings that let you pass additional command-line arguments to the gcc compiler. The Other C Flags are passed to the compiler when compiling C and Objective-C source. The Other C++ Flags are passed when compiling C++ and Objective-C++ source.

It should be noted that the default setting for `OTHER_CPLUSPLUSFLAGS` is `$(OTHER_CFLAGS)`, so if you want to add arguments to C and Objective-C compiles that you *do not* want passed to the C++ compiler, you'll need to edit both settings.

Other Compilers

Other compilers also use build settings. The two described in the following table let you pass arguments to the lex and yacc compilers.

BUILD SETTING	DESCRIPTION
`LEXFLAGS`	Command arguments passed to the lex compiler.
`YACCFLAGS`	Command arguments passed to the yacc compiler.

Linker Settings

Linker settings control the `ld` linker, invoked for any compiler that produces object code files that need to be linked to create a binary executable. The following table describes these settings.

BUILD SETTING	DESCRIPTION
Library Search Paths (`LIBRARY_SEARCH_PATHS`)	See the earlier "Search Paths" section.
Other Linker Flags (`OTHER_LDFLAGS`)	Like the "other" compiler flags setting, this set of settings let you pass whatever additional command-line arguments you need to the linker.

Kernel Modules

If you're producing a Kernel module, you'll probably need to use some of the settings described in the following table:

BUILD SETTING	DESCRIPTION
Module Version (`MODULE_VERSION`)	The version declared in the module's stub.
Module Identifier (`MODULE_NAME`)	The module's unique identifier.
Module Start Routine (`MODULE_START`), Module Stop Routine (`MODULE_START`)	The names of the module's start and stop functions.

Deployment

Deployment settings control the deployment phase of a build. This is the final phase, where the finished products are cleaned up, polished, shrink-wrapped, and generally made ready to ship.

Deployment post-processing is performed whenever the `DEPLOYMENT_POSTPROCESSING` build setting is set to `YES`. This setting is also set to `YES` if you build a project using the `xcodebuild` tool and pass it the `install` argument. Deployment post-processing consists of:

➤ Stripping the binary of debugger symbols and unnecessary linkage information.

➤ Running any copy files or script phases that have the "only run when installing" flag set. (See Chapter 16 for more about copy file and script phases.)

➤ The ownership and permissions of the final product are set.

The following table describes the deployment settings:

BUILD SETTING	DESCRIPTION
Deployment Postprocessing (DEPLOYMENT_POSTPROCESSING)	If set to YES, deployment post-processing is performed.
Deployment Location (DEPLOYMENT_LOCATION)	If this is set to YES — note that this is a Boolean flag, not a path — the products are built in the deployment location instead of the normal build location. This setting is also YES if xcodebuild is run with the install command. See the INSTALL_PATH and related build settings to control where the deployment location is.
Installation Directory (INSTALL_PATH)	The path where the products for this target should be placed. This path is relative to $(DSTROOT). For example, the install path for a BSD tool might be /usr/bin. The install path for a framework would be /Library/Frameworks.
Strip Debug Symbols from Binary Files (COPY_PHASE_STRIP)	If this is set, the executable binaries are stripped of debugger information *when they are copied to their deployment folder*. Normally you don't have to set this, because stripping of deployed products should happen automatically. Set this if you are including code built by some external process or outside of Xcode altogether.
Strip Linked Product (STRIP_INSTALLED_PRODUCT)	If YES, the normal product stripping performed by post-processing is, instead, *not* performed.
Skip Install (SKIP_INSTALL)	If this and Deployment Location are both set, products are deployed instead to $(TARGET_TEMP_DIR)/Uninstalled Products. Use this for targets that generate products that are used by, but not included with, the final deployed products. This could include, for example, a static library.
Installation Build Products Location (DSTROOT)	The destination folder for installed products. Products are "installed" within this folder using relative paths to their final location. For example, a BSD tool that installs a tool might be installed in $(DSTROOT)/bin. You might think that the normal value for DSTROOT would be /, but you'd be wrong for two reasons. It would be very surprising to novice Xcode users if in the process of building a project they started overwriting installed system components. Also, most of the locations in / are not writable unless root privileges are obtained, and Xcode does not normally run as root. Instead, this folder is a "picture" of what the final installation should look like. For normal builds, this is a temporary location or a folder within the build folder. To build and install a product directly in the system, set DSTROOT to / and run the xcodebuild tool as root.

BUILD SETTING	DESCRIPTION
Install Owner (`INSTALL_OWNER`) (`INSTALL_GROUP`) (`INSTALL_MODE_FLAG`)	When `DEPLOYMENT_POSTPROCESSING` is on, these Install Group settings determine the owner, group, and UNIX Install Permissions access privileges of the deployed product. These default to `$(USER)`, `$(GROUP)`, and `a-w, a+rX`, respectively.

Most of these settings are enabled, or only control steps that are performed, when `DEPLOYMENT_POSTPROCESSING` is on. If changing a deployment or installation build setting doesn't have the desired effect, check to see if it is dependent on `DEPLOYMENT_POSTPROCESSING`.

Build Information

The rest of the build settings covered here are informational. That is, you shouldn't try to set these in the build settings in an attempt to influence how Xcode builds your product. Instead, most of these are build settings that are set by Xcode based on its environment, other information you have already configured in the project, or reflect specifically what Xcode is doing. For example, Xcode sets the `TARGET_NAME` build setting to the name of the target currently being built. You can use this information in custom scripts or external build tools, or refer to it in other build settings. What you shouldn't do is try to redefine it.

Because of this, most informational build settings do not show up in the Build tab where project and target build settings are edited. The following table describes the informational build settings. (Also refer to Chapter 17 about the build settings that are defined when custom scripts or build rule scripts are executed.)

BUILD SETTING	DESCRIPTION
`ACTION`	This setting will be either `build` or `clean`, depending on what kind of build Xcode is performing.
`PROJECT_NAME`	The name of the project being built.
`CONFIGURATION`	The name of the build configuration that is active.
`TARGET_NAME`	The name of the target being built.
`TARGET_BUILD_DIR`	The path in the build folder where the products of this target should be written.
`TARGET_TEMP_DIR`	The path used for temporary files while building a target. Custom build scripts should write any temporary files they generate into this directory.
`PROJECT_TEMP_DIR`	A temporary folder for use by any build process in the project.
`SRCROOT`, or `PROJECT_DIR`	The project folder.

continues

(continued)

BUILD SETTING	DESCRIPTION
SDKROOT	Described earlier in the "Cross-Development" section.
OBJROOT	The top folder where intermediate object files are written.
SYMROOT	The "symbol-rich" product location. This is where products are written before they are stripped.

Tools

To avoid having to hard-code the path of various build tools and to have the ability of redefining which tool to use for all phases of a build, the following build settings are defined:

ASM	GATHERHEADERDOC	MKDIR	REZ
CC	HEADERDOC2HTML	MV	RM
CD	JAR	NMEDIT	RPCGEN
CHMOD	JAVA_COMPILER	OSAC	SED
CHOWN	JAVACONFIG	OSAL	SH
CP	LD	OSAS	STRIP
DITTO	LEX	PBXCP	TOUCH
ECHO	LIBTOOL	RANLIB	UNZIP
EGREP	LN	REGGEN	XARGS
FIXPRECOMPS	MAKEPSEUDOLIB	RESMERGER	YACC
FIND	MERGEINFO	RESOURCE_ PRESERVING_CP	ZIP

Each of these settings contains a path to the executable tool of the same name. Thus, if you wanted to invoke the Java compiler in a build script, use the statement ${JAVA_COMPILER} instead of /usr/bin/javac. If at some point you decide to use a different Java compiler, both your scripts and Xcode will still be using the same one.

Standard System Locations

The build settings described in the following table may be useful for defining installation locations and for locating tools, plug-ins, templates, or other resources in your build scripts. Each gets defined with a path to one of the standard locations defined by the system or the current installation of the Xcode tools. If you've installed Xcode in some directory other than /Developer, these paths will be adjusted accordingly. There are actually more settings than are listed, but these are the major ones.

BUILD SETTING	PATH
SYSTEM_APPS_DIR	/Applications
SYSTEM_ADMIN_APPS_DIR	/Applications/Utilities
DEVELOPER_DIR	/Developer
DEVELOPER_APPLICATIONS_DIR	/Developer/Applications
DEVELOPER_BIN_DIR	/Developer/usr/bin
DEVELOPER_TOOLS_DIR	/Developer/Tools
SYSTEM_LIBRARY_DIR	/System/Library
LOCAL_LIBRARY_DIR	/Library
USER_LIBRARY_DIR	~/Library
XCODE_APP_SUPPORT_DIR	/Library/Application Support/Apple/Developer Tools

THE XCODEBUILD TOOL

The development tools include an xcodebuild command-line tool for building Xcode projects. The xcodebuild tool is installed in your /usr/bin directory by the developer tools installer, so you do not have to add the /Developer/Tools directory to your shell path to use it. The installer also installs a man page for xcodebuild.

Having the ability to build Xcode projects via a command-line tool provides a great deal of flexibility in your development workflow. You can build complex shell scripts to build different product configurations automatically. You could schedule nightly builds of large projects. You can integrate Xcode projects into other make tools, like gnumake or Ant. It's also used to define custom build commands in the Organizer (see chapter 22). Besides being able to drive the build process externally, you can also use xcodebuild to add a layer of intelligence inside Xcode. Using custom build scripts and external build targets, you can invoke scripts that make decisions, and then build another target or project using xcodebuild. Here's an example: one limitation of Xcode targets is that you can't change the input files to a target based on a build configuration. That is, you can't have a target that links to one library when built using one build configuration and a different library for another. You could easily create two targets: MyApp-Release and MyApp-Debug. A custom script can examine the build settings and build the appropriate target using something like xcodebuild -target MyApp-${CONFIGURATION}. The possibilities are almost limitless.

Using the xcodebuild Tool

To use the xcodebuild tool, the working directory must be set to the project folder. The tool does not accept a path to a project folder or document elsewhere. When you execute xcodebuild, you can optionally specify the name of the project, the target, and the build configuration to be built as arguments. If any are omitted, xcodebuild will choose a project, target, and build configuration for you.

`xcodebuild` *reads and respects the Xcode preferences you've defined. However, preferences are stored on a per-user basis. If you run* `xcodebuild` *under a different user ID, namely root, the Xcode preferences used will be those of that other user. Unless you've run and configured the Xcode application while logged in as that user, there will be no Xcode preferences file, and* `xcodebuild` *will use the defaults for all settings.*

A project name can be specified using the `-project projectname` argument. This name is the complete filename of the project document, including its extension. If this argument is absent, `xcodebuild` finds and builds the one and only project document in the folder. If there is more than one project, `xcodebuild` throws an error and stops. This argument is only needed for project folders that have multiple project documents.

You can choose a target using the `-target targetname` argument. If this argument is omitted, the first target defined in the project is built. For projects you intend to build using `xcodebuild`, arrange your targets so that your top-level aggregate target is the first target in the Targets group. That way, you don't have to specify a target for your most common builds. Alternatively, you can use either the `-activetarget` or `-alltargets` switch. The `-activetarget` switch builds the last active target set in the Xcode application. The `-alltargets` switch builds all of the targets in your project; something you can't do in Xcode, except for clean builds.

The `-configuration configurationname` switch selects a build configuration to use. You can specify the build configuration or use the `-activeconfiguration` switch instead. These switches select either the named build configuration or the last active build configuration set in the Xcode application. If both are omitted, the default build configuration is used. Go to the Configurations tab of the project's Info window to set the default build configuration for your project.

Two additional arguments are used to modify the build. The first is the build action. This can be one of the values described in the following table.

COMMAND	DESCRIPTION
build	Builds the target or targets.
clean	Runs a clean build on the target or targets.
install	Performs a build, enabling all deployment postprocessing phases. This option sets the DEPLOYMENT_POSTPROCESSING build setting. You should define the DSTROOT location if you want the final products installed someplace other than the build folder.
installsrc	Copies the source of the project to SRCROOT. Rarely used.

If you don't specify any action, `build` is assumed. You can specify more than one action. The actions will be executed in order, just as if you had invoked the `xcodebuild` tool multiple times. For example, `xcodebuild clean build` first runs a clean build followed by a normal build.

You can also pass build settings to the xcodebuild tool using the following guidelines:

➤ Build settings passed as arguments to xcodebuild supersede any other build settings defined elsewhere. See "The Scope of Build Settings," earlier in this chapter.

➤ The syntax for a build setting is SETTING_NAME=value.

➤ Each setting is a separate argument.

➤ The shell may require you to quote the contents of some build settings.

➤ You can include as many build settings as will fit on the command line.

The following listing shows xcodebuild being passed two build settings: DSTROOT and DEPLOYMENT_LOCATION:

```
xcodebuild DSTROOT=/ DEPLOYMENT_LOCATION=YES install
```

There are many other miscellaneous xcodebuild options. Three you might be interested in are listed in the following table:

OPTION	DESCRIPTION
-version	Outputs the version of the xcodebuild tool to stdout.
-list	List the names of the targets and the build configurations defined in the project. The active target and both the active and default build configurations are all noted. No build is performed.
-help	Outputs a concise summary of xcodebuild's argument syntax.

Compatibility

xcodebuild is capable of building .xcodeproj (Xcode 2.1 and later) documents as well as earlier .xcode project documents. If you run xcodebuild without specifying a project document name, it first searches for an .xcodeproj document and reads that if found. If there are no .xcodeproj documents present, it looks for an .xcode document. In the latter case, xcodebuild internally upgrades the .xcode document, turning it into an .xcodeproj document, and then builds using that .xcodeproj document. The intermediate .xcodeproj document exists only in memory, and is discarded once the build is complete.

XCODE AUTOMATOR ACTIONS

In addition to the xcodebuild tool, the Xcode Development Tools also install a suite of Automator actions, shown in Figure 17-37.

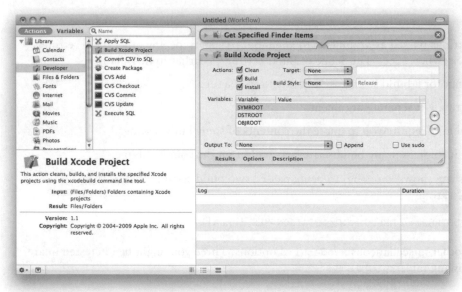

FIGURE 17-37

There are actions to perform CVS source control actions (see Chapter 21), create installation package, and perform builds. The Build Xcode Project Action is just a wrapper that ultimately invokes the xcodebuild tool to perform the build, but the Automator action interface makes it far easier to configure and integrate the build with a larger workflow.

The Build Xcode Project action expects an Xcode project document as its input. The action options let you choose the action (clean, build, and so on), specify a target, choose a build configuration, and supply an arbitrary set of build settings.

DISTRIBUTED BUILDS

One of the more amazing features of Xcode is distributed builds. It's not so much the technology that performs it, which is sophisticated to be sure, but how incredibly easy it is to set up and use.

Distributed builds allow the compilation of source files to be distributed among a group of computers, where they can be compiled in parallel. Every build can call upon the resources of two or — if you have them — more than a dozen computers to simultaneously compile the files in your project. This allows a single developer to harness the power of other (probably) idle machines on his network, such as file servers. Teams of users can share and make more effective use of their resources. It's also a great equalizer. A team member developing programs on a single-core MacMini can harness nearly the same power for his builds as the next developer, who's using a multi-processor, multi-core system.

Here are a few prerequisites and limitations to using distributed builds:

➤ All machines must be accessible via TCP/IP.

➤ All systems must be running the *exact* same version of the operating system and compiler. When you're upgrading your operating system or Xcode, perform the upgrade on all of your development machines simultaneously. This ensures that there is no difference between compilers and the system frameworks between distributed machines.

➤ All computers must be of the same architecture. Intel computers can only distribute builds to other Intel-based systems.

➤ Distributed building only distributes the Compile Sources phase of native targets for C language files. This includes C, C++, and Objective-C. Java, AppleScript, Link, Copy Files, custom scripts, and Jam-based targets can't be parallelized. Precompiling headers, linking, and product packaging are all performed on the local machine.

➤ To be effective, you need a fairly high-speed network. 100MB Ethernet is considered a minimum, with 1GB Ethernet or better preferred. You won't get much benefit from distributed builds over a wireless network. Remember too that FireWire can be daisy-chained to create a very high-speed TCP/IP network.

➤ Firewalls can block distributed builds. Computers employing firewalls must allow traffic on ports 3632 and 7264.

Using distributed builds couldn't be easier. Every machine with Xcode installed can be a provider (will compile files for other developers), a client (will distribute builds to other providers), or both. Each client can also be selective about machines to which it distributes builds.

Open the Distributed Builds pane of the Xcode Preferences of each development machine on the network. The Distributed Builds pane is shown in Figure 17-38.

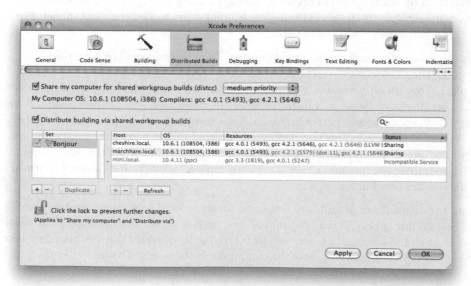

FIGURE 17-38

Sharing Your System with Others

In order to share your computer — offer to compile files for other developers — you must first unlock the padlock in the lower-left corner. You are asked to supply an administrator username and password. Authenticating as an administrator allows Xcode to install the background services that provide distributed building.

Check the box next to the Share My Computer for Shared Workgroup Builds option to make this computer available on the network to perform builds for other developers. The pop-up menu next to the option allows you to choose a process priority for the distributed build process. If you regularly perform time-sensitive, CPU-intensive, tasks such as multi-media processing, you might consider setting this to medium or low priority. Lowering the priority also gives local builds an edge over builds for other developers. Remember that process priority only comes into play when two or more processes are competing to use the CPU. If the computer is idle, it doesn't matter what the priority is; the build will use all of the available CPU time.

Xcode uses the distcc *tool and* distccd *daemon to perform distributed builds. When you share your system with a workgroup, Xcode starts up a* distccd *daemon for each processor core in your CPU. These daemons run all the time; you don't have to be running the Xcode application in order to build products for other workgroup members.*

Distributing Your Builds to the Workgroup

In the lower portion of the pane is a list of computers you can distribute builds to. Available computers are organized into sets, listed on the left. The Bonjour set is a smart set that lists all active build providers on the local subnet. This set is assembled using the Bonjour (ZeroConfig) protocol, and automatically adjusts to reflect the available build providers on the local subnet. For most installations, this is the only set you will need.

The computers in the list display their status and suitability. The Host column contains the IP address of the system. The OS and Resources columns list the versions of the provider's operating system and compilers. You can only distribute a build to a computer with the same version of OS and compiler. The compiler in question will be the compiler required by the target being built. In the example in Figure 17-38, the computer marchhare.local has a compatible version of gcc 4.0.1, but an incompatible version of gcc 4.2.1. This computer could accept builds for targets that use the gcc 4.0.1 compiler, but not ones that required gcc 4.2.1. The computer mini.local, on the other hand, is running an older operating system and cannot accept any builds. Incompatible computers, tools, and Xcode installations are listed in red.

If you want to limit the distribution of builds to a specific subset of local computers, or if you want to add computers that do not appear in the Bonjour list, you need to create a custom set. Click the + button below the list of sets to create a new set, and then give the set a name. You can also duplicate an existing set. Selecting a set, or sets, lists only the computers in those sets. The list is always a union of the sets selected, so computers in multiple sets are listed only once. To delete a set, select it and click the − button. You cannot delete the Bonjour set.

To add a computer to a custom set, either drag a computer from the list into the set, or click the + button below the list with that set selected. Enter the address of the new system, using either a domain name or a numeric address. Xcode adds the new system to every set currently selected and automatically queries the system to discover its status and suitability. To remove a computer from a set, select it in the list and click the − button. You cannot add or remove computers from the Bonjour set. Consequently, having the Bonjour set selected disables both the add and remove buttons for all sets. To add or remove computers from the list, select only custom sets.

To distribute your builds to other computers, check the box next to Distribute Building Via Shared Workgroup Builds, and then check the box next to each set that you want Xcode to include in distributed builds. The computers in all of the checked sets will be considered when Xcode distributes builds to other computers.

That's all there is to it. If you've elected to distribute your builds with other computers, your next build will employ distributed building. Figure 17-39 shows the build of a large project on a laptop computer. Normally, it would only compile one or two files at a time, but with distributed building, it can now compile a score of files simultaneously by exploiting the other computer systems in its workgroup.

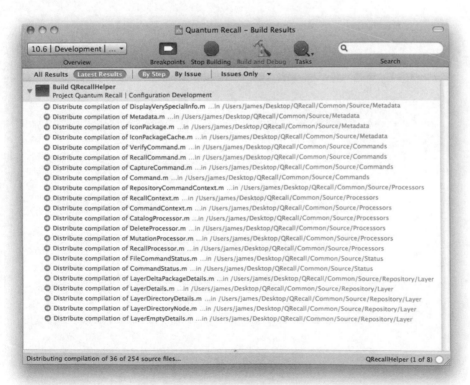

FIGURE 17-39

SUMMARY

Controlling the build process is a critical step in any successful development project. You should now be able to start and stop builds at will, examine the results of the build, and locate errors that occurred while building. Using build settings and build configurations, you can customize many features of the compiler, linker, and Xcode itself. Using build setting layers and build configurations, you can create complex sets of build settings, allowing you to customize specific features of specific targets for specific variations.

Just as important as control is the speed of your development. By learning to enable such features as prefix headers and distributed builds, you can radically reduce the amount of time it takes to build and test your application.

Even after building your project successfully, you're still not quite done. The next chapter shows you how to run and test your application from within Xcode.

18

Debugging

WHAT'S IN THIS CHAPTER?

➤ Running your application

➤ Starting your application under the control of the debugger

➤ Setting breakpoints and creating smart breakpoints

➤ Examining, changing, and customizing the display of variables

➤ Debugging a program running on a remote system

Getting your project to build is sometimes only half the battle. OK, let's be honest; it's often much less than half the battle. It's a cruel fact of programming that your application will have bugs, design flaws, and unexpected behavior. Object-oriented languages, modeling, good design, rigorous coding standards, and unit testing can reduce the number of bugs that creep into your code, but unless your application is trivial, it doesn't matter how careful you've been, how many code reviews you've done, or how many "best practices" you've employed. Someday your application is simply not going to work the way you want it to, and you'll have to find out why. The tool of choice to answer that question is the debugger.

The debugger is a magic window into your application. You can literally watch the internals of your program at work. You can stop your application, examine the values of variables, the state of other threads, and much more. Xcode even allows you to alter values and fix some code while your application is still running — the equivalent of performing a heart transplant on an athlete who's in the middle of running a marathon.

RUNNING YOUR APPLICATION

Before getting into debugging, this section covers the trivial case of simply running your application. You can launch your program, more or less as it would be launched from the Finder or shell, using these commands:

➤ Build ➪ Build and Run (Command+Return)

➤ Build ➪ Build and Run - Breakpoints Off (Command+R)

➤ Run ➪ Run (Option+Command+Return)

➤ Run ➪ Run - Breakpoints Off (Option+Command+R)

All of these commands launch the active executable produced by the most recent build. You choose the active executable much as you do the active target and build configuration, described in the "Choosing the Active Executable" section.

If your "Run" command has turned into a "Debug" command, it's because you have breakpoints enabled. With breakpoints enabled, Run ➪ Run becomes Run ➪ Debug, Build ➪ Build and Run becomes Build ➪ Build and Debug, the Run toolbar button becomes a Debug button, and so on. Breakpoints are globally enabled and disabled by the Run ➪ Activate/Deactivate Breakpoints command.

The run commands that also say "Breakpoints Off" first deactivate all breakpoints before running the executable, equivalent to first choosing Run ➪ Deactivate Breakpoints.

The two Build and Run commands build the active target before starting your program. This is the most common way of running an application — notice that they have the simpler key combinations. It first ensures that the target is fully built before starting your program. Remember to save your source files first, or set the Always Save setting in the Building tab of Xcode's preferences.

The run commands are also accessible via your toolbar in the form of the Run/Debug button and the Build and Run/Debug buttons, shown in Figure 18-1. The Option key changes the action of the buttons from running with (breakpoints enabled) and without (breakpoints disabled) the debugger.

FIGURE 18-1

Monitoring Your Process

Running a program opens the Debugger Console window, shown in Figure 18-2. You can reopen this window at any time using the Run ➪ Console (Shift+Command+R) command. When your executable is launched via Xcode, this window is connected to the stdout, stdin, and stderr pipes of the process. In Xcode, the run window is sometimes referred to as a Pseudo Terminal and acts as a surrogate shell for the process, capturing any output or error messages and supplying any keyboard input to the program's stdin pipe. For command-line tools, this is the main window for your application. For GUI applications, this window captures what would normally be sent to the System Console. For example, messages written using NSLog(...) are captured by the debugging console window when the application is started from within Xcode.

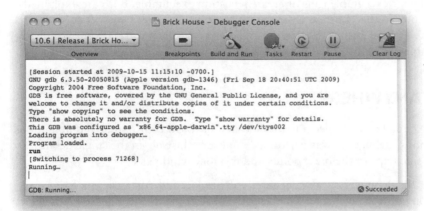

FIGURE 18-2

You can modify these I/O connections, along with many other aspects of your program's execution environment. See the "Custom Executables" section later in this chapter for more details.

Stopping the Executable

Whenever the executable is running, the Run/Debug button changes into a Stop button. You can unceremoniously terminate the running program (equivalent to a kill -KILL command or a Force Quit) using the Stop button or by choosing the Run ➪ Stop (Shift+Command+Return) command.

Choosing the Active Executable

The active executable determines what program is launched when you choose any of the run or debug commands. You can change the active executable using the Project ➪ Set Active Executable menu or using an Active Executable control that's been added to any toolbar. In each menu, there is an item for every executable your project produces. Normally, changing the active target also changes the active executable. If your project produces two applications, Client and Server, changing from the Client target to the Server target also switches the active executable from Client to Server.

In a number of circumstances this might not happen automatically. This is especially true when switching to or from an active target that does not produce an executable. Switching from an application target to an aggregate target (which produces nothing) or a framework target (that doesn't produce anything that can be executed on its own) does not change the active executable. In these circumstances, you'll need to choose the active executable yourself.

You may sometimes want to launch a different executable from the one produced by the target. Say you are working on the Server application, but need to test it using the Client application. Select the Server as the active target and then switch the active executable to the Client. When you Build and Run, the Server gets built, but it's the Client that gets launched.

For the vast majority of projects, the executable produced by your application target is the executable that you want to run or debug. If you have a special situation, you may need to modify the environment in which your executable runs or create a custom executable. Both are explained toward the end of this chapter in the "Custom Executables" section. For now, you'll concentrate on debugging simple executables produced by application and command-line targets. Everything here applies to custom executables as well.

DEBUG ANYTIME, ANYWHERE

The past few versions of Xcode have revealed a noticeable trend toward transparent and ubiquitous debugging. In earlier versions, debugging was performed almost exclusively in the single debugger window, with occasional side trips to the breakpoints and memory windows.

Now, Xcode tries to bring the debugger to you whenever you need it, and wherever you happen to be, rather than making you go to the debugger. Xcode doesn't even open the debugger window by default anymore.

You can debug your applications in the same editor window that you write your code. You can set and modify breakpoints, view variables, and control execution. You can still utilize the traditional debugger window — which is still exceptionally useful for some debugging tasks. Furthermore, it provides some additional, and rather interesting, debugging interfaces. All of these interfaces are described in detail in later sections of this chapter, but I'll summarize them here.

Xcode 3.2 provides three primary debugging interfaces:

> ➤ In-Editor debugging
> ➤ The Debugger window
> ➤ The mini-debugger

In-Editor debugging controls appear in all of your editing panes whenever a debug session is in progress, as shown in Figure 18-3.

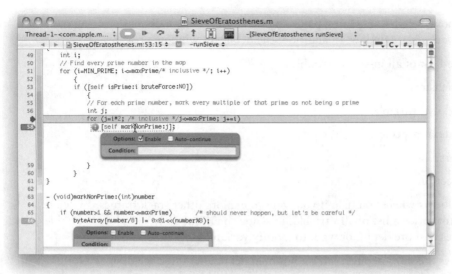

FIGURE 18-3

From your source file editing pane, you can:

➤ Set, enable, disable, and delete breakpoints

➤ Control program execution (pause, run, step over, step into, set out of, and so on)

➤ Examine variables

➤ Switch to a different task or stack frame

The second big interface is the debugger window, shown in Figure 18-4.

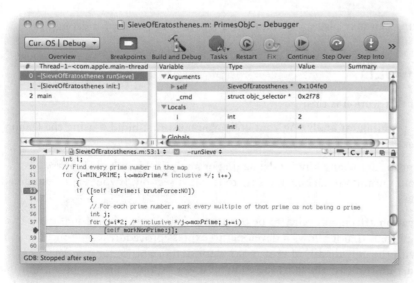

FIGURE 18-4

The debugger window includes an editing pane, so everything you can do in an editing pane can also be done in the debugger window. In addition, the debugger window provides:

➤ A structured list of all in-scope variables

➤ The CPU registers

➤ Access to global variables

➤ Advanced data inspectors

➤ A stack frame list

➤ Thread selection

The debugger window is where you turn if you want to explore other stack frames, switch to another thread, want to see a list of all variables in scope simultaneously, see global variables, want to examine variables in more detail, or want to modify variables.

The third interface is the mini-debugger. It's a minimal debugging interface designed for use with full-screen applications and other situations where getting to the debugger window is awkward or inconvenient. The mini-debugger is described in later sections.

You can see where you can debug from almost anywhere in the Xcode interface, but you can also debug your application anytime; you can launch your application normally and then *later* decide that you want to debug it; Xcode will interrupt the process, attach its debugger, and hand over control to you.

In fact, that's really the primary reason for the Run ⇨ Run - Breakpoints Off (Option+ Command+R) command. After starting your application, all you have to do is create, enable, or reactivate (Run ⇨ Activate Breakpoints) a breakpoint; Xcode will invoke the debugger, have it attach itself to your running executable (if needed), set the requested breakpoints, and let the debugger take over — just as if you had started your application under the control of the debugger in the first place. In Mac OS X 10.6 (Snow Leopard), Xcode keeps the GDB debugging running all the time, so it's even more responsive.

Before any serious debugging can take place, you must first prepare your project for debugging.

BUILT TO BE DEBUGGED

The take-home message of this section is this:

➤ Before debugging, profiling, or analyzing your code, you must first build it using the Debug build configuration.

It's an essential requirement for doing any kind of debugging or analysis. If you're in a hurry, switch your active build configuration to Debug and skip to the next section. If you're interested in knowing why, keep reading.

How you build your application affects its ability to be debugged. The quintessential quality of a modern programming language is that it allows a developer to express procedures symbolically, letting the compiler deal with the ugly details of how to accomplish those procedures in machine code. Listing 18-1 shows just how obtuse the machine code for a few "simple" lines of programming source can be. The source code is shown in the listing, followed by the resulting Intel machine code.

The debugger has the unenviable job of reversing this process — it must examine the raw machine code and translate that back into something that corresponds to the functions, methods, code blocks, classes, structures, and variable names defined in your source code. (You see this process at work later in Figure 18-6.)

Available for download on Wrox.com

LISTING 18-1: Compiled source code

SOURCE CODE

```
- (void)dealloc
{
    free(byteArray);
    [super dealloc];
}
```

COMPILED ASSEMBLY CODE

```
pushl     %ebp
movl      %esp, %ebp
pushl     %ebx
subl      $36, %esp
movl      8(%ebp), %ebx
movl      4(%ebx), %eax
movl      %eax, (%esp)
call      _free
movl      %ebx, -16(%ebp)
movl      L_OBJC_CLASS_SieveOfEratosthenes+4, %eax
movl      %eax, -12(%ebp)
leal      -16(%ebp), %edx
movl      L_OBJC_SELECTOR_REFERENCES_2, %eax
movl      %eax, 4(%esp)
movl      %edx, (%esp)
call      _objc_msgSendSuper
addl      $36, %esp
popl      %ebx
leave
ret
```

To accomplish this feat, the debugger needs a lot of help. That help comes in the form of debugger symbols produced by the compiler. Debugger symbols are a kind of massive cross-index. They contain information like "the machine instruction at byte offset 12,738 corresponds to line 83 of the source file breakme.c." If you set a breakpoint at line 83 of breakme.c, the debugger knows it needs to stop your program at the instruction found at offset 12,738. If your program crashes at (or near) the machine instruction at offset 12,738, the debugger can tell you that your program crashed at (or near) line 83 of breakme.c.

The debugger symbols contain similar information about data structures, classes, automatic variables, and so on. You must request that these debugger symbols be produced when your application is compiled. If you have created your project using one of the Xcode templates, you should have a Release and a Debug build configuration. The Debug build configuration, shown in Figure 18-5, for your program's target has the following build settings:

➤ Generate Debug Symbols: On

➤ Debug Information Format: DWARF with dSYM File

➤ Optimization Level: None

➤ Fix & Continue: Off

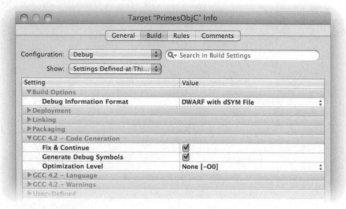

FIGURE 18-5

Generate Debug Symbols enables the full array of debugger symbols in the compiler, detailing every aspect of your code for the debugger. Without it, the debugger is next to useless. This information is produced when each source file is compiled, it takes a little extra time to compile, and produces a lot of data — quite often more data than your actual program — which the debugger has to load. All of this slows down both compilation and launch time. If you are debugging a massive amount of code, you may elect to generate debug symbols only for some modules and not others. For example, you may generate debugger symbols for your main application code but not some well-tested library routines. This speeds up building and debugging, but limits your debugging to the portion of your code that has debugger symbols.

The Debug Information Format defines which file format to use to write the debugging information. DWARF with dSYM File is the modern format and should be your first choice. DWARF and Stabs are older formats that embed the debugging information in the executable.

If you're using the modern DWARF with dSYM File debug symbols format, the legacy build settings Strip Linked Product and Strip Debug Symbols During Copy are largely superfluous. Legacy debugging symbols were stored in the executable files themselves, and later stripped off during the deployment phase of your Release build configuration. The modern dSYM file writes the debugging information to a separate symbol file, so the executable is essentially already "stripped" of its debug information.

If you're developing a legacy application created with an earlier version of Xcode, update your debug format to DWARF with dSYM File and make sure the Strip Debug Symbols During Copy build setting is set to NO. Leaving Strip Debug Symbols During Copy on will interfere with code signing, which is critical to iPhone and modern Mac OS X applications.

While you're debugging, the optimization of your code should be set to None. The reason why goes back to how debuggers work. Optimization, by its very nature, is logic in the compiler that reorganizes, reorders, rewrites, and often eliminates code that it finds to be inefficient or redundant. Take the following code fragment as an example:

```
Line 100: int i=0;
Line 101: for (i=1; i<argc; i++)
```

With optimization turned on, the compiler eliminates the statement i=0 because the result of that assignment is never used. In the debugger, it now becomes impossible to set a breakpoint at line 100 because the code that corresponds to that line of source code doesn't exist in your compiled application. More advanced optimization techniques, such as loop unrolling or instruction reordering, can produce even more bizarre aberrations, such as programs whose statements execute out of order (for example, line 101, then 103, then 102). It might be impossible to stop an application at a certain point in your source code, or step through your code one line at a time. Skeptical readers are invited to enable full optimization and then attempt to debug their application.

Fix & Continue is a feature, covered later in "The Magic Fix," that allows you to make limited code changes in your application while your application is running. That is, you don't have to stop your program, change your code, rebuild, and restart. You simply change your code and keep executing. To use this feature, your compiled object code must contain additional information that the Fix & Continue feature needs. If you leave this build setting off, you can still debug your code, but the Fix & Continue feature is disabled.

The Release build configuration for new projects has the opposite build settings: no debug symbols, symbols stripped, normal optimization, and no Fix & Continue. If you have created your own targets or build configurations, you'll need to set them up accordingly.

Note that Xcode project templates define many of these settings in the *target's* build settings. If you have a multiple target project, you can easily misconfigure the settings in one target and not realize it. Or, you can set them in the project build settings, where they will be promptly ignored. For these reasons, I recommend moving these basic debug settings into the project build settings level for multi-target projects, and then override these settings only in those targets that require something different (which is rare). This way, you can adjust the level of debugger symbols produced (for example) with a single build setting, rather than having to change this setting in every target.

TIP TO REMEMBER

If you think you're having problems getting your build settings right, create a temporary build configuration to experiment with. After you have everything working, you can compare that to the original, or just delete the one that doesn't work. If you've made a lot of changes and really want to know what the differences are, export all of your build settings by copying and pasting them into two separate text files. You can then compare them visually or using a diff tool.

DEBUGGING EXECUTABLES

With the preliminaries out of the way, you're ready to debug your application. Getting started is as easy as running your program. Choose any of these commands to start your application under the control of the debugger:

➤ Build ➪ Build and Debug (Command+Return)

➤ Build ➪ Build and Debug - Breakpoints On (Command+Y)

➤ Run ➪ Debug (Option+Command+Return)

➤ Run ➪ Debug - Breakpoints On (Option+Command+Y)

As mentioned in the "Running Your Application" section, the two unqualified "Debug" commands change to "Run" commands when breakpoints are inactive. The two "Breakpoints On" commands simply activate breakpoints and start debugging, identical to Run ➪ Activate Breakpoints, followed by Build/Run ➪ Debug.

All of these commands start your program under the control of the debugger. The time from which the debugger starts your program until it finishes is referred to as the *debug session*.

An alternative is available in the targets group if you would like to build and then run or debug a target that is *not* the active target or executable. Right/Control-click the target's icon in the target smart group and choose either the Build and Start or the Build and Debug command. The effects are the same as changing the active target to the one selected, issuing a Build and Run/Debug command, and then switching the active target back to what it was originally.

You can have only one debug session active for a project. However, you can have concurrent debug sessions from separate projects. A Client and a Server application, both built using separate projects, could each be running in separate debug sessions simultaneously.

The Process Behind the Curtain

Like most modern integrated development environments (IDEs), the Xcode application doesn't perform the actual debugging — or compilation, or linking, or profiling — of your application. Xcode simply provides an intelligent interface to the command-line tools that do the bulk of the work. In the case of debugging, the work is usually done by gdb, the GNU Debugger.

I say usually, because Xcode can also use other debuggers. It understands the JavaBug and AppleScript debuggers, but if you're doing Mac OS X or iPhone OS development, you'll be using gdb.

Xcode doesn't try to hide the debugger; there are plenty of places where you can interact with the debugger directly. What it tries to do is eliminate much of the tedium of using command-line debuggers by replacing the command line with an interactive, graphical user interface.

So while you're working your way through this chapter, keep this in mind:

➤ Almost every debugging task you undertake in Xcode is eventually translated into a command sent to gdb, or whatever debugger you're using.

Debugger Spoken Here

Another great advantage to using an intermediate debugger is that your debugger interface remains largely the same regardless of the target application environment. Xcode can debug an application in any of the following environments:

➤ A local process running in Mac OS X

➤ A remote process running on another Mac OS X system

➤ An iPhone application running in a local simulator process

➤ An iPhone application running on a remote device

Debugging an application running on the same computer system is the most common scenario, but by no means the only one. The section "Remote Debugging," later in this chapter, shows you how to debug a process interactively that is running on a different computer system.

iPhone application development would seem like it is worlds apart from desktop application development. While the design and implementation might be substantially different, the development tools remain almost identical.

You might have expected a substantial portion of this chapter to be dedicated to the iPhone simulator and iPhone native debugging, but there's really very little to say. Though there's some prerequisite configuration required before an iPhone or iPod Touch can debug applications (see Chapter 22), there is virtually no difference between debugging an iPhone application running on an iPod Touch and debugging a Cocoa application running on your development system. Almost everything in this chapter applies to both.

ATTACHING TO RUNNING EXECUTABLES

As mentioned earlier, the Xcode debugger can *attach* itself to an already running process on your local system, extracting debug information and taking control of its execution. Xcode may do this for one of four reasons:

➤ You create a new breakpoint or enable an existing breakpoint

➤ You reactivate existing breakpoints

➤ An application you started in Xcode crashes or encounters a trap

➤ You choose a process from the Run ⇨ Attach to Process menu

The first three all apply to the currently running executable started via Xcode, but the behavior is a little different depending on which operating system you're running. If you're running Mac OS X 10.5 (Leopard) or earlier, your application is launched normally and the gdb debugger is started and attached when requested. If your running Mac OS X 10.6 (Snow Leopard) or later, Xcode preemptively starts gdb when it launches your application, but lets your application "run free." When you enable breakpoints, gdb steps in, enables breakpoints, and assumes control of your application's execution. The primary advantage is speed; gdb is launched quietly in the background, and springs instantly into action when requested.

Whether gdb *is preemptively started ahead of time or launched post hoc is largely immaterial, except in a few circumstances. Some of the system frameworks include anti-piracy code that either resists being debugged or disables certain features in the presence of the debugger. If you're working with QuickTime or similar libraries, you may have to manually launch your application and then use the Run ⇨ Attach to Process command at some strategic time.*

Once your application is running, creating or enabling any breakpoint signals to Xcode that you want to take control of the application with the debugger. The workflow you'd typically use this in looks something like this:

1. Write some code.

2. Build and run the application.

3. Discover that something's not working right.

4. Start the debugger and have it attach to the already running application.

5. Debug the problem.

The Run ⇨ Attach to Process menu lets you attach the Xcode debugger to a process that Xcode didn't launch. In this menu are all of the running applications. If you need to attach to a background process, choose the Run ⇨ Attach to Process ⇨ Process ID command and enter the process ID you want to debug. These commands are useful when you want to debug a process that you started outside of Xcode (say, from the Finder) or for processes started programmatically; for instance, you've written a Cocoa application that executes a command-line tool.

When attaching to a running process, Xcode does its best to match the executable with a target in the current project. If it can't it will still attach to the process, but the amount of useful debugging information will be extremely limited.

The third reason Xcode will attach to your running application involves a trap, uncaught signal, or other exception that would normally cause the process to exit immediately. Xcode automatically intercepts these exceptions and — rather than letting your application terminate — attaches the debugger. You are left in a debug session with the program suspended at the location that caused the fatal problem. You can examine the threads, stack, variables, and other information in an attempt to determine what went wrong.

You might find it useful to intentionally cause a trap programmatically. To do this, you can add a debugger trap or a hard trap instruction to your code. The `Debugger()` or `DebugStr()` functions request the debugger. For the most part, they act like programmatically defined breakpoints. They will cause the debugger to stop the application, or attach the debugger to an already running application. If left in your code and run in the absence of a debugger, these functions will write a message to the system console every time they are executed — but they won't terminate your application.

A machine trap instruction is essentially a programmatic crash. It can be inserted using an assembly directive, as depicted in the following listing:

```
#if defined(__ppc__) || defined(__ppc64__)
    asm { trap }
#endif
#if defined(__i386__) || defined(__x86_64__)
    __asm { int 3 }
#endif
```

These machine language trap instructions cause your application to immediately stop. If launched from Xcode, Xcode will attach the debugger as it would for any unrecoverable exception. If a trap is executed outside of Xcode, your program will immediately terminate. The system will treat your application as if it had crashed.

Also see the "Custom Executables" section. Whether Xcode stops for `Debugger()` calls or automatically attaches itself when the process crashes can be disabled for individual executables.

IN-EDITOR DEBUGGING

Xcode's in-editor debugging tools let you perform basic and common debugging actions right in your editing window. This means that in many situations you can edit, compile, run, and debug your application without ever switching to another Xcode window or view.

When a debugging session starts, the debugger strip appears at the top of your editor pane, as shown in Figure 18-6. Combined with breakpoint controls in the gutter (which, more than likely, were already visible) and additional symbol inspectors (called *datatips*), the in-editor debugging controls allow you to do three things:

➤ Modify breakpoints

➤ Control execution

➤ Inspect variables

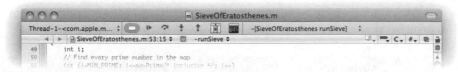

FIGURE 18-6

 A setting in the debugging pane of the Xcode preferences enables the in-editor debugging controls. If you don't see the in-editor debugging controls, check your preferences.

Editing Breakpoints

Breakpoints are described in detail in the "Breakpoints" section of this chapter, but here's the short lesson:

➤ Click a line number in the gutter to create a breakpoint

➤ Click a breakpoint to enable/disable it

➤ Drag a breakpoint to a new line to relocate it

➤ Drag a breakpoint out of the gutter to delete it

➤ Double-click a breakpoint to reveal it in the breakpoints window

Controlling Execution

The red arrow in the gutter, shown in Figure 18-3, indicates the line of code containing the CPU's program counter. This is, essentially, where your program is executing — with some caveats that I'll get to in a moment.

Selecting the Thread and Stack Frame

The debugger strip appears in the editor pane above the navigation ribbon. On the left is a pop-up control that selects the thread with which you want to work. On the right is another pop-up control that lists and selects the stack frame with which you want to work. In between are a series of debugger control buttons.

The gutter's program counter indicator is for the selected stack frame of the selected thread. If you switch threads using the left-hand control, the program pointer moves to indicate where that thread is currently executing. If you choose a different stack frame, it shows where execution will continue when that stack frame is restored — in other words, the code that called the code in the subsequent stack frame.

Running and Stepping Through Code

In between the task and stack frame pop-up menus are the debugger actions. These are listed, from left to right, in the following table:

ACTION	COMMAND	SHORTCUT
(De)activate Breakpoints	Run ⇨ (De)activate Breakpoints	Control+Command+\
Continue	Run ⇨ Continue	Option+Command+P
Step Over	Run ⇨ Step Over	Shift+Command+O
Step Into	Run ⇨ Step Into	Shift+Command+I
Step Out	Run ⇨ Step Out	Shift+Command+T
Debugger Window	Run ⇨ Debugger	Shift+Command+Y
Console Window	Run ⇨ Console	Shift+Command+R

The first five actions are described in detail in the "Controlling the Debugger" section. The last two simply open the debugger window (see "The Debugger Window" section) or the debugging console window (already mentioned in the "Monitoring Your Process" section).

Hover Step Controls

If you hover your cursor over a line number in the gutter that corresponds to executable code, or over a function or method name in the code, one of a number of step controls appears.

Hovering the cursor over the currently executing code line reveals a tiny *continue* button, as shown underneath the cursor in Figure 18-7. If you carefully slide the cursor over to the button and click it, Xcode lets the program continue executing.

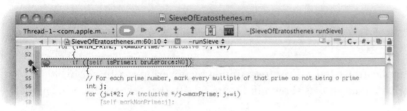

FIGURE 18-7

Hovering the cursor over any other executable line in the gutter reveals a *continue to here* button, as shown in Figure 18-8. The continue to here action sets a temporary breakpoint and then continues execution. Assuming the application doesn't encounter another breakpoint first, the process will run until it gets to the line over which you were hovering.

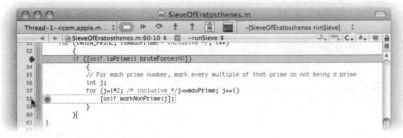

FIGURE 18-8

 The Continue to Here command can also be found in the contextual menu when you Right/Control-click a line the gutter. This can be faster than trying to use the hover controls.

Hovering over a function or method call, as shown in Figure 18-9, reveals a targeted *step into* button. Much like the continue to here action, it sets a temporary breakpoint at the beginning of the function you're hovering over and then lets the application continue execution. The program runs until it steps into the function you targeted.

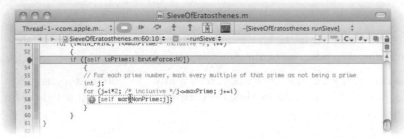

FIGURE 18-9

Viewing Variables

Variables in your running application can be examined simply by hovering the cursor over the variable name. This displays a *datatip*, as shown in Figure 18-10, that reveals the type, name, and value of the variable.

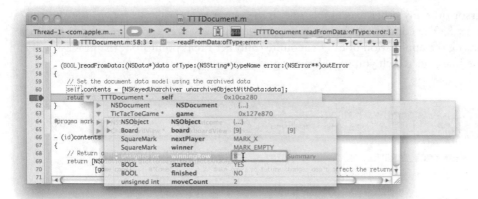

FIGURE 18-10

Simple variables display a single row describing its type, name, and current value.

Complex variables, like objects and structures, include a disclosure triangle that expands to reveal its individual instance variables or fields. Complex instance variables can themselves be expanded, letting you "drill down" in search of the variables for which you're looking.

Datatips only appear for variables in the scope of the current stack frame of the currently selected thread. Changing the thread or stack frame from the debugger strip brings a new set of variables into scope. The section "The Threads Pane" illustrates this in more detail.

By default, the expansion of subvariables is automatic, but you can turn that off. Clicking the disclosure triangle of an expanded variable collapses it again.

A datatip row may contain one of two active controls. One is a value editor. Most mutable scalar values can be changed simply by clicking its value in the datatip, also shown in Figure 18-10.

The other control is a datatip menu, which appears as two arrows on the left-hand side of the datatip. Clicking the arrows pops up the a datatip menu, as shown in Figure 18-11.

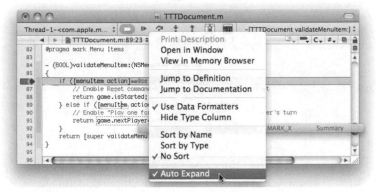

FIGURE 18-11

From the datatip menu you can dump (print) the variable's value to the debugger console, open the variable in its own window, jump to the symbol's definition or documentation, enable/disable data formatters, control the order in which subvariables are displayed, and turn datatip auto-expansion on or off.

Variable windows, memory browser windows, types, and data formatters are all described later in the "Examining Data" section.

THE DEBUGGER WINDOW

The debugger window, shown in Figure 18-12, is the master control center for debugging. Debugging controls in the editor or mini-debugger are designed to be unobtrusive or appear only when requested. The debugger window is just the opposite; it presents as much information about the variables and state of your application as possible. The debugging features accessible from the editor pane or the mini-debugger are all duplicates of the features in the debugger window, so the detailed descriptions of each are included in these sections.

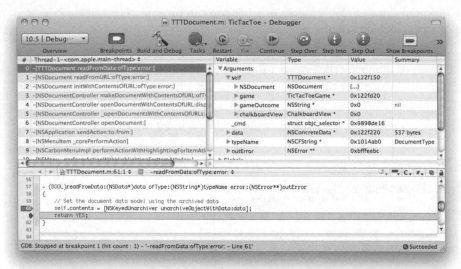

FIGURE 18-12

Each project has its own debugger window. You can open the debugger window at any time using the Run ➪ Debugger (Command+Shift+Y) command. You can minimize or close the debugger window — if only to get it out of your way — without upsetting the debug session. Reopen the debugger window again and resume where you left off.

The debugger window has three main panes: the threads pane, the variables pane, and the listing or editor pane. The debugger pane has an alternate vertical layout to the one shown in Figure 18-12. Use the Run ➪ Debugger Display ➪ Vertical/Horizontal Layout command to switch between the two. The vertical layout splits the window vertically, with the threads and variables panes on the left and the entire vertical pane on the right dedicated to the listing or editor pane. Choose the style that you find most comfortable.

You can resize all three panes by dragging the small grey thumb bar that appears at the nexus of the three panes.

The Threads Pane

The threads pane displays the stack of the active thread, as shown in Figure 18-13. Each entry in the list represents a single stack frame, and the selected entry defines the active stack frame. A frame contains the return address of the caller and all of the function's automatic variables. If the address of the function can be translated into a name, the function's name is displayed. Otherwise the address of the function is listed.

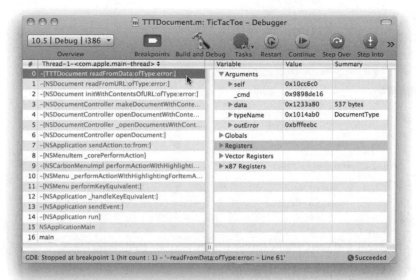

FIGURE 18-13

When you stop an application in the debugger, the debugger stops all threads, but the pane displays the call stack of the thread that hit the breakpoint. The left column indicates the relative depth of each function in the call stack. The name of the function currently executing is displayed at the top of the list and always has a stack depth of 0. The name of the function that called the currently executing function is listed underneath that and has a stack depth of 1, and so on all the way back to the function that started the thread.

 For the debugger, there are only functions, structures, and variables. Different languages refer to subroutines using various terminologies: procedure, function, member function, method, subroutine, or message handler. Ultimately, each becomes a block of code at an address in memory. When this book uses the words "function" or "subroutine," substitute the term of your preferred paradigm.

The contents of the variables pane and the initial contents of the editor pane are determined by the current selection in the threads pane. When you stop an application, the current (top) function in the call stack of the stopped thread is selected. Select another function in the call stack, and the variables and editor pane change to display the variables and execution location in that function. This allows you to examine not only the variables of the current function, but also the variables and calling address of the functions that called the current function.

You can view another call stack by selecting a different thread from the pop-up menu at the top of the pane, as shown in Figure 18-14.

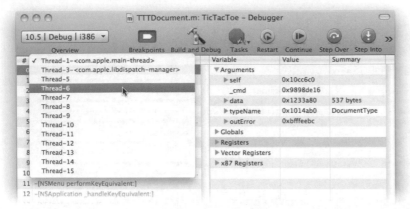

FIGURE 18-14

You can also step through the threads in your application using these two commands:

➤ Run ➭ Next Thread (Control+Option+Command+↑)

➤ Run ➭ Previous Thread (Control+Option+Command+↓)

Change to another thread, and you can examine the local variables and calling address of any frame on that thread's stack. Depending on the language and run time library used, threads may or may not have readable descriptions. If they do, the description will appear next to the thread's identifier.

The Run ➭ Sync With Debugger command is a kind of navigation "home" for the debugger window. It reselects the thread and top-most stack frame that caused the debugger to stop, and jumps to the program's execution location in the editor pane.

The Listing or Editor Pane

The listing or editor pane displays the source code of your application, a disassembly listing, or both. The latter combination is shown in Figure 18-15. The debugger chooses a view automatically when it needs to display a breakpoint or calling location. If the debugger can correlate the program location with a source file, it displays the source code in an editor pane.

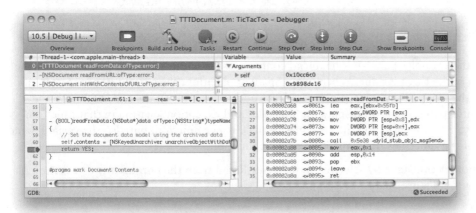

FIGURE 18-15

This is a full-featured editor pane, allowing you to edit your source code right in the debugger window. It also contains all of the breakpoints, hover step controls, and datatips described earlier in the "In-Editor Debugging" section. The only thing it doesn't have is the debugging strip, because all of those functions are provided elsewhere in the debugger window.

You can choose an alternate source code view using one of the following commands:

➤ Run ⇨ Debugger Display ⇨ Source Only

➤ Run ⇨ Debugger Display ⇨ Source and Disassembly

➤ Run ⇨ Debugger Display ⇨ Disassembly Only

If the debugger cannot determine a source file that corresponds to the program's location, there is no source view; it displays only the disassembly of the machine codes and the disassembly display commands have no effect. Similarly, only languages that compile directly into assembly language have a disassembly view; Java and AppleScript programs do not show a disassembly view of their byte code or tokens.

Breakpoints and the current execution location are indicated in the gutter of the editor pane. Breakpoints appear as dark blue (enabled), light blue (disabled), or yellow (invalid) markers. The program counter (PC) indicator appears as a red arrow. The breakpoint and location indicators are so critical to the effective use of the debugger that the gutter display is turned on whenever you are in a debug session. If your Xcode Preferences are set not to display the gutter in the editor, the gutters disappear again at the end of your debug session.

The program-counter indicator always points to the current execution location for the selected thread and stack frame. In a source file, it points to the source line most closely associated with the program-counter position. In the disassembly listing, it points to the exact instruction. If the top (level 0) stack frame is selected, the arrow indicates where the current thread is executing. Select another stack frame in the list and it indicates the location where the stack frame above it was called.

> *Because the meaning of the PC indicator is relative, make sure you pay attention to what stack frame you have selected. If you choose another stack frame, the PC indicator points to where the current execution location was called from, not where it is. Using a command like Step Over does* not *step to the next instruction after the PC indicator. It steps to the next instruction in the top stack frame, where the program is actually stopped.*

The Variables Pane

The variables pane displays the known data variables for the selected stack frame. The key word here is *known*. The debugger *must* have debug symbol information that describes the structure for the selected stack frame. If there is no description available, it cannot interpret or display any data values on the stack and the pane is empty. You will encounter this most often when you stop an application in a system framework or library routine.

Variable Groups

Variables in the display are organized into a hierarchy of groups. The top-level groups are listed in the following table:

VARIABLE GROUP	DESCRIPTION
Arguments	The parameters passed to the current function.
Locals	The automatic variables allocated in the stack frame.
File Statics	Local static variables allocated in the same module.
Globals	Potentially, any global variable in the application.
Properties	AppleScript properties.
Registers	The CPU's hardware registers.

If there are no variables of a given type, the group containing that type is not displayed: a simple C function with no parameters does not display an Arguments group. A method with no automatic variables has no Local group.

Although the Arguments group is technically just more local variables, Xcode groups them for convenience. In object-oriented languages, the arguments include the implied variables such as `this` or `self`. Expand the `this` or `self` object to view the instance variables of the current object.

The Locals group contains the local (also known as automatic or stack) variables allocated on the stack frame.

The File Statics group contains any static variables defined in the code's module. The scope is immaterial; the defined variables may be local or global.

The Globals group contains any global variables you want to examine in the applications. Because this could, potentially, contain hundreds if not thousands of variables (remember that every library and framework that your application is linked to can declare globals), this group must be manually populated with just the symbols you want to examine. This is explained later in the "Viewing Global Variables" section.

The Registers group, or groups, depends on the architecture of the assembly code and your current processor. Interpreted languages like Java and AppleScript won't have a Registers group. CPUs with vector processing units, floating-point calculation units, or CPUs that have a separate set of 64-bit registers may display addition register groups.

Exploring Variables

Variables are listed by name. Structures, arrays, and objects appear as groups in the listing. Expose the contents of a group to examine its member variables, just like you did with the datatips. The Value column shows the interpreted value of the variable. For simple types (integers, floats, strings) it's the textual representation of the value. For arrays, structures, and objects it's a summary of its content. The summary can be very generic or quite specific, as you'll soon see.

Pointers or references display the address or id of the object to which they are pointing but act like the object to which they refer. Thus, you can expand a pointer to a structure so it shows the member values of the structure. Change the pointer and all member values change accordingly. Xcode dynamically determines the structure of objects when it can. The most obvious example is a generic reference of an id or Object type. Variables of this type impart no information about the class or structure of the object they might reference. When Xcode displays an object reference, it examines the type of the object and adjusts its display to reflect the structure of the *actual* object. Thus, you will see the member variables of an id or Object reference change, depending on the type of object to which it refers.

Similar to datatips, you can change the scalar value of variables. Simply double-click in the value cell of the variable and edit its value.

Value Summaries

The Summary field is an intelligent interpretation of the variable's contents. Using a system of data formatters, the field can display a more human-readable summary of the object or structure's contents. Xcode has numerous data formatters built in. A simple example is the NSCalendarDate object. Without data formatters, an NSCalendarDate reference would display as an object at a particular address. Exposing its member values would display several variables, shown on the left in Figure 18-16. The `_formatString` variable contains something cryptic, the `_timeZone` value contains a pointer to an opaque object, and the `_timeIntervalSinceReferenceDate` variable contains a big floating-point number. Unless you can convert seconds-since-the-epoch to a calendar date in your head, none of these values are particularly informative.

FIGURE 18-16

This is where data formatters come to the rescue. Xcode includes data formatters for strings, dates, and even the time zone object. Turn data formatters on and the display changes to something far more useful, shown on the right in Figure 18-16. The format string and time zone values are now easily readable, and the date object reference itself displays a practical representation of the date and time encapsulated by that object. You learn how to create your own data formatters, which is even more powerful, later in the "Data Formatters" section. You can enable and disable data formatters using the Debug ⇨ Variables View ⇨ Enable Data Formatters command.

Variable Types

There is also an optional Type column that you can display using the Run ⇨ Variables View ⇨ Show Type Column command. This column shows the type of each variable. For objects, this field shows the type of the object the debugger believes it to be — which is not necessarily the type of the reference. If the debugger cannot determine the type of the object, typically because the reference is invalid or set to `nil`, the type displayed is the type declared for the variable.

Showing the Type column is probably the first thing I do after opening the debugger window for the first time. Alternatively, you can also Right/Control-click any variable and choose Show/Hide Type Column from the pop-up menu. Sadly, Xcode doesn't preserve this setting between Xcode sessions.

There's a lot more to examining data in the debugger. This brief overview should give you some idea of what you're looking at while you progress to the more practical topic of controlling the debugger and setting breakpoints. Until you can stop your application, there's no data to examine.

CONTROLLING THE DEBUGGER

One of the most elementary, and often most effective, methods of debugging an application is simply to stop it and examine its state. Look at the value of local variables and objects, and see what functions have been called and in what order. You may then want to step through the code one line at a time to witness its order of execution. This, rather passive, method of debugging is often all that's required to determine what your code is doing wrong or unexpectedly.

You control this kind of immediate and interactive debugging through a set of debugging commands. None of these commands (except the Pause command) is available until the debugger has suspended your application. This happens when the execution of your program encounters a breakpoint, some exceptional event, or when you use the Pause command. The most predictable method is to set a breakpoint. It's possible to stop your program using the Debug ➪ Pause command, but it's rarely that useful. Pause stops your program wherever it is at that moment — usually in some framework or kernel call.

Breakpoints can do many sophisticated things, and you can set them in a variety of ways, all of which is covered later in the "Breakpoints" section. For now, all you need to do is set and enable simple breakpoints by clicking in the editor pane gutter of any source file. A breakpoint appears as a blue marker that indicates the position of the breakpoint in the source code. Clicking an existing breakpoint toggles its state between enabled (blue) and disabled (grey). Only enabled breakpoints interrupt program execution. To delete a breakpoint, drag the breakpoint out of the gutter or use the Right/Control-click menu to select the Remove Breakpoint command.

After the execution of your program has been suspended, a set of execution control commands becomes available. These are listed in the following table:

COMMAND	SHORTCUT	DESCRIPTION
Continue	Option+Command+P	Resumes execution of your program. Your program will run until it encounters another breakpoint or terminates.
Pause	Option+Command+P	Immediately suspends execution of your program. This is the only command that will stop your program without setting a breakpoint.

COMMAND	SHORTCUT	DESCRIPTION
Step Into	Shift+Command+I	Executes one line of source code. If the line contains a call to another function, execution is stopped again at the beginning of that function, which is what gives this command its name — you are stepping *into* the function being called. If the source line does not call another function, this command is equivalent to Step Over.
Step Over	Shift+Command+O	Executes one line of source code and stops before executing the line that follows. If the line contains calls to other functions, those functions are allowed to execute in their entirety.
Step Out	Shift+Command+T	Resumes execution until the current function returns to its caller.
Step Into Instruction	Option+Shift+Command+I	Equivalent to Step Into, but steps through a single machine instruction rather than a full line of source code, that might translate into dozens of machine instructions.
Step Over Instruction	Option+Shift+Command+O	Equivalent to Step Over, but steps over only a single machine instruction.
(continue to here)	Option+click in gutter	Sets a temporary breakpoint and starts the program running.
Sync With Debugger		Returns the debugger window's view to showing the current thread, current stack frame, current function, and current PC indicator where the debugger last suspended your process.
Stop	Shift+Command+Return	Forcibly terminates your program's process.

Pause and Continue

The Pause and Continue commands are immediate and self-explanatory. They share the same menu item, toolbar button, and keyboard shortcut. The Pause command is active whenever the process is executing, and the Continue command is active whenever it is suspended.

Generally, the Pause command isn't very useful for working GUI applications, because it tends to suspend the application in a run loop. You will probably find it most edifying when your application is stuck in an endless, or seemingly endless, loop. It can also be helpful to suspend your application while you think about your next move or contemplate where to set a breakpoint. You don't have to stop the program to set a breakpoint, but you don't necessarily want your application running amuck while you decide where it should go.

Step Over and Into

Step Over and Step Into are the two most commonly used debugger control commands. Step Over lets you walk through the logic of a single function, ignoring the details of other functions that it might call. Step Into traces the execution of the program one step at a time, regardless of where that leads.

Step Into, Step Over, Continue to Here, and many other debugger commands work by setting temporary breakpoints. A temporary breakpoint is one created by the debugger for some ephemeral purpose, which it then deletes as soon as it's reached. For example, the Step Into command works by setting a temporary breakpoint at the beginning of the function that you want to step into. It then lets the process execute. Most of the time this works as expected.

You may, however, encounter unexpected behavior if the code encounters another breakpoint first (possibly in another thread) or if there's an exceptional event; the debugger will stop there instead.

A different situation arises if a function exits abnormally (via a longjmp, *by throwing an exception, or by terminating a thread) — the program may never execute the code wherein the temporary breakpoint was set. In this situation, the program avoids the breakpoint and continues running indefinitely.*

The Step Over command is intelligent about recursive functions. Stepping over a function that calls itself does not stop until all nested iterations of the function have executed and returned, even if that entails executing the same code position that you are stepping over.

If your editor pane is in disassembly view, Step Into and Step Over behave exactly the same way, but they each execute a single machine instruction — instead of the group of instructions generated by the single line of source code.

If the source line contains multiple calls, the Step Into command steps into the first function called. This is significant if a function passes parameters that are obtained by calling other functions. The example in Listing 18-2 illustrates this. If the debugger first stopped at this line and you issued the Step Into command, the debugger would step into getDefaultMode(), not setMode(). That's because the getDefaultMode function is called first to obtain the value of setMode's single argument.

LISTING 18-2: Nested function calls

Available for download on Wrox.com

```
setMode(getDefaultMode());        // reset the mode
```

After you return from `getDefaultMode` (see the Step Out command), the debugger again returns to this line of source code, but the CPU's program counter is now poised at the call to `setMode`. This time the Step Into command steps into the `setMode` function.

 This is the situation where the hover step controls are exceptionally useful. Hover your cursor over the function or method name you want to step into and click its step into button. Xcode will step into that specific function, allowing any prerequisite functions to execute without interruption.

Step Into only steps into functions that have debug information and have local source files associated with them. You cannot step into library functions, framework APIs, or kernel code that was not compiled with full debug information. Attempting to step into such a function is treated like a Step Over.

Stepping Out

Step Out is convenient for letting the current function complete its execution and return again to the point where it was called. It's common to step into a function simply to examine the values of its arguments. After you are satisfied the function is behaving correctly, you can then use Step Out to let the function finish and return to where it was called. The same issues about exceptional exits that apply to Step Over also apply here.

Stepping Over and Into Single Instructions

The special Step Into Instruction and Step Over Instruction perform the same actions as the Step Into and Step Over, but each only executes a single machine instruction. These functions work in either source or disassembly view, but are most useful when you're viewing both the source and disassembly of your program's code where the meaning of Step Into and Step Over becomes ambiguous.

Step Into Instruction is also away around the Step Into command's self-imposed limitation of never stepping into a function that doesn't have source information (like a library function). If the function being called has no source code available, Step Into Instruction still steps into it, automatically switching to a disassembly-only view, as required.

Continue to Here

The continue to here command doesn't appear in the menu and has no keyboard shortcut. A continue to here button appears when you hover over an executable line number in the gutter. You can also use this, much quicker, shortcut:

➤ Option+click a line number in the gutter

The continue to here action creates a temporary breakpoint and starts your application running, just as if you had set a regular breakpoint and issued the Continue command. A breakpoint indicator is not visible in the gutter or anywhere else in Xcode, and the breakpoint is deleted as soon as it is hit. This makes it extremely easy to skip through blocks of code or around loops by simply clicking where you want to stop next. The same caveats about temporary breakpoints mentioned earlier apply here.

THE MINI-DEBUGGER

The mini-debugger is a compact debugger control window that's intended to be used in situations where switching between your application and Xcode is awkward or impossible. This is particularly true of applications that present full-screen multimedia, games, animation, screen savers, and similar environments.

You open the mini-debugger with the Run ⇨ Mini-Debugger (Control+Command+Home) command. It opens a small floating window, shown on the left in Figure 18-17. The mini-debugger window floats above all other window layers, including the menubar, so it stays visible regardless of what application you switch to or what other windows are displayed.

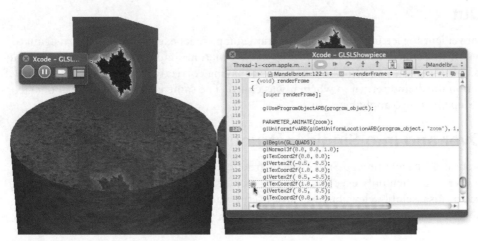

FIGURE 18-17

While the application is running, the mini-debugger window has four buttons:

➤ Stop

➤ Pause

➤ (De)activate Breakpoints

➤ Xcode

The stop, pause, and toggle breakpoints button each perform their respective action. The Xcode button simply returns you to the Xcode application — often handy in applications where all of the Xcode windows and the menubar are obscured.

Whenever the application is paused, the mini-debugger window expands to show a small editor pane, as shown on the right in Figure 18-17. The pane has all of the in-editor debugger controls described in the "In-Editor Debugging" section.

If you like the mini-debugger, you'll probably want to set the On Start Open Mini Debugger setting in the debugging preferences pane.

BREAKPOINTS

Breakpoints are locations in your program where you want the debugger to take control. Formally, a breakpoint is set at a particular address in memory. When the CPU's program counter matches the address of a breakpoint — that is to say at the instant before the instruction at that breakpoint's address is to be executed — the CPU stops executing your program and passes control to the debugger.

So far you've created only basic breakpoints. The default action of a breakpoint is to halt the execution of your program, hand over control to the debugger, and wait for instructions, but breakpoints are capable of much more.

Before getting into more advanced techniques for defining breakpoints, here's a quick review of the methods for creating a basic breakpoint — one that simply stops the program when encountered:

> ➤ Click in the gutter of a source file.

> ➤ Right/Control-click in the gutter of a source file and choose the Add Breakpoint command.

> ➤ Choose the Run ➪ Manage Breakpoints ➪ Add Breakpoint At Current Line (Command+\) command when the active text cursor is in a source file.

> ➤ Use any of the debugger commands to create a temporary breakpoint and start the program running.

When you're setting breakpoints graphically, Xcode allows you to set a breakpoint on just about any line of the source file. A lot of times this doesn't make any sense, but Xcode can't tell that. When you set a breakpoint in a source file, you're actually setting the breakpoint at the first executable instruction produced by the source file at, or following, the line you clicked. Figure 18-18 shows three breakpoints set in a source file. All three of these breakpoints point to the same address location. The first one is set on a declaration statement that produces no code, and the second one is set on a completely blank line. Only the source code on line 30 produces any executable code in the application. Ultimately, you could set a breakpoint on line 28, 29, or 30 with the same results. The breakpoint is set at the instruction that implements the `switch` statement.

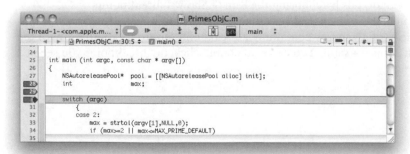

FIGURE 18-18

In a similar vein, source code that you might not think of as producing code often does. A good example is the closing brace of a C++ function. All functions have to return, and the closing brace of the function body produces code that destroys any automatic objects, pops the stack frame, and returns to the caller. This happens even in void functions. Consequently, you can set a breakpoint at the closing brace of a function if you want to catch the function after the body of the function has executed, but before it returns to the caller.

The concept that this section is trying to express is that there is not always a simple one-to-one correlation between the source code statements and the executable code with which the debugger deals. The debugger does its best to translate between the two, but inconsistencies do occur. Just be prepared for this and understand what's going on.

Breakpoint Types

There are two kinds of breakpoints: source breakpoints and symbolic breakpoints. So far, this chapter has only dealt with source breakpoints. Source breakpoints are associated with a particular line in a source file. You set and see source breakpoints right in the gutter of the source file's editor pane.

Symbolic breakpoints are breakpoints that have been created for a particular symbol — that is, at the address of a symbol defined in the program. There are two important differences between a symbolic breakpoint and a breakpoint set at a line in a source file.

The most obvious is that you don't have to have the source file. Using symbolic breakpoints, you can set a breakpoint at the entry point of any library routine or framework API. For example, you could set a symbolic breakpoint at the `free()` function. Any code that calls the `free(...)` function would break into the debugger.

The other important difference is that the breakpoint address is not associated with a line in a source file. You could cut the function from one file and paste it into another, and the breakpoint would still work.

You find out how to create symbolic breakpoints shortly.

Breakpoints Window

Breakpoint management gets far more interesting when you open the breakpoints window, shown in Figure 18-19. You can do this by choosing the Run ➪ Show ➪ Breakpoints (Command+Option+B) command — which is also available as a button in many toolbars. The toolbar button has an icon of a window containing a breakpoint (not to be confused with the *other* breakpoints button that has a + sign). You can also double-click any breakpoint you see in a source file.

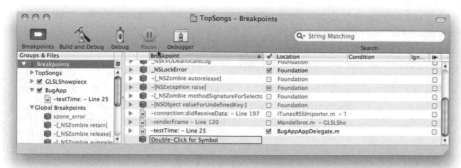

FIGURE 18-19

The Breakpoints window has two panes: a Groups & Files pane containing the Breakpoints smart group and a details pane listing the individual breakpoints. It should be noted that this is really just an abbreviated view of your project window, without the editor pane. Everything you can do in the Breakpoints window can be accomplished in the Breakpoints smart group and details pane of your project window.

Breakpoint Groups

The Breakpoints smart group has two subgroups. Each open project creates a group that contains all breakpoints specific to that project. The group might be simply named Project Breakpoints, or if multiple projects have been opened you will see a group named for each project. When you create a source file breakpoint in an open project, it's added to its group. These breakpoints are saved (per user) in the project document, so your breakpoints will persist between Xcode sessions.

The Global Breakpoints group contains breakpoints that are available to all projects. This is particularly useful for complex symbolic breakpoints that you want to use in different projects. Possibly, you could keep breakpoints in a common library that you use in several projects. Global breakpoints are saved in your Xcode Preferences.

Breakpoint Details

The list in the details pane shows the breakpoints selected in the Groups & Files window, or all the breakpoints contained in a selected group or groups. To limit the list of breakpoints to a particular subset, select only that subgroup in the Groups & Files pane. To see all of the breakpoints defined, select the top-level Breakpoints group.

Each breakpoint listed displays an icon, description, enabled check box, location, condition, and continue option. By Right/Control-clicking the column header of the table you can optionally choose to display the (normally hidden) Comments, Last Modified, and Hit Count columns. You may also hide columns that don't interest you.

The icon indicates the type of the breakpoint. Source breakpoints have a source file icon, and symbolic breakpoints have a 3D cube. Source breakpoints are described by the function name and line number within the source file, shown in the Location column, where they are set. Symbolic breakpoints are described by the symbol of the breakpoint address, possibly with a qualifier to distinguish between similar symbols. The location of a symbolic breakpoint is the library or module where it resides.

The name or address of a symbolic breakpoint is editable — double-click the name to change the symbol. Source breakpoints are not. Double-clicking a source breakpoint in the list jumps to that location in the source file. This is the complement of double-clicking a breakpoint in a source file, which jumps to that breakpoint in the breakpoint window.

The Comments column contains a text field for recording your comments about, or a description of, the breakpoint. If you have a lot of comments, open the Info window for the breakpoint and edit the comments there. The Last Modified field records the last time the breakpoint was altered. The Continue column is explained later in the "Breakpoint Actions" section, and the Condition field is explained in the "Iffy Breakpoints" section.

A breakpoint's detail line can be expanded to display the its actions, described later in the "Breakpoint Actions" section.

Breakpoint Details in an Editor Pane

You've seen breakpoints in editor panes more than a dozen times so far, but there's a somewhat obscure command for displaying some details about the breakpoint right in the editor pane, as shown in Figure 18-20.

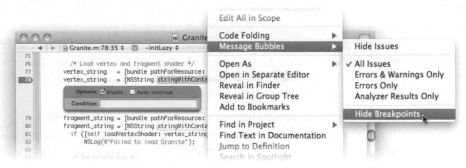

FIGURE 18-20

The View ➪ Message Bubbles ➪ Show Breakpoints command reveals breakpoint bubbles containing some details about each breakpoint. This same command is accessible via the Right/Control-click menu in the editor pane, also shown in Figure 18-20.

The enabled, auto-continue, and breakpoint condition can be edited right in the editor pane. This can be particularly handy when using the mini-debugger.

Deleting Breakpoints

To delete one or more breakpoints in the breakpoints window, select the breakpoints in the window and press the Delete key. You can also select a group of breakpoints in the Groups & Files pane and choose the Delete command from the Right/Control-click contextual pop-up menu.

To delete a source breakpoint from within a source file editor, click and drag the breakpoint out of the gutter. You can also Right/Control-click the breakpoint and choose the Remove Breakpoint command.

Enabling and Disabling Breakpoints

The check mark column in the breakpoints list shows whether that breakpoint is enabled. You can enable or disable an individual breakpoint by ticking its check box. This is synonymous with clicking the breakpoint's indicator in the source file. Enabled breakpoints are dark blue; disabled breakpoints are light blue.

Selecting breakpoints in the Groups & Files pane lets you to enable and disable breakpoints en masse. Select any combination of breakpoints and breakpoint groups in the Groups & Files pane — these commands do not work in the details list. Right/Control-click one of the selected items and choose either the Enable Breakpoints or the Disable Breakpoints command from the contextual menu. Enabling or disabling a group sets the state of every breakpoint contained in that group.

Hold down the Option key and the Enable Breakpoints command turns into the Enable Only These Breakpoints command. This command enables the selected breakpoints, and then disables all other project breakpoints. This is a quick way of enabling a strategic group of breakpoints you want to focus on while simultaneously disabling all others.

> *You may notice that some breakpoints display a – sign in their enabled check box. These are enabled breakpoints that the debugger can't set for some reason. Examine the debugger console output (covered later) to find out which breakpoints are having problems. This is most commonly encountered with symbolic breakpoints that the debugger can't resolve. Beyond the obvious reason that the symbol simply doesn't exist in the application's name space, it can also happen when you're using ZeroLink or lazily loaded libraries. These technologies defer the loading and linking of functions until they are actually called, which means that the code for many functions won't be loaded into memory when the program starts executing. Until the debugger can turn a symbol name into an absolute memory address, it can't set a breakpoint.*

Creating Symbolic Breakpoints

To create a symbolic breakpoint, first select the Breakpoints group in which you want the breakpoint created. At the bottom of the details pane list is a special placeholder breakpoint with a border around the name Double-Click For Symbol. To create a new symbolic breakpoint, do just what it says, as shown in Figure 18-21.

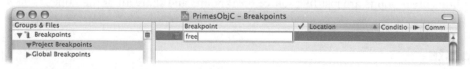

FIGURE 18-21

The symbol can be any function name known to the linker. This can be a function in your own application or any system API or library to which your application is linked. For C function calls, just the name of the function is sufficient. If there is any ambiguity, Xcode prompts you to choose the specific symbol that you meant. In Figure 18-22, a breakpoint is set on the `free` symbol, and Xcode wants to know which "free" it's referring to.

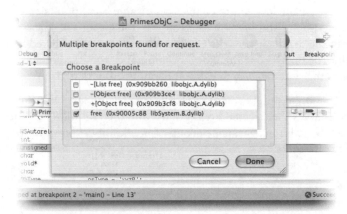

FIGURE 18-22

Objective-C and C++ methods must be expressed in their complete form. To set a symbolic breakpoint at the `isPrime:` method of the SieveOfEratosthenes class, create a breakpoint for the `-[SieveOfEratosthenes isPrime:]` symbol. Note that the symbol must have a + or – sign indicating a class or member method. In this example, : indicates that the method takes a single parameter. Just like when you're using the `@selector` operator, `isPrime` and `isPrime:` are two different methods. If the method took a second `BOOL` parameter, the symbol would be something like `-[SieveOfEratosthenes isPrime:ignoringMap:]`.

In C++, the symbol should be a complete, fully qualified, prototype of the method. If the NestOfBugs class contained a member function named `catchMe` that took a single integer as a parameter, the symbol to use would be `NestOfBugs::catchMe( int i )`. Unlike the Objective-C symbol, the name of the parameter is included exactly as it was declared in the class statement. `gdb` will not find the function without a complete copy of its declaration. The return type of a function is not part of its name.

Symbolic breakpoints do not appear as breakpoint indicators in the gutter of the source file editor pane, even if the symbol identifies a function in your source code. Other than the visual differences, symbolic breakpoints are just like source breakpoints and share all of the same capabilities and traits.

Iffy Breakpoints

One of the first things you'll notice about breakpoints is that they always work. Although it might be gratifying to know that the technology is reliable, you may soon discover that it can be a curse as well. Setting a breakpoint in a function that gets called a million times is enough to wear out the button of any mouse if you have to click the Continue button 999,999 times. Furthermore, quite often the problem with a loop will be found at the end, not the beginning. Placing a breakpoint in the middle of a loop can be a study in tedium.

What you really want to do is break at the moment your application is doing something interesting or suspicious. For example, you want to break a loop on its *last* iteration or just when a parameter is NULL.

You can accomplish this by using a breakpoint conditional. In the Condition field of the breakpoint, enter any C Boolean expression. If the breakpoint is enabled and the conditional expression evaluates to true when the breakpoint is encountered, the breakpoint stops the program. Otherwise, the breakpoint is ignored and the program continues to run.

Conditional Breakpoint Example

The best explanation is an example. The following function calculates a factorial:

```
static long long int factorial( long long int n )
{
    if (n>=1)
        n *= factorial(n-1);
    return (n);
}

int main (int argc, const char * argv[])
{
    printf("20! = %lld\n",factorial(20));
    return 0;
}
```

You build and run the application, and it produces the following output in the debugging console window:

```
20! = 0
```

Clearly, that's not the correct answer. You suspect that the problem is when n is small, so you set a breakpoint at the first line of the factorial() function (the line if (n>=1)). You start the program under the control of the debugger, and it immediately stops in the factorial function. The variable n has a value of 20.

You click Continue and the program recursively calls factorial again, causing the breakpoint to stop again; this time n equals 19.

You can see where this is leading. You'll have to restart the application another 18 times before you get to a value of n that's interesting. Though 18 isn't so bad, 180 would be, and 18,000 would be ridiculous in the extreme.

What you really want to know about is what happens when n is small (2 or less). To find out, you set a breakpoint condition, as shown in Figure 18-23. Now the breakpoint stops only when n is less than or equal to 2.

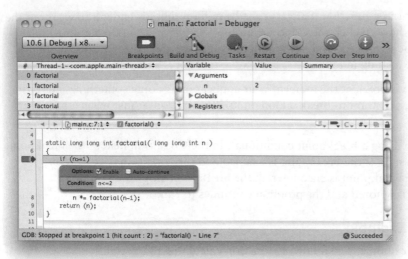

FIGURE 18-23

With a single breakpoint condition, you've skipped to the 19th invocation of the factorial function in a single debugging step. Now that you're here, you use the Step Over and Step Into commands to walk through the next few invocations of `factorial` and immediately see what the problem is: When n is 1, the `if` condition is still true, `factorial(n-1)` is called, which returns 0, and the multiplication zeros out the total.

The solution is change the conditional to `if (i>1)`.

Conditional Expressions

A breakpoint's conditional expression can contain only primitive C statements. It can't employ preprocessor macros or make use of any variables beyond what appears in the variables pane. In other words, it can only evaluate expressions based on what the debugger knows about your program.

As an example, take the C variable `char string[MAX_LEN]`. Assuming `MAX_LEN` was 100, you could test to see if the string buffer contained a character near the end of the array using the expression `string[98]!='\0'`. However, you could not use the expression `string[MAX_LEN-2]!='\0'` because the debugger doesn't normally know about preprocessor macros.

If there is a problem with the expression, Xcode displays a warning symbol next to the condition in the Breakpoints window. Sometimes this is normal, because an expression might refer to local variables that aren't in scope when the condition is defined. The debugger reevaluates the breakpoint condition when the breakpoint actually occurs, but if the expression is still invalid, it is ignored and the breakpoint acts as if it has no condition. The debugger also notes the problem with a message in the debugger console like "warning: Error parsing breakpoint condition expression."

Be very careful about expression side effects. The expression i==0 *activates the breakpoint when the value of* i *is zero, and ignores the breakpoint if it is any other value. The expression* i=0 *sets the value of i to zero and continues executing. Assignment, increment, and decrement operations all have their normal effect on values. Be careful of expressions like* o[++k]!=NULL *that alter the value of* k *when the debugger evaluates them. The equivalent expression without side effects would be* o[k+1]!=NULL.

Be conservative and defensive when you're using expressions. Don't make assumptions that will cause your expression to miss problems, or cause more problems itself. The following table describes a few examples:

EXPRESSION	RESULTS
i>1000000	Poor. The variable is a signed integer. If the value exceeds MAX_INT, the value will be negative and the condition will never be true. If you're looking for a problem where this integer exceeds its nominal range of 0 to 1,000,000, this expression could miss it.
!(i>=0 && i<=1000000)	Better. The range of the integer is bounded at both ends.
ptr->m!=0	Poor. ptr is a pointer that could be NULL, causing the expression evaluation itself to throw an address error.
(ptr!=0 && ptr->m!=0)	Better. The member value m will not be tested if the ptr is NULL, avoiding possible access errors.
(ptr==0 || ptr->m!=0)	Best. If you really never expect ptr to be NULL, the breakpoint should break on that condition as well.

If your condition requires something to be computed, consider adding some code to your application to help your debugging. Here's an example that assumes that you have defined a DEBUGGING macro and set it to a non-zero value when compiling your code for testing:

```
#if DEBUGGING
    int actualStrLen = strlen(str);
#endif
    strncpy(buffer,str,1024);
```

You can now set a breakpoint at the strncpy statement with the condition actualStrLen>=1024.

Breakpoint Ignore Count

A common breakpoint condition is to simply ignore the next few hits. If you hit a breakpoint in a loop that's going to repeat 1,000 times and you want to know what happens toward the end of the loop, you just want to skip over the next 998 occurrences of that breakpoint. This is easily accomplished by setting a breakpoint's ignore count setting.

In the breakpoint window, find the Ignore Count column for the breakpoint and enter a non-zero integer. The next occurrences of that breakpoint will be ignored. To reactive the breakpoint, set the ignore count back to zero.

Breakpoint Actions

In addition to just stopping the program, breakpoints can also perform actions when they are encountered. When a breakpoint is taken, the program stops and control is passed to the debugger. If the breakpoint has breakpoint actions, the debugger immediately performs those actions.

To add or edit actions, expose the breakpoint's contents in the Breakpoints window. For source breakpoints, double-click the breakpoint in the gutter of the source file and Xcode takes you to that breakpoint in the Breakpoints window. Click the + button to add a new action. Click the − button to delete an action. You can't reorder actions, so when you're adding actions, use the + button above the point where you want to new action inserted.

After you've added an action, choose the type of action from the pop-up menu at the top. There are five kinds of breakpoint actions, as listed in the following table:

ACTION	FUNCTION
Log	Logs a message to the system console.
Sound	Plays a sound.
Debugger Command	Executes a command in the debugger.
Shell Command	Executes a shell command.
AppleScript	Executes an AppleScript.

Log a Message

The Log command enables you to generate a message when the breakpoint occurs. How you receive this message is controlled by the two check boxes in the lower-right corner of the action, shown in Figure 18-24. Log outputs the message to the debugger console, and Speak uses the Macintosh text-to-speech technology to say the message out loud.

FIGURE 18-24

The message can contain any of the following special character sequences:

MESSAGE TOKEN	REPLACED WITH
%B	The name of the breakpoint
%H	The number of times this breakpoint has been tripped
%C	The comments attached to the breakpoint
@expression@	Any gdb expression

The open-ended @expression@ form permits you to include anything that the debugger can evaluate at that moment in the program. The example in Figure 18-24 shows a breakpoint that logs the following message:

```
testTimer fired, userInfo has 3 entries
```

The expression [[timer userInfo] count] is executed and the resulting value is inserted into the log message. Again, be very careful of side-effects when using expressions.

Make a Sound

The Sound action plays the system sound selected from the pop-up menu.

Have the Debugger Do Something Else

The Debugger Command action is where the power of breakpoint actions really begins to reveal itself. This action enables a breakpoint to execute almost any other gdb command. There's a lot of potential here, but some all-time favorites are the print, backtrace, and breakpoint commands.

> *Two* gdb *commands that you should never use in a breakpoint action are* jump *and* continue. *Using* jump *or* continue *can interfere with Xcode's ability to execute other breakpoint actions. See the "Breakpoint Continuation" section for information about the action you want your program to continue after hitting a breakpoint.*

The print command prints the value of an expression to the debugger console, similar to the Log action. The backtrace command dumps a summary of the call stack.

The log action and the print and backtrace commands are extremely useful, to be sure, but they're all relatively passive. Executing gdb commands automatically opens up a universe of possibilities — or Pandora's box, if you're not careful.

The power of debugger command actions can be illustrated using breakpoints that create and clear other breakpoints. One common problem is trying to debug the behavior of a function when it's called under specific circumstances; circumstances that can't be easily described in a breakpoint conditional. This kind of situation occurs often in complex object-oriented applications where seemingly innocuous methods get called under unusual situations, or at unexpected times. The reason these problems are so difficult to isolate is that the function encountering the problem might be called hundreds, if not millions, of times under normal conditions where the problem doesn't manifest itself; so simply setting a breakpoint at the problematic method is out of the question.

The following example illustrates this kind of puzzle. You're developing an iPhone application with a custom view defined in a nib document. You create many instances of this view, configure it via a -setValues: message, display it, and then discard it.

```
 1 @interface QuickView : UIView {
 2     // ...
 3 }
 4 - (void)setValues:(id)info;
 5 @end
 6
 7 @implementation QuickView
 8
 9 ...
10
11 - (void)setValues:(id)info
12 {
13     // Configure view to display values...
14 }
15
16 @end
```

So far, so good. While analyzing the performance of your app, you discover that loading every new view from the nib document is taking too much time. You would get better performance if you loaded a few of these view objects from the nib document, and then reused them again later, so you create a simple pool of view objects:

```
 1 @class QuickView;
 2
 3 @interface ViewPool : NSObject {
 4     @private
 5     NSMutableArray *pool;
 6 }
 7 - (QuickView*)view;
 8 - (void)recycleView:(QuickView*)view;
 9 @end
10
11 @implementation ViewPool
12 ...
13 - (QuickView*)view
14 {
15     // Return an existing view from the pool, or load a new one.
16     QuickView *freshView;
17     if ([pool count]!=0) {
18         freshView = [[[pool lastObject] retain] autorelease];
19         [pool removeLastObject];
20     } else {
21         // Load the NIB and extract the single top-level object
22         freshView = [[[NSBundle mainBundle] loadNibNamed:@"QuickView"
23                                                    owner:nil
24                                                  options:nil]
25                     lastObject];
26     }
```

```
27      return (freshView);
28 }
29
30 - (void)recycleView:(QuickView*)staleView
31 {
32      [pool addObject:staleView];
33 }
34
35 @end
```

While testing your program, you discover a problem. The correct order of use should be:

1. Create a bunch of QuickView objects.

2. Configure their content using -setValues:.

3. Display the views.

4. Return all of the views to the pool.

What's happening in your application is that something is calling -setValues: *after* the view has been returned to the pool. You suspect that some object is still trying to use the view after it has been recycled, but you can't determine when or why.

This kind of problem can be trapped using breakpoints and breakpoint actions:

1. Create two breakpoints in ViewPool.m at lines 27 and 32.

2. Add a breakpoint action to the breakpoint at line 32. Set the action type to Debugger Command, and enter the following gdb command:

    ```
    break QuickView.m:13
    ```

3. Add a breakpoint action to the breakpoint at line 27. Set the action type to Debugger Command, and enter the following gdb command:

    ```
    clear QuickView.m:13
    ```

4. Build and start the program under the control of the debugger.

Your program runs normally until a QuickView object receives a -setValues: message between being returned to the pool, but before being pulled out again. The sender is the likely culprit.

Here's how the solution works: the breakpoint action in the -recycleView: method creates a breakpoint in the -setValues: method. If any code should invoke -setValues: after one or more view objects have been returned to the pool, the program will stop. Once new view objects are requested again, it's assumed that -setValues: messages are acceptable again, so the breakpoint in the -view method clears (deletes) the -setValues: breakpoint. The result is a breakpoint that only exists between calls to -recycleView: and -view:.

The one annoying aspect of this solution that the breakpoints in -view and -recycleView: still stop execution of your application. The solution to that is to set their continue flag, described later in the "Breakpoint Continuation" section.

Note that the automatically created breakpoints may not appear in Xcode because Xcode didn't create them; but they're fully functional breakpoints nevertheless. Using the debugger command action requires an understanding of the gdb debugger commands and their syntax. Documentation for the gdb debugger is available online at http://www.gnu.org/software/gdb/documentation/.

Run a Script

The Shell Command and AppleScript breakpoint actions can be used to execute any arbitrary command-line program or AppleScript program file.

The usefulness of these actions depends entirely on what you're trying to accomplish. Say you have a database program that is corrupting record data. You could create a breakpoint action to execute a MySQL query statement that would dump the contents of suspect records at strategic points in the program. Another clever trick is to use Mac OS X's screen capture tool (screencapture) to take a snapshot of your display at a critical moment.

The Shell Command action takes a command file and a list of arguments. This must be an executable command file — a binary program or an executable script. You can enter the path directly, or click the Choose button to browse for it. The path can be an absolute or project-relative path. Arguments are space-separated, just as if you executed the command using the shell, and you can include gdb expressions enclosed between two @ characters just like the Log action. Normally, the debugger executes the command asynchronously. That is, it starts the command executing and immediately returns control to the debugger. If you want the debugger to wait until the command is finished before continuing, check the Wait Until Done option.

The AppleScript action accepts an AppleScript in the action pane. The script does not need to be in a handler block. You can compile your script and check for syntax errors using the Compile button and try out your script using the Test button. The AppleScript executes in the context of the gdb process, so interactive AppleScript commands like display can't be used. Commands like delay, beep, and say work just fine. The script can also contain gdb expressions enclosed between @ characters.

Breakpoint Continuation

The earlier example of using breakpoints to set breakpoints glossed over a serious problem. The breakpoints with the actions will still break. After the breakpoint has been hit, and all of its actions have been executed, the debugger still stops your program and waits for instructions. In the example of trying to trap a call that occurs during a destructor, this defeats the purpose of having breakpoints created and deleted automatically. What you really want is for the breakpoint to execute its actions and immediately resume execution of your program. This is exactly what the continue option does.

The continue option is the CD-player-style "play" column in the breakpoints list, as shown in Figure 18-25. Checking this option for a breakpoint means that the breakpoint does not return control to you. The actions of the breakpoint are executed, and the program continues executing exactly as if you had clicked the Continue button.

FIGURE 18-25

The continue option makes all manner of debug automation and checking possible. There are, however, some hazards. Debug actions are executed asynchronously. That is, the debug action merely starts the action. The debugger does not normally hang around waiting for them to complete, so be careful about creating breakpoints that will start, or queue up, hundreds of breakpoint actions. This can be particularly annoying when you're using audio feedback.

The Shell Script breakpoint action has the Wait Until Done option that suspends the debugger and your program until the Shell Command completes. Breakpoint actions can be combined with a breakpoint condition. The breakpoint and all of its actions are executed only if the condition evaluates to true.

Importing and Exporting Breakpoints

Pretend that you are working on a project with another programmer. You've isolated a problem using a complex set of breakpoints. How do you send those breakpoints to your team members so that they can reproduce the problem and fix it? Project breakpoints are saved on a per-user basis in the project, so you can't just give them a copy of the project document. When they load the project, they won't see any of the project breakpoints you've set. And scrawling breakpoint descriptions on napkins doesn't sound particularly efficient either.

The solution is to export the breakpoints to a file using the Export Breakpoints command. Select any set of breakpoints or breakpoint groups in the Groups & Files pane and Right/Control-click the selection. Choose the Export Breakpoints command to export the selected breakpoints to a text file.

The Import Breakpoints command creates a new subgroup with the name of the breakpoint export file and populates it with its contents. Rename and reorganize the imported breakpoints as you see fit.

As a single developer, you can use these commands to archive a collection of breakpoints for some future purpose or move some breakpoints between projects without resorting to making them global breakpoints.

Breakpoint Templates

Xcode provides a number of preconfigured breakpoints that you can insert by Right/Control-clicking a line in your source code and then selecting any of the breakpoint templates from the Built-In Breakpoints menu. You can also create your own breakpoint templates, which will appear in the same menu.

To create a reusable breakpoint, create and configure a breakpoint. Once you are happy with it, create a breakpoint group in the Groups & Files pane named Template Breakpoints (Right/Control-click and choose Add ⇨ New Group). This group can be a subgroup of your project breakpoints or the global breakpoints. You can even have both. Now drag the breakpoints you want to reuse into this group.

Any breakpoints that appear in the Template Breakpoints group also appear in the Right/Control-click contextual menu in any source file's gutter. Creating a breakpoint from one of the templates inserts a breakpoint that's a copy of the breakpoint in the template. The only thing that is different is its location.

EXAMINING DATA

Now that you've learned all about controlling the flow of your application while debugging, let's return to examining the content of variables. "The Variables Pane" section briefly introduced the variables pane of the debugging window. Now look at that pane in a little more detail and look at other ways of examining the contents of memory.

To recap, the variables pane (previously shown in Figure 18-4) displays the known variables within the scope of the selected stack frame. Variables are grouped by type. Structures and objects appear as groups, forming a hierarchy of containers and values. These are described by the debug symbol information attached to your program.

As you step through your program, the debugger compares the values that were displayed when your program was last started against the values that appear when the debugger stopped it again. Any values that are different are highlighted in red, as shown in Figure 18-26 — it may be difficult to see in this black-and-white illustration, but the value of variable j is red.

FIGURE 18-26

The code was stopped at line 57 where the value of j was undefined. The Step Over command was issued. The debugger allowed one statement (the for statement) to be executed and stopped the program again. The value of j is now 4 and Xcode highlights the change in the display. Using the Step Over command again returns the value to black again, because that statement did not alter its value. It doesn't matter how much the program executes between stops. As long as the variables pane is showing the same set of variables at the next stop, Xcode highlights whatever values are now different.

Scalar Formats

The Value column displays the primitive value of each variable. For scalar values, this is a numeric value. For structures and pointers to structures, it is the address of the structure or the value of the pointer. The default display format for scalar values is Natural. For signed integers and floating-point numbers, the column displays a signed decimal value. Unsigned integers display an unsigned decimal number. Character types display both the decimal and Unicode representations of the value. Pointers and structures are shown as hexadecimal memory addresses. The natural format is usually sufficient, but you can manually choose a different representation. The choices are as follows:

- Hexadecimal
- Decimal
- Unsigned Decimal
- Octal
- Binary
- OSType

You can find these formats in the Run ➪ Variables View menu, or in the Right/Control-click contextual menu of the variables pane. Select one or more variables in the pane and then choose one of these fixed formats to force the expression of the value, or values, into the desired format. Choose Natural to return to Xcode's automatic formatting. The first five formats are self-explanatory. The OSType format displays a 32-bit integer as a four-character string. This data type is used by many system APIs.

Viewing Data in Another Window

You can also choose to examine the contents of a value or structure in a separate window. Double-click the variable name, choose the Run ➪ Variables View ➪ View Variable In Window command, or from the Right/Control+click contextual menu. This can be particularly useful for viewing large or complex objects. It is also handy because the variable's value continues to be displayed as long as the variable exists. You can place a local structure pointer in a separate window and continue to examine its value while stepping though other functions. After the variable is no longer in scope or its stack frame is released, the window containing the value closes.

If a variable type isn't even close to the type of data it represents, you can use the Run ➪ Variables View ➪ View Value As command, also available via the Right/Control+click contextual menu of the variables pane. Select a variable in the list and choose this command. Xcode prompts you to enter a cast for the variable's value, as shown in Figure 18-27.

FIGURE 18-27

Xcode then attempts to interpret the value of that variable using the type cast. This is particularly useful for generic types such as void*. As shown in Figure 18-27, the pointer to a string was assigned to a void* variable. By using the View Value As command, you can coerce the debugger to interpret the void* value as if it was a char* variable, shown on the right.

Sometimes you just need to look at memory. Using the Debug ⇨ Variables View ⇨ View As Memory command, you can open the memory browser window shown in Figure 18-28.

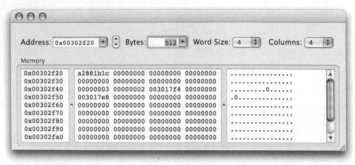

FIGURE 18-28

The browser displays a block of memory in hexadecimal and ASCII formats, much like the hexdump command. The Address field determines the starting address of the display. Initially, this is the address of the selected scalar, structure, or object in the variables pane. If the selected variable is a pointer or object reference, the address is the value of that pointer (a dump of what the pointer points to, not a dump of the pointer's value). The Bytes menu lets you select how much memory is disassembled in the window. Choose one of the preset values or enter your own. Use the up and down arrows between the Address and Bytes field to move one page of memory forward or backward. The Word Size and Columns menus control the number of bytes in each column of hexadecimal values, and the number of columns in each line, respectively.

There is only one memory browser window. Selecting a new address using the View As Memory command simply changes the address in the Address field. The Address field has a pop-up menu that keeps a short history of previously viewed addresses. If you need to follow a pointer to another address that you find in a block of memory, simply copy the address from the hexadecimal listing and paste it into the Address field (prefixing it with 0x).

If you try to view memory that is outside the address space of your application, the memory browser displays *A*'s for the bytes it can't access.

Viewing Global Variables

The Globals group in the variables pane contains a selected set of global variables that you want to examine. Normally, this group has nothing. It's impractical for this group to contain every global variable in your application's process space. The group could contain hundreds of variables, be impossible to navigate, and place a huge burden on the debugger display.

Instead, the group starts out empty. Use the global variables window, shown in Figure 18-29, to add variables to this group or merely browse the global variables in your application. You can open this window using the Run ⇨ Show ⇨ Global Variables command or by attempting to expand the Globals group when it is empty.

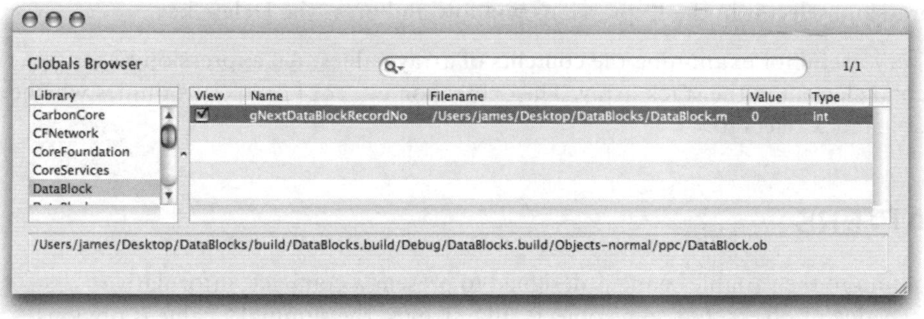

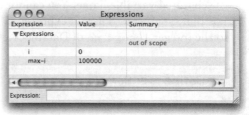

FIGURE 18-29

The global variables window is divided between a list of modules on the left and the list of global variables in each module on the right. Select a module, and Xcode lists all of the global variables that your application has access to on the right. To search for a particular variable name, enter some fragment of the variable's name in the search field at the top of the window.

Figure 18-29 examines the global variables declared in a program named DataBlock. The listing tells you the filename the variable is declared in, its current value, and its type. By selecting the box in the View column, this variable is added to the Globals group in the variables pane. The viewed global variables are recorded in the user preferences of the project document. After these variables are added, they will always appear in the Globals group of your variables pane until they are removed or until the variable itself no longer exists.

Expressions

Another way to view variables is through expressions. Expressions appear in the Expressions window, shown in Figure 18-30. You can open this window using the Run ⇨ Show ⇨ Expressions command. To add an expression in the window, type the expression in the input field at the bottom of the window, or select any variable and choose Run ⇨ Variables View ⇨ View Variable As Expression.

FIGURE 18-30

These are debugger expressions and are subject to all of the limitations and caveats of breakpoint conditions. In the Expressions window, each expression acts like a variable. You can alter its display format or open it in a separate window. You can also add type casts to an expression to coerce the interpretation of the expression's value.

Expressions are interpreted within the context of the currently selected stack frame, and those expressions retain that context. In the example previously shown in Figure 18-30, there are two expressions that resolve to value of the integer i, but these two variables are from different stack frames. Each was added to the window and a different stack frame was selected in the threads pane. The first one was added while a function was executing, but that function has now returned. Therefore, the context that defined that variable no longer exists and the expression is marked as "out of scope."

To delete an expression, select it in the Expressions window and press the Delete key.

Expressions are very useful for examining the contents of array values. An expression like `stack[1]` examines the second element in the stack array. The expression `buffer[index]` examines whichever element the variable index refers to.

DATA FORMATTERS

The summary column in the variables pane is designed to present a compact, informative explanation of the value or object. For some objects, like strings, the summary value is obvious. For objects like a collection it might display the size of the collection — not a lot of detail, but still informative. For an opaque FSRef structure, it might convert that structure into a readable filename — very informative, indeed. This descriptive transformation is done using data formatters.

Xcode includes many data formatters, but they won't help with any object that you define. You can create your own data formatters to summarize complex data structures and objects in the debugger.

Creating a Custom Data Formatter

Creating your own data formatters is very easy. It is really nothing more than a format string with placeholders for values or expressions derived from the variable being summarized. Any regular text in the data formatter is displayed verbatim. There are two kinds of placeholders: references and expressions.

References are delimited by two percent characters (`%reference%`). A reference can refer to a single member variable by name. If the variable is contained in a substructure, use the appropriate period (.) separated variable name. You cannot use operators such as pointer dereferences or array indexes. For that, you need to use an expression. Taking the class that's defined in Listing 18-3, the reference to the integer `record_no` of DataBlock class would be `%header.record_no%`.

LISTING 18-3: Sample class

Available for
download on
Wrox.com

```
typedef struct {
    int record_no;
    unsigned long checksum;
} BlockHeader;

@interface DataBlock : NSObject
{
    @public
        BlockHeader     header;
        NSMutableData*  data;
}
```

An expression is any debugger expression; the same kind of expression that you can add to the Expressions window. In fact, it's good to think of an expression in a data formatter as an expression in the Expressions window, as you'll see in moment.

Expressions are contained between matching braces (`{expression}`). Unlike references, expressions do not assume the context of the value being examined. To refer to the object being examined, use the $VAR macro in the expression. $VAR will be replaced with the name of the variable when the data formatter is evaluated. Using the previous class as an example again, the expression to access the record_no value would be {$VAR.header.record_no}. If you're now guessing that you can refer to other variables in the context of the current stack frame, you're correct. However, this isn't a good idea, which is explained later. Limit your evaluation to the structure or object being examined.

The advantage of expressions over references is that they are more expressive. You can perform math, include conditionals, and even call member functions. Again using the class defined in Listing 18-3, here are some valid expressions:

➤ {$VAR.header.record_no}

➤ {$VAR.header.checksum&0x0000ffff}

➤ {$VAR.data?(int)[$VAR.data length]:0}

Combining these two techniques, you can now create a data formatter for the DataBlock object type. Start by running the program and stopping the debugger with an instance of the DataBlock class in scope. Make sure that Run ➪ Variables View ➪ Enable Data Formatters is checked. Select the DataBlock variable in the variables pane and choose the Run ➪ Variables View ➪ Edit Summary Format. The debugger lets you edit the data formatter for the variable. Now you can enter the data formatter string shown in Figure 18-31.

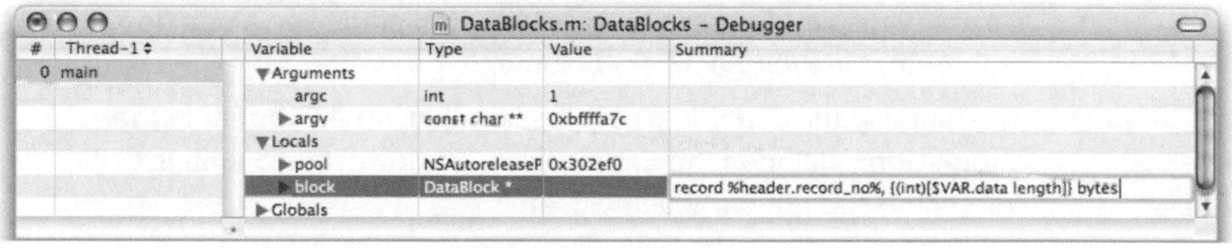

FIGURE 18-31

After it has been entered, this text becomes the data formatter used for every instance of the DataBlock class. The debugger resolves the references and expressions for each instance, creating the more informative summary shown in Figure 18-32.

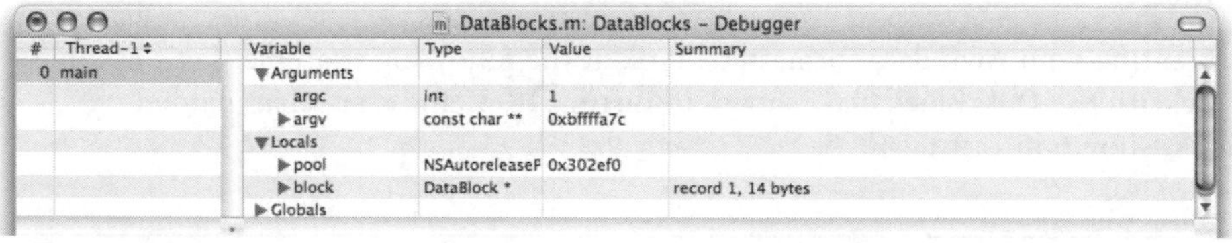

FIGURE 18-32

The syntax used for references and expressions can be extended to obtain other information about the value or expression. The final display value can be something different from the value to which the expression evaluates. The other types of information that can be extracted from an expression are chosen using one of the column selectors listed in the following table. The "column" you are selecting is one of the columns in the variables pane or the Expressions window. In essence, the result of a reference or expression is treated as if it had been entered into the Expressions window. The column selector lets you choose which column in the window will be used as the result of the expression. You can think of an expression result as an object with four properties (value, name, type, and summary) — the column selector lets you choose which property to display.

COLUMN SELECTOR	DESCRIPTION
`{expression}:v`, `%reference%:v`	The value of the expression — that is, the primitive numerical value that would appear in the Value column of the Expressions window. This is the default column. Omitting the column selector is equivalent to using `:v`.
`{expression}:t`, `%reference%:t`	The type of the final data object to which the expression evaluates. A numerical expression would result in a primitive data type, such as int or double. The type of an expression that refers to a member variable, or calls a function, will be the type of the expression's result. For example, the expression `{[$VAR owner]}:t` would display the type of the object returned by the method owner.
`{expression}:s`, `%reference%:s`	This selector results in the text that would appear in the Summary column of the expression. Because the Summary column can be formed using data formatters, this is a way of using other data formatters in portions of your data formatter. You can only use this on expressions that have a summary display. Expressions that result in primitive values do not have any content in their Summary column.
`{expression}:n`, `%reference%:n`	The name of the variable or expression that would appear in the Expression column of the Expressions window. The column is self-referential and not particularly useful.

The type column (`:t`) can be useful for displaying the type or class of a member value. For example, if you have a class that manages a collection of homogenous objects, a data formatter of `collection of {[$VAR lastObject]}:t` would tell you what kind of objects your collection contains.

The summary column selector is the most useful. You can use it to construct data formatters from other data formatters.

To get a feel for creating your own data formatters, look at the following example. Let's assume you have a project with the DataBlock class shown in Listing 18-3, and a subclass named StampedDatablock, shown in Listing 18-4.

Available for download on Wrox.com

LISTING 18-4: DataBlock subclass

```
@interface StampedDataBlock : DataBlock
{
    @private
        NSCalendarDate*     createdDate;
        NSCalendarDate*     modifiedDate;
}
```

To create a custom data formatter for these two classes, follow these steps:

1. Build the application, start it under the control of the debugger, and stop at a breakpoint where a DataBlock and StampedDataBlock object are in scope, as shown in Figure 18-33.

2. Set the data formatter for the `block` variable to `record %header.record_no%, {(int)[$VAR.data length]} bytes`.

3. Set the data formatter for the `trackedBlock` variable to `{(DataBlock*)$VAR}:s, created %createdDate%:s`.

4. Continue stepping through the program.

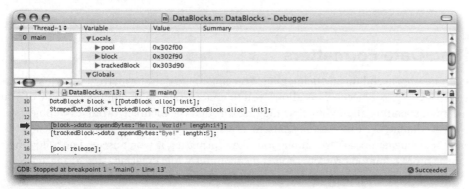

FIGURE 18-33

The first data formatter created for the DataBlock class summarizes its contents by accessing its `record_no` and data instance variables. The debugger now presents a much friendlier summary of the object's state.

The StampedDataBlock formatter is a little trickier. The StampedDataBlock class does not inherit the data formatter for DataBlock. Data formatters for each type are independent of one another.

Two problems are inherent in creating a data formatter for the new subclass. First, you don't want to repeat everything you wrote for the DataBlock formatter. Secondly, you don't want to write a formatter for the NSCalendarDate member object. The summary column selector lets you avoid both of these problems by setting the data formatter for the StampedDataBlock class to `{(DataBlock*)$VAR}:s, created %createdDate%:s`. The first expression casts the object to an instance of its superclass and obtains text that would appear in its Summary column, effectively calling the data formatter you created for the DataBlock class. The second reference obtains the value of `createdDate` and inserts what would appear in its Summary column, essentially using Xcode's built-in data formatter. The final result, shown in Figure 18-34, is a data formatter that extends the data formatter of its superclass using a built-in data formatter supplied by Xcode.

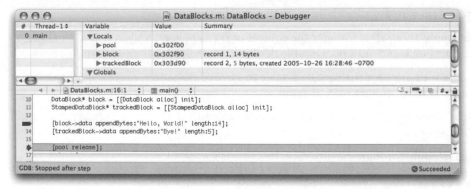

FIGURE 18-34

Troubleshooting Data Formatters

Data formatters can be very useful during debugging. You can create data formatters that quickly summarize the state of complex objects. This allows you to concentrate on the high-level logic of your application, rather than spending all of your time digging through the member variables of objects trying to decode their content. Writing data formatters, however, can be a frustrating experience. If there is *anything* the debugger doesn't like about your data formatter, it won't use it. The following table lists some of the more common problems you can encounter while creating data formatters:

TYPE OF PROBLEM	SOLUTION
Syntax	Be extra careful about the syntax of your expressions and references.
Quotes	Double quotes in the body of an expression must be escaped with a backslash. Example: `name "{[$VAR getProperty:\"name\"]}:s"`. Notice that the quotes inside the expression are escaped, but not in the text outside the expression.
Unknown types	The debugger often does not know the data type of values returned by functions. If you have any doubts, cast the result: `author {(NSString*)[$VAR authorName]}:s`
Execution problems	Expressions that call functions have to function perfectly. The formatter `name {[$VAR name]}:s` will fail if the method name throws an exception, tries to access a `NULL` variable, can't allocate memory, or any of a limitless number of similar run time problems. The functions that you call using data formatters should be extremely defensive.
Null summary	You cannot use the `:s` column selector if the expression results in a data type that has no summary column content.
Invalid references	Expressions that use other variables in the current stack frame context will fail when interpreted in a different stack frame or execution context where those variables don't exist. Data formatters should concern themselves only with examining the contents of the structure or object.

TYPE OF PROBLEM	SOLUTION
ZeroLink, dynamically loaded libraries	This is yet one more situation where dynamically loaded libraries can trip you up. Expressions executed in the debugger will *not* cause unreferenced symbols to load. If your application hasn't caused a symbol or function to load yet, a data formatter that uses that function or type will fail.
Temporary Objects	(For Objective-C programmers) Be warned that creating auto-released objects in your data formatters may result in memory leaks. An example would be `{ (NSString*) [NSString stringWithCharacters: $VAR.uStr.unicode length:$VAR.uStr.length] }:s`. The problem here is that the NSString object is created in the context of the debugger and has no auto-release pool. You will see a "leak" message in the debugger log.
Side Effects	Data formatters can call functions in your application. Side effects, such as altering instance variables or releasing objects, can have unexpected consequences in your application and your debugging efforts.

If you are having problems getting a formatter to work, break it down into its individual components and subexpressions and try each one at a time. Slowly build up the expression until you get it working or find the element that thwarts your efforts. Try expressions without the column selector. Cast return values liberally. Replace macros and function calls with constants. Turn off ZeroLink. Add the same function call to your code and try debugging it.

Data formatters you define are stored in the `~/Library/Application Support/Apple/Developer Tools/CustomDataViews/CustomDataViews.plist` file. Data formatters are global to all projects and are not stored in the project document. Sharing data formatters with other developers will require some copying and pasting, or you may just want to exchange `CustomDataViews.plist` files.

Beyond Data Formatter Strings

Although data formatters can do a lot, they are limited to what can be expressed in a format string. If you need a data formatter that exceeds these capabilities, you can develop your own data formatter plug-in. The descriptions for doing so are in the `DataFormatterPlugin.h` file, buried inside the Xcode application itself at `/Developer/Applications/Xcode.app/Contents/PlugIns/GDBMIDebugging.xcplugin/Contents/Headers/DataFormatterPlugin.h`. This file contains detailed information about formatter strings, the format of `CustomDataViews.plist`, and how to create a data formatter plug-in, among other topics.

In brief, you create a data formatter plug-in by creating a bundle. The bundle contains its own `CustomDataViews.plist` file. Unlike data formatter strings that you type into the debugger window, the data formatter strings in the bundle's `CustomDataViews.plist` file can call any of the functions defined in the plug-in bundle. The sample ManagedObjectDataFormatter project produces a data formatter plug-in for managed objects. You can find it by searching the Xcode documentation for ManagedObjectDataFormatter. Use this project as a template for creating your own data formatter plug-ins.

Object Descriptions

Like data formatters, many object-oriented languages have adopted conventions for converting any object into a textual representation. In Java, this is the `toString()` function. Objective-C uses the `-[NSObject description]` method. If you are using an object that supports one of these standards, you can use the Run ⇨ Variables View ⇨ Print Description to Console command. The debugger invokes the standard "to string" function on the object and sends the result to the debugger console.

WATCHPOINTS

Watchpoints are breakpoints for data. You can make any variable a watchpoint. Whenever the debugger detects that the value of that variable has changed, it stops your application.

Watchpoints sound great, but they are fairly limited. The biggest problem is that your application can't execute any code where the watchpoint variable is out of context, so they are mostly useful for global variables that are always in scope and for catching state changes in a loop.

You set a watchpoint by first selecting a variable in the variables pane. Choose the Run ⇨ Variables View ⇨ Watch Variable command. This places a magnifying glass icon next to the variable as shown in Figure 18-35. Start the program executing again, and it breaks at the point just before the variable is altered with a dialog box explaining what is about to happen, also shown in Figure 18-35.

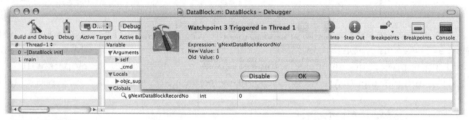

FIGURE 18-35

You can choose to acknowledge the event and leave the watchpoint set, or disable the watchpoint by clicking the Disable button. Watchpoints are automatically deleted whenever your application exits the context where the watchpoint variable exists. Watchpoints are not retained between debug sessions.

 You can create an effect similar to a watchpoint using a breakpoint conditional like `i!=0`. *It's not as convenient as a watchpoint, but it's more durable.*

To remove a watchpoint, select the variable being watched and choose Run ⇨ Variables View ⇨ Watch Variable again to remove the check mark.

CHANGING DATA AND CODE

So far, this chapter has taken a rather passive approach to debugging. You've viewed code and variables in countless ways, but you haven't actually changed anything. Xcode lets you alter both data and code while your application is executing. This can be a huge time-saver when you're debugging. You can change the values of parameters to test specific cases, or correct a value that was miscalculated and continue testing.

Changing variables is easy. Select a primitive variable and choose the Edit Value command from either the Run ⇨ Variables View menu or the Right/Control-click contextual menu in the variables pane. You can also double-click the value of the variable right in the variables pane. Edit the value and press Return. The only acceptable forms are decimal, octal (beginning with a zero), or hexadecimal (beginning with 0x). To enter a character you need to translate that character into a decimal or hexadecimal value. The Code Table view of the system's Character Palette is particularly useful in looking up character code values.

If the variable is a pointer, you can change the address of the pointer or you can expand the variable and Xcode allows you to change any primitive values to which the pointer points.

The Magic Fix

It's simple enough to poke a new value into a variable and continue executing, but what if the code itself is incorrect? Xcode allows you to fix that too.

This bit of magic — and it really is something close to magic — is a feature called Fix & Continue. As the name implies, it enables you to recompile code in your application and continue debugging it *without restarting your program*. Use of this feature depends on some prerequisites. The debug version of your application must be built with the following:

➤ The Fix & Continue (GCC_ENABLE_FIX_AND_CONTINUE) build setting checked

➤ Compiled using gcc version 3.3 or later

➤ Full debug symbols

➤ No optimization

If, for any reason, the debugger can't use Fix & Continue, the Fix command will be disabled while debugging.

Using this feature is deceptively simple. Say, for example, you discover a bug in your source code while you're debugging. Listing 18-5 shows a common programming mistake: a loop with a missing increment statement.

Available for download on Wrox.com

LISTING 18-5: Bad loop

```
Token findOneToken( const char* s )
{
    while ( *s!='\0' && isspace(*s) )
        s++;
```

continues

LISTING 18-5 *(continued)*

```
        Token token;
        token.word = s;
        token.length = 0;
        while ( *s!='\0' )
            {
            char c = *s;
            if (isspace(c))
                break;
            token.length++;
            }

        return (token);
    }
```

After stepping through the second loop a few times, it becomes obvious that it gets stuck because the statement c = *s should have been c = *s++.

To correct this code, simply edit the statement so that it reads c = *s++ and choose Run ⇨ Fix or click the Fix button in the debugger's toolbar. The source for this file is recompiled, the new code is loaded into your application's code space replacing the old version of findOneToken, and the program counter changes to point to the equivalent line in the new code.

If that was all that needed to be done, you could continue debugging the application. Replacing the buggy code has, unfortunately, created another situation. Before you added the increment operator, the s variable wasn't being incremented — but token.length was. The length value now has a non-zero value and won't agree with the length of the string when the function returns.

Can you continue debugging your application without having to restart it? You have two ways of addressing this. The first would be to use the variables pane and simply edit the value of token .length, setting it back to 0. Another way is to alter the program counter so that the program continues executing at a different location in the code. Here the PC indicator is being dragged back up to the token.length = 0 statement so that the entire second loop starts over from the beginning, as shown in Figure 18-36.

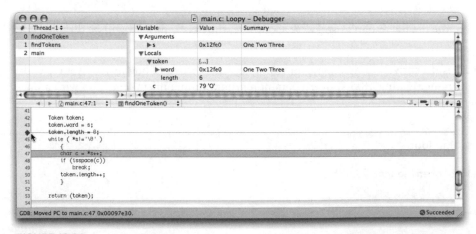

FIGURE 18-36

When the execution is continued, the program starts again at the top of the (now bug-free) loop, reinitializes `token.length` to `0`, and executes correctly.

Magic Fix Limitations

Fix & Continue does have some limitations. Here are a few:

➤ Fix is not supported by all debuggers. Support for Fix & Continue comes and goes in `gdb`.

➤ You cannot redefine `typedef` variables, data structures, classes, or function arguments.

➤ You cannot redefine the automatic variables on the stack frame.

➤ You cannot redefine global data variables.

➤ You cannot make any change to your application's resources, such as icon or nib files.

➤ You cannot fix a bad reference to a function by renaming the function.

In short, you can make any change that alters *only* the executable code of one or more functions. You can't make a fix that alters the data types or linkages that are, or could be, used anywhere else in the application.

You should be aware of a couple other caveats about how Fix & Continue works. Fix & Continue replaces the code of a function that was executing and changes the current program counter so that execution continues in the new code. However, it does not change the program counter in any other stack frame. Say that Function A calls Function B. If you stop the program in Function B and fix Function A, when Function B returns it will return to the *old* Function A, not the corrected one. The corrected Function A won't be called until something else calls Function A again.

Fix & Continue only compiles and replaces the in-memory image of a single file. If you make changes in several files, you will need to perform a Fix & Continue on each one.

Also note that Fix & Continue only patches the memory image of the running application. It does not alter the original executable file that was produced by the last build. If you restart your application the old (bug-ridden) version is executed. Worse, the executable code is now out of sync with the modified source files. Make sure you follow each debugging session where you use Fix & Continue with a new build to incorporate the changes you made into the final product.

DEBUGGER CONSOLE

The debugger console has been mentioned several times in this chapter. To access it, choose the Run ⇨ Console (Shift+Command+R) command, or click the Console button in the debugger window's toolbar. This opens the debugger console window, shown in Figure 18-37.

Like many of Xcode's interfaces, the debugger window is just a graphical front-end to the gdb (or Java, or AppleScript) debugger that runs underneath it. The debugger console window is a shell window that interacts with the debugger process directly. When you click the Continue button in Xcode's debugger window, Xcode just sends a `continue` command to gdb. Any information that gdb outputs is visible in the debugger console window.

If you are having problems with the debugger, the debugger console window is the first place to look. Problems setting breakpoints, resolving symbols, or evaluating expressions are logged there.

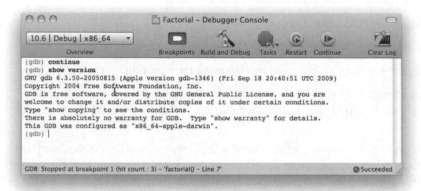

FIGURE 18-37

More interesting is that the debugger console window is a fully interactive terminal window. Through this window you can type commands directly into the debugger. The debugger provides many features that are not available through the graphical interface provided by Xcode. Of course, this requires an understanding of the gdb (or Java debugger) commands and their syntax. You can learn the basics by entering the help command at the (gdb) or JavaBug> prompt. The AppleScript debugger has no interactive commands.

SHARED LIBRARIES

One miscellaneous debugger tool is the shared library window, shown in Figure 18-38. Opened with the Run ➪ Show ➪ Shared Libraries command, it shows the status of the shared libraries that your application is linked to. Most of the information here concerns how many of the debugging symbols for each library have been loaded into the debugger.

FIGURE 18-38

The Module column shows the name of each shared library. The Address column shows the address in the application's memory space where the library has been loaded. If the field is blank, the library has not been loaded into memory yet. The complete path to the selected library is shown at the bottom of the window.

The Starting Level and Current Level columns show what level of debugging symbols should be loaded for each library when the debugger starts and right now, respectively. The debugger can avoid loading symbols for a library, load only the external declarations, or read all debugging symbols including source file line information. The less debugging information loaded, the faster the debugger starts up and runs — and the less it knows about your application.

Normally, the debugger loads only the external declarations. This is the superficial information about the library. Whenever it needs to know more detailed information, it automatically loads any remaining debugger symbols that describe data structures, source file line numbers, and so on. You can watch this process at work. Start an application and set a breakpoint very early in the application, like at the first line of main(). Open the shared library window and the global variables window. Start looking through the libraries in the global variables window. As you browse each library for global variables, the status of the loaded symbols in the shared library window changes from None or External to All as you force the debugger to load additional debugging symbols for each library — debug symbol information that the debugger needs to display the global variables in each library.

You can manually load the symbols for a library into memory by changing the setting in the Current Level column. The change occurs immediately. The Starting Level column determines what the Current Level column will be set to when the library is initially loaded. You can set this to a particular level or use the Default setting. If set to Default, the level used will either be the Default Level for System Libraries or User Libraries, as appropriate, set with the two global pop-up menus at the top of the window. The default level of External is known as "lazy" symbol loading; the idea is to get your application running in the debugger as quickly as possible by loading only the minimal amount of information and worrying about the details later. You can disable Lazy Symbol Loading in the Debugger pane of the Xcode Preferences. Disabling Lazy Symbol Loading changes the User Libraries default from External to All.

The Reset button at the bottom sets the Starting Level of all libraries to Default.

You can manually add or remove libraries from the list by clicking the + and – buttons at the bottom of the window. To add a library, browse to the location of the library and open it. Remember that in the file browser, the Shift+Command+G key combination opens the Go To sheet, allowing you to enter a path to normally invisible directories like /usr/lib.

The shared libraries window is mostly informational, but it can be used to give hints to the debugger telling it to load — or avoid loading — debug symbol information at strategic times. If you are debugging a very large application, this can speed up the debugger by not loading unnecessary symbols or speed up your debugging workflow by preloading symbols you need. You cannot use this window to force libraries to load or unload or to force symbol information that the debugger is using out of memory.

CUSTOM EXECUTABLES

So far you've been running and debugging simple applications without much thought to the environment in which those applications were running. When you created a target to produce your application, Xcode also created a matching product and an executable. The executable, which appears in the Executables smart group of the Groups & Files pane, defines the execution environment for your application. It defines what binary program will be executed when it is launched, what parameters and environment variables will be passed to it, and what its I/O file descriptors will be attached to. You can customize the environment settings of an executable created by Xcode, or you can create your own.

You may want to customize or create a custom executable for several reasons. For example:

➤ You need to pass command-line parameters to the process when it is started.

➤ You need to set environment variables for the process, or choose a different working directory before the process is started.

➤ You want to redirect the input or output of the tool to something other than the run or debugging console windows.

➤ You need to debug an executable that Xcode didn't produce or for which Xcode doesn't automatically create a product and executable, such as a program produced by an external build process.

➤ Your executable is launched via a script or some other process.

➤ The project you are developing is a plug-in or a framework that can't be executed on its own. You need to launch an application that will load the plug-in and exercise it.

General Settings

Open the Info window for an existing executable, or choose the Project ⇨ New Custom Executable command to create a new one. The General tab of the executable's Info window, shown in Figure 18-39, controls the environment for that executable when it is run.

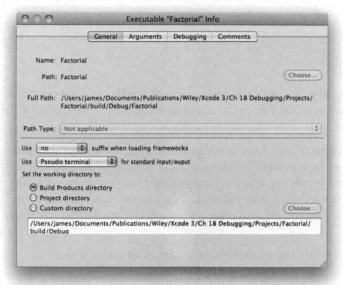

FIGURE 18-39

The Path option is the path, relative to the build product's directory, to the program that will be launched when the executable is started. Normally this is the binary application produced by your target. Change this if you want a different program executed instead. An example would be a UNIX program that is started by a shell script that checks the state of the program, gathers configuration information, and so on, before launching the binary program. If your product is started by such a script, enter the path to the script here.

At the bottom of the window is the current or working directory that will be set before the executable is launched. This is important to some executables that expect to find resources or perform work on files relative to the current directory. Normally this is set to the build directory for the product. That is, the current directory will be the same directory that contains the executable. The build product directory will change depending on which build configuration is active. You can alternatively choose the project directory or a custom directory. Enter the custom directory path, or click the Choose button to browse for a folder.

The Use Suffix When Loading Frameworks option passes a special flag to the dynamic linker. It tells the system's run time library loader to search for alternate versions of framework libraries. Many libraries are provided in alternate versions designed to aid in debugging or profiling. They may include additional integrity checks or log informational messages to the system log that are useful during development. When set to No, the loader links your application to the standard system libraries.

The Use For Standard Input/Output option determines where the stdout, stdin, and stderr file descriptors will be connected when the executable is launched. The Pseudo Terminal connects your application to the run or debugging console you've been using throughout this chapter. The Pipe choice is only useful for remote debugging, as described later. The System Console choice directs the program's output to the system console. Macintosh applications launched by the user, and command-line programs launched without a shell, normally have their output redirected to the system console log. You can review the system console log using the Console utility provided with Mac OS X. When set to the System Console choice, stdin is connected to null.

Arguments and Environment

Use the Arguments pane to pass additional arguments and environment variables to your program. This can be extremely useful for testing command-line applications or setting special features of the run time system.

To add an argument, click the + button beneath the Arguments pane and type in the argument value, as shown in Figure 18-40. You can later edit arguments by double-clicking their values and reorder them by dragging. The check box in the left column is an enabled setting. Only arguments that are enabled are passed to the executable. This makes it easy to keep several commonly used arguments in the list and quickly select just the ones you want. Select an argument and click the – button to delete it entirely.

The environment variables pane works exactly the same way as the arguments, except that this pane defines named variables that are defined in the environment of the process. The values of environment variables can also reference any of the following build settings: SYMROOT, SRCROOT, OBJROOT, BUILT_PRODUCTS_DIR, and TARGET_TEMP_DIR. Chapter 17 covers referencing build settings in general and the meaning of these build settings in particular.

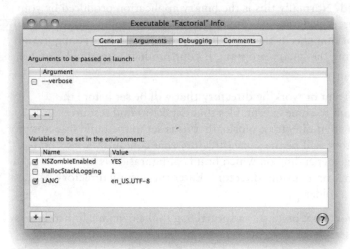

FIGURE 18-40

Debugging

The Debugging pane, shown in Figure 18-41, controls additional settings that affect the execution environment of your program when you launch it under the control of the debugger. The When Using option controls which debugger Xcode will start to debug your application. The debugger chosen must be capable of debugging the kind of application that the executable produces. The Java debugger cannot debug a binary executable. Xcode sets this appropriately for executable products produced from targets. For custom executables, you need to tell Xcode which debugger is appropriate.

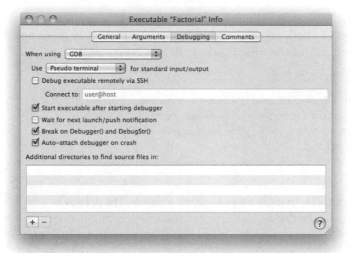

FIGURE 18-41

The Use For Standard Input/Output option controls the connections to the program's I/O. You may want to set this to System Console if the output of the program is obscuring the output of the debugger itself in the Debugger Console window. It is also possible to distinguish between the output of the debugger and your program by coloring their text differently in the Debugger Console window. (See the Debugger pane settings in the Xcode preferences.) If you are doing remote debugging, this option must be set to Pipe.

The next two options configure the gdb debugger for remote execution. The "Remote Debugging" section in this chapter explains how to configure a program for remote debugging.

The Start Executable After Starting Debugger option automatically starts your application running as soon as the debugger is loaded. Normally this is checked, but you may not want this to happen. Turning this option off launches the debugger, but performs no further action. This permits you the opportunity of making special adjustments in the debugging environment, such as setting breakpoints or editing static variables, before the program starts running. You can even use the debugger command to attach to an already running instance of your application, rather than launching a new one.

The Break on Debugger() And DebugStr() option sets the USERBREAK environment variable before your application is started. The presence of this environment variable causes the Debugger() and DebugStr() functions defined in Core Services to send a SIGINT signal to your program if either of these functions are called. Without this setting, these functions do nothing or just log a message to the console. When running under the debugger, a SIGINT signal suspends your program just as if it hit a breakpoint. This option sets this environment variable only when the executable is launched for debugging. To have it set all of the time, set the USERBREAK environment variable to 1 in the Arguments pane.

The Auto-Attach Debugger on Crash option causes the debugger to attach to the executable's process should it crash. This is equivalent to stopping your executable immediately after it crashes, but before the process is terminated, and issuing the Run ⇨ Attach To Process command.

 The Auto-Attach Debugger on Crash option is really only meaningful in Mac OS X 10.5 (Leopard) and earlier. In 10.6 (Snow Leopard), Xcode preemptively starts the gdb *debugger every time you launch your application from within Xcode, so in effect it's already attached.*

The Additional Directories to Find Source File In pane lists the paths to where the debugger can find the source file used to build the executable being debugged. Normally you don't need to add anything here because Xcode automatically searches all of the source directories in your project. However, if you have included source files outside your project or the executable was built from source files that Xcode doesn't know about — files in an externally built target, for instance — add those directories here. You can click the + button and type in the path, or drag a folder from the Finder and drop it into the list.

Selecting an Executable

The active executable that you select using the Project ⇨ Set Active Executable menu is the executable that will be launched when you choose any of the Run or Debug commands. This is typically the product produced by the active target, but it doesn't have to be. After selecting a target, you can change the active executable to an executable produced by another target or to a custom executable that you've created.

When you switch targets, Xcode examines the active executable. If the active executable is the one created for the product produced by the current target, and the target you are switching to produces an executable product, the active executable is changed to match the new active target. For most projects, this means that the active executable will "follow" the active target as you change between them. However, if you have targets that don't produce an executable, or have created and made custom executables active, changing the target may not change the executable. You need to be especially watchful if you have created aggregate targets. An aggregate target that builds both a client and server application will not select an active executable when you make that target active. You must specify which executable, the client or the server, needs to be launched when you choose Run or Debug.

DEBUGGER PREFERENCES

You can use the Debugging pane of the Xcode preferences, shown in Figure 18-42, to configure a few common debugging features.

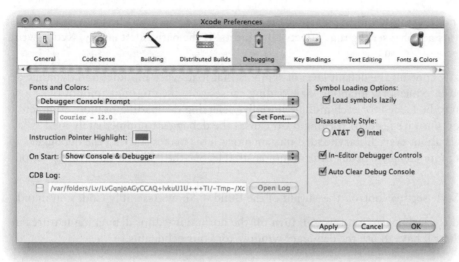

FIGURE 18-42

Starting on the left are the Fonts and Colors preferences. Select a category of text from the pop-up menu, and then change the font, style, and color of the font using the Set Font button. With these settings, you can alter the appearance of text that appears in the run and Debugger Console windows. This makes it possible, or at least easier, to differentiate between the text output by the debugger and the text output by your program. By default, Xcode colors the debugger's prompt and bolds the text sent to the debugger. All output appears the same.

The Instruction Pointer Highlight color is the color used to highlight the currently executing line of source code in the debugger. If you prefer to see a different color, click the color well or drag a color into the color well to change it.

The On Start setting lets you choose to automatically open certain windows when you start your application using the debugger. The choices are:

➤   Do Nothing

➤   Show Console

➤   Show Debugger

➤   Show Console & Debugger

➤   Show Mini Debugger

If you tend to use the in-editor debugging controls, set this to Show Console. Otherwise, choose Show Debugger or Show Console & Debugger so that the debugger window will automatically open when you begin debugging.

If you are using the mini-debugger, the best choice is to open it automatically; by the very nature of programs that you'd want to use the mini-debugger with, opening it after you've started your application can be awkward.

The GDB Log setting will optionally write an extremely detailed log of your debugging session to a text file for later analysis. This is particularly useful if you're trying to diagnose a problem with gdb commands, breakpoint actions, and so on. Enter the path to where you want the file written — just remember that this is a global setting that affects all projects. If the path is left empty, Xcode writes to a temporary file.

Load Symbols Lazily controls the default level of symbols that load when modules and dynamic libraries are loaded into memory. Enabling lazy loading causes only the minimal amount of debug information to be loaded for each module initially, deferring the loading of more complete symbol information until it's needed. Turning it off causes the debugger to immediately load everything it knows about every library loaded into memory. This makes starting the debugger slower, but makes more complete debug information available. See the "Shared Libraries" section for more details.

The Disassembly Style setting controls the output of the Build ⇨ Show Assembly Code command.

Clearing the In-Editor Debugger Controls will turn off the normal in-editor debugging features in each editor pane. You'll have to use the debugger window for your debugging.

REMOTE DEBUGGING

The gdb debugger supports remote debugging. The debugger runs on one computer, while your application runs on a different computer. What actually happens is that another copy of the debugger is started on the remote computer along with your program, and the two debuggers communicate via a network connection. The remote instance of the debugger transmits all of the pertinent information about your application to the local debugger so you can see what's going on. Commands issued to the local debugger are, similarly, forwarded to the remote debugger for execution.

Remote debugging permits you to test your application in an environment different from that of your development system. A typical requirement is the need to debug your application using an earlier version of the operating system. Xcode, and even the computer you're developing on, may not be compatible with the OS you need to run under. Even if it were, building your application and then rebooting your computer into an older version of the OS to test it is both tedious and unproductive.

Remote debugging is also useful for debugging interactive code. Video games and drag-and-drop handlers can be nearly impossible to debug on a single machine, because the sequence of user events needed to test the problem are interrupted by the debugger itself. The mini-debugger is a great tool, but it still requires user interaction on the same system running the application.

Debugging your application remotely requires some special configuration of both computers. Specifically, you must:

- ➤ Pre-authorize an ssh login account on the remote computer.
- ➤ Create a shared build location accessible by both computers via the same path.
- ➤ Configure the executable for remote debugging.

Remote debugging works through the Secure Shell (ssh) remote login facility built into Mac OS X. ssh provides secure communications paths using a public-key encryption system. The primary reason for using ssh for remote debugger communications is not security — although that's valuable if you need it. Instead, Xcode leverages a powerful feature of ssh called *tunneling* that lets it communicate with a remote debugger process as if it were running locally. But the side effect of using ssh is that it requires a secure connection to be established first, and that requires authentication. Normally this is done interactively using a password. For debugging, this is awkward. To get around the need for a password, you need pre-authorized access to the remote machine so that the local computer can connect directly to the remote computer without any human intervention.

You create pre-authorized ssh logins by manually generating and exchanging parts of a public/private key pair. (If you are curious, a typical ssh login authenticates a user and then spontaneously generates a temporary public/private key pair for that session. Pre-creating a public/private key pair skips both of these steps.) To create a pre-authorized login on the remote computer, follow these steps (the commands you would enter are in bold):

1. On the local computer, open a Terminal window and generate an RSA public/private key pair using the ssh-keygen tool:

   ```
   local:~ james$ ssh-keygen -b 2048 -t rsa

   Generating public/private rsa key pair.
   Enter file in which to save the key (/Users/james/.ssh/id_rsa):
   Enter passphrase (empty for no passphrase):
   Enter same passphrase again:
   ```

2. Press Return when Xcode asks for a filename. This uses the default RSA filename for your account. If Xcode asks to overwrite the file, answer with a **y**. Enter a passphrase or press Return to leave it blank. (A blank passphrase is less secure, but is still acceptable and more convenient in a low-security environment.) Confirm the passphrase by entering it again. If you are successful, a new private key is written to ~/.ssh/id_rsa and your public key is written to ~/.ssh/id_rsa.pub, as follows:

   ```
   Your identification has been saved in /Users/james/.ssh/id_rsa.
   Your public key has been saved in /Users/james/.ssh/id_rsa.pub.
   ```

3. On the remote computer, make sure Remote Login is enabled in the Sharing pane of the System Preferences. This allows ssh connections from other computers.

4. Log in to the remote computer using the account you plan to debug under. This verifies that the network connection works and that the remote computer is configured to accept ssh logins. In this example, I'm logging in to the computer whiterabbit using a special account I created just for testing. Use the account name and address of your remote computer in place of test and whiterabbit.local.

   ```
   local:~ james$ ssh test@whiterabbit.local
   Password:
   Last login: Wed Sep 21 15:39:42 2005
   Welcome to Darwin!
   whiterabbit:~ test$
   ```

5. You now need to transfer the public key you just generated to the remote computer. One way is to use ssh 's file transfer capability to send the id_rsa.pub file to the remote computer. Open a second Terminal window (you still have more work to do in

the remote shell you just connected to, so leave that alone for the moment) and enter the following command:

```
local:~ james$ scp ~/.ssh/id_rsa.pub
test@whiterabbit.local:development_rsa.pub
Password:
id_rsa.pub                                    100% 1123      1.1KB/s
00:00
```

Again, supply the password of the remote account and substitute the correct account name and computer address. This command copies the id_rsa.pub file from the local .ssh directory into the development_rsa.pub file in the home folder of the remote computer.

6. Return to the Terminal window with the ssh shell session on the remote computer. Use the ls command to verify that the development_rsa.pub file was transferred.

7. You now need to append the public encryption key in the development_rsa.pub file to the list of authorized computers for this account. To do this, use the following commands:

```
whiterabbit:~ test$ mkdir ~/.ssh
whiterabbit:~ test$ cat ~/development_rsa.pub >> ~/.ssh/authorized_keys
whiterabbit:~ test$ rm ~/development_rsa.pub
whiterabbit:~ test$ chmod go-rwx ~/.ssh/authorized_keys
```

The .ssh directory and authorized_keys file may already exist, in which case you don't want to overwrite them. You just want to append the new key to the existing file. This is a text file, so it can also be edited using nano, vim, or your favorite text editor. The last two commands delete the public key file that was transferred and rescind all non-user access to the authorized_keys file for security purposes.

8. The remote computer is now pre-authorized to accept secure connections from your current account on the local computer to the account you just configured on the remote computer. Verify this by logging out of the current remote session and connecting again, like this:

```
whiterabbit:~ test$ exit
logout
Connection to whiterabbit.local closed.
local:~ james$ ssh test@whiterabbit.local
Enter passphrase for key '/Users/james/.ssh/id_rsa':
Last login: Tue Oct 25 09:49:46 2005 from marchhare.local
Welcome to Darwin!
whiterabbit:~ test$
```

This time, ssh prompted for the passphrase used to generate the key, not for the password of the test account on the local computer. If successful, you know that ssh used the key for this computer to connect to the test account on the remote computer. If you want to change any of these variables in the future — you want to connect from a different development machine or from a different account or to a different account — you must repeat these steps.

The next step is to create a shared build location accessible to both computers. Both the development and remote computer must have direct access to the entire build folder containing both the final product as well as all intermediate build files. More importantly, the UNIX path to the folder must be identical on both computers. You have three easy ways of accomplishing this.

➤ The first, and probably simplest, solution is to employ a third-party file server. Create a build folder on a file server separate from your local or remote computer. (The "Build Locations" section in Chapter 17 discussed different ways of relocating your project's build folder.) You can now mount the build folder on both the local and remote computer using the same path.

➤ The second is a hybrid approach. Configure your project to build to a local folder in a common, publicly accessible folder like /Users/Shared/Projects/DistantBugs. Turn on the file sharing services of OS X and connect to it from the local machine. Now create a symbolic link on the remote computer so that the build folder can be reached on both machines using the same path. You must use the command-line tools to create symbolic links. The following example mounts the main volume of a development system (Griffin, in this example) as a network volume on a remote computer, and a symbol link is created in the remote computer's Shared folder that links to the same folder on the development system:

```
ln -s /Volumes/Griffin/Users/Shared/Projects /Users/Shared/Projects
```

Now, any build folders that are created in the development computer's /Users/Shared/Projects folder will appear at the same location in the remote computer's file system.

➤ The third method of getting both computers access to the same build folder would be to simply copy the entire build folder to the remote computer. For a one-shot test, this might be the easiest solution. However, if you were constantly rebuilding the project, this would be both inconvenient and inefficient. You could automate the process by creating a target script phrase to copy the contents of the build folder to the remote computer. If you decide to go this route, consider using a utility like rsync to quickly transfer only the portions of the build folder that change after each build. Remember that the location of the copy must reside at the same location as the original, or at least have an equivalent UNIX path.

The last step in this process is to configure Xcode to start the debugging session remotely. You do this is in the Debugging pane of the executable's Info window, previously shown in Figure 18-41.

Check the Debug Executable Remotely Via SSH option. When you do this, the Standard Input/Output option changes to Pipe. Leave it that way; this choice *must* be set to Pipe for remote debugging to work.

Start your debugging session as you normally would. The first time you do, Xcode asks for your passphrase to decode the private key you generated earlier, as shown in Figure 18-43. Once it has your private key, it connects to the remote computer and starts the debugging session. After this point, debugging your application remotely isn't significantly different from debugging it locally.

FIGURE 18-43

If anything goes wrong — problems connecting to the remote computer, accessing the product on the remote computer, or starting the debugger — consult the debugger console window for clues. Both the ssh client and the debugger output copious diagnostic messages to the console. Anything that goes wrong should be documented there.

DEBUGGING AIDES

A number of miscellaneous tools and features are scattered around the debugger, Xcode, and the operating system itself that will help you find bugs in your code. The "Custom Executables" section covered loading the debug variant of frameworks and enabling Debugger() and DebugStr() calls. The following sections describe a few more Xcode facilities.

Catching a Throw

The command Run ⇨ Stop on Objective-C Exceptions command enables an implied breakpoint whenever an Objective-C exception is thrown. You can enable or disable this breakpoint at any time during your debugging.

Stopping for Debugger() and DebugStr()

The Run ⇨ Stop on Debugger()/DebugStr() command sets an implied breakpoint whenever your application calls the Debugger() or DebugStr() commands. Normally these function calls are ignored. The command in the Debug menu enables this feature for all of the executables in your project. If you want to have Debugger() and DebugStr() break only in certain executables, disable the menu item and enable the same setting for selected executables in their Debugger pane.

Guard Malloc

A very useful debugging feature for C programmers is the Guard Malloc library. Choosing the Run ⇨ Enable Guard Malloc command before you start the debugging session causes your executable to be linked against the Guard Malloc (libgmalloc) library instead of the normal malloc routines provided by the system. The Guard Malloc library uses the virtual memory features of the CPU to map every block of memory allocated using malloc(...) into its own address space. If your program attempts to access any data outside the immediate boundaries of the allocated block, an EXC_BAD_ACCESS error occurs, crashing your program at the exact point where the illegal access occurred.

It should be noted that Guard Malloc can *significantly* slow down your application, but the additional execution time is usually worth it, because out-of-bounds memory accesses are particularly difficult to debug.

Debug Variables

Debug variables are either environment variables or preference property values that invoke special behavior in the libraries and frameworks and are useful for debugging.

There is also a wide range of debugging support functions that your application can call directly, but a discussion of those is beyond the scope of this book. The best resource is Apple's Technical Note #2124, Mac OS X Debugging Magic. You can find it in the Xcode documentation.

Environment variables can be set using the Arguments pane of the executable's Info window. Preference values can be set using the defaults command-line tool. You can read the man page on the defaults tool for the details of setting user default values, but here's a simple example:

```
defaults write com.my.SimpleApp NSShowAllViews YES
```

The com.my.SimpleApp file is the user preferences file associated with the application. By default, this is the Identifier set in the target's Properties pane. The command sets the NSShowAllViews property to YES, which causes the AppKit framework to draw a colored border around every NSView. Setting property values only works for Carbon and Cocoa applications that use the user defaults framework.

The following table describes a few environment variables useful for C programming:

ENVIRONMENT VARIABLE	DESCRIPTION
MallocScribble	Fills deallocated memory with 0x55s. If your program reads the data again, it should be obvious in the debugger that the data is from a stale block.
MallocGuardEdges	Adds guard pages before and after large allocation blocks. This will catch attempts to access data well beyond the edge of each allocated block. It can be used independently of the Guard Malloc library.
MallocStackLogging	Logs the stack state for each allocated block. There are tools that will read this log and assist you in debugging memory allocation problems, especially memory leaks.

If you think you have a problem with loading dynamic libraries, try some of the environment variables described in the following table:

ENVIRONMENT VARIABLE	DESCRIPTION
DYLD_IMAGE_SUFFIX	Searches for libraries with this suffix first. Use this to load alternate variants of libraries. A lot of the system libraries include debug versions that can be loaded by setting the suffix to _debug.
DYLD_PRINT_LIBRARIES	Logs the names of each library, as it is loaded. If you think you're loading the wrong dynamic library, set this variable to 1.
DYLD_PRINT_LIBRARIES _POST_LAUNCH	Logs the names of loaded libraries, but it only starts logging after your application has started executing. This avoids logging a lot of the core libraries.
DYLD_PREBIND_DEBUG	Logs pre-binding diagnostics information about your application.

If you're debugging memory leak or retain/release problems in Cocoa, consider setting some of the environment variables described in the following table:

ENVIRONMENT VARIABLE	DEFAULT	DESCRIPTION
NSZombieEnabled	NO	If this is set to YES, NSObjects are "zombified" instead of being deallocated. A zombie object has all of its message handlers replaced with a call that will break into the debugger. This will catch an attempt to send a message to an object that has already been released and deallocated.
NSDeallocateZombies	NO	Set this to YES and the memory for zombie objects will actually be released. The NO setting is the safest, but can result in memory leaks that themselves may cause your application to misbehave.
NSHangOnUncaughtException	NO	Normally an uncaught NSException will cause a Cocoa application to terminate. Set this variable to YES and it will simply hang instead, allowing you to break into it using the debugger and examine its state.
NSEnableAutoreleasePool	YES	Setting this value to NO defeats the functionality of auto-release pools. Use this if you want to keep around all of the objects that an auto-release pool would normally release.
NSAutoreleaseFreedObject CheckEnabled	NO	This is a very handy setting for finding double-release bugs. Setting this variable to YES will cause the auto-release pool to log an error message if the pool contains an object that has already been released.
NSAutoreleaseHighWaterMark	0	This is a useful diagnostics tool to check for situations where you are putting an excessive number of objects into an auto-release pool. Set it to a number other than 0 and the system will log a warning whenever more than that number of objects have been added to the pool.
NSAutoreleaseHighWater Resolution	0	Use this setting to log a warning message for every *N* number of objects above the high-water mark level. The high-water mark level emits a single warning when the number exceeds that value. This setting emits a warning for every increment. Setting the high-water mark to 1000 and the resolution to 50 would log a message when there were 1000, 1050, 1100, 1050, . . . objects in any auto-release pool.

The two preference settings described in the following table are useful when you're debugging an AppKit application that is having drawing or layout problems. You must set preferences in the preference file of the application before you launch it.

PREFERENCE KEY	DESCRIPTION
NSShowAllViews	Define this preference and set it to YES and the AppKit window manager will draw a colored border around each NSView in the application. This makes it very easy to see spacing and layout problems.
NSShowAllDrawing	Define this preference and set it to YES and AppKit will draw a colored rectangle before drawing each NSView. This makes it very easy to see what components in your windows are drawing, when, and in what order. Also check out the various Quartz Debug features.

This is just the tip of the iceberg. There are literally hundreds of variables, system calls, and development tools to help you track down and debug your application. Most are collected and maintained in *Apple Technical Note #2124, Mac OS X Debugging Magic*, which you can find in the Xcode documentation or read online at `http://developer.apple.com/mac/library/technotes/tn2004/tn2124.html`.

SUMMARY

You should now have at your disposal a cornucopia of tools and techniques for isolating, trapping, examining, and correcting any aberrant behavior in your application. You are likely to spend a lot of time using the debugger. Knowing how to harness the debugger's capabilities can save you hours of time.

Getting your application to build and execute correctly may be all you intended to accomplish. For some applications, even this isn't the end of the development process. You may not be satisfied that your application merely runs. You want it to run *fast* — and that is the subject of the next chapter.

19

Performance Analysis

WHAT'S IN THIS CHAPTER?

➤ Performance analysis best practices

➤ Analyzing code-level performance with Shark

➤ Analyzing everything else with Instruments

➤ Solving common performance problems

Whether it's a rollercoaster ride or a visit to the dentist, a lot of times you just want things to go faster — and the applications you build with Xcode are no exception. Speeding up an application entails finding and eliminating inefficient code, making better use of the computer's resources, or just thinking differently. Neither Xcode nor I can help you with the last one. Sometimes the most dramatic improvements in a program are those that come from completely rethinking the problem. There are, sadly, no developer tools to simulate your creativity.

The more mundane approaches are to reduce the amount of waste in your application and to harness more of the computer system's power. To do that you first need to know where your application is spending its time and learn what resources it's using. In simple terms, to make your application run faster you first need to know what's slowing it down. This is a process known as performance analysis, and for that, Xcode offers a number of very powerful tools.

Recent versions of Xcode consolidate a wide variety of performance analysis tools that, in prior versions, were individual applications. In Xcode 3.2, the former rag-tag band of developer gizmos has been gathered together under a single umbrella called Instruments. I do not exaggerate when I say that Instruments is the single greatest advancement in Macintosh debugging ever, but it hasn't replaced every tool. You'll still make regular use of the debugger (Chapter 18) and you'll also want to use Shark, a dedicated code-level analysis tool.

This chapter discusses some of the principles of performance analysis, Shark, and Instruments. The manual for Instruments is excellent — just search the Xcode documentation for "Instruments" — so this chapter won't go into too much detail about every instrument and display option. Instead, I show you how to use Instruments in an Xcode-centric workflow and walk you through the solution to three very common performance problems.

PERFORMANCE BASICS

The term *performance* means different things to different people. This chapter concentrates on the simplest and most direct kind of performance enhancement: getting your application to run faster. In general, this means getting your program to work more efficiently, and therefore finish sooner.

In the real world, this is too narrow of a definition, and performance solutions are sometimes counterintuitive. A graphics application that draws a placeholder image, and then starts a background thread to calculate successively higher resolution versions of the same image, might actually end up drawing that image two or three times. Measured both by the raw computations expended and by clock time, the application is doing much more work and is actually slower than if it had simply drawn the final image once. From the user's perspective, the *perceived performance* of the application is better. It appears to be more responsive and usable, and therefore provides a superior experience. These are the solutions that require you to think "different," not just think "faster."

When considering the performance of your application, keep the following principles in mind:

- ➤ Optimize your code only when it is actually experiencing performance problems.

- ➤ People are notoriously bad at estimating the performance of a complex system.

- ➤ Combining the first two principles, you probably have no idea what or where your performance problems are.

- ➤ Set performance goals for your program and record benchmarks *before* starting any performance enhancements. Continue making, saving, and comparing benchmark results throughout your development.

If It isn't Broken . . .

The first principle is key; don't try to optimize things that don't need optimizing. Write your application in a straightforward, well structured, easily maintained, and robust manner. This usually means writing your application using the simplest solution, employing high-level routines, objects, and abstractions. Given the choice of using a neatly encapsulated class and a collection of C functions that do the same thing, use the class.

Now run your application and test it. If, *and only if*, its performance is unacceptable should you even consider trying to speed it up. Your current solution might be taking a simple 4-byte integer, turning it into a string object, stuffing that into a collection, serializing that collection into a data stream, and then pushing the whole mess into a pipe — whereupon the entire process is promptly reversed. You might recoil in horror at the absurd inefficiency used to pass a single integer value, but computers today are mind-numbingly fast. All that work, over the lifetime of your application, might ultimately consume less CPU time than it takes you to blink.

In addition, optimization makes more work for you now and in the future. Optimized code is notoriously more fragile and difficult to maintain. This means that future revisions to your project will take longer and you run a higher risk of introducing bugs. So remember, don't fix what ain't broke. Every optimization incurs a cost, both today and in the future.

Embrace Your Own Ignorance

Modern computer languages, libraries, and hardware are both complex and subtle. It is very difficult to guess, with any accuracy, how much time a given piece of code will take to execute. Gone are the days where you could look at some machine code, count the instructions, and then tell how long it would take the program to run. Sure, sometimes it's easy. Sorting a hundred million of anything is going to take some time. Those kinds of hot spots are the exception, not the rule. Most of the time the performance bottlenecks in your application will occur in completely unexpected places.

Another common fallacy is to assume you can write something that's faster than the system. Always start by using the system tools, collections, and math classes that you have available to you. Only if those prove to be a burden should you consider abandoning them. You might think you can write a better sorting routine, but you probably can't. Many of the algorithms provided by Apple and the open source software community have been finely tuned and tweaked by experienced engineers who are a lot smarter than you or I.

Combining the first two principles, you can distill this simple rule:

> ➤ Don't try to guess where your performance problems are.

If you have a performance problem, let the performance analysis tools find them for you.

Improve Performance Systematically

The last bit of advice is to have a goal and measure your progress. Know what the performance goals of your application should be before you even begin development. Your goals can be completely informal. You may simply want your application to *feel* responsive. If it does, then you're done. Most of the time you will not need to do any performance analysis or optimization at all.

If your application's performance seems sub-optimal, begin by measuring its performance before you try to fix anything. If you accept the earlier principles, this is a prerequisite: you must measure the performance of your application before you can begin to know where its problems are. Even if you already know, you should still benchmark your application first. You can't tell how much (or if any) progress has been made if you don't know where you started from.

Continue this process throughout the lifetime of your application. Applications, like people, tend to get heavier and slower over time. Keep the benchmarks you took when you first began, and again later after optimization. Occasionally compare them against the performance of your application as you continue development. It's just like leaving a set of scales in the bathroom.

PREPARING FOR ANALYSIS

Most of the performance analysis tools, especially ones that analyze the code of your application, need debug symbol information. They also need to analyze the code you plan to release, not the code you are debugging. If you've been building and testing your application using the debugger (covered in Chapter 18), you probably already have a build configuration for debugging. The debugger needs debugging symbols on and all optimization turned off. Your released application should be fully optimized and free of any debugger data. Performance analysis sits right between these two points. It needs debugging symbols, but it should be fully optimized. Without the debugging symbols, it can't do its job, and there's no point in profiling or trying to improve unoptimized code.

If you're using the modern DWARF with dSYM file debug information format, set up your Release build configuration as follows:

➤ Debug Information Format (DEBUG_INFORMATION_FORMAT) = DWARF with dSYM

➤ Generate Debug Symbols (GCC_GENERATE_DEBUGGING_SYMBOLS) = YES

The DWARF with dSYM file format writes the debugging information to a separate dSYM file that's not part of your final product. The end result is a finished application that's (mostly) stripped of any debugging information, along with a companion dSYM file that provides the debugger and performance analysis tools with all of the information they need. This is the build configuration you'll find if you created your project using any of the modern Xcode project templates.

If you've inherited an older project, created one with an earlier version of Xcode, or can't use the DWARF with dSYM file format for some reason, you're going to need a special build configuration for performance analysis. Create a new build configuration specifically for profiling by doing the following:

1. In the Configurations pane of the project's Info window, duplicate your Release build configuration, the configuration used to produce your final application. Name the new configuration "Performance."

2. In the Performance configuration for all of your targets and/or the project, turn on Generate Debug Symbols. Turn off Strip Debug Symbols During Copy.

Switch to this build configuration whenever you need to do performance analysis and enhancements. If you change the code generation settings in your Release configuration, remember to update your Performance configuration to match.

SHARK

Shark is a code performance analysis tool, and is the premier tool for optimizing your code's raw execution speed. It works by periodically sampling the state of your application from which it assembles an approximate overview of its performance. Though Instruments has similar tools, Shark is purpose-built for optimizing code and is my first choice when that's my singular focus.

Shark can be used on its own in a variety of modes, but you're going to start it directly from within Xcode. First, build your target using your performance build configuration. From the menu choose Run ⇨ Launch Using Performance Tool ⇨ Shark.

 Remember that the items in the Run ⇨ Launch Using Performance Tool menu do not build your project first. Get into the habit of performing a build (Command+B) before starting any performance tool, or you'll be analyzing old code.

When Xcode starts Shark, it tells Shark which executable to analyze and describes its environment — saving you a lot of configuration work in Shark. The initial window, shown at the top of Figure 19-1, selects the type of analysis that Shark will perform. The useful choices are:

SHARK CONFIGURATION	BEST USE
Time Profile	Optimizing the raw performance of your code
Time Profile (All Thread States)	Speeding up your application by looking for delays caused by either your code or system routines your code calls
Time Profile (WTF)	Same as Time Profile, but analyzes a fixed time period ending when Shark is stopped

Shark can perform many different kinds of analyses, but only a few make sense when you're launching a single process from Xcode. Many of Shark's other modes also overlap those in Instruments, and for those cases you'll probably be better served by the latter.

 All the choices in the analysis menu are named, editable configurations supplied by Shark. You can change these configurations (Config ⇨ Edit) or add your own (Config ⇨ New), much the way you redefine batch find options in the Project Find window.

The Time Profile measures the performance of your application's code. The All Thread State variant includes time spent waiting for system routines. Think of it as optimizing process time versus optimizing elapsed time.

Normally, Shark captures a fixed number of samples or for a fixed time period — parameters you can change by editing the configuration — stops, and then performs its analysis. The Windowed Time Facility (WTF) mode captures samples indefinitely into a circular buffer. When stopped, it analyzes the latest set of samples. In other words, regular analysis starts at some point and analyzes a fixed time period beyond that point. WTF analysis ends at some point and analyzes the time period up to that point.

To profile a Java application, choose one of the Java-specific analysis modes in Shark and pass the -XrunShark argument to the Java command that launches your program. The easiest method of accomplishing this is to add a -XrunShark argument in the Arguments pane of the executable's Get Info window. You might want to create a custom executable just for Shark profiling, or just disable this argument when you are done.

Java and Xcode have an on-again, off-again romance — Apple alternately breaks Java support in Shark and then fixes it again. Some combinations of the Java run time and Xcode analysis tools don't work well together, if at all. Consult the Java release notes or inquire on the Xcode-users discussion list if you are having problems.

To start a Shark analysis of your application simply click the Start button, or press Shark's hot key (Option+Esc), and a launch process configuration dialog box appears, as shown in Figure 19-1. The dialog has been preconfigured by Xcode, so you shouldn't have much to do. Before beginning your analysis, you can choose to modify the command-line parameters or environment variables passed to your application. This example passes an argument of "150000" to the program for testing. The menu button to the right of the Arguments field keeps a history of recently used argument lists.

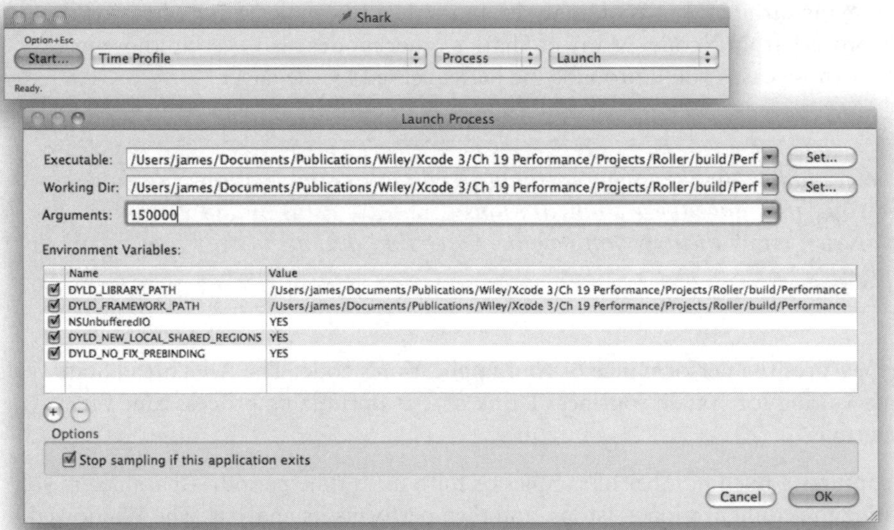

FIGURE 19-1

You can also attach Shark to a currently running application. If you've already started your application from Xcode, launch Shark and choose your running process from the menu at the right of Shark's control window. Click the Start button, or switch back to your application and use Shark's hot key (Option+Esc) to start sampling at a strategic point.

Profile View

Your program runs while Shark is analyzing it. Shark stops its analysis after your program has terminated, when you stop it yourself using the Stop button, by pressing Shark's hot key (Option+Esc), or when Shark's analysis buffer fills up — typically 30 seconds' worth. Shark then presents its profile of your application's performance, as shown in Figure 19-2.

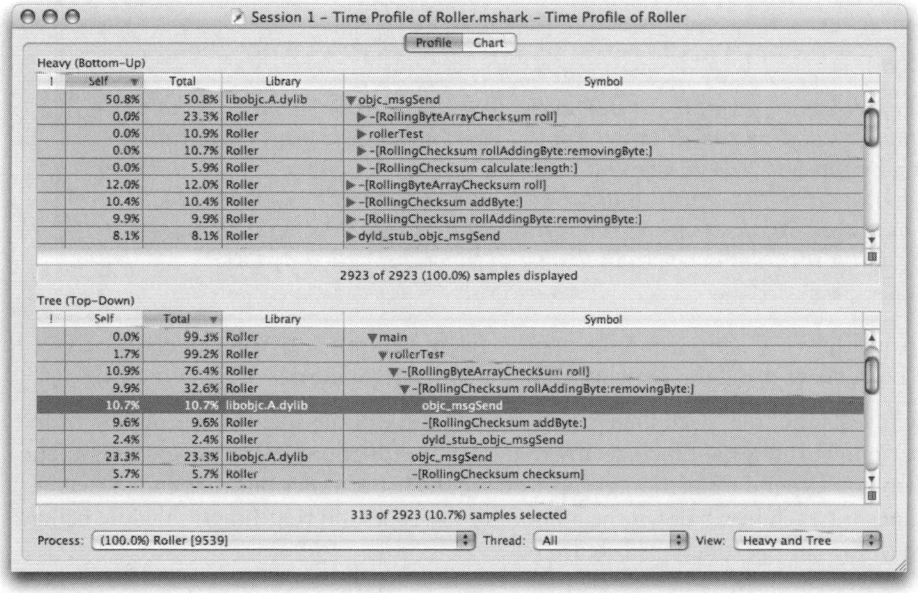

FIGURE 19-2

Figure 19-2 shows the Tree (Top-Down) view of your application's performance in the lower pane. The columns Self and Total show how much time your program spent in each function of your application. The Self column records the amount of time it spent in the code of that particular function. The Total column calculates the amount of time spent in that function and any functions called by that function. The organization of the tree view should be obvious, because it parallels the calling structure of your application. Every function listed expands to show the functions that it called and how much time was spent in each.

The compiler's optimization can confuse Shark as well as the debugger. Take the following code as an example:

```
main()
{
    calc();
}

int calc( )
{
    return (subcalc());
}

int subcalc( )
{
    return (x);
}
```

The compiler may convert the statement `return (subcalc())` *into a "chain" rather than a function call. It might pop the existing stack frame before calling* `subcalc`, *or jump to* `subcalc()` *and let it use the stack frame for* `calc()`. *Either way, it has avoided the overhead incurred by creating and destroying a stack frame, but when Shark examines the stack, it thinks that* `main` *called* `subcalc` *directly, and it includes* `subcalc` *in the list of functions called by* `main`.

The Heavy (Bottom-Up) view is shown in the upper pane of Figure 19-2. You can choose to see the Tree, Heavy, or both views using the View menu in the lower-right corner of the window.

The Heavy view inverts the tree. Each item is now the amount of time spent executing the code within each function. This does not include any time spent in functions that this function might have called. When you expand a function group, you see the list of functions that called that function. The times for each break down the amount of time spent in that function while being called from each of the calling functions listed.

The Tree view gives you a bird's-eye view of where your application is spending its time, starting with the first function called (where it spends all of its time), and subdividing that by the subroutines it calls, the subroutines called by those subroutines, and so on. The Heavy view determines which functions use up the most of your program's CPU time. This view works backward to determine what functions caused those heavily used functions to be called, and how often.

You can use this information in a variety of ways. The typical approach is to use the Heavy view to see which functions use the most time. Those are prime candidates for optimization. If you can make those functions run faster, anything that calls them will run faster too. Both the Heavy and Tree views are also useful for finding logical optimizations. This usually entails reengineering the callers of heavy functions so that they get called less often or not at all. Making a function faster helps, but not calling the function in the first place is even quicker.

At the bottom of the window are the Process and Thread selections. These two menus enable you to restrict the analysis to a single process or thread within that process. Set one of these menus to something other than All, and only samples belonging to that thread or process are considered. Because Xcode launched Shark for this particular application, there is only one process. If the application you launched runs in multiple threads, select the thread you want to analyze. The status line above these two controls displays the number of samples being considered.

STATISTICAL SAMPLING

At this point, you might be wondering how Shark obtained all of this information. Shark is one of a class of tools known as *samplers*. Shark interrupts your application about a thousand times every second and takes a (very) quick "snapshot" of what it's doing. After these samples have been gathered, Shark combines all of the samples to produce a statistical picture of where your program spends its time.

Think of trying to analyze the habits of a firefly. You set up a high-speed camera in the dark and film the firefly as it flies around. After you've got several thousand frames, you could compose all of those frames into a single picture like a single long exposure. Points in the picture that are very bright are where the firefly spent most of its time, dimmer spots indicate places where it visited briefly, and the black portions are where it (probably) never went at all. This is exactly what the Heavy view shows — the accumulated totals of every snapshot where Shark found your application in a particular function at that moment.

The word "statistical" is important. Shark does not trace your program nor does it rigorously determine exactly when each subroutine was called and how long it took to run. It relies entirely on taking thousands of (essentially) random samples. Functions that execute very little of the time may not even appear. Shark can only be trusted when it has many samples of a function — which is perfect, because you're usually only interested in the functions that take up a significant amount of time. The ones that don't aren't worth optimizing.

Code View

The profile view is useful for identifying the functions that are candidates for optimization, but what in those functions needs optimizing? Double-click any function name and Shark switches to a code view of that function as shown in Figure 19-3.

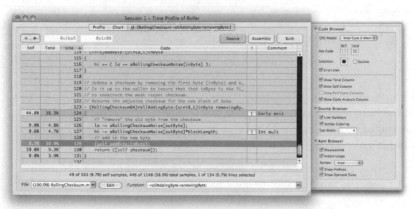

FIGURE 19-3

The code view shows the amount of time your application spent in each line of your function, or, to put it more precisely, it shows the percentage of time that it found your application at that line of source code when it captured a sample. Source view requires that you compiled your application with full debug information, and that information was not stripped from the executable. If there is no debug information available, you'll see the machine code disassembly of the function instead. If you really want to get into the nitty-gritty details of your code, change the listing to show the machine code, or both the machine and source code side-by-side, using the buttons in the upper-right corner.

Shark highlights the "hot spots" in your code by coloring heavily used statements in various shades of yellow. This shading continues into the scroll bar area so you can quickly scroll to hot spots above or below the visible listing. Even though the window will scroll through the entire source file that contains the function you are examining, only the statistics and samples for the function you selected are analyzed. If you want to scrutinize samples in a different function, return to the Profile tab and double-click that function.

The truly amazing power of Shark really becomes evident in the code view. Shark analyzes the execution flow of your code and makes suggestions for improving it. These suggestions appear as advice buttons — small square buttons with exclamation points — throughout the interface. One is shown in Figure 19-4. Click an advice button and Shark pops up a bubble explaining what it found and what you might do to improve the performance of your code.

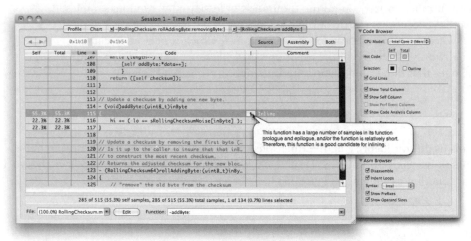

FIGURE 19-4

The advice feature is quite sophisticated; many of its suggestions require the analysis of code flow, instruction pipelining, and caching features of various processors. Shark can recognize when you are dividing where you might be better off with a bit shift instead, or where loops should be unrolled, aligned, and so on. It's like having a CPU performance expert in a box.

Every time you link to a code view from the summary window it creates another tab at the top of Shark's analysis window. Close the tab or navigate back to the profile pane. Jumping from one function to another within a code view, however, replaces the contents of the pane much like a browser. Use the history buttons (upper left) to navigate back to previous functions.

Stack View

When you switch to Chart, the view changes from the accumulated statistics to a temporal graph of your program's execution, as shown in Figure 19-5. The table at the bottom shows the samples taken by Shark — essentially the frames of the movie. The chart above it depicts the stack depth at each sample. Clicking a sample in the list or at the same horizontal location in the chart highlights its corresponding sample and displays the calling stack that was active at that moment in the program's execution. Using the right and left or up and down arrow keys, you can literally "scrub" back and forth through the execution of your application. When you select a function name in the chart or the stack frame list, Shark highlights the duration of every function executing at that moment. You can see in the chart not only how long it took for the selected function to run but how long functions that called that function ran.

The graph can be quite dense, depending on how many samples you have. Use the slider bar at the left to magnify the graph, and then scroll to the right and left through it using the horizontal scroll bar. You can hide the stack frames to see more of the chart by clicking the small join-pane button in the lower-right corner of the chart. Click it again to reveal the stack frames once more.

The squiggly lines between samples indicate a thread switch. The samples after the line are code executing in a different thread than the previous sample. As with the profile view, you can choose to restrict the graph to just those samples from a single process or thread.

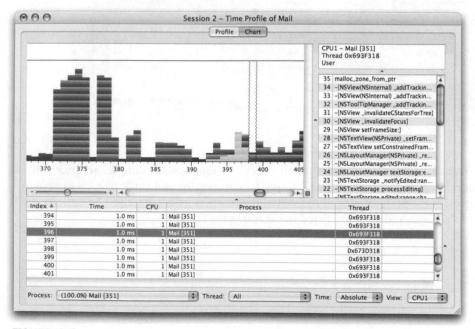

FIGURE 19-5

Refining the Analysis

Shark has a number of controls for refining what samples you choose to analyze and how. Unfiltered sample data can be overwhelming and obscure the real problem. Overly filtered data can also be misleading, hiding the very thing you're looking for. Shark includes some filtering and analysis options that help you find the right balance.

To see these controls, open the advanced settings drawer using the command View ➪ Show Advanced Settings (Command+Shift+M). The advanced settings for the profile and chart views are shown in Figure 19-6.

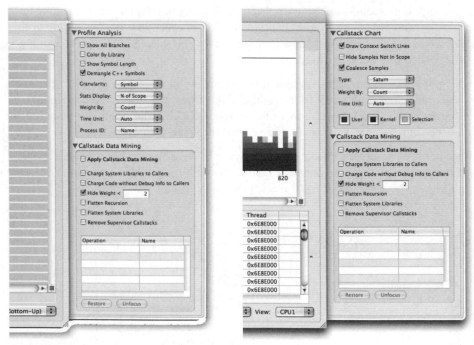

FIGURE 19-6

The Callstack Data Mining section applies to all views and adjusts what samples are included and how they are accounted for. Callstack Data Mining reinterprets the call stack of each sample in an effort to represent the performance of individual functions more accurately. The options you'll probably want to change, and why, are listed in the following table:

CALLSTACK DATA MINING OPTION	EFFECT
Charge System Libraries to Callers	The amount of time calculated for function will include the time spent executing system calls. Use this to zero in on time-consuming functions, even when the time spent in the function itself might be small.
Charge Code Without Debug Info to Callers.	Similar to the first option, assume that any function without symbol information is opaque code and can't be analyzed. Warning: if your application lacks debug symbols, this option will make all your samples disappear!
Hide Weight	Great for filtering out noise functions — functions with only a few sample hits — from large samples. If you don't have any heavy hotspots, this can hide too much. Turn it off if you can't find the functions you're looking for.
Flatten Recursion	If your functions use recursion, this option applies the cost of the recursive call to the function's weight.
Remove Supervisor Callstacks	Ignores any samples that occur in the kernel (supervisor) state. This includes interrupt handling.

The Charge System Libraries to Callers option adds the time spent in system library calls to the function that called it. Similarly, the Charge Code Without Debug Info To Callers accumulates the time spent in calls compiled without debug information to the caller. Use these options when you want to assume that you can't optimize any of the system library code or code that you didn't write (and have no debug information for). This simplifies the profile and lets you concentrate on locating hot spots in your code.

The Profile Analysis and Callstack Chart panels let you customize the display of the profile and chart views, respectively. Using these settings you can:

➤ Color function calls by the library that they are in

➤ Demangle C++ function names so they are easier to read

➤ Change how the time and sample units are displayed

➤ Change the color of the chart

Play with these settings to get the display features you prefer.

Saving and Comparing Shark Sessions

The beginning of the chapter explained that it's important to keep track of your progress as you optimize your program. You will also want to review the performance of your application in the beginning, and compare that to what it is now.

The Save (Command+S) and Save As (Command+Shift+S) commands save the sample data in a file for later perusal. When you save a Shark session, it presents the dialog box shown in Figure 19-7.

If you choose to embed the source file information, you'll be able to browse the code view with the original source at a later date. If you strip the information, you will have all of the statistical data but won't be able to examine code listings that include source (unless the original source is still available when you load the session). To load an old session, open the session file from the Finder or use Shark's File ⇨ Open or File ⇨ Open Recent command.

You can also have Shark compare two sessions. Choose the File ⇨ Compare (Command+Option+C) command and open two Shark session files. Shark presents a single profile browser showing the changes in the profile values instead of absolute values for each function.

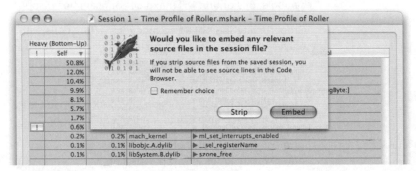

FIGURE 19-7

Merging Shark Sessions

In addition to saving and comparing sessions, you can merge two sessions. This is useful if you made two samples of the same code under different circumstances. You can save each of these sessions as a separate file, and then merge them together and analyze the data as if all of the samples occurred in a single session.

To merge two sessions, choose the File ⇨ Merge (Option+Command+M) command. Shark will present two open file dialogs. Choose the first session file in one and the second session file in the other. Shark merges those samples into a new untitled session. This can take a while, so be patient.

If you need to merge more than two sessions, save the merged session as a new file, close it, and then merge the merged session with a third.

Using Shark to Analyze Remote and iPhone Applications

Shark can be used to analyze an iPhone app or other process running on a remote system. Xcode, however, won't set this up for you automatically. If you need to do code performance analysis on an iPhone or a remote application, first consider using the CPU Sampler template in Instruments. The CPU Sampler instrument is like a baby version of Shark that runs as an instrument, and Xcode will automatically set up and connect Instruments to an iPhone application. Instruments is by far the easiest solution, if not the most powerful.

If you really want to use Shark instead, connect to your iPhone or remote process using the Sampling ⇨ Network/iPhone Profiling command. See the Shark help document for the details.

Learn More About Shark

This introduction to Shark only scratches its surface. Full documentation for Shark is available within the application itself in the Help menu. There is a user's guide, profiling and data mining tutorials, as well as interactive processor instruction references.

Shark can analyze multiple processes and applications that are no longer responding. You can start and stop its sampling from within your application, the keyboard, or using command-line tools. It can debug memory bandwidth issues, processor cache hits, and virtual memory paging. Read the documentation for a complete description of all of these features. If you still have questions, consider joining the Performance Analysis and Optimization mailing list (PerfOptimization-dev) at http://lists.apple.com/.

INSTRUMENTS

Instruments is an application for doing performance analysis. Instruments replaces a hodgepodge collection of older utilities (Sampler, Big Top, Spin Control, ObjectAlloc, Thread Viewer, and others) with a uniform, flexible, and coordinated set of modular testing tools. Using Instruments, you can quickly assemble a custom set of analysis modules that will target, and hopefully illuminate, exactly the problem you're trying to solve.

To use Instruments, you assemble a deck of customized data collection modules (called *instruments*) that gather information about your application, the entire system, or both. The arrangement, as shown in Figure 19-8, comes out looking something like Garage Band. Each track records a different aspect of your application or the system. You can examine the details of an individual track, correlate different tracks, replay your application's performance, compare the performance of different runs, and much more.

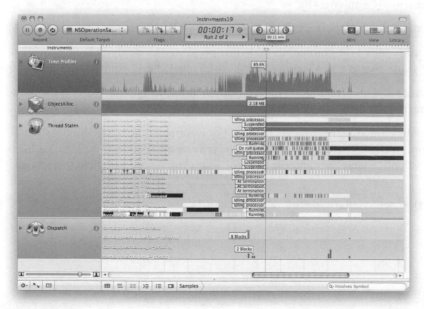

FIGURE 19-8

The *Instruments User Guide* is quite good. You can find it by searching for "Instruments" in the Xcode documentation or online at http://developer.apple.com/mac/library/documentation/ DeveloperTools/Conceptual/InstrumentsUserGuide/. The user guide, however, focuses mostly on what Instruments can do and how to use it as a standalone application. This chapter focuses more on how to use Instruments in an Xcode workflow, and demonstrates using Instruments to solve some typical development problems. The two are complementary, and I encourage you to read both.

Terminology

The following table defines the vocabulary used by Instruments:

TERM	DEFINITION
Instruments	The Instruments performance analysis application and testing suite
instrument	An individual data collection module
track	The data set collected by a single instrument
Trace Document	A document containing a set of instruments *and* the data they collected
Template	A document containing a configuration of instruments
playhead	A position control that shows/selects a common point in time

Recording Trace Data

Running your application under the watchful gaze of Instruments is very simple:

1. Build your application (Command+B).
2. Choose an Instruments template from the Run ➪ Run With Performance Tool menu.

The first step is important. None of the commands that start performance analysis builds your project first, so if you've made changes and want to test those changes, build your project first.

Xcode launches Instruments in the correct mode for your target application, configures it using the selected template, and starts your application running.

Not all Instruments templates are available for every target. For example, iPhone OS 3.0 does not provide garbage collection, so the GC Monitor template is grayed out for iPhone apps. Here's a list of the more popular Xcode-supplied templates and the kinds of issues you would use them to analyze:

XCODE INSTRUMENTS TEMPLATE	INSTRUMENTS	USE
Object Allocations	ObjectAlloc, VM Tracker	Look for Objective-C memory leaks, possibly ones that cause excessive VM memory usage.
Leaks	ObjectAlloc, Leaks	Look for object, and non-object, memory leaks.

XCODE INSTRUMENTS TEMPLATE	INSTRUMENTS	USE
Zombies	ObjectAlloc with Zombies detection	Find under-retained/over-released Objective-C objects.
Time Profiler	Time Profiler	Analyze code performance, much like Shark.
CPU Sampler	Sampler, CPU Monitor	Compare application CPU utilization with overall system CPU utilization.
Threads	Tread State	Examine thread creation, switching, and state history.
Multicore	Thread State, Dispatch	Examine thread states and Grand Central Dispatch queues looking for CPU utilization, bottlenecks, and stalls.
GC Monitor	Object Graph, ObjectAlloc, Garbage Collection	Look at the high-level picture of object allocation, lifespan, and garbage collection activity.
File Activity	File Activity, Reads/ Writes, File Attributes, Directory I/O	A combination of instruments that monitor all high-level file activity. Use it to look for file access problems, ordering, or inefficient I/O.
Core Data	Core Data Fetches, Core Data Cache Misses, Core Data Saves	Track down poor Core Data performance looking for excessive fetches, poor caching, or slow saves.

Instrument collection continues as long as the application is running. Quitting your application, or pressing the Stop button in Instruments, terminates data collection — and your application.

Instruments' interface is live. You can browse, dig into, and analyze data as it's being collected. When you're done, either leave the trace document window open, save it, or close as you wish.

 Be careful of trying to do too much in Instruments while simultaneously gathering instrument data that involves system resources, like the CPU Sampler or Multicore templates. Instruments is, itself, using CPU, memory, and file system services to do its job. This can skew the results of your application's performance.

Accumulating and Discarding Traces

After terminating your test application, leave the trace document open and do one of two things:

➤ Press the Record button to restart the application.

➤ Start the application from Xcode again, using the same Instruments template.

Instruments will, again, start your application and begin recording. The recording creates a second data set, called a *run*, in the trace document. Every time you restart your application in the same trace document, Instruments accumulates another run. Figure 19-9 shows four instruments with three runs of accumulated data.

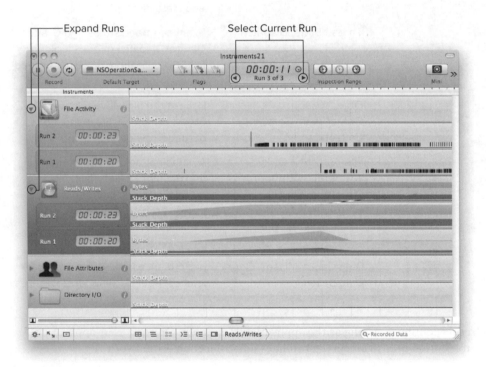

FIGURE 19-9

You have two ways of browsing runs:

➤ Expand an instrument

➤ Choose a run in the time control

Expand an instrument to examine and compare the results of individual runs simultaneously. The current run is always shown on the instrument's main track.

You can also page through the runs using the time control in the toolbar. Click the arrows to select the current run. This run becomes the data that appears in the main track of every instrument. Use the run selector to review the entire results of a previous run.

Run data can consume a lot of file, memory, and screen space. If you have a run that you don't find interesting anymore, make it the current run using the time control and then choose Instrument ⇨ Delete Run N. Instruments will delete the nth run of samples from all instruments.

The Run Browser

Another way to review multiple runs of analysis data is to use the run browser, shown in Figure 19-10.

FIGURE 19-10

The run browser presents a cover flow style display of each run of instruments, along with some summary information. Here you can make comments about each run, delete a run, or click Promote Run to switch immediately to that run in the trace document window — equivalent to using the run selector.

The return button, at the lower right, returns you to the trace document window.

Analyzing Trace Data

The data gathered from each instrument is organized into panes of successively more detailed information. You start by perusing the tracks, which compactly summarize the data gathered by that instrument. To examine the data of a single instrument in more detail, select the track and expand the details pane. The details pane typically provides numerous filter, analysis, and exploration tools. The details of individual samples can be explored even further in the extended details pane. Each of these is described in the following sections.

Tracks

Tracks present a graphical summary of the trace data for each instrument. What information is displayed, and how, is controlled by the inspector tab of the instrument. You get to the inspector tab by clicking the small i button at the right edge of each instrument, or by choosing File ⇨ Get Info, as shown on the left in Figure 19-11.

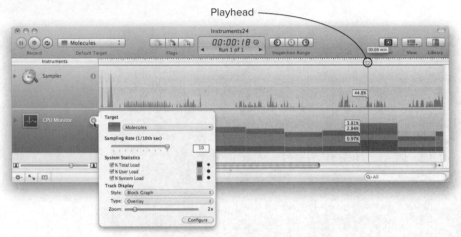

FIGURE 19-11

The inspector for each instrument varies, but in general you can choose the target (normally all instruments target the same process, but that's not a requirement), various instrument-specific settings, and the format of the track's graph. The Style and Type controls determine what metric is displayed in the track and how it's drawn.

The Zoom control increases or decreases the vertical size of the track, setting the resolution of the graph. You can also zoom the scale of the selected track using the View ⇨ Increase Deck Size (Command++) and View ⇨ Decrease Deck Size (Command+–) commands.

The Zoom control at the bottom of the window determines the horizontal magnification of all of the tracks. Use the two zoom controls to zoom in on details, or zoom out to look for overall trends.

You can peek at individual data points in the graph using the playhead control, as shown on the right in Figure 19-11. When you drag the playhead control across the track, datatips show the values of the data points in each track at that specific time. Depending on the horizontal zoom, a single pixel might represent several samples. You may have to zoom in to review discrete data points.

More Detail

After you've narrowed down the region of sample data you want to explore, it's time to use the details pane that appears at the bottom of the trace document window, as shown in Figure 19-12. The details pane is normally already visible by default, but you can collapse and expand it using the details button in the lower-left corner of the window, or by choosing the View ⇨ Detail (Command+D) command.

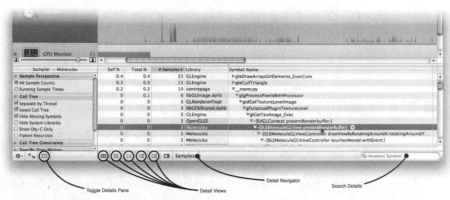

FIGURE 19-12

Each instrument has its own details pane format, but generally it displays a tabular view of the instrument's individual samples and a structured view of its analysis. It may alternatively present graphs, other organizations of the same data, console messages, or even the source code associated with the samples. Each view is selected using the icons at the bottom of the details pane.

If you're trying to find something specific, enter a search term in the search field. The term might be a symbol name, address, or library name, depending on the type of information displayed. You can usually narrow the scope of the search using the search field's menu.

Even More Detail

When the detail in the details pane isn't enough, you may need to open up the extended details pane either by clicking the extended details view button to the right of the other detail views, or by choosing the View ➪ Extended Detail (Command+E) command from the menu. The extended detail pane appears on the right side of the trace document window, as shown in Figure 19-13.

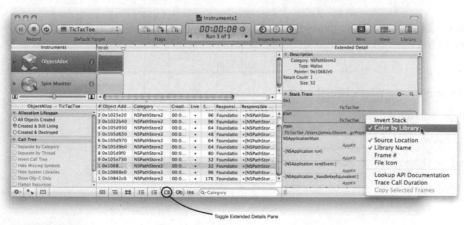

FIGURE 19-13

The extended details pane is about as close as you're going to get to the raw data collected by the instrument. Samples may include a variety of information, depending on the instrument and how it's configured. Some instruments don't show any extended detail at all. Three types of extended data are very common:

EXTENDED DATA TYPE	DESCRIPTION
Description	A textual summary of the sample. This is where you'll find most of the simple properties of each sample. This might include the address of the object, the file system function called, the size of the memory allocation, the entity name that caused the cache miss, and so on.
Stack Trace	Many instruments capture a stack trace each time they take a sample. The stack trace group shows state of the call stack when that sample was taken.
Timestamp	Almost every sample includes a timestamp, which is shown in the timestamp group.

Right/Control+clicking the stack trace presents a configuration menu, shown on the right in Figure 19-13, where you can:

➤ Change the order in which stack frames are listed

➤ Color the functions by library

➤ Choose how much information about each stack frame function is displayed

➤ Jump to the API documentation for a function

Timeline

The timeline, shown in Figure 19-14, shows the temporal relationship of events in the tracks. You can use the timeline to:

➤ Peek at data points in a track

➤ Jump to samples at a particular time

➤ Mark locations with a flag

➤ Navigate between flags

➤ View and analyze a subset of the trace data

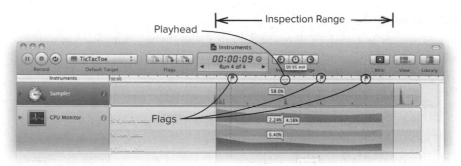

FIGURE 19-14

Peeking and Navigating Using the Playhead

You've already seen how you can peek at data points in the track by dragging the playhead to a time.

In detail views that list data points by sample/time, the playhead and the detail list are usually synchronized; dragging the playhead to a time selects that sample in the details pane, and selecting a sample in the details pane moves the playhead to that location in the timeline.

Using Flags

You can mark interesting locations in the timeline using flags. Flags are set and removed at the current playhead location, and you can jump the playhead to a previously set flag. You can do this using the flag controls in the toolbar, or with the following commands:

- ➤ Edit ➪ Add Flag (Command-↓)
- ➤ Edit ➪ Remove Flag (Command-↑)
- ➤ View ➪ Next Flag (Command-→)
- ➤ View ➪ Previous Flag (Command-←)
- ➤ View ➪ Inspect Flag

The Next and Previous commands jump the playhead to the next or previous flag in the timeline. The Inspect Flag command opens an inspector panel that allows you to name the flag and record comments for future reference, as shown in Figure 19-15.

FIGURE 19-15

Setting the Inspection Range

Normally, instruments present and analyze all of the data in a run. If you're interested in only a portion of that data — specifically, just the samples between two events — you can set the inspection range of the instruments using the Inspection Range controls in the toolbar. To set an inspection range:

1. Move the playhead to the first sample to include in the analysis.

2. Click the left button in the Inspection Range control.

3. Move the playhead to the last sample to include.

4. Click the right button in the Inspection Range control.

All of the details and analysis performed by all instruments will now be constrained to just the data collected between those two time periods, also shown in Figure 19-14.

To reset the inspection range to include all samples again, click the center button in the Inspection Range control.

Sample numbers are relative. That is, sample 0 is the first sample in its data set. When you change the inspection range, you change the sample data set and sample 0 will be the first sample in the new range. If you're using the sample number to identify a data point, remember that its number will change if you alter the inspection range. Also note that while sample numbers change, time stamps don't.

Customizing Instruments

Instruments can be customized in a myriad of ways. Most instruments are customized through their inspector pane, which you've already seen. Other analysis and view settings are usually found in the details pane containing the instrument's data.

When you edit instrument or display settings, those settings are part of the trace document. Settings are preserved when you save a trace document or continue to use a modified trace document for future runs.

Using Instruments via Xcode adds a wrinkle to changing instrument settings. When you launch Instruments from Xcode you do so by selecting a template. Normally, this creates a new trace document and initiates a recording. However, if Instruments already has a trace document open *and* that document was created with the same template selected in Xcode, Instruments will reuse the open document and accumulate another run. Thus, as long as you continue to select the same Instruments template in Xcode, Instruments will continue adding runs to the same trace document. Choose a different template and Instruments will create a new document — bypassing any changes you've made to instrument settings.

This has implications if you customize your instruments or trace document after starting Instruments for the first time. To customize instruments in an Xcode workflow, use one of the following workflows:

➤ Start Instruments using an Xcode template. Customize the instruments and leave the trace document open. Start Instruments again from Xcode using *the same template*. Instruments will reuse the already open trace document and accumulate another run using the customized settings.

➤ Start Instruments using an Xcode template. Customize the instruments and leave the trace document open. Start another recording by clicking the Record button in Instruments or choosing File ➪ Record Trace (Command+R). Instruments restarts your application and begins recording. This works as long as the location and run time environment of your test application remains unchanged — that is, you don't change build configurations.

➤ Create a trace document (through any means), customize the instruments, and then save it as a new Instruments template. See the section "Creating Instrument Templates" later on for the details. Use the newly created template for future analysis.

Adding Instruments

Instruments are easy to add; just drag an instrument from the library into your trace document, as shown in Figure 19-16.

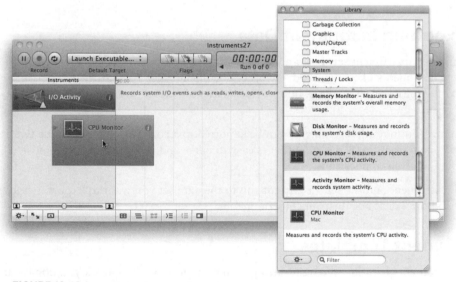

FIGURE 19-16

Open the library palette by choosing the Window ➪ Library (Command+L) command. The library palette in Instruments bears more than a passing resemblance to the library palette in Interface Builder. Almost everything you can do in Interface Builder's palette can be done in Instruments' library palette. This includes changing the list style, creating custom groups, creating smart groups, and searching. See the sections "Library Palette" and "Customizing the Library Palette" in Chapter 13, and substitute the word "instrument" for "object."

Be frugal when adding instruments. Instruments can gather a tremendous amount of data in a very short period of time — you can quickly overwhelm your computer system with too much data. I have personally created (what I thought was) a simple instrument set that within 30 seconds had ballooned the Instruments process to 56 gigabytes of virtual memory. Even on a machine with 16 gigabytes of physical RAM, the data set was tediously slow to work with. My time would have probably been better spent developing a more targeted analysis.

Removing Instruments

Removing an instrument couldn't be easier; select an instrument and choose the Instrument ⇨ Delete Instrument command or press the Delete key.

Removing an instrument removes it and all the data associated with that instrument. If you want to refer to the data for that instrument, consider saving the trace document first or exporting the data to a file.

Saving and Exporting Instrument Data

All of your instruments, instrument settings, and trace data is stored in the trace document; save and open trace documents like you would any other document type. You can also export trace data as a text file for external analysis, import trace data, and create your own instrument templates.

Trace data from many (but not all) instruments can be exported to a comma-separated value (CSV) file. This is a simple, common, text file format that is easy to parse and is compatible with most spreadsheet and data analysis applications.

Select the desired instrument and the set the current run to the data set you want to export. Choose the Instrument ⇨ Export Track For 'Instrument' command.

Creating Instrument Templates

Creating sets of instruments with just the right settings can be a lot of work — work you don't want to have to repeat every time you start a new analysis session. One way to preserve that work is to save a deck of configured instruments as an Instruments template.

Creating the template is easy: set up a trace document with the instruments and settings you want. Choose the File ⇨ Save As Template command and choose a location, description, and icon, as shown in Figure 19-17. Opening that template document creates a new trace document with your preconfigured set of instruments.

FIGURE 19-17

To add your customized template to Xcode, place your template document in your `~/Library/Application Support/Instrument/Templates` folder. Templates in this folder automatically appear in Xcode's Run ⇨ Run With Performance Tool menu, as shown on the right in Figure 19-17.

Using Instruments by Itself

Xcode makes it extremely convenient to use Instruments to analyze your application, but there may be times when you want to use Instruments on its own. Personally, I tend to take a hybrid approach. I usually begin by launching Instruments from Xcode, then I may stay in Instruments, refining its settings and my tests, until I've found my problem, ultimately returning to Xcode to address it.

Here are a few ways in which Instruments can be used on its own and why you might want to do so.

Choosing the Target Process

Each instrument has a target that describes the source process, or processes, that it's going to sample. Most instruments sample a single process whereas others monitor the state of the entire system.

When started from Xcode, instruments that sample a single process will all be configured to launch and sample your application. Most of the time this is exactly what you want, but there's much more latitude in what Instruments can be configured to monitor:

➤ Launch and sample a new process — this is the default when started from Xcode.

➤ Attach to an already running process.

➤ Configure all instruments to observe the same process or configure them to analyze different processes simultaneously.

Launching a process is how Instruments comes configured when you start it from Xcode. From the Default Target control in the toolbar you can change the setting from Launch Executable to either Attach to Process or Instrument Specific, as shown in Figure 19-18.

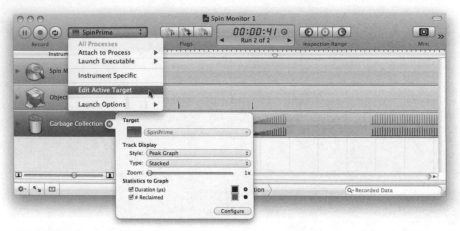

FIGURE 19-18

Choose Attach to Process when the process you want to analyze is already running. Let's say you've been testing your application for hours and it suddenly becomes unresponsive. You certainly don't want to have to stop it, start it again in Xcode, and spend an hour reproducing the problem. Instead, launch Instruments, configure some instruments, and choose your running application from the Attach to Process menu. Once attached, choose File ➪ Record Trace (Command+R) to begin recording.

The other option is to choose Instrument Specific. That setting enables the Target setting in each individual instrument, also shown in Figure 19-18. Use this arrangement when you need to monitor two or more related processes simultaneously. For example, to improve the performance in a client/server system you might create two Time Profiler instruments. One Time Profiler can sample the client while the other samples the server. You can now compare the load and performance of each process as they interact.

Both the Default Target control and the individual Target controls for each instrument have an Edit Active Target command. This presents a dialog where you can select the executable, set command arguments, and establish environment variables. Again, if you launched Instruments from Xcode all of this has been preconfigured for you. If you're setting up a target on your own, you may need to configure its environment.

Using Quick Start Keys

Instruments has a hot key combination called its Quick Start Key. You can choose the key combination you want to use in the Quick Start pane of Instruments' preferences. Select the instrument template you want to use and click in the Key column to assign a hot key combination to that template. You can assign different key combinations to different templates, just don't use key combinations that you're likely to encounter in other applications.

Once a hot key has been assigned to a template, you can sample a running process using these steps:

1. Position the cursor over a window belonging to the target process. This is important.

2. Press the quick start key combination for the template you want to use.

3. To stop sampling, either position the cursor over a window belonging to the same process and press the quick start key combination again, or simply switch to Instruments and stop recording.

Because the target process is selected based on the position of the cursor, you can use it to start sampling multiple targets simultaneously.

Mini Mode

Like the mini-debugger, Instruments has a mini mode too. Switch to mini mode by choosing the View ⇨ Mini Instruments command. All open trace documents are reduced to a compact status display, as shown in Figure 19-19.

FIGURE 19-19

Close the mini instruments window, or choose the command again, to restore the display.

Analyzing an iPhone Wirelessly

Xcode and Instruments make debugging and profiling your iPhone or iPod Touch application nearly effortless. Behind the scenes, these tools are actually communicating with a remote debugging service running on the target device, gathering information, and analyzing it on your development system.

This puts hardware developers in a unique quandary. Xcode and Instruments normally use the USB communications port to upload, launch, and monitor your iPhone application, but if your iPhone or iPod is plugged into a hardware device, the USB port is occupied.

To work around this you can attach Instruments to your application using its wireless network capabilities. To analyze an iPhone app wirelessly, follow these steps:

1. Enable wireless networking on your iPhone or iPod Touch device. Configure both the device and your development system to communicate via the same wireless zone.

2. With the USB cable connected to your device, build and install your application as you normally would.

3. Launch Instruments, choose a template, and create a trace document.

4. While holding down the Option key, choose the Default Target control, as shown on the left in Figure 19-20. The device command will change to Enable Device-Name — Wireless. Choose the command and Instruments will start a second instruments server using the wireless network for communications.

5. After a few moments, a second device appears in the menu — representing the second remote instruments server — as shown on the right in Figure 19-20. Choose this device as the target.

6. Disconnect the USB cable, connecting whatever accessory you want to test.

7. Start the program and sample it using Instruments.

FIGURE 19-20

Typical Scenarios

The following four scenarios are typical problems during application development. They are used to illustrate how Instruments integrates into an Xcode workflow and highlight the functionality of some of the more popular instruments. The problems tackled are:

➤ Slow code performance

➤ A memory leak

➤ An unresponsive application

➤ Automating a test that requires user interaction

Code Performance

The first problem is one of raw code performance. I have a much larger application that uses a rolling checksum algorithm implemented by two classes, RollingChecksum and RollingByteArrayChecksum.

To simplify testing — and this example — I copy the two classes and use them to create a simple command-line executable that calculates a series of rolling checksums for a buffer filled with random data. It repeats the test several thousand times so that my sampling tools can get a statistically accurate picture of their performance.

Because this is purely a code performance analysis, I choose to do it in Shark. I begin by following these steps:

1. Build the command-line test program.

2. Choose Run ➪ Run with Performance Tool ➪ Shark.

3. Click Start to start the test program running.

4. Let Shark sample the test program until it stops (about 8 seconds).

The initial analysis, shown in Figure 19-21, shows that Shark has identified my heaviest functions.

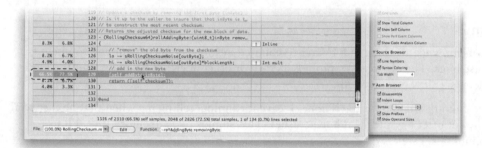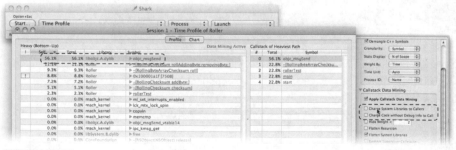

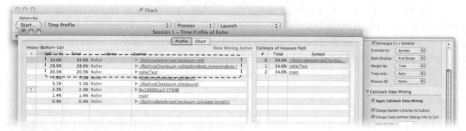

FIGURE 19-21

The second one, `-[RollingChecksum rollAddingByte:removingByte:]` is my higher-level checksum calculation routines, so I double-click the name of the function to see where it's spending its time. Shark opens a source code pane, as shown in Figure 19-22.

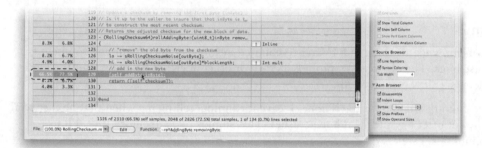

FIGURE 19-22

I see that much of the time is spent in the `[self addByte:inByte]` statement, but that seems unlikely because the `-addbyte:` method is only one line of code with minimal calculations. I close the source tab and return to the profile tab. Here I change the data mining options so that they don't hide library functions without symbol information, and lo and behold the real culprit appears, as shown in Figure 19-23.

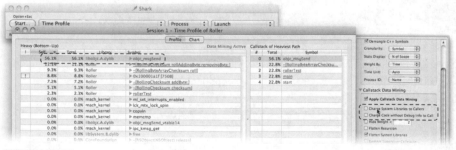

FIGURE 19-23

It turns out that `obj_msgSend` is responsible for over 57 percent of my application's CPU time. The function `obj_msgSend` is the Objective-C run time function that dispatches messages to objects. My conclusion is that message dispatching is eating up all of my performance because I'm sending millions and millions of messages that only do tiny little things.

The solution is to avoid the Objective-C messaging overhead. One solution is to cache the address of the method and call it directly. This solution speeds up my application about 350 percent. Another solution is to avoid the method call altogether and create preprocessor macros to perform the low-level checksum calculations in-line. The in-line macro solution resulted in a 700 percent performance improvement for this application. Not bad, for 10 minutes of work.

> *Shark will often identify functions as having an "early exit." What this means is that Shark finds a lot of samples in the code that sets up and returns from the function, but not so many samples in the function itself. This often occurs with functions that do very little, so the overhead of the call dwarfs the work that they perform. If the function is a performance bottleneck, in-lining its functionality using macros or other techniques is one way to improve performance.*

Retain Problem

A persistent problem when working in a reference-counted memory management environment is retain and release bugs. The obvious symptom is a crash or other aberrant behavior, but the more insidious problem is a slow memory leak.

I wrote a simple countdown app for the iPhone. I leave it running, telling me when that next special event will occur, but after a while my iPhone crashes. This sounds like a memory leak. I'll use Instruments to find out. I start by:

1. Selecting the iPhone Simulator target SDK.

2. Build the application.

3. Choose Run ➪ Run With Performance Tool ➪ Object Allocations.

Xcode starts Instruments with an ObjectAlloc instrument and launches the app in the simulator. I elect the ObjectAlloc instrument and watch as the application runs, as shown in Figure 19-24.

FIGURE 19-24

Sorting by number of living objects, I immediately notice that the NSStrings count continues to grow. Every second about 10 new NSStrings are created — but not destroyed. To find out where these objects are being created, I click the exploration arrow next to the CFString symbol name. This expands the display to show the history of all NSString objects created in the application, as shown in Figure 19-25.

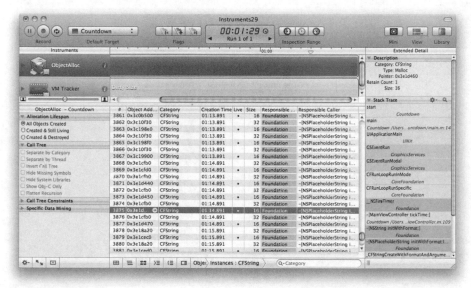

FIGURE 19-25

I scroll down toward the end — I'm not interested in the string objects created during application startup. I find a likely candidate that's still alive and click its exploration arrow to drill down into the object's history, as shown in Figure 19-26.

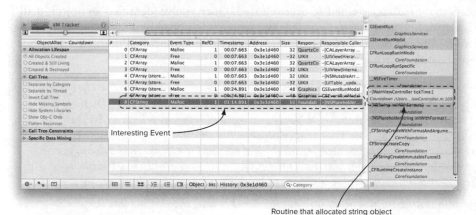

FIGURE 19-26

I'm now looking at the history of this object. Or, more precisely, I'm looking at the history of this memory location. Notice that over time many different objects have occupied this memory location, but the last one allocated is the stray NSString object. It has one Malloc event and nothing else, which means that it's been allocated but never released. To find out who allocated this string, I select it and look at the event's stack trace in the extended details pane. Here, as shown in Figure 19-26, I find that the -[MainViewController tickTime:] method allocated this string somewhere near line 109. Double-clicking that frame in stack jumps to the source view, shown in Figure 19-27.

FIGURE 19-27

I can immediately see the problem. The string allocated in line 108 is never released or auto-released. The solution is to add the statement [partStr release]; immediately after the -setText: message.

ObjectAlloc is an invaluable tool for tracking down retain and release problems. First, use it to identity the objects that are over-retained or over-released. Once you've identified an object, drill down into its history to find where it was created, and where it has been retained, auto-released, and released. This audit trail of memory management events should quickly illuminate what code is failing to manage the object properly.

Enabling NSZombies is an extremely useful debugging technique. It disables the normal deallocation of Objective-C objects and instead replaces released objects with so-called "zombie" objects — empty objects that throw an exception when sent any message. It's easy to catch messages sent to zombie objects in the debugger or ObjectAlloc. I showed you how to set the NSZombies environment variable in Chapter 18, and the ObjectAlloc instrument has a Zombies option built in.

The problem with zombies in iPhone applications is that the iPhone has very little memory and no virtual memory swap, so zombie objects can quickly consume all of the device's free memory; zombies are essentially the ultimate memory leak. The best use of zombies on the iPhone is in those situations where the problem can be reproduced quickly and definitively — before you run out of memory — or in the iPhone simulator.

Spinning Pizza of Death

It's happened to everyone. You try to click or type something into an application and instead of something happening, your cursor turns into a spinning rainbow. Euphemistically called the *spinning pizza of death*, and sundry similar names, it's the operating system telling you that the application has become unresponsive. Technically, it means that the application's main event loop isn't processing new user events, probably because it's blocked or performing some calculation.

To simulate this kind of problem, I wrote a simple application called SpinPrime. It takes a number from the user and determines if it's prime when the user clicks a button. The button action occurs on the main event loop; if the calculation is time consuming, it can cause the application to become unresponsive.

When I test the application with a few large numbers, it becomes unresponsive. The question I want answered is "where is the application spending its time when it is unresponsive?" In this sample application, the answer is obvious, but in most situations it isn't. That's where the Spin Monitor instrument is so handy. I'm going to use Spin Monitor to find the code that's causing my application to hang. I begin by:

1. Building the SpinPrime application.

2. Choosing Run ⇨ Run With Performance Tool ⇨ Time Profiler.

3. Stop the sampling of the application (Command+R).

4. Open the library palette and add a Spin Monitor instrument.

5. Remove the Time Profiler instrument.

6. Choose File ⇨ Record Trace (Command+R) to restart the application and recording.

7. Enter a relatively large number and click the Test button.

8. Click again and wait for the application to begin spinning.

The Spin Monitor instrument samples your application, much like the Time Profile or Sampler, but it only does so when the application is unresponsive. After stopping the application, I switch to the call tree view, as shown in Figure 19-28, and Instruments shows me that a lot of the time my application's spin time was in the method -[SpinPrimeAppDelegate checkPrime:]. I'm not surprised.

I started with the Time Profiler template because Xcode doesn't ship with a template that includes Spin Monitor. I work around it by choosing any template, then replace the instruments with those I want. Be careful not to remove the old instruments before adding your new ones, or Instruments will forget the target process information that Xcode so kindly configured for you. If you regularly use an instrument group, save your setup as a template in ~/Library/Application Support/Instrument/Templates.

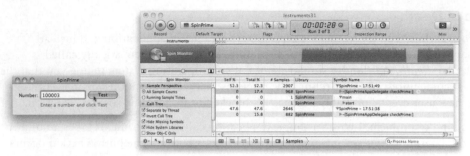

FIGURE 19-28

I double-click the name of the method and Instruments switches to its source view, as shown in Figure 19-29.

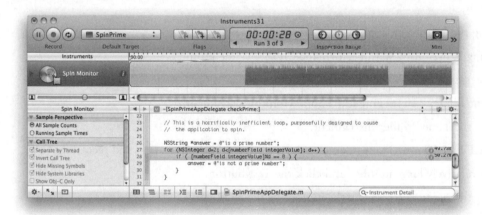

FIGURE 19-29

In the source view, the infotips tell me that almost 99 percent of the time the code was in either line 27 or 28. My application's performance bottleneck is clearly localized to these two lines — which are in desperate need of optimization.

Repeating a User Interface Test

One of the principles of performance analysis, cited at the beginning of this chapter, is to record the baseline performance of your application before starting any optimization, or else you have nothing to measure your progress. For GUI applications, this presents a problem. To reproduce the behavior of your application accurately, you have to reproduce the user events that occurred accurately, and you have to reproduce them every time you test your application. For complex sequences of events, this is nearly impossible to do yourself.

What you need is an automated testing tool that will do exactly the same sequence of events every time. Instruments has one, and it's called the User Interface instrument. It's a user events recorder and playback instrument. Here's how I use it:

1. Build the SpinPrime application.

2. Choose the Run ➪ Run With Performance Tool ➪ UI Recorder template.

3. Xcode starts Instruments with a single User Interface instrument.

4. In the application, I type in a number and click the Test button.

5. After SpinPrime is finished calculating the answer, I stop recording.

The User Interface instrument has recorded my mouse and keyboard actions in the application, as shown in Figure 19-30. Once the User Interface instrument has recorded a sequence of user interface events, it turns into a player, repeating those same events for every subsequent recording. The Record button changes into a Drive & Record button.

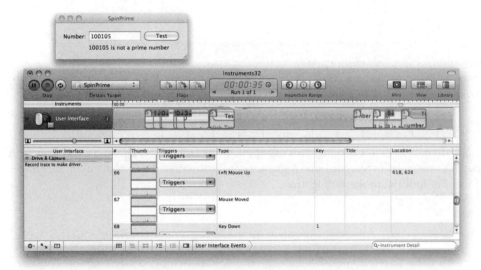

FIGURE 19-30

To use this recording, I need some additional instruments. I add a Time Profile instrument from the library and click the Drive & Record button. Instruments restarts my application and immediately begins replaying the user interface events, this time sampling the application with the Time Profile instrument, as shown in Figure 19-31.

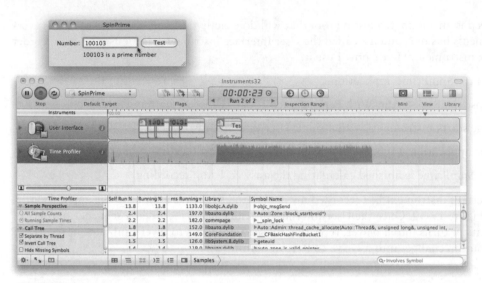

FIGURE 19-31

The User Interface instrument depends on the assistive technologies framework to observe and replay user events. To use it, you must have the Enable Access for Assistive Devices option enabled in the Universal Access panel of the System Preferences.

I can repeat this as often as I need. I can improve the application and then replay the exact sequence of events, comparing subsequent runs for improvements in performance. I can also add and change instruments if I feel I'm looking in the wrong area.

SUMMARY

Xcode integrates with some powerful performance, profiling, and memory analysis tools. This goes well beyond just stepping through your code looking for logic mistakes. It means analyzing how much memory is allocated, when, and who's cleaning it up. It means taking a look at what functions your application is calling, how often, and how much time that takes. All of these tools are here to give you a different perspective into how your application behaves, and hopefully provide some insight into what you can do to make it better.

The next chapter explores yet another approach to finding and eliminating bugs from your application: don't let those bugs slip into your application in the first place. This might seem like a ridiculous statement, but unit testing strives to accomplish just that.

20

Unit Testing

WHAT'S IN THIS CHAPTER?

➤ Learning how unit tests work

➤ Adding unit tests to your Objective-C project

➤ Configuring unit tests for an iPhone app

➤ Adding unit tests to your C or C++ project

Unit testing is a way of validating the run time behavior of your code at build time. In other words, you can test and verify the functionality of individual modules before you assemble them into a working application.

In addition to writing your application's classes, you also write one or more *unit tests* that exercise those classes and verify that they perform as expected. These tests are not part of your application and live in a separate *unit test bundle*. You can elect to have these tests performed on your code whenever you build your product, ensuring not only that your code compiles and links but that it behaves correctly as well.

Unit testing is a fundamental part of Test Driven Development (TDD), a development philosophy popularized by the Extreme Programming movement. In TDD, you develop the test for your function or class first, and then write your function to meet the expectations of the test. In essence, this is what rigorous designers have done for years. They first develop a detailed specification of exactly what a function should do, write the function, and then verify that the function behaves as designed. The quantum leap provided by unit tests is that the "specification" is now an automated test that verifies the design goals of the code rather than a paper description that must be interpreted by the programmer and verified by a quality assurance engineer. Because the test is automated, it can be run every time the application is built, ensuring that every function still conforms to its specification, or immediately alerting the developer if it does not.

Whether or not you subscribe to the principles of Extreme Programming, unit tests provide a powerful tool for avoiding issues like the so-called "forgotten assumption" bug. The typical scenario goes like this:

1. You develop a complex application.

2. You then decide to add a new feature to some core class.

3. You make the change in what you think is a completely transparent manner, only to discover that some other part of your application now fails miserably.

This is invariably a result of one of two problems: either you inadvertently introduced a bug into the core class, or you forgot about an assumption made by the client code that uses the class. Unit tests can help avoid both of these pitfalls.

Xcode supports unit testing of C/C++ and Objective-C applications using two different technologies. Although the concepts and initial steps are the same, most of the details for creating and using unit tests differ for the two languages. After you get past the basics, skip to either the Objective-C or C++ section, as appropriate, for integrating unit tests into your application.

HOW UNIT TESTS WORK

Unit tests are little more than code — which you write — that exercises the classes and functions in your project. You are entirely responsible for determining what and how your code is tested. Your tests are compiled into a unit test bundle, which is produced by a unit test target added to your project. The collection of tests in a unit test target is called a *test suite*. To run the tests, all you do is build the unit test target. The target first compiles your tests. It then runs a special build script phase that loads your test code, runs all of the tests, and reports the results. If any of your tests fail, the build process reports these as errors and stops. Figure 10-1 shows the build log from a project with unit tests.

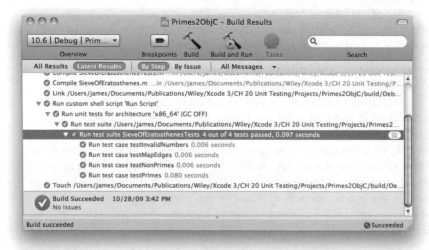

FIGURE 20-1

Unit test bundles are part of the build process. The code associated with unit testing is compiled into the unit test bundle and should never be included in your final product.

GETTING STARTED WITH UNIT TESTS

There are four basic steps to adding unit tests to a project:

1. Create a unit test target.

2. Configure the target and your application for unit tests.

3. Write some tests.

4. Integrate the tests into your development workflow.

How you approach each step depends on a number of decisions. The biggest decision is whether to create *independent* or *dependent* unit tests. Each has its own advantages and disadvantages. The one you choose will determine how you configure your unit test target, your application target, and how your tests can be integrated into your development workflow.

Don't confuse dependent unit test with target dependencies. Although a dependent unit test target typically depends on its subject target, the term "dependent" has to do with the fact that unit test bundle is not self-contained. Both dependent and independent unit tests may depend on other targets, or not.

Independent Unit Tests

Independent unit tests are the simplest to create and use, but they have a couple of drawbacks. An independent unit test bundle includes both the tests *and* the code to be tested. All are compiled and linked into the unit test bundle. At build time, the bundle is loaded and all of the tests are executed.

➤ Advantages:

  ➤ Self-contained

  ➤ No special code required

➤ Disadvantages:

  ➤ Doesn't test actual product

  ➤ Code must be compiled twice

The advantage to independent unit tests, and where they get their name, is that the target and unit test bundle are entirely self-contained. All of the code to be tested is compiled by the target. That is, the target is *independent* of any other applications or products that your project produces. In fact, the code doesn't even need to be compiled elsewhere. You could, conceivably, create a project that only tests code and produces no products whatsoever.

The disadvantage is that the code being tested is compiled separately from the same code that gets compiled when your application is built. One consideration is the fact that the code could be compiled differently for the unit test bundle and the application. Build-setting differences between the unit test target and your application's target could easily cause subtle differences in the code the compiler produces, which means that your tests are not actually testing the same code that will run in your application. For most code, this probably won't matter, but a difference in, say, the signedness of character variables, optimization, or the size of enums could cause your tests to miss bugs in your application's code or fail tests that should pass. If you are rigorous, or just paranoid, you'll want to test the actual code that your final application will be executing — not just a reasonable facsimile.

The other, potential, disadvantage to recompiling all of the same code is that it takes time. All of the code you intend to test will have to be compiled twice — once for the application and again for the unit test bundle. If your code base is large, or it depends on a lot of other code that must be compiled, then compiling everything twice will slow down your builds.

Dependent Unit Tests

Dependent unit tests perform their tests on the actual code produced by your product. A dependent unit test bundle contains only the test code. When it comes time to perform your unit tests, the program or library that your project produced is loaded into memory along with the unit test bundle. The references in the unit test bundle are linked to the actual classes and functions in your application and then executed. The unit test bundle *depends* on another product to accomplish its purpose.

- ➤ Advantages:
    - ➤ Tests actual code
    - ➤ Code only compiled once
- ➤ Disadvantages:
    - ➤ Test environment may be awkward
    - ➤ Dependent on other targets

As you might guess, there's more than just a little sleight of hand involved here. The unit test framework uses two techniques, depending on what kind of product you're testing. The method used to test libraries, frameworks, and independent unit tests is pretty straightforward: the unit test target executes a testing program that loads the unit test bundle (containing the test code and possibly some code to be tested) along with any dynamic libraries or frameworks that need testing. The tests are executed and the testing utility exits.

Testing an application is decidedly more bizarre. The unit test target runs a script that launches the actual executable produced by your project. Before the executable is started, several special environment variables are configured. These settings are picked up by the system's dynamic library loader and cause it to alter the normal sequence of binding and framework loading that occurs at run time. The settings instruct the loader to first load a special unit test framework into the application's address space. This process is known as *bundle injection*. The testing framework causes your unit test bundle to also be loaded into memory. Initialization code in your unit test bundle intercepts the execution of your application, preventing it from running normally. Instead, the unit test bundle's code links directly to the functions defined in the application and executes all of the tests. It then forces the application to terminate.

However convoluted, the beauty of this process is that your unit tests will test the actual, binary code of your application; the same code that will run when your application launches normally. The disadvantage is that this process is complex and requires a number of concessions from your application. Mostly these are restrictions on how your application is built. In the case of some C/C++ applications, you are also required to add code to your application to support dependent unit testing.

iPhone Unit Tests

The iPhone SDK supports unit testing too. The techniques are very similar to the Objective-C unit testing under Mac OS X — in fact, they both use the same testing framework — but with the following differences:

➤   Independent unit tests are called *logic tests* in iPhone parlance, and are executed using the iPhone simulator.

➤   Dependent unit tests are called *application tests* in iPhone parlance, and are preformed on an actual iPhone or iPod Touch.

➤   Setting up an application test suite for the iPhone is significantly different than setting up a dependent test suite for a Mac OS X application.

Except for those configuration differences, you can follow the guidelines and instructions for writing Objective-C unit tests when developing for the iPhone, substituting the terms "independent test" and "dependent test" with "logic test" and "application test."

iPhone unit testing requires iPhone OS 3.0 or later.

ADDING A UNIT TEST TARGET

The first step in adding unit testing to a project is to create a unit test target. Choose Project ➪ New Target and choose a Unit Test Bundle template. Choose the Unit Test Bundle template from the Carbon group to test a C/C++ product, from the Cocoa group to test a Mac OS X Objective-C product, or from the Cocoa Touch group to create an iPhone unit test. An example is shown in Figure 20-2.

Some releases of the Xcode Development Tools, particularly those intended for iPhone development, do not include the older Carbon and C++ target templates, so your installation might not have a Carbon Unit Test Bundle template. You can "borrow" one from an older Xcode installation or try installing the Mac OS X Xcode package.

Give the target a name and select the project it will be added to. Choose a name that reflects the subject of the test. For example, if you were writing tests for a target named `HelperTool`, you might name the unit test target `HelperToolTests`.

FIGURE 20-2

Xcode creates a new unit test target and adds it to your project. You now need to configure it properly and populate it with tests. How you configure your unit test target depends on what kind of unit test it is and what kind of product it tests.

 You might be anxious to try out your new unit test target, but you can't until it is configured and you have added at least one test; a unit test bundle will fail if it doesn't contain any tests. The "Creating a Unit Test" section, later in this chapter, tells you how to add tests to your unit test bundle.

Unit Test Target Dependencies

Unit tests are part of the build process. Target dependencies are used to integrate unit tests into your build. What target dependencies you create (if any) will depend on the kind of unit test you are creating.

Independent Unit Test Dependencies

Because independent/logic unit tests are self-contained, they do not (technically) need to be dependent on any other targets. All of the code that needs to be tested will be compiled when the target is built. Whenever you want to run your unit tests, simply build your unit test target.

One of the main tenets of test driven development is that your unit tests should be performed automatically every time you build your project. To do that, follow these steps:

1. Set the active target to your application target.

2. Make your application target dependent on your unit test target.

Now every time you build your application, Xcode will first build and run all of the unit tests.

Alternatively, you could make the unit test target dependent on your application target; then you have the choice of just building your application or building your application and running all of your unit tests. You could also leave your application and unit test targets independent of each other and create an aggregate target that builds both. As you can see, independent unit test targets are pretty flexible.

Dependent Unit Test Dependencies

Dependent Mac OS X (but not iPhone) unit test targets must depend on the target, or targets, that produce the products they test. Otherwise, there is no guarantee that the tests will be performed on up-to-date code. If you want unit tests run every time you build your product, follow these steps:

1. Set the active target to the unit test target.

2. Set the active executable to the results of the product target.

Now every time you build, the application is built followed by a run of all of the unit tests. The build will only be successful if both the build and the unit tests pass muster.

Using this arrangement, you can easily ignore unit tests by building just the product target, or making another target dependent on the product target directly. In a project with many product and unit test targets you could, for example, create two aggregate targets: one that depends on all of the product targets for "quick" builds and a second that depends on all of their respective unit test targets for "full" builds.

An iPhone unit test target's dependencies are inverted from those used by dependent unit test targets. The section "Configuring an iPhone Application Test" shows you both how to configure the iPhone application unit test target and set up its dependencies.

Configuring an Independent/Logic Unit Test

Independent unit tests require no special configuration. All you need to do is make the source code for both the tests and the code to be tested members of the target. The compiler build settings for the target should match those of your product target as closely as possible, so that the code produced when you're compiling the unit test target is as close as possible to the code that will be compiled into your final product.

Add the source files to the target by dragging them into the Compile Sources phase of the unit test target, or by opening their Info window and adding them to the unit test target in the Targets tab. You can add the source for the actual tests in a similar manner (if the tests already exist), or by adding them to the unit test target when you create them. The section "Creating a Unit Test" shows how to write and add a new test.

The target SDK for an iPhone logic test (independent unit test) must be set to the iPhone Simulator.

Configuring a Mac OS X Dependent Unit Test

A dependent unit test needs to know where to load the application or libraries to be tested.

Testing an Application

For applications, you accomplish this by setting the Bundle Loader (BUNDLE_LOADER) and Test Host (TEST_HOST) build settings. These should both be set to the executable you want to test. Follow these steps to quickly set both values:

1. In the Info window of the unit test target, select the Build tab. Choose All Configurations. Arrange the windows so that Groups & Files list in the project window and the Info window are both visible. Expand the Products group in the project source group.

2. In the target's Info window, find the Bundle Loader setting — you'll find it in the Linking group — and click in its value field to edit it. In the Products smart group, locate the executable product to be tested and drag it into the value field of the Bundle Loader setting. Xcode inserts the full path to the executable. For application bundles, you need to locate the application's binary executable — the folder with the extension .app is not an executable. You can manually supply the path, or follow these steps:

  a. Right/Control+click the product and choose Reveal in Finder.

  b. In the Finder, Right/Control+click the application and choose Open Package Contents.

  c. Open the Contents folder.

  d. Open the MacOS folder.

  e. Drag the application's executable into the Bundle Loader setting's value cell in the target's Info window.

3. Select the beginning of the path that represents the build location for the current build configuration. Typically this is /path/to/project-folder/build/build-configuration name/, but it may be different if you have altered the default build locations. Replace this portion of the path with the $(CONFIGURATION_BUILD_DIR) macro. In a project that produces a simple command-line executable, the final Test Host path will look like $(CONFIGURATION_BUILD_DIR)/*ProgramName*. For a bundled Cocoa or Carbon application, the Bundle Loader path will look something like $(CONFIGURATION_BUILD _DIR)/*AppName*.app/Contents/MacOS/*AppName*.

4. Locate the Test Host setting — you'll find it in the Unit Testing group — and double-click its value field to edit it. Enter $(BUNDLE_LOADER) as its value. This sets the TEST_HOST build setting to the same value as the BUNDLE_LOADER setting.

The Bundle Loader setting tells the linker to treat the executable as is if were a dynamic library. This allows the tests in the unit test bundle to load and link to the classes and functions defined in your application.

The Test Host setting tells the unit test target's script phase the executable that will initiate testing. When testing an application, it is the application that gets loaded and launched. The injected testing framework and bundle intercepts the application's normal execution to perform the tests.

Preparing Your Application

A few concessions are required of applications being tested by dependent unit test bundles. You must make these changes in the target that produces your application, not the unit test target. These requirements do not apply to independent unit tests or when you're testing dynamic libraries or frameworks.

Open the Info window for the application target and choose the Build tab. Choose All Configurations and set the following:

➤ Set ZeroLink to NO (uncheck the box).

➤ If your project is a C++ program, find the Symbols Hidden By Default setting and turn it off (uncheck the box).

ZeroLink must be turned off for your application. The ZeroLink technology is incompatible with the techniques used to intercept the application at run time. ZeroLink has been deprecated in Xcode 3, so you may not even see it in your build settings, but projects from prior versions of Xcode may still have it set.

The Symbols Hidden By Default option must be disabled for C++ applications so that all of the classes and functions defined by your application appear as external symbols. The unit test target must link to the symbols in your application, so these symbols must all be public. Objective-C tests are all resolved at run time by introspection, so they don't require any public symbols at link time.

Testing Libraries and Frameworks

When you're constructing a unit test to test a dynamic library or framework, leave the Bundle Loader and Test Host settings empty. This is because the "program" to be loaded for testing will be the unit test bundle itself. If the Test Host setting is blank, the script launches the otest (for Objective-C) or CPlusTestRig (for C/C++) tool instead. The testing tool loads the unit test bundle and runs the tests it finds there, with the assumption that the unit test bundle either contains (in the case of independent tests) or will load (in the case of dependent tests for libraries and frameworks) the code to be tested.

For dependent unit tests that test libraries or frameworks, the unit test bundle *is* the client application. Configure your unit test bundle exactly as you would an application that uses those libraries or frameworks, adding the frameworks to the target and including whatever headers are appropriate to interface to them. The dynamic library loader takes care of resolving the references and loading the libraries at run time.

Configuring an iPhone Application Test

Testing an iPhone application is different from testing a Mac OS X application, and requires a different organization in Xcode. In Mac OS X development (described in the previous section), you tell the unit test bundle what product you want tested. It takes on the responsibility of loading that target, injecting itself into the application, and performing its tests.

In iPhone development, the roles of the application and unit test bundle are reversed. You create a custom version of your application that includes the unit test bundle product. You load and run your test app on your iPhone or iPod Touch device like any other app. Once started, your app loads the unit test bundle, which takes over and performs its tests.

To configure an iPhone app for unit testing, follow these steps:

1. Add a Unit Test Bundle target, using the Cocoa Touch Unit Test Bundle template, as described in the beginning of this section. This is your *unit test target*.

2. Duplicate the target that builds your app. Give it a descriptive name like MyAppTesting. This is your *test app target*.

3. Make your test app target dependent on your unit test bundle target.

4. Add the product of the unit test target (the `MyTests.octest` bundle) to the Copy Bundle Resources phase of your test app target. This will include the compiled suite of unit tests in your app's resource bundle.

5. Set the active target to the test app target.

6. Set the Target SDK to iPhone Device 3.0 or later.

7. Build and run your test app target. The test results will appear in your console window.

Unlike all other kinds of unit tests, iPhone application tests aren't run during the build phase. You must build and run your test application, which downloads both it and the unit tests to your iPhone for execution. This introduces a number of limitations to using iPhone application tests:

➤ Application tests can't be made an automatic part of your build process.

➤ The application test bundle must also be provisioned to run on your iPhone. The "correct" way to do this is to create a provisioning profile that includes both the application and the application test bundle (see Chapter 22). I admit that I'll often simply set the Bundle

Identifier build setting in the unit test bundle to the same ID as the application. It seems sleazy, but it works.

➤ The unit test bundle will take over your app, run its tests, and exit. You can't use your application interactively during testing.

➤ The code in the unit test can't link directly to the application. This is because the unit test target builds before the application, so it can't link directly to the application's code.

You might be scratching your head about the last one. You're probably asking "If the unit test code can't link to the code in the application, what use is it?"

One solution is to include the code in both targets. At run time only one implementation of the class will be used — most likely the one in the application (because it loaded first), but the Objective-C run time doesn't specifically guarantee this. Regardless, this is an acceptable solution in most cases and gives your unit tests direct access to iPhone hardware and its application environment.

Another solution is introspection. Instead of referring to application classes directly, do it indirectly in the case where the test will be running on an actual iPhone. Listing 20-1 shows an example. This code will compile, link, and run — as long as something in the same process actually implements the SieveOfEratosthenes class, which our application does.

LISTING 20-1: Using soft class references in an iPhone application test

Available for
download on
Wrox.com

```
- (void)setUp
{
#if TARGET_OS_IPHONE
    testSieve = [[NSClassFromString(@"SieveOfEratosthenes") alloc]
                initWithMaxPrime:UNIT_TEST_MAX_PRIMES];
#else
    testSieve = [[SieveOfEratosthenes alloc]
                initWithMaxPrime:UNIT_TEST_MAX_PRIMES];
#endif
    STAssertNotNil(testSieve,@"Unable to create SieveOfEratosthenes");
}
```

 The most significant pitfall in iPhone application testing is the same problem inherent in logic tests (independent unit tests). Namely, that you run the risk of testing code that's different from the code in your final product. You must remember to update your test app target scrupulously so that it has the same build configuration as your primary app target. If you have any doubts, simply discard the test app target and reproduce it using the steps listed previously. This will guarantee that all of your test app target settings are identical to those in your production app target.

CREATING A UNIT TEST

Once you have your unit test target created and configured, adding unit tests is simple. Here are the basic steps:

1. Create a unit test class and add its source file to the unit test target.

2. Add test methods to the class.

3. Register the tests with the unit testing framework.

Unit test class files can go anywhere in your project, but I suggest, at the very least, creating a group for them named "Tests" or "Unit Tests." In a larger project you might organize your unit test files in a folder, or you might group them together with the code that they test. The choice is yours.

Each class that you create defines a group of tests. Each test is defined by a test method added to the class. A class can contain as many different tests as you desire, but must contain at least one. How you organize your tests is entirely up to you, but good practices dictate that a test class should limit itself to testing some functional unit of your code. It could test a single class or a set of related functions in your application.

Once defined, your tests must be registered with the unit testing framework so that it knows what tests to run. For Objective-C tests this happens automatically. Objective-C test methods must adhere to a simple naming scheme — basically they must all begin with the name "test." Objective-C introspection is then used to locate and run all of the tests you defined. For C++ unit tests, you add a declaration for each test you've written. The exact requirements for each are described in the "Objective-C Tests" and "C++ Test Registration" sections, respectively.

Each test method should perform its test and return. Macros are provided for checking the expectations of each test and reporting failures. A test is successful if it completes all of its tests and returns normally. An example test is shown in Listing 20-2.

Available for download on Wrox.com

LISTING 20-2: Sample C++ unit test

```
void SieveOfEratosthenesTests::testPrimes( )
{
    // Test a number of known primes
    static int knownPrimes[] =
        { 2, 3, 5, 11, 503, 977, 12347, 439357, 101631947 };

    SieveOfEratosthenes testSieve(UNIT_TEST_MAX_PRIMES);
    for (size_t i=0; i<sizeof(knownPrimes)/sizeof(int); i++)
        CPTAssert(testSieve.isPrime(knownPrimes[i]));
}
```

In this example, the `testPrime` function defines one test in the SieveOfEratosthenesTests class. The test creates an instance of the SieveOfEratosthenes class, and then checks to see that it correctly identifies a series of numbers known to be prime. If all of the calls to `testSieve.isPrime()` return `true`, the test is successful; the `testPrimes` object is destroyed and the function returns. If any call to `testSieve.isPrime()` returns `false`, the `CPTAssert` macro signals to the testing framework that the test failed. The testing macros are described in the "Objective-C Test Macros" and "C++ Test Macros" sections.

Common Test Initialization

If a group of tests — defined as all of the tests in a TestCase class — deal with a similar set of data or environment, the construction and destruction of that data can be placed in two special methods: setUp and tearDown. The setUp method is called before each test is started, and the tearDown method is called after each test is finished. Override these methods if you want to initialize values or create common data structures that all, or at least two, of the tests will use. The typical use for setUp and tearDown is to create a working instance of an object that the tests will exercise, as illustrated in Listing 20-3. The test class defines a single instance variable that is initialized by setUp and destroyed by tearDown. Each test is free to use the object in the instance variable as the subject of its tests.

For Objective-C tests, the methods your test class should override are - (void) setUp and - (void) teardown. For C/C++ tests, the functions to override are void TestCase::setup() and void TestCase::tearDown().

LISTING 20-3: Objective-C unit test using setUp and tearDown

Available for download on Wrox.com

SieveOfEratosthenesTests.h

```
#define UNIT_TEST_MAX_PRIMES  100000

@interface SieveOfEratosthenesTests : SenTestCase
{
    SieveOfEratosthenes* testSieve;
}
```

SieveOfEratosthenesTests.m

```
@implementation SieveOfEratosthenesTests

- (void)setUp
{
    testSieve = [[SieveOfEratosthenes alloc]
                init:UNIT_TEST_MAX_PRIMES];
}

- (void)tearDown
{
    [testSieve release];
    testSieve = nil;
}

- (void)testInvalidNumbers
{
    // These should all return NO
    STAssertFalse([testSieve isPrimeInMap:-1],
                @"-1 is not a prime number");
    STAssertFalse([testSieve isPrimeInMap:0],
                @"0 is not a prime number");
    STAssertFalse([testSieve isPrimeInMap:1],
                @"1 is not a prime number");
}
```

The setUp and tearDown methods are called before and after every test. This allows tests to perform destructive tests on the object — that is, tests that alter the object's state — because the object will be destroyed at the end of the test and re-created anew before the next test is run.

Unit test classes have standard constructor and destructor methods. *Do not use the constructor to create test data.* If your test structures are expensive to create and destroy, you may be tempted to create them in the constructor and let them persist for the duration of the test class. Don't do this. Your next approach might be to turn the setUp method into a factory that creates a singleton object when called the first time. Sorry, but that probably won't work either. Some testing frameworks create a separate instance of the test class for each test.

Instead, make a single test that creates the expensive object and then calls a series of subtests itself. Remember *not* to name your Objective-C subtests "test…" or the testing framework will run them again.

Because so many of the minor details of creating tests for Objective-C and C/C++ differ, the steps for creating your own tests have been separated into the following two sections, "Objective-C Tests" and "C++ Tests."

Objective-C Tests

To create an Objective-C test class and add it to a unit test target, start by selecting the File ➪ New File command. The new file assistant presents a list of new file templates. Choose the Objective-C Test Case Class, as shown in Figure 20-3, from either the Cocoa Class or Cocoa Touch Class group, as appropriate.

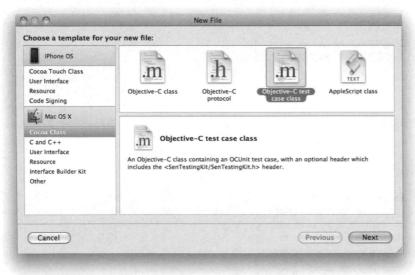

FIGURE 20-3

Click the Next button and give the test case class and file a name. The name should be descriptive of its purposes, such as StudentTests for a set of tests that validate the Student class. Make sure you create a matching .h file. Select the working project and add the test to the desired unit test target, as shown in Figure 20-4, making sure you don't include the test class file in any other target. Click the Finish button.

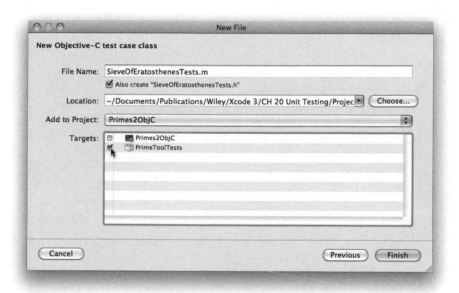

FIGURE 20-4

Xcode creates a skeletal test class definition and implementation, similar to the one shown in Listing 20-4. All of your test classes for Objective-C must be direct subclasses of the SenTestCase class.

Available for download on Wrox.com

LISTING 20-4: Example Objective-C test case

```
#import <SenTestingKit/SenTestingKit.h>

@interface StudentTests : SenTestCase {

}

@end
```

Xcode has created the framework for your class and has already added it to your unit test target. The only thing you need to do now is to write one or more test methods. Each test method:

> ➤ Must begin with "test" in lowercase, as in -testNegativeCoordinates
>
> ➤ Must return void
>
> ➤ Must not take any parameters

An example of three such tests is shown in Listing 20-5.

Available for
download on
Wrox.com

LISTING 20-5: Example Objective-C tests

```objc
#import "StudentTests.h"

@implementation StudentTests

- (void)setUp
{
    student = [[Student alloc] initWithName:@"Jane Doe"];
    STAssertNotNil(student,@"Unable to create Student");
}

- (void)tearDown
{
    [student release];
    student = nil;
}


- (void)testNameConstructor;
{
    STAssertTrue([[student name] isEqualToString:@"Jane Doe"],
                @"Student.name property incorrect");
}

- (void)testNamePartsParsing;
{
    STAssertTrue([[student firstName] isEqualToString:@"Jane"],
                @"Student.firstName parsing incorrect");
    STAssertTrue([[student lastName] isEqualToString:@"Doe"],
                @"Student.lastName parsing incorrect");
}

- (void)testNamePartsReplacement;
{
    STAssertTrue([[student name] isEqualToString:@"Jane Doe"],
                @"Student.name property incorrect");

    [student setFirstName:@"John"];
    STAssertTrue([[student name] isEqualToString:@"John Doe"],
                @"Student.name first name replacement incorrect");

    [student setLastName:@"Smith"];
    STAssertTrue([[student name] isEqualToString:@"John Smith"],
                @"Student.name last name replacement incorrect");
}
@end
```

Amazingly, you are all done. The introspective nature of Objective-C allows the unit test framework to discover automatically all classes that are subclasses of SenTestCase in the bundle, and then find all void methods that begin with the name "test." The unit test framework creates your test object and then executes each test method one at a time.

Objective-C Test Macros

When you write your test, you will employ a set of macros to evaluate the success of each test. If the assertion in the macro fails to meet the expectation, the test fails and a signal with a description of the failure is passed back to the unit test framework. Test failures appear as an error in the build log.

Each macro accepts a description of the failure. The description argument is a Core Foundation format string that may be followed by a variable number of arguments, à la `NSLog(description,...)` or `-[NSString stringWithFormat:format,...]`. The unit test macros available are listed in the following table. The `STFail` macro unconditionally records a failed test. Use it in a block of code where the program flow has already determined that a failure has occurred. All of the other macros are assertion macros. The test is successful if the parameters meet the expectations of the assertion. If they do not, a failure is recorded using the description constructed using the format string (`@"..."` in the table) and the remaining arguments.

UNIT TEST ASSERTION MACRO	DESCRIPTION
`STFail(@"...",...)`	This is the basic macro for unconditionally recording a test failure. This macro always causes the described failure to be recorded.
`STAssertTrue(expression,@"...",...)`	The test is successful if the statement `expression` evaluates to `YES`. Otherwise, a description of the failed test is logged.
`STAssertFalse(expression,@"...",...)`	The test is successful if the statement `expression` evaluates to `NO`.
`STAssertNil(reference,@"...",...)`	The test is successful if the statement `reference` evaluates to `nil`.
`STAssertNotNil(reference,@"...",...)`	The test is successful if the statement `reference` evaluates to something other than `nil`.
`STAssertEquals(left,right,@"...",...)`	The test is successful if the numeric value of the statement `left` equals the numeric value of the statement `right`. Both statements must evaluate to the same primitive type. That is, they must both be long int, float, and so on. You may cast them if necessary. If the values are not the same type or value, the test fails.

continues

(continued)

UNIT TEST ASSERTION MACRO	DESCRIPTION
`STAssertEqualsWithAccuracy(left,right, accuracy,@"...",...)`	The test is successful if the absolute difference between the numeric value of the `left` statement and the numeric value of the `right` statement is equal to or less than the value of `accuracy`. Both `left` and `right` must evaluate to the same primitive type. If the values differ by more than `accuracy` or are not the same type, the test fails.
`STAssertEqualObjects(left,right,@"...", ...)`	The test is successful if the object reference in the `left` statement is equal to the object reference in the `right` statement, according to the `[left isEqual:right]` method. Both object references must be of the same type and the `isEqual` method must return normally with a Boolean result. If the object references are not the same type, the `isEqual` method returns `NO`, or the `isEqual` method throws an exception, the test fails.
`STAssertThrows(statement,@"...",...)`	The test is successful if `statement` causes an exception to be thrown.
`STAssertThrowsSpecific(statement,class, @"...",...)`	The test is successful if `statement` causes an exception of the class `class` to be thrown.
`STAssertThrowsSpecificNamed(statement, class,name,@"...",...)`	The test is successful if the `statement` causes an exception of `class` with the `name` exception name to be thrown.
`STAssertNoThrow(statement,@"...",...)`	The test is successful if `statement` does not cause an exception to be thrown.
`STAssertNoThrowSpecific(statement, class,@"...",...)`	The test is successful if `statement` does not cause an exception of `class` to be thrown. Note that the test is still successful if the statement causes some other class of exception to be thrown.
`STAssertThrowsSpecificNamed(statement, class,name,@"...",...)`	The test is successful if `statement` does not cause an exception of `class` with the `name` exception name to be thrown.

After you have added your tests, you are ready to build the unit test target.

C++ Tests

To create a C++ test class, follow the instructions for adding an Objective-C Test Case Class to your project, with the one exception that you'll start by choosing the C++ Test Case Class template from the Carbon group. Once you've selected the correct targets and added the class files to the project, return here.

Even if your application is written in pure C, the C/C++ testing framework still requires C++ objects to define and drive the test process. Write your tests by creating the appropriate C++ class. The test member functions you add can then call your application's C functions.

Xcode creates a skeletal test class definition and implementation, as shown in Listing 20-6. All of your test classes for C++ must be direct subclasses of the TestCase class.

Available for download on Wrox.com

LISTING 20-6: Example C++ test case

```
#include <CPlusTest/CPlusTest.h>

class StudentTests : public TestCase {
public:
    StudentTests(TestInvocation* invocation);
    virtual ~StudentTests();
};
```

Xcode has created the framework for your class and has already added it to your unit test target. The only thing you need to do now is to write one or more test methods. Each test method:

➤ Must return `void`

➤ Must not take any parameters

Unlike Objective-C, C++ test method names do not have to conform to any naming convention, but it is more readable if you retain the habit of starting each method name with "test." An example of two such tests is shown in Listing 20-7.

Available for download on Wrox.com

LISTING 20-7: Example C++ tests

```
#include "StudentTests.h"

StudentTests::StudentTests(TestInvocation *invocation)
    : TestCase(invocation)
{
}
```

continues

LISTING 20-7 *(continued)*

```
StudentTests::~StudentTests()
{
}
void StudentTests::testNameConstructor( )
{
    Student student("Jane Doe");
    CPTAssert(strcmp(student.getName(),"Jane Doe")==0);
}
void StudentTests::testNameProperty( )
{
    Student student();
    CPTAssert(student.getName()==NULL)
    student.setName("Jane Doe");
    CPTAssert(strcmp(student.getName(),"Jane Doe")==0);
}
```

C++ Test Registration

C++ does not include the kind of introspection that Objective-C uses to discover the test classes and methods that you've defined. Consequently, you must tell the C++ unit test framework exactly what tests you've defined. You accomplish this by registering the tests using static constructors, as shown in Listing 20-8.

Available for download on Wrox.com

LISTING 20-8: C++ test registration

```
StudentTests studentTestsNameConstructor(TEST_INVOCATION(StudentTests,
                                            testNameConstructor));
StudentTests studentTestsNameProperty(TEST_INVOCATION(StudentTests,
                                            testNameProperty));
```

For every test you want run, you must create an instance of your test class, passing a TestInvocation object to its constructor. To make this easier to code, the unit test framework provides a TEST_INVOCATION macro, which creates a configured instance of the TestInvocation class for you. The macro parameters are the name of your TestCase subclass and the test function. You can give the static variable any name you want, but it is more readable if you give it a name that describes the test. Remember that these object names are public, so generic names like test1 are likely to collide with similar names from other TestCase classes.

Each invocation object is constructed when the application starts up. The constructor for the TestCase class registers the test with the unit test framework. Thus, as soon as the application is ready to run, the testing framework has a complete list of the tests to be executed.

C++ Test Macros

When you write your test, you will employ the CPTAssert macro to evaluate the success of each test. If the argument to the macro evaluates to a non-zero value, the test was successful. If not, the test and a signal with a description of the failure is passed back to the unit test framework. Test failures appear as an error in the build log. Examples of using CPTAssert were shown in Listing 20-7.

C++ Test Execution

In addition to registering the tests, a C/C++ application being tested by a dependent unit test needs to invoke the unit tests at the appropriate time. Unlike an Objective-C application, C applications can't be automatically intercepted to prevent their normal execution. You must add code to your application to run the tests and exit — but only when your application is being run for the purposes of unit testing. This section describes the code you need to add to non-Carbon applications — that is, any kind of process that doesn't use a Carbon run loop — and a less invasive method you can use with Carbon (run loop) applications.

For command-line applications, this is simply a matter of inserting some code into your `main()` function. You insert this code after the point in your application where your unit tests can be run — typically after any required initialization — but before the application actually starts running. Assuming your application has no special initialization, the example in Listing 20-9 shows what you need.

Available for download on Wrox.com

LISTING 20-9: Unit test hook for main()

```cpp
// Conditional support for C/C++ unit tests
#ifndef UNIT_TEST_SUPPORT
#define UNIT_TEST_SUPPORT    1
#endif

#if UNIT_TEST_SUPPORT
#include <CPlusTest/CPlusTest.h>
#endif

int main (int argc, char * const argv[])
{
    //Perform any required initialization here...

#if UNIT_TEST_SUPPORT
    TestRun run;
    // Create a log for writing out test results
    TestLog log(std::cerr);
    run.addObserver(&log);
    // Get all registered tests and run them.
    TestSuite& allTests = TestSuite::allTests();
    allTests.run(run);
    // If the TestSuite ran any tests, log the results and exit.
    if (run.runCount())
        {
        // Log a final message.
        std::cerr << " Ran " << run.runCount()
                << " tests, " << run.failureCount() << " failed."
                << std::endl;
        return (0);
        }
    // Otherwise, run the application normally.
#endif
    ...
```

The code creates a TestRun object, gets all of the registered tests, and then runs them. In a dependent unit test, the registration code for the tests exists in the unit test bundle. Unless the unit test bundle was loaded and initialized before the startup code called `main()`, there will be no tests to run. In this case, the application assumes that it is running in the absence of the unit test bundle, falls through, and executes normally. If tests are registered and run, the code reports the success or failure of those tests and exits immediately.

The definitions of the TestRun, TestLog, TestSuite, and related classes are included in the special unit testing framework that was added to your system when you installed the Xcode Developer Tools. These classes do not normally exist in a standard installation of Mac OS X, and your application will fail to start without them. Do not include this testing code in your final application. Ensure that the release build of your application is devoid of any references to the unit testing classes and framework. Using the previous example, the Release build configuration of this project could define the `UNIT_TEST_SUPPORT=0` *preprocessor macro to ensure that no unit test code is compiled in the final version.*

For Carbon applications, you can intercept the start of program execution far more elegantly. Any technique (like the one just demonstrated) that runs the unit tests after initialization, but before regular program execution, is acceptable. The dynamic nature of the Carbon event loop, however, allows your unit testing bundle to intercept the execution of the application without making any changes to the application itself. This avoids having to add conditionally compiled code to your application.

Listing 20-10 shows how to use a Carbon timer to accomplish this. This code should be added to the unit test target, not your application.

Available for download on Wrox.com

LISTING 20-10: Unit test hook for Carbon application

UnitTestRunner.h

```
#include <Carbon/Carbon.h>

class UnitTestRunner
{
private:
    EventLoopTimerUPP timerUPP;
    EventLoopTimerRef timerRef;

public:
    UnitTestRunner();
    virtual ~UnitTestRunner();

protected:
    static void testTimerFired(EventLoopTimerRef timer, void* userData);
    void runTests(EventLoopTimerRef timer);
};
```

UnitTestRunner.cpp

```cpp
#include <CPlusTest/CPlusTest.h>
#include "UnitTestRunner.h"

UnitTestRunner installTimer;    // static constructor to create timer

UnitTestRunner::UnitTestRunner() : timerUPP(NULL), timerRef(NULL)
{
    // Get the UPP for the static bridge method.
    timerUPP = NewEventLoopTimerUPP(UnitTestRunner::testTimerFired);
    (void)InstallEventLoopTimer(GetMainEventLoop(),0,0,timerUPP,this,&timerRef);
}

UnitTestRunner::~UnitTestRunner()
{
    // Destroy the timer
    if (timerRef != NULL) {
        RemoveEventLoopTimer(timerRef);
        timerRef = NULL;
        }
    if (timerUPP != NULL) {
        DisposeEventLoopTimerUPP(timerUPP);
        timerUPP = NULL;
        }
}

// Static method to bridge the call to the local instance.
void UnitTestRunner::testTimerFired(EventLoopTimerRef timer, void* userData)
{
    ((UnitTestRunner*)userData)->runTests(timer);
}

void UnitTestRunner::runTests(EventLoopTimerRef timer)
{
    if (timer == timerRef) {
        // We're done with the timer
        RemoveEventLoopTimer(timerRef);
        timerRef = NULL;
        // Create the test run
        TestRun run;
        // Create a log for writing out test results
        TestLog log(std::cerr);
        run.addObserver(&log);
        // Get all registered tests and run them.
        TestSuite& allTests = TestSuite::allTests();
        allTests.run(run);
        // If tests were run, log the results and terminate the application
        if (run.runCount()) {
            // Log a final message.
            std::cerr << " Ran " << run.runCount() << " tests, "
                    << run.failureCount() << " failed."
                    << std::endl;
            QuitApplicationEventLoop();
            }
        // Else, fall through and continue running the application
        }
}
```

The static constructor for `installTimer` causes an instance of this object to be created during the initialization of your application. Because the constructor is part of the code in the unit test, the UnitTestRunner object is only created when your application is running in the presence of the unit test bundle. The class creates a timer with a 0 interval and registers it with the Carbon event manager. As soon as the application has performed its basic initialization and the event loop is ready to run, the timer fires. The `testTimerFired()` function catches the timer event and invokes the `runTests()` function. This function runs all of your unit tests and quits the application.

In the absence of the unit test bundle, there is no constructor, no timer object is created, and your application starts running normally. The beauty of this scheme is that it requires no modification to your application. There is no possibility of accidentally producing a version of your application that contains any unit test support, and you can test the final application binary you intend to release.

DEBUGGING UNIT TESTS

Who watches the watchers? Sometimes a unit test, designed to keep your application free of bugs, has bugs itself. When this occurs, you need to bring the power of the debugging tools to bear on the unit test code, rather than your application. The problem is that unit tests run during the build phase, not the debug phase, of the Xcode environment. The tests themselves are never the target of a Debug or Run command, and you have the added catch-22 of trying to build an application whose unit tests fail.

Debugging iPhone Application Tests

However awkward an iPhone application (dependent) unit test is to set up and use, it is stunningly simple to debug.

Remember that an iPhone application test is a regular copy of your iPhone app that includes a unit testing bundle. To debug your application tests, simply run your test application target under the control of the debugger (Run ⇨ Debug). Figure out what's wrong and then return to running your application normally.

Debugging Dependent Mac OS X Unit Tests

Debugging dependent unit tests for an application requires that you reverse the normal order of targets and trick the application target into running your unit tests instead of executing your application normally, all under the control of the debugger. Here's how:

1. Open the Info window for the project (Project ⇨ Edit Project Settings). In the General tab, change the Place Intermediate Build Files In setting to Build Products Location.

2. Remove the application target dependency from the unit test target.

3. Set the active target to the application target and build it (Build ⇨ Build).

4. Add the unit test target as a dependency for the application. This reverses the normal dependency between the unit test and the target.

5. Disable the run script phase of the unit test target. Expand the dependent unit test target and double-click the final run script phase. Edit the script by adding an `exit` command at the beginning, as shown in Figure 20-5, essentially disabling the script.

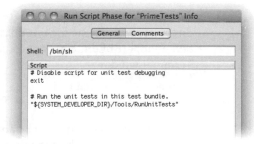

FIGURE 20-5

6. Open the Info window for the application's executable (in the Executable smart group). Select the Arguments tab. If this is an Objective-C application, add the argument `-SenTest All`.

7. In the environment variables pane:

   a. Add a `DYLD_INSERT_LIBRARIES` variable and set its value to `$(DEVELOPER _LIBRARY_DIR)/PrivateFrameworks/DevToolsBundleInjection .framework/DevToolsBundleInjection`.

   b. Add a `DYLD_FALLBACK_FRAMEWORK_PATH` variable and set it to `$(DEVELOPER _LIBRARY_DIR)/Frameworks`.

   c. Add an `XCInjectBundle` variable and set it to `UnitTestBundlenName.octest`. If this is a C++ testing bundle, the extension will be `.cptest` instead of `.octest`.

   d. Add an `XCInjectBundleInto` variable and set it to `AppName. app/Contents/MacOS/AppName`.

8. Your application executable should now look like the one in Figure 20-6. Set your active build configuration to Debug.

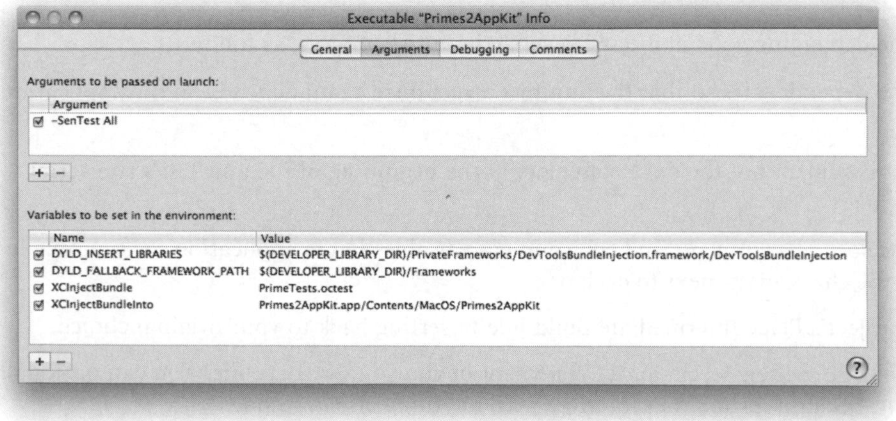

FIGURE 20-6

9. Add the statement `set start-with-shell 0` to the invisible `.gdbinit` file in your home directory, creating the file if it doesn't already exist. You can do this using a number of text editors (BBEdit, emacs, pico, and so on) or by issuing the following commands in a Terminal window:

```
echo '' >> ~/.gdbinit
echo 'set start-with-shell 0' >> ~/.gdbinit
```

Now build and debug your project. The application target causes the unit tests target to build, but not run (because you disabled the unit test's run script). Note that there's a quirky circular dependency here — the unit test target still tries to link to your application's binary. If your application hasn't been built, the unit test target will fail to build with a link error. That's why I had you perform step 3 before proceeding, so the unit test bundle has a product to satisfy its link phase.

Xcode then launches the executable under the control of the debugger. The environment variables trick the application executable into acting as if it were being run for the purposes of unit testing. The system loads the unit test bundle and executes the tests, allowing you to set breakpoints in the unit test source and debug them.

> **TIP TO REMEMBER**
>
> There are so many steps involved in setting up a dependent unit test for debugging that it's easy to mess up your project in the process. Before you begin, make a copy of your project document or check it into source control. After you've debugged your problem — and assuming that the fix didn't involve changes to your project document — simply discard the test document and replace it with the saved one. You should always close the project before copying, replacing, or renaming your project document.

When you are done debugging your unit tests, reverse the entire process, as follows:

1. Reverse the dependencies so that the unit test target once again depends on the application target.

2. Remove or comment out the `exit` statement at the beginning of the unit test's run script phase.

3. Disable the special arguments and environment variables in the application's executable by removing the check mark next to each one.

4. Set your project's Place Intermediate Build File In setting back to your original choice.

5. Remove the `set start-with-shell` statement in your `~/.gdbinit` file. You can optionally just leave it, because it shouldn't interfere with anything else in Xcode.

Debugging Independent Unit Tests

Debugging independent tests is a little simpler. It requires that you create an executable from the unit test bundle so that the debugger knows how to launch it under its control. The executable is actually the test harness utility and its arguments tell it what unit test bundle to load and execute. Follow these steps to create the executable:

1. Create a custom executable. Give it the same name as your independent unit test target. (The "Custom Executables" section in Chapter 18 has the details.)

2. Set the executable to `$(DEVELOPER_TOOLS_DIR)/otest` for Objective-C unit test bundles, or `$(DEVELOPER_TOOLS_DIR)/CPlusTestRig` for C++ unit test bundles.

3. In the Arguments tab, add the `$(CONFIGURATION_BUILD_DIR)/`*NameOfUnitTest*`.octest` argument for Objective-C bundles. The bundle extension will be `.cptest` for C++ bundles.

4. Disable the unit tests in the independent unit test target by adding an `exit` statement to the beginning of the run script phase, as previously shown in Figure 20-5.

Set the active target to the unit test and the active executable to the custom executable you just created. You can now set breakpoints in the unit tests and launch it under the control of the debugger just like any other application. When you are done debugging, restore the run script phase of the unit tests by removing the `exit` statement in the run script phase. This permits the tests to run during the build phase once again.

SUMMARY

Unit tests can be powerful allies. They permit you to codify the behavior of your code and integrate the validation of that behavior directly into the build process. Incorrect handling of a parameter value, or the failure to throw an exception under certain circumstances, is now as easily caught as syntax errors in your source code.

Effective use of unit testing is a discipline, encompassing a variety of philosophies and a broad range of styles and techniques. If you are serious about integrating unit testing into your development, you should get a good book on test-driven design or Extreme Programming.

21

Sharing Source

WHAT'S IN THIS CHAPTER?

➤ Creating source trees

➤ Configuring source control

➤ Adding a project to source control

➤ Checking out a project

➤ Sharing, checking in, comparing, and merging project files

Software development has always been characterized as a rather solitary vocation. The stereotype of a single programmer working into the wee hours of the night, isolated in a basement or attic room, is now mostly the purview of fiction writers. Most modern development is done in teams — even when those teams are scattered across the globe and connected only by the Internet. Members of a team need ready access to the assets of projects they are working on. They need to collaborate on changes and distribute their work to other team members.

Software projects themselves may also need to share resources. A suite of applications developed for a single corporation might need to include a common set of graphics, or share a set of preprocessor definitions. It's impractical to put all of the applications into a single project, and (as you saw in Chapter 5) source file references outside the project folder can be problematic. Projects need a way to share common assets rationally.

Closely related to the subject of sharing source files is the concept of *source control management* (SCM), or just *source control*. Source control systems store and track the changes made to source files over time. It is usually the basis of a collaboration system among multiple developers, acting as a mediator between developers, arbitrating changes, and communicating those changes to others. Individual developers have come to appreciate the discipline, security, and accountability that source control systems bring to their development. Even if you are a single programmer working on a single project, you may still want to set up a source control system.

Source control is used for many, if not most, open source projects. If you want to participate in an open source project, you'll want to plug your Xcode project directly into the source control system used by that project. After it is configured, you'll be able to browse the comments and revisions for the project right in the Xcode interface. You can see what new files are available and immediately update your local copy.

SHARING VIA XCODE

Xcode provides two facilities for sharing source files between projects and developers: *source trees* and source control.

Source Tree Basics

Source trees define folder locations where shared source files reside. There is no restriction on where these are located or on how the source files are maintained. An earlier chapter mentioned a suite of application projects that all need to include the same corporate artwork; a source tree folder could be defined for those graphic files.

Any number of projects can refer to the files in a source tree's location. Changing the location of the source tree changes *all* of the references in *all* of your projects simultaneously. For example, if the graphics art department sends you a new CD with updated artwork, all you have to do is pop the disc into the CD-ROM drive, point that source tree to a folder on the CD, and rebuild your projects. Source tree locations are defined individually for each user, so a different programmer can use the same project with source tree locations specific to their environment.

Source Control Basics

Source control, often referred to as version control, is the principal method of tracking historical changes made to source files and sharing source files among a group of developers. It provides three important services:

- ➤ A centralized repository
- ➤ Security
- ➤ Change history

The first service stores the master copy of all source files in a central repository. Changes made to a source file by one developer are sent back to the central repository, where those changes can then be distributed to other developers. This allows multiple developers to work on the same project in a rational manner.

The second service provides a degree of security, protecting against accidental damage to local project files and providing a point for centralized backups.

The third service, and probably the most important, keeps a record of all changes made to a project over time. Developers can quickly see exactly what has changed in each file, and review comments made by the programmer that explain why. Source control can also be used like a time machine. You can reconstruct the state of a project at any point during its lifetime. You don't need to archive a copy of your entire project at every point in its development. For example, if you're working on version 1.6 of your application, but suddenly need to debug version 1.2, simply query the source control system for a copy of your project as it existed on the day you finished version 1.2.

Source trees and source control serve different needs and each is designed to solve a different problem. Some aspects overlap, but generally they complement each other. They can be used independently or in combination. For example, a project from one source control repository can refer to files in a source tree that's being maintained in a different source control repository. What source file sharing and control techniques you employ will depend entirely on your needs and work environment.

SOURCE TREES

A source tree is a named path to a folder on your system. A source tree consists of a

➤ Symbolic name

➤ Display name

➤ Path to the tree's location on your system

Any source file reference in a project can be relative to a source tree location. The location of the tree is independent of the location of the project folder.

For example, if you define a source tree named "buttons" and set it to the location `~/Development/Common/Buttons`, any project that has a source reference relative to the "buttons" source tree will look for that file in the `Buttons` folder inside your local `Development` folder. If you move that folder, or decide to use a different folder, you simply redefine the "buttons" source tree and every source file reference based on that tree changes.

The "your" in "a source tree . . . on your system" is important. Source trees are defined individually for each user account. For someone else to use a project that refers to files in the buttons source tree, they must also have defined a source tree named "buttons." It doesn't have to have the same display name or be the same path, but it does have to have the same symbolic name. In fact, it makes sense that it wouldn't have the same path — another developer wouldn't have access to your `/Users/yourname/Development/Common/Buttons` folder.

The source trees defined for your account are global to all Xcode projects that you open. Consider this when deciding on a name for your source tree.

Define a Source Tree

Open the Source Tree tab of the Xcode Preferences, as shown in Figure 21-1.

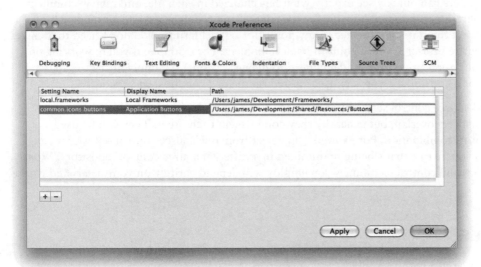

FIGURE 21-1

Click the + button below the list to define a new source tree. Give it a symbolic name or key, a display name, and a path where the tree can be accessed on your system.

The symbolic name is how Xcode identifies a source tree. It should be simple and must be unique. I prefer to use so-called "reverse DNS" notation, like `com.wiley.proXcode3.shared`. The symbolic name is stored in each project file reference that's relative to a source tree. Any other developers you share the project with must define a source tree with the exact same symbolic name, or their project file references will be broken.

The display name is how the source tree will appear in the Xcode user interface. It can be anything you want, should be descriptive, and can be changed later. Different users can have different display names for the same source tree.

To delete a tree, select it in the list and click the − button.

Source Tree References

After you've defined a tree, use it to refer to source files in your project. The source trees you've defined automatically appear in all dialogs that add an existing file, folder, or framework to your project, as shown in Figure 21-2.

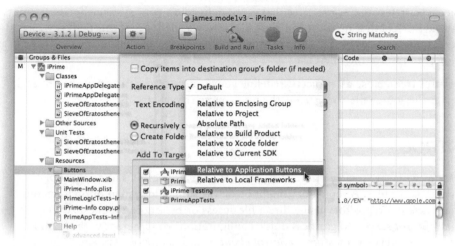

FIGURE 21-2

Source trees also appear in the reference section of every source file's Info window, as shown in Figure 21-3. You can make any source file's path type relative to any source tree that you've defined. If you are reorganizing a project to use source trees, select a group of source file references and change their path type to the new source tree as a group. Typically, you would set the path type of a group folder to that of a source tree, and leave the members of that group as Relative to Enclosing Group.

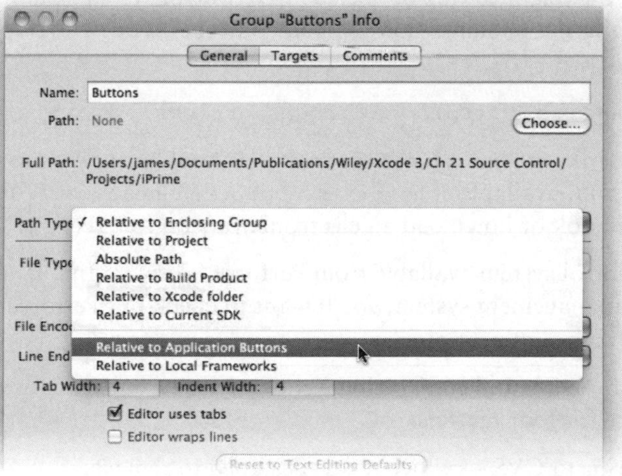

FIGURE 21-3

If you open a project that refers to a source tree that is not defined on your system, Xcode attempts to locate the file at the same path it used the last time that tree was defined. If this path is wrong, the file will turn red, indicating that it cannot be located. Define the required source tree, then close and reopen the project to resolve the reference.

To redefine your source trees, close all projects, redefine your source trees, and open the projects again. Xcode resolves the source file paths using the new source tree locations.

SOURCE CONTROL

Source control systems work by storing the master copies of your project files in a *repository*. A repository is a database of files. A repository might be on the same file system or on a remote system. Xcode might access a repository using direct file access or by sending requests over a network to a *source control server*. Regardless of the configuration, you interact with the source control system through Xcode or via a *source control client* installed on your system.

A file stored in a repository is called a *managed file*. When you want to work with a managed file, you *check out* the file from the repository. The copy of the file you checked out is called the *working copy*. If you make changes to the working copy, you later *check in* the file to record those changes in the repository.

After the changes have been recorded, other developers can check out the file to incorporate your changes into their working projects. You can compare your working copy with other versions in the repository to see exactly what has changed. You can also check out an earlier version of any file and use it instead — maybe because you don't like the changes made by another developer.

Xcode has integrated support for three major source control systems: Concurrent Versions System (CVS), Subversion, and Perforce. CVS was the reigning king of open source control systems but has since been usurped by Subversion. An installation of Subversion is included in the Xcode Developer Tools.

➤ You can get more information about CVS at `http://www.nongnu.org/cvs/`.

➤ Learn more about Subversion at `http://subversion.tigris.org/`. You'll also want to read *Version Control with Subversion*, available at `http://svnbook.red-bean.com/`. You can purchase a printed copy of the book or download an electronic version for free.

➤ Perforce is a commercial source control system available from Perforce Software Inc. If you need a commercial source control management system, you'll want to check out Perforce at `http://perforce.com/perforce/products.html`.

This chapter concentrates on setting up Subversion and configuring Xcode to use it. Subversion was chosen for this book over CVS and Perforce for four reasons:

➤ Subversion is, in many ways, superior to CVS — which it was designed to replace.

➤ Subversion is less expensive than Perforce (it's free).

➤ Subversion is very popular among open source projects.

➤ Subversion comes pre-installed with Snow Leopard and is the de facto standard for Xcode source control.

That's not to say that CVS or Perforce are bad choices. If you already have a CVS or Perforce repository, then your best choice is clear.

SOURCE CONTROL BEYOND XCODE

You're not limited to using the source control systems that are integrated into Xcode, and you're not limited to using your source control system via Xcode.

The Git SCM system has attracted a lot of attention lately, and may someday overshadow Subversion. You can use Git — or any other source control system — to manage your project's files; you just can't use it from within Xcode (unless your SCM has a Subversion or CVS emulation mode).

Source control systems also provide many features and commands that Xcode doesn't support. Xcode's source control commands focus on common tasks you're likely to perform during development (check out, check in, compare, merge). Regardless of whether you use a source control via Xcode, you will still need to reach for your favorite source control client to perform advanced activities like repository creation, branching, tagging, migration, and filtering.

Even for those actions that can be performed from within Xcode, you may still prefer using your source control client or a third-party application. For example, when I'm about to release a product I use a third-party Subversion utility for collecting, organizing, and reviewing the changes made since my last release. Though the same information can be found in the Info window of my project, it's not nearly as easy to sift through.

Using Source Control

Using source control through Xcode can be broadly divided into three phases:

1. Define a repository.

2. Check out a project from a repository.

3. Use source control from within the project.

The next section describes how to define a repository. The sections starting with "Browsing Repositories" describe how to view the contents of a repository and check out an Xcode project. Once you have a project checked out under source control, all of your subsequent interaction will be through the project, described starting in the "Source Control Interface" section.

Defining a Repository

As mentioned earlier, a repository is a centralized collection of managed files. Before you can use source control, you must define the location and characteristics of the repository, or repositories, that you want to use. Just like source trees, each developer must create an equivalent repository definition if they expect to share the same set of managed files. The definitions might be the same or different. For example, you might create a source control repository on your local drive. Later, you decide to collaborate with another programmer and open access to that repository via the Internet. Your repository definition would still refer to your local file system while his would refer to a remote repository.

All of the repositories you use are defined in the SCM tab of the Xcode Preferences (Command+,), as shown in Figure 21-4.

FIGURE 21-4

Each repository definition has three parts:

➤ The source control client used to access the repository

➤ The access method and parameters

➤ A path to the root directory within the repository

Click the + button below the list of repositories to define a new repository. A dialog sheet will prompt you for a repository name and the client that will be used to access the repository. The client you choose — SVN, Subversion, or Perforce — will determine what settings are needed to define the repository. The name identifies the repository definition in Xcode and can be changed later.

Clicking OK creates a new repository definition. Fill in the settings as required. What those settings are is entirely dependent on how the repository was created and where it resides. If you didn't set up the repository, contact the administrator of the repository for the correct settings. In some situations they may need to create a user account and password for you, or you might have to register an SSH key.

For Subversion repositories, the settings to configure are:

SUBVERSION SCM SETTING	DESCRIPTION
Scheme	http, https, file, svn+ssh, and so on
Host	Host name or IP address of server (for network schemes)
Path	Path to root directory in repository (may include the path to the repository itself)
Port	Network port to use (for network schemes)
User	User account name (if required)
Password	Password for user (if required)

The URL setting and the other settings mirror each other. Whatever you enter for the other settings is combined into a single URL, and whatever you enter into the URL setting is decomposed into its individual settings. If your Subversion administrator or open source project provides an URL to the repository, paste that into the URL field; Xcode will fill in the settings for you. Conversely, if you need an URL to access your repository via the source control client or some third-party tool, Xcode has already constructed it for you. Copy the URL and paste it into your client.

The path setting defines the top-level directory within the repository where this repository definition is anchored. You may create a single repository definition that points to the top-level directory in the repository, or you can define multiple repository definitions that point to individual subdirectories within a single repository. Which you choose is a matter of personal preference, style, and any security restrictions that might be in place. I tend to define a repository definition for each set of related projects, even if more than one set shares a single repository. When I browse that repository, I'm not distracted by unrelated directories.

The path setting might also describe the location of the repository itself. That is, the first part of the path is the location of the repository database, and any remainder is a path within the repository structure. It's not obvious where the path to the repository ends and the path within the repository begins, but it's usually immaterial.

Repository on a Local File System

If you've created a Subversion repository on a local volume, you can use the file scheme to access it directly. Set the following two settings:

➤ Scheme: `file`

➤ Path: `/Complete/Path/To/Repository/Subpath/To/Root`

The `file` scheme path defines the location of the repository database and must begin with an absolute file system path to the repository database. Any remaining path components are interpreted as subdirectories within the repository.

Creating a local repository is best when you need source control for archiving and version tracking. If you plan to collaborate with other developers, you'll probably want to create your repository on a networked server.

If you don't have access to an existing Subversion repository, or just want to get started using Subversion for your own projects, jump ahead to the "Creating a Subversion Repository" section, and then come back here to define it in Xcode.

Repository Access via a Web Server

Subversion repositories designed for wide consumption are often set up behind a web server, such as Apache. Source control requests are made through the web server and passed along to the source control server. This is very common with open source projects. If you don't have a URL for the project's repository, you will need to configure the following settings:

➤ Scheme: `http` or `https`

➤ Host: `www.host.net` or `10.0.254.1`

➤ Path: `/path/to/repository/root/directory`

➤ Port: alternate port (optional)

➤ User: account name (optional)

➤ Password: account password (optional)

Setting up Subversion to work behind a web server is a non-trivial exercise. You're most likely to encounter this for repositories that have already been created.

Subversion Server via a Network or SSH

Subversion supports a couple of its own client/server schemes. The `svn` scheme lets you set up a Subversion server on a computer and interact with it via a dedicated IP port. This is useful for development groups on a local area network, and is much easier to set up than a web-hosted

Subversion server. It has the disadvantage of limited security, and the non-HTTP IP port might be blocked by firewalls, neither of which are typically concerns on a private LAN.

To set up a Subversion server, see the "Server Configuration" chapter of the *Version Control with Subversion* book.

A less well-known scheme is svn+ssh — also described in *Version Control with Subversion*. This scheme performs Subversion actions by executing source control client requests on a remote computer via SSH. The remote computer doesn't need to be running a Subversion server, but it does need to be transparently accessible via SSH. This usually means that you've installed pre-authorized SSH keys for the remote account on the server.

Because there's no server process involved, the svn+ssh scheme is easy to set up — not that much more difficult that setting up a local repository. You will also want to install pre-authorized SSH keys so that Xcode doesn't prompt you for a password or passphrase every time it needs to interact with the repository. If you followed the instructions for setting up remote debugging in Chapter 18, you're already done. Security in svn+ssh is excellent, because it's supplied by SSH.

The primary disadvantage to svn+ssh is performance; invoking the source control client via SSH is slower than a dedicated server would be. Nevertheless, I highly recommend this configuration for small, geographically scattered teams that need secure source control with modest performance and minimal maintenance.

Checking Your Repository Definition

The repository definition pane automatically tests the settings as you enter them. A status indicator at the bottom of the pane shows Xcode's success in using those settings. The possible results are:

- ➤ Incomplete Configuration
- ➤ Authenticated
- ➤ Error: Description of error

The first message means that your definition is still missing some required setting or settings.

A green "Authenticated" message means that Xcode has successfully accessed the described repository using your settings. Congratulations, you are ready to start using your repository!

A red "Error" message indicates that the settings are wrong or that some other configuration or communications issue is preventing Xcode from accessing the repository. Read the error description for clues and carefully review your settings.

Source Control Options

Before running off to use your newly defined repository, take a quick look at the Options tab of the SCM preferences pane, as shown in Figure 21-5.

FIGURE 21-5

I recommend checking the Configure SCM Automatically option. When you check out a project via source control, the working files are under the influence of the source control system — but the project will not necessarily be configured to use source control. Turning this option on allows Xcode to configure your project automatically to use source control when it detects that it's appropriate. Otherwise, you'll have to configure the project manually as described later in the "Configuring a Project for Source Control" section.

The Save File Before SCM Operations automatically saves your files to disk before performing any source control action (check in, check out, and so on). I recommend setting this option for the same reasons I recommend setting the Always Save Files option in the Building pane.

The remaining options control how files are compared in Xcode. Most often this is when you want to compare the working version of your file with a different version in the repository. Some of these settings also apply to comparing files in snapshots.

The Comparisons Handling option selects the application and layout used when comparing two files. Xcode will obtain both versions of the file and pass them to the application for side-by-side comparison. Your choices are:

- ➤ Xcode
- ➤ FileMerge
- ➤ BBEdit
- ➤ Other

Using Xcode is the fastest, but also the least capable. Xcode's built-in comparison window is adequate for comparing two files but is awkward if you want to selectively replace individual sections of your working files with those from the revision.

The FileMerge application is a standalone file comparison utility included in the Xcode Development Tools package. If you own Bare Bone's BBEdit application, you can use its excellent file comparison interface instead.

The Other setting lets you select any third-party comparison tool that accepts two filename arguments and compares them.

Xcode can also compare files using the traditional POSIX diff tool. The settings under Differencing define some format arguments that Xcode will pass to diff. See the diff man page for a complete description of these settings.

Your SSH Certificates

If access to your repositories requires a private SSH encryption key, those keys will appear in the SSH tab of the SCM preferences pane.

The keys that appear here will be any keys installed in your account's .ssh directory and any SSH keys in your keychain.

You can add security by entering a passphrase for one or more keys. Xcode will prompt you for this phrase whenever it needs to use the selected SSH key. Leave the passphrase field empty to bypass the prompt.

Creating a Subversion Repository

If you're setting up Subversion for your own personal use, or just want to try out source control, the simplest solution is to create a local repository. The following Terminal command creates an empty repository named Subversion in your Documents folder:

```
svnadmin create ~/Documents/Subversion
```

Now go to Xcode's SCM preferences pane and create a repository definition, as described in the "Defining a Repository" section. For the example given, your settings will be:

- ➤ Client: Subversion
- ➤ Scheme: file
- ➤ Path: /User/*youraccount*/Documents/Subversion

You can elect to use a different repository name and location as you see fit. Note that you can't use a user-relative path (~/Documents/...) in the repository definition setting.

Filtering Out Noise

Ideally, your source control repository should contain only the files needed to build your project. This includes your project document, source files, resources files, and so on. It should *not* contain any intermediate products (object files, compiled data models, help indexes), superficial files (code sense index, disassembly files), or any final products (applications, bundles). There are a number of techniques for excluding these so-called noise files from your repository.

 The "no products" rule isn't universal. Repositories are sometimes used to store finished products. This is particularly true of frameworks, libraries, and other products that are source files for other projects. A finished framework that's used by a large number of developers can be checked into a repository and treated like any other immutable project resource. This spares the project from having to check out, and maintain a dependency on, the project that produces the framework.

Xcode's default folder organization conveniently places all intermediate files, project indexes, and products inside the project's `build` folder. Wow, that makes it easy! All you have to do is leave the `build` folder out of your repository and 98 percent of your noise files have been eliminated. There are basically two approaches to this, and which one you take determines whether you address other noise files at the same time.

Omitting the build Folder

The simplest technique — as long as you consistently remember to do it — is simply to leave the `build` folder out of repository. With no `build` folder in the repository, your project's `build` folder will not be a working folder (that is, managed by source control), and the source control system will ignore its content. To accomplish this, make sure the project has no `build` folder when it's first imported (see the "Adding a Project to Source Control" section). Do this by either:

➤ Closing the project and deleting the `build` folder before importing it into the repository

➤ Redefining the location of the `build` folder so that the intermediate files and products are written to a location outside the project folder

Either of these will eliminate the `build` folder from the project when it is imported, so there will be no `build` folder in the repository. After that, just be careful not to do anything that would inadvertently add or import the `build` folder.

Excluding the build Folder

A more rational approach, in my mind, is to configure Subversion so that it automatically ignores the `build` folder. Once that's done, you don't have to think about it. Whenever you import a project or check in files, Subversion will automatically ignore the contents of the `build` folder. To do that, set Subversion's `global-ignores` property in the `~/.subversion/config` file. An excerpt of my `~/.subversion/config` file is shown here:

```
### Set global-ignores to a set of whitespace-delimited globs
### which Subversion will ignore in its 'status' output.
# global-ignores = *.o *.lo *.la #*# .*.rej *.rej .*~ *~ .#* .DS_Store
global-ignores = .DS_Store build *.mode* *~.nib *~
```

I commented out the default definition of global-ignores and replaced it with my own. The global-ignores property is a space-separated list of filename patterns (globbing) that Subversion will exclude/ignore on your entire system. The patterns I defined exclude the following:

PATTERN	FILE DESCRIPTION
.DS_Store	The hidden .DS_Store file used by Mac OS X to manage the appearance of folders in the Finder
build	Any file or folder named 'build'
.mode	Window position, toolbar, and other superficial layout information stored per-user inside the project document
*~.nib	Backup .nib files created by Interface Builder
*~	Generic backup files created by some editor applications

These patterns automatically exclude all intermediate, product, and noise files from my repository.

The hazard of setting an exclude pattern like "build" is that you might someday encounter a project that has a subdirectory named build *that contains source files. It's unlikely, but if it did happen Subversion would dutifully ignore that folder too, probably to the detriment of the project.*

You can configure per-folder filters in Subversion. These can add additional ignore rules for a specific project or override the global rule. See the Version Control with Subversion *book for the details.*

Excluding Other Noise Files

Generally, noise files are files that are not significant to building the project. It's not that they don't contain any useful information, but deleting them won't affect the build. The advantage of checking noise files into source control is that they often contain information that you want to preserve or share. When I check out a project, it would be nice if that project remembered all of my settings and preferences.

The disadvantage is that noise files tend to change often. The source control system will want you to check any modified files back into the repository along with a change comment. This often results in many revisions to the repository that don't represent significant changes to the project. This can be annoying to other developers who must constantly wade through repository changes that have no real impact on their work.

The noise files I exclude are .DS_Store and the *.mode* files found inside the project document. These are classic noise files because they store window position and other ephemeral layout information that has little bearing on my workflow. If I export a project, and it doesn't save the size of the project window, it won't cause me any grief.

The noise files that are most contentious are the per-user *.pbxuser files stored inside the project document. Each *user*.pbxuser file stores preferences and other settings for that developer, such as breakpoints, smart groups, and bookmarks. If you've worked on a project for a significant amount of time, this can represent a lot of customization that you might not want to lose when the project is checked in. On the other hand, every time you set a breakpoint your project document will have appeared to have changed, which can result in a lot of extraneous project document updates that other developers must deal with.

As a rule, the more developers working on the same project the more problematic noise files become. You and your other developers will have to decide whether the noise is worth the extra data.

Browsing Repositories

Once you have one or more repositories defined, you can open the Repositories window by choosing the SCM ⇨ Repositories command. The repository window, shown in Figure 21-6, is where you can browse the content of a repository, perform some maintenance, and where you will ultimately check out a project under source control.

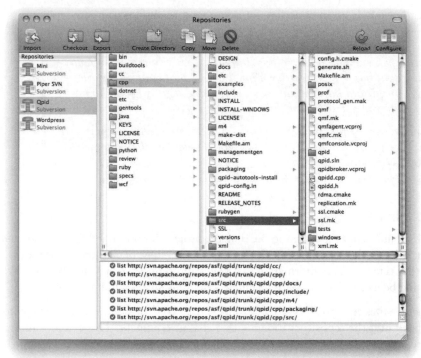

FIGURE 21-6

On the left are the repositories that you've defined. Select one and the browser in the upper pane will let you navigate through the most recent content of each repository directory. The lower pane shows a running log of the actual SCM commands that Xcode is issuing in order to perform whatever actions you request.

The Reload toolbar button re-fetches the information from the repository and refreshes the display. The Configure button jumps to the SCM pane of the Xcode preferences — the one you've been using in the previous sections.

You don't typically spend a lot of time in the repositories window. The significant actions you'll perform here are checking out and importing/exporting entire projects, which are all described in subsequent sections. Once you do that, almost everything else is done through the project.

The repository window does provide a basic set of repository commands. Besides perusing the contents of a repository, you can:

- ➤ Create a new repository subdirectory
- ➤ Copy a repository file or directory
- ➤ Move (rename) a repository file or directory
- ➤ Delete a repository file or directory

These commands are all self-explanatory. Just remember that you're modifying the content of the repository, not the files in your file system.

While the command set looks simple, there's actually a lot you can do with it. If you've taken time to skim the *Version Control with Subversion* book, you already know that Subversion doesn't use metadata (a.k.a., tags) to demarcate releases or branches. Instead, it uses a convention of subdirectories. The main development files are stored in a `trunk` directory. Releases are defined by copying the entire trunk into a subdirectory of the `tags` directory. Similarly, copying a project folder into a `branches` subdirectory creates a branch. Thus, tagging milestones and branching are simply matters of copying one repository directory into another.

Speaking of subdirectory conventions, if you've just created a new Subversion repository for a single project, you'll want to start by creating a `trunk` subdirectory, as shown in Figure 21-7. You can create `tags` and `branches` directories when you need them.

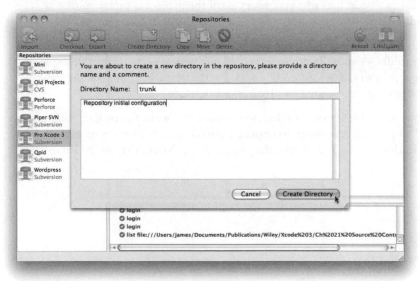

FIGURE 21-7

When you create the subdirectory, Xcode prompts you for a comment. Every change to the repository is recorded, annotated with an explanation that you provide, and no information is actually destroyed. Deleting a repository folder doesn't delete it from the repository; it simply means that, in the most current version of the repository, the directory no longer exists. Its previous incarnations are still, and will always be, available.

If you plan to store multiple projects in a single repository, I recommend creating top-level folders for each project, and then creating `trunk`, `tags`, and `branches` subfolders within each project folder. Other developers prefer to create single top-level `trunk`, `tags`, and `branches` directories and then have subdirectories for each project within those. There are advantages and disadvantages to each. Consult the *Version Control with Subversion* book before embarking on any major repository design.

Adding a Project to Source Control

So far, you've created a repository, defined it in Xcode, and can browse the repository in the repository window. Now you want to place your project under source control. The basic steps for putting a project under source control are:

1. Create the project.

2. Import the project into the repository.

3. Check out the project under source control.

4. Configure the project to use source control.

The first two steps are required because placing a project under source control presents a bit of a chicken-and-egg problem; a project can't be under source control until it's been checked out of the repository, and it can't add files to a repository until the project is under source control. To get around this conundrum, you begin by *importing* a project into the repository.

Importing takes a project folder — actually any arbitrary file or folder — that *is not under source control* and adds it to the repository. You can do this with anything at any time, but the most common reason is to get a project into source control in the first place.

In the repositories window, select the repository directory where you want the project folder copied into the repository, or select just the repository to import it into the repository's root directory. Click the Import button in the toolbar and choose the project folder to import, as shown in Figure 21-8.

FIGURE 21-8

Click the Import button and Xcode copies the entire project directory into the repository as a new subdirectory.

 Before checking in your project, make sure you have either deleted your build *folder, relocated your* build *folder, or followed the directions in the section "Filtering Out Noise," so that the files produced by your project aren't copied into the repository. Only the documents in a project that produce something should be under source control — not any of its results.*

You might think that all you have to do now is flip a switch in the project and start using source control, but you're not there yet. You must now check the project back out of the repository — only then do you have a set of *working* files that are under source control.

Checking Out a Project

Checking out a project (or any set of files) from source control creates a working copy of the managed files in the repository. Working files are special. The source control system maintains additional information about the file and its relationship to its managed counterpart in the repository. Before you can use source control from within an Xcode project you must first check the project out.

Somewhat counterintuitively, you must check out your project to someplace *other* than its original project folder. Either checkout the project to a new location, or first trash, move, or rename the original project folder. I wouldn't delete it yet — just in case something goes wrong.

In the repositories window, select the repository folder you want to check out. If you want to check out the entire repository, select only the repository. Click the Checkout button and select a location where the working project files will be written, as shown in Figure 21-9.

FIGURE 21-9

The default name for the enclosing folder will be the repository or folder you're checking out. If you want to change it, do so now. The reasons you might want to change it are varied, but one common reason is that Xcode and traditional Subversion repositories don't use the same directory structure.

In an "old school" Subversion repository, a project folder named `MyProject` would appear in the repository as `/MyProject/trunk`, `/MyProject/tags`, and `/MyProject/branches`. When you check out `trunk`, the folder "trunk" becomes the project folder. This is probably not what you wanted. The solution is to check out `trunk` from the repository, but rename it to `MyProject` before clicking Checkout.

HOW SOURCE CONTROL MANAGES WORKING FILES

When you check out a set of files from a repository, the source control system writes additional metadata about each file. This includes information like:

➤ The location of the managed file in the repository

➤ The revision number of the working file

➤ A copy of the original file

➤ Status and history

The presence of this metadata is what allows source control to track and manage the working files; this is what it means to be "under source control."

In a Subversion system, this information is stored in invisible .svn directories that you'll find in every folder of your working project. As a rule, don't delete or otherwise disturb these hidden directories. Their integrity is crucial to the smooth operation of the source control system.

All of the files in your project have now been checked out, and all of the working copies of those files are under source control. You can now skip ahead to the "Configuring a Project for Source Control" section.

Exporting a Project

Exporting a project is the inverse of importing one, and is the complement to checking one out. Exporting a project produces copies of the managed files in the repository, but does not create working files. In other words, it simply copies the files in the repository to your local drive without any of the source control metadata required to manage them. An exported project is *not* under source control.

Use the export command when you simply want to obtain an unencumbered copy of a project or some files. For example, let's say there's an open source project that you're interested in looking at. You're not a contributor to the project (yet), and have no need to track changes or compare files to older revisions. You would use the export command to fetch a copy of the project sans any source control information or ties to its originating repository.

Similarly, you might be working on version 1.6 of your application and need to build version 1.2. If you have no intention of creating a new branch or reviewing changes, simply export the project from the 1.2 tag directory into a new folder and build it.

Configuring a Project for Source Control

The last step is to configure the project to use source control. Open the Info window for the project group, choose the Project ➪ Edit Project Settings command or choose SCM ➪ Configure SCM for this Project. At the top of the General tab, you will see the Roots and SCM settings, as shown in Figure 21-10.

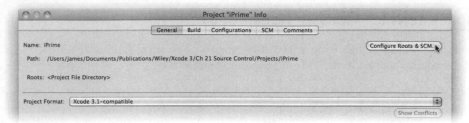

FIGURE 21-10

This portion of the project's Info window describes the project's name, location, and the roots of the project. The project roots is a list of directories that encompass the assets of the project. For most projects, everything is contained within the project's folder, which appears in the list as `<Project File Directory>`.

Because you just checked the entire project out from source control, the first order of business is to enable source control for the project folder. Click the Configure Roots & SCM button. A sheet appears listing all of the roots of this project and the source control repository each is associated with. For now, all you are interested in is the repository for your `<Project File Directory>`. If the Configure SCM Automatically preference is on and Xcode was able to unambiguously determine which repository the project came from, the repository for your project may already be configured. If that's the case, you can skip to the next section and start using source control from within your project.

If SCM has not been configured for your project, do so now. First, select the source control management system you're using from the pop-up menu at the top of the sheet. All of your project roots must use the same source control system. For example, you can't have one root managed by Subversion and another by Perforce.

Now select the repository from where your project was checked out, as shown in Figure 21-11. Here, Xcode plays matchmaker; it compares the source control information in your working directories with the definitions of your repositories, and suggests which repositories appear to be valid choices.

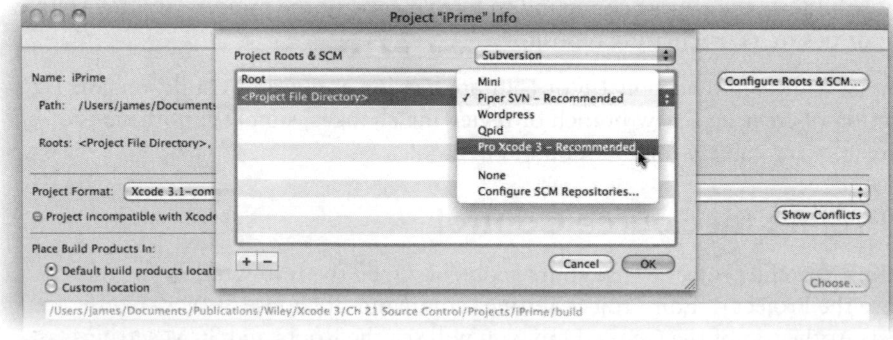

FIGURE 21-11

Click OK to accept your changes. Once at least one project root has been configured to use source control, the source control interface within Xcode is enabled. If this is a single, self-contained project, move on to the "Source Control Interface" section.

Setting a root's repository to none disables source control management for that directory tree.

The Configure SCM Repositories command at the bottom of the menu jumps to the SCM pane of the Xcode preferences, which you used at the beginning of this chapter to define the repository.

Project Roots

A single project can administer source control in multiple directory trees by defining additional project roots. As a rule, you should always define the repository for your project's folder. If your project incorporates assets outside your project folder, those assets are under source control, and you want to manage them from within your project, add each top-level directory as a project root by following these steps:

1. Click the Configure Roots and SCM button.

2. Click the + button at the bottom to define a new root.

3. Choose the top-level folder that contains the working (checked out) assets.

4. Choose the repository that the working files came from.

Naturally, if your additional root directories were checked out of repositories other than the one your project is in, you'll first have to define those repositories in the SCM pane of the Xcode preferences.

There are a number of scenarios in which a project would have multiple roots:

➤ The project builds several subprojects and you want to have source control over the files in those subprojects from within your project.

➤ Your project uses the files in a source tree directory that is checked out from a repository.

➤ Your project includes a shared development asset, like a framework, and you'd like to be able to update it via source control from within the project.

The paths to your project roots are all always relative to your project folder. If you add roots to a project and then change anything that invalidates this relationship — relocating a source tree, for example — the source control features for those files will simply stop working until you update your root paths.

Source Control Interface

Interaction with source control in Xcode is done primarily through the commands in the SCM (Source Control Manager) menu and the SCM tab in various Info windows. File-specific commands apply to either the selected file or group of files in the project window, or to the currently active editor pane. This chapter often refers to "selecting a file" before executing one of the SCM commands. It's implied that the same command would apply equally to the file in the active editor pane.

As soon as you enable source control for a project, a new SCM tab appears in the project's Info window, as shown in Figure 21-12. A similar SCM tab appears in the Info window of all project files that are under source control.

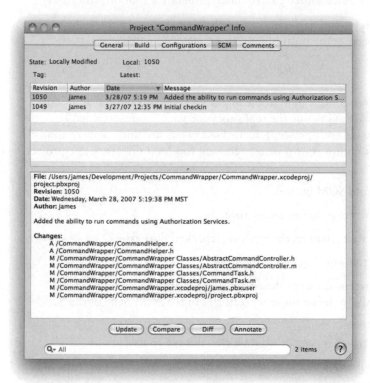

FIGURE 21-12

The State field shows the current status of the project document or source file. This tells you if the file is up-to-date (that is, it is the same as the most recent version of the file stored in the repository), if it has been modified locally, if it needs to be updated, and so on. The Local field shows the version of the file that you last checked out of the repository — also called the *base revision* — and the Latest field shows the most recent version stored in the repository.

Below the file's status is the list of revisions. Each revision has a number, an author, a date, and a comment. Select one to show the full details of the revision in the lower pane of the window.

Use the four buttons below the detailed description to update or see the annotation view of a selected revision in the list. You can select one revision in the list and compare or diff it against the working copy of the file, or you can select two revisions in the list and compare them to each other. All of these commands are explained later in this chapter.

SCM Smart Group and Window

The SCM smart group in the Groups & Files pane lists the pending source control operations for the project, as shown in Figure 21-13. The details pane for the SCM smart group displays an additional source control status column — the left column, next to the document icons shown in Figure 21-13.

FIGURE 21-13

The SCM column shows the status of any pending source control actions or conflicts. When you make changes to a project in Xcode, you are only changing the local copy of the project. None of the changes you make propagate back to the source control repository until you *commit* those changes. As you work on the project — adding, removing, and editing files — Xcode keeps track of all of the changes that you've made. These appear in the SCM smart group. When you commit your changes, Xcode executes the pending actions in the SCM smart group, dutifully adding, removing, and modifying files in the repository to mirror those in your project.

You can also view the SCM status of files in any other details pane by enabling the SCM column, as shown in Figure 21-14. Right/Control+click the column titles to show or hide the SCM column.

FIGURE 21-14

The SCM column contains a single character that indicates the status or pending SCM operation of each file, as described in the following table:

SCM STATUS	DESCRIPTION
(blank)	The file is up to date. It is the same file as the latest version in the repository. You have not modified it, nor are there any newer versions available to be checked out.
M	The file has been modified locally. The changes will be written to the repository the next time the file is committed.
U	The file needs updating. The file has not been modified locally, but the repository now contains a newer version of the file than the one you have checked out.
C	The modifications to the file are in conflict. There is a newer version of this file in the repository *and* you have modified the local copy of the file. This usually occurs when two or more developers are making changes to the same file simultaneously. The "Resolving Conflicts" section tells you how to merge your changes with those in the repository.
A	The file will be added to the repository. The file is not currently in the repository or under source control, but you have instructed Xcode to import it when you commit it or the entire project.
R	The file will be removed from the repository. You have deleted (or renamed) the local file. The next time you commit the project, the corresponding file in the repository will also be deleted.
?	The repository has no information about this file. This is usually because it is a new file whose status hasn't been changed to "add" yet.
– (hyphen)	The file is in a directory that does not exist in the repository. When you're adding folders to your project, you first add them to the repository using your source control client. After the enclosing folder is added, you can add files to the repository using either Xcode or your client tool.

Choose the SCM ➪ Refresh Entire Project to update the SCM status of every file in your project.

Double-clicking the SCM smart group or choosing the SCM ➪ SCM Results (Shift+Command+V) command opens the SCM results window, as shown in Figure 21-15.

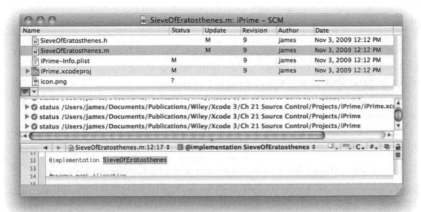

FIGURE 21-15

This window shows more detailed information about the SCM status of each file. Like the SCM smart group and details pane, it lists the name and status of each file. It also lists:

➤ The base revision of the working file

➤ The author of the base revision

➤ The check-in date of the base revision

➤ Update status, if there's a newer version of the file

 The base revision *is the version of the file you checked out of the repository. It's the original version of your working copy, before you made any changes. It is not necessarily the current version of the file or the latest version in the repository.*

In the lower-left corner of the window are a small log button and a pop-up menu. Clicking the log button toggles the display of the SCM transaction log, as shown in the middle of Figure 21-15. The log shows the commands issued to, and the results from, the source control client used for this project.

The menu button next the log button selects one of three display modes for the SCM window:

➤ All

➤ Interesting

➤ Flat

The All setting displays all of the files in your project. The Interesting and Flat settings show only pending SCM actions (modified files, new files, files that need updating, pending deletes). The Interesting choice organizes items hierarchically, whereas Flat lists them alphabetically.

At the bottom of the window is a standard editor pane, which you can collapse by dragging the pane divider to the bottom of the window.

Committing Changes

No change occurs in the repository until you commit it. Choose the SCM ⇨ Commit Entire Project command to commit all pending changes in the project. Alternatively, you can select individual files in a source group or details pane and commit just a subset of files using the SCM ⇨ Commit Changes command. You can only commit pending actions, such as add, modify, or remove. Files that display no status or a conflict status cannot be committed either because there's no action to perform or agreed Xcode doesn't know what to do with them. You must first tell Xcode what to do with the file, and then commit the change.

Committing individual files is usually safe, as long as you are sure the changes being checked in will be valid in the absence of other changes that you have yet to commit. Whenever a commit includes the addition or removal of files, you should endeavor to commit those actions along with the corresponding changes made to the project document. The safest action in this situation is to commit the entire project. The "Source Control and the Project Document" section explains this in more detail.

> *In general, your goal when checking in changes should be to maintain the integrity of the project in the repository. If you make changes in two files that depend on each other, check both of those files in together. If you don't, you'll have a version of the project in the repository that won't build because a change made to a source file was checked in, but the matching change made in its header file was not.*

When you commit a change, Xcode prompts you for a comment, as shown in Figure 21-16. You should be descriptive and complete. The comments you enter will be attached to every transaction required to complete the commit. Source control comments are another form of documentation. The modifications made in your project are only comprehensible if you explain what you changed and why, both clearly and accurately.

FIGURE 21-16

Discarding Changes

If, for whatever reason, you decide to abandon the changes that you've made to a file, you can discard them and revert to the base revision — the version you originally checked out from source control. This is not necessarily the latest version of the file in the repository. When you discard changes to a file, Xcode presents the warning dialog shown in Figure 21-17.

Discard all changes?

All local changes will be lost.

Cancel   Discard Changes

FIGURE 21-17

You can't discard changes by simply checking out a different revision of the file (as discussed in the "Updating Files" section). Xcode won't overwrite your local file with a revision from the repository until you explicitly discard your changes. This prevents you from accidentally wiping out hours, if not days, worth of work. If you do try to update a modified file, you will only end up changing the base revision associated with that file. This action will either associate the file with the latest revision (containing as-yet uncommitted changes), or it will put the file in conflict mode. The "Resolving Conflicts" section explains how to merge conflicting changes.

Adding Files to Source Control

Adding a file to the project involves first adding the file to the project and then adding it to the repository. How you add the file to the project is entirely up to you. You can use any method discussed in the book so far for adding an existing file or creating a new one. (Chapter 5 contains detailed instructions on adding files to a project.) After the file is added to the project, the SCM status of the file may be ?, -, or blank, indicating that the file, or the folder that contains the file, is unknown to the repository.

In the case of an unknown file (?), select the file in the source group or details pane and choose the SCM ➪ Add to Repository command. This creates a pending action in the SCM smart group that will add that file to the repository when committed. The file then becomes the working copy of the soon-to-be-added file in the repository

If you've accidentally created a pending add (delete, rename, or similar) action, you can usually cancel it using your source control client. In Subversion, use the catch-all revert *command, as in* svn revert Help. *The pending add action for the Help folder is forgotten, essentially taking you back to the time before you added it. Revert only works with pending actions; once you've committed an action, the change becomes part of the repository — forever.*

If you've created files inside a folder that is not in the repository, you'll need to add that folder to the repository before Xcode will pay any attention to its files. Use one of these two methods to add a folder to your project:

➤ If the folder is represented by a source item in the project, select it and use the SCM ⇨ Add to Repository command to add it and its contents to source control.

➤ If the folder does not appear as a source item in Xcode, use your source control client to add the folder, and optionally its contents. For example, the Subversion command to add an existing Help folder is:

```
cd ~/Development/MyProject
svn add Help
```

If you add just the folder, the status of the files in that folder will change to ?, indicating that Xcode now sees them as unknown files. You can now use Xcode to add those files to the repository.

 If you find yourself tempted to import *the new file or folder, don't. The folder that contains the new file is under source control, but the new files aren't — thus, the ? status. If you import the files into the repository you now have a local file (not under source control) that duplicates a managed file in the repository. Subversion treats this situation as a conflict and will refuse to check the file in or out until it's resolved. If you find yourself in this situation, discard the local copy and check out the file from the repository. Now you have a working copy under source control.*

Whenever you make source control changes using the client tool, the repositories window, or through any other means outside the project, choose SCM ⇨ Refresh Entire Project to update Xcode's status of the working files.

Deleting Files under Source Control

Deleting a file requires that you remove it from both the project and the source control repository. When you delete a file reference from a project, Xcode gives you the option of removing just the file reference or physically deleting the source file. If you choose the latter, and the file exists in the repository, Xcode presents a second dialog, shown in Figure 21-18.

FIGURE 21-18

If you choose to remove the file, a repository remove action is added to the SCM smart group and the file is removed from the repository when the action is committed. If you choose not to remove the file, the file is deleted locally but remains in the repository. If you choose to remove the repository file as well, the project displays a grey (disabled) reference to the file in the project, indicating a reference to a file that has been deleted. After the action has been committed and the file in the repository has been removed, the phantom reference to the deleted file will disappear.

Renaming Files under Source Control

Renaming a file in a source control repository is as simple as renaming the source item in your project. In the repository, the action consists of removing an existing file and adding a new file with a different name. When you rename a source file in Xcode, it presents the dialog box shown in Figure 21-19.

FIGURE 21-19

If you choose to rename the file in the repository, Xcode creates two SCM actions: the first action removes the old file, and the second action adds the same file back into the repository with its new name. Commit these two actions together to complete the rename.

Updating Files

When a newer version of a file exists in the repository, Xcode displays a U as the SCM status for the file. This indicates that you must update this file if you want the latest version.

If you want to retrieve the latest version of a file, select one or more files in the project window and choose the SCM ⇨ Update To ⇨ Latest (Shift+Command+L) command. This checks out the most recent version of the files from the repository, replacing your working copies.

You can also retrieve an earlier version of a file. Select a single file and choose the SCM ⇨ Update To ⇨ Revision command. This presents a sheet, similar the one shown in Figure 21-20, listing the history of the file. Highlight the revision of the file you want to retrieve and click the Update button.

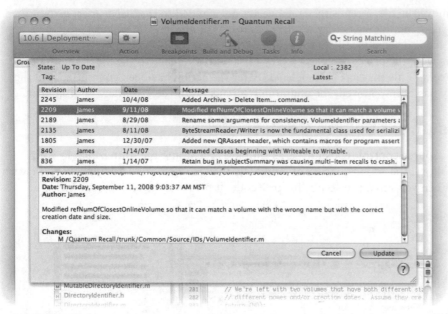

FIGURE 21-20

You can also update (check out) multiple files at or near a specific revision using the SCM ➪ Update To ➪ Specific Revision command. Enter the desired revision number into the dialog box and click the Update button. Xcode checks out either that specific revision of the file, or the most recent revision that is older than that revision. For example, assume there are two files in the repository. File A has revisions 1, 3, and 5. File B has revisions 1, 2, 4, and 6. If you update both to specific revision 4, Xcode checks out revision 4 of file B and revision 3 of file A.

> *When you revert to an older revision of a file, the SCM information about that file may revert as well. This depends on which source control system you are using. If it does revert, the file's SCM history appears to be current when it isn't, listing only the revision information up to the revision you retrieved. The file does not display a U indicating that a newer version of the file is available. Use the SCM ➪ Refresh Entire Project command to fetch the latest source control information from the repository. The information about the more recent versions of the file reappears and the file status changes to U.*

You can bring an entire project up to date by selecting the project group in the Groups & Files pane of the project window and choosing the SCM ➪ Update To ➪ Latest (Command+Shift+L) command or by choosing the SCM ⇨ Update Entire Project command. Xcode retrieves the most recent revision of the project document and every file in the project.

 Whenever you update the project document itself, close the project and reopen it. Changes made to the project document by updating will not be "seen" by Xcode until it is forced to reread the project document.

Comparing Revisions

You can compare the files in your project with other revisions using the SCM ⇨ Compare With and SCM ⇨ Diff With commands. The Compare With commands employ a graphical utility to compare, and possibly merge, the differences between the two files. The Diff With commands use the UNIX `diff` tool to compare the files.

Choose the file you want to compare, and then choose the Latest, Base, Revisions, or Specific Revision command from either the Compare With or Diff With submenu:

➤ Latest compares your working file against the latest revision in the repository.

➤ Base compares your working file against the base revision that you most recently checked out, which may or may not be the most recent revision.

➤ Revisions presents a list of file revisions, along with their comments, for you to choose from.

➤ Specific Revision prompts for a revision number — which Xcode assumes you already know — and then retrieves that revision, or the most recent revision that's older than that revision.

If your working file is already the same as the latest or base revision, the appropriate commands are disabled. If you want to browse the revisions and their comments, choose the Revisions command.

All of the various Compare With commands use the comparison utility selected in the SCM preferences pane (see the "Source Control Options" section, earlier in this chapter). I recommend using FileMerge or BBEdit (if you own it). This chapter demonstrates using FileMerge.

You've already used Xcode's built-in comparison editor when comparing files in snapshots. This choice has the advantage of being fast, and it doesn't launch another application, but Xcode's tool is significantly limited in its ability to selectively borrow and undo changes from the other file, which I feel makes it more of a hindrance when working with source control.

When launched by Xcode, FileMerge shows a side-by-side comparison of the two files, as shown in Figure 21-21.

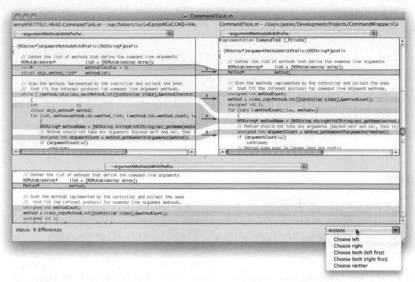

FIGURE 21-21

The window graphically illustrates the changes made between the two files. In the example shown in Figure 21-21, four groups of changes (visible in the window) were detected. Scroll through the file to see other differences, or use the Find ➪ Go To Next ➪ Difference (Command+Down Arrow) and Find ➪ Go To Previous ➪ Difference (Command+Up Arrow) commands. The window may have a third pane at the bottom, which shows a merged copy of the two files. To collapse this pane, use the pane divider. The "Resolving Conflicts" section discusses how to merge files.

The Compare With commands give you one additional command not available in the Diff With submenu. SCM ➪ Compare With ➪ File enables you to select an arbitrary file and compare it with your working source file.

If you use one of the Diff With commands, Xcode opens a text window that displays the output of the diff command, as shown in Figure 21-22. The SCM options, described in the "Source Control Options" section, let you choose a number of diff formatting options.

```
                 Diff HEAD vs. Local — CommandTask.m
      ◄ ►   Diff HEAD vs. Local — CommandTask.m:1:1 ◆
 5  282,283c282
 6  < void*                    methodIterator = 0;
 7  <     struct objc_method_list* methodList;
 8  ---
 9  >     Method*              method;
10  287,291c286,289
11  < while ( (methodList=class_nextMethodList([controller class],&methodIterator)) != NULL )
12  <     {
13  <         int              i;
14  <         struct objc_method* method;
15  <         for (i=0, method=methodList->method_list; i<methodList->method_count; i++, method++)
16  ---
17  >     unsigned int methodCount;
18  >     method = class_copyMethodList([controller class],&methodCount);
19  >     unsigned int i;
20  >     for (i=0; i<methodCount; i++, method++)
21  293c291
22  <         NSString* methodName = [NSString stringWithCString:sel_getName(method->method_name)];
23  ---
24  >     NSString* methodName = [NSString stringWithCString:sel_getName(method_getName(*method)) encoding:NSUTF8StringEncod
25  295c293
26
```

FIGURE 21-22

Merging Changes

The file comparison and merge utilities can also be used to combine the differences between two files. This is useful in a number of situations. One of the very liberating aspects of working with a source control system is the freedom to make experimental changes to your code. If you decide that you don't like the changes, you can compare your working copy with an earlier version of your source code stored in the repository. The file comparison utilities let you "undo" your changes by selectively moving blocks of code from the earlier version back into your working one. This is a much more surgical correction than merely discarding all of the changes in a file.

Both the FileMerge utility and BBEdit's compare files function place both old and new versions of the file on the screen side by side. Both highlight the blocks of text that differ between the two. For each difference, you can choose whether to keep it as it is or revert to the alternative version in the other file.

The FileMerge utility does this with a merged file pane at the bottom of the window. The merged file contains all of the common elements of both files and selected blocks of text from either the right or the left file pane. To create the merged version, select each difference and choose what to include in the merged version from the following table:

ACTION ITEM	KEYBOARD SHORTCUT	RESULT
Choose left	←	Use content from left file
Choose right	→	Use content from right file
Choose both (left first)		Include contents of left file followed by the right file
Choose both (right first)		Include contents of right file followed by the left file
Choose neither		Ignore the contents of both files

Using the ↑ and ↓ keys, navigate to the next change and then use ← or → to select which change you want to keep. When you are finished, save the file as a new document, or replace one of the existing files with the merged version.

BBEdit works a little differently. In BBEdit there is no third file. It presents the two files in a separate editor windows (see Figure 21-23). A third window displays the list of differences between the two. Select a difference to highlight the corresponding regions in both files. From the differences window, you can replace the block in either file with the contents of the other using the Apply to New or Apply to Old button. When you are done, save the modified files back to their original locations, or use the File ➪ Save As command to save the changes to a new file.

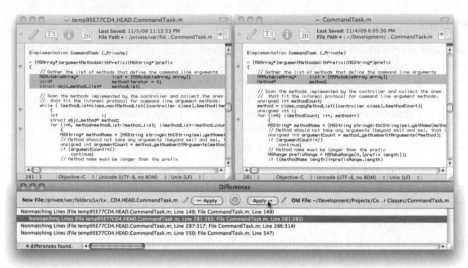

FIGURE 21-23

Viewing Annotations

Another way of seeing how a file has evolved is to look at its annotation view. Select a file and choose a command from the SCM ➪ Get Annotations For submenu. The choices are Latest, Base, Revision, or Specific Revision. You can also select a revision of a file in the SCM tab of the Info window for the files and click the Annotate button.

The annotated listing of a file, shown in Figure 21-24, displays the revision number in which each line was added and the author of that line. In this example, you can see that the maxPrime property was added by daphne in revision 10 of the file. The rest of the file was from the original when james first checked it in. Annotated listings do not show lines that have been removed, nor do they show the previous versions of lines that have been altered.

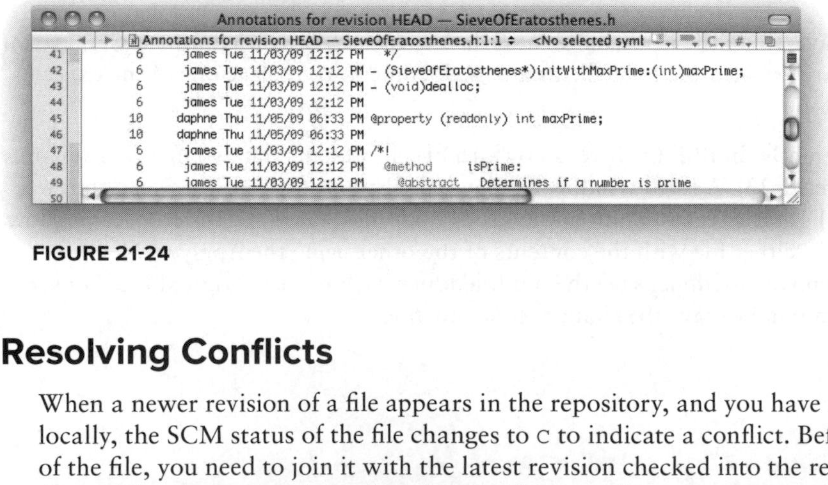

FIGURE 21-24

Resolving Conflicts

When a newer revision of a file appears in the repository, and you have modified that same file locally, the SCM status of the file changes to C to indicate a conflict. Before committing your version of the file, you need to join it with the latest revision checked into the repository to add, combine, or discard the changes made by the other developer with yours — or not.

When a conflict occurs, you have two choices. You can abandon the changes that you've made, replacing them wholesale with the changes made in the latest revision of the file. To abandon your changes, select the conflicting file and choose SCM ⇨ Discard Changes.

The other choice is to merge your changes manually with those checked into source control. Select the file and choose the SCM ⇨ Update To ⇨ Latest (Shift+Command+L) or SCM ⇨ Update To ⇨ Revision command. Instead of overwriting your changes with the latest revision of the file in the repository — which you obviously don't want — your version and the latest version of the file are combined. If the sections that were changed in each file don't overlap, Xcode merges your changes with those in the repository and updates your working file.

If the changes conflict, the overlapping sections of the file that are different are noted by comments, as shown in Figure 21-25. The SCM status for the file changes to a green C, indicating that the file is in conflict resolution.

FIGURE 21-25

Edit the file, removing or combining the differences, until you have successfully integrated your changes with those of the other developer. If you are using Subversion, choose the SCM ⇨ Resolved command to let the repository know that you are done merging the changes.

You can now commit your combined changes, creating a new revision that contains the changes from both versions. When you commit your merged file, document your changes and the fact that these were combined with changes from the previous revision.

Going Offline

At some point, you may find yourself working on a project without access to the source control system or repository from which it was checked out. For example, you might have moved the project to another computer, or are using it on laptop that is no longer in contact with your source control server.

You can temporarily disable SCM control of your project using the SCM ⇨ Go Offline command. This disables most SCM menu commands and the SCM status column. History and revision information that Xcode has already obtained for files is still available, but none of the commands that operate on those revisions will function.

You can continue to edit, add, and rename files in your project. These actions simply create pending SCM actions. When you are back in touch with the source control repository, restore SCM functionality by choosing the SCM ⇨ Go Online command, and then commit or update your project as needed.

Source Control and the Project Document

The project document requires some special handing when a project is under the control of a source control system. The project document is a package containing several files. The `project.pbxproj` file contains the structure and common settings of the project document bundle. This includes source file references, target definitions, and build settings. If you change any of these values, the `project.pbxproj` file appears in the SCM smart group as a modified file, as shown in Figure 21-26. The changes made to the project won't be stored in the repository until you commit this file.

FIGURE 21-26

Each user has a personalized settings file in the project document package. These were described in the "Excluding Other Noise Files" section. When, and whether, you check these files into the repository is up to you. Being part of the project document, modifications to these files will make it appear that the project document has changed — unless they are explicitly excluded from the repository. Here are some points to keep in mind:

➤ Whenever you add, remove, or rename files in a project, commit the changes to the project document and *all* of the add and remove actions simultaneously, or check in the file changes before the project document. This will avoid the situation where the project has file references to files that are not (yet) in the repository.

➤ Whenever you update the project document files from the repository, close the project and reopen it from the File ➪ Recent Projects menu. Replacing the project document on disk does not force Xcode to reread the project settings in all cases. Closing the project and reopening it does. After you update a project document, you may get a warning that the project file has changed. Choose the option to reread the document from disk.

➤ To make the most of personal settings in the `.pbxuser` files, make sure all of the developers working on a project have distinct account names. If you work on a project from different systems, use the same account name on both or you will be treated as a different developer.

SOURCE CONTROL VS. SNAPSHOTS

As explained in the sidebar "How Source Control Manages Working Files," a project under source control contains hidden metadata that keeps track of the state of the working files.

Snapshots work by making a literal copy of every file in your project folder. I think you can immediately see the potential conflict.

Interleaving source control actions with snapshot restores can result in stale source control information. Restoring a snapshot after performing some source control action also restores the now obsolete source control metadata. This will result in inconsistent and erroneous SCM status information.

If you need to restore your project from a snapshot, be mindful of restoring old source control metadata by using one of these techniques:

➤ Avoid performing any source control action between taking a snapshot and restoring from it.

➤ If source control actions have occurred, then either:

➤ Restore individual changes or files from the snapshot without restoring the entire project.

➤ After a restoring from a snapshot, immediately perform an SCM ⇨ Refresh Entire Project command.

SUMMARY

Source control management allows Xcode to become a member of a community. It also provides important tools for tracking, auditing, documenting, and protecting your hard work. Source trees let projects share common assets, maximizing their reuse, in a manner that won't break your projects when they're moved to another location or environment. Together, source control management and source trees allow you to benefit from the value of work that has already been done, and the work of your colleagues, in a portable and interactive manner.

The next chapter explores the multifaceted Organizer window, where you can automate your projects, keep notes, and configure test devices. Interestingly, it's a great place to add source control scripts.

22

Using the Organizer

WHAT'S IN THIS CHAPTER?

- ➤ Adding items to your organizer
- ➤ Using, editing, and creating custom organizer actions
- ➤ Making snapshots of organizer items
- ➤ Managing iPhone/iPod devices
- ➤ Configuring your iPhone/iPod for development
- ➤ Using iPhone/iPod developer utilities

The organizer window, shown in Figure 22-1, is a recent addition to Xcode. It encompasses an eclectic collection of ad hoc functionalities, and could have easily been named the "Doesn't Belong Anywhere Else" window. Nevertheless, it performs a number of vital functions, particularly for iPhone and iPod Touch developers. It acts as a gathering point for disparate resources, furnishes a framework for automating and scripting your workflows, provisions and authorizes devices for development, aids in iPhone app debugging, and even provides a means of managing non-Xcode projects.

Choose the Window ➪ Organizer (Control+Command+O) command to open the organizer window. There is only one organizer window; it doesn't belong to any project. The organizer window has a set of predefined groups on the left. Click the details button at the bottom of the window to expand or collapse the optional details pane on the right.

FIGURE 22-1

The first part of this chapter focuses on the Projects & Sources group. Here you can manage projects, folders, documents, and other file items, attach custom scripts to those items, and perform basic manipulations like editing, moving, and renaming them.

The later sections deal with the Devices and iPhone Development groups. These are specialized features designed specifically for iPhone and iPod Touch development.

PROJECTS & SOURCES

The Projects & Sources group lets you collect projects, folders, and files in a single location. Once you have added items to the organizer, you can:

➤ Open or edit items

➤ Rename, move, and copy files

➤ Build, clean, and run projects

➤ Execute custom scripts

➤ Search folders

➤ Take snapshots

These actions are available via the add menu or action menu in the lower-left corner of the window, the action buttons in the toolbar, and the Right/Control+click contextual menu for each item. All four menu locations are illustrated in Figure 22-2.

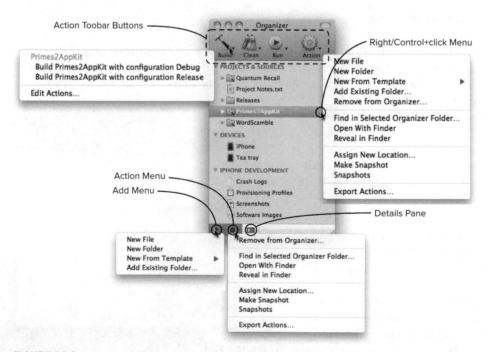

FIGURE 22-2

Adding Items to the Organizer

The first step in using the organizer is to add some items to it. Though you can add almost any item (document or folder) to the organizer, its capabilities bloom when you add folders, particularly project folders. Use any of these techniques to add items to the organizer:

➤ Drag a document or folder into the Projects & Sources group.

➤ Choose Add Existing Folder from either the add or Right/Control+click menu.

➤ Create a new file or folder and add it to the organizer using any of the following action menu commands:

  ➤ New File

  ➤ New Folder

  ➤ New From Template ➪ *Template Name*

Once you have an item in the organizer, what you can do with it depends greatly on what kind of item it is. The following table lists all of the things you can do with an item directly from the organizer, but not all actions apply to every type of item:

TO DO THIS	DO THIS
Open document or folder in Finder	Double-click the item or choose the Open With Finder command
Open project folder	Choose the Open With Finder command
Open project in project folder	Double-click the item
Edit a file that Xcode understands	Select the document
Reveal item in Finder	Choose the Reveal In Finder command
Edit folder location	Choose the Assign New Location command
Rename item	Select, and then single-click the item's name
Build a project in a folder	Choose a build action from the Build button
Clean a project in a folder	Choose an action from the Clean button
Run an executable in a folder	Choose an action from the Run button
Run a custom action script for a folder	Choose an action from the Action button
Search the contents of a folder	Choose the Find In Selected Organizer Folder command
Take a snapshot of a folder	Choose the Make Snapshot command
Manage the snapshots of a folder	Choose the Snapshots command
Remove a top-level item	Select it and then press the Delete key or choose the Remove from Organizer command

Xcode provides very basic actions for documents, significantly more for folders, and even more for project folders. The basic actions — open, edit, rename, and reveal in Finder — should all be self-explanatory.

 Items in the organizer are much closer to the "real thing." You might be tempted to treat them like source items in a project — that is, quasi-independent objects that abstractly refer to a real item in the file system — but organizer items act much more like items in the Finder. If you rename any item, drag an item into a folder, drag an item out of a folder, or delete an item in a folder, you're initiating a real action in the file system — the item will be renamed, moved, copied, or trashed. About the only non-destructive action you can take in the organizer is to delete a top-level item in the Projects & Sources group. This merely removes the organizer's reference to the item, but does not delete the source item.

The organizer makes a subtle distinction between a folder and a project folder that contains a project document. For example, double-clicking a project folder opens the project in Xcode, not the project folder in the Finder.

In a somewhat ironic twist, Xcode largely ignores project documents that you add to the organizer; it prefers that you add the project folder that contains it. You are free to add a project document, but Xcode will treat it like a generic document, not a project.

Any folder in the organizer can be associated with *actions*. Folders that have one or more actions are stamped with the Xcode "tool" icon. The Build, Clean, Run, and (the eponymous) Action actions that you can invoke are described in the "Using Organizer Actions" section.

Embracing Foreign Projects

The organizer is a great place to manage foreign — that is, non-Xcode — projects. As you'll see in later sections, you can define custom actions for organizer items; actions like make, clean, and install. Adding a project that's built using make or ant (a Java build tool) lets you manage that project from within Xcode. You can define actions to build various targets, perform source control, or anything else you need.

The add menu includes a number of templates for Java projects that are built with ant. Use these as starting points for subsuming your non-Xcode projects into the organizer, then automate them using organizer actions.

Searching Organizer Folders

You can search all of the files within a folder in the organizer using the multi-file search window. To search the contents of a folder, follow these steps:

1. Select a folder in the organizer.

2. Choose the Find in Selected Organizer Folder command in the actions menu.

3. Perform your search using the multi-file search window.

The multi-file search window is described in Chapter 8. It's identical to using the project find window, except that the target file set is permanently set to In Selected Organizer Folder.

Taking Snapshots

You can take and restore snapshots of any top-level folder in the organizer. To take a snapshot, choose Make Snapshot from the action menu. To review, compare, restore, or delete a snapshot, choose Snapshots from the action menu.

Using snapshots in the organizer is identical to using snapshots in a project, described in Chapter 11. When taking snapshots from within your project, the project folder gets copied. In the organizer, the snapshot is whatever top-level folder you've selected in the organizer.

> *Organizer snapshots and project snapshots are maintained independently. That is, making a snapshot of a project folder in the organizer does not add a snapshot to that project's snapshot window, and vice versa.*

USING ORGANIZER ACTIONS

The action buttons in the toolbar execute action scripts that (can potentially) perform an almost unlimited variety of tasks. Actions can only be defined for folder items in the organizer. A newly added non-project folder will (probably) have no actions defined. Xcode automatically generates a number of useful actions whenever you add a project folder to the organizer. You are free to use, modify, remove, and add your own actions, as you'll see in the next few sections.

Each action toolbar button is a combination of a button and a menu. Click and hold the button — don't Right/Control+click the button, you'll only get the toolbar menu — to reveal its action menu, as shown in the upper left of Figure 22-2. It lists the actions defined for the selected folder along with an Edit Actions command.

Notice that one of the actions in the menu is checked. This is the *default action*. If you simply click the action button, this is the action that will be performed. Executing a different action in the list also makes it the new default. Just remember that clicking the button will perform the last selected action again.

Automatically Created Actions

When you add a project folder to the organizer, Xcode generates a number of actions automatically — the exception to this is described in the "Preserving and Sharing Actions" section later in this chapter. The actions it generates are based on the project documents found in the project folder. After adding a project folder you will find:

➤ The Build button has a build action for each build configuration in the project.

➤ The Clean button has a clean action and a clean all action for each build configuration in the project.

➤ The Run button has a run action and a debug action for each build configuration in the project.

➤ The Action button has an install action for the project.

Normally, a project folder only has a single project document. If your project folder has multiple project documents, a complete set of actions is added for each project. Thus, a folder with two project documents, each with three build configurations, will result in six actions being generated for the Build button and 12 actions in each of the Clean and Run buttons.

The progress and output of the Build, Clean, and Run buttons appear in a separate organizer window. The output of Action button actions is determined by the action (described later). All organizer actions run scripts — either shell scripts or Automator actions — that run, more or less, independently of Xcode. The build actions are performed by the xcodebuild tool (see Chapter 17). Starting a build action does not open the project in Xcode, nor will it start building an open project in Xcode. The build runs in a separate process and an organizer build window collects the results.

Notice also that's there's no mention of targets, or the active executable in the automatically generated actions. The actions generated by Xcode build the default target and use the default executable. If you want some control over those, you'll want to customize your actions, as described in the next section.

Creating Custom Actions

Choose the Edit Actions command from the action toolbar button's menu to redefine its actions. The Edit Actions command presents an action sheet, as shown in Figure 22-3.

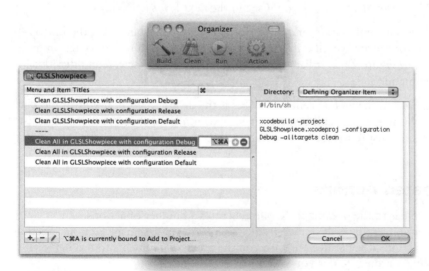

FIGURE 22-3

The action sheet lists the actions defined for the button. Here you can:

➤ Rename, reorder, and delete actions

➤ Assign action to a keyboard shortcut

➤ Edit the definition of an action

➤ Create new actions

Rename the action's name in the menu by clicking its name. Reorder it by dragging items in the list. Choose the New Separator command from the Add button menu in the lower-left corner of the window to insert a gray menu separator. Choose Edit ➪ Delete or click the – button at the bottom to delete an action or separator.

To assign an action a keyboard shortcut, select the shortcut cell in the ⌘ column and type the key combination you want to assign. If the combination you've chosen conflicts with one already assigned, Xcode will alert you at the bottom of the window, as shown in Figure 22-3. Choose a different combination and press it (the key combination). Click the – button next to the shortcut to delete a key combination — pressing the Delete key simply assigns the Delete key to the action. To assign multiple shortcuts to the same action, click the + button.

Keyboard shortcuts are only active when the folder item that owns the action is selected in the organizer. Thus, you can assign the same keyboard shortcut to one action of every top-level folder in your organizer without creating any shortcut conflicts.

The definitions of actions are edited in the right side of the action sheet. What appears there depends on the type of action, explained in the next section. The actions automatically generated by Xcode are all shell script actions. The script of the action is displayed in an editing pane, where you are free to customize it in any way you see fit. For example, you may want to add a `-target` argument so that the action consistently builds the same target, rather than relying on the project's last active target setting. Just remember to update the action's title appropriately if you significantly alter what it does.

You can create a new action by choosing New Shell Script, Add Script File, or Add Automator Workflow from the Add menu button. The different types of actions and how they can be customized are described in the next few sections.

The Anatomy of an Action

Every action has four attributes:

➤ The shell script or Automator action to execute

➤ A working directory

➤ An input source

➤ An output destination

The script is what defines the action. You have all of the POSIX and Automator tools at your disposal, which gives you an immense amount of latitude in designing your action.

To some degree, the distinctions between the Build, Clean, Run, and Actions menus are purely taxonomic. You can attach a script that builds your project to the Action button and a script that cleans your project to the Build button. The different buttons do impose different constraints, consistent with their intended purpose, but your scripts are in no way limited to the implied purpose of the button to which they're attached.

The Directory setting of the script is the working (default) directory that's set before the script is run. Action directories are described after the section "The Action Folder Hierarchy."

The input and output sources are different depending on which button you attach the action to. Actions in the Build, Clean, and Run buttons have no input and their output is always directed to the details pane or a new organizer window. Scripts in the Actions menu have an optional input source and a number of choices for output destinations.

Action Types

The three types of actions are described in the following table:

ACTION TYPE	DESCRIPTION
Shell Script	Executes a shell script that's part of the action definition.
Script File	Runs an existing executable script file.
Automator Workflow	Runs an existing Automator workflow document.

The script of either a shell script or script file action can be any executable POSIX script. The script interpreter is typically the default shell (/bin/sh), but could just as easily be bash, tcsh, perl, or ruby.

The Run button is an exception; the settings for a shell script in the Run button menu allow you to choose an executable and provide it with a list of command-line arguments — presumably the executable that you want launched. You can choose an optional debugger to attach to the process. To run an arbitrary script, use a script file action or direct the shell to launch an existing script.

The Build, Clean, and Run buttons distinguish themselves by setting the ACTION environment variable before they start a script. Your script can test this environment variable for the values BUILD, CLEAN, or RUN and adjust its behavior. This allows you to create a single script that behaves differently depending on which organizer button it's attached to. For example, a script attached to the Build button could build a complex product and stop, but when attached to the Run button could perform the same build and then immediately launch it.

The Action Folder Hierarchy

Actions can be attached to any folder in the organizer. When you select a folder in the organizer, the actions that appear in the action toolbar buttons are an aggregate of the actions attached to that folder and all of the actions attached to any of its enclosing folders. Take the example project shown in Figure 22-4.

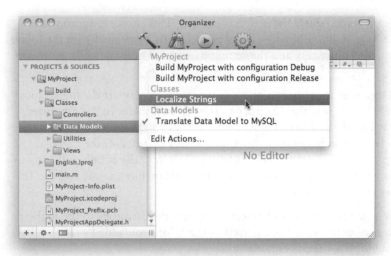

FIGURE 22-4

The MyProject project folder contains a Classes subfolder, which itself contains Controllers, Data Models, Utilities, and Views subfolders. Actions have been attached to the MyProject, Classes, and Data Models folders — these folders appear with a "tool" stamp on their folder icon.

When you select the Data Model folder and open the Build action menu, as shown in Figure 22-4, the menu includes all of the actions defined for the MyProject, Classes, and Data Models folders, organized by the folders that define them. If you had selected the Classes or Controllers folder, only the actions for the MyProject and Classes folders would have been listed.

When you're editing the contents of an action toolbar button, a navigation bar appears at the top of the action sheet. Use this to navigate to the actions attached to enclosing folders. An example is shown at the top of Figure 22-5.

Action Directory

The working directory is set to a specific path before the action's script or workflow executes. By default, it's the directory of the item that owns the action, but can be any of the following:

ACTION DIRECTORY	DESCRIPTION
Defining Organizer Item	The folder in which the action is defined
Selection	The selected folder in the organizer
Top-Level Organizer Item	The highest enclosing folder in the organizer; the folder item you added to the organizer
Home Directory	Your account's home folder
File System Root	The root directory

The Defining Organizer Item is the folder where the action is defined. This choice is appropriate when the action performs something — like a build — that's permanently associated with the folder to which it's attached. This is the default setting and the setting used by all automatically generated actions.

The Selection and Top-Level Organizer Item choices allow your action to play off the hierarchical organization of action folders. Selection sets the directory to the selected folder in the organizer, which might not be the folder where the action is defined. This allows you to create an action that can be individually applied to different subfolders. In the example in Figure 22-4, the Classes folder defines a Localize Strings action. By setting its directory to Selected, the action will run on the selected folder. This allows you to choose an individual source folder (like Views) and run the enclosed action (from Classes) on just the contents of that folder.

The Top-Level Organizer Item is just the opposite of Selection. It sets the directory to the highest enclosing folder in the organizer, essentially anchoring itself in the folder you added to the organizer — never any of the subfolders that it contains.

Home Directory and File System Root are alternatives that ignore the organizer folder structure and set the working directory to your home folder (~) or the POSIX file system root (/).

Input and Output

Only actions attached to the Action button can specify where they get their input and what happens to the script's output. For all other action buttons, scripts receive no input (/dev/null) and their output is captured in a build window (Build and Clean) or a console window (Run).

Action input can be set to either Selection or No Input, as shown in Figure 22-5.

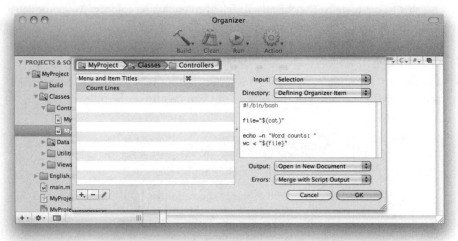

FIGURE 22-5

Selection doesn't mean that the contents of the selected item are piped to the script. It means that *the path* of the selected item is piped to the script. This allows you to write action scripts that act on individual files, but might require some finesse in obtaining that information.

The example shown in Figure 22-5 presents a simple action that counts the lines, words, and characters in the selected file. To accomplish this, it obtains the path of the selected file in the organizer using the statement file="$(cat)". This bash statement pipes the contents of stdin into a literal string, and then assigns it to the file variable.

The output of an action script (stdout) can be directed to any of the following destinations:

➤ Discard Output

➤ Display in Alert

➤ Place on Clipboard

➤ Open in New Document

➤ Open as HTML

The default is Open in New Document and presents the output of your action in either the organizer details pane or a new window.

The remaining choices are self-evident. Be careful when choosing Display in Alert that the output of your script is never too verbose.

Xcode can optionally direct any error messages (stderr) from your script to one of the following destinations:

➤ Ignore Errors

➤ Display in Alert

➤ Place on Clipboard

➤ Merge with Script Output

Ignore Errors discards the stderr output. Merge combines stderr with stdout. The rest take independent action with any error messages. Note that setting both output and errors to either Display in Alert or Place on Clipboard is equivalent to setting errors to Merge with Script Output.

Preserving and Sharing Actions

Deleting a top-level item from the organizer discards all actions defined for it, or any of its enclosing folders. If you add the folder back to the organizer, only the automatically generated actions will appear. This is a shame, because you might have put a lot of thought and effort into those actions.

You can preserve your actions, automatically restore them in the future, and share your actions with other developers by first exporting your actions to an .xccommands file. To export a set of actions, follow these steps:

1. Define the actions for an organizer folder.

2. Select the folder in the organizer.

3. Choose the Export Actions command from the actions menu.

4. Give the .xccommands file a name and save it in a folder — the obvious choice being the one where you exported the commands, but it can be any folder.

Importing and sharing your actions is devilishly simple. Place the exported .xccommands file in a folder. The next time you add a folder to the organizer, here's what happens:

➤ Xcode looks for an .xccommands file in each folder it adds to the organizer.

➤ If it finds an .xccommands file, the file is imported and defines the actions for that folder.

➤ An .xccommands file overrides any automatic actions that would normally be generated by Xcode.

➤ Only the first .xccommands file found is imported per folder.

To preserve the actions you've defined for a project, simply export your actions to an .xccommands file and save it in that project's folder. The next time you, or anyone, adds that project folder to the organizer, your custom set of actions will appear.

Action Ideas

The use of actions is almost unlimited, but here are a few of my favorites:

➤ **Clean builds of a specific target and configuration:** The script performs a clean build, immediately followed by a full build.

➤ **Release builds:** Perform a clean build of the project, and then package the resulting product in a disk image, archive, or Installer package. If your product release process isn't completely automated, it should be.

➤ **Tag releases in source control:** My script, shown here, extracts the product version from a header file in the project, then uses that value to tag the entire project in the Subversion repository. Once I've built my release product and am happy with the results, I use this action to tag it in source control.

```bash
#!/bin/bash

PROJ_DIR="${PWD}"
PROJ_NAME="$(basename "${PROJ_DIR}")"

# Extract the short version string from the source file
VERSION=$(awk '/#define.*VERSION_SHORT[ \t]/ { print $3 }'↩
"${PROJ_DIR}/Version.h")
echo "version ${VERSION}"

REPOS="svn+ssh://mini.local/Users/Shared/Subversion/${PROJ_NAME}"
TAG=$(tr '.' '-' <<< ${VERSION})
echo "creating tag release-${TAG}"
svn copy -m "Release ${VERSION}" "${REPOS}/trunk" "${REPOS}/tags/↩
release-${TAG}"
```

Automating your workflow will make you more productive and your development more consistent. The organizer is the perfect place to collect and manage those processes.

DEVICES

The Devices and iPhone Development groups in the organizer are designed specifically to support the special needs of iPhone and iPod developers. Much of the information in these two groups overlap. The difference is in their perspective; the Devices group displays information about actively connected devices, whereas the iPhone Development group — described in a later section — aggregates historical development information from all of your devices.

Adding and Removing Devices

iPhone and iPod Touch devices are automatically added to the organizer whenever you connect one to your computer while Xcode is running. Once added, they persist until removed from the organizer. The organizer shown in Figure 22-6 has had two devices added. The device named "iPhone" is currently connected, as indicated by the green dot next to its name, whereas the device named "Tea tray" is not.

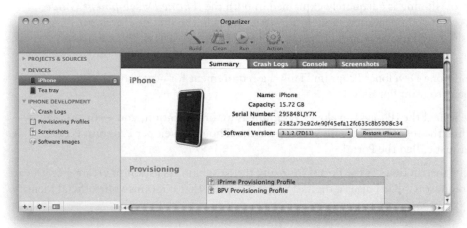

FIGURE 22-6

The activities in the Devices group interact directly with the connected device. A device that's not connected does little but display the message "This device is not currently connected." You'll see the identity of the device and you can browse previously downloaded crash reports — but that's about it.

To remove an obsolete device from your organizer, Right/Control+click the device name and choose the Remove From Organizer command. You can also have Xcode ignore a particular device, such as a personal iPod that you do not use for development. To do that, plug in the device and choose the Ignore Device command from the same menu.

You interact with your development device by connecting it to your computer, selecting it in the organizer, and then choosing the desired tab that appears in the details pane. The tabs are Summary, Crash Logs, Console, and Screenshots. The functions of each are described in the next few sections.

The Summary tab shows the name, serial number, unique device identifier (UDID), and the version of the operating system installed on your device. You'll need the UDID to register your device for development. You can obtain it by copying text from the details pane, or by Right/Control+clicking the device name in the Devices group and choosing the Copy Device Identifier command.

For the sake of brevity, both the organizer and this book use the generic term "iPhone" to mean any iPhone, iPod Touch, or similar device that's supported by Xcode. This is not a slight to any iPod Touch users nor is it meant to exclude any future Apple devices.

Installing Provisioning Profiles

Before you can get started doing any kind of iPhone development — or more precisely, before you can begin to do any Apple-sanctioned iPhone development on an Apple device — you must provision your iPhone. Provisioning is basically the installation of a set of digital signatures, some that you generate and others obtained from Apple, that authorize your iPhone to execute your application for the purposes of development. The iPhone will refuse to install or launch an application that has not been digitally signed by both its author (that's you) and Apple.

The process of provisioning is adequately explained in both the *iPhone Development Guide*, included in the Xcode documentation, and in the instructions in the iPhone Developer Program Portal, the web site you'll use to obtain provisioning profiles. Nevertheless, I'll summarize the steps here:

1. Join the iPhone Developer Program. This is a requirement for accessing the iPhone Developer Program Portal.

2. If you've joined the iPhone Developer Program as an organization, you — or someone — must define the team members allowed to use the iPhone Developer Program Portal, hereafter just called the Portal.

3. Follow the instructions at the Portal for using the Keychain Assistant to create a certificate signing request (CSR). This is a digitally signed request that contains your official identity.

4. Upload your CSR to the Portal. Review the request and approve it.

5. Apple then creates a *development certificate*, which is digitally signed by both you and Apple. An iPhone uses these signatures to determine the authenticity of an application.

6. Download the development certificate and install it on your keychain. If you need to do iPhone development using other computers or accounts, you will have to transfer copies of your private key (the one used to create the CSR) and your development certificate to those computers.

7. Make backups of your private key and development certificate and put them in a safe place, or places.

8. With the development certificate in place, you can now authorize individual devices for development. Plug each device into Xcode and use the organizer to obtain its Unique Device Identifier (UDID). Copy your device's UDID to the clipboard by selecting the ID in the Summary tab, or Right/Control+click on the device name and choose the Copy Device Identifier command. Register your device in the Portal.

9. Create an application identifier for the application you want to run on your registered development iPhone. Your application's identifier is a combination of a reverse-DNS name that you assign and a Bundle Seed ID generated by the Portal. An example would be `8E945J6902.com.wiley.proxcode.iPrime`. In the Properties tab of the app target of your project, set the Identifier field to be the same identifier, without the Bundle Seed ID. In this example, the application identifier must be set to `com.wiley.proxcode.iPrime`.

10. Register you application ID with the Portal.

11. With all the preliminaries out of the way, you can now use the Portal to generate provisioning profiles. A provisioning profile combines your development certificate, developer identity, device identity, and application identifier. It defines what combination of developers and devices your application is permitted to run on, to be debugged on, and similar development privileges.

12. Download the provisioning profile from the Portal.

Once you've obtained one or more provisioning profiles, you need to install them into your development device. Plug in and select the device in the organizer. Either drag the provisioning profile document into the Provisioning list of the Summary tab, or click the + button below the list of provisioning profiles, as shown in Figure 22-7, and choose the provisioning profile to install.

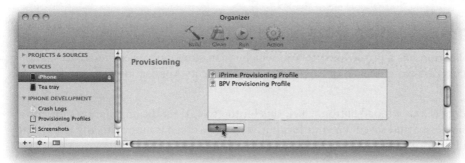

FIGURE 22-7

You're likely to create a new provisioning profile for each application you develop, although it's possible to create a wildcard profile that provisions multiple applications with similar IDs.

To remove a provisioning profile from the device, select it and click the – button.

Managing Development Applications

The next section in the Summary tab lists the applications that you have installed on your device, as shown in Figure 22-8. This list includes applications from Apple and other vendors, in addition to the applications that you've installed during development. The only applications that you can affect here are those that you've installed for development purposes. To remove any commercial applications, do so using the device or iTunes.

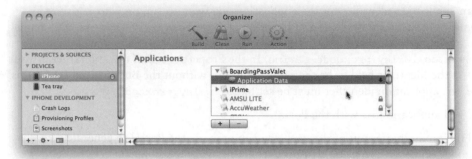

FIGURE 22-8

Normally your applications get installed on your device as a consequence of development. Whenever you run or debug an iPhone app on a device, Xcode first downloads and installs the application before starting it. For whatever purpose, you can also install applications you've built (and provisioned) manually. Click the + button and select the application bundle to install. The application is installed immediately.

The more useful feature is the ability to remove applications that you're done developing. Select an application and click the − button. After removing the application, you'll probably want to remove its provisioning profile as well.

Downloading Application Data

Each iPhone application has a private directory in which it can store data, user preferences, and resources. To access this data, expand the application to expose its Application Data package, also shown in Figure 22-8.

Next to the package is a download button. Click this button to extract the application's private directory from the device and save it on your local drive. The package is automatically expanded and appears as a folder of files.

Installing Alternate Operating Systems

During development, you will want to test your application against different versions of the operating system. The currently installed operating system on your device appears in the pop-up menu in the Summary tab.

If you have other iPhone OS SDKs installed, select one from the menu. Apple also makes pre-release or seed versions available to developers from time to time. If you've downloaded one of these software seeds, select it by choosing the Other Version command in the OS version menu, as shown in Figure 22-9.

FIGURE 22-9

After choosing a new OS, click the Restore iPhone/iPod button next to it. Xcode will erase your device — deleting all applications and data — and install the selected operating system. You can now install and test your application.

 Installing a different OS erases everything on your device. If you have applications or data you want to preserve, first synchronize your device with iTunes. iTunes will make a backup of your device. After testing, launch iTunes again. In the Summary tab for the device, click the Restore button and do not request another backup. After your device has been reset, select an existing backup. iTunes will restore your device and all of its data.

Reviewing Crash Logs

The Crash Logs tab lets you examine any crash logs or panic reports that have been downloaded from the device, as shown in Figure 22-10. Crash logs are automatically downloaded by the organizer and iTunes.

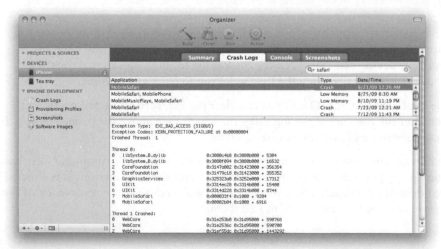

FIGURE 22-10

You can browse a report by selecting it in the list. Right/Control+click a report to delete it or reveal its text file in the Finder.

Monitoring the Device's Console

Like Mac OS X, the iPhone OS also has a console log. This is the collection point for diagnostic messages emitted by iPhone applications and other processes.

The Console Logs tab, as shown in Figure 22-11, reads the console log from the device.

FIGURE 22-11

This is the actual running console log, downloaded from the connected device. If you have an application running on your device, you can check the console log for messages in real time. The console log doesn't update automatically; click the Reload button to fetch any new messages.

Much like the Console application in Mac OS X, you can clear the log, save a selected portion of the log to a text file, or filter the contents of the log using the search field above the pane. The search field performs both case-sensitive and case-insensitive searches.

Use the console to find diagnostic messages output by your application while it's running. Note that when you run or debug an app via Xcode, the output of NSLog() and similar functions is redirected to the Run Console window of the project. These messages will also appear in the console log of the device, but you don't have to open the console log to find them.

Capturing Screenshots and the Default Image

The Screenshots tab displays the screenshots that been captured for this device, lets you take a screenshot, and will automatically install a screenshot as the default — that is, launch screen — for an iPhone application.

Screenshots are useful for documenting your application, sharing results with other developers, and examining interface anomalies.

The Screenshots tab is divided into two panes, as shown in Figure 22-12. One the left are all of the screenshots collected for this device. On the right you can view a selected screenshot or take a new screenshot.

FIGURE 22-12

To take a screenshot, run your application and arrange the screen to your liking. In the Xcode organizer, click the Capture button. Xcode instructs the device to take a screenshot and then downloads it into the organizer.

You can browse previously taken screenshots on the left. Select a screenshot to view it full size. You can also do any of the following:

➤ Drag a screenshot into the Finder to copy the screenshot file.

➤ Press Delete, or Right/Control+click and choose the Delete Screenshot command, to delete a screenshot.

➤ Install the screenshot as the Default screen for an iPhone application.

The default screen of an iPhone application is an image file that appears while the application is still loading. It can be used to present an entertaining splash screen or annoy users with crass advertising, but it's often used to make the application appear to load faster than it really does. This last trick is accomplished by making a screenshot of the initial view of your application with no content, and then installing that as the default image. When the user taps your app, a full-fledged interface appears (without content) almost immediately. What's really happening is the application is still launching while the user is looking at the default image. As soon as the app starts up, the display seamlessly refreshes.

To create this bit of prestidigitation, follow these steps:

1. Open your iPhone application project.

2. Run your application on the device and wait until its first window appears, with no content.

3. In the organizer, take a screenshot.

4. Click the Save As Default Image button and choose your Xcode project.

The Save As Default Image button adds a `Default.png` file to your project's Resources group. Of course, you could have done this yourself, and you're free to provide any kind of `Default.png` file that you want.

 Screenshots taken in the organizer and screenshots taken using your device are not intermingled. If you've taken a screenshot on the device — by holding down the sleep and home buttons — use iPhoto to download the image file. You can then import it into your project.

iPHONE DEVELOPMENT

The iPhone Development group is largely a rehashing of local and historical information that you've already seen in the Devices group. The key difference is that the information in the iPhone Development group is obtained from your local system and applies to all of your devices, connected or not.

Crash Logs

The Crash Logs group is an aggregate list of all the crash logs from all of your devices. It functions the same way the Crash Logs tab in the Devices group does.

Provisioning Profiles

This group lists the status of all of the provisioning profiles you've installed on your system, as shown in Figure 22-13.

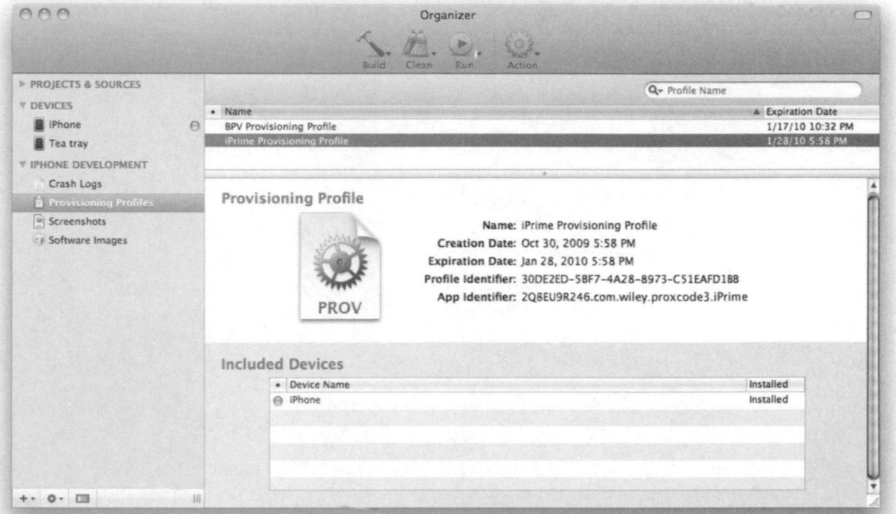

FIGURE 22-13

Select a profile to display its details and the list of devices where it is currently installed.

Press Delete or Right/Control+click a profile and choose the Delete Profile command to permanently delete a provisioning profile from your system. You can also choose the Reveal Profile in Finder command to locate the file.

Screenshots

This group is identical to the Screenshots tab of an individual device, except that it shows all of the screenshots captured in the organizer.

Software Images

Finally, the Software Images group lists the operating system packages that are installed on your system. These are the packages that allow you to install different versions of the iPhone OS on your device. See the "Installing Alternate Operating Systems" section, earlier in this chapter.

SUMMARY

The organizer is a powerful new addition to Xcode that lets you organize your project, devices, and tasks at a level above your individual projects. By customizing and sharing actions you automate repetitive workflow and can share those solutions with other developers. You now know how to connect, register, and interact with your iPhone and iPod Touch devices.

The final chapter turns to what many consider to be an endless source of joy and entertainment: tweaking obscure options and settings in Xcode, customizing it to suit your every whim.

23

Customizing Xcode

➤ Setting expert preferences

➤ Changing command key shortcuts and editor key bindings

➤ Using alternate editor applications

➤ Creating custom text macros and command scripts

➤ Making your own project, file, and target templates

Apple is famous for developing spare and elegant software. Rare indeed is the Apple application that suffers from "featurosis" — a malady of ever-expanding specialized features that eventually smother an application in an incomprehensible maze of commands and options.

Developers, however, are not consumers. At least they don't think of themselves as consumers. Developers are professionals that expect, nay demand, that almost every aspect of the tools they use be under their control to alter, repurpose, and tweak as they see fit. I have personally worked with a developer who, dissatisfied with the warnings produced by a compiler, downloaded its source code, corrected the perceived flaw, and built his own personalized version to use. Although the wisdom of his actions are debatable, the spirit of "if you don't like the way it works, build your own" runs deep and strong through the developer community.

For this reason, Xcode is a departure from most software produced by the engineering teams at Apple. Xcode has a dizzying array of customizable options, as witnessed by the monstrous Xcode Preferences window. Using the Xcode interface, you can completely customize the keystrokes used to invoke every Xcode command and motion. The extensive set of build settings enable you to specify any of the innumerable switches passed to compilers, linkers, and other tools employed by Xcode. You can completely reorganize the build process, and even assume complete responsibility for it. You are free to use a different text editor. You can even alter seemingly inconsequential interface details, such as the highlight colors used by the debugger.

Surprisingly, the list doesn't stop there. There are scores of hidden and undocumented customizations in Xcode. Most are application settings that you can alter by editing the Xcode preferences file, as discussed in this chapter. You can also create your own templates and customize the Xcode application by adding your own commands.

 Most undocumented features are unsupported by Apple and the Xcode development team. I've tested every customization presented in this chapter, but that doesn't mean they will work in future versions of Xcode. Customization features that turn out to be popular are often re-implemented and appear in future versions in a friendlier and better-supported form. Check the release notes for the feature you are looking for.

XCODE PREFERENCES

If you came to this chapter looking for the meaning of a particular Xcode preference setting, most of them are discussed in the chapter that the setting applies to. For example, the options in the Code Sense tab are discussed in the "Code Sense" section in Chapter 7. To point you in the right direction, the following table lists the tabs in the Xcode Preferences window and the chapter where those settings are explained.

PREFERENCE TAB	CHAPTER
General	3 and 6
Code Sense	7
Building	17
Distributed Builds	17
Debugging	18
Key Bindings	23
Text Editing	6
Font & Colors	6
Indentation	6
File Types	6

PREFERENCE TAB	CHAPTER
Opening Quickly	6
Source Trees	21
SCM	21
Documentation	12

The Xcode documentation also describes the preference settings for each topic. Chapter 12 of this book provides assistance in browsing the Xcode Help documents.

KEY BINDINGS

The only preference tab not covered in the other chapters is Key Bindings. The Key Bindings pane, shown in Figure 23-1, allows you define the keystroke combination associated with just about every command and action that Xcode performs. You will also see that a few actions are inaccessible in Xcode's default configuration and can only be accessed by assigning them a key binding.

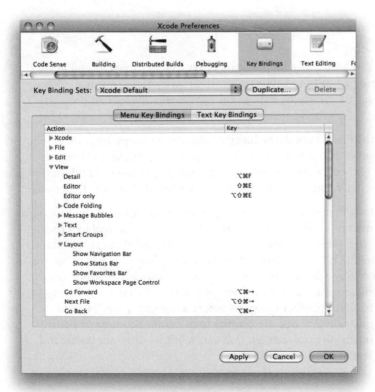

FIGURE 23-1

Key bindings are stored in sets. Use the Key Binding Sets pop-up menu to switch between any of the predefined sets that ship with Xcode, or any sets that you've defined. Choose a set and click the Apply or OK button, and the new bindings take effect immediately. If you want to create a new binding set, select a base set and click the Duplicate button. Give the key binding set a name, as shown in Figure 23-2. To delete the selected set, click the Delete button. You cannot edit or delete predefined sets. To customize one of the predefined sets, duplicate it and edit the new set. If you try to edit a predefined key binding set, Xcode offers to first duplicate the set.

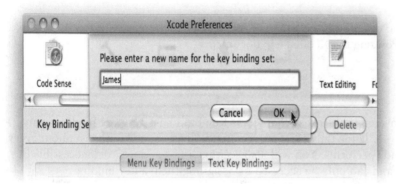

FIGURE 23-2

Menu Key Bindings

The Key Bindings pane has two tabs: Menu Key Bindings and Text Key Bindings. Menu key bindings, previously shown in Figure 23-1, bind keyboard shortcuts with the items in the Xcode menus. Menus items that are created dynamically, such as the list of recently opened projects, cannot be bound.

To edit a menu key binding, find the menu item in the hierarchy of menu groups and double-click its Key cell in the table. The menu item's current binding turns into an editable field, as shown in Figure 23-3. This is not a normal text edit field; it captures any single keystroke or combination you press. You've used it most recently in Chapter 22 when assigning keyboard shortcuts to actions.

To bind Command+P to the Xcode ➪ Preferences command, press Command+P on the keyboard. Instead of invoking the File ➪ Print command, Xcode captures the shortcut and replaces the previous key binding. Also shown in Figure 23-3 is a warning at the bottom of the pane that "~CM-P is currently bound to Print." This is a warning that the key binding that you chose for this command is currently assigned to another command. If you accept this key binding, the binding on the other command will be removed. This is your only warning that a conflicting key binding will be removed, so check for conflict messages before assigning a binding and immediately enter a shortcut combination that doesn't conflict with another command before going on. Unless, of course, your intention is to reassign that shortcut to a different command, in which case that's exactly what you'll get.

FIGURE 23-3

To accept a key binding change, click outside the edit field. There is no keyboard shortcut to accept a binding, because any keystroke you press will be captured as the new binding. To remove a key binding, double-click the binding to enter edit mode and then click the grey – button to the right of the cell.

Traditionally, key bindings for menu items are Command key combinations. However, you are free to assign any keystroke combination you want. Existing examples are commands like Edit ➪ Next Completion, which is bound to Control+., or Edit ➪ Select Next Placeholder, which is bound to Control+/. Be judicious in these assignments — for example, assigning the Tab key to the Xcode ➪ Quit command is *not* recommended.

Letter keys have no sense of case in key bindings. Command+A is one key combination, and Command+Shift+A is a different key combination. The state of the Caps Lock key has no influence on key bindings.

When editing key bindings, Xcode displays the symbols listed in the following table for special keys:

SYMBOL	KEY
~CM	Command
~OP	Option
~SH	Shift
~CT	Control
←	Left Arrow
→	Right Arrow
↑	Up Arrow
↓	Down Arrow
→ǀ	Tab
↺	Esc
⌫	Delete (backspace)
⌦	Delete (forward)
‡	Page Up
‡	Page Down
↖	Home
↘	End
↵	Return
⌤	Enter
Space	Space

Text Key Bindings

Text key bindings are the keystrokes that the text editor interprets as actions. By altering the text key bindings, you can change the behavior of the Xcode text editor.

Editing a text key binding is almost identical to the procedure for editing menu key bindings, as you can see in Figure 23-4. The only significant difference is that you can assign multiple key bindings to the same action. Any of the key combinations listed will invoke that action.

To alter a key binding, double-click the Keys field of the binding. Set the first, or replace the existing, key combination by typing the desired combination. To add additional key combinations to the same action, click the + button to the right side of the edit field, as shown in Figure 23-4. To delete a specific key combination, click the combination in the list to select it and then click the – button.

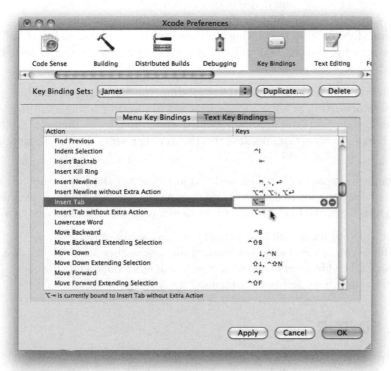

FIGURE 23-4

In the editor, any regular character key that is not assigned an action is inserted literally into the text — assuming the encoding of the document permits it.

To give you an idea of the kind of subtle change you can make to the editor, I'll step you through the process of turning off the automatic indenting that normally occurs when you press the Tab key.

Pressing the Tab key in most text editors simply inserts a tab character into the text. If you look at the key bindings for Xcode, you'll see that the Tab key is tied to the Insert Tab action. On the face of it, it would appear that Xcode does the same thing. In reality, Insert Tab adds an additional level of convenience; it automatically re-indents the line after inserting the tab.

The insert tab action that does nothing but insert a single tab character is named, cleverly, Insert Tab Without Extra Action. Normally, the automatic re-indenting of your text is a huge convenience, but you might find yourself in a situation where you just want a tab to be a tab. You can fix this in the key bindings for the editor, as follows:

1. Open the Key Bindings tab of the Xcode Preferences. If you don't have your own key bindings set already, duplicate the current key bindings set and give it a new name.

2. In the Text Key Bindings table, find the Insert Tab action and double-click its current binding (usually the Tab key).

3. Hold down the Option key and press the Tab key. Click outside the field to set it.

4. Click the OK button to adopt the new key bindings.

Editing the text key bindings changes the key combinations that Xcode will use in all text editor panes. In steps 2 and 3, you replaced the key binding for the Insert Tab action — the action with the extra features — with Option+Tab. Because the Option+Tab was previously bound to Insert Tab Without Extra Action, Xcode warned you of the conflict (see the bottom of Figure 23-4) and deleted that binding when you accepted the new one.

Now the Tab key (alone) has no binding. Without a special key binding, the Tab key is treated like any other character. No special reformatting or navigation is attached to inserting a single tab character any more. Alternatively, you could have accomplished the same thing by binding the Tab key to the Insert Tab Without Extra Action action. Because the Tab key represents the tab character, both are equivalent.

Key bindings are global, and both the menu key bindings and text key bindings share the same table. A key combination can only be assigned to a single menu command or editor action. Keep this in mind when you're assigning non-Command key combinations to menu commands and vice versa.

Key bindings are stored by name in your local `~/Library/Application Support/Xcode/Key Bindings` folder as `.pbxkeys` files. You can exchange key binding files with other users. To install a key binding file, quit Xcode, copy a key bindings file into the `Key Bindings` folder, launch Xcode, and select the new set from the Key Bindings Sets pop-up menu.

USING AN EXTERNAL EDITOR

Is customizing the editor keystrokes and command shortcuts not enough? What if your favorite editing feature isn't included in Xcode's editors? What if Xcode doesn't even have an editor for the kind of file you've added? Fear not; you can elect to use a third-party editor, instead of the built-in editors provided by Xcode, for some or all of your editing needs.

Although Xcode's editors are powerful, Xcode has a relatively limited feature set when editing certain types of source files, like XML and HTML. The ability to plug a dedicated HTML editor into Xcode adds a powerful new dimension to your development environment.

Xcode has several different built-in editors. What you have been exposed to most in this book is the Source Code editor. There is also a Plain Text editor, an RTF (Rich Text File) editor, an XML Properties List editor, an Xcode Configurations Settings File editor, an AppleScript Dictionary editor, an Image editor, a Data Model editor, and a few others. The editor that is used when you open a file is determined by the settings in the File Types tab of the Xcode Preferences (see Chapter 6). Each file type that Xcode understands is associated with an editor. This can be one of the editors built into Xcode, an external application, or the decision can be deferred to the Finder.

Using an Alternate Editor Once

At any time, you can open a file using an alternate Xcode editor. Right/Control+click the source item and choose an editor from the Open As menu. The menu contains the list of Xcode's internal editors that are capable of editing that type of file. This is particularly useful when you need to edit or examine a file in a less structured way. For example, open a property list file (`Info.plist`) using the Plain Text editor if you want to edit the raw XML.

The Open With Finder command, found in the same menu, opens the file just as if you had opened the file in the Finder. For Xcode source files, it's very likely that this will be Xcode itself. To force a file to open in another application, use the Reveal In Finder command to locate the file. Drag the file to an application in the dock or open it using the Finder's Open With command. Alternatively, switch to the other application and use its File ⇨ Open command or drag a source item directly from the project window into the editor's dock icon.

Specifying the Default Editor

Changing an editor choice in the preferences changes the default editor for that file type for all projects. For each file type, there are essentially four possibilities:

- ➤ One of Xcode's built-in editors
- ➤ A specific external editor
- ➤ The default application the document is associated with in the operating system
- ➤ The default for the super-type

In Figure 23-5, the default editor for AIFF audio files is being changed from its default — open it using the Finder, which would most likely open iTunes — to launch the Sound Studio audio editing application.

FIGURE 23-5

The choice of Xcode editors is always limited to the editors that understand that file type. A `text.html` file can be edited using the Source Code editor or the Plain Text editor; the RTF editor does not understand HTML and is not a choice. The `text.rtf` file type can be set to use the RTF editor, the Source Code editor, or the Plain Text editor.

File types are arranged in a hierarchy. When a type is set to Default, it defers the choice to its enclosing supertype. The top-level types have pre-programmed choices based on what editors are available for that type. In general, if you set the editor for a supertype and set a subtype to Default, the subtypes will use the editor of the supertype. In the example shown in Figure 23-5, the editor for the `audio.aiff` type is being set to Sound Studio. If the editor for the `audio` supertype had been set instead, *all* of the audio subtypes (`audio.mp3`, `audio.au`, `audio.aiff`, and so on) would open using Sound Studio.

Using an External Editor

When External Editor is specified, Xcode tells that application to open the file instead of opening it in a separate window. The selection of an external editor does not affect single-pane operations, such as simply selecting a source file in the project window. The editor pane in the project window, the class browser, the Project Find window, and others will continue to use Xcode's internal editor to immediately display a file in the same window. Only double-clicking a source item or using the Open in Separate Editor command opens the file in its external editor.

External editors are not synchronized to the changes made in Xcode. Whenever Xcode is reactivated, it checks to see if any files were altered. Xcode cannot detect changes made in an external program before they are saved. Get in the habit of saving all of your changes before switching back to Xcode. If it detects changes, Xcode rereads the file and updates its display.

In the unfortunate situation where changes have also been made in both the Xcode editor and the external application, the dialog box shown in Figure 23-6 is presented. You can choose to keep the changes made in Xcode, ignoring the changes that were written to disk, or vice versa. Xcode does not have a merge function and cannot combine the changes made in two places. If you have inadvertently made important changes in both places, use the Keep Xcode Version choice. Reopen the file in the external editor, and then copy and paste the changes made there to the editor pane in Xcode. Save the file within Xcode to commit the combined changes. Another approach is to use Xcode's File ⇨ Save a Copy As (Shift+Option+Command+S) command to make a new file of the Xcode version, then use a utility like FileMerge to compare and combine the changes.

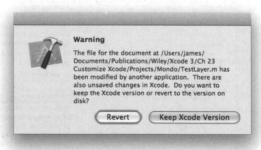

FIGURE 23-6

Because of the hazard of editing source files in both the external editor and Xcode, I recommend using the Condensed layout or leaving the editing pane in the project window collapsed. This reduces the temptation to make a quick edit in a file that might be opened elsewhere.

Supported External Editors

Xcode provides full support for BBEdit, Text Wrangler, SubEthaEdit, Emacs, xemacs, and Interface Builder. Only those installed on your system will appear in the menu of external editors. You can also select any other application, but Xcode will only provide limited support for it.

Full support means that Xcode communicates with the external editor and tells it to save files when appropriate. For example, when you build a project, you can have Xcode tell your external editor to save all of the unsaved files before compiling, just as it does for internally edited files. Similarly, closing a project saves all files in an external editor.

External editors with limited support means once the file is open, Xcode has no more interaction with the application. It is your responsibility to save and close the file in the editor as needed.

External editors do not use the file and line encodings, tab, or indent settings of the source item. Some editors, like BBEdit, either automatically detect the format or store that information in the resource fork of the file. Use the external editor to change the encoding. Then change the settings in the project's source item to match.

TEXT MACROS

In the "Text Macros" section of Chapter 6, you learned how to insert text macros using the Edit ➪ Insert Text Macro menu and via Code Sense. These macros can be great timesavers when using common programming idioms. If you regularly use the text macros, you may find that you want to customize the macros provided by Xcode or invent your own.

This is the first of the non-sanctioned Xcode customizations. At one time, Apple supported user-created text macro files and appeared to be moving toward formally documenting them. Since then, Apple has retreated and now states that custom text macros are not (officially) supported. Nevertheless, creating your own isn't difficult and all currently available versions of Xcode will honor user-defined text macros.

Apple has made a recent concession to its "not supported" position. Xcode 3.2 has an XCCodeSenseFormattingOptions expert setting that allows you to override text macro values using your user defaults. The "Expert Preferences" section, later in this chapter, explains how to set Xcode's user defaults. The "Sanctioned Text Macro Customization" section describes what text macro properties you can redefine. But first, it helps if you understand how text macro definitions interact with one another.

Creating Text Macro Definitions

Adding or altering text macros is accomplished by defining your own text macro definitions. Definitions are written using a simple C-like structure syntax and stored in plain text files with an extension of .xctxtmacro. You can create new definitions, or replace any of the existing definitions that come bundled with Xcode.

When Xcode starts, it assembles all of the text macro definitions by searching two locations: the Xcode application bundle and the /Developer/Library/Xcode/Specifications folder. Xcode no longer looks in your home folder's ~/Library/Application Support/Xcode/Specifications folder, so it's no longer possible to install per-user custom text macros. Xcode scans both of the locations and reads every `.xctxtmacro` file that it finds. All of the `.xctxtmacro` files are read and digested before reading the files in the next location.

 If you've created a custom text macro file and your macros don't appear in Xcode, check the Console application. Xcode will record problems parsing an `.xctxtmacro` file in the system log.

Every definition contains an `Identifier` property. This property is the unique identifier for each definition. Definitions with a duplicate `Identifier` completely replace any previously read definition; Xcode essentially ignores any previously read definition with the same `Identifier`. Thus, definitions defined in your custom files can selectively override any definition found in the Xcode bundle.

Macro Definition

An `.xctxtmacro` file consists of a comma-separated list of definition blocks. The entire list is surrounded by parentheses, with each definition block contained between curly braces. Thus, the high-level structure of an `.xctxtmacro` file is:

```
(
    {
    definition
    },
    {
    definition
    },
    …
)
```

A definition is an arbitrary collection of properties written as key/value pairs using the syntax *key* = *value*; . The value can be any text, a list, or another block of properties. A text value can be "naked" if it doesn't contain any special characters (such as whitespace) that would confuse the parser. If it does, it can be surrounded by quotes like a literal C string. Quoted strings can use the backslash to escape special characters.

Xcode defines a number of keys that have special meaning, some of which are required. You are free to add your own keys and use them as values in other definitions. The following shows an example definition:

```
{
    Identifier = c.printf;
    BasedOn = c;
    IsMenuItem = YES;
    Name = "Printf() Call";
    TextString = "printf(\"<#message#>\");";
    CompletionPrefix = printf;
}
```

The `.xctxtmacro` file also supports C (`/* … */`) and C++ (`// …`) style comments.

Text Macro Properties

Each definition block must include an `Identifier` key. This key is used both to uniquely identify each definition and to refer to it in other definitions. By convention, it should be a reverse domain name that mirrors the hierarchy of the definition — this will make more sense when I explain about inheritance — and it should not contain any special characters that would require it to be quoted. Each `Identifier` is unique and a definition with a duplicate `Identifier` value will completely suppress any previously defined definition with the same `Identifier`.

The remaining properties of a definition shape its purpose. You can use any combination of properties you wish, but only certain combinations make any sense. To help you, the text macros built into Xcode contain a set of macros that expand to prototype definitions for new text macros — yes, they're macro macros. You can find these in the Edit ➪ Insert Text Macro ➪ Text Macro Specifications menu.

The properties recognized by Xcode's text macro interpreter are listed in the following table:

MACRO PROPERTY	DESCRIPTION
Identifier	This is the unique identifier for the definition, and is a required property. The `Identifier` is not inherited.
Name	This is the descriptive name of the definition. For menu items, this is the name that will appear in the menu. When using Code Sense, the completion list will include this text as a description of the macro. The `Name` property is not inherited.
BasedOn	This property is the `Identifier` of the definition that this definition inherits. Most properties in the `BasedOn` definition are inherited; the exceptions are noted.
IsMenu	If set to YES, this definition creates a submenu in the Edit ➪ Insert Text Macro menu. The `Name` defines the title of the menu. Submenu items are not macros and are solely for organizing text macros into groups. The `IsMenu` property is not inherited.
IsMenuItem	If set to YES, this text macro creates a menu item in the Edit ➪ Insert Text Macro menu. If the definition is `BasedOn` an `IsMenu` definition (directly or indirectly), it will appear in that submenu group. Otherwise, it will appear as a top-level item in the Edit ➪ Insert Text Macro menu. The `IsMenuItem` property is not inherited.
TextString	The body of the text macro. This property defines the characters that will be inserted when the text macro is inserted. It can contain placeholders, described later, and variable references.

continues

(continued)

MACRO PROPERTY	DESCRIPTION
CompletionPrefix	This property is the "symbol" used to select the text macro using Code Sense. This is independent of the Name or TextString property of the text macro. For instance, a text macro that inserts a "do forever" loop could have a completion prefix of "forever". You could select this macro using code completion by typing as little as "fore". The CompletionPrefix property is not inherited.
IncludeContexts	A comma-separated list of the contexts where the definition is enabled. The root context, xcode, would enable the definition in any Xcode editor pane. The more specific context, xcode.lang.c, would enable the definition only when Xcode is editing a C or C-like language.
ExcludeContexts	A comma-separated list of the contexts where the definition should be disabled. Used to refine the IncludeContexts by excluding sub-contexts. For example, if IncludeContexts was (xcode.lang.c) and ExcludeContexts was (xcode.lang.c.comment, xcode.lang.c.string), then the definition would be active in all C source contexts, except when you're editing the text of a comment or in the middle of a literal string.
OnlyAtBOL	If set to YES, the macro will only appear as a Code Sense suggestion when the cursor position is at the beginning of a line.
CycleList	This property is a comma-separated list of definition identifiers. This list is used to order multiple text macros that share a single menu item. This allows you to associate multiple variants of macro with a single menu item. The first time you choose the menu item, the first macro in the list is selected. If you immediately select the text macro menu item again, the first macro is removed and replaced with the second macro in the list. The list is circular and will continue to substitute the different variants until you settle on the one you want. This property does not control the order in which text macros appear in the completion list — or cycled using Control+. — when using Code Sense. Only the first definition should define a CycleList.
DefaultSettings	This property is a block of properties that define default property values for inherited definitions. Any definition that inherits from a definition containing a DefaultsSettings property will inherit all of the properties defined therein.

Placeholders

Including placeholders (<#name#>) in the TextString property makes it easy to jump immediately to the places in the macro that need to be replaced with valid code or other content. After a text macro is inserted, the first placeholder is automatically selected. Text macros support a special form of placeholder that surrounds the name of the placeholder with exclamation marks: <#!name!#>.

If text in the editor pane is selected when the text macro is inserted, this special placeholder is automatically replaced with the selected text. If no text is selected, or the macro was inserted using code completion, the special placeholder acts like any other placeholder. A text macro can only include one special placeholder. If your text macro does not contain a special placeholder, and the user has text selected when the macro is inserted, the macro text replaces the original text.

Property References

Definitions can also include any other property name you wish to invent. Property names, either defined or inherited, can be inserted into any value using the syntax $(*key*), where *key* is the name of the property. In addition to any property values defined, you also have access to any of the macros listed in the "Template Macros" section, later in this chapter. For example, the reference $(FULLUSERNAME) will be replaced with the long account name of the current user.

The ability to define arbitrary property values, refer to property values in other properties, and inherit property values creates a flexible framework for designing modular text macro definitions. The following shows a simple example:

```
(
    {
        Identifier = james.main;
        TextString = "// main()\n// Written by
$(FULLUSERNAME)\n$(MainDecl)\n{\n\t\n\treturn (0);\n}\n";
        IsMenu = YES;
        Name = "James";
        ExcludeContexts = ( "xcode.lang.string", "xcode.lang.character",
                            "xcode.lang.comment", "xcode.lang.c.preprocessor" );
    },

    {
        Identifier = james.main.c;
        BasedOn = james.main;
        MainDecl = "int main( int argc, char** argv )";
        IncludeContexts = ( "xcode.lang.c" );
        OnlyAtBOL = YES;

        IsMenuItem = YES;
        Name = "main()";

        CompletionPrefix = main;
        CycleList = (
            james.main.c,
            james.main.java
            );
    },

    {
        Identifier = james.main.java;
        BasedOn = james.main;
        MainDecl = "public static int main( int argc, String[] argv )";
        IncludeContexts = ( "xcode.lang.java" );
        OnlyAtBOL = YES;
```

continues

(continued)

```
        IsMenuItem = NO;
        Name = "main()";

        CompletionPrefix = main;
    }

)
```

In this example, the `james.main` definition creates the generic definition for a text macro that inserts an empty `main()` function. It also creates a submenu in the Edit ➪ Insert Text Macro menu named "James."

The `TextString` property refers to the (as yet undefined) `MainDecl` property. The two definitions that follow, `james.main.c` and `james.main.java`, define actual text macros that appear in the text macro menu and code completion. Both inherit the `TextString` property defined in `james.main` (via the `BasedOn` property). The individual variants — one for C and the other for Java — define the `MainDecl` property that will replace the `$(MainDecl)` reference when the `TextString` property is resolved.

The end result is two macros that appear in the text macro menu and code completion as "main()". When invoked while editing a C source file, it inserts a `main()` function using the declaration `int main ( int argc, char ** argv )`. When inserted in a Java source file, it emits the same function but has a declaration of `public static int main( int argc, String[] argv )` instead.

You can find more complex examples of inheritance and property references in the `.xctxtmacro` files supplied with Xcode. Use the following Terminal command to ferret out the text macro files that come bundled with Xcode:

```
find /Developer -name '*.xctxtmacro'
```

Open these files in Xcode, or any text editor, to get a feel for how text macros are structured and organized. The text macros in Xcode are both elaborate and sophisticated, and because text macros are not officially explained anywhere, these files and the comments they contain are the closest thing you'll find to documentation.

Sanctioned Text Macro Customization

The text macros built into Xcode make extensive use of inherited properties that allow you to globally customize their formatting. For example, the `TextString` property defined by Xcode's try/catch macro looks like this:

```
TextString = "try$(BlockSeparator){\n\t<#!statements!#>\n}$(PostBlockSeparator)
catch$(PreExpressionsSpacing)($(InExpressionsSpacing)<#exception#>
$(InExpressionsSpacing))$(BlockSeparator){\n\t<#handler#>\n}
$(PostBlockSeparator)finally$(BlockSeparator){\n\t<#statements#>\n}";
```

The reason the macro is so complex is because all of the macros included in Xcode use a number of variables to define common formatting elements, such as the spacing before and after an expression. By overriding selected properties, you can redefine the formatting of every Xcode text macro with just a few lines.

This used to be done by creating your own text macro definition files. But now that Apple has shied away from supporting per-user text macro definitions, one of the most common reasons to do so is also cut off. Apple has, instead, provided the same functionality via an expert preference. The "Expert Preferences" section explains how to define these special settings.

The expert preference setting that affects text macros is named XCCodeSenseFormattingOptions. The value is a dictionary — this is one setting that's easier to edit using the Properties List Editor, rather than via the command line. It can contain values for any, or all, of the following text macro property values:

PROPERTY	DEFAULT	DESCRIPTION
BlockSeparator	""	Whitespace after the parenthesized expression of an if, for, or while statement and its opening brace.
PostBlockSeparator	"\n"	Whitespace after the closing brace of a block.
FunctionBlockSeparator	"\n"	Whitespace after a method or function name and argument-list declarations and its body.
PreExpressionsSpacing	" "	Whitespace between an if, for, and while keyword and the opening parenthesis.
InFunctionArgsSpacing	""	Whitespace inside a parenthesized function argument list (after the opening parenthesis and the closing parenthesis).
InExpressionsSpacing	""	Whitespace inside a parenthesized expression (after the opening parenthesis and the closing parenthesis).
PreFunctionArgsSpacing	""	Whitespace between a function name and the opening parenthesis.
PreCommaSpacing	""	Whitespace before a comma inside a function argument list.
PostCommaSpacing	" "	Whitespace after a comma inside a function argument list.
PreMethodTypeSpacing	" "	Whitespace before the parenthesized return type in an Objective-C method declaration.
PreMethodDeclSpacing	" "	Whitespace between the parenthesized return type and the method name in an Objective-C method declaration.
InMessageSpacing	""	Whitespace inside an Objective-C message expression — after the opening bracket and before the closing bracket.

continues

(continued)

PROPERTY	DEFAULT	DESCRIPTION
PreColonSpacing	""	Whitespace before a colon in an Objective-C method name or message expression.
PostColonSpacing	""	Whitespace after a colon in an Objective-C method name or message expression.
MessageArgSpacing	""	Whitespace between the parenthesized type and argument name in an Objective-C method declaration.
CaseStatementSpacing	"\t"	Relative indentation of a case keyword inside a switch block. A tab ('\t') character indents by the tab indentation width.

For example, if you want all code blocks inserted by Xcode text macros to place the opening curly brace on the next line of code, redefine the BlockSeparator property to "\n". The following command accomplishes this from the command line:

```
defaults write com.apple.Xcode XCCodeSenseFormattingOptions
-dict BlockSeparator '\n'
```

This command creates a dictionary in the Xcode user properties with a single key/value pair of BlockSeparator = '\n'. Note that this also replaces any previous dictionary that might have been set, another reason why using the Properties List Editor is a better idea.

EXPERT PREFERENCES

Expert Preferences are additional, often obscure, preferences for which there is no direct user interface for changing it. You set expert preferences by directly altering the settings in the preferences file for the Xcode application. This file is com.apple.Xcode.plist, located in your ~/Library/Preferences folder. There are two simple ways of changing these settings. However you alter them, remember that the Xcode application should not be running when you do. Changing some values while Xcode is running may have unpredictable consequences. It's best to first quit the Xcode application, make your changes, and then launch Xcode again.

The first method is to use the defaults command from a Terminal window. The syntax for setting a value in the Xcode preferences is as follows:

```
defaults write com.apple.Xcode key -type value
```

The write command tells the defaults command to set a value in the file. The last three arguments specify the symbol, the type of the value, and the value it will be set to. (Refer to the man page for the defaults command for more options.) For example, the drag-and-drop delay used by Xcode's text editor can be adjusted by setting the value for the NSDragAndDropTextDelay key. The command to set this value to 500 (milliseconds) is as follows:

```
defaults write com.apple.Xcode NSDragAndDropTextDelay -integer 500
```

To avoid any ambiguity in how the value is interpreted, it's recommended that you include a *-type* option that casts the value to a specific property list value type. The types that are most useful are:

- ➤ -string (the default)
- ➤ -int or -integer
- ➤ -float
- ➤ -bool or -boolean

When setting Boolean values, the defaults tool is very flexible. It will accept 0, 1, false, true, NO, and YES.

If you ever need to delete a preference value, returning it to its default value, use the delete command, like this:

```
defaults delete com.apple.Xcode key
```

The second method is to use the Property List Editor application included with the Xcode development tools. Figure 23-7 shows setting the same value by editing the com.apple.Xcode. plist property list file. Remember not to open the file until *after* you have quit the Xcode application. The Property List Editor makes setting complex values, like dictionaries and numeric types, much easier. Remember that the com.apple.Xcode.plist file contains *all* of Xcode's preferences and state settings; be mindful not to alter other internal settings indiscriminately, because it may affect Xcode's stability.

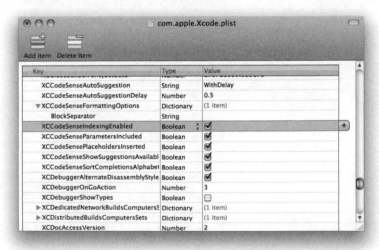

FIGURE 23-7

The following sections list some of the more useful expert preferences settings, grouped by subject. Apple has documented most of these in the Xcode User Defaults document. Search for it in the documentation, or read it online at http://developer.apple.com/mac/library/documentation/DeveloperTools/Reference/XcodeUserDefaultRef/. These hidden settings change from one version of Xcode to the next, so consult this list or the release notes if you can't find what you're looking for here.

Projects and Files

The following table lists the projects and files settings:

SETTING	DEFAULT	DESCRIPTION
PBXCustomTemplateMacroDefinitions	(none)	A dictionary of values used to replace variables in project and file templates. The canonical example is the (now obsolete) __MyCompanyName__ value.
PBXDontWarnIfProjectSaveFails	NO	Setting this to YES suppresses Xcode's warning that there were problems saving the project documents. Project documents are constantly being updated, and Xcode warns you if the file cannot be written. This occurs repeatedly if you have no write access to the document, such as a project on a CD-ROM.
PBXPreservePosixPermissionsOnSave	YES	If set to YES, Xcode tries to restore the POSIX file permissions whenever it saves a file. You may want to change this to NO if you are writing project files to a non-native or networked file system.
NSRecentDocumentsLimit	10	The maximum number of projects to keep in the File ⇨ Open Recent File and File ⇨ Open Recent Project menu.
XCOpenProjectFilesInsideFolders	NO	Setting this to YES lets you open a project document by opening its project folder. In the Open dialog, open a project folder and Xcode will find the first project document and open it instead. Useful if you open a lot of projects that have lots of files in the project folder. This option is known to cause problems with keyboard navigation of the Open dialog.

Editing

The following table lists the editing settings:

SETTING	DEFAULT	DESCRIPTION
NSDragAndDropTextDelay	500	The delay, in milliseconds, that you must hold the mouse button down without moving it before a click in a text selection becomes a text drag. If you are constantly selecting instead of dragging text, reduce this delay. Increase it if you find yourself dragging text when you wanted to select it. Set the delay to 0 (or a negative number) to disable text dragging altogether.
PBXIndentOnPaste	YES	Normally, when you're pasting text into a syntax-aware editor pane, Xcode automatically re-indents the text. If you find this annoying, change this setting to NO and pasted text will be inserted literally. You can always manually re-indent the text using the Format ➪ Re-Indent command.
PBXBeepOnNoMatchingBrace	YES	Set this to NO to suppress Xcode's habit of playing the system "beep" sound when it can't find a matching brace. The editor looks for matching braces whenever you type a closing brace or parenthesis, or if you double-click a brace or parenthesis.
XCShowUndoPastSaveWarning	YES	Xcode warns you whenever you are about to undo a change that occurred before the file was last saved. If you find this warning annoying, change this setting to NO.
XCColorUnknownLanguages	NO	The Xcode editor normally provides syntax coloring only for languages that it understands. Setting this to YES will cause text that appears to be comments (lines beginning with #, text between /* … */, and so on), URLs, and string literals to be colored in any text file.
XCCodeSenseAllowAuto CompletionInPlainFiles	NO	Normally, auto-completion is only active in files that Xcode understands. Setting this option to YES enables auto-completion for all file types. Auto-completion will consist of language keywords and text macros.

continues

(continued)

SETTING	DEFAULT	DESCRIPTION
XCScrollToEndOfMatchingBrace	YES	When you double-click a quote, brace, or parenthesis, Xcode scrolls so that the matching brace is visible in the editor pane. Set this to NO to leave the scroll position alone.
XCMatchIndentWithLineAbove	YES	When Syntax-Aware Indenting is disabled, or when you're editing a non-syntax-aware source file type, this setting still causes auto-indenting of a new line to the same tab position as the previous line. Setting the value to NO disables auto-indenting of new lines, in the editor's Insert Newline action.
XCSmartInsertDeleteEnabled	NO	Set this to YES and Xcode will try to be "smarter" about how it inserts and deletes spaces around words when inserting and deleting within a source file.
XCCodeSenseFormattingOptions	(none)	A dictionary of text macro property values that override those defined by the text macro definition files (.xctxtmacro). See the "Sanctioned Text Macro Customization" section for a description of the values in the dictionary.
XCShowNonBreakingSpace	YES	Xcode normally displays a non-breaking space (Unicode 0x00A0) as a dot (•). Change this setting to NO and non-breaking spaces will display as whitespace.
XCShowControlCharacters	YES	Xcode normally displays control characters that it finds in text files as an inverted question mark (¿). Change this setting to NO and control characters in source files will be invisible.

Functions Menu

The following settings control what kinds of items are included in the Functions menu of the editor's navigation bar. The Show Declarations setting in the Code Sense tab of the Xcode Preferences controls the inclusion of function and method definitions. To include, or exclude, other types of items from the menu change these settings to YES or NO as desired.

SETTING	DEFAULT
PBXMethodPopupIncludeMarksDefault	YES
PBXMethodPopupIncludeClassDeclarationsDefault	YES
PBXMethodPopupIncludeClassDefinitionsDefault	YES
PBXMethodPopupIncludeMethodDeclarationsDefault	YES
PBXMethodPopupIncludeMethodDefinitionsDefault	YES
PBXMethodPopupIncludeFunctionDeclarationsDefault	YES
PBXMethodPopupIncludeFunctionDefinitionsDefault	YES
PBXMethodPopupIncludeTypesDefault	YES
PBXMethodPopupIncludeDefinesDefault	YES
PBXMethodPopupIncludeWarningsDefault	NO

Building

The following table lists the building settings:

SETTING	DEFAULT	DESCRIPTION
BuildSystemCacheSize InMegabytes	1024	The "trim" size of the precompiled headers cache. Precompiled headers are cached and reused whenever possible. If the size of the cache is larger than this value in megabytes, Xcode deletes the oldest precompiled headers to recover disk space. Note that this happens only once, when the Xcode application is first launched. Setting this value to 0 disables this check, allowing the cache to grow unabated. Also see the BuildSystemCacheMinimumRemovalAgeInHours setting.
BuildSystemCacheMinimum RemovalAgeInHours	24	This is the number of hours a precompiled header must have been in the cache before it can be removed. Even if the BuildSystemCacheSizeInMegabytes setting tells Xcode it's time to delete old headers in the cache, headers that are younger than this setting will never be removed, even if it means not trimming the cache down to the requested size.

continues

(continued)

SETTING	DEFAULT	DESCRIPTION
PBXBuildSuccessSound	(none)	Set this to the path of a sound file you want played when a build is successful.
PBXBuildFailureSound	(none)	Set this to the path of a sound file you want played whenever a build fails.
PBXNumberOfParallelBuildSubtasks	(none)	The number of parallel tasks the build system will try to keep running while building. If not set, the build system uses the number of processors installed in your computer. Set this to a number greater than the number of processors if your builds are I/O bound. Reduce the number to keep Xcode from using all available CPU resources.
PredictiveCompilationDelay	30	The number of seconds before a predictive compile is performed. If a source file in an editor pane hasn't been modified for a while, Xcode attempts to compile it in the background. Increase this delay if background compilation is using too many resources, or reduce it to be more aggressive. This feature requires that predictive compilation is enabled in the Xcode Preferences. Xcode ignores this setting if you try to set it to 10 or less.
UsePerConfigurationBuild Locations	YES	Build locations are normally separated into subfolders by build configuration. This avoids the need to rebuild the entire project when switching build configurations, but uses considerably more disk space. Set this to NO, and the build products of different build configurations will be written to the same folder.

Distributed Builds

The following table lists the distributed builds settings:

SETTING	DEFAULT	DESCRIPTION
XCMaxNumberOfDistributedTasks	25	The maximum number of tasks to distribute to other computers when you're using distributed builds.
XCDistributedBuildsVerboseLogging	NO	Change this setting to YES to enable diagnostic messages from the distcc tool. If you are having problems with distributed builds, these messages may provide some insight as to why.
DistributedBuildsLogLevel	0	Controls the amount of detail produced by Xcode's distributed build manager. This is useful for debugging distributed build problems. The value must be 0, 1, or 2.

Debugging

The following table lists the debugging settings:

SETTING	DEFAULT	DESCRIPTION
XCAutoClearRunDebugStdIOLogs	NO	Set this to YES and Xcode will clear the run, debug, and standard I/O windows at the beginning of each debugging or run session. Normally, Xcode preserves the results of the previous run or debug session, allowing the output of those to accumulate until you quit Xcode or manually clear the log windows with the Debug ⇨ Clear Logs command.
PBXGDBPath	/Developer /usr/bin/gdb	The path to the gdb debugger. Change this setting to use an alternate version of the gdb debugger. Note that for remote debugging, Xcode's default is /usr/bin/ssh.

continues

(continued)

SETTING	DEFAULT	DESCRIPTION
PBXGDBDebuggerLogToFile	NO	If you think you need to debug the communications between Xcode and the debugger, change this setting to YES. This causes Xcode to log all communications between Xcode and the gdb tool to a file in /var/tmp/folders.*<uid>*/ Temporary Items. The name of the file is determined by the PBXGDBDebuggerLogFileName setting. If you are having problems with the debugger, Apple requests that you include this log file in any bug reports.
PBXGDBDebuggerLogFileName	(none)	If left undefined, the name of the debugger log file will be XCGDB-*name-pid*, where *name* is the name of the executable and *pid* is its process ID. Setting this to a fixed value causes the log to be written to the same file for every debug session, overwriting any previous file. This setting requires that PBXGDBDebuggerLogToFile is set to YES to have any effect.

Snapshots

This single setting determines where snapshots are stored. If you have a scratch drive you may want to direct the snapshot repository to there. If you've previously taken snapshots, remember to relocate the SnapshotRepository.sparseimage file to its new location before launching Xcode, or else Xcode will forget all of your snapshots.

SETTING	DEFAULT	DESCRIPTION
XCSnapshotDiskImagePath	~/Library/Application Support/Developer/ Shared/ SnapshotRepository. sparseimage	Path to the sparse disk image document that Xcode uses to store snapshots.

Source Code Management

The path setting specifies the path to the Perforce source control client tool. The CVS and Subversion client tools are fixed.

SETTING	DEFAULT	DESCRIPTION
PBXPerforceToolPath	/usr/local/bin/p4	The default path to the Perforce client tool.
XCSMLogSize	500	The maximum amount of text (in K) that will be kept in the SCM log, and that can be viewed in the SCM Results window.

Documentation

The following table lists the documentation setting:

SETTING	DEFAULT	DESCRIPTION
XCDocWindowSharesGlobal FindString	YES	When this is set to YES, the search field for the help window automatically picks up the value of the global find string. This is a system-wide resource shared by Xcode's find windows and other find-savvy applications. If you make a search in Mail, for instance, switching to Xcode automatically picks up the last term you searched for. Change this setting to NO to suppress this behavior.

TEMPLATES

Although this is not officially documented, it's also possible to customize Xcode by adding your own project and file templates. Templates are installed in the File Templates and Project Templates folders found in the /Developer/Library/Xcode folder. You can customize the existing one or add your own here. Like text macros, Xcode no longer searches the system (/Library) or user (~/Library) domains for templates, so if you want to customize them you'll have to hack the set that comes installed with Xcode.

The hierarchy and names of the subfolders within the templates folder determine the grouping and order of the templates that will appear in the New File or Project assistant. The easiest way to see this is to compare the file structure of a template folder with the new file assistant, shown in Figure 23-8.

FIGURE 23-8

You can group your templates however you want, simply by placing them into a subfolder of related templates, with one exception: some groups have a `.plist` file that defines additional information about the group, selection options, and so forth. If a folder contains a `.plist` file you will have to edit it to include your template definition or else Xcode will ignore it. If the folder doesn't have a `.plist` file, just drop in your template and it will appear in Xcode.

File Templates

File templates can be a single file or a file template bundle. The simplest way to add a file template is to place a plain document file in the `File Templates` folder. The next time you start Xcode and use the File ⇨ New File command, the name of the file appears in the list. Select it and Xcode reads the file and use its contents to fill in your new file.

File template bundles are a little more sophisticated. File template bundles are not real bundles, but are folders that mimic the bundle structure. A file template bundle has an extension of `.pbfiletemplate`. The name of the folder is the name of the template, as it will appear in the New File assistant. Inside the folder is a `TemplateInfo.plist` file and one or two document files. `TemplateInfo.plist` contains a number of properties, described in the following table:

PROPERTY	DESCRIPTION
MainTemplateFile	This property is required. It is the name of the primary template file in the bundle.
CounterpartTemplateFile	This property is the name of a companion file that can be created by the template. This property is optional. If present, Xcode displays a check box option in the new file dialog box that asks if the user wants to create the companion file at the same time they create the main file.
Description	Text that describes the template. This description appears in the lower pane of the new file assistant when the user selects this template in the list. This property is optional, but highly recommended. If omitted, Xcode displays "No description available."

Create the template file or template bundle, name it appropriately, and place it in the `File Templates` folder or in a subfolder if you want it to be in a group of templates. Relaunch Xcode and your new template appears in the new file assistant.

Template Macros

Templates can contain variable names that are replaced with a value when the template is read. The macro names are surrounded by double-angle quotes (`«NAME»`). The following table lists the macro variables defined by Xcode when a file template is read.

The double-angle quote characters, which are Unicode characters 0x00AB and 0x00BB, respectively, require that the file be encoded correctly — "Correctly" being defined as whatever Xcode expects the encoding to be. Open the template file in Xcode. If the double-angle quotes appear as one or two strange characters, then the encoding is mismatched. First note the current encoding. Now, try switching to a different encoding using the View ⇨ Text ⇨ File Encoding menu and choose the Reinterpret option. If the double-angle quote characters appear correctly, you've discovered their encoding. Switch back to the original encoding, this time choosing the Convert option, and save the file. You can type these characters using Option+\ and Option+Shift+\ on a U.S. Standard keyboard. If you are using a different keyboard layout, you may have a different key combination. Refer to the system's Keyboard Viewer palette if you have difficulty finding them, or use the system's Character palette to insert the characters directly.

MACRO	EXAMPLE	DESCRIPTION
DATE	11/17/05	Today's date, short format.
YEAR	2006	The year.
FILENAME	My File.txt	The complete name of the new file.
FILEBASENAME	My File	The filename given to the file by the user, without its extension.
FILEBASENAMEASIDENTIFIER	My_File	The base filename, suitable for use as a language identifier. The same as FILEBASENAME, but with all non-alphanumeric characters replaced with underscores.
FULLUSERNAME	James Bucanek	The current user's full account name.
PROJECTNAME	Tom & Jerry	The name of the project.

continues

(continued)

MACRO	EXAMPLE	DESCRIPTION
PROJECTNAMEASIDENTIFIER	Tom___Jerry	The name of the project, suitable for use as a language identifier. The same as PROJECTNAME, but with all non-alphanumeric characters replaced with underscores.
PROJECTNAMEASXML	Tom & Jerry	The name of the project encoded using XML entities to escape any special characters.
USERNAME	james	The current user's UNIX account name.
UUID	89E2FBF6-9B88-40EB-BFCF-4550CA9F54CA	A Universally Unique Identifier. This value will be different every time.
ORGANIZATIONNAME	Genius, Inc.	A common macro defined in the expert preferences.

The UUID value is interesting and might be useful if the documents you are creating need to be managed by a database or identified in some fashion.

The ORGANIZATIONNAME macro was described in the "Who's __MyCompanyName__?" section of Chapter 4.

The PROJECTNAME and related macros are defined for project templates or if the file is being added to a project. If you create a new file using a template but select "none" as the project to add it to, these variables are replaced with nothing. In fact, any undefined or unrecognized macro name is replaced with nothing in the new file.

Project Templates

You can also create your own project templates. If you want to create a simple project template that gets duplicated verbatim when created, follow these steps:

1. Create a new project. Configure the project the way you want it: Add source files, frameworks, targets, special settings, and so on.

2. Close the project. Delete the build folder and any other intermediate files that might be in the project folder.

3. Rename the project folder to the name of the template as you want it to appear in the new project assistant.

4. Move the project folder to a location in the /Developer/Library/Xcode/Project Templates folder where you want it to appear in the new project assistant list. Like file templates, some of these groups have .plist files that define the templates for that group. Copy

your template to a folder without a `.plist` file, such as the `Other` folder, or edit the `.plist` file to include the new template.

5.   Quit Xcode. Relaunch Xcode and create a new project using your template.

Project Templates with Macros

Simple project templates are easy, but boring. What you really want are project templates like those that ship with Xcode. These include files, class names, and project settings that magically alter themselves to match the name of the project you just created.

Making a project template that will customize itself is considerably trickier than what's involved in making a file template. How much of your project gets dynamically configured depends on how much work you want to put into it. The key to configuring a self-customizing project template is to create a `TemplateInfo.plist` file and embed that in your project document package. The `TemplateInfo.plist` file should contain three properties: `Description`, `FilesToRename`, and `FilesToMacroExpand` as described in the following table:

PROPERTY	TYPE	DESCRIPTION
Description	String	This optional property is a string that describes the template. This description appears in the lower pane of the new project assistant window when a user selects this template from the list.
FilesToRename	Dictionary	This optional property is a list of key/value pairs. Each pair consists of the name of the original file in the project and the name it should be renamed to when the new project is created.
FilesToMacroExpand	Array	This optional property is a list of file name paths, relative to the new project folder, of the files that should be scanned for replicable template macro names.

You should definitely supply a description string. It makes the template more pleasant to use, and is useful for debugging (explained later).

The `FilesToRename` property is a translation table that renames certain files in the project as the project template is being duplicated. The values in this dictionary can include template macros, which allow you to give files in your project dynamic names. In the example shown in Figure 23-9, the `Template_Prefix.pch` file in the project template will be renamed to «PROJECTNAME»_Prefix.pch. PROJECTNAME will be replaced with whatever filename was given to the new project by the user.

You can use any of the template macros listed previously in the "Template Macros" section in the project document or in the source files of your project template. The files in the project document package are automatically scanned for template macro names. This is how the macro names in the `TemplateInfo.plist` file are expanded. Also scanned is the `project.pbxproj` document. Thus, any build settings in the project that contains a template macro name will be replaced. This allows you, for example, to set the Prefix Header build setting to «PROJECTNAME»_Prefix.pch so it will match the name of the renamed Template_Prefix.pch file in the new project.

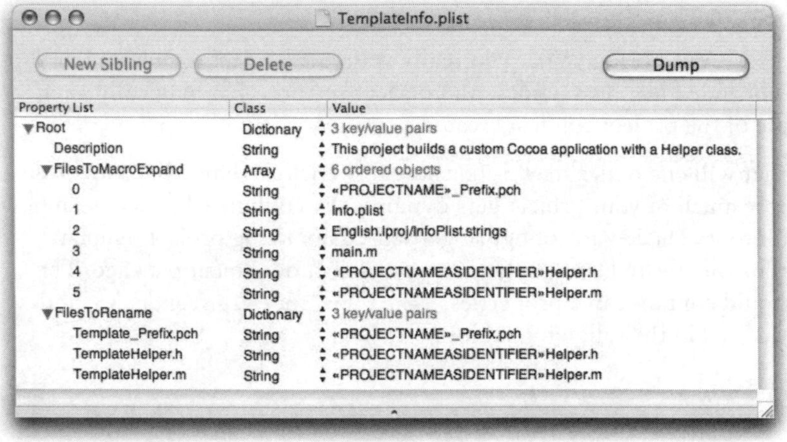

FIGURE 23-9

Other files in the project are not automatically scanned for template macro names. To replace template macro names in any other files requires that you add its path to the FilesToMacroExpand property. The names in the list are the files in the new project, not the template, so if you want to process a file that you've also renamed, use the name the file was changed to — which itself will probably involve template macros.

In the example previously shown in Figure 23-9, the «PROJECTNAMEASIDENTIFIER»Helper.h files are scanned for template macros. The original file in the TemplateHelper.h template looks like this:

TemplateHelper.h

```
//
//   «PROJECTNAMEASIDENTIFIER»Helper.h
//   «PROJECTNAME»
//
//   Created by «FULLUSERNAME» on «DATE».
//   Copyright «YEAR» «ORGANIZATIONNAME». All rights reserved.
//

#import <Cocoa/Cocoa.h>

@interface «PROJECTNAMEASIDENTIFIER»Helper : NSObject
{

}

@end
```

Not only will the file be renamed to match the project, but the class it defines will also get a matching name.

File References in Project Templates

The `FilesToRename` property renames files in the project folder. The macro replacement can be used to generate names dynamically in files and project properties. Unfortunately, these two mechanisms don't work closely with each other or with the project itself. The `FilesToRename` property just renames files. It doesn't alter or fix up any of the project references to those files. If nothing else is done, the project will contain bad references to the original files. To fix this, you must manually insert template macros into the `project.pbxproj` file. You can do this in Xcode or the Property List Editor by temporarily giving the `project.pbxproj` file an extension of `.xml` or `.plist`, or you can use another text editor like BBEdit.

 If you edit template property files with BBEdit, make sure you use the correct encoding. Property list files typically have an encoding of UTF-8. If you open one of these files using ASCII encoding, the double-angle quote characters will not be encoded correctly. Use BBEdit's File ⇨ Reopen Using Encoding ⇨ Unicode command to reinterpret the file as UTF-8.

You'll have to find and replace the filename paths in the property files by hand, because there is no facility for entering these dynamic names in the Xcode interface. The format for the project document file is not intended to be "user friendly." Nevertheless, it's pretty safe to search for the file names you want to make dynamic and replace them with template macros. Just be careful not to make any other structural changes in the file, or you'll likely end up with a corrupted project document.

For example, here's a fragment of a `project.pbxproj` file that contained references to the `TemplateHelper.h`, `TemplateHelper.m`, and `main.c` source files:

```
1AAE3664092E3E8c23412C87 /* TemplateHelper.h */ = {isa = PBXFileReference;
fileEncoding = 4; lastKnownFileType = sourcecode.c.h; path =
«PROJECTNAMEASIDENTIFIER»Helper.h; sourceTree = "<group>"; };

1AAE3665092E3E8c23412C87 /* TemplateHelper.m */ = {isa = PBXFileReference;
fileEncoding = 4; lastKnownFileType = sourcecode.c.objc; path =
«PROJECTNAMEASIDENTIFIER»Helper.m; sourceTree = "<group>"; };

29B97316FDCFA39411CA2CEA /* main.m */ = {isa = PBXFileReference;
fileEncoding = 4; lastKnownFileType = sourcecode.c.objc; path = main.m;
sourceTree = "<group>"; };
```

The file has been edited so that the first two source file names are now altered dynamically to match their renamed versions in the new project.

Problems with Project Templates

Template project problems can be difficult to isolate, because there are no overt errors or warnings produced by Xcode to tell you that something is wrong.

The first thing to check in your new template is that its description appears in the new project assistant window when you choose your template in the list. If it does not, then Xcode didn't read your `TemplateInfo.plist` file. Make sure the location, syntax, and encoding of the file is correct. You might find that the easiest way of doing this is to open the file using the Property List Editor and forcing the file to be resaved. The Property List Editor usually corrects any inconsistencies when it writes a new file.

If you have macros in source files that aren't being expanded, make sure they have been written using the default encoding expected by Xcode for that file type. Follow the steps for fixing the encoding in the earlier "Template Macros" section. Also double-check that you've added the file to the `FilesToMacroExpand` property. If the file is one that gets renamed, make sure you specified its new name — not its original name — in the template.

Look at the system console log. Some problems encountered during template processing are logged here and may give you some clue as to what is wrong.

Last, but not least, study (or just copy) the Xcode templates that come preinstalled. They demonstrate a wide range of customizations. Learning how they work may illuminate what's not working in yours.

Project Template Portability

If you are creating project templates for your own consumption, you're pretty much done. However, if you want to create sophisticated templates to share with other developers, there are a couple of additional details you should consider.

You'll want to delete your user settings files from the project document package. These documents are stored inside the project document package and are named using your logged-in UNIX account name. Other users don't need these documents in their projects.

Target Templates

You may also find it useful to create custom target templates. These are the templates used by the new target assistant when you're adding a new target to your project. Target templates are defined by the target template files found in the `/Developer/Library/Xcode/Target Templates` folder. A target template file is a property list fragment with an extension of `.trgttmpl`. Several properties must be set correctly for the target template to be functional. The important elements are the `Class` and `ProductType` properties. The easiest way to create a new target template is to copy a template file that creates the correct target type and edit its other properties. This listing shows the target template file for a Cocoa application target:

```
{
    Class = Native;
    ProductType = "com.apple.product-type.application";
    Description = "Target for building an application that uses Cocoa APIs.";
    CustomBuildSettings = {
        INSTALL_PATH = "$(USER_APPS_DIR)";
        INFOPLIST_FILE = "«PRODUCTNAME»-Info.plist";
        OTHER_LDFLAGS = "-framework Foundation -framework AppKit";
        GCC_PREFIX_HEADER = "$(SYSTEM_LIBRARY_DIR)/Frameworks/
```

```
AppKit.framework/Headers/AppKit.h";
        GCC_PRECOMPILE_PREFIX_HEADER = YES;
        PRODUCT_NAME = "«PRODUCTNAME»";
        PREBINDING = NO;
        GCC_GENERATE_DEBUGGING_SYMBOLS = NO;
        GCC_MODEL_TUNING = G5;
    };
    CustomProductSettings = {
        CFBundleExecutable = "«PRODUCTNAME»";
        CFBundleInfoDictionaryVersion = "6.0";
        CFBundleVersion = "1.0";
        CFBundleIdentifier = "com.yourcompany.«TARGETNAMEASIDENTIFIER»";
        CFBundleDevelopmentRegion = English;
        CFBundlePackageType = "APPL";
        CFBundleSignature = "????";
        NSMainNibFile = "MainMenu";
        NSPrincipalClass = "NSApplication";
    };
    BuildPhases = (
        {
            Class = Resources;
        },
        {
            Class = Sources;
        },
        {
            Class = Frameworks;
        },
    );
}
```

After you make a copy of the template file, edit the Description, CustomBuildSettings, CustomProductSettings, and BuildPhases properties. The CustomBuildSettings can define any build settings you want and can refer to template macro values. The PRODUCTNAME and TARGETNAMEASIDENTIFIER template macros are defined while creating a new target and can be used to refer to the new target's name.

The CustomProductSettings are present for targets that produce an Info.plist file and contain a list of customized values that will appear in the Properties pane of the target's Info window.

The BuildPhases property lists the build phases for the new target. The possible BuildPhase types are

- Aggregate
- Application
- Bundle
- CopyFiles
- Frameworks
- Headers

- ➤ JavaArchive
- ➤ Legacy
- ➤ Library
- ➤ Native
- ➤ Resources
- ➤ ShellScript
- ➤ Sources
- ➤ Tool

Refer to other templates, or first create a target of the desired type and add your desired phases to it, to ensure that the target can accept a particular build phase type. You should not include a build phase in a target type that does not normally accept that build phase type.

Name your target template file and place it where you want it to reside inside the Target Templates folder. Relaunch Xcode to use the new template.

USER SCRIPTS

User scripts are custom actions that appear in the Xcode menu. Each script is an executable text file that can optionally interact with the content of your active editor pane, essentially allowing you to extend the editor with your own commands. You can write your scripts using a shell language, perl, python, ruby, awk, or any other interpreter you want.

> *Although the script is in the form of an executable file, you cannot substitute a binary executable. The file must be a text file encoded using UTF-8. However, there is nothing stopping a script from launching another binary executable or script. For example, a custom script could start an AppleScript using the* osascript *tool.*

Xcode preprocesses script files before they are executed. Scripts contain additional properties and commands that enable them to communicate with the Xcode application — in a fashion. Because of the subtle differences between regular executable scripts and custom Xcode scripts, the following sections use the term "custom script" to indicate an executable script that employs special Xcode syntax.

The StartupScript

When Xcode starts, it looks for the custom script /Developer/Library/Xcode/StartupScript and executes it. This script is a custom script that can employ any of the special custom script extensions explained later — at least those that make sense in the absence of an editor context. You can modify this script to automatically perform any action you want every time Xcode starts.

The `StartupScript` is worth mentioning, from an historical perspective, because this is where you used to install custom scripts in the Xcode menus. That ability has been formalized, as you'll see in the next section, so the `StartupScript` is no longer the appropriate place for customizing Xcode's interface. If your `StartupScript` creates menu items or keyboard shortcuts, now would be a good time to remove those and add them back using the Edit User Scripts interface.

Creating a User Script

Choose the Edit User Scripts command from the script menu — that's the menu that looks like a scroll. This command opens the Edit User Scripts window, shown in Figure 23-10.

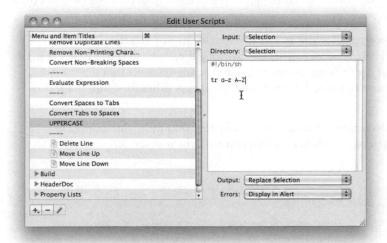

FIGURE 23-10

The Edit User Scripts window is almost identical to the actions window used to define custom organizer actions. The only significant differences are that the Add menu includes a New Submenu command and user scripts have different options than action scripts. This is where you create, add, name, arrange, and assign keyboard shortcuts to user scripts. See Chapter 22 if any of this seems unfamiliar. The user scripts window maintains a hierarchy of submenus, which you can edit and reorganize.

User Script Options

User scripts can be invoked while editing and are intended to augment the capabilities of the Xcode editors. User scripts can do anything, but they typically process the file or text selection by digesting the text in the editor pane and replacing it with its output. The user script's options determine how the script interacts with the document. Some of these options duplicate menu script variables, described later.

A user script has four options:

- ➤ Input
- ➤ Directory
- ➤ Output
- ➤ Errors

The Input option determines what information will be piped to the script on its `stdin`. The choices are None, Selection, and Entire File. Unlike the organizer, Selection in this case means exactly what it says: the span of text currently selected in the editor. Use this when you want your script to filter or process the current selection. The Entire File choice pipes the entire contents of the current editor pane to the script, and of the current editor pane, and None doesn't supply anything at all.

The Directory option sets the working directory to one of three locations: Selection, Home Directory, or File System Root. These choices will set the working directory to the one that contains the file in the editor pane (.), your user's home directory (~), or the file system's root directory (/), respectively. This is usually only useful for scripts that need to process other files, and the setting isn't normally significant.

The Output and Errors settings determine what happens to any text output by the script. The following table lists the Output settings and what will happen with the text the script sends to `stdout`:

OUTPUT	DESCRIPTION
Discard	The output of the script is discarded. This is the default.
Replace Selection	The output of the script replaces the current selection in the editor pane.
Replace Document Contents	The output of the script replaces the contents of the entire editor pane.
Insert After Selection	The output of the script is inserted into the active file immediately following the current selection or insertion point.
Insert After Document Contents	Appends the output of the script to the end of the editor pane.
Open in New Window	Opens a new editor window and writes the output of the text to it. The original source file is not affected.
Open as HTML	Same as Open in New Window, but the output is interpreted and displayed as a web page.
Place on Clipboard	Transfers the output of the script to the clipboard. The original source file is not affected.
Display in Alert	Displays the output of the script in an alert dialog.

Similarly, the Errors setting determines the disposition of text output to `stderr`. The choices are Ignore Errors, Display in Alert, Place on Clipboard, and Merge with Script Output.

Anatomy of a User Script

A custom script is, above all else, an executable script file. The first line of the file must be a "shebang" line that informs the system of the application that will be used to interpret the script. The first line of a `bash` script would be as follows:

```
#! /bin/bash
```

The file must be encoded using UTF-8 or an encoding that is compatible with UTF-8. UTF-8 is a superset of the plain ASCII encoding, so any interpreter that requires ASCII source will be compatible.

A custom menu script can contain special tokens that enable it to interact, in a fashion, with the Xcode application. These consist of menu script definitions and custom script variables. Custom script tokens are surrounded by the character sequences `%%%{` and `}%%%`. An example is the expression `%%%{PBXFilePath]%%%`. This user script variable will be replaced with the path of the file being edited when the script is preprocessed. You can think of user script variables as shell macros, except that they are substituted prior to the script's execution. From the script's perspective, they appear as a literal value.

> *Prior to the introduction of the Edit User Scripts interface, user scripts were added to the menu by the StartupScript using special user script declarations that defined the script's name in the menu, its keyboard shortcut, its input and output options, and so on. If you're incorporating an older user script, remove declarations like PBXName=, PBXKeyEquivalent=, PBXInput=, and PBXOutput=. Use the values from those declarations to set equivalent options when configuring the script in the Edit User Scripts window.*

Scripts can also call a number of utilities provided by the Xcode tools framework. These are executable programs and scripts that can be called by your custom script. See the "Script Helpers" section for the script utilities you can use.

User Script Variables

User script variables are replaced by the value obtained from the currently active editor pane. Again, this substitution happens prior to the beginning of script execution, so treat these variables as constants in your script. Here's an example that uses the `PBXSelectionLength` variable that contains the number of characters in the user's current text selection when the script is executed:

```
if [ %%%{PBXSelectionLength}%%% == 0 ]; then echo "No Selection"; exit; fi
```

If the value of `PBXSelectionLength` is 8, the actual line of text in the script that is executed by the interpreter will be:

```
if [ 8 == 0 ]; then echo "No Selection"; exit; fi
```

PBXFilePath

The `PBXFilePath` variables expand to the complete pathname of the file in the editor pane. You can use this instead of, or in addition to, piping the contents of the document to the script's input. It's also useful for writing scripts that perform some action on the file itself — like a source control script — instead of the contents of the editor pane.

 This variable works reliably when used in an editor pane displaying an existing file. In other situations — like a text selection in the build transcript or a text file window that's never been saved — its behavior is erratic. It may evaluate to nothing, a path that isn't a file, or a path to a temporary file. Code defensively when using this value.

PBXSelectedText and PBXAllText

The `PBXSelectedText` and `PBXAllText` variables expand to the contents of the current text selection or the contents of the entire editor pane, respectively. You can use these variables instead of, or in addition to, the Input option of the script.

These can be rather dangerous to use in a script. They are replaced, verbatim, with the contents of the selection or editor pane. There is no protection from special characters that might be inappropriate at that location in your script. In other words, the substitution may result in portions of the editor text being interpreted as part of the script. For example, the following shell statement appears harmless, but it will cause the script to fail with a syntax error if the currently selected text contains a double quote character:

```
SELECTION="%%%{PBXSelectedText}%%%"
```

One way to avoid this kind of problem in the shell is to use a so-called "here document," like this:

```
cat << END_OF_SELECTION
%%%{PBXSelectedText}%%%
END_OF_SELECTION
```

Most shells and interpreters like `perl` support some kind of "here document" syntax. It's more robust than trying to quote the value, but still isn't foolproof. Consider an editor pane where the text "END_OF_SELECTION" is the current selection.

PBXTextLength, PBXSelectionStart, PBXSelectionEnd, and PBXSelectionLength

These four variables, described in the following table, report the number of characters in the file or current text selection and the index into the current document where the text selection begins and ends.

VARIABLE	DESCRIPTION
PBXTextLength	The number of characters in the active editor pane.
PBXSelectionLength	The number of characters in the current text selection. This will be 0 if the text selection is an insertion point.
PBXSelectionStart	The position within the editor pane where the current text selection or insertion point begins.
PBXSelectionEnd	The position within the editor pane where the current text selection ends.

Using these variables, your user script can treat the contents of the editor pane as a whole. A common scenario is to set the script's Input option to Entire Document and its Output option to Replace Document Contents. The script reads the entire document into a variable and then uses these four user script values to identify the selected text. The script has the entire contents of the document, knows the location of the current selection, and can change anything within the document.

These variables are typically more useful when used with interpreters, like perl and ruby, that provide more sophisticated string and character functions.

PBXSelection

The PBXSelection variable is replaced by a special marker — some obscure sequence of characters known only to Xcode. The Xcode editor looks for this special marker, or markers, in the text output by the user script. If it finds these markers in the text, it uses them to set the text selection in the editor pane. This only applies when the output of the script is being used to replace or insert text in the editor pane.

Including one PBXSelection marker in your script's output causes the insertion point to be placed at that position. Including two PBXSelection markers causes everything between the two to be selected. This listing shows a custom script that inserts a HeaderDoc comment and leaves the class name selected:

```
#! /bin/bash

cat << END_OF_HEADERDOC
/*!
    @class       %%%{PBXSelection}%%%Class%%%{PBXSelection}%%%
    @abstract
    @discussion
    */
END_OF_HEADERDOC
```

The two selection markers in the output text are caught by Xcode and used to establish a new text selection in the editor pane, as shown in Figure 23-11.

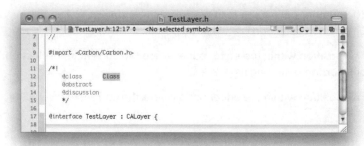

FIGURE 23-11

Script Helpers

Xcode — or more precisely the Xcode developer tools framework — provide a number of utility programs that can be called by a custom script to programmatically interact with Xcode and the user.

These tools are in a framework bundle added by the Xcode Developer Tools installer. Use the path supplied in the PBXUtilityScriptsPath custom script variable to locate the tools. The following script demonstrates using the PBXUtilityScriptsPath variable to execute the AskUserForExistingFileDialog tool:

```
TOOLSPATH='%%%{PBXUtilityScriptsPath}%%%'
"${TOOLSPATH}"/AskUserForExistingFileDialog "Choose a text file"
```

Prompt for a String

The AskUserForStringDialog tool prompts users for some text, which they can enter interactively via a dialog box. The single, optional, argument specifies the default text value that will appear in the dialog box when it is opened. The text entered by the user is returned via stdout. The following example bash script prompts for a username, supplying the current account's short name as a default, and captures the results in the variable NEWNAME:

```
NEWNAME="$('%%%{PBXUtilityScriptsPath}%%%/AskUserForStringDialog' ${USER})"
```

Ask for an Existing File or Folder

AskUserForExistingFileDialog and AskUserForExistingFolderDialog prompt the user to select an existing file or folder, respectively. Each takes a single, optional, prompt argument that will be visible in the dialog box. The path to the selected file or folder is returned via stdout. If the user clicks the Cancel button in the dialog, the return value is empty. You have no control over the type of file the user can select. The dialog displays, and allows the user to choose, invisible files and folders.

Prompt for a New File

The `AskUserForNewFileDialog` tool prompts the user to choose a filename and location for a new file. The path to the new file is returned via `stdout`. The tool takes two, optional, arguments. The first is a prompt string that will be visible in the dialog box. The second is a default filename for the new file. To specify a default filename but no prompt, pass an empty prompt like this:

```
'%%%{PBXUtilityScriptsPath}%%%/AskUserForNewFileDialog' "" "New.txt"
```

Ask for an Application

`AskUserForApplicationDialog` presents the user with an application picker dialog. This dialog, shown in Figure 23-12, enables the user to choose an application known to launch services, or browse the file system in search of an unknown one. The tool returns the full path to the application's program file or bundle folder, as appropriate.

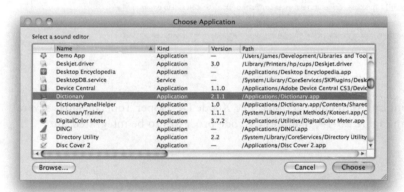

FIGURE 23-12

The command takes two, optional, arguments. The first is the title used for the dialog, normally "Choose Application." The second argument is a prompt string, normally "Select an application."

APPLESCRIPT

In addition to the many ways in which Xcode can run automated scripts, the Xcode application itself can be driven programmatically using AppleScript. Open the AppleScript dictionary for Xcode, shown in Figure 23-13, and you will find a rich and complex set of objects and command to work with.

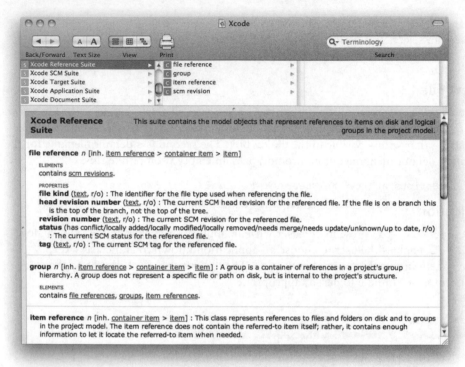

FIGURE 23-13

Closely related to AppleScript are Automator actions. The Xcode Developer Tools includes several Automator actions, shown in Figure 23-14, that allow Xcode processes to be integrated into Automator workflows.

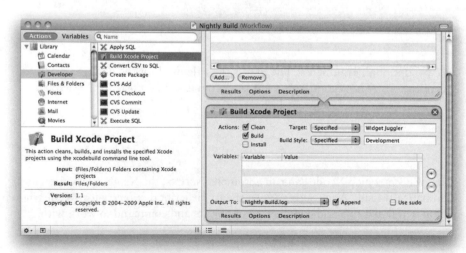

FIGURE 23-14

Although you can build a project using the xcodebuild tool, that's about all you can do with it. AppleScript provides the ability to automate Xcode by accessing the data and structures within projects and the Xcode application itself. For example, your company may have a set of target settings that need to be uniform across multiple projects. You can write an AppleScript program to quickly check, and possibly correct, those properties in dozens of projects containing potentially hundreds of individual settings. Or maybe you just like your windows stacked up in certain way. The possibilities are almost endless.

Remember too that AppleScripts are supported directly by the organizer (see Chapter 22). Once you write and save your AppleScript, you can attach it to a project in the organizer as an action.

AppleScript programming is beyond the scope of this book, but here are a few tips for using AppleScript with Xcode:

➤ A shell script can start an AppleScript using the osascript tool. This enables you to utilize AppleScript in build phases and custom commands. You can also use AppleScript to integrate applications that couldn't normally be controlled by a build script, such as an audio or image conversion program.

➤ The AppleScript Standard Additions allow an AppleScript program to run a shell script, meaning you can freely mix AppleScript and shell scripting technologies.

➤ Although Xcode lets you create AppleScript Studio applications, debugging an AppleScript application that is trying to interact with Xcode at the same time can be problematic. If you can't debug your script because the script is trying to use Xcode at the same time, switch to another AppleScript editor or debugger like the AppleScript Editor application included with Mac OS X.

RESETTING YOUR XCODE CUSTOMIZATIONS

If you ever want to wipe all of your customizations and put Xcode back the way it came when you first installed it, then close the Xcode application, open up a Terminal window, and issue the following two commands:

```
defaults delete com.apple.Xcode
rm -rf ~/Library/Application\ Support/Xcode
```

This will reset all per-user customizations and restore Xcode to its factory defaults for the logged-in user.

SUMMARY

In earlier chapters, you learned to customize your project and how it is built. In this chapter, you learned to customize your Xcode environment beyond the many options already exposed in the Xcode Preferences window. You can set invisible features, add your own processing scripts to any editor pane, and develop your own file, project, and target templates to make repetitive tasks in Xcode easier and more productive.

This brings us to the end. I sincerely hope that this book has provided you with a well-rounded introduction to Xcode, a clear explanation of its core concepts, and an appreciation of those facilities and features that you might not have known existed. My only remaining desire is that you take what you've learned here and use it to create award-winning, bug-free, software for one of my favorite computer platforms.

INDEX

powered by
books 24x7

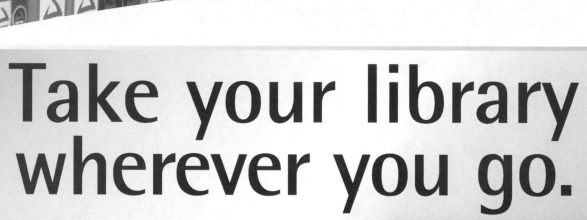

Take your library wherever you go.

Now you can access complete Wrox books online, wherever you happen to be! Every diagram, description, screen capture, and code sample is available with your subscription to the Wrox Reference Library. For answers when and where you need them, go to wrox.books24x7.com and subscribe today!

Find books on

- ASP.NET
- C#/C++
- Database
- Java
- Mac
- Microsoft Office
- .NET
- Open Source
- PHP/MySQL
- SQL Server
- Visual Basic
- Web
- XML

www.wrox.com